ELIZABETH & JOHN

ALAN ATKINSON is an Australian historian who first graduated in 1970. He has written a number of books, including *The Europeans in Australia*, in three volumes, the third of which won the Victorian Prize for Literature. He is an honorary professor and Doctor of Letters with The University of Sydney, and an emeritus professor with The University of New England.

The Amaryllis Josephine, shown on the front cover (artist Pierre-Joseph Redouté), was a bulb originating in southern Africa. The Macarthurs' amaryllis was brought to New South Wales from the Cape of Good Hope by Thomas Hobbes Scott in 1825. First planted in Scott's garden at the cottage at Elizabeth Farm, it was moved to the main garden in 1827, 'together with many others equally beautiful and extraordinary', as Elizabeth Macarthur said, and bloomed there for the first time later that year: EM to Edward, 31 May 1828, ML A2906.

Praise for
Elizabeth & John

Based on fifty years of research and reflection by one of this country's most original and creative scholars and finest writers, here is the story of the world made by settler Australia's greatest family, the Macarthurs. No Australian historian has ever explored the inner lives of a married couple, their family and their milieu with such skill, passion and intensity. No one has brought to any subject in Australian history deeper insight into dreams, ambitions and tragedy that the British occupation of this continent entailed. *Elizabeth & John* is a stunning achievement by one of Australia's greatest-ever historians.
Frank Bongiorno

Professor Atkinson's portrait is intimate and affectionate. It reads well while maintaining the highest standards of academic rigour.
The Canberra Times

Through this remarkable study of two key figures in the history of early colonial New South Wales and especially of their marriage, Alan Atkinson here conducts a master class in connecting the personal, the intimate and the local with worldwide processes of colonisation, migration and capitalist expansion. In his capacious historical vision, family life and connections in all their complexity become the thread that holds colonial history, and perhaps history generally, together.
Ann Curthoys

This magisterial work takes us into a captivating world of 19th-century Australia through a compelling, eloquent, and beautifully drawn study of the remarkable lives of John and Elizabeth Macarthur.
Joy Damousi

Nobody sees as far into the minds and hearts of the early Australian colonists as Alan Atkinson. In this fascinating double-portrait, based on a lifetime's research, he reveals Australia's first power-couple as never before: together and apart; as they saw themselves and as they were seen by their friends and enemies; at the apex of a fast-developing colony and at the far edge of global networks of family affection, commercial ambition and imperial power. A tour de force of scholarship, imagination, and literary power.
Graeme Davison

With trademark lyricism, Alan Atkinson builds a rich and moving picture of the social, intellectual and material world of the Macarthurs. *Elizabeth & John* transforms our understanding of early New South Wales and two of its most significant figures.
Lisa Ford

The Macarthurs have long been the subjects of caricature, even wilful distortion. In this superb book, Alan Atkinson has restored their humanity, exploring their characters, their relationships between themselves and with others, the ideas and influences that shaped them and how they in turn helped shape colonial Australia. This is history at its best, based on vast research and deep understanding.
Stephen Foster

This was evidently a labour of love and a fascination for Atkinson. The reader is treated to such a detailed level of knowledge and understanding that one could easily think Atkinson knew Elizabeth and John, personally. Possibly, after all his research, Atkinson felt he did.
Hearsay

As with a novel, I found myself wondering what the characters were doing while I was away from the book.
Inside Story

Enthralling and powerful. Alan Atkinson writes with the easy, lyrical elegance that comes of deep historical understanding and fine, slow history. In *Elizabeth & John* he weaves together the lives of the Macarthurs with the life of the mind, and brilliantly navigates the mysterious mirror maze between them.
Grace Karskens

Elizabeth & John is a truly amazing work of history. A triumph. This is historical scholarship at its dazzling best. Beautifully produced and written, Alan Atkinson's intimate portrait of Elizabeth and John Macarthur's marriage also opens windows on to the wider worlds of 19th-century England, the European Enlightenment and early New South Wales during the years of the British invasion and occupation. Attentive to his subjects' inner selves and sensibilities and the imperatives of an imperial and patriarchal order, Atkinson's book is truly a tour de force.
Marilyn Lake

At once intimate and epic, inspired and deeply compassionate, this is the kind of book that can only come from a lifetime of close reading. Meticulously researched, imaginatively conceived and breathtaking in its ability to retrieve past worlds – both private and public. An exceptional work of biography and history written by one of Australia's most original historians.
Mark McKenna

Against the clamour and rancour of modern 'history wars', Atkinson gives us exactly the type of story we need right now – nuanced, poetic and intellectually graceful. He lures us, dreamlike, into the complex thoughts and feelings of people who mattered, and allows us to visit the world they inhabited. Atkinson's style and sensibility is a refreshing reminder of how we might sincerely assess the great men and women of the past, instead of tearing down their statues, or even building them in the first place.
David Roberts

Atkinson cares equally about the history of ideas as he does about the Macarthurs and these two preoccupations produce a book delightfully dizzying in breadth and scope. This is a history that soars and swoops between mammoth global processes and exquisitely personal sentiments.
Sydney Morning Herald/ The Age

Elizabeth & John presents a new way of understanding Australian cultural history. It rereads the lives of its subjects against the wealth of primary source material now available online. The result gently requests a reappraisal of Australian colonial society.
Marian Quartly

For Scarlett

ELIZABETH & JOHN

THE MACARTHURS *of* ELIZABETH FARM

ALAN ATKINSON

NEWSOUTH

UNSW Press acknowledges the Bedegal people, the Traditional Owners of the unceded territory on which the Randwick and Kensington campuses of UNSW are situated, and recognises the continuing connection to Country and culture. We pay our respects to Bedegal Elders past and present.

A NewSouth book

Published by
NewSouth Publishing
University of New South Wales Press Ltd
University of New South Wales
Sydney NSW 2052
AUSTRALIA
https://unsw.press/

© Alan Atkinson 2024
First published 2022

10 9 8 7 6 5 4 3 2 1

This book is copyright. Apart from any fair dealing for the purpose of private study, research, criticism or review, as permitted under the *Copyright Act*, no part of this book may be reproduced by any process without written permission. Inquiries should be addressed to the publisher.

A catalogue record for this book is available from the National Library of Australia

ISBN   9781761170317 (paperback)
        9781761179143 (ebook)
        9781761178276 (ePDF)

Internal design Josephine Pajor-Markus
Cover design Alex Ross
Cover image Lithograph drawn by Pierre-Joseph Redouté, of the flower *Amaryllis josephinae*, named for Empress Josephine of France. Scanned from plates 370–371 in Redouté's *Les liliacées*, published in Paris by the author and printed by Didot jeune in 1813. Lithographed by Lemaire. Courtesy of University of Southern California, on behalf of the USC Libraries Special Collections
Printer Griffin Press

All reasonable efforts were taken to obtain permission to use copyright material reproduced in this book, but in some cases copyright could not be traced. The author welcomes information in this regard.

CONTENTS

Note about names   xiii
Introduction   1

PART 1

1   The first border   15
2   The stepfather   21
3   Elizabeth   27
4   A locomotive disposition   35
5   John   46
6   The joint design   55

PART 2

7   The far side of the earth   65
8   Everyone thinks   77
9   Ginger group   85
10   Inspector of public works   93
11   'A maneuvering business'   103
12   Cloth, a family concern   111
13   The meaning of happiness   118

PART 3

14	Trust and lack of trust	129
15	1801, a gateway year	139
16	Answers from the edge of Empire	149
17	A new story	157
18	The golden fleece	161

PART 4

19	'Our first universe'	173
20	The importance of Miss Lucas	184
21	Tjedboro	189
22	Curiosity	193
23	Exactitude	204

PART 5

24	Suddenly larger limits	219
25	Insurrection	222
26	The parlour scene	234
27	Variegated truths	242
28	John's self-reflection	251
29	Elizabeth's judgment	262
30	Commanding the long term	272

PART 6

31	The supposed point of invasion	283
32	Intrigued by the young	289
33	A daughter grows up	299
34	The excellence of Madeira	309
35	Mind over mind	321
36	Vicissitudes of convict reform	330

PART 7

37	La révolution morale	341
38	Hobbes Scott	347
39	Justice at every step	357
40	Rebuilding home	367
41	Nemesis was Greek	375

PART 8

42	John's misted horizon	387
43	A type of divorce	397
44	The breach made by widowhood	409
45	Old age	420
46	The end	428

Epilogue	433
Acknowledgments	436
Select bibliography	441
Notes	449
Index	507

NOTE ABOUT NAMES

In this story, there has been no ideal way of referring to members of the Macarthur family. I have made a rule of using first names – 'Elizabeth', 'John', 'Edward' and so on. This is to save confusion and to make sure that there is no impression of ranking among them. Only very rarely have I referred to John Macarthur simply as 'Macarthur'.

It is true that in their own day only immediate family and very close friends would have used first names like this. As a result my usage undoubtedly suggests a lack of critical distance. My excuse is that life stories nearly always have that problem anyway. It is very hard to enter thoroughly into someone else's world view without at least seeming to take their side. The problem cannot be skirted around so I have chosen to take it head-on.

Secondly, I have used the now conventional spelling 'Macarthur' throughout, although for more than half their lives – until about 1817 – Elizabeth and John wrote 'McArthur'. Their son John seems to have led the changeover – see Chapter 32 – and even after that, the second 'a' was often capitalised, making 'MacArthur', or at least a little enlarged. Elizabeth, especially, found it hard to give up the old way.

I have used the newer spelling also for John's nephew Hannibal, but not for any of the previous generations or for their kinsman in England, John McArthur of Hinton Lodge. Him I call 'Hinton McArthur'. The other old spelling, 'M'Arthur', never adopted by family members but sometimes by others, I do not use at all.

ELIZABETH & JOHN

I do not use 'sic' in this book, and all misspellings and also all indications of emphasis (italics), where they appear within quotation marks, are to be understood as belonging to the original source.

INTRODUCTION

The Macarthurs, the family at the heart of this book, had a strong sense of their own historical importance. We can be thankful for that. It means that they kept an enormous quantity of their own records – letters, account books and so on – that otherwise might have been lost. It is for that reason I have been able to tell their story in the way I have.

The Macarthurs were pioneers of the Australian wool industry, which, even before John Macarthur died in 1834, was bringing enormous wealth to New South Wales. However, wool was only part of their story as I tell it here. There are larger and deeper questions, as they knew very well themselves. For one thing, the wool industry was part of the process of invasion and occupation. It was thanks to sheep and cattle that so much of the country was overrun so quickly, with devastating impact on Australia's First Nations.

The Macarthur family papers, now in the State Library of New South Wales, are like a great forest of voices. Get well into that forest and the voices start calling from all sides. It takes a long time to work through even a fraction of the whole, but it is certainly worth the trouble. Thanks to the wealth of documentation, the two main characters in this book, Elizabeth Macarthur (1766–1850) and her husband John (1766–1834), can be seen – and heard – far more fully and vividly than most men and women of that time and place.

The first thing that strikes the wanderer in this forest is that Elizabeth and John must have been a careful and persevering couple. There was no way otherwise, in the small spaces they lived in in New South Wales, that they could have filed away so much, so efficiently and over so many years. What they did with their sheep, in preserving the breed, they also did with their bits of paper.

Their eldest son, Edward (1789–1872), was an especially active paper collector. Edward left home at seven and he spent most of his life in Europe. A need to keep up the connection with his parents and siblings might explain why, even in his travels, he took so much trouble to keep letters together, even copying out a good number of old ones so as to make up a complete record. He was most careful with his mother's letters. With Edward, for reasons hard to unravel, the family's historical importance seems almost to have centred on Elizabeth. It is largely thanks to his efforts that we know as much as we do about her thoughts and movements over the whole period of her life in New South Wales.

It was one thing to hang onto the records. It was another thing to know and to show what they mean. In this case, the third son, James Macarthur, was the first to try. James's earliest effort seems to date from the 1840s and only one page of it survives, noting his father's birthday, 13 August, and the old story about family participation in the Battle of Culloden, 1746 – a memory reinvigorated by the battle's centenary. In the 1840s Elizabeth, his mother, was still alive and it may be that James made a deliberate effort to find out what she knew about events before his own birth. If so, he gleaned only snippets – see Chapter 4. With such material, in the 1850s he put together a complete biographical account of his father, for the 16-volume *Imperial Dictionary of Universal Biography*, published in London in 1863.[1]

In 1866–67 James began to think of building on this effort with the publication of selected family records relating especially to the foundation of the wool industry. However, he died in April 1867 and the work was taken over by his daughter, Elizabeth

INTRODUCTION

Onslow. Under her auspices, one extremely valuable new document was discovered, Elizabeth Macarthur's shipboard journal, 1789–90, which turned up among the papers of Emmeline Parker, the Macarthurs' youngest daughter, when she died in 1888. So far, family research had concentrated on John. With this document the record dramatically changed, and Elizabeth's voice emerged in a highly distinctive, heartfelt way.

Extracts were published from the journal, together with some of Elizabeth Macarthur's early letters, in Frederick Bladen's *Historical Records of New South Wales*, volume 2 (1893). Elizabeth Onslow herself died in 1911 and the larger work of producing the family publication, initiated by her father James, was completed by her daughter Sibella. *Some Early Records of the Macarthurs of Camden*, a groundbreaking work among its kind, was published by Angus & Robertson, in Sydney, just before the outbreak of World War I.[2]

EVEN WITHIN TEN YEARS OF HIS DEATH JOHN Macarthur had been called 'the Father of the Australian Fleece', the sort of man, in other words, who deserved a public statue or some other memorial. Wool was a national staple and he was therefore one of Australia's 'great men'. Elizabeth's journal and letters brought John's wife onto the stage, but still very much in a secondary role. 'Her life was a life of service,' said a women's journal in 1933, 'service to her husband, her family and her adopted country.' For that, it said, she deserved to share some of the credit as a wool pioneer.[3]

And yet, it was hard to read that material and to believe that Elizabeth's life was wholly subservient. *Some Early Records*, making such prominent use of her journal and letters, and produced by her granddaughter and great-granddaughter, both of them women of commanding authority, complicated the story of the 'great man'. From the later 1930s, with the rise of the Country Party, the Country Women's Association and, during World War II, the Women's Land Army, Elizabeth Macarthur began to be thought of as a pioneer countrywoman. In retrospective imagination she began to appear with her own distinctive strength of character. That is clear enough in the first good sketch of her life story, by Marjorie Barnard and Flora Eldershaw, in Eldershaw's edited collection, *The Peaceful Army* (1938).[4]

Even this was hardly enough to answer the questions lurking within the evidence published so far. What sort of marriage was it? How did Elizabeth and John work together as husband and wife? What, exactly, was the emotional connection and how did it evolve over the 45 years of their life together? Who contributed what to their obvious success in New South Wales? For a long time, even for a century and a half, it had been clear enough that John Macarthur was a clever, enigmatic man – 'the ingenious Mr McA—', as a visiting seaman called him in 1793, '[that] complex character', 'that strange genius', as the historian Thomas Dunbabin said, in 1941.[5] Where did that leave Elizabeth?

In 1940 the first collection of the Macarthur family papers, making up 111 volumes, was presented to the NSW Public Library (now the NSW State Library). A second collection, almost twice that size, was to follow in 1957, but it dealt less immediately with Elizabeth, John and the very early years. Using only the first collection, the historian M.H. Ellis wrote his biography, *John Macarthur*, published in 1955. Ellis had his own ideological idiosyncrasies – he was obsessively anti-Communist. However, his book was by far the best study of John, and even perhaps of Elizabeth, up to that point.

Malcolm Ellis was a fine stylist, he had a good grasp of character and in describing John Macarthur he managed some wonderfully telling passages. John, Ellis said, 'had an explosive quality. He seemed always to be feeling the construction of his

INTRODUCTION

surroundings, to be forever hunching his shoulders, so to speak, as if involuntarily trying to burst his way out of some invisible cell.' And yet, Ellis made a habit of stopping short at such insights, as if frightened to plunge too deep. What was the imagined world John wanted to burst into? 'He was a born planner and organizer', says Ellis again, but for what purpose, beyond making money?[6]

In just the same way, Malcolm Ellis stopped short in his approach to Elizabeth. Taking the family as a whole, he said, Elizabeth was 'the soundest in judgment and least emotional of them all', and the one 'best endowed with serenity of mind'. With perfect ease, she could 'translate his [John's] views and intentions from the visionary to the practicable ... [and] sketch his moods discreetly'.[7] But what exactly, we might ask, did she add in the course of translation? What did translating from the visionary to the practicable really mean? Most of all, what did she think and what did she initiate herself? And again, how, for both of them, did it feel? All those questions hover about Ellis's story.

FROM THE 1960S THE REPUTATIONS OF ELIZABETH AND John were refashioned. I began researching and writing history about that time too, so that I have watched the process underway for the last five decades. It has had its own powerful momentum, which I have sometimes – not always, by any means – found hard to agree with.

From the 1960s to the 1980s there was a deep shift in historical sensibility in Australia, typical of the world as a whole. In New South Wales, from the first years of invasion, there had always been an oppositionist, sometimes radical understanding. Now that was woven into a new postwar Australian nationalism. According to this understanding, some of the invading population truly belonged to the new country and others were interlopers and exploiters. The latter group were typically people with secure resources, ongoing British connections and a self-perceived right to power. From the 1790s that group clearly included the Macarthurs. Indeed, over time the Macarthurs became the quintessential type of that group. Self-seeking and suspiciously successful, they did not and could not belong.

The new historical sensibility fastened in detail on this line of thought. It also drew on some innovative and brilliant methods of history writing coming mainly from overseas, which paid particular attention to questions of gender, race, the arrogance of empire and the deep human damage involved in British colonialism since 1788.

In the immediate postwar period, research psychologists also began to write history, or rather to use historical figures in an effort to understand what had led them to rise above the crowd. Their conclusions were not usually flattering to their subject matter, by tending to discount creativity, generosity of spirit and largeness of vision, or at least these things became contingent on psychological wounds. Erik Erikson's book, *Young Man Luther: A Study in Psychoanalysis and History* (1958), was a pioneering example. In Australia, the first two volumes of Manning Clark's great work, *A History of Australia* (1962 and 1968), did much the same, though the wounds for Clark were lesions of the spirit.

So Malcolm Ellis's quizzical portrait of John Macarthur, including his sketch of Elizabeth, was superseded. In 1967 the second volume of the new *Australian Dictionary of Biography* appeared, with Margaret Steven's account of John's life and character. It included a psychological assessment in which he appeared more or less as an emotional cripple. '[H]umourless and a stranger to self-criticism', Steven called him, with 'no gift for personal relationships and few resources to spare for friendship'.[8]

There might be faint hints of truth in this. However, an accurate story of John Macarthur's marriage and family life makes him very far from an emotional cripple. Beyond that, as the following story shows, most of what he managed to do throughout his life was a result of deep and reliable friendships.

Ideas about Elizabeth have always been shaped by ideas about John, which is, in itself, a pity. She deserves to be approached as an independent being. In 2020, for instance, the novelist Kate Grenville gave her reason for writing a story about Elizabeth Macarthur – fiction dressed as fact – as her wish to imagine what it would be like to be married to 'one of the most difficult men on the planet', a man, she said, with no redeeming features other than his skill with 'bullying, flattery and fibs'. The publicity for Grenville's book took all this to its extreme. In doing so, it sketched John Macarthur as he lives on in popular understanding, cut loose from evidential moorings. Legend has evolved into fact and, according to the publicity for the book, John is best remembered now as a sociopath, a 'ruthless bully' and a 'colonial monster'.[9]

The 21st century is an age of 'fake news', manipulated photographs and disinformation. For both Elizabeth and John, fiction and fact have now been so completely entangled and confused that we might wonder whether the truth can ever be known again.

In this respect, I like the angle used by Michelle Scott Tucker in her biography, *Elizabeth Macarthur: A life at the edge of the world* (2018). However, the story I offer in the pages that follow is an effort to take everything back to the beginning, so as to start inquiry afresh. Everything we think we know about the lives of Elizabeth and John needs to be reconsidered. I have been surprised, in meeting this need, what a difference it makes to the larger story of British occupation and settlement in New South Wales during those years.[10]

I have been working on this material, on and off, for the last 50 years or so and still, in going more deeply into it during the writing of this book, I have been struck by the way so much of the old understanding is based on pure guesswork. The guesses can be traced back to the 1790s, when ex-convict settlers began telling each other that John Macarthur was an extortionate rum-trader. Malcolm Ellis rightly said that there is no evidence of that. '[N]evertheless,' Ellis added, 'the charges live', surviving into the mid-20th century, when he wrote, and, of course, beyond.[11] Just as some soil produces apparently indestructible weeds, some lives create a wilderness of hearsay that no amount of good evidence to the contrary can root out. Long live the man we love to hate.

Again, all this affects our understanding of Elizabeth, as the woman who chose to spend her life with this 'complex character', this 'strange genius', this 'ruthless bully', this 'colonial monster'. How should we come to terms with a marriage in some ways just as complex and just as strange? If we take it for granted that John Macarthur was a bad man then all the surviving evidence takes on a colouring to match. If we think that, then every word he wrote is suspect. On the other hand, leave the question of character open and the evidence takes on a new richness altogether – a deeper and more complex humanity. That is what I aim to do in this book.

IN PIECING TOGETHER THIS STORY OF ELIZABETH AND John, I have had one advantage denied to most of the people who have written about them before. The internet has transformed the writing of history. It makes vastly more information easily available and the implications of that are profound. In the first place, important new sources of evidence can be turned up much more easily and quickly than they could in the past. I could never have foreseen how much difference all this would make to my understanding of the past. It is not only more convenient. It makes vastly more research possible, without undue effort, for every story we want to write.

The sheer quantity of such detail translates into *a difference of quality*. This is where the revolution in history writing can be

INTRODUCTION

really felt. I have been startled by the possibilities pretty much every day during the writing of this book.

Family history sources, available on the internet, create for individual men, women and children alive during the last few hundred years, in seemingly limitless numbers, a network of kin. That matters profoundly, because the choices made in every life, past and present, have overwhelmingly depended on family – on parentage, on upbringing, on material inheritance, on the example and support of older relatives, and on the tensions and responsibilities of marriage and parenthood.

Also, we can now, in many cases, have a better understanding of the way particular individuals in the past talked and thought. We can have a stronger sense of the ordinary life of the mind. Words uttered, especially as they appear in distinctive phrases, can be understood to echo things read. I can often imagine what books John or Elizabeth Macarthur read by reading their letters, because certain phrases can be traced to some previously published and – now – digitalised source. So far the life of the mind has figured little in accounts of early colonial New South Wales. That ought to change now.

These two things – feeling and intellect – add up to a good deal. They are more than the sum of their parts. Knowing so much more from individual to individual makes a quantitative difference to the kind of stories we can tell about the past. Thanks to the internet it is, or ought to be, far easier now to imagine past lives *from within* – what it was like to live in a faraway time, as a thinking, feeling being, and as one of a kind.

I want to suggest too that when so much can be revealed about so many people in the past, history ceases to be history in a conventional sense. It becomes a kind of memory – a more vivid and personal thing than history, as we usually understand it. Historians have always pretended that they have no kind of feeling relationship with the people they write about. They pretend that they treat them with a kind of scientific detachment. As an ideal, that is impossible, of course. No-one writing about other people can put aside their sense of human connectedness altogether. With 'history from within' – stories of subjectivity and self – it is harder still.

The stories that result from this enlarged approach can be a revelation. I hope there are some fragments of revelation in what follows.

FINALLY, THE STORY TOLD IN THIS BOOK BELONGS TO the long-term evolution of historical understanding in Australia. It will be clear by the end of the book that I see the early invasion period, the lifetime period of Elizabeth and John, rather differently from other Australian historians so far. I see possibilities culminating especially in the 1820s, with instructive echoes for the present.

It has been normal to think about those few decades, from the 1790s to the 1830s, with at least a hint of condescension, if not outright contempt. A few able men and women in colonial New South Wales tried hard – so the story goes – but even those few must seem mediocre from our point of view. They were not clever by the standard of more democratic days. They belonged to a generation obsessed with questions of social rank, and who spent their energies squabbling. At best they were 'colourful'. At worst they were ridiculous, or else, like John Macarthur, 'colonial monsters'.

Are monsters self-aware? One of the main aims of this story is to show what Elizabeth and John – and other individuals, where I can manage it – thought about themselves. As I say in the opening chapter, one of the central achievements of the European Enlightenment, was a widespread skill in introspection – in the business of keeping an eye on 'self'. Elizabeth and John were

INTRODUCTION

natives of the Enlightenment and they were, both of them, adept in self-awareness, self-assessment and self-dramatisation. They heard themselves speak. They watched themselves act. To follow their movements from that point of view is to turn upside-down – or rather, inside-out – our understanding of their lives, their marriage and the time and place they lived in. They deserve a voice in their own story. So I have tried to prove in this book.

PART 1

I

THE FIRST BORDER

This is an Australian story but it wanders often to Europe. It begins there too, in the valley of the Tamar, one of the main rivers of the English West Country, peninsular country with Cornwall at its tip. The Tamar nearly cuts the peninsula in two. Its trickling start is in Woolley Moor, about 6 kilometres south of the Bristol Channel. It then takes its course further southward, through 98 kilometres of uneven green countryside, cherry plantings white in spring and deeply shaded oak woodland, to Plymouth and the English Channel.

Elizabeth and John, though they did not know each other as children, both grew up within walking distance of the sound, sight and cool smell of this river.

The Tamar made up most of the border dividing Cornwall from Devon. It was a potent border. Grey rock, carboniferous sandstone and shale, coloured the river depths and the word 'Tamar', like 'Thames', echoed the Celtic word for 'dark water'. The Sanskrit *tamasa*, used for a tributary to the Ganges, meant much the same. Celtic and Sanskrit, Cornwall and the Indies, both places part of this story, were linked in this way by men and women feeling their way through the mysteries of deep time.[1]

What a depth of meaning is there. What an inter-layering of the lucid and opaque. What a mass of overlapping, interconnecting ripples of local association, across two continents and many centuries. In the glittering dark Tamar itself, the river of Elizabeth and John, how many generations of salmon, pink flesh and silver scales, bred in annual succession? Tamar salmon, Daniel Defoe testified in the 1720s, swam in abundance and were 'exceeding fat and good'. And where the salmon swam, how many human individuals met their end year by year? It was said that the god of the river demanded as tribute, each 12 months, a drowning in that liquid plenty. The forfeit failing one year meant two next time.[2]

The mass of the Cornish were poor. In 1791 the wandering geologist-clergyman Edward Daniel Clark gave a vivid account of place and people. Clark had entered Cornwall by a highway in the south, where the river met the sea. Stepping from the ferry – there was no bridge – you find, he said, that 'every object wears the rugged aspect of penury', and yet, 'with all this appearance of the most miserable poverty, like a rich miser in a threadbare coat, it [Cornwall] possesses immense hoards of treasure.' He meant its tin, lead and copper. These metals had been mined for many centuries and had created a distinctive way of life, a self-reliance, over time. Now the business was greatly speeded up by the use of steam power to bring up the metal. The British government's newly invented copper coinage, supplementing gold and silver, came from Cornish mines.[3]

Dressed in miners' clothing, greasy with old sweat and alive with 'creepers' – things that live on unwashed human bodies – Clark descended a copper and tin mine to a depth of about 240 metres. Geology was a new science with apparently vast potential and Clark's generation was drawn to such adventures, thinking to penetrate the solid infrastructure of Creation. Stunned by the heat and closeness, at the lowest point Clark heard the miners singing in their strange tongue, like offspring of the earthy deep. How often did Elizabeth and John, as children, hear snatches of the same in the open air? Another traveller summed up the Cornish as altogether 'a very strange kind of beings … hard as the native iron'. Some found it difficult to think that they were really members of 'a great and enlightened nation'.[4]

Who, in the late 18th century, could doubt that England was otherwise enlightened? That century, even more intensely since about 1760, was an age of enormous change, the age of the Enlightenment. Throughout Europe new light fell on human understanding, and the British archipelago felt the fresh breath and abundant energies of a great movement of ideas, a new morning for civilisation. The impact of the Enlightenment drove technological progress, material prosperity, emotional sensibility and cultural refinement. It shaped global power. At the main centres of European population, especially the big cities, the movement had deep roots, but in border country such as Cornwall and in overseas outposts such as Britain's colonies the impact was patchy. Old and new mingled in raw contrast.

The Industrial Revolution, with the Enlightenment, drew on the needs of men, women and children in the mass. It created needs. Take clothing. Everywhere there was more clothing to buy, and more choice – it was a happy time for drapers – and the old materials, such as linen and wool, kept up with the new, such as cotton. Vast quantities of raw cotton were now arriving from plantations worked by enslaved men and women – the Enlightenment was an extraordinary combination of good and evil – on the other side of the Atlantic, for manufacture mainly in northern England. Devon and Cornwall had wool mills specialising in broadcloth, a medieval manufacture, thick, plain and weather-resistant. Like the local mines, West Country cloth manufacture was already being reshaped by technological innovation. Newly invented flying shuttles, fitted to the looms, doubled productivity by halving the number of weavers per machine, so as to cater for the growing market in Britain and abroad.[5]

Devon and Cornwall had their own native breeds of sheep, the Exmoor, the Bampton Nott and so on. Sheep were valued for both mutton and wool, and by the 1760s these old breeds were being crossed with New Leicesters – itself a new breed – so as to yield more meat and a longer, stronger fleece.[6] Better machinery and better livestock made more money, but they were also signs of a new kind of organised, practical, hands-on intelligence, and of a need to manage the complexity of Creation, to take up the handiwork of God by sorting, classifying and improving. Elizabeth and John Macarthur were devoted life-long to that great agenda. These were hallmarks of 'a great and enlightened nation'.

The manufacture of textiles was one of the main drivers of the Industrial Revolution. The technology was cutting edge, replete with ingenuity and profit. However, this was also a time of nearly continuous war. The Enlightenment saw violence reimagined so that war itself, and technologies of violence, drew on ingenuity too. Entire nations had to be armed for survival. By the 1780s gun manufacture, like cloth manufacture, was central to British prosperity. Guns were also needed to safeguard more and more private property, and the gun industry, mainly in Birmingham in the English midlands, built up great wealth.[7] Wealth from clothing, from weapons and much else was all deeply intertwined: productivity with credit, credit with law, law with government – abundance with bloodshed, at home and abroad.

Like the internet revolution two centuries later, the Enlightenment offered new ways of pooling material resources, energy and ideas. There were new habits of civility, new forms of knowledge and new ways of killing en masse. Coal mining, much increased, turned pleasant landscapes into raw energy. There was a mighty shift in the impact of people working together in an able, focused way, for whatever purpose. There were new forms of shared knowledge so as to create a new layer of networked, collective intelligence. Businessmen found ways of accumulating enormous sums of money for capital investment – banking and the share market took off, and so did the mass commodification of

THE FIRST BORDER

human beings. The Enlightenment was largely funded by slavery, a point this story comes back to later on.

Often in stark contrast with slavery, the simplest human energies were more tightly amalgamated, in coffee houses and learned societies, in salons, gentlemen's clubs and the first labour unions, in every kind of workplace and in national armies. Historians speak of an 'associational culture'.[8] Everywhere human power, beyond the individual, took on a sharper edge.

There was new human order. That meant new ideas about humanity itself. The sciences of humanity – psychology, anthropology, linguistics and so on – flourished. This was also the first great age of the novel, an extraordinary method of laying bare the mysteries of human thought and feeling. Men and women began to see themselves as managers of other minds, in schools, prisons, armies – wherever true enlightenment seemed lacking.

The Enlightenment changed the way people looked inward on themselves. So they explored their own inner darkness. It was an age when educated Europeans sought self-knowledge and self-awareness, often with the awkward enthusiasm of pioneers. Again, results were patchy but here and there, more and more, men and women were drawn into themselves, and yet at the same time lifted out, by new cognitive skills. In their quiet moments the enlightened few marvelled at the result.

Just as Edward Daniel Clark explored the Cornish copper mine, descending into places normally impenetrable, individuals such as Elizabeth and John Macarthur were drawn to the mysteries of their own internal life. Elizabeth, especially, found a connection between self and the natural environment, as if each echoed the other. She was to love what she called her 'solitary rambles' in the Australian 'forest'. From her earliest years in New South Wales the 'native scenery', as she said, touched a chord with her. Several of her children were to show the same intensely romantic frame of mind. With it went ideas about the deep interconnection of all the natural world, over space but also over time – from past into future. Elizabeth and John were to be among the invaders and supplanters of ancient Australia. And yet – ironically – arguments about environmental conservation and sustainability, so urgent later on, can be traced back to the lucid self-consciousness of men and women like them.[9]

There have been many generational turning points, going back thousands of years, when humanity has given fresh value to the idea of getting beyond self – a 'mirror moment' (is that me?), a leap of imagination, moral, intellectual and spiritual too. The late 18th-century was such a time. Every kind of human relationship was touched, from the face-to-face to the global. I suggest this highly complicated human event, this new skill in looking inward, made more difference than anything else.

Jean-Jacques Rousseau in his *Confessions*, published in the original French in two parts, 1782 and 1789, spelt out the transformation – like some later guru from the East. Rousseau, as a contemporary put it, 'offer[ed] valuable instruction in the art of observing ourselves, penetrating to the most hidden motives of our conduct and actions'.[10] Such refashioning – self-felt and self-heard as it happened – was pure enchantment.

This way of thinking about yourself, and on top of that thinking about yourself thinking, mirrors on mirrors, has been called 'radical reflexivity'. It became a habit among the well-read and it gave the Enlightenment a distinctive glory, even among blood and suffering on a new industrial scale.[11]

For Elizabeth and John, brought up in border country, this was their excitement.

2
THE STEPFATHER

All over Europe the Enlightenment proved its power with buildings of great architectural and engineering sophistication. As a small example, take Whiteford House, near the village of Stoke Climsland, on the Tamar's right bank. The house and estate were the creation of John Call, who made his fortune in India in the service of the East India Company, a British mercantile operation with a presence throughout much of the subcontinent. In India, John Call had risen to be chief engineer for the company at Fort St George (Madras, now called Chennai), with a seat on the governor's council. He was particularly good with the manipulation of water (hydroengineering). He came home aged 38, married an heiress, was a Fellow of the Royal Society at 43, a member of parliament at 52 and a baronet at 59.[1] Meanwhile he built Whiteford.

John Call's sole purpose in going abroad had been to make money, with an original target of £10 000. Properly invested he thought he might get that up to £15 000, but he had in fact done better by joining a three-man syndicate to lend funds to a prodigal Indian prince, the Nawab of Arcot. That alone brought him something like £25 000. Thus funded, John Call laid out the grounds at Whiteford in the latest style, with a small canal and lake, cascades, islands, bridges and sluicegates.[2] Nearby he owned Kit Hill, with views to the sea, a site marked by Neolithic barrows, or burial mounds. On it he built a 'Saxon castle' to heighten the effect.[3]

New, improved gaols were being built here and there throughout England. John Call designed one for Bodmin, in central Cornwall, with individual cells, the first anywhere, plus infirmary, baths and chapel. The great penal reformer John Howard was impressed. This fine example of up-to-date humanity was due mainly, he said, to the 'unwearied pains' of John Call.[4] Call also joined a group of gentlemen and clergy wanting to build a canal beside the Tamar so as to connect the north and south coasts. Most of the river was not navigable and a canal could be useful in carrying farm produce to southern markets, and in distributing the lime from the shells on northern beaches to farmers wanting it as fertiliser.

The men behind the canal scheme came from two sections of the Tamar, its source in the north and midway downstream. In the north the leading names were Call's friend and confidante Wrey J'Ans of Whitstone House and John Kingdon, vicar of Bridgerule. These two figure largely in the early story of Elizabeth and John, but so does the surveyor employed to mark out the direction the canal might take. This was Call's neighbour at Stoke Climsland, Edmund Leach. Ingenious and enthusiastic, Leach had a small farm at Hampt on the river's edge. Surveyors like Leach, self-taught mathematician-geometers, earned a good living in country places, measuring, valuing and laying out new roads. They were men essential to the physical infrastructure of the Enlightenment. Many, Leach included, knew just how important they were.

The canal included a succession of different water levels and Edmund Leach's work set him wondering about the way vessels might be best moved from one to the next. He invented an engine to obviate the need for locks, by lifting them from one level to the next. It might also, he said, be used in drawing heavy loads out of Cornwall's deep mines. Leach admitted his own lack of 'scholastic

THE STEPFATHER

education'. He put his faith instead in gigantic mathematical tables, working models and close to 1000 hands-on experiments.[5]

With its enabling legislation passed by the British parliament the canal project unluckily stalled, but Leach did not give up. He persisted with the canal, repositioned according to his own ideas, and his wonderful engine. His survey work had taken him to the home territory of Wrey J'Ans and John Kingdon, where the river began, and there he met with the family of Elizabeth Macarthur or, as she was then, Elizabeth Veale. Leach and Elizabeth's mother, Grace Veale, had both been recently widowed and they were married at Bridgerule when Elizabeth was 12. Grace brought to the farmhouse at Hampt a small income from her previous marriage, all the more for Leach to invest in his great scheme. The next two years were characterised, as he put it, by 'innumerable losses and disappointments'.[6]

Eventually he had his model finished, plus an explanatory 'treatise'. It had been a 'Herculean task', he said, completed 'by the Divine assistance, [and] with an infinite deal of labour and time', but he was sure it would achieve more than anything else Britain now could boast.[7] However, he had failed to find local support, even from John Call. During the autumn of 1780 he took his work to London to show the Society for the Encouragement of Arts, Manufactures and Commerce, a body set up to foster new inventions and giving influential publicity and money prizes, sometimes as much as £100, for good ideas.[8] Nothing eventuated and Leach returned disappointed to Cornwall. He was now 64 and Grace had just given birth to another baby, her third and Leach's first, all girls.

He pressed ahead. The ten-year expiry date of the 1774 *Canal Act* was approaching and further progress depended on the Act's renewal. That was a major challenge. Leach needed to publish his treatise but it cost money, and he was already, he said, 'reduced to very indigent circumstances'. Late in 1785, leaving wife and baby

– Elizabeth, now 18, was probably living in Bridgerule – he went again to London, and by mid-November he was able to present his treatise, in expanded form and properly printed, to the Society for the Arts. Badly in debt, he needed donors to carry him through. 'If your Honours,' he said, 'could do me the favour of procureing me a few subscribers ... you would do me an immense favour.' He also handed in a second working model, 'an indifferent homely jobb', but the best he could now manage.[9]

Again, he failed. Publication of his treatise was abandoned and he started looking for any source of income at all. He was now in his late sixties. 'Would to God,' he said, 'I could find a frind that could procure for me some little imployment if ever so mean.' His spelling betrays his accent. The great men of Cornwall had abandoned him. Now so did his wife. Grace Leach followed Elizabeth back to Bridgerule, taking child and income, and when Edmund Leach died in March 1791, aged 75, there was nothing to save him from the last indignity, a pauper's grave. Whether he knew it or not, his treatise had just been published, in London. This was probably thanks to the third Earl Stanhope, who had just come into some property near Bridgerule. It was immediately reviewed in at least three journals and Leach's name was made, though it took another 30 years for any canal to be built, much too late for the man himself.[10]

The Tamar canal project was designed to extend horizons in true Enlightenment fashion, but Leach's horizons were narrow. The most penetrating review of his treatise spoke of his off-putting verbosity and his vast mechanical calculations, which unhappily made no allowance for friction. His mind, the reviewer said, was obviously shaped by 'the circle of society with which he has been more immediately connected', a circle too small for such an ambitious project.[11] Edmund Leach was not just a self-educated farmer from a distant corner of England. He was obsessive, a dreamer and a man without friends.

THE STEPFATHER

Sometimes, it seemed good to think unaccompanied. Jean-Jacques Rousseau wrote his *Reveries of a Solitary Walker* about the time Edmund Leach married Grace Veale. Published in Paris in 1782, it was immensely popular. Twenty years later William Wordsworth did nearly as well with his poem 'Daffodils' ('I wandered lonely as a cloud'). But these men cultivated loneliness so as to know themselves better. Sublimely self-aware and self-knowing, they also made loneliness marketable. For Edmund Leach, loneliness was a weeping wound, and in the end it killed him.

The Enlightenment gave its best rewards to men and women who knew how to be sociable, how to consult and listen, and how to weave their skills into some larger pattern. Edmund Leach fell short. On the whole, the story of Elizabeth and John is a story of sociability. It has been said by a 20th-century writer that John Macarthur 'had no gift for personal relationships'.[12] That is certainly not true. Both paid a good deal of attention to collaboration and trust. Carefully patterned conversation was part of the mix and so was the liveliness of shared silence. In fact, if this story is about any one thing beyond all others it is the shifting quality of that kind of silence. It is woven in from start to finish.

John Call, of Whiteford House, unlike Edmund Leach, was a good collaborator. He had learnt his methods as a servant of the great company in India. While Leach was struggling against his final disappointment, Call, now in his fifties, was taking on ever larger projects, mainly connected with naval supplies. Throughout the 18th century a mighty collective effort of nation-building was underway, an accumulation of order, productivity and military power. The navy, which was all about teamwork, was the jewel in Britain's crown – a source of power but also a catalyst for experiment, discovery, invasion and control. John Call joined the effort by leading a government inquiry into the state of Crown lands throughout England, especially the forests, a vital supply of timber for ship-building. The result was 17 reports and immediate legislative action.[13] At the same time – the detail comes later – Call joined in a related scheme for bringing ships' masts and sailcloth from the far side of the globe, from a country newly discovered and further even than India. This was Norfolk Island in the Pacific Ocean.

To start with, the government saw too many problems with the Norfolk Island idea, but the arguments used by Call and his colleagues opened the way for an expedition, in 1787, and for the invasion and settlement of the nearby mainland, called New South Wales. Two years later again, in 1789–90, Elizabeth and John Macarthur, not long married, were to take that path.

3
ELIZABETH

Edmund Leach's stepdaughter, Elizabeth Veale, afterwards Elizabeth Macarthur, saw personal ruin at first hand when she was young. Even before Leach's downfall, within her own lifetime, there was trouble with money.

Her mother had been born a Hatherly. Both Hatherlys and Veales were families with good-sized farms near Bridgerule, a village straddling the Tamar. The Hatherlys lived at Tackbeare, to the south-west. Built long ago as a manor house, with spacious windows, curiously moulded plasterwork and heavy Jacobean furniture, Tackbeare by this time qualified only as a large farmhouse. The Veales lived in the south-east, at Lodgeworthy, or Lugworthy, where they had farmed for 100 years or more, first as tenants and then as owners.[1]

Grace Hatherly and Richard Veale, her first husband, had married at Bridgerule on 8 August 1764, when Grace was 17 and Richard probably a good deal older. Their marriage settlement included 40 acres (16 hectares) set aside by the bridegroom to provide a small income for his wife (£8 per annum) in case he died first, and in turn, at their marriage, he received from John Hatherly, her father, 'a considerable [but unspecified] marriage portion'. Richard Veale was called 'Squire Veale', but probably more because of what he spent than what he owned. According to a later family story, thanks to 'a taste for field sports and too great hospitality' he fell deeply in debt.[2]

ELIZABETH & JOHN

Debt might in fact have been Richard's reason for marrying, because of the 'considerable' sum that came with his bride. Two of his particular friends, Daniel Hewett and Richard Hawke, had married with profit the year before, Hawke to the daughter of the lately deceased vicar of Bridgerule. Richard Veale had had a hand in wrapping up the late vicar's estate and in sorting out his friend's marriage settlement. Now, at his own marriage, Hewett and Hawke were both trustees for his settlement, together with Grace's father.[3]

Grace and Richard Veale had two children. Elizabeth was born on 14 August 1766, and named, apparently, after a Hatherly great-aunt, Elizabeth Chapman.[4] Her sister Grace was born sometime in 1769 (christened in May), but three years later both the younger child and their father died. Lodgeworthy then passed to John Veale, apparently a nephew. Or it may be that the bulk of it had belonged to John Veale all along, with Richard looking after it until John grew up. Richard's death left Grace and Elizabeth with £8 a year from the dowry, secured as that was by the marriage settlement.[5] So they remained for six and a half years until Grace Veale, still only 31, married Edmund Leach and went to his home downriver, at Stoke Climsland.

On Richard's death, though the income belonged to his widow, title to the dowry lands passed to Elizabeth, his only surviving child. So Elizabeth grew up with a marriage portion of her own, managed for the time being by her grandfather, because the other trustees, Hewett and Hawke, had also died.[6] Otherwise, she learnt to look after herself, moving apparently among several households. At the same time she acquired a steadiness of character that made her wonder at her somewhat feckless remaining parent. 'My mother,' she said once, in exasperation, 'is a truly surprizing woman.' She spent long enough in her stepfather's house at Stoke Climsland to make one good friend there, a farmer's daughter, Mary Parson, but she otherwise divided her time between ackbeare, with her grandfather, and the Bridgerule vicarage, with another friend, the new vicar's eldest, Bridget Kingdon.[7]

This shifting among several different types of household was a training in patience, adaptability and tact, even in a certain detachment. Like a novelist or an analyst of emotion, Elizabeth watched the feelings of others, and yet she was not interested in questions of blame. 'I do not … trouble myself,' she once said, 'by "motive hunting".'[8]

At the same time she learnt two fundamental rules of behaviour. Avoid talking about 'self'. Men might do it. Not women. Also, avoid gloomy thoughts. Even more, avoid telling gloomy thoughts to others. 'I will not dwell upon this, it makes me sad', 'I hasten from this subject', 'sorrow and regret … can be of no avail', were to be the refrain of her life.

Kingdons, Hatherlys, Veales, Hewetts and Hawkes were interwoven, connected by blood, marriage and various forms of mutual trust. Bridget Kingdon's father had succeeded Richard Hawke's father-in-law as vicar of Bridgerule in September 1765, and he and his wife had moved into the vicarage newly married. Bridget was their firstborn. She, Bridget, long remembered Elizabeth as her first friend, just that little bit older, half within and half-beyond her own family, and 'the lov'd companion of my early hours'. When suitors gathered 'there is not a person in the world', Bridget told her, 'I wou'd so soon disclose every sentiment of my heart as yourself'. Elizabeth might have felt the same but in her own way she was also close to the three eldest Kingdon boys, John, Roger and Charles.[9]

Much of England, especially the granite moorland of the West Country, was wild still and uncolonised. In such places nature predominated, its sounds, as the novelist Joseph Conrad puts it, 'completely foreign to human passions'. In Cornwall even the villages were penetrated by such sound. Elizabeth's childhood was full of it, and it had the sort of freshness and strangeness – of naked difference – that always delighted her. Her later memories of the vicarage included sea wind beating on the upper windows, and it blew in her face just as often. She, Bridget and the boys were ramblers, making excursions across country through those wild vacancies, and bringing home shells from the seacoast at Bude, a morning's walk away.[10] She was to take her walking habits eventually to New South Wales.

The Kingdons had eight sons and three daughters, and all grew up but Griselda, the middle girl, who drowned at five years old at the Tamar bridge. That abundant river and that bridge, like the salt air, haunted Elizabeth's fancy too. She was to have moments on the other side of the world when its image held her thoughts. So, 30 years after she left England she wrote to Eliza, the vicar's last-born, about her dreamlike longings – 'sit[ting] myself down beside you, at the bridge so often passed and repassed in my younger days'.[11]

Among the Kingdon children, all younger than her, Elizabeth was a remarkably strong presence, making herself memorable too. Well into middle age, one of the brothers was to let loose a torrent of grief to his 'dear friend' on the world's far side, unseen for 50 years, about the loss of his own daughter, as if he found even the thought of Elizabeth reading what he wrote a source of comfort.[12]

The children's mother, born Jane Hockin, daughter of another West Country clergyman, had her own inheritance, and the Kingdons' accumulated property included several local manors and the power of appointment to five parishes, including Bridgerule.[13] Jane Kingdon we know very little about, except that she was rarely well.

John Kingdon, on the other hand, the vicar himself, was lively and eccentric – 'active and busy about many things', as Bridget put it. Somewhere in the house there was 'always some machine or other in motion', which suggests he made household gadgets

ELIZABETH

or toys. Taken with the energies of the young, he was not above entertaining small boys on the sea-windy hills near the vicarage chasing a hare. He also admired the cleverness of girls and women. See, for instance, the will he made in his old age. At that point all eight sons were still alive, and yet as sole executor of his large estate he named Eliza, his last born and barely grown up.[14]

The Kingdon boys seem to have gone to school at Bideford, a port town 24 miles away. John, the eldest, certainly did. The old Bideford grammar school, taking boarders, was managed by William Walter, a highly regarded clergyman-landowner-magistrate, like John Kingdon. William Walter appears again later in this story. Elizabeth and Bridget must have been taught by Bridget's father, absorbing at the same time habits of gentry housekeeping from her mother and the servants. The vicar, a learned man himself, paid particular attention to the intellectual life of his children, and learning at home was normal for girls of the Kingdons' rank in life.[15]

In the vicarage Elizabeth also learnt to drop the West Country accent of her parents and to speak as educated people did in Oxford and London. The same thing was happening all over England, with the beginning of a wholesale effort to teach children 'pure' forms of English grammar and pronunciation. Elizabeth conformed, though not perfectly, either in soul or tongue. It might be startling and yet 'refreshing', she once said, to find a man 'gentlemanly in his habits and feelings' speaking still with the accents of the West Country.[16]

The education Elizabeth had from John Kingdon might have been different had she been a boy but she ended up all the same with what was called a 'masculine' intelligence.[17] She was also decisive, and she had an instinct for setting things in order, whether objects, words or ideas, so as to make them work for her. John Kingdon did not teach her up-to-date accounting but with him or with someone else, maybe Edmund Leach, she apparently learnt enough mathematics to make a brief effort with trigonometry later on.

There was a network of regular visiting from the vicarage, especially with the J'Ans family at Whitstone House. Wrey J'Ans and John Kingdon had both supported the original scheme for a canal across the peninsula, on which Leach spent his livelihood, and they sat together as magistrates. Wrey J'Ans was a truly memorable man, bound to impress intelligent children. Whether from the magistrates' bench or otherwise, 'his sound judgment, clear conception, and great abilities ... render[ed] his opinion almost a law.' He was also a senior officer in the Cornwall militia. Elizabeth and Bridget called him 'the Major'.[18]

He was a romantic figure too, and Elizabeth's imagination had a romantic edge. It was not long since Wrey J'Ans's forebears had fought for England's expelled Catholic kings, and more recently still a nearby cousin had spent vast sums on 'ideal societies' in Florida and the Bahamas, designed to give livelihoods to the poor. Strangest of all, Mrs J'Ans (Fanny Rawleigh), mother of his seven children, was not his lawful wife. Nor was he always faithful to her. And yet it was a close family, the four daughters speaking with the learned wit of one parent and the Tamar-bred accents of the other.[19]

The Major was a careful agricultural improver, which might be how he made his most vivid impression on Elizabeth Veale. His advice on the planting and cultivation of apple trees, so as to produce good cider, was read nationwide. At Whitstone the main enemy of Wrey J'Ans's trees was the hard salt wind.[20]

ELIZABETH VEALE WAS WIDE AWAKE TO THE GREAT changes of her day. She could see how different her girlhood was from her mother's. There were better roads, because turnpike trusts raised money to build and maintain them. During the 1750s and 1760s turnpike mileage throughout England had increased by 50 per cent. As a result, the quantity of mail sent throughout England quadrupled even while Elizabeth grew up, and girls like her were encouraged to write to friends near and far, because letter-writing was central to a good education. Printers and booksellers multiplied, linked by their own publishing networks so that slowly, step by step, a national readership came into existence.[21]

Among the educated minority the minds of the young, open to novelty, women as well as men, were transformed. A young woman, if she was literate at all, might read more than her mother had ever done and communicate more through the post. Her thoughts were deliberately shaped by writing. She could find a sense of community even with women she did not know. She could see herself over and over, in refreshing ways, as a woman among women.

Women's publications multiplied, both novels and periodicals, from the intellectual *Ladies' Diary* – though read at least equally by gentlemen – with a circulation of 30 000 at mid-century, to the *Ladies' Pocket Magazine*, which sold 14 000 a month.[22] Women wrote books, pamphlets, songs and music, and other women read and played them. Print illuminated so many different ways of being a woman and of understanding what being a woman might mean.

'Sensible' was a word the new generation used over and over. To be sensible was to feel in a 'civilised', self-conscious way about the joys and sufferings of others, real or fictional. A man or woman of sensibility knew how to talk about feeling. Without egotism – without dwelling unduly on 'self' – Elizabeth also learnt to explore the territory of mind. Mimicking Jean-Jacques Rousseau was like travelling to the far side of the earth. Everything felt in the business of growing up could be seen from an angle strange to older people, especially in an out-of-the-way place such as Cornwall.

Imagining herself as she grew up, Elizabeth Veale shifted between shyness and enthusiasm, candour and command. In behaviour and language, she watched herself well. She was the sort of girl who valued what she called 'retirement', routine without bustle. Curious about many things, she was especially curious about her own feelings.[23] She told small stories about them, which are part of the larger tapestry of this book.

The way forward was marriage, for her as for all girls. Marriage was the only possible method of breaking into a fully sensible life, and of ridding self from childhood's blindness. 'Marriage', as Jane Austen said, 'is a great Improver.'[24] The question now is why Elizabeth married as she did, and what sort of improver and what sort of adventure, for herself and for the other party, her marriage turned out to be.

4
A LOCOMOTIVE DISPOSITION

The word 'locomotive' was fashionable, at least among the learned, when Elizabeth and John were children. With roads so much multiplied and ocean-going vessels so much improved, with horizons so much expanded, it was time to reflect on what all this new movement meant. According to the poet Thomas Gray, 'there was no other way of learning things' than by moving about, especially if books were hard to come by. And yet maybe a 'locomotive disposition' was dangerous to faith and virtue. A taste for variety, said one English writer, a Quaker, was 'the Opposite of Bigotry', and yet it could be just as bad as bigotry. Did not the prophet Jeremiah say that a good man lets himself settle like wine, 'on his lees', so that like wine his taste remains 'and his scent is not changed'? Only by attaching ourselves to the spot where we truly belong do we come to terms with who we are.[1]

Elizabeth Veale's family had lived for generations in one small corner of the West Country. The Kingdons, apart from periods in Oxford and Exeter, had done much the same. John Macarthur's family, on the other hand, had been on the move for some time, crossing borders and seas, and even the broad Atlantic. His parents and relations dealt in distance for a living. Whatever that meant for their own self-knowledge, their 'locomotive disposition' makes it hard to know them now as we might like to. Evidence of their movements is often scarce.

In history, as in archaeology, it can be useful to work from certainty, things we know for sure, to uncertainty and speculation. Archaeologists might examine a vacancy, such as a hole in the ground, as a way of deciding what once filled it. In this story, and especially in this chapter, I build on probabilities as an archaeologist might do, making guesses from a few thin and scattered threads of certain knowledge.

John's father, Alexander McArthur – the usual spelling at that point – was born in the 1720s, almost certainly in his ancestral territory in the Scottish Highlands, namely at the edge of Loch Fyne in southern Argyll, two days by road and sail across the firth of Clyde from Glasgow, Scotland's doorway to the Atlantic. The McArthurs were a sept of Argyll's dominant clan, the Campbells, and were therefore attached by feudal loyalty to the Campbell chiefs, the dukes of Argyll. Successive dukes were patrons of Presbyterianism and the Scottish Enlightenment in this part of the Highlands. Their influence was immense and men and women from Highland families were deeply bound by such loyalties, even into John Macarthur's lifetime and at the far end of the earth.

Campbells and McArthurs had a foot in two camps. They belonged partly to the world of Gaelic tradition, of old language and inspirited land, and partly to the world of the Enlightenment and of European and transatlantic trade. They were a shrewd combination of old and new. Alexander McArthur seems to have been the grandson of another Alexander, who had prospered during the Protestant coup that ousted the Catholic king, James II, whose leader in Scotland was the first duke, then earl, of Argyll. This was the so-called Glorious Revolution of 1689, and that earlier Alexander McArthur had been among Argyll's leading local men.[2]

The supporters of the Hanoverian king, George I, took power and the McArthurs were among them. The original Alexander was given the job of confiscating weapons from recalcitrant clansmen. Afterwards he gathered taxes, calculated by the number of hearths in each house, for the new regime. The Highlands had never been taxed before and Alexander McArthur's effort involved 'many horrid and difficult passages', but the result was a marvellous bureaucratic effort and a good fee for the collector. With it he secured a respectable landed estate at Soccoch, overlooking Loch Fyne and the village of Strachur, and so began the family fortunes.[3]

This was a clever, thrusting family. In or about the 1740s yet another Alexander McArthur, possibly the tax collector's grandson, set up as a retailer of wine and spirits in Glasgow and, by trading across the Atlantic, rose to call himself 'merchant'. His son and heir, John McArthur (1755–1840), best remembered as the biographer of the naval hero Lord Nelson, figures largely in this story. By right of lineage, wealth and/or strength of character this John McArthur was a type of McArthur family head, no small thing in Highland tradition.[4] The story of Elizabeth and John would have been very different without him.

Through this thicket of Alexanders we come again to John Macarthur's father. Highland men, it was said, were known for their fidelity and perseverance, but also for their marked sense of personal honour, 'a large share of *vanity* and disposition to *dash* [or showing off]'.[5] This might be a hypothetical sketch of the third Alexander. He was a linen draper and like his cousin he might have learnt his trade in Glasgow, the obvious starting place for any McArthur wanting a commercial career. The growing of flax and the making and marketing of linen, sailcloth and so on, were the most important of Scotland's home industries, and the trade was centred on Glasgow. At this point strenuous efforts were underway to improve quality, variety and saleability, which partly meant copying methods used on the European mainland, where the business of cloth production was highly advanced. The best models were to be found in the Netherlands, western Germany and some of the western parts of Switzerland.

The early life of Alexander McArthur the linen draper was interrupted in 1745–46, when the men of Argyll were called to fight against invasion. Prince Charles Edward Stuart, grandson of James II, landed on the coast of the Highlands with a small army in an effort to take back the throne for his family, and the Duke of Argyll's adherents, apparently including Alexander and some of his brothers, fought for King George at the decisive Battle of Culloden, in April 1746. Afterwards, according to family memory, Alexander crossed the North Sea to 'the Continent'.[6]

Given that he was young man beginning his career, this expedition must surely have had something to do with the cloth trade. So we might guess – guess only – that Alexander went to places where he could learn about linen, its manufacture and its sale.

WHERE EXACTLY? CHARLES EDWARD STUART'S INVASION was part of a much larger European conflict, the war of the Austrian Succession, and Alexander McArthur is not likely to have travelled in enemy territory, including France. He very likely began at Rotterdam, in the Netherlands, a place crowded with commercially minded Scots. From there it was possible, though expensive, to travel up the river Rhine through various small German-speaking states to linen manufacturing territory in Switzerland. During some such journey Alexander found a wife.

Alexander McArthur's family was Presbyterian. Presbyterians were Calvinists and as such belonged to a communion of faith scattered across western Europe. In some countries, Scotland, Holland, and several of the Swiss cantons, Calvinism was the majority faith supported by government. In England, by contrast, Calvinists (Presbyterians and others) counted as Dissenters – dissenting, that is, from the mainstream Church of England. Largely excluded from Oxford and Cambridge, English Calvinists had their own academies and their own intellectual leadership, including a few men of enormous influence in England and elsewhere. Everywhere, indeed, Calvinism was interwoven, enriched by and enriching, Enlightenment thought.

The new questions asked during the European Enlightenment led men and women to reimagine their dealings with God, and across western Europe Calvinists took a particular approach to such questions. Calvinists of the Enlightenment insisted that the human individual was a moral being and a creature of duty. All goodness lies in duty, so said the great Scottish Presbyterian moral philosopher Thomas Reid, and duty comes in three parts, 'to God, to ourselves, and to our neighbour'. Here were heavy responsibilities. In meeting them it was crucially necessary, even in childhood, to cultivate a deep strength of soul and a power to persevere in God's name.[7]

This was Christianity reinvented. There was more prudence in it, more regard for self, than the New Testament original. Jesus said, 'If thou wilt be perfect, go and sell that thou hast, and give to the poor ... and come and follow me.'[8] But surely, said Calvinists, it was better to manage our lives, our wealth and intelligence, all of it God-given, so as to do what we can *continuously* for the poor and our neighbour? In our mind's eye, they said, we must think of our lives as a road to the future, as a pilgrimage of duty.

It was unusual for men and women to marry outside their own denomination, but the single communion of Calvinism eased the way for marriage across national boundaries. A man and woman might come from different language communities – French and English, for instance – and yet marry because faith was more fundamental than language or secular loyalty. If they agreed on matters of religion there might be little else to divide them.

John Sheldon, an English Calvinist, trained for the ministry among dissenting intellectuals in central London. He lived close to the chapels used by French-speaking Calvinist merchants from Switzerland and France, and three of his sisters married such men. Stationed afterwards at Canterbury, south-east of London, it was Sheldon who baptised Alexander McArthur's son James, at the Dissenters' meeting house in Guildhall Street, Canterbury, on 20 January 1752.[9]

The baptismal record made by John Sheldon is the earliest surviving reference to Alexander McArthur, and it also names the baby's mother, Catherine. This was 14 years and seven months before the birth of John Macarthur, younger son of Catherine and Alexander, and future husband of Elizabeth Veale.

In January 1752, when this christening took place at Canterbury, Catherine and Alexander McArthur, still a young couple, seem to have been on a journey. There is no evidence that they spent much time at Canterbury, though it is possible. Canterbury was the main stopping point for travellers to London from Dover, and Dover, as a seaport, received travellers especially from France – in 1752 the war with France was over – and, beyond France, from Switzerland and Italy. Catherine and Alexander had probably come across the water from Calais, Boulogne or Dunkirk, on the French coast. If so, Catherine had taken this journey, wave-tossed and pregnant, during a bitter winter. Daytime temperatures were under zero (Celsius) in Paris and they must have been much the same all the way. In Canterbury the McArthurs seem to have quickly found John Sheldon, so that their baby James was only eight days old when he felt the minister's sanctifying touch.[10]

WHO WAS ALEXANDER MCARTHUR'S WIFE CATHERINE? Everything about her life before January 1752 is uncertain and given the amount of work that has already been done searching for information it is not likely now that anything will ever be found.

She holds in her hands many of the threads of the following story and yet, like a puppet-master, she stands behind a screen. The only certain knowledge comes from what appears for the baptism of her three sons – the youngest died early – and the record of her own burial, in 1777. Put this together and remember the normal age period for childbearing, and it appears that Catherine was born in the 1730s and that she married when she was little more than a girl.[11]

The rest of her story comes to us in more roundabout, arguable ways. Every mother leaves a mark, a certain duplication of character, on her children and in this case – guessing again – it is certainly possible to read back from the imprint to the original. Catherine can be known partly through the character of her two surviving sons, especially from the way they dealt with women. John's wife Elizabeth was powerfully self-reliant, and it is hard to imagine the partnership between them working as well as it did – with such intricate success – if John had not had a mother just as strong. Such then, by my conclusion, was Catherine McArthur.

No-one remembered her family name. Why not, and why do none of her blood relations appear in the written record? Why did her two sons, James and John, have nothing to say about her and where she came from, or nothing that anyone of the next generation could remember? How much of all the forgetting did Catherine herself impose, by setting her face against the past?

A few whispers of other information come, second- or third-hand, from a grandson, who was born after Catherine's death. She had been 'a foreign lady,' so he had been told, 'said to be of great beauty and accomplishments but of what country I know not'. Others said she spoke a language other than English. Among the old Macarthur family books in New South Wales there was once a mysteriously large number of volumes from the early 1700s, the period of Catherine's lifetime or before, in French and published in France. Some of them might have been hers – the only material inheritance, perhaps, from her earlier life, and evidence in black and white of her 'accomplishments' and of her background among educated people.[12]

Then again, she married Alexander, it was said, 'in opposition to the wishes of her family'.[13] If this was in any way true, it might explain all the other silences. Divorcing herself from the people she had grown up with, she locked all her recollections away, in a strange manifestation of toughness and pride.

Finally, there is the question of religion. Alexander was Calvinist and almost certainly Catherine was too. On top of that, a Canterbury christening suggests a journey into England from France and/or Switzerland. Altogether then, I suppose in this story that Catherine grew up in a Calvinist family in France or in the western parts of Switzerland – Geneva, Neuchâtel or Lausanne. There was copious English traffic with those places. John Sheldon's ties, for instance, were mainly with the French-speaking Swiss.

Whatever the facts, it is easy to see John Macarthur as the product of a Calvinist upbringing, in his way of looking inward, in his rigid self-regard, but also in his understanding of the world at large. The Calvinist God was a god of tough love. He was almighty and merciless, and yet he was a Father who could be known and relied on. The Calvinist God also honoured the virtues of his chosen few. As John himself said once in a moment of painful struggle, those few, those men and women justifiably certain of their 'innocence, integrity and honor', might always rely on 'the favor and protection of a just God'.[14] Who taught him that?

ALEXANDER MCARTHUR MIGHT HAVE LEARNT A GOOD deal from his European journey. Swiss linen, for instance, was a luxury item in Britain. If he did go to Switzerland he might have watched Swiss flax-spinners, women working in their own homes, drawing thread into unprecedented lengths and weaving it into

3-yard-long sheets (about 3 metres), exceptionally fine and fit for bed or table. Swiss weavers also specialised in linen gauze, for sale in the far-off, mosquito-ridden parts of the world.[15] Cloth was an international commodity. Whether linen, cotton, wool or silk, cloth could be carried in bulk at low cost over long distances. In some form or other, it could be sold to anyone anywhere. It only needed traders to understand human needs in all their variety, and if possible to conjure up new needs through good advertising. The more money there was in any population the more of it went on clothes.

For 15 years after the christening of James at Canterbury in January 1752 the family disappears again from all surviving record. Much later, James passed on a story that when he was little his father went – and he seems to have meant he went alone – to 'America, and the West Indies'. Other kin spoke, just as vaguely, of 'an adventurous career in the West Indies'.[16] Large numbers of Europeans, Scots included, crossed those waters just to earn a living and at this time, especially, the cloth trade was one way of doing it. Men sent by Glasgow merchants to manage sales in the West Indies and southern mainland of North America, the slave colonies, with a wage of, say, £100 a year, might do well, trading for themselves on the side. However, they needed to stay for some time and Alexander McArthur might have been away during most of the 1750s and 1760s.[17] In some such way, including a long and painful absence, he seems to have gathered enough capital and/or credit to fund the rest of their lives.

JOHN SHELDON'S SISTER MARY MARRIED JEAN-LOUIS Bonhôte, one of a family from Neuchâtel that sent several young men to seek their fortunes among the international trading network of central London. Among the network of Jean-Louis's kin left behind was the international lawyer Emer de Vattel, son of a Swiss pastor. De Vattel's *Le droit des gens* (1758), translated into English as *The Law of Nations*, was one of the great books of the age. For de Vattel, all sovereign states, worldwide, were to be thought of, in law at least, as equal participants in the business of the world. Like good Calvinists, sovereign governments should each be governed by conscience in their dealings nation to nation, aiming always for prudential balance and ever weighing self-interest and the wider good. In short and in principle, at least, a locomotive disposition did lessen bigotry.

God's creation was to be observed and understood with a wondering but impartial eye. Among the old books written in French, possibly Catherine McArthur's, were three matching sets, the best known works of the great Enlightenment intellectual and populariser of new knowledge Bernard Le Bovier de Fontenelle (1657–1757). Here is a passage from one of them, Fontenelle's most famous essay, the *Entretiens sur la pluralité des mondes* (*Conversation on the Plurality of Worlds*).

I give it here in contemporary translation. Fontenelle's philosopher can be heard explaining to an inquisitive friend his vision of humanity, in which the mighty theatre of Creation is laid before an audience of one, and that one is himself – the human individual, a mind alone, the singular unchanging I:

> [S]ometimes [he said], I fancy myself suspended in the air, without any motion, while the earth turns round me in twenty four hours; I see, I know not how many different faces pass under me, some white, some black, and some tawny; sometimes I see hats, and sometimes turbants; now heads with hair, and then bald pates; here I see cities with steeples, some with spires and crescents, others with towers of Porcelain; and, anon, great countries with nothing but huts; here I see vast oceans, and there most horrible desarts;

in short, I discover the infinite variety which is upon the surface of the earth.[18]

Was this really Catherine McArthur's book? However it reached the shelves of Elizabeth and John, that sense of infinite variety – that airy vastness, a little chill and quite new to Europeans, but full of humanity and surprise – worked through their joint existence.

5
JOHN

John Macarthur was born on 13 August 1766, one day earlier than Elizabeth Veale.¹ As children, one at each end of the River Tamar, Elizabeth Veale and John Macarthur both learnt to imagine the wider world through writing. But as they watched and read, moving into their teenage years, their habits developed differently. Elizabeth, with print or handwriting, had a way of deliberately conjuring up her own feelings, while John had an instinct for performance. The more he read the more he felt, even as a type of physical sensation, the nobility of language.

Later on, with his own family around him in New South Wales, John was to regale them with high-sounding passages from the things he read – a carnival of voices, from Edmund Spenser's bright fantasy (*The Faerie Queene*) and Samuel Butler's jaunty cynicism (*Hudibras*) to John Milton's vast imaginings (*Paradise Lost*) and the elegant common sense of Joseph Addison's essays. Addison might have taught him in his own youth – and so he might have passed the lesson on – about the importance of 'the whole Man', the integrated human being, rich or poor, who knows that there is a world of obligation, a 'publick Good', beyond 'his own Necessities and Passions'. Whenever he forgets that world he makes himself a lame man, '[he] is hopping instead of walking, he is not in his entire and proper Motion.'²

John Macarthur did not forget. From boyhood, he read in order to answer one large question. How might a man make himself shine? In answer, he 'formed himself', so one of his own sons remarked, 'almost too much upon the old Roman model'. John Macarthur's favourite heroes, inherited from boyhood, were the Roman republican generals Coriolanus and Scipio Africanus (Scipio the Elder), as they appeared in current literature, types of the Roman ideal – severe, self-denying, men of iron principle.[3] Such images flattered his youth. They looked like the Stoic model of human character but in some ways they were no more than a boyish version of the good Calvinist, who relied in silence on the justice of God.

IT IS IMPOSSIBLE TO SAY HOW LONG JOHN'S FAMILY HAD been settled in that neighbourhood before his birth, but probably no more than a couple of years. The town of Plymouth Dock, sometimes known simply as Dock and later called Devonport, not far from Plymouth, sat on the Devon–Cornwall border and had been built to service one of Britain's great naval dockyards. Government dockyards of this sort existed also at Portsmouth and in the Thames estuary at Deptford, Chatham, Woolwich and Sheerness. They were part of a mighty effort to build a navy unbeatable on the oceans of the world.

John Macarthur always read carefully the world around him. In an intellectualised way, he chased complexity and the complexities of Plymouth and Plymouth Dock shaped his thinking as he grew up. In this way, at some point in his youth he was alerted to the newly devised science of political economy, one of the Enlightenment's best examples of the way system permeated God's creation. Political economy explored the interweaving of material prosperity and human welfare, and it explained, in a practical, materialist sense, how statesmen and men of capital might secure the happiness of humankind. It matched exactly John Macarthur's habits of thought, and Plymouth and Plymouth

Dock, sites of tantalising experiment and wide geographical reach, gave him an excellent start.

Private trade in those places was booming. Following the Seven Years' War against France and Spain (1756–63) the Newfoundland herring fishery had been opened to English fishermen and boats went out in numbers from Plymouth and Dartmouth. David Jardine, a Scot, probably from Dumfriesshire, south of Glasgow, had settled in Plymouth during the war. Starting as a cloth merchant, he had prospered through the manufacture of sailcloth, using Scottish methods, and had sold to the dockyard, along the coast and across the Atlantic. To his warehouse Jardine added a mill for the manufacture of sheathing paper – paper coated with tar and used for ships' insulation.[4] It might have been Jardine's commercial success at Plymouth that drew the McArthurs to Plymouth Dock.

William Shepherd, locally born, similarly grew rich with his wool factory at Plymouth, specialising in baize, a thick flannel. Shepherd also dealt in sheepskins. He eventually employed hundreds of men, women and children, with wages totalling over £1000 a week. Trading like Jardine to North America, he had his own wharf, including a warehouse used by William Cookworthy, inventor of English porcelain. Cookworthy also sold in the colonies. By returning vessels Shepherd brought in tar, turpentine and ships' masts.[5]

Plymouth and Plymouth Dock were hurried and hybrid places, a little like colonial frontiers themselves. Trust was instrumental and ad hoc, strangers were everywhere and violence was common. Soldiers passing through fought with seamen from the King's ships, and men from different regiments fought each other. A shootout between two bodies of militia in 1783 killed several participants.[6]

Plymouth Dock's tradesmen made as much money as they could from the dockyard, conspiring together to control tenders, prices and profit. They also pooled their capital in more or less ephemeral partnerships and for various purposes, say in sending raw wool of local growth across the Atlantic and woollen cloth to western Europe. At the same time they depended on London for capital and finished goods. There is some slight suggestion, for instance, of Alexander McArthur's involvement with a London supplier of military and naval clothing, William Prater of Charing Cross. He might have died in Prater's debt. West Country debts were often long-term, more than elsewhere in England, and a trader's personal credit, or 'honour', was a vital asset. Attacks on credit had to be defended as attacks on life itself. But then the prudent trader also knew how to move on from argument, in search of peace and future profit.[7]

At Dock, talk about the duties of life and the regulation of conscience was led by a 'Calvinistic Methodist' minister, Andrew Kinsman, who gave sermons in and out of doors, though accosted, at least in his early years, with brutal abuse. Kinsman aimed his remarks at men and women who, every day, met with human difference. That may be why he spoke often about religious freedom. Variety was the work of the Almighty, he said, and in all our diversity each must deal directly and independently with the Lord. '[I]t is almost as hard a thing to find two Christians alike in all things, as it is to find two things alike in nature.' This, again, was the Calvinism of the Enlightenment.[8] Long-term trust, even despite difference, was the foundation of human society – trust between self and God, trust between self and neighbours, trust at home, trust in habits of work, trust in making money.

William Shepherd was an enthusiastic Presbyterian and Kinsman's close friend. Shepherd lived by biblical principle, including St Luke's rule for the prosperous – 'unto whomsoever much is given, of him shall be much required'. He gave secure employment, he paid well, every year he set aside a tenth of his profits for the poor and he made easy loans to young men on the make. He lectured his workers on their faith and they answered him, so it was said, with 'affectionate zeal'. Shepherd's was a living Calvinism, a merging of self-interest and larger benevolence. Trust drove profit.[9]

VERY DIFFERENT FROM SHEPHERD'S BUSINESS BUT JUST as enterprising was the government dockyard at the bottom of the McArthurs' street. It had a workforce of several thousand and it was impossible, so a guide book said (1803), for a visitor to leave the yard unimpressed with '[t]he diversity of employments, ingenuity, and manual activity, exhibited in the various departments'. Here was 'human industry on a grand scale' – a rare scale – with ramifications worldwide.[10]

The dockyards of England have been called 'the first factory-like industrial organisations' (factory-like in a modern sense). They were certainly experimental, too much so for some. During John's school years, the men who built the ships in that and other government yards held out against a new arrangement whereby they were paid for the job done (task-work) rather than by the hour. They also found themselves subject to a stricter time discipline and more careful inspection. Wartime pressure forced change and so did the Enlightenment hunger for system, but the men responded with talk of revolution. The same 'constant noise of liberty' was heard everywhere. Thomas Paine's manifesto for democracy, *Common Sense* (1776), was a runaway bestseller in Britain and America, and it gave a sharp point to just this kind of discontent.[11]

The town of Plymouth Dock was built from an interweaving of old capital and new. The land was held on long leases from the lord of the manor, and the period of lease for town allotments was usually three lives. That meant that three named individuals, usually members of a single family, could hold it until death, one after the other, an arrangement that encouraged long-term investment and subletting. By 1783, and maybe from the time he arrived, Alexander McArthur was subtenant of a large corner building in Fore Street, Dock's main thoroughfare, a few minutes' walk from the dockyard gates. It had once been the home of the principal officer of the dockyard and it was a prime site. The tenancy was worth £25 a year but as subtenant Alexander must have paid rather more than that.[12]

Plymouth and Dock were also full of new lessons about credit, currency and investment. Metal currency, traditionally gold and silver, was in short supply throughout Britain, and barter and paper credit were used instead, mostly in combination. That is to say, paper was given in payment for labour and goods. At Dock, householders found long-term certainty in the dockyard. The yard's credit was anchored in the government treasury in London and its payments were in the form of navy bills, interest-bearing statements of credit managed by the Bank of England. The local currency at Dock was therefore tied to the national debt, the vast system of long-term trust on which rested the military and naval power of Enlightenment Britain. The empire could not have existed without such a system of credit and nor could Plymouth Dock.[13]

Throughout Britain there was an ongoing, highly sophisticated debate as to what currency really was, a question deeply interesting to John Macarthur in later years. The new political economy taught that all material value was relative, depending less on substance than on how parties agreed among themselves, so that even gold, and any amount of it, might be worth less than a good signature. As one great innovator, the French banker John Law, put it, money 'has no value in itself except in its action and movement'. 'To gain from it,' he said, 'you have to get rid of it.'[14]

Merchant banks, beginning in England in the 1760s, under-pinned new ideas about currency. They gave institutional force to credit and promises. In Plymouth Dock another Fore Street linen draper, Richard Nelson, began operations as a banker from 1790. Such 'country banks' dispensed trust and credit. In places like Dock they also looked after the funds of seagoing men. Step by step, promises themselves became currency.

In fact, John Law's remarks applied not just to money but to everything that goes to and fro among human beings – feeling or fortune, words or silence, gunshot or glances. In that way Law's remarks sum up the whole story, as I tell it, of Elizabeth and John. Everything comes back to human connection and the way individuals acted together. Beyond that, it depends on our connection with our world. The polymath Johann Wolfgang von Goethe sensed that when he said – more or less – that colour is what we do with light.[15]

Not only with money but in all the common dealings of life, more and more, it was not substance that really mattered. It was perception. It was commitment. It was not what parties did but the spirit in which they did it. It was relationship and the integrity of communication. Again, it was trust. With a certain minimum of mutual understanding, value was captured and held in talk, in the shake of a hand and in the measured dance of a pen nib. This was a change with very deep implications. Fumbling as best he could at its outer edge, it fascinated John Macarthur.

PLYMOUTH DOCK COULD EDUCATE IN OTHER WAYS too. This part of the West Country had one newspaper, the *Exeter Flying Post*, and the bookseller Patrick Ferdinand Maurice, in Fore Street, near the McArthurs' house, was both agent and correspondent. A man of adventurous mind, Maurice stocked 'Books in different Languages' – a few he published himself – as well as stationery, ledgers and mathematical and navigational instruments. There was also a theatre on the other side of the marketplace, popular with army and navy men. Its young manager knew the Kembles, a theatrical family of nationwide repute – the great actor Sarah Siddons was one – so as he grew up John might have seen some of the best acting England could offer.[16]

Further off, in Plymouth, lived John Mudge, an eminent maker of telescopes. Mudge was also a physician and a published expert on smallpox and its prevention, a subject interesting to the McArthurs because John, at least, caught smallpox as a child. He carried facial scars for the rest of his life. Such subjects divided the local population and Mudge struggled against those who were sure that the cause of smallpox was bewitching. Men like Mudge who suggested other causes were called, even 50 years later, 'a pack of fools'.[17]

John Mudge's sister Elizabeth was married briefly (she soon died) to John Garrett, master of the 'free grammar school' at Chudleigh, near Exeter. This was apparently the school John Macarthur went to, probably from about seven years old. Free grammar schools were places managed independently of the Established Church, and they might be more open to experiment than better known schools. Garrett was a famously successful teacher, sensitive to the more down-to-earth needs of tradesmen's sons. His second wife Mary (Finnemore), who must have looked after the boarders, John Macarthur included, came from a family of forward-thinking Dissenters. 'Grammar' meant Latin and Greek, but Garrett might have expanded his teaching to history, rhetoric and so on. In later life, John Macarthur never used his school Latin but his admiration for the 'shining characters' of ancient Rome might well have begun in Garrett's classroom.[18]

Besides his elder brother James, John seems to have had a sister, of whom nothing is known beyond the name of her husband – Thomas Kerr – and a younger brother, William, who died at about two. Catherine, their mother, herself died in August 1777.[19] John had just turned 11. Imagine Mary Garrett taking him aside at school to give him the news. He rarely if ever mentioned his mother in later life, but it is impossible to know what that silence means. At 11 such a wound might be damagingly deep.

John came to the end of his schooldays at about 14 (1780), at which stage a boy needed to start preparing for his life's career. Dock offered plenty of examples of young men rising fast. Evan Nepean, a friend of his brother James, was the son of a leading citizen of Saltash, directly across the river from Dock. The father was involved in local parliamentary politics, so much so that he took secret service pay and the Admiralty looked after Evan. Starting at sea as a captain's clerk, official patronage plus his own quick intelligence made for meteoric promotion. Shortly after John left school, Evan, at 29, was named undersecretary in the Home Office in London, second only to the minister himself.[20]

Andrew Kinsman, the Calvinist minister, was a mentor for such young men, possibly for Evan, possibly for the brothers James and John. Lively, candid, hopeful, Kinsman charmed the young, or at least the brighter few, and his ideas touched John's on many points. He was an uncompromising fighter and yet he was also delicately self-aware, a man alert to his own voice, like an actor on stage. So, in the midst of a sermon, Kinsman might be struck, as he said himself, by 'that liberty of speech which filled my own soul with wonder'.[21]

Kinsman spoke with a fine rhythm, he wore his heart on his sleeve and even in London he drew great crowds. In timbre alone his voice must have been commanding. Similarly, it was said of John Macarthur that his lungs were a Stentor's, which in Greek myth implied a voice equal to 50.[22] At about 14, going out into the world filled with the lessons of Plymouth Dock, it must have seemed time to speak up.

6
THE JOINT DESIGN

Elizabeth Veale and John Macarthur were married by John Kingdon in the parish church at Bridgerule on 6 October 1788. Marriages in England, to be valid in law, had to be celebrated within the Church of England, the Established Church of government, and the promises prescribed were set out in the Church's *Book of Common Prayer*. One promise in particular went to the heart of their future living, breathing, tangible joint existence. The man had to say to the woman, '[W]ith my body I thee worship, and with all my worldly goods I thee endow.' In this world of goods he offered her everything, not just the reverence of the flesh – not just an honourable desire for her alone – but everything material that his energy and skills could get together.

And yet this promise was deeply misleading. The woman in return promised to serve and obey, and that promise was backed up by the Common Law of England and enforced by English courts at every level. Unlike the *Book of Common Prayer*, the Common Law spoke not of the husband's need to give but of his right to take. According to the Common Law the man had absolute authority over the 'worldly goods' he brought to the marriage and everything the woman owned too, unless some of it had been deliberately set aside for her by mutual and signed agreement. *Common Prayer* talked of bodily 'worship', but the Common Law said that even her body was his to command, short of serious injury.

Women especially had to find their own way through this thicket of contradictions, day by day, night by night, moment by moment. Then, as now, marriage could turn into mutually assured destruction. At best, even when it was loving and lovely, marriage was, as Jane Austen said in *Mansfield Park*, 'a maneuvering business'.[1]

Marriage was about tangible things. It was about the joining of needs to assets, present to future. At least one party, if possible, should bring some 'fortune', saved or inherited. How else were the couple and any future children to live? Elizabeth Veale's fortune was the capital attached to her mother's dowry. John's fortune, as this story now relates, was an army commission. On a dual foundation of that kind a couple might build in many ways. Their aim must be material decency, comfort and security for the long term, but they also had to put together what a later age was to call social capital, and the more the better. The labour and responsibilities of the two parties might be different but the decisions they made about livelihood were interwoven. A husband and wife, well matched, could give each other larger hopes.

John's schooling might have ended, say, in summer 1780. He then, very likely, took some small part in the business in Fore Street. However, by August 1782, at 16, he was old enough for an army commission. He was appointed to the bottom of the hierarchy, as an ensign, one rank down from lieutenant, two down from a captain, in a Plymouth-based Independent Company of Foot. It was the last year of the American Revolutionary War, parliament had just voted to bring the conflict to an end and this company was new, one of several raised to defend port towns such as Plymouth and Dock during the uncertain interim. Just as they had supported Charles Edward Stuart's invasion in 1745–46, the French had helped the revolutionaries in America. It was hard to know what they would do at this juncture.[2]

An ensign's commission cost £400, plus about £100 for uniform and equipment – heavy scarlet, white and gold, high hat, boots

THE JOINT DESIGN

and sword. All this John had to buy himself. However, money and credit were suddenly available because his brother James had lately married and the bride, Catherine Hawkins, a local maltster's daughter, had a fortune of £600, a great prize. It was to come in fragments over the years, as the maltster himself put it, 'for the benefit and improvement of his [James's] trade', but the promise changed everything.[3]

John's Independent Company was almost immediately merged with six others to form a new regiment under Major Benjamin Fish, and then moved to Devon's north coast, near Barnstaple. There the first and only regimental muster took place. So, on 17 March 1783, as the earliest immediate record of the man, or boy, himself, John Macarthur added his signature, characteristically firm and neat, to a list of his assembled men. His military experience this time was brief. The war was nearly over, everyone knew that Fish's Corps was to be disbanded and the mayor of Barnstaple had already written to London reporting local fears of 'such fellows being left at large without any provision'.[4]

He meant the ordinary soldiers, many of them Irish, because the officers were well looked after. As usual in such cases, they all moved from full to half-pay so as to be on call for future emergency. Ensigns were guaranteed £33.9s.2d (33 pounds, 9 shillings and twopence) per annum. It was not much – a good book could cost two or three pounds – but still ten times more than the income of labouring men. This, and whatever he might have saved from his full pay, was the beginning of John's independent fortune.

He could now start to train for his real ambition, which was a career in the law, and the bar in particular. His voice was strong, his enthusiasms were impassioned and his brain was hungry. In love with language and declamation, he aimed to rise at the heart of affairs. In Britain, as in revolutionary North America, the best speech-makers were heroes now. It was an age of theatre, and rhetoric was theatre of the most glorious kind. As never before among English-speaking peoples, men's voices, raised in parliament, pulpits, law courts and public meetings, were tools of daring and power.

Young men aiming to go to the bar might spend several years in informal study before enrolling at England's 'judicial university', the Inns of Court in London. John Macarthur chose to begin this process by reading books of law and history, and by mixing with the sort of country gentlemen who presided as honorary magistrates at courts of petty and quarter sessions. Barnstaple, where Fish's Corps ended up, and nearby Bideford, were the justice centres for north Devon, both with courts of quarter sessions. Circumstantial evidence suggests that John Macarthur attached himself to William Walter, a landowner-magistrate at Bideford, and headmaster of its grammar school. So far, then, it is fair to imagine John living at this point in Bideford, reading Walter's books and living among his boarders in his schoolhouse beside the River Torridge.[5]

John Macarthur was certainly interested in schooling. Elizabeth, his future wife, was to remember how sorry he was that her half-sister Isabella Leach, at eight or nine, was barely literate. Probably through the same kind of interest – a fascination with the opening up of minds – John came to know one of William Walter's boys at Bideford. This was Tom Kingdon, eight years his junior, the clever fifth son of the vicar of Bridgerule, Walter's brother-magistrate.[6] It was a connection that changed his life.

It must have soon become clear that John Macarthur's half-pay was not enough to get him to the bar. For men without university degrees training at the Inns of Court took five years. Meanwhile, as well as paying fees at his chosen Inn, the student had to support himself. John might hope to put together a lump sum by selling his half-pay entitlement to another new officer, or else go back to full pay, at some expense, and eventually sell out. Either way, the gap between assets and likely outlay was obviously too big.

THE JOINT DESIGN

In due course he might also have started to wonder whether it was wise to try. He had no feel for the law. His habits of thought ran in other directions altogether. These two large problems might explain why he waited much longer than was usual for aspiring lawyers. So, for four years, from 17 to 21, critical years in any life, he paused.

IF HE DID START AT BIDEFORD WITH WILLIAM WALTER, at some point John Macarthur moved west, nearer Tom Kingdon's family. Walter had close family connections around Holsworthy and for a time John lived, as his family afterwards recalled, 'in a farmhouse near Holsworthy', finding a livelihood, maybe, among them. Somehow, during his later youth, he learnt to handle some of the larger promises of the Enlightenment and it would be worth a great deal to know who guided him at this turning-point time. Some mentoring mind made all the difference to his habits of thought.

At Sheepwash, near Holsworthy, the astute gentleman linen draper Edward Bound, William Walter's brother-in-law but a Presbyterian, is one possibility.[7] So are the Reverend William Holland Coham, of Coham House, another brother-in-law, and the landowner-attorney Benedictus Marwood Kelly, of Holsworthy. Holland Coham took the lead locally with experimental farming. His interests included sheep breeding, mainly with Merinos, Ryland and New Leicester, and his efforts were instructive for the whole neighbourhood.[8] John Macarthur had no reason at that point to take much notice of Holland Coham's sheep, but he might have remembered them later on. Such gentry networks, well read and enterprising, gave him glimpses of a world very different from Plymouth Dock.

There was fox-hunting across the sea-windy country west of Bridgerule, apparently meeting at Tintagel, some way down the

Cornish coast, a delight John long remembered. In all of this he made himself noticeable. Wrey J'Ans at Whitstone foresaw an interesting future, and Elizabeth's friend, Tom Kingdon's sister Bridget, kept her eye on him during drawing room chat. '[I]t ever was my opinion,' Bridget said, 'that Mr M. wou'd make an excellent husband, if he met with a woman whose disposition and accomplishments suited him.'[9]

Elizabeth Veale obviously thought so too and by about March 1788 she and John Macarthur seem to have been publicly committed to marriage. At first sight they seemed strangely matched, as Elizabeth afterwards remembered, her quiet self-containment as against his steely self-regard. 'I was considered indolent and inactive; [and] Mr Macarthur too proud and haughty for our humble fortune, or expectations.'[10] In fact, John's hauteur was partly play-acting and Elizabeth's fortune, though humble, was not negligible. Her strength of character was less sharp-edged than his but it was just as luminous and, like him, she enjoyed risk. At the same time, there was a solidity in his self-assurance that she must have welcomed after the uncertainties of life so far.

John Macarthur aimed to fund his married life partly by means of his commission. Its sale price, whether full pay or half-pay, was set by government and so was the cost of movement from half to full. John arranged first to move back to full pay, at the prescribed cost, £98.17s.6d, and in April 1788 he was gazetted as an ensign in the 68th or Durham Regiment of Foot. Commanded by Major-General John Lambton, the 68th was currently on garrison duty in Gibraltar but Macarthur immediately applied for leave, continuing on full pay. His intended next step was to sell his full-pay commission so as to retrieve most of what he had spent so far. Elizabeth's contribution was to come from her own small property, her mother's dower. This she sold to a neighbour, another of William Walter's in-laws, for £340, subject, apparently, to the continued payment of the dowry.[11]

THE JOINT DESIGN

Whenever John's part of the plan came through they could look forward to a combined capital of £700–800, with which to start their life together, but how they meant to use it is impossible to know. Full of hope, on 15 May, in what might have looked like a shadow-marriage, Elizabeth and John stood together in the church at Bridgerule as godparents to the vicar's last-born, another Elizabeth – always called Eliza.[12] By August the prospective bride was pregnant and on 6 October she and John were married at Bridgerule. There is no suggestion that anyone looked askance at the ordering of these last two events, though it might have been different even 30 years later.

By New Year 1789 John's leave had long expired, Elizabeth's pregnancy was six months gone but still his commission was unsold. His commanding officer seems to have doubted the correctness of John's methods, the Secretary at War was consulted and in due course the bad news came. 'His Majesty', General Lambton was informed, 'does not allow officers to be brought from the half pay for the purpose of selling entirely out.' Lambton passed that decision straight on to John Macarthur. He would have to join his regiment at Gibraltar or else go back to half-pay.[13]

John had no intention of doing either. He immediately took one of the new rapid coaches direct to London. The journey might have taken two days except that Elizabeth, now awkwardly large – was it his idea or hers? – went with him. On 18 March their son was born at the White Hart Inn in Bath, after what must have been a single day on the road. Small, fragile and apparently premature, they called him Edward. Arriving in London, John wrote himself to the Secretary at War, but the same answer came back. Persistence only brought two curt replies.[14]

Anyone else might have bent to the bureaucratic will. John Macarthur would not be controlled. Authority used against him in this blunt way always brought a response that was visceral and unyielding. Partly as a result, his life was to be punctuated by hard awakenings, crises that forced him to know himself and to measure his self-regard. This was the first. As for Elizabeth, here was evidence that as a provider, every husband's main reason for existence, John was not all-wise.

PART 2

7

THE FAR SIDE OF THE EARTH

During the 1780s the most bustling, ambitious power in Asia was a British joint-stock company working from Leadenhall Street, in the heart of London. The Honourable East India Company, founded in 1600, held a chartered monopoly over British trade through two oceans, from Cape Horn to the Cape of Good Hope, but its activities were mainly in India, where its wealth and geographical reach expanded by the month. During most of the 18th century young Englishmen and Scots flooded to its service there. It was so much easier to make money quickly in India with the company than anywhere at home.

John Call had left Cornwall for India when he was 17, in 1749. Another who went at that age, a year after Call, was Warren Hastings, from Oxfordshire, and the two had served together on the company's council at Madras (now Chennai). That done, Call went home but Hastings rose to supreme authority as governor of Bengal, 1772–85.

As a boy John Macarthur must have wondered about seeking his fortune in India, but by the time he was the right age the East India Company was in trouble. Ministers in London were making it accountable as never before for its use of power in India. Service there no longer looked like a high road to riches. A deep shift in public attitudes was underway, as a group in the House of Commons led by Edmund Burke pressed the question of British tyranny and greed on the subcontinent. 'Young men (boys almost) govern there,' Burke told the Commons, 'without society, and without sympathy for the natives', entirely selfish, ignorant and irresponsible. Their sole interest was 'a sudden fortune'.[1] Governor Hastings personified the larger evil. As soon as Hastings came home Burke launched his impeachment in parliament. For 148 days stretched over seven years – while Edmund Leach was sinking into poverty, while John Macarthur was learning the ways of landed families, and while Elizabeth Veale was making herself into a woman of the Enlightenment – Edmund Burke argued about British iniquity in the East.

Burke's speeches challenged imagination. Those parts of India devastated by British rule were, he said, about the same size as the land Britons knew and loved: '[F]igure to yourself the form and fashion of your sweet and cheerful country from Thames to Trent, north and south, and from the Irish to the German sea, east and west, emptied and embowelled (May God avert the omen of our crimes!) by so accomplished a desolation.'

And more. He asked his audience to imagine, if they could, a public order, a public faith, more ancient and venerable even than their own. 'Whatever fault they may have, God forbid we should go to pass judgment upon people who formed their Laws and Institutions prior to our insect origins of yesterday.'[2]

Strange to say, Warren Hastings had been imagining such things for years. Thanks partly to Hastings, work was already underway for the better understanding of ancient India. Hastings had taken legal advice from leading Brahmins, ordered the translation of al-Marghinani's great legal commentary, *The Hedaya*, founded a madrasa (college) for teaching Islamic law and helped to start the Asiatic Society in Calcutta (now Kolkata), which built up a large collection of venerable writing.

And yet Hastings believed in 'the right of conquest'. The British won that right by coming to terms with the ancient laws of the Indian people and with their sense of justice, because in doing so, he said, we would have 'a more generous sense of feeling for their natural rights'. So a conqueror wins the 'distant affections' of the conquered. Conquest must work through duty, justice and expertise.[3] Here was a vital reinterpretation of imperial power, theoretical, paternalistic and deeply destructive in new ways.

Most of the ancient cultures of the world, East and West, included what was called the Golden Rule. In Judaism it was 'Love your neighbour as yourself'; in Shia Islam, 'Do good to others as you would like good to be done to you'. The Hindu *Mahabharata* said the same, and the *Sutrakritanga* of the Jain. So did Christianity and many others. But the Golden Rule was invented for face-to-face societies, where everyone knew everyone else almost as they knew themselves. Now there were problems.

How were even the best of Christians to hold back a momentum of power, the upshot of Enlightenment, beyond anything the world had ever seen? Surely that power was given by God himself – by Providence? If so they had a right to conquer, but how to conquer – how to remake their own societies and how to prevail worldwide with something like justice – was another question. Many hardly cared. For many more the question made no sense. However, for a few it was painful and perplexing.

This story tells of a puzzling among people such as the Macarthurs as to how to follow the logic of enormous power in ways that conscience could justify. In this new age, full of unfamiliar possibilities, what did it mean to be just?

JUST AS THAT QUESTION WAS FIRST SERIOUSLY TACKLED the British began to interest themselves in New Holland, the vast territory beyond India lately revealed to Europeans as a result of new navigational technology. There the turning point events happened while Elizabeth Veale and John Macarthur were still children. In August 1768 (at this point, at either end of the Tamar, Elizabeth and John were learning to walk) the naval barque *Endeavour*, commanded by James Cook, had set off from Plymouth Dock for those parts. After circumnavigating New Zealand, it had travelled northward along New Holland's eastern coast, which Cook called New South Wales. A brief visit to one inlet, during April–May 1770, led to glowing reports about the richness of the soil. Cook called it Botany Bay. The Eora and Tharawal people, who lived there, called it Kamay. On a second voyage (1772–75; Elizabeth and John were learning to read), with two ships this time, Cook discovered an ocean outcrop between New South Wales and New Zealand, which he named Norfolk Island, noting its abundant tall pine trees and flax plants. Such trees might be useful for ships' masts and the flax, he thought, could be made into hemp, the raw material of sailcloth and ropes. The navy needed both.

When the revolutionary war in North America ended in 1783 (Elizabeth and John turned 17) the British government was urged to make use of Cook's discoveries. The relevant department of state was the Home Office, where James McArthur's friend Evan Nepean was undersecretary, or junior minister. The American-born James Matra, a midshipman on the *Endeavour*'s first voyage, made the first move on behalf of a group of propertied American Loyalists needing a new home, sending in a detailed proposal for their resettlement in New South Wales. Matra had the backing of the eminent botanist Joseph Banks, who had been with him on the *Endeavour*, and he was on friendly terms with Nepean. However, he soon found that Nepean's chief, Lord Sydney, was less interested in settling Loyalists than in solving another problem created by the independence of the American colonies.[4]

Before the revolution, men and women who had been criminally convicted in the higher courts and sentenced to transportation had been sent to those colonies, mainly Virginia and Maryland. In England and Ireland transportation was the most common punishment handed down by such courts and the war and its outcome made a new destination increasingly urgent. The gaols were packed. Alerted to Lord Sydney's main concern, Matra said that New South Wales might take convicts too. However, failing to make progress he eventually stood aside for the naval captain Sir George Young, a man with even better connections.[5] Young was John Call's brother-in-law.

Sir George Young, a veteran naval hero, perfectly understood the obstacle in Matra's way. He knew that the East India Company was likely to block any new settlement that seemed to threaten its monopoly across the two oceans. Through Call he might have hoped to pull strings with the company. Also the brothers-in-law had a new plan, less objectionable to the company, with a convict settlement on the mainland and, on Norfolk Island, their own privately funded operation getting timber and flax for British ships. There would be no trade in either place.[6]

However, the East India Company would not budge. During 1785–86 Lord Sydney and Evan Nepean looked for other places to which convicts might go. Only when their shortlist was quite exhausted did they turn back, in August 1786, to New South Wales. Matra, Young and Call, however, were sidelined and rules were made to keep the company happy. There was be no substantial private enterprise at all and, to prevent long-distance trade, no ship-building except for coastal vessels.[7]

Could such a settlement succeed? Nothing like it had ever been tried before – the carriage of hundreds of men, let alone women, to a destination so far away and so little understood, and, to make things even more risky, with no large private capital to draw on and no prospect of any. What would happen once they got there? Where was funding to come from later on? Could such a community survive, except at vast, open-ended government expense? It was an experiment built from urgent need, political pressure, ignorance and hope.

THE FIRST FLEET, SO-CALLED, WITH SIX CONVICT transports, three supply vessels and two naval escorts, arrived at Botany Bay in January 1788, but a much more promising site for settlement was found straightaway, a little to the north at Port Jackson. There an inlet they called Sydney Cove became the centre of operations. Everything so far was straightforward. The convicts put ashore totalled 543 men and 189 women, shipboard deaths had been less than 6 per cent, the governor, naval captain Arthur Phillip, kept good order, and hopeful reports were sent back with the first returning ships.

The Home Office had looked after the chartered rights of the East India Company, but it had been less careful about the claims of the people already in possession in New South Wales. Even before the fleet left, writers in London newspapers had condemned the scheme as unworthy of a Christian and civilised people, and an obvious assault on 'the common rights of mankind'. Violence seemed certain. However, there was also a naive optimism. Surely, a scheme so limited would do minimal damage? Joseph Banks, remembering what he had seen with James Cook on the *Endeavour* two decades earlier, said that the people there were 'very few'. They might be expected to make room so that the outcome would be good for both sides. The current inhabitants, said one writer, would be formed 'into a more civil community, so as that they and our countrymen may reciprocally contribute to the felicity of one another'.[8]

Their poverty too would protect them. Unlike the people of India the people of New South Wales apparently owned too little to tempt fortune-hunters and thieves. That country, so another writer said, was 'a perfect blank in nature so far as the productions of art go'. The governor was ordered to treat the people with 'amity and kindness', leaving them in penurious peace. They must not be 'wantonly destroy[ed]', nor suffer 'any unnecessary Interruption in the exercise of their several occupations', and anyone doing so was to be punished.[9]

THE FAR SIDE OF THE EARTH

ELIZABETH AND JOHN, WITH EDWARD, THEIR NEW-born, had reached London at the beginning of April 1789. John's argument with the War Office about the sale of his commission in the 68th Regiment took up the rest of that month. In this time they got to know the Thompsons, a family with a house in London, near Leicester Square. Thomas Thompson was an army broker – a go-between in the buying and selling of commissions – and from now on he was to be John's London agent. Almost certainly, John and Elizabeth also went to Portsmouth to see John's kinsman, the naval purser John McArthur. This John McArthur had lived in India and served in American waters. He might have been a crucial advisor. He certainly was later on.

The first news of the arrival of the convict fleet in New South Wales had reached England at the end of March. It included a book-length account by Watkin Tench, an officer with the garrison of marines, which was published in June.[10] In government offices the scheme now took more permanent shape, plans were made for another cargo of convicts and the whole business of law, order and collective security was better pinned down.

The garrison had to be replaced because most of its officers, after their three-year tour of duty, wanted to come home. In early May it was decided to raise a new foot regiment as a fixed garrison. As an inducement to long-term service at such a remarkable distance its officers were to be given an immediate step up in rank, and there was talk of cost-free promotion thereafter.[11] Major Francis Grose of the 96th Regiment was called from half-pay to take command. The New South Wales Corps was to have 300 men, divided, like the marines, into four companies. Each company commander (a captain) had to find his own officers (a lieutenant and ensign each) and men.

Nicholas Nepean, the undersecretary's younger brother, was the first captain named and he asked John Macarthur to come in as his lieutenant. John and Elizabeth made their decision in

July. It was a bold but obvious way out of their current dilemma. Like so many before them – like John Call, for instance – they aimed to go to the outer limit of European understanding and to find the means to live as they wanted in England. Elizabeth assured her mother that a spell in New South Wales promised 'the most material advantages'. 'The new settlement,' she said, 'is an immediate object with government, and every effort will be made to promote its success.' She and John expected to hear of his further promotion almost as soon as they arrived.[12] They might then come home and sell out at considerable profit.

There was the thrill of adventure too. The mind-toppling distance terrified Elizabeth at first, but she was, she knew, an educated woman. She looked at the world, she was pleased to think, in a free-minded way. Blinded to start with, she said, 'by common and vulgar prejudices', she soon found the prospect irresistible. Curiosity drove her to it, 'and believe me', she told her mother, 'I shall be greatly disappointed if anything happens to impede it'.[13]

Women were starting to travel in small numbers from England to India, but New South Wales was far more remote. Nothing Elizabeth ever did was so remarkable. Nothing she and John ever did together shows more clearly the confidence they gave each other.

JOHN, ELIZABETH AND EDWARD, NOW EIGHT MONTHS old, and his nurse, Sarah Richardson – there is more about her later on – went aboard the *Neptune*, a ship for women convicts, in the Thames in November 1789. This Second Fleet to New South Wales included four other transports and a storeship. Briefly then the *Neptune* was moved to Plymouth Sound and Elizabeth made a last quick visit to her mother and friends at Bridgerule.

This journey was to take both John and Elizabeth, pregnant again, to their physical and emotional limits. It was the same perhaps for Sarah the nurse, but of her feelings at this point there is no record. Their first problem, as they headed for Plymouth Sound, was their ship's captain, Thomas Gilbert. John complained about stench from the women convicts' latrine buckets, Gilbert heard about it and abused him, and John answered in kind. Gilbert demanded a duel and, having anchored, they met by arrangement near John's old home in Plymouth Dock. From there they and their seconds went to high ground called Mount Wise, topped by a new stone-built octagonal fortress, a windy spot with sweeping ocean views. John Macarthur might have come there as a boy, to gaze across the chilly deep.

During his life John Macarthur fought three duels. This was his first. Sometimes duellists shot deliberately wide of their target but this could be taken as an admission of fault. John never did. In duelling, he felt himself unalterably right and deadly serious, though he must have known that pistols being what they were – highly inaccurate – the outcome was up to God. His bullet passed through Gilbert's coat. Elizabeth heard only 'distant hints' of this event, but when she found out the truth she weighed with care her own feelings. At first, other difficulties made the news hard to take in. Then she found herself trembling to think of it. She had only God to thank, she said, 'that a more lasting cause does not oblige me to consider it with horror'.[14]

Their ship then doubled back along the south coast and the whole fleet assembled at Portsmouth, before finally leaving in January 1790. Nicholas Nepean had written to the ship's contractors about Gilbert and they found a new captain, Donald Trail, but he was worse. Brutal to convicts and soldiers alike, he blocked the way from the Macarthurs' cabin to the gallery where Elizabeth went each day with Edward for fresh air. He was, she said, 'a perfect sea-monster'.[15]

John could spend each day in the open but Elizabeth, Edward and Sarah had no escape from the stench and clamour. Oil of tar did little to sweeten the air. In the hotter latitudes the smell got worse, while on two sides, beyond thin walls, the 'dreadful imprecations and shocking discourses [of the women convicts] ever rang in my distracted ears'. And then there were the cries of her own child, who was not doing well, and her fears for the approaching birth of her second.[16]

Elizabeth rarely complained but now she spoke of 'a set of monsters whose triumph and pleasure seemed to consist in aggravating my distresses'. At her urging, in mid-Atlantic they changed places with an officer on the *Scarborough*, where they shared what she called 'a small cabin' with John's friend, Lieutenant Edward Abbott. Their new captain was much kinder, but Edward suffered to the journey's end, 'so very ill', she said, 'that I could scarcely expect him to survive a day'. They reached the Cape of Good Hope at the end of April and there, bringing drunken soldiers back to the ship, John got wet in the surf, which brought on a paralysing fever. '[E]very sense was lost,' Elizabeth said, 'and every faculty but life destroyed.' Their new baby, a girl, was born and died in the same cluttered cabin.[17]

Except for one transport wrecked on the way, the Second Fleet anchored in Port Jackson on 28 June. John continued helpless for some time even there.

THE SELF, THE 'I' OF EACH HUMAN BEING, IS A TYPE OF globe, separate and entire. It is open to discovery just as the Earth is. In travelling to a new hemisphere, with such trials in transit, Elizabeth and John must have been drawn to make the effort of discovery many times. Hard experience makes both world and self visible from new angles.

At the Cape and again at Sydney Cove, Elizabeth had no sooner come ashore than she put aside thoughts of her babies, though Edward was still struggling to survive, and started looking and learning, watching her own sensations. As she said many times in life, sorrow and anxiety were no help to anyone. She liked to move her mind to other things. Things of nature drew her first. At the Cape, she told her journal, '[i]n every plant I see something new'. At Sydney Cove, as she said in a letter to Bridget Kingdon, 'everything was new to me, every bird, every insect, flower, etc.; in short, all was novelty around me, and was noticed [by me] with a degree of eager curiosity and perturbation.'[18]

So challenged, so early and in so many ways, Elizabeth built her own strong place from which to make sense of the world. She always hungered to understand the pattern of activity that held communities together, the ant-heap intricacy of human labour and enterprise, and she took delight in arranging the detail in a comprehensive way in her own mind. In New South Wales she made a point of learning from young officers already there. She never saw Norfolk Island herself, for instance, but she sent home a mass of detail about it, as part of a letter to Bridget finished nine months after their arrival, which was obviously meant for reading aloud to everyone interested. There might have been great gatherings at the vicarage to hear Elizabeth's letters.

In writing home to Bridgerule, Elizabeth's main topic to start with was the people of this country. Several officers had already collected information, and Elizabeth added her own gloss. 'Their [fish]hooks', she told the vicarage family, 'they grind into form from a shell. They perform this with great dexterity upon any rough stone. Their canoes are made of the bark of some of their gum trees, taken off in a particular form for that purpose. These they paddle about the coves, and bays, very dextriously.' The vicar might have winced at her spelling. She wrote too of the 'wonderful ingenuity' of the spear-throwing and the complexities of 'their language (if it may be so called)'.[19]

She told the story of the Cadigal man Colebee and the Wangal man Bennelong, their capture and their escape. Governor

Phillip had hoped that these two men, if they were treated well, might act as go-betweens in building up friendly relations between the newcomers and their own people. It had all happened before she arrived and yet she traced in detail the feelings and shifts of thought she imagined for the two men. 'When they were taken to the governor's house and immediately cleaned and clothed their astonishment at every thing the[y] saw was amazing. A new world was unfolded to their view at once.'[20]

She looked deeply into these – to her – strange faces. Daringa, wife of Colebee, came to show her her newborn baby girl. 'I ordered something for the poor woman to eat, and had her taken proper care of for some little while.' They got on so well that Daringa kept coming back. 'The child thrives remarkably well,' Elizabeth reported, 'and I discover a softness and gentleness of manners in Daringa truly interesting.' And yet, Daringa seemed abused and Watkin Tench testified to Colebee's beating her about the head. Altogether, Elizabeth remarked, 'the women appear to be under *very great* subjection.' They were 'more or less slaves to their husbands'.[21]

These men at the far side of the world were 'certainly not a very *gallant* set of people, who take pleasure in escorting their ladies. No,' she said, 'they suffer them humbly to follow Indian file like.'[22] In this way many miles of ocean, lately covered with months of pain, were cancelled by a homely joke. This young woman's jibe at the vanity of men cannot have been the first for Australia, but it must have been the first shared in Europe too.

8

EVERYONE THINKS

In New South Wales for the first dozen years of invasion it was impossible to make much money by growing and making things. The East India Company and the London government blocked large investment and every worthwhile market was a long way away. It might be possible one day to get rich with the forced labour of convicts but, as yet, it was hard to know how. There were fears that the convicts would scatter, and that 'the contagion of English vice, and English villainy, will be disseminated in the space of a few years, throughout every country, situated in the South Seas'. In 1789–90, when John and Elizabeth Macarthur were making their plans for New South Wales, that had not happened, or not much, but everything remained uncertain.[1]

Besides, forced labour, Black slavery in particular, was under attack. Within a fortnight of the First Fleet's departure, in May 1787, the Society for the Abolition of the Slave Trade was formed in London. At the same time Warren Hastings had been charged with the abuse of British power in India. Momentarily, at least, the public conscience was concentrated on evils Empire-wide, but especially on slavery, on which so much of its wealth and power depended. Even among the cynical, that added a new complication to making money abroad. Few doubted that men and women of Christian ancestry had a right to make money wherever they saw fit, worldwide, but there had to be new ways of doing it.

The horrors of slavery were palpable. Where it did not kill it stung the flesh. Imagine your own body attacked and degraded. Imagine a life of hard physical labour in an alien country among alien people, with no hope of escape and no appeal. Imagine! – that was the message now. In New South Wales, Elizabeth Macarthur tried to imagine how Colebee and Bennelong had felt, suddenly cleansed and clothed. In England other men and women challenged themselves – if only as a kind of intellectual game – with thinking what it must be like to be carried from a bright African beach to the stinking horrors of a slave ship, and to a very different land. That single question, 'What must it be like?', summed up the new sensibility. A famous Wedgwood medallion made in 1787 showed a Black slave chained at wrists and ankles, and surrounded with the words, 'Am I not a man and a brother?'[2] And again, clear though implicit, 'Do I not feel as you do?'

But then, making that medallion was an act of power too – taking that man, and carrying him, caught within caricature, into your own imagining. His own reality remained alien and unknown. It was in this spirit that the British of the new generation went abroad.

The Scotsman Adam Smith, professor of moral philosophy at Glasgow University, was one of the chief luminaries of the Enlightenment. In his best-selling *Theory of Moral Sentiments* (1759), Smith explored this new sensibility; this need, as he called it, for 'changing places in fancy with the sufferer'. Plymouth was a slave-trading port and people there and at Plymouth Dock, while many profited from it, were well aware of the iniquities of the system. Some of them were very ready to change places in fancy just as Smith described. An abolition committee was formed at Plymouth in 1788. As part of its propaganda this committee published the immediately famous drawing of a slave ship, a cut-away plan showing men and women packed side by side under deck, with room only to lie down. It was an image bound to horrify. 'What must it be it like?' One Quaker family in London, the Hoares, pinned that picture to their dining room wall so that they could see it, seated side by side as they took their meals.[3]

Slavery had long been part of Scottish notions of making money. Some in John Macarthur's family still profited by it. Eighteenth-century Glasgow had grown rich on colonial rum, sugar and cotton, all slave-grown, and Glasgow merchants, their kinsmen and agents went backwards and forwards across the water, keeping an eye on assets. No enterprising Scot could well avoid it.

The question 'What must it be like?' had implications for every kind of human employment, not just slavery. All sorts of labour, free, unfree or partly free, were rearranged under the impact of Enlightenment. The point and purpose of change was explained by Adam Smith in his even more famous book, *An Inquiry Into the Nature and Causes of the Wealth of Nations* (1776). Everyone who worked could also think. It was a fine thing to change places in fancy with those who suffered slavery. But why not imagine the feelings of all men and women simply trying to survive and do well? '[T]he uniform, constant, and uninterrupted effort of every man to better his condition,' said Adam Smith, '[is] the principle from which publick and national, as well as private opulence is originally derived.'[4] Why not sympathise, in a practical, down-to-earth way – for your own good – with that extraordinary universal effort? Why not harness the hopes of all who build the wealth of others?

This is where Elizabeth Macarthur shone, in seeking out skeins of interconnected labour and imagining the inner effort of everyone who had a part in them. That habit of mind had already appeared in her early letters back to England, where she explained the new communities in New South Wales and Norfolk Island as a type of fabric woven by shared work. She was onlooker and participant at the same time.

ELIZABETH & JOHN

BONDED AND FORCED LABOUR WAS SO IMPORTANT IN settlements abroad because free labour was scarce and inclined to wander. For a long time, not only enslaved Africans but also convicted criminals from England, Scotland and Ireland had been sent to those places to serve their time. The convicts who had gone to Maryland and Virginia in the decades before 1775 had been bought – or rather, their labour power had been bought – by settlers from the captain of their ship. It was all privately done. The shipowner's profit was the price paid by the settler minus the cost of transportation. The settler's profit was the value of the convicts' unpaid labour, normally over a seven-year period, minus the cost of their purchase and upkeep.[5]

Government made nothing out of it. By the 1780s, however, at the same time as the American Revolution, a sharper concern for the national economy threw up the idea that convict musclepower ought to be used for the public good. Edmund Leach's scheme for building a canal beside the Tamar had included convict labour. Leach had imagined the convicts well fed – coarse barley or rye bread, meat and cheese – looked after by a surgeon and a chaplain, rigorously managed and under military guard. 'Each convict,' Leach added, '[might] be branded in some conspicuous place', or else chained. They might be shot if they tried to escape.[6]

In New South Wales the governor, Arthur Phillip, hated slavery, at least in principle. He understood that free settlers would come some day to New South Wales, but he believed that when they did the labour they employed must be free. Meanwhile, the convicts would work for the public good, growing food for the public store. To Phillip's mind, that was not slavery. Slavery, for Phillip, was rooted in greed and cruelty – casual beatings, rape – while the convicts would be managed with all possible humanity and for the public good. '[T]here can be no slavery in a free land,' he said, 'and consequently no slaves.'[7] He therefore called the convicts 'servants of the Crown', but under his government they were to be bound for the full period of their sentence or until they were pardoned. And yet his instructions said nothing about that and, whatever he thought, it looked very like slavery.[8]

From the start there was another point of view. Convicts were creatures of mind as well as muscle. Robert Ross was commanding officer of the garrison, the marines, and Phillip's lieutenant-governor. Shortly after the landing at Sydney Cove a second settlement was made on Norfolk Island and from March 1790 Ross was in charge there. With a few exceptions, under his command Norfolk's convicts were partly freed – in practice, not in law – and put in a position where they could think for themselves and get ahead, at least a little. Large numbers were given the use of a few hectares each on which to grow whatever they could, with free time for a good part of each week. A sow went with each allotment. She remained government property – the settlers were barred from killing and eating her – but they owned all the piglets they could raise.[9]

Major Ross was a Scot. On Norfolk he seems to have drawn on Scottish farming experience and on Scottish ideas about the clever use of the soil. Throughout Britain, changing life on the land was partly about new techniques and new machinery, but in Scotland especially it was also about self-reliance among the humbler sort and on their teaching each other. Farmers' clubs were common in Scotland, setting standards from year to year and awarding prizes.[10] Farmers proved to each other the value of looking ahead, into the long term.

Take the piglet part of Ross's scheme. It involved critical choices. Do you eat your piglet? Do you sell your piglet? Do you wait for your piglet to breed other piglets? These piglets were like interest on capital. A similar experiment with livestock was worked out in the Dutch settlement at the Cape of Good Hope. The Dutch East India Company sent from the Netherlands to the Cape several fine-woolled Merino sheep, ewes and rams, originally from the flock of the King of Spain, and a dozen years later the same number was sent back to the Netherlands, leaving a many-times multiplied progeny for the Cape settlers to breed further and grow rich with.[11] Piglets in one place. Lambs in the other. We meet these sheep again later on.

THE ENLIGHTENMENT, FOR MANY WHO ENGAGED WITH it, was all about investment and experiment over time. This was the essence of the unfolding science of political economy, John Macarthur's guide to all things. In the field of political economy the two leading British authorities were, once again, both Scots, Sir James Steuart and, eleven years his junior, Adam Smith. Steuart's conclusions were best spelt out in his *An Inquiry into the Principles of Political Oeconomy* (1767), Smith's, as I say, in his *An Inquiry Into the Nature and Causes of the Wealth of Nations* (1776).

Sir James Steuart has a larger part in this story than Adam Smith. Smith thought more about questions of national trade, including manufacturing, customs and tariffs. Steuart made everything turn on land and agriculture, and on effort that looked inwards. Smith hunted for equilibrium, a certain balance in making, buying and selling. Steuart left room for ingenuity and creative change. What if clever invention or executive action could bring communities out of poverty or even get them started from scratch? What might be achieved by the singular touch of human beings, overseeing large numbers, judging for the long term and cultivating by degrees a certain collective 'spirit' – Steuart's word – among the people? Much the same questions recur in the 21st century, dealing with challenges Steuart could never have imagined. With those challenges comes a renewed attention to land. Economists like Steuart matter again now, this time on a global scale.[12]

Steuart drew partly from French thought and experience,

including the ideas of Richard Cantillon, as publicised after his death in *The Analysis of Trade, Commerce, Coin, Bullion, Banks, and Foreign Exchanges* (1759). Cantillon, Irish-born but based in France, had been involved in funding French settlement in North America. Lease hundreds of acres each to prospective farmers, Cantillon said, rent-free for 50 years. Give those farmers what they needed for building. Leave room among them for villages, with land likewise rent-free. Trade would gather, skilled men would settle and civilisation would take root. From executive action 'rightly applied', as Cantillon put it, would come independent life.[13]

For Adam Smith, prosperity depended on an almost accidental magic, the 'invisible hand' adjusting individual effort to meet the market. For Cantillon and Steuart there had to be ingenious, conscientious people in charge. Their gaze had to be everywhere. They had to use public money to 'preserve in vigour every branch of industry' and they had to create and keep up 'a certain fund of subsistence for all' – 'food, other necessaries, and employment'. They had to make sure that everyone rose together.[14]

Even labouring men must be shown how they could manage for themselves:

> [C]onvince them [Cantillon said] that they are to enjoy the Fruits of their Labour unmolested, and be protected by equal and universal Justice in the Possession thereof; this will raise a Spirit and a Desire in them to acquire the Product of other People's Labour, in Exchange of which their own must be given: This creates an Ambition, and even a Necessity in them to exert that Spirit.[15]

In short, appeal to their hopes and ambitions, to their energy of mind. Each governor of humanity must be overseer and teacher, but with an infinite lightness of touch.

Cantillon and Steuart were a neat fit for the experiment in New South Wales and for the time being this small world, with everything and everyone close by, tangible, audible, odoriferous, was John Macarthur's mental workshop. He and Elizabeth turned instinctively to this mind-centred method. For John it was the answer to every puzzle.

How then, in New South Wales, was settlement to be perpetuated? During the Macarthurs' first years, answers were already springing up. Two methods had already been tried. There was Phillip's tightly run ship, in which only the captain understood where they were headed, and there was Robert Ross's distributed initiative, his calculated, shared investment in time. It was an open question as to which would eventually prevail.

9
GINGER GROUP

Elizabeth Macarthur missed being able to talk with other women. At Bridgerule she and Bridget Kingdon had been bred not just to a knowledge of the wide world but also to self-knowledge, a kind of knowledge they could form between them. She loved that. Here at Sydney Cove, so she wrote home to Bridget, she had 'no female friend to unbend my mind to, nor a single woman with whom I could converse with any satisfaction to myself'.[1] And yet she also liked to talk with clever men. They were drawn to her too.

During their first three and a half years abroad John and Elizabeth lived at Sydney Cove, except for four months up-harbour at Rose Hill. Their friends were other officers, none of them with wives. Many had homes or connections in Devon and Cornwall, and were glad, Elizabeth told her mother, to raise a glass to 'The banks of the Tamar'. That was one comfort. The marines stayed until December 1791 and their officers included several well-read young men who had been drawn by the extraordinary novelty of the original expedition. They met with them often. Besides these, there were two naval surgeons among the Macarthurs' particular friends: George Worgan, 'a man of extensive reading', who had come with Governor Phillip on the *Sirius*, and John White, an eager naturalist whose book about that expedition was already in the London shops.[2]

Highly literate men on the move normally carried with them boxes of books. Some of the officers at Sydney Cove shared their books with Elizabeth and John, so that by accident or intention volumes stayed on the Macarthurs' shelves when their owners went home. Some survive there today. Watkin Tench, captain-lieutenant of marines, left his copy of Caesar's *Commentaries*, which John Macarthur must have been glad to have, and Lieutenant Thomas Timins left Samuel Johnson's *Works of the English Poets*, in 59 small volumes. Lieutenant William Dawes, astronomer and mathematician, left at least two books, one algebra, the other botany.[3]

Women's intelligence can give a fresh slant or provocation to men's, and vice versa, and the meeting of groups such as this one, small as it was, might make a deep and lasting impact. Meeting, say, at day's end in the Macarthurs' cottage of logs and bark, and on picnics and other outings, these few officers shaped the way Elizabeth and John thought about this strange spot. Tench and Worgan were especially lively talkers, and Tench, elaborately literate, lucid, cheerful, eight years older than the Macarthurs, was an inspiration to them all. He dropped in nearly every day.[4]

Tench's story of the journey to New South Wales had been published before the Macarthurs left England, predating John White's book, and he was already writing another, *A Complete Account of the Settlement at Port Jackson, in New South Wales*, which was to be published in London in 1793. He had every reason to wrestle with and talk about his subject matter as he translated it to paper. The Macarthurs had the benefit of that.

Wherever he was, Watkin Tench could not help seeing events all around him as part of a larger, longer story. In writing and talk, backwards and forwards, thinking and listening, listening and thinking, he was always on the lookout for meaning. On his return to England, for instance, he was to be caught up in the war with revolutionary France and his third book was to be about his six months as a prisoner of war in Brittany.[5] Tench gleaned and sorted everything of value in voices he heard – manner, information, points of view – everywhere. All good books come from talk. Tench's second book, at least, must owe a good deal to the meetings at Sydney Cove.

William Dawes did not visit so often. 'He is so much engaged with the stars,' said Elizabeth, 'that to mortal eyes he is not always visible.' However, Dawes reinforced Tench's opinion on many matters. Dawes had been part of the anti-slavery campaign in England and Tench knew slavery first-hand because he had cousins in Liverpool who were rich slave traders with a plantation in Grenada. One of them, Banastre Tarleton, a hero of the fight against American independence, now MP for Liverpool, was a loud, taunting enemy of the anti-slavery movement. Visiting the family plantations as a younger man, Tench, on the other hand, had been shocked. He was still in touch with Tarleton but he was convinced that whatever the cost, such cruelty must end. It may be that 'the opulence of England' depended on slavery, but what of that? 'I do not hesitate to exclaim – "Perish our commerce"; let our humanity live!'[6]

The thoughts of those who met and talked with Elizabeth and John turned also to the ancient possessors of the land roundabout. By 1790, while these people seemed less strange to the settlers than they had at the beginning, their larger secrets were elusive still. The invaders believed that all human beings were to be understood in connection with their Creator. What 'notions ... of the Deity', as William Dawes put it, did these peoples have? They did not apparently worship the sun, moon or stars, as might be expected. '[A]nd yet', as Elizabeth reported to Bridget Kingdon, 'they say all who die go up to the clouds.' 'Certain it is,' said Tench, '... that they believe the spirit of the dead not to be extinct with the body.' Clearly too, he added, they had some idea of 'a living intellectual principle', a 'superintending deity'. They felt something sublime in touch with themselves, much as Christians did. Indeed, in most things, Tench decided – the minds of his listeners marching with him for the moment – there was no real difference. Europeans enjoyed 'the fortuitous advantage of birth alone'.[7]

ANOTHER SUBJECT OF CONVERSATION, JUST AS PRESsing, was the future of the invasion project. So far that depended completely on the governor, Arthur Phillip. Phillip spoke of founding a new civilisation in this part of the globe, and yet he seemed to have no agenda for making his creation move of its own accord – no systematic idea of the way communities can be persuaded to use their own energies and intelligence in order to do well. Remember Major Ross's piglet principle. In other words, the governor had no sure grasp of the main principles of political economy. He did not seek advice from his officers on questions of government. Watkin Tench circled around this problem in both his books, and it must have been one the group often tackled too.

A ginger group is a small collection of people within a larger body that thinks at a more fundamental level than the rest. They might look for better ways of doing the job in hand. They might see a deeper purpose in the job itself. These few, now including Elizabeth and John, did both those things, or so it seems from the way Watkin Tench, calling in nearly every day, set down his candlelight thoughts for publication.

As everyone knew, English colonies were typically the work of joint-stock companies, which could draw on shareholders for all necessary funds, at least in getting the business underway. Most of the early Atlantic Ocean settlements had started like that and in eastern seas the East India Company remained the great exemplar. And yet in New South Wales the ban on any sort of large private investment meant that everything expensive had to come from the government itself. That was the main long-term issue.

In his first book (1789) Watkin Tench had called the settlement 'an experiment, no less new in its design, than difficult in its execution'. That word, 'experiment', says a lot. Experiment was one of the core activities of the Enlightenment, but it was usually in physics, chemistry and so on. This was an experiment with human beings, and for that political economy offered the only rules so far.

The soil near Sydney Cove was not good, said Tench in this first book. There must surely be better elsewhere, but even then, he said, the human material must be right. Everything must depend on those who did the work and Tench was sure that convicts alone, untaught, unwilling, with very limited resources, could not succeed.[8] The fundamentals of the experiment were wrong. There was no substitute for skill, prudence, a will to succeed and at least a little capital, besides the land itself.

By the time Elizabeth and John Macarthur arrived Tench had decided that the 'large tracts' he had hoped for did not exist. The settlement would therefore, he thought, have trouble even in supporting itself, let alone providing anything useful for export. These conclusions he set out in his second book. No able managers had turned up either. That meant that the best prospect imaginable now was scratch-farming by the semi-competent. There was a lack of common prudence, surely, in 'settling, with convicts only, a country so remote and extensive'. With all due tact he blamed the government.[9]

He wrote more frankly to his cousin, Banastre Tarleton, who quoted his complaints in a speech in the House of Commons. This new British territory, Tench had told Tarleton, 'could not produce anything serviceable for the mother country, or even for the maintenance of those who were unfortunately sent there'. Tarleton used this information in a campaign by the parliamentary opposition to prove that the NSW experiment was rash, ill-advised and cruel to the convicts, and that it ought to be abandoned.[10]

Those who waited in New South Wales, knowing how Tench and others had written home, had good reason to doubt the future. Elizabeth and John Macarthur certainly did. '*If*,' Elizabeth said, writing home herself, 'the British government think fit to continue the colony …'. I stress the 'if'. Whatever happened, she and John had no need to worry for their own sake. Their main hope so far was for John's promotion to captain. When that happened they could go home and start the life they wanted.[11]

In 1792, that hope was postponed but not abandoned when Major Grose made John Macarthur acting paymaster to the regiment. The additional salary was equal to a captain's and, on top of that, regimental funds could be invested more or less as the paymaster liked, for private profit. Macarthur and Grose were personally liable for overall loss, so they had to be careful. However, by now, at Sydney Cove, more ship arrivals created a real chance of good returns.[12]

Meanwhile, time passed. The world the Macarthurs had left behind moved on. They probably heard of the death of John's father by ships arriving in October 1791. Edmund Leach died too and the news of Grace Leach's remarriage came sometime in 1793. Alexander McArthur might well have died in debt – he left no will – and Elizabeth judged her mother's third husband to be an 'idler', which suggests scant money there too. By this time Edward, their firstborn, had another sister, who survived. They called her Elizabeth, and another addition was due in autumn 1794. Altogether then, with more children themselves, the liabilities of the young couple multiplied. They were doing well, but only as long as they stayed where they were.

In December 1792, however, when it was still unclear whether the settlement would continue at all, Governor Phillip went on leave. He did not resign and it was understood that he aimed to come back. He did not and it was nearly three years before his successor arrived. Major Grose was acting governor to start with, although Grose understood soldiering and little more. 'I cannot but be alarmed,' he told the minister in London, 'at all I purchase and everything I do, being unaccustomed to business.' He was 'fearful', he said, 'of acting so much from my own discretion.'[13] Then Grose also left and for ten months more the even more hesitant William Paterson, the Corps' second-in-command, was in charge.

This period of acting governors might have spelt the end for the settlement experiment. However, Governor Phillip's vessel had barely reached the open sea before his ways had been abandoned and everything had taken a new direction. There was in fact a way to survive, and even a way to do well. This sudden move had in it a kind of doctrinaire boldness, an echo of Richard Cantillon and Sir James Steuart, introduced in the previous chapter. Someone among the invaders clearly believed, like Cantillon, that livelihoods for all might be created by executive action, 'rightly applied'.[14]

During the three years after Phillip's departure John Macarthur was 'inspector of public works', an appointment with no exact precedent in any British colony, vague in its purpose and vague in limits. He was stationed at Parramatta, the main grain-growing district, where there was a public storehouse for produce from government and private farms. Parramatta was crucial for the whole economy, and from his base there John Macarthur took charge of the convicts employed in government farming, of the problems of ex-convict settlers, and of managing the grain supply in the store. Though still a lieutenant, he was also given command of the Parramatta detachment of the NSW Corps.[15]

It was John Macarthur, then, who was responsible for the deep and sudden post-Phillip changes. He was already in charge of regimental funds. Now he was in charge of the grain supply, on which survival itself depended. More than that, he was the acting governor's right hand, with a right, as he thought, to interfere in everything the government did. Neither Grose nor Paterson welcomed the responsibility of governing. John Macarthur, on the other hand, was bold, self-dramatising, supremely self-confident and patently clever. His voice can certainly be heard in some of Grose's more preemptory official letters.[16] His mind ran ahead of others, ever forming larger patterns, sometimes much larger. He was also sharply dogmatic. He was hard to resist, especially in crisis.

10

INSPECTOR OF PUBLIC WORKS

Officially, John Macarthur became inspector of public works in February 1793. He resigned exactly three years later. His most urgent duty was to make sure that the settlement did not starve and, given the cost and uncertainty of supplies from abroad, that meant making it as far as possible self-sufficient. Five or six years before he started, Evan Nepean, considering that question at his desk in the Home Office, had drawn largely on wishful thinking. With the soil yielding as it should, Nepean imagined that farming would flourish straightaway. As a result, he said, 'after the first year, one half of the expence of victualling the convicts and marines may be saved'. Self-sufficiency would come soon after that. The first year of settlement was therefore fully rationed but no provision was made beyond the second.[1]

However, four years after first settlement, when John Macarthur became inspector, self-sufficiency was still a far-off dream. On the government farms progress had been slow. Farming by individuals had barely begun. Those who had land were working hard, so they said, because '[w]e are now working for ourselves', but they were still too few.[2]

Even working for yourself depended on government supply. Starting up, settlers could expect to be given tools and building materials, grain for sowing and livestock for eating and breeding. They were also entitled in the long-term to convict labourers, with all necessary food and clothing. The distribution of all this bounty was now up to John Macarthur. Settlers, John thought, should look after themselves as much as possible as quickly as possible, but he also believed that in any country, new or otherwise, the government had a crucial part to play in expanding prosperity. There was a balance to be struck, continuously adjusted over time, between giving support, opening up opportunity and enforcing independence.

As inspector of public works, John Macarthur managed through a small hierarchy, just as Governor Phillip had done, headed by three superintendents of convicts, at Sydney, Parramatta and nearby Toongabbie, two storekeepers, at Sydney and Parramatta, and a few others with more specialised skills and duties. Phillip's men remained in place. Except for the master bricklayer James Bloodsworth, who had built Government House, all had arrived free. The few who were added thereafter were also free arrivals, most of them recommended from England. John Macarthur made his mark mostly in the use of the soil. The political economists he seems to have followed – Richard Cantillon, Sir James Steuart – made agriculture the foundation of all progress. So did he.

In New South Wales the area of government farming was a little over 1000 acres (410 hectares) when Phillip left. As inspector, Macarthur reduced that by more than half, most of the remnant being at Toongabbie. At the same time the granting of land became markedly more diverse and experimental. Phillip's method of giving land to former convicts was continued but two new methods were introduced, one straightaway and the other with more caution. At the beginning of the new regime about 280 convict men had served their terms and of those about a fifth had title to their own small estates, typically 30 acres (about 12 hectares) for single men and more for married. Phillip gave no land to women. It was the same with Macarthur, except that a few women were included and also some men who had not finished their terms.[3]

INSPECTOR OF PUBLIC WORKS

However, with Phillip's departure, almost immediately, large grants of land, usually 100 acres each (about 40 hectares) began to be given to civilian officials and to the officers of the NSW Corps. These were men with good government incomes, which meant that they could be expansive in planning ahead – breeding livestock, for instance, for the long term. The poor were more inclined to kill and eat their animals while they could. These larger grants were very quickly more successful than the ex-convict ones. By the end of Macarthur's time, in terms of total acreage, they added up to only a fifth of the whole and yet they carried more than half the colony's grain and nearly all its livestock. The Macarthurs took possession of Elizabeth Farm at Parramatta under this arrangement in February 1793, and John gave himself a second 100 acres in April 1794. It was good soil and about 25 kilometres inland from Sydney Cove, a distance that could be travelled by land or – more cheaply and quickly – by way of Port Jackson and the Parramatta River. This was what Watkin Tench had argued for – the distribution of land to individuals who could use it with profit.

This new method carried the whole process while John Macarthur was inspector. For the first time the future seemed secure. After just 18 months, the judge-advocate, David Collins, declared that things had never looked so hopeful. The country seemed rich after all, and the general mood had given way to 'a spirit universally prevalent of cultivating it'. Anyone trying to energise community can measure success by the number trying to join in. So, in October 1793, a convict named James Wilkinson offered to build a flour mill. 'His abilities as a millwright,' said Collins, 'had hitherto lain dormant.' Now he wanted to share in the unfolding economy. Arriving in September 1795, Governor Hunter found remarkable improvement, including, he said, with some exaggeration, 'not the smallest appearance of distress'.[4]

JOHN MACARTHUR'S THIRD METHOD WAS PURELY experimental and the most interesting of all. British troops stationed in North America before the American Revolution had had their own company and regimental gardens so that they could be sure of vegetables. Some gardens could expand into small farms. The same happened in New South Wales at the very start. The soldiers of the marine detachment had 17 acres (nearly 7 hectares) under cultivation and Nicholas Nepean's company, which included John Macarthur, had a shared farm.[5] These plots not only fed the soldiers themselves. Any surplus could be sold to the government to feed the convicts.

Under the new regime, 1793–95, this system was taken to a new level. Soldier-cultivators were offered legal title, by way of shared grants. The men of the Corps could now own land just as the officers and officials did, and, as two of them said themselves, 'Every soldier that applied for it had it.' Already the soldiers had been given the chance to become independent householders, living not in barracks, as they usually did in garrison towns, but in huts they built themselves. Even that was unwise, so David Collins said, because with a house of his own a man 'might, in course of time, think of himself more as an independent citizen, than as a subordinate soldier'.[6] Now land grants gave the men, or some of them, independence in law.

It was good for morale. It reminded soldiers why they were in New South Wales and that everything depended on them, but it also helped to entrench a hard-fisted, tightly bound core group, an entitled few, among the invaders. That was risky, but of course entitlement and violence had been there from the beginning. That was what invasion meant.

The scheme started with six senior non-commissioned officers – the regimental sergeant-major, the quarter-master and four other sergeants – being given grants side by side on the Parramatta River. Two more sergeants were added at the same place soon afterwards and then, in increasing numbers, grants were made to the lower ranks. During Macarthur's three years, just under a third of the soldiers of the NSW Corps were given freehold title, 122 in total, compared with 129 sometime convicts. Added up, the soldiers' freehold acreage easily topped the officers'.

This scheme took its energy from the soldiers themselves, but it was energy harnessed by John Macarthur. The soldiers carried over habits of shared effort typical of regimental life and in groups that were apparently self-selected. During these three years 28 groups took up grants and more probably worked the soil without the same certified reward. Most groups were of two, three or four men each, but a few had as many as 13 or 14. A few included men who were not soldiers at all – the provost marshall, for instance, and the government storekeeper at Parramatta.

There is a good deal of mystery about this scheme. Some grants were made 'in common' and all of them might have been collectively managed, with convict labourers doing most of the harder work. Within each group the men might have made any number of arrangements balancing shared effort and individual rights, but all must have depended somehow on a living, shifting internal economy, shaped by the men's knowledge of each other and by what they felt about the land and its promise.

The original site for this experiment, midway between Sydney and Parramatta, was called 'Concord'. '[P]lenty is the fruit of concord.' So said Joseph Addison, one of John Macarthur's favourite authors, in a description of life in republican Rome – Rome before the empire. In that idealised age, Romans of every degree were thought to have worked in harmony. Romans were all labourers then, said another writer, 'and all the labourers were soldiers'.[7] The experiment in New South Wales, illicit and unorthodox, is hard to gauge, but during 1793–95 it gathered momentum and it was fine-tuned over time, lasting even beyond John Macarthur's time as inspector.

There was never such a solitary spot, a new settlement in the blue abyss, where so much room was made for unlettered ambition. Where it succeeded the soldiers' experiment must have been inspired by mutual trust, patience and a willingness to take risks – not just risk with the land but risk with the ordinary priorities of military life. It is evidence of the sort of authority John Macarthur enjoyed among the men of the Corps, something that appears again later on. It is also the first evidence of his originality in fitting his ideas about political economy to real life, echoing also in this case his love of Roman history.

John Macarthur had not turned 30 when this three-part project came to an end. As a mixture of success and failure, the experience left a deep mark on him. With some justification, he could now see himself as a key figure for the future prosperity of New South Wales. The whole exercise, to his mind, proved what he could do if he had a free hand.

ELIZABETH MACARTHUR GAVE BRIDGET KINGDON a neat summary of the colonial economy during these years. '[S]ome thousands of persons,' she said, 'are fed from the public stores, perhaps between three or four thousand.' They were clothed like that too and the settlers used this publicly funded labour to grow the grain they sold to the government store, receiving in return government receipts.

> [T]hese receipts [Elizabeth explained] pass current here as coin, and are taken by masters of ships and other adventurers who come to these parts with merchandise for sale. When any number of these have been accumulated in the hands of individuals they are returned to the Commissary, who gives a bill on the Treasury in England for them.

INSPECTOR OF PUBLIC WORKS

In much the same way navy bills were issued from the naval yard at Plymouth Dock so as to pass current in town and roundabout. In New South Wales, however, the cumulative cost was enormous. 'These bills,' Elizabeth said, 'amount to thirty or forty thousand pounds annually. How long government may continue so expensive a plan it would be difficult to foresee.'[8]

Elizabeth echoed John, and it was John's great aim to scale back that cost. When the new governor, John Hunter, Phillip's successor, arrived in September 1795 John Macarthur, still inspector of public works, informed him that the officers and civilian officials were now growing enough grain to feed their own people themselves. His project had succeeded so far. Hunter took no notice, but then, in early February 1796, a complaint arrived from London about continuing expense and John Macarthur seized the moment. He persuaded the officers of the Corps and the civilian officials to put their names to a statement announcing that they were now largely self-sufficient, and offering to supply their own labourers not only with grain for grinding into flour but also with meat and clothing. Each of them, they said, might make his own arrangements with government because their means varied, but all would take any future support as a loan, to be paid back from harvest profits.[9]

This scheme was pure Macarthur. Like the experiment with soldiers' farming, it was an effort to marry diversity and system, individual effort and mutual trust. It was very different from Governor Phillip's approach. John Macarthur's habits of thought prefigured, ever so slightly, the 'managed complexity' of 21st-century ecological engineers, who look for single-minded programs to secure ongoing infinity of life. In thinking about how things ought to work he always looked less to sustainability than to resilience, less to steady-state than to evolutionary change, managed carefully enough but at arm's length.[10] That was the way he thought about education too – a point for later on.

At this point he aimed to keep his brother officers and the civilian officials together while he brought the governor onside. He had already led the same two groups, military and civilian, in the business of imports and retail prices – as we will see in another chapter. However, Hunter was wary. He and his inspector had lately quarrelled on another policy question. The governor thought that small farmers should grow more maize and he had promised that the public store would buy maize even if it was not needed. For John Macarthur that meant a waste of grain (30 000 bushels of maize), a waste of public money (£8000) and a 'false and dangerous' application of political economy. Thus indulged, the farmers would learn 'to look always to the gov[ernmen]t for support instead of relying on their own energies'. Only through being squeezed a little and by being forced to look about them would they try new things. The colony badly needed a safer meat supply, for instance. With surplus grain on hand the farmers might feed more pigs.[11]

This quarrel came to a head at just the wrong moment. John Macarthur resigned in disgust and his self-sufficiency scheme was heard of no more. Hunter had once trusted him in everything. Now, as he, Hunter, told the minister in London, the Duke of Portland, he could see through his former inspector. John Macarthur was 'restless, arrogant, [and] overbearing', and his 'theoretical schemes' were impractical and absurd.[12]

John Macarthur made his own appeal to London. For three years he had worked to create independent life in New South Wales. Writing to Portland himself, he spelt out the way things ought to be. His explanation used logic and language – economic modelling – like that of Sir James Steuart. For argument's sake he assumed a population of male householders and labourers, with their relative numbers in realistic proportion. He assumed that every year one cultivated acre would produce from 15 to 30 bushels of wheat and that each individual would consume

12 bushels. In that case, at the very least, he said, a single acre would support one man. However, each landowning householder with one labourer might easily cultivate at least 6 acres. Therefore, with good and consistent policy on the part of government it would be fair to expect more than enough grain to feed the population, and for each landowning householder to have time to diversify, with livestock, for instance.[13]

The purpose and principles built into John's calculation for the Duke of Portland were to crop up several times during his life. He later turned to questions of export too, but so far he was more interested in the fact that in good seasons in New South Wales the people could now grow more grain then they needed. How could the excess be made into a permanent blessing? His best answers were to come later. For the time being he was out of office and even the fundamentals were going wrong. The governor, unguided, gave land to men unlikely to succeed on their own and if a certain minimum of unpromising men were to waste their time on unpromising land then there must be gross waste. '[T]he labour of one half of the people,' he told Portland, must be 'directed to purposes which can never be of the smallest utility or advantage.'[14]

John Macarthur's letter to the Duke of Portland looks starkly bold but it was part of a conversation backwards and forwards across the world involving various individuals – a fabric of correspondence now largely lost. In May 1797, in London, Sir John Sinclair, president of the government's Board of Agriculture, made an effort to find out about farming in New South Wales during John Macarthur's time as inspector, including 'certain experiments' he had heard about. Sinclair's source was probably John McArthur, the Highland-born kinsman already mentioned in this story.[15] The Sinclair–McArthur connection comes later on.

In August 1796 John Macarthur sent Governor Hunter yet another calculation. This time he offered to lead by example at

Elizabeth Farm. He would take 100 additional convict labourers, he said, and feed them from his own grain harvest, and he promised that within a year, or 18 months at most, he would also take on the cost of their meat and clothing. If, within that time, he could not pay for those items, he would, he said, 'give grain in lieu – valuing both what I receive and what I give at the English market prices'. It was a plan, he said, 'founded on reason and experience'. It was also roughly a repeat of the proposal made by officers and officials at the start of the year, but limited to himself. He was sure, he said now, that others would follow his example when they could.[16]

John Macarthur was certainly free, so the governor replied, to feed his own people if he liked, but he doubted whether anyone else would want to do the same. As a retort verging on the petty, Macarthur then demanded 10 000 nails from the government store, when, as he must have known, nails were so scarce that they were being made out of scraps of iron.[17]

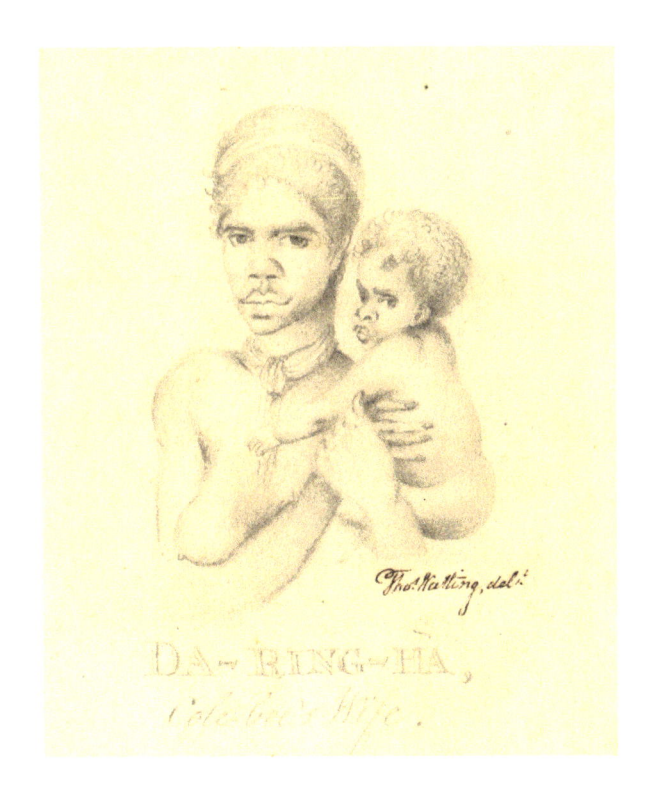

Daringa (c 1770–1795), wife of Colebee, a portrait drawn in 1792–95 by Thomas Watling. Daringa was the first of the Indigenous people of the Port Jackson area to befriend Elizabeth Macarthur.

John McArthur (1756–1840), the 'ingenious Highlander', called in this story Hinton McArthur, was an expert on the reach and power of the British Empire – a portrait painted in 1795 by George Romney.

Watkin Tench (1759–1833), officer of marines and author. He called on Elizabeth and John nearly every day in the months after their arrival. Artist and date unknown.

Elizabeth Paterson (1770–1839), one of Elizabeth Macarthur's early women friends in NSW, a portrait by the London artist William Owen, painted 1787–99.

John Macarthur (1766–1834). This miniature portrait was probably painted in London in 1803–04, when John was about 39, to mark his triumph with the organisation of wool exports from NSW. The artist, now unknown, has left out apparently obvious small-pox scars. The distinctive jaw and bottom lip appear again in John's son Edward (next page), but in milder form.

Edward Macarthur (1789–1872), eldest son of Elizabeth and John, a portrait by an unknown English artist about the time he first joined the army (1808), at 19 years old.

Mary Macarthur, afterwards Bowman (1795–1852) (?). The two portraits, here and on the next page, are almost certainly the sisters Elizabeth and Mary, painted by a colonial artist in about 1817–23.

Elizabeth Macarthur (1792–1842), eldest daughter of Elizabeth and John (?). Of the two matching portraits, I suggest this is young Elizabeth, given the less robust figure, the more lively expression, the bright droplet earrings and the roses in the bonnet. The jewellery at stomach and waist might be 'the gold Indian chain [here attached to a pendant watch] and ... silver waist buckle' listed as Elizabeth's by her mother, 23 December 1843 (ML A2907).

Elizabeth Macarthur (1766–1850), a water-colour dating from 1845 when she was 78 or 79, by the Sydney artist William Nicholas. Nicholas must have visited Elizabeth Farm to do this work, at a time when Elizabeth was relatively well and happy, and 'very comfortable', as she said, 'with my son-in-law and dear Emmeline' (to Edward, 15 August 1845, ML A2907).

James Macarthur (1798–1867). A water-colour sketch done in London to mark his marriage in June 1838 to Emily Stone. He had proposed in April, been accepted in May and left for New South Wales with his new wife in November. The artist was R.B. Scanlan (apparently not to be confused with his much better known contemporary, R.R. Scanlan).

Elizabeth Farm, the house in about 1823, a hand-coloured engraving by the colonial artist Joseph Lycett. This was before the alterations of 1826, which extended the main house a little to the east (the left). Also, in the picture the garden and orchard, afterwards enlarged, appear only on the slope to the west.

II

'A MANEUVERING BUSINESS'

I remember when I was about ten years old watching two builders making some changes to the house we lived in. Each went about his own part of the job, taking as given the other's skill and effort, each adding bit by bit to the whole. I thought then, or rather I felt because I was not yet up to thinking about it, what a blessed and mysterious condition that was. There is a word for it in Spanish: 'confianza'. I have found that sort of mutual feeling – self-confidence and shared confidence interwoven – endlessly interesting ever since.

There was 'confianza', deeply felt, in the way Elizabeth and John worked together during their first ten years in New South Wales. They lived with trust but each had interests of their own. Also, each was a creature of will. On first arrival, having made a journey that could only be called heroic, Elizabeth's mood was buoyant. She trusted this place to do wonderful things for her and she made several efforts to drive herself even further, to reinvent herself – as if crossing the world amounted to being born again.

Their friend the ships surgeon George Worgan, who had come on the First Fleet, was from a family of musicians in London. He had brought his piano with him, a square, campaign-style instrument by the London maker Frederick Beck. Even in England, pianos and piano-playing were a novelty, still slow to penetrate Cornwall, for instance. Worgan taught Elizabeth Macarthur to play, starting with 'God Save the King' and a beginner's tune called 'Foot's

Minuet', and, although she was not a natural musician she boasted now of reading musical notes 'with great facility'. This piano Worgan left with her when he went home.[1]

She also tackled new types of book-learning or, as she modestly told Bridget, 'some easy science to fill up the vacuum of many a solitary day'. In this case her teacher was the marines officer William Dawes, astronomer and mathematician, and, from her first home at the head of Sydney Cove, Elizabeth took pleasant walks to Dawes's house on what was later called Dawes Point. Besides algebra, Dawes showed her how to make models of the solar system, 'explaining to me the general principles of the heavenly bodies'. Among the family papers from this time there is an exercise book briefly used for trigonometry, a discipline useful for astronomy. Two unfinished diagrams, circles and triangles intertwined, might be Elizabeth's, but nothing more appears.[2]

She moved through this varied subject matter as if she were looking for something to match the bent of her brain. She needed to know about organic change, reproduction and growth, and she turned from astronomy to botany, a lifelong favourite, though it interested Dawes less.

> No country [she exclaimed] can exhibit a more copious field for botanical knowledge than this. I am arrived so far as to be able to class and order all common plants. I have found great pleasure in my study; every walk furnished me with subjects to put in practice that theory I had before gained by reading.[3]

The theory she spoke of came from one of Dawes's textbooks, *An Introduction to Botany* (1776 edition), by James Lee. As with Worgan's piano, Elizabeth kept that book when Dawes left.

James Lee was a leading interpreter of the immortal classifier of animal and plant life, the Swede Carl Linnaeus (1707–78), and

'A MANEUVERING BUSINESS'

Lee's book explained in detail Linnaeus's method of universal classification – his 'sexual system'. Linnaeus saw reproductive method as the defining feature of species and genera among plants. Understanding how it worked seemed to open doors to an all-inclusive understanding of the plant world. '[T]he whole Process of Nature,' Lee said, was revealed 'in the propagation of the various Species of Vegetables.' Hopeful botanists must hunt out the stamina, the male parts of each flower, and the pistilla, the female parts. The male was active and the female receptive – seemingly, a universal truth – and so the story of life among the plants might be pieced together in all its particulars.[4]

At the Cape, on the way out, Elizabeth was struck with the sight of uncultivated Africa – 'Africa in its native dress', as she said – and in New South Wales she found the same primeval freshness. During her early walks in the bush, she hunted out the neatly gendered intricacies that would make everything fit into Linnaeus's great system.

Every new challenge beckoned to the next. All these ventures – music, the stars, algebra, botany – belonged to Elizabeth's first nine months in New South Wales. The novelty she saw everywhere was part of her settling into a new sense of self. Mastering it was pure joy. '[S]ince I have had the powers of reason and reflection,' she told Bridget, 'I never was more *sincerely* happy *than at this time*.'[5]

Then there was her garden and orchard, a fundamental aspect of settlement at Elizabeth Farm. Garden growth, with its various vicissitudes, its trial and error, its skill and patience, its fast and slow, its long and short term, encapsulates the whole story of Elizabeth and John. A garden is all about keeping to a certain space, asking yourself questions and looking forward. Surrounding their home, framing so many of their movements, their garden was essential to their way of life, though for the time being it touched Elizabeth most.

The science of plants was the science of both gardening and agriculture. In Cornwall, the Kingdons' neighbour Wrey J'Ans had been a keen apple grower, publishing advice on the positioning and layout of orchards, choice of stock, planting, irrigation, mixing with other crops – peas for compost – and pruning and manuring. At the Cape of Good Hope in 1790 Elizabeth visited the Dutch East India Company's great garden – the Cape was still a Dutch possession – and she almost certainly met Robert Jacob Gordon, who was largely responsible for it. Gordon was commander of the garrison and as a descendant of Scots he welcomed all British passers-by. He was also an explorer and plant collector, and his own garden at the Cape was a showplace. Elizabeth might have seen it too.[6]

Colonel Gordon's companion on some of his earlier African expeditions was William Paterson, another Scot and a British officer. Paterson was now second-in-command of the NSW Corps. Stationed first at Norfolk Island, from 1793 he lived on the mainland and for most of 1795 he was acting governor, while the settlements waited for Arthur Phillip's successor. His wife Elizabeth was Elizabeth Macarthur's first woman friend in New South Wales. A 'love of the beauties of nature,' she said, made Mrs Paterson 'a most agreeable companion', while Captain Paterson was another keen amateur botanist, with some horticultural experience.[7]

Kitchen vegetables were Elizabeth's first priority, but for the rest of her life she gathered exotics from Europe and Asia, especially flowers, and Paterson might have advised her there. As for indigenous plants, this country, she said, was dense with 'fine shrubs, trees, and flowers which by their lively tints afford a most agreeable landscape'. The native rose, a boronia, was her favourite – or so she said later on when she was better at distinguishing species.[8] Natives, however, were hard to transplant.

At Elizabeth Farm, management was variegated like a garden, full of overlapping method, tone and purpose. That included the management of marriage itself. It was a play of wills, in which John's will was scripted to prevail, at least in anything relating to the long term and the large scale. With 1000 sheep, Elizabeth told Bridget, '[y]ou may conclude … that we kill mutton, but hitherto we have not been so extravagant. Next year, Mr. Macarthur tells me, we may begin.'[9]

Because he was a man, but also because of the sort of man he was, his feelings made a much greater impact than hers. At home and abroad, John offered continuous theatre – selfishness and unselfishness, pettiness and sacrifice, intensity and unpredictability – and yet their lives together were punctuated with moments of vulnerability on both sides.[10] Elizabeth might not have read political economy, but she had a strong sense of the way different forms of work fed into each other at the ground level – a networked understanding. A slave to duty, she was useful in her handiwork, useful in her management, useful in her feelings, useful in her intelligence and curiosity; altogether deliberately, precisely useful. She knew that in John's mind she could not fail. She also knew that occasionally he could.

In both feeling and productivity Elizabeth Farm was a type of unfolding economy. There was a shifting pattern of need, obligation, questions and answers, mutual adjustment and shared understanding. The sense of it all, the noise, the physical closeness, the smells of the garden, orchard, dairy and so on, the novelty and surprise, the disruptions, the disappointment, the sunshine and breeze felt by Elizabeth and John in and about those few small rooms – the gazing outward from that vantage point onto the world – are all long forgotten now, but traces survive.

IN ONE OF HER LETTERS TO BRIDGET KINGDON, Elizabeth Macarthur shared her husband's pride in what they had done in house, garden and beyond by transcribing part of a letter he had written to his brother James at Plymouth Dock. This was early spring 1794, when John had been inspector of public works for about 18 months. Not long ago, he told James, and Elizabeth therefore told Bridget, this settlement had languished in 'a state of desponding poverty and threatened famine'. The improvement since, he said, is 'scarcely credible'. John was much younger than James, and younger brothers have a good deal to prove. In England five years earlier John had been landless and moneyless. Here, already, he told his brother, '[o]f this year's produce I have sold £400 worth, and I have now remaining in my granaries upwards of 1800 bushels of corn.'[11]

In short, £400, the price paid for his commission in 1783, was now one part of his annual income. Livestock, living assets, said at least as much about a man's prospects and position in the world, and here he had much to boast about.

> My stock [John said] consists of a horse, 2 mares, 2 cows, 130 goats, upwards of 100 hogs. Poultry of all kinds I have in the greatest abundance. I have received no stock from government, but one cow, the rest I have either purchased or bred. With the assistance of one man and half a dozen greyhounds, which I keep, my table is constantly supplied with wild ducks or kangaroos. Averaging one week with another these dogs do not kill less than 300 lb. [136 kilograms] weight.

The glory of all that.[12]

The cow, dismissed by John as the only animal not won by his own effort, was a milker, given by Major Grose in 1793, when their family included a small boy, a baby and another on the way. For Elizabeth, it was her own cow, 'of which I am very proud'. The dairy, with the garden and orchard, were among the first things outside the house for which she took direct responsibility. Four years later she had added more cows. 'I have now,' she told Bridget, 'a very good dairy, and in general, make a sufficiency of butter to supply the family.' By this time too they had their own plough, the first in New South Wales, instead of the customary hoe, and they were also trying out white clover, a prized method of improving English pasture. Both might have been sent from Cornwall, where white clover grew unaided, and possibly by their friend George Worgan, now a Cornish farmer. Worgan loved his machinery.[13]

Generally speaking, whatever they produced was either for household use, for sale or for reinvestment – say, as seed grain or breeding stock – and Elizabeth and John took particular care in sorting and classifying. Secure preservation and good record-keeping were crucial in carrying the work forward. Each year had to be married to the next, and to the next after that. This was progressive farming. Wrey J'Ans might have inspired one or both of them in this habit of thinking ahead, and in making clear distinctions as to quality and purpose. In growing apples, J'Ans said, everything depended on sorting. In planting, look for 'hardiness' and shape in each seedling, and pay attention to soil quality, exposure to winds and so on. And keep in mind the ultimate purpose of your stock – with apples, whether eating or pressing for cider – because that will also determine early choices.[14]

In just the same way, with livestock, sorting – paying meticulous attention to quality, with good fences and regular inspection – shaped the generations to follow. An 1800 report of the Macarthurs' farm animals listed a flock of sheep, 50 head of cattle, most of them of a 'very superior' English breed, and ten horses, including six Indian mares and a valuable American stallion, all 'in very good order'. Much depended too on trustworthy herdsmen and shepherds, and in that case too their rule was choose carefully and keep only the best. Among the convict workforce at Toongabbie, as inspector of public works, John Macarthur 'did not find it difficult', he said, 'to select good overseers from amongst the prisoners'.[15] He and Elizabeth seem to have been just as adept in spotting the ingredients of trust in their own men and women.

On English farms, so it was said, 'The Art of Oeconomy is divided … between the Men and the Women'. 'Oeconomy' was an art and Elizabeth and John were collaborating artists. It was work like the weaving of cloth, and yet the law made the whole fabric, in principle, his. 'Mr McArthur,' Elizabeth told Bridget in 1798, 'has frequently in his employment thirty or forty people.' But then she suddenly put herself in the picture – '*we* pay [them] weekly', and '*we* both feed and clothe [them]' (my emphasis of 'we'). Or rather, she said, '*we* furnish them with the means of providing clothes for themselves'.[16] Title was his. Action belonged to them both.

Elizabeth said 'we' because this was her area. She was therefore central to the great question John tackled as inspector of public works. Convict labourers were fed and clothed by government rationing. How much might that be done by their own employers? In thinking that question through he had to work from calculations Elizabeth made every day as she looked into their own cupboards, casks and sacks. 'In Mr Macarthur's society,' she told Bridget, 'I experience the tenderest affections of a husband, who is instructive and cheerful as a companion.'[17] His bounding brain intrigued her, but instruction went both ways. Her system translated into his. She must have seen that.

As the Scottish scholar John Millar said at the time, women were 'respected upon account of their diligence and proficiency in the various branches of domestic economy'. Therefore, Millar went on, housewives 'naturally endeavour to improve and extend those valuable qualifications'. And again, as Jane Austen said, marriage was 'a maneuvering business'.[18] So there was a grey area, a place of interwoven decisions, of everyday give and take, which a married woman might dominate more or less.

12
CLOTH, A FAMILY CONCERN

Cloth and needlework preoccupied every woman, more or less. Also, the marketing of cloth, wholesale and retail, was the business John Macarthur had been brought up in. Cloth, in all its tangible, multi-textural reality, was also one of the great drivers of the Industrial Revolution. The making of cloth, its transportation, its sale and its range of uses were all issues of constant change. With cloth, change in any one part of the manufacture and marketing seeped in time through all the others.

There was no end to the contingencies that had to be understood by anyone who hoped to command the mysteries of cloth. Think of air. What happened in the air, due to variations of weather and climate, affected the quality of the raw product – wool, flax, cotton. Weather and climate also affected what was worn and what would last. Medical opinion was beginning to stress the many ways clothing affected the access of air to the skin, depending on age, gender and prior state of health. Disagreement among growers and manufacturers, at every stage, from soil type to the wording of advertisements and the cutting of hems, made complications infinite.

You were what you wore. Clothing was a precise sign of individual identity and self-respect. In New South Wales clothes offered the most obvious, urgent point of difference between old inhabitants and new. Also, material for cloth had been central to the way the invasion of New South Wales had happened in the first place. In 1783–85, before there was any government plan, John Call and Sir George Young had suggested a base on Norfolk Island for making cloth from its indigenous flax, so as to build up the supply of sailcloth for the British navy. And then, flax cultivation was one of the official purposes of the 1787–88 expedition to the island, second only to the transportation of convicts. The naval lieutenant Philip Gidley King was therefore sent straightaway to make a settlement there, although by this time the immediate purpose was not sailcloth but clothing for the convicts. Their current standard issue was a light canvas called 'duck'.[1]

Elizabeth Macarthur was surprised when she first landed to find no cloth being made at Sydney Cove. However, a start had in fact been made on Norfolk Island. Philip King was the son, grandson and nephew of clothiers in Cornwall, and as commandant he made cloth manufacture a leading project. He put convict women to work with a few skilled men. He was also keen to find out how, in New Zealand, Māori worked their flax, and he collected a long list of Te Reo Māori words to bridge the informational gap.[2]

King's family, at Launceston, Cornwall's county town, and John Macarthur's father and brother at Plymouth Dock called themselves linen drapers, but they probably stocked cloth of all sorts, and especially wool. Wool-bearing sheep were everywhere around Launceston and Bridgerule, and the spinning of woollen yarn was a common sight in farmhouses. The yarn might be used for knitting into guernseys and socks, sold at market or passed on for weaving by industrialised looms in the bigger towns, Launceston included.[3]

Wool grew on sheep but not all breeds of sheep grew wool. They were valued instead for their meat. In New South Wales, the first settlers' sheep, imported from the Cape of Good Hope and from Bengal, only grew hair but, interbred, their flesh was very good, 'delicate fine meat', according to Governor Hunter.[4]

Elizabeth and John had owned Bengal sheep since 1793 and as John Macarthur told his brother James, they did particularly well. He seems to have written in similar terms and about the same time to his friend, the India merchant Michael Hogan, who was then in England. Hogan had already sent speculative cargo to New South Wales and he now decided to commit himself more deeply. In February 1796 his ship, the *Marquis Cornwallis*, commanded by himself, arrived at Sydney Cove. Hogan had called last at Cork, where, under contract from government, he had loaded 233 Irish convicts. He was Irish himself and he had also taken on board Irish livestock, including sheep, for the land he aimed to take up in New South Wales, as an absentee owner.[5]

The Macarthur–Hogan connection seems to have been long-standing, predating the Macarthurs' journey to New South Wales. They trusted each other. Hogan very quickly put together one of the largest acreages in the colony then departed with Edward Macarthur, who was starting school in England, while John Macarthur kept an eye on his land and on the final disposal of his cargo. Edward was seven, the age at which children normally moved up from elementary learning to the next stage – grammar school for boys and perhaps a ladies' boarding school or some form of advanced home learning for girls – and there was nothing like that in New South Wales. Half a century later Elizabeth could still feel the pain involved in sending her firstborn into the void.[6]

Hogan's ram and several ewes were kept with particular care at Elizabeth Farm. They were all of the Galway breed, derived from English Leicesters, and they were the first wool-bearing sheep in New South Wales. Hogan had probably valued them for their mutton, but the ram was put among the Macarthurs' ewes and its first crop of antipodean lambs appeared in early spring 1796. Their bright pink skin, as it dried after birth, soon showed up a coat of tiny crimped fibres, each curly-tipped and altogether yieldingly soft, that were the beginnings of wool.[7]

ELIZABETH & JOHN

EVEN AFTER HE RESIGNED AS INSPECTOR OF PUBLIC works, in February 1796, John Macarthur kept on wrestling with the self-sufficiency question. His brain, caught in such a puzzle, found it hard to let go. To the governor he sent his ideas about meat. The settlers must be encouraged to keep more grazing animals, he said. He meant mainly cattle and sheep, but he also sketched a way of building up pig numbers. If settlers grew enough meat, including pork, they could feed their convicts with that instead of depending on the government. Also, when other sources of food failed, the colony would be better placed to avoid starvation.[8]

Work at Elizabeth Farm had already proved that diversity helped income and added to general value. If everyone could do the same, so that general prosperity increased, land values must go up too. However, in the real world of New South Wales there seemed to be little hope of that. He and Elizabeth must therefore sell soon, before everything got worse. John, at least, was seriously concerned as to how much capital they would be able to take back to England so as to justify a decade of service in this place.

In 1794 they had been full of hope. Moderate riches had seemed assured, thanks to a rapidly growing population. But the influx of convicts had since slowed because of the war with France. As usual in wartime, men in England had been absorbed into the army and navy, crime was less and fewer convicts had been transported. Here the market for foodstuffs suffered accordingly. In spring 1798 Elizabeth told Bridget Kingdon how very happy they were and yet at the same time John wrote dismally to Michael Hogan. The settlers, he said, were all growing grain and paying no attention to anything else. At the same time the market stood still. '[U]nless immense numbers are shortly sent into the colony,' he said, 'there will be more grain than there can be any demand for … As the labor of [one] man will at least feed four, what is to become of the [grain] surplus; no one can tell.'[9]

One thing, he said, was certain. The price of grain must collapse. 'What then shall I do with my farm, you will ask? Where shall I find a purchaser? This I cannot answer.'[10] Had service in New South Wales all been a terrible mistake, as with his hopes in England ten years before for the sale of his army commission? Could he afford another such setback?

A biting anxiety might well explain the Macarthurs' interest in the Hogan lambs. Within easy view of their house, these animals offered a new theme for their thoughts about diversity and about the likely selling price of Elizabeth Farm. So far, local cloth manufacture had been all about flax for the making of duck. Why not wool for some fabric just as serviceable, such as blankets or broadcloth, made on the spot for local use?

Soon after the lambs from Hogan's ram were born – the same springtime – two naval vessels, under captains Henry Waterhouse and William Kent, left for the Cape of Good Hope with the governor's orders to buy cattle. On the same ships were Philip Gidley King, his wife Anna Josepha, and William and Elizabeth Paterson, all going home on leave. As previously mentioned, eight years earlier a cargo of wool-bearing sheep had arrived at the Cape from the Netherlands. They were Merinos, a breed originally Spanish, and at the Cape they had been entrusted to William Paterson's friend Colonel Gordon. Gordon had kept them by themselves on Robben Island in Table Bay, where their numbers grew. Paterson himself remembered seeing them there.[11]

Gordon had since died, having distributed most of the progeny, but a few remained with his widow. The Patersons must have called on Susanna Gordon at her house in Cape Town, with the Kings, Waterhouse and Kent. Philip King at this point hoped to return to Sydney Cove as Governor Hunter's successor and for him wool was just as interesting as flax. He therefore had reason to notice Mrs Gordon's sheep. In the event, Waterhouse and Kent, who were the only ones returning straightaway, were persuaded to buy some for New South Wales, with the idea that they would get their money back by sales at Sydney Cove.[12]

Unluckily, most of the sheep – including all of Kent's – died en route, the survivors were expensive to look after, and in New South Wales demand was small. John Macarthur offered 15 guineas for the lot, which was a small fraction of the original cost, and Waterhouse chose instead to sell to various buyers. The Macarthurs bought two rams and four ewes. A neighbour at Parramatta, the government chaplain Samuel Marsden, who came from Yorkshire's West Riding, another great wool-growing district, also bought some, and perhaps with a better sense of what he might do with them.[13] John Macarthur's interest in sheep, including these sheep, was scant. As he told a committee in England not long after, he had taken them for their mutton, not their wool. All the same, once he had them, he said, 'I considered them as so valuable that I never killed one.'[14]

He said nothing about them in the letter he wrote to Michael Hogan a year after their purchase, though he did mention the Irish sheep Hogan had left behind. Their number had grown, he said, but one ewe was barren, one had been killed by a dingo and a third had died from disease. Hogan's Hawkesbury property also needed attention. Hogan, he said, must find either a trustworthy resident manager or a tenant prepared for serious risk, or else he must sell. Whatever he chose, so John implied clearly enough, he would lose. No-one here with land had much to hope for.[15]

It might have been Elizabeth, rather than John, who thought the Cape sheep too valuable to kill. Though the profit in money terms might well be nil, the way wool replaced hair from one generation to the next was interesting to a mind like hers. Here was another way of thinking about Linnaeus's link between classification and procreation – another way of finding patterned change, cyclical or progressive, beneath apparently static nature. It was just what Elizabeth liked.

Then things changed. Philip Gidley King, the great promoter of local cloth, who had been with Waterhouse and Kent when they bought Mrs Gordon's sheep, was named as Hunter's successor. He arrived in 1800 and the government was soon employing 30 convict women to spin and 17 men to weave whatever wool was available, mostly for ordinary coarse blanketing. Their output in 1801 was about 1000 yards (a yard is slightly less than a metre).[16] Also, width was limited to a yard because loom-width matched weavers' reach, but altogether it was a promising start.

Here was a market for home-grown wool. Fineness was not an issue. Increasingly, the Macarthurs' hopes of selling up with a fair return seemed likely to come good. Wool-bearing sheep would add diversity and value. Edward was now at school at Chudleigh near Exeter, spending holidays at Bridgerule with the Kingdons. Thoughts flew backwards and forwards across the globe. At Elizabeth Farm, as Elizabeth told Bridget, 'We often remember and talk over in the evening the hospitalities which we have both received in Bridgerule vicarage.' She hinted only vaguely at the possibility of them all coming home, but Edward must have already carried back stories of his father's determination to leave New South Wales.[17]

Expectation gathered. Or so it seems from the way Bridget Kingdon answered Elizabeth's letters now. How she looked forward, she said, to seeing her old friend again, the antipodean adventure over, and to chatting as they had always done, happy and easy as girls.[18]

13
THE MEANING OF HAPPINESS

When she had been nine months in New South Wales, Elizabeth Macarthur, still in the morning of her adult life, told her friend Bridget Kingdon, '[S]ince I have had the powers of reason and reflection I never was more *sincerely* happy *than at this time*.' She said much the same seven years later.[1] Why the overflowing happiness?

There was her curiosity and sense of adventure. More important even than that, she and John were deeply attached. But as Elizabeth said herself, her happiness was also tied to her 'powers of reason and reflection'. They had crossed with great difficulty to the far side of the world. They had since settled into 'this retirement', as she called it – retirement from normality – in a way that challenged imagination.[2]

The meaning of 'happy' has shifted a little. In Elizabeth's day it meant not just 'glad' but also 'lucky' and 'well provided for'. Happiness could be measurable, as in the phrase 'the greatest happiness of the greatest number'. Samuel Johnson, in his great *Dictionary* (1755), said happiness was, among other things, a 'state in which the desires are satisfied'. 'It is true,' Elizabeth said, 'I have some wishes unaccomplished, that I th[ink] would add to my comfort, but when I consider this [life on earth] is not a state of perfection I am *abundantly content*'.[3]

Happiness came from the close fit between what had to be achieved and the resources on hand, including resources of mind and body. 'The gratifications of life,' said John Farquhar, a Scot and a leading sermoniser, 'arise to man from the consonance between certain powers of his mind, and certain objects that are adapted to them.' John Macarthur, unlike Elizabeth, was never quite happy because he usually lived in a gap between imperfect present and perfect future. Elizabeth needed only a place to work by her own direction, her family and interesting things about her. Happiness, she said at another time, came from 'health [and] industry with the blessing of God'. God tied labour to achievement and it was an awareness of Providence that justified fortitude, and made happiness secure.[4]

In this way the trials of life were turned to good. Popular literature – plays, novels and ballads – told many stories of the trials of women. There was the familiar legend of 'patient Griselda', a woman of humble background whose heroic virtues are tested by her husband, a great lord. He pretends he has killed their children but still she does a wife's duty, 'Hoping the Best, and to the Worst resign'd; / Such was her Force, and Confidence of Mind'.[5] The fortitude of women, like the authority of men, belonged to a God-given order. Women supposedly lived for others and through their power to endure they promoted the general happiness as well as their own. John Kingdon, at Bridgerule, clearly impressed with the moral of this story, christened his middle daughter Griselda.

Griselda's was an old story. The same moral in more modern dress appeared in newer ones. Charlotte Smith's best-selling *Emmeline* (1788) told of the heroine's 'sense of rectitude' and 'force of understanding', which gives her strength to manage the greed and wilfulness of various men. Like Griselda, Emmeline is happy at the end.[6] Patience had its reward.

What happened when husband and wife seemed equal, or at least comparable, in 'force of understanding', rectitude and moral strength? That possibility was pondered rather more often during the high Enlightenment, the years of Elizabeth and John. The radical political philosopher William Godwin, in London, wrote novels too. In one of them he told the story of an ideal marriage. 'We had each our separate pursuits,' says Godwin's hero, 'whether for the cultivation of our minds, or the promotion of our mutual interests.' Husband and wife, working apart, learnt mutual respect and so they 'enter[ed] with fresh ardour into society and conversation'. Altogether, he says, it was 'perfect happiness'.[7]

All this came from Godwin's memory of his own brief marriage with the pioneer feminist Mary Wollstonecraft. When Elizabeth said, 'no two people on Earth can be happier than we are' she hinted at the same, an ideal state realised to her mind in New South Wales.[8]

IN COASTAL NEW SOUTH WALES THUNDERSTORMS stunned the ear. Much more violent and noisy than storms in Europe, thunder was another of the deeply disorienting things about this country. 'The Thunder and Lightning,' said George Worgan, 'are astonishingly awful here.' Surely a sound so vastly sublime must issue from the greatest power of all. 'Now hark!', wrote the convict poet John Grant, 'The voice of the Most High / In awful accents rends the sky.' But Elizabeth Macarthur, with her Kingdon intelligence, heard no such thing. For her the thunder was unimaginable to anyone who had not heard it, but it was only 'a violent concussion of the elements'. Even with familiarity it shocked her, and yet it was open to reason all the same.[9]

A Christian missionary, stationed at Parramatta in the late 1790s, reported talking with local officers, such as John Macarthur, about religion. He was an Evangelical, eager to convert others to his faith. His name was William Henry. In talking to such people, Henry said, it was useless to cite the Bible, 'as its authority was of no consequence with them'. With these people nothing worked except 'principles of philosophy'.[10] However, he was wrong. In imagining God, John, and Elizabeth likewise, had limited trust in the 'principles of philosophy'. Elizabeth took some satisfaction in her 'powers of reason and reflection', but they both knew that human intelligence could reach only so far. They – Elizabeth especially – had a clear sense of the unknowable, in nature, in other people, in themselves and in God.

At some point, even in daily life, reason must always give way to feeling. Hugh Blair, greatest of Scottish sermonisers, explained that however powerful reason might normally be, in extremity it easily fails. When sudden action was called for, for instance, it could vanish like smoke. It was feeling, he said, that led to final truth.[11] Thunder was not for Elizabeth the voice of God. All the same, it was proof of God's power of creation, from moment to moment in the life of the world.

There were few things more impressive and comforting, said Thomas Kingdon, the Kingdons' fifth son and a clergyman himself, than the idea of the Almighty 'in every point of time, graciously engaged in directing the operations of the natural and moral world'. Encircled in the ocean's isolating vastness, Elizabeth Macarthur had felt God close to her on the way to New South Wales. Seven years after that great journey, in England, Samuel Taylor Coleridge wrote his famous 'Rime of the Ancyent Marinere':

> Alone, alone, all all alone
> Alone on the wide wide Sea;
> And Christ would take no pity on
> My soul in agony.

However, Elizabeth's thoughts in transit had echoed lessons from the Bridgerule vicarage and from her devout grandfather John Hatherly of Tackbeare. Early in the voyage she wrote about Hatherly to her mother. 'Tell him,' she said, 'with my love, that

I have not forgotten his counsel to have ever present to my mind the duty due by us to our Maker.' And again, even more definitely, when she reached Sydney Cove: 'Tell him … that he need be under no apprehension for my religion.' The trauma of the journey had driven his advice home. John Hatherly died within months of getting this news.[12]

'Alone, unfriended,' Elizabeth told her journal, 'and in such a situation, what do I not owe to a merciful God for granting me support and assistance in these severe moments of affliction.'[13] The whole experience had been fraught with isolation and danger, including the death of her second baby and the likely death of little Edward, John's illness, and the chance of shipwreck, starvation and disappearance into the oceanic void. She had every reason to turn to the Almighty.

In her first letter to Bridget after arrival she had given a graphic account of the sufferings of the men and women of the First Fleet who had gone even further, to Norfolk Island, that far-off speck in the Pacific. After some time on the island, as their supplies ran out, apparently deserted on the wrong side of the world, they faced death. Elizabeth's letter echoed her own recent fears.

> [B]ut before hope was quite extinguished, a ship appeared and brought them a long expected supply, believe me, my d[ea]r friend, that in writing these faithful tracts of the pitiable situation of the inhabitants of Norfolk Island, a chill seems to overpower my faculties, my mind has so truly entered into their distresses that a dread comes over me, which I am unable to describe, but it is succeeded by so firm a reliance on the merciful dispensations of an Almighty, whose hand I think we may here trace without presumption; that I can only admire in silence.[14]

Here is the innermost Elizabeth, drawn to the surface by shared terror. She was intrigued as usual with her own feelings but she found those feelings infected by the fears of others. A suddenly connecting magic chilled her, but once again the story ended with safety under God.

THAT WORD 'ADMIRE' – 'I CAN ONLY ADMIRE IN SILENCE' – holds a world of mystery. For Elizabeth, it implied then a mix of fear and attraction hard to grasp in later days. Admiration drew her towards the mighty and infinite, and in apprehensive wonder her soul was overwhelmed. Scientific learning was an aid to reason but at the same time, as her botany textbook told her, the more we learn the harder it is to avoid 'admiring the Creator in his wonderful Creation'.[15] Admiration of that sort made us better men and women.

Admiration might make religious ceremony almost redundant. Elizabeth and John married during her first pregnancy, and with all their babies, one after another, they saw no urgency in christening. Edward, poised over the grave, was two before he was christened. So was James, born in 1798. And yet their children were all taught to know God – the Kingdons' God and John Hatherly's God – and to pray, especially at bedtime.[16]

God's power, said Tom Kingdon, was beyond 'any thing that we can imagine'. It followed from that that we must admire it by any means we can, and there could be no singular and perfect method. '[T]he body is one,' he said, 'and hath many members.' At Plymouth Dock, Andrew Kinsman, the Calvinist, had said the same. Some ways of worship might be more 'reasonable' than others but none was supremely true. '[T]he human mind,' wrote James Anderson, a Scottish luminary like Hugh Blair and John Farquhar, 'is radically the same in all nations.' That disruptive notion, that new conception of mind, had reached New South

Wales with the invaders. All peoples worldwide, said Watkin Tench, 'shall one day ... be assembled before the "living throne", of a common Father'.[17]

When Elizabeth agreed to go to New South Wales she was driven by the conviction that God could carry his blessings everywhere. 'The same Providence,' she told her mother, 'will watch over and protect us there as here.' The voyage was painful, lonely and dangerous, but from such risk, successfully negotiated, sprang a sense of deep renewal and in three years more Elizabeth could say, 'I thank God we enjoy all the comfort we could desire.' Thanking and admiring God was part of happiness as she understood it.[18]

TOM KINGDON WROTE HIS OWN SERMONS. HIS ELDER brother John, also a clergymen but not as clever as Tom, did not. Like most clergy, in preaching John Kingdon cut and pasted from the published sermons of others. His favourites included Hugh Blair, the most popular sermoniser of his day, and George Carr, an Englishman with an Episcopal (Anglican) congregation at Edinburgh.[19] Echoing these two, John Kingdon told his flock that happiness came from the understanding that, under God, our lives were in our own hands. 'All the advantages of nature or of fortune ... are ... intrusted to our management.' '[A]ttention, industry and a due cultivation of our minds' are therefore among the necessary tasks of life. While we live they ought to be second nature. Expect happiness as a result, he said – he was mouthing George Carr at this moment – 'in proportion to the measure of our virtue, and the improvement of our talents'.[20]

With this agenda – 'attention, industry and a due cultivation of our minds' – Elizabeth and John put down roots in New South Wales, even from the moment of arrival. After only eight years, thinking of their return to England, Elizabeth spoke of a lasting connection with this place. When she said this, they had four children, Edward, Elizabeth, John and Mary, and she was pregnant with James. Learning of England, one after the other, each imagined it as a place of perfection. '[T]he little creatures all speak of going home … with rapture', but she was sure they would think differently when they had lived in both countries, as she had done. 'I shall much wonder', she said, 'if some of them make not this place the object of their choice.'[21]

Some of the invaders had wondered from the start at the ways in which the ancient owners had come to terms with their own physical environment, adapting what they found about them to human need. The babies of the Eora were wrapped in a curiously soft paperbark, 'a kind of mantle', Elizabeth said, 'not much known in England I fancy'. 'Some of their manufactures,' said Watkin Tench, 'display ingenuity, when the rude tools with which they work, and their celerity of execution, are considered.' The shafts of their fish-gigs and spears, he went on, were made from the long shoot rising from the heart of the local grass trees, barbed with kangaroo bone or the stingray's 'prickle'. With the same sort of detail Bennelong of the Eora explained, so Tench said, 'all the details of his family economy'.[22] So Bennelong spelt out the method of his own happiness.

Ultimately, of course, happiness must be beyond explanation. For the invaders, Bennelong's certainly was. Elizabeth was happy in a difficult place, far from all the friends and familiarity of her early life. Something about its very remoteness and its newness to European knowledge touched her deeply. She did not enjoy bustle. Living at Elizabeth Farm, she even avoided Sydney if she could. She loved her visitors, as messengers from beyond, possibly for the way they confirmed her isolation – her self-sufficiency. As a child she had belonged to no particular spot, no single household. Now, she thanked God, she did.

PART 3

14

TRUST AND LACK OF TRUST

Among the great questions of the European Enlightenment, perhaps the most vexed in terms of everyday life was the question of trust. During the lives of Elizabeth and John few things were talked and fussed over more. Trust, private and public, trust among honourable enemies, trust among friends, trust in trade, trust in the workplace, trust between governments and people, seemed to be the rock on which everything worthwhile rested, so that without it all failed. '[W]here men act without regard to fixed principles,' – principles that others could rely on – so John said, 'and make expediency alone the rule of their conduct it is impossible to say what they may or may not do.'[1]

Self-discipline filled the house at Elizabeth Farm. Mutual trust penetrated the corners and pervaded the air. It was a type of spiritual geometry, reflected in the precise and settled form of gardens, orchards, crops and livestock.[2] The Macarthurs' 'very good order', as Governor King called it, was a thing of enormous power. Elizabeth never tried to take its magic beyond home territory. John did, with a brilliance fumbling and visionary, naive and acute.

In dealing with the unprincipled and untrustworthy, John Macarthur told John Piper, our best weapon is confidence in ourselves. Inner strength was all, and John Macarthur was proud of the way he marshalled his own thoughts, avoiding pain and pointlessness. Physical pain, he said to Elizabeth, 'you know I do not mind'. In Bridgerule, according to Elizabeth, people had thought he was 'haughty'. It was to be the same in New South Wales and he was hated for it. He drew intense loyalty, especially from among the soldiers, but to many his gaze seemed cold. A 20th-century historian once referred to him as 'that strange genius'. He knew he was strange.[3] In his mid and late twenties, step by step, discovering himself, John Macarthur made his instincts match his circumstances, feeling his way by trial and error, and at the same time feeding his ego – adjusting as best he could to the continent without, and laying deeper claim to the continent within.

John Macarthur spent 22 years as an army officer, joining at 16 and resigning at 38. More than a third of that time he spent on half-pay or on leave, and during most of the rest he was also an active farmer and, for three years, inspector of public works. From his first commissioning in 1782 to his transfer to the NSW Corps and finally his resignation in 1804, he never saw military life as an end in itself. It started as a way of putting together money to fund his real ambitions. It ended when new income was assured. Someone – probably William Balmain, principal surgeon – said that John Macarthur had the spirit of a soldier but lacked a soldier's circumspection.[4] That was always true.

All the same, soldierly spirit, individual and shared, meant a good deal for his sense of who he was. John Macarthur was deeply interested in the way soldiers identified with each other and in the way an officer such as himself could be part of that bond. For a while these were the questions that obsessed him almost more than any other.

He took a strong line in making sure that his men had their entitlements and more. Twice on the way from England, on the *Neptune*, he had started arguments on the soldiers' behalf about their rations. '[T]he sergeant,' Elizabeth said, 'complained to him of an attempt made to cheat him of several pounds of the men's allowance of meat, which he had scarcely heard when the chief mate of the ship (who was close by) exclaimed he was a d[amne]d rascal.' Macarthur's retort was quick. '[He] told the mate with some severity that the sergeant would do well to punish him for his insolence.'[5] Such interventions, sincerely angry, sometimes risky, were bound to make an impression on the men.

While John Macarthur was inspector of public works it must have seemed to the soldiers that the settlement belonged to them. Their officers were in charge, convicts were ordered to give way to soldiers and, against all precedent, they were offered legal title to land of their own. 'Every soldier that applied for it had it.'[6] Just as telling, John Macarthur gave the soldiers an ongoing drama they could make their own. The lead role was his. He was a disciplinarian and he made that obvious, but he also told them what they wanted to hear, that the Corps was a law unto itself, and that they could look to him as that law's interpreter.

Very obviously and with deep conviction, he acted out the role of a morally upright man, master of all he touched, orderly, prosperous, and standing for a code of personal honour beyond the civil power. He also exposed, very often, a little of the delicate underside of self, as the best drama and the most effective kind of instruction always do.

The Corps' position was peculiar and fragile. Their isolation was extreme and long-term. In England, medical specialists worried about 'nostalgia' – the name they gave to the suffering of soldiers forced to serve for long periods far from home. Remote British outposts were usually staffed by a succession of regiments, so as to limit the risk, and yet the men of the NSW Corps had been sent to this extraordinary place for life.[7] In the circumstances it was surprising how orderly they were. John Macarthur might have taken some credit for that.

OTHERWISE, TRUST WAS UNCERTAIN IN NEW SOUTH Wales. Men and women, banished from their homes and families and taken under guard to the ends of the earth, carried in conditions usually associated with slavery, endlessly telling each other to fear the worst, were not likely to trust those they held responsible. Also, apart from Governor Phillip and the chaplain, Richard Johnson, it is not likely that anyone in authority did much to win them over.

Trust and the lack of trust affected survival. During the first years of invasion and settlement, trust of some sort was obviously urgent and the officers of the garrison and the civilian officials, together referred to as the 'officers of the settlement', made some effort to keep it up. In Governor Phillip's time the supply of food and clothing had been a crisis question and in tackling it Phillip had consulted with these gentlemen, individually and as a body. They met, for instance, in April 1790 when the food situation was at its worst. From December 1792, when Phillip left, the NSW Corps was in charge. However, with respect to questions affecting general survival, military and civilian officers continued in uneasy partnership, with John Macarthur, as paymaster, and John Palmer, as commissary, speaking for each group. Three years later – but it is a story I have told already – at the end of John Macarthur's time as inspector of public works, came the proof of their success, when the 'officers of the settlement', both military and civilian, proposed to Governor Hunter that they start supplying their own convict servants with food and clothing.

The only other means of survival apart from growing their own was buying from abroad. The 'officers of the settlement', military and civilian, cooperated there too. The most effective method of import involved the NSW Corps using its government credit. In each British regiment, wherever it was, the paymaster managed the fund voted by parliament for its support. As capital he and his fellow officers could invest it as they liked, though they were liable for losses. John Macarthur was paymaster of the Corps, keeping accounts with its London agent, Cox and Greenwood. John Palmer and other civilians were also part of the importing effort and Palmer's contribution seems to have been crucial. During 1792–94, though the officers of the Corps were now the public face of government, they and the civilian officials together used more than £16 000 of Corps funds in this way, bringing in supplies from abroad.[8]

In doing so, they made use of the storeship and whaler *Britannia*, sending it under charter to the Cape and Bengal for livestock and goods. Governor Phillip had authorised this arrangement towards the end of his time, and he had also set up a 'market house' at Sydney Cove and established a mark-up limit of 100 per cent. High mark-ups were unavoidable when payment, or the real value of payment, was uncertain and few markets anywhere in the world were as uncertain as this one. Even honest buyers could not be trusted to repay. Coin hardly existed and small payments were made or promised in kind, such as food or drink, or by scribbled notes acknowledging debt. Value itself was hard to pin down. Phillip's 100 per cent (double wholesale cost) was many times more than the highest English rates but then the Corps' chances of getting its money back was many times more doubtful. Underpinning everything was the paymaster's credit, via the London agent, with the British treasury.[9]

There was another problem, less often mentioned. No-one could doubt that the local government had a right to grant land. The King's instructions and various administrative arrangements made that clear. It was much more doubtful whether it had any control over buying and selling – interfering, that is, with the property dealings of free men and women. As far back as 1786–87, when planning started, there had been doubts about the legal underpinning of government in New South Wales. These doubts continued into the 1790s and beyond. On Norfolk Island in

1794 Philip Gidley King wondered out loud whether men and women who had served their term and stayed on were still, strictly speaking, under the law.[10] The same question returned with a vengeance on the mainland under Governor Bligh, 1806–08.

As a result, there was reason to hesitate in pushing government control over import and distribution. Phillip had taken strong action but he had done so in a time of genuine emergency. Also, in Phillip's time wholesale and retail had been merged, so that everything was fairly simple. Post-Phillip, business boomed, more and more convicts finished their term, population multiplied and questions about the reach of government became far more challenging. Now, every wholesale purchase, having been negotiated with ships' captains, was divided up by the 'officers of the settlement' in prearranged shares, and after that, every officer sold his share as he liked through convict and ex-convict dealers, who quickly multiplied. Profit at wholesale, or promised profit, seems to have been kept at Phillip's 100 per cent, but profit at retail was now added, and at both stages mark-up was swollen by greed as much as by prudence. The joint burden was borne by the helpless consumer.[11]

A sailor on the *Britannia*, Robert Murray – he was apparently 17 when he arrived – was shocked by what he saw of the officers' 'meanness'. He meant especially the officers of the Corps. In the privacy of his journal he took them to task. To the poor, he said, 'you owe your all! And can you thus persecute your fellow creatures; Can you thus debase human nature? Ask yourself by what means did I become possessed of the property I have? Conscience will answer you – if you have any.' In Europe at just this time grain monopolies and high prices were a serious grievance among the poor, causing riots in England and revolution in France. When Murray talked about propertied people owing their all to the poor he was using the radical language of the time.[12]

Murray thought that all the officers of the Corps were to blame – 'I know not of any exception' – but that is questionable. Evidence is scanty. He also noted that every one of them lived with 'a prostitute, and illegitimate offspring', and yet John Macarthur was one obvious exception. The officers were not all the same. In terms of ethical respectability they differed among themselves. '[S]everal,' according to William Balmain, who knew much more about it than Murray, were 'low bred ignorant men' and some were 'young and inexperienced', but some, he implied, were neither.[13] They might well have varied in the way they chose to buy and sell.

As for John Macarthur, despite 200 years of guessing, there is no good evidence either way. John's favourite play, William Shakespeare's *Coriolanus*, seems to have been for him a kind of philosophical text. In it the hero is advised by his mother Volumnia to live through a combination of 'Honour and Policy', and this was John's rule too.[14] Policy might involve playing on the weakness of others, using unfair advantage, as with conflicts of interest, and occasional bribery. Honour meant physical and moral courage, keeping your word and paying your debts, whatever the rank and condition of the other party. It involved a strong sense of long-term justice. As he had obviously learnt at Plymouth Dock, it did not include taking shortcuts with money.

The officers' control of wholesale buying lasted about two years. By then the worst crisis had passed. Convict and ex-convict dealers, gathering wealth, were pushing them aside, and ships' captains began to see that they could make more money by dealing directly with such men, who sold incoming cargoes at public auction. Simeon Lord, who had been transported for stealing muslin and calico in bulk, was one of the first auctioneers and before long he and his connections dominated the trade.[15]

This was not a happy outcome for the men and women who were the end-consumers, including small ex-convict settlers. The dealers also worked as middlemen, buying up the settlers' grain at low prices and delivering it to corrupt government storekeepers for as much as they could get. As a result many settlers fell into disabling debt. In 1796 the 'officers of the settlement', once again military and civilian, made an effort to take back control by combining against the ex-convicts in the purchase of supplies from three ships from Calcutta, possibly by arrangement beforehand with the captains.[16] One of these vessels was the *Marquis Cornwallis*, on which Michael Hogan, owner and captain, also brought the fine-wooled sheep that ended up on Elizabeth Farm.

Michael Hogan was particularly close to David Collins, the settlement's judge-advocate. Besides his judicial duties Collins did a good deal of the background work of government and as long as he stayed in New South Wales (1788–96) he helped in knitting together something like a fabric of trust. Collins took an interest in Hogan's fortunes, and it might have been mainly thanks to him, Collins, that these various cargoes were kept out of the dealers' hands. With the *Cornwallis*, and possibly the other two, onselling to retailers had to be authorised by John Palmer, John Macarthur or some senior officer of the Corps.[17]

Their purpose, according to Collins, was to prevent the 'unjust and unreasonable prices' currently paid by settlers, and there was talk of Hogan organising regular supplies from England on the same basis. Collins helped him to a waterside lease, suitable for a wharf and warehouse, and John Macarthur became his agent on the spot. Governor Hunter was persuaded to agree, and Collins hoped that the British government might take the business further by subsidising freight, as the East India Company did with its shop on St Helena, in the mid-Atlantic. So, he said, they could hope not only for lower prices but also for quality goods from home instead of 'the sweepings of the Indian bazars'.[18]

The British government, mindful, perhaps, of the East India Company's trade monopoly in the Pacific and Indian oceans, vetoed this scheme, or else Hogan changed his mind. Instead, the small settlers themselves made an effort to get around the ex-convict dealers – the 'opulent traders', as Collins called them – by forming their own cooperative, which might buy on their behalf at the water's edge. This effort collapsed before it could achieve anything. However, the 'officers of the settlement' then straightaway stepped in themselves.[19]

This was their last try. Elizabeth Macarthur explained it to Bridget Kingdon. 'The officers in the colony,' she said, 'with a few others possessed of money or credit in England' acted to prevent 'impositions'. William Balmain and John Macarthur put together a written agreement, signed by the officers of the Corps, civilian officials and others. In it the signatories committed themselves to buying cargoes as a group, with a self-imposed ban on any one of them taking articles the group had rejected. With a newly appointed agent in Calcutta, in August and September the Corps alone, from their shared fund, committed over £15 000 to this scheme, by far their biggest outlay so far.[20]

The *Hunter*, with their first and largest cargo, arrived in Sydney Cove in January 1800. According to a passenger on board, it found general shortage, high prices and a few individuals making themselves rich. Now, to some extent at least, prices came down. The dealers had been giving as much as 50 shillings a gallon for rum, which the settlers used to pay wages, and selling it on with considerable interest. The officers gave the *Hunter*'s captain only 8 shillings. However, the end result was mixed. How much sale and resale happened between the unloading of the rum and its final bibulation it is impossible to say, but the eventual retail prices, according to the smaller settlers, were 20 shillings or even 60 – far from cheap.[21]

Nothing can be more fragile than the reputation of a cartel, well intentioned or not. In this case, the smaller settlers only saw their rich neighbours joining the dealers in cruel exploitation, with

John Macarthur and William Balmain as extortioners-in-chief. The latter, offended, as they said, by these 'unfounded charges', brought their scheme to a sudden end, but nothing could prevent the small farmers' suspicions passing intact to posterity.[22] Trust could be engineered at the officer level. It could not exist between the officers and the suffering poor.

15

1801, A GATEWAY YEAR

With John Hunter's arrival as governor late in 1795 – noted in a previous chapter – the military men had ceased to be supreme in New South Wales. Civilian magistrates had been appointed and the soldiers found their special standing undermined. There were a few reactionary explosions. In February 1796 a group of soldiers destroyed the house of John Baughan, carpenter and millwright, on Dawes Point, Sydney Cove. Several were ex-convicts newly enlisted and Baughan heard one, who had been his servant, libelling him. As payback he took the man's unattended firearm and handed it in, and revenge followed with an attack on him, his wife and his home.[1]

This group were from John Macarthur's company and John, on hearing about it, sent Baughan an apology on the soldiers' behalf and offered reparation. Baughan agreed – Mary Baughan thought he would be murdered otherwise – and withdrew the criminal charge he had made against the men. The matter might have rested there except that William Balmain, who was one of the new civil magistrates, told Baughan that if he overlooked the crime he would be breaking the law himself.[2]

Balmain appeared in the last chapter, cooperating with John Macarthur on imports. That was in 1798. The trouble with Baughan and the soldiers occurred two years before that, when Macarthur and Balmain were not on good terms. Balmain received a letter, one of John Macarthur's high-sounding compositions, accusing him of 'shamefully malevolent interference' in the business of the Corps. Ostensibly, it was from the officers as a whole and Balmain confronted them head-on. He had a high regard, he said, for some of them but Captain Macarthur he challenged to a duel. The officers, again through their ventriloquist, told him they would fight him one by one, 'untill there is not one left'. Balmain, bullied into submission, could only say that he would 'maintain to his last breath the character of a gentleman in defyance of every unmanly mode of detraction that Mr McArthur is capable of using', and the two agreed to peace.[3] After that they fell back into a kind of mutual respect.

There was an echo of the same thing, again in 1796, with Richard Atkins, another of the new magistrates. Atkins was the well-read, high-minded son of a Buckinghamshire baronet, but he was also childishly incompetent with money, plagued by debt and addicted to drink.

Several months after the Balmain episode Atkins wrote as a magistrate to John Macarthur, notifying him that his soldiers were taking vegetables from the government garden at Parramatta. He sent the name of the latest offender, suggesting forgiveness. Another soldier, he said, he had let go. John Macarthur asked for the second name – 'It was never my practice to conceal fraud or to screen offenders' – but Atkins refused to give it because he had promised forgiveness. Again, military order clashed with the restored civilian government. John Macarthur called this response 'a gross insult to me in the execution of my duty'.[4]

He complained to the governor but this time it was his opponent who took steps to finalise their quarrel. Richard Atkins tried to provoke a duel by sending John Macarthur the most insulting letter he could manage. Atkins was about to take over as acting judge-advocate and he wanted to stop future trouble by settling matters now, with honour. However, as with Balmain, John Macarthur wanted to avoid a fight and he wrote again to

Governor Hunter asking him to charge Atkins with criminal libel – that is to say, with a libel likely to create a breach of the peace. It was an impossible request. Atkins, the only judge available, could not try himself, as John Macarthur must have known.[5]

OVER THE NEXT FOUR OR FIVE YEARS A GREAT DEAL changed in New South Wales. John Macarthur's easy dominance among the brotherhood of garrison officers, evident especially in the argument with Balmain, slipped away. Women were part of the reason. During the 1790s most of the officers of the NSW Corps lived with convict women, who might be servants as much as partners. However, William Paterson, commanding officer from December 1794, was married and the Patersons and Macarthurs saw a good deal of each other. Then, from about 1800, more officers acquired English wives. Edward Abbott married while on leave and William Minchin arrived as a new appointment with his wife Ann.[6]

Philip Gidley King, the new governor, unlike Phillip and Hunter, was also married. A woman presiding at Government House changed the way the whole system worked. Anna Josepha King built herself a drawing room, a space where ladies might meet, talk and organise their own events and projects, pre-eminently the new Female Orphan School, managed by herself and Elizabeth Paterson.[7] Suddenly, as well as the brotherhood of officers, there was network of women committed to decorous family life. With its own share of civilities and tensions, it had two main centres, Elizabeth Farm and Government House.

The presence of officers' wives in a place like New South Wales raised old problems of military discipline. Where did an officer's first obligations lie, to family or regiment? Edward Abbott had joined the Corps well aware of the difficulty. His father, an artillery captain and lieutenant-governor of Detroit, had been dismissed from the army when family ties made him baulk at transfer from North America to the Caribbean.[8] Now, the war with France led to officers and men being forced into an even tighter discipline and the unregulated distractions of private life were whittled back further. It was a particularly vexed issue in New South Wales because so many officers, like the soldiers, had households, farms and trading interests to attend to.

Governor King was all in favour of tighter military discipline, but he also wanted the government more in tune with family and neighbourhood life. Unlike the previous governors he understood the ways of trade and industry, and the work of women. The making of cloth was something he had started on Norfolk Island, and he was keen to work on a larger scale on the mainland, especially with wool. A government brewery was soon underway too, with the hope of replacing 'that poisonous fire', imported spirits, with locally made beer.[9] In the same spirit, the new governor planned to build up the government flocks and herds, a scheme pivotal to the Macarthurs' story.

So things stood in winter 1801, when Elizabeth and John entered what was so far their worst crisis in New South Wales. It was nine months since Governor King had taken office. Already there had been telling shifts in loyalty. The Patersons' attentions were now divided between Elizabeth Farm and Government House. The Abbotts and Minchins were drawn mainly to Elizabeth Farm.

The second half of the year, June to December, saw a series of high-level arguments, best summarised as the James Marshall affair and the affair of Mrs Paterson's letter. It was all very complex and mysterious, involving little-documented private loyalties, wives and women's friendships, so that, once again, elucidating the story depends on some guesswork.

In June the convict transport *Earl Cornwallis* – not Michael Hogan's *Marquis Cornwallis* – arrived in Sydney Cove. Henry Crawford, a young officer coming to join the NSW Corps, had been drowned on the way. His possessions had been watched over by James Marshall, a naval lieutenant who was serving as agent for the Transport Board. Army rules meant that Crawford's default executor was the Corps' commandant, but William Paterson was away exploring when the *Earl Cornwallis* arrived and the second-in-command, Joseph Foveaux, was at Norfolk Island. The next in line, John Macarthur, was therefore Crawford's executor. His inquiries proved that Marshall, as custodian of Crawford's property, had taken Crawford's good quality gun and bedspread, replacing them with his own.[10]

James Marshall was physically large and emotionally volatile. Ordered into arrest, Marshall abused John Macarthur, who, this time, demanded a duel. John Macarthur's second was Edward Abbott. Marshall's second was the young acting purser on the *Earl Cornwallis*, John Fitzpatrick Jefferie. It was the duty of seconds to agree on all arrangements for the duel but Abbott refused to deal with Jefferie. Duelling was a business for gentlemen and Jefferie, he said, was not a gentlemen. He had seen him selling goods like a shopkeeper.[11]

James Marshall grew impatient for action. Armed with a 'large stick' or 'bludgeon', he tracked down Abbott first, hit him and then confronted Macarthur. He was tried for each attack and the bench of the Criminal Court consisted, as usual, of the judge-advocate, Richard Atkins, and six officers. In this case five of the six were from the Corps and three were John Macarthur's particular friends, namely William Paterson, back from his expedition, John Piper – no visitor at Elizabeth Farm was better loved by parents and children – and Piper's younger brother Hugh.[12]

In criminal trials such as this, victims were prosecutors. John Macarthur therefore conducted his own case so as to give his first prepared speech in a court of law. He had once wanted to go to the bar but in this case he ignored all questions of law. He said nothing about criminal guilt.

Instead, everything turned on his own feelings on seeing 'this Monstrous Mass of Matter' – Marshall was a big man – come at him with a stick:

> Let me intreat of you [he told the court] to look upon this Man, view his gigantic Stature, examine his tremendous Club, imagine that you see him advancing ... intoxicated with Fury, breathing Mischief, and looking Destruction to the Object of his Search, and you will be enabled to form some Idea of the Danger of my Situation.

Lacking any legal argument, hearing only melodrama, the bench was at a loss. It fined and imprisoned Marshall for striking Abbott but the Macarthur case it referred to London.[13]

Marshall complained about partiality in both cases and the governor asked for an inquiry by the bench. This, however, was refused in what the governor called a 'public insult' to his own authority. He ordered James Marshall back to England with his sentence suspended and turned to making the most of the still unfolding quarrels in New South Wales.[14]

IN SPRING 1801 JOHN MACARTHUR WAS AGAIN IN SYDNEY and as usual he stayed with the Patersons. While he was there he organised an officers' boycott of Government House and Paterson agreed to write to the commander-in-chief in England, the Duke of York, about King's shortcomings as governor.[15] Signed by Paterson but, as King said, 'indited' by John Macarthur, this letter to the duke argued among other things for the removal of army and naval officers from the criminal court. It was a curious letter, proof of John's strangely random intelligence. He was quite capable of exploiting weaknesses in public institutions while at the same time looking for ways to mend them. He had apparently talked over the flaws in the criminal court with William Balmain because Balmain, who was going to England on leave, not only took the letter with him but offered his own opinion when he got there. He thought the bench only needed a few civilians added – some 'respectable inhabitants', he said – by way of balance.[16]

All this had nothing to do with John Macarthur's overriding ambition, his anxious desire to sell up at a good price and go home himself. That, in fact, now seemed likely. Major Foveaux, before sailing for Norfolk Island, had persuaded King to buy all his cattle for the government herd and John had immediately offered his stock too. The governor was impressed. The Macarthurs owned 50 cattle, of a much better breed than the government's, ten horses, including an excellent American stallion, and 600 mostly Spanish sheep. King looked forward to turning out woollen cloth on a large scale at Parramatta and for that the Macarthurs' sheep would be 'a great acquisition'. As samples, John gave him eight fleeces from the latest clip, which King sent home for expert assessment. However, the overall price was high: £4000 overall. The governor, having written home about Foveaux's offer, now asked for permission to buy Macarthur's as well.[17]

Those eight fleeces were more proof of the orderly methods used at Elizabeth Farm. Each was labelled, in much the same way, perhaps, as Elizabeth kept listings of her garden, so that one by one they told a story of generational change. Three of the eight showed primitive beginnings, taken from a Bengal ewe (hair only), an Irish ewe and a Cape ewe, four were from the second generation by various mothers (Bengal, Irish and Cape), and one from the third generation. A sample of the best would have been enough. Elizabeth, if it was she, did more. She deliberately told a tale of her own curiosity, with the arrangement and annotation of eight stages of unfolding life.

Foveaux had more sheep than the Macarthurs. His had been bred for mutton as well as wool but now, following the Macarthurs' offer, Foveaux offered his sheep too. Again, King had to get the minister's permission.[18] It now seemed possible that the governor would make do with Foveaux's sheep, and John Macarthur was persuaded that Elizabeth Paterson, the colonel's wife, was using roundabout means to bring that about.[19] Why and how is one of the mysteries of this tortuous series of events.

THE OFFICERS WHO HAD SAT IN MARSHALL'S CASE HAD all agreed to boycott Government House, but William Paterson was wavering. On 22 August John Macarthur asked him what he meant to do and the colonel declared that he could not desert the governor. Thus exposed, John decided that his only hope lay in persuading King that Paterson was really his enemy. Unluckily, King had confidence in William Paterson and none in John Macarthur.[20]

John Macarthur was better with bold strokes than underhand cunning. Talking with Samuel Marsden, his neighbour at Parramatta, he said he would do all he could to be on good terms with the governor. Paterson, he said, only pretended to be the governor's friend and as evidence he showed Marsden a letter Elizabeth Paterson had written to his own wife at Elizabeth Farm. This was a rash move. Neil MacKellar, lieutenant in John Macarthur's company, was also the governor's secretary and aide-de-camp, and like Paterson he had taken the governor's side. MacKellar now spread accounts of John Macarthur broadcasting Mrs Paterson's correspondence – a tale 'greatly exaggerated and in some instances premeditatedly false', so John himself said. Then, on 13 September, the governor tested the officers' boycott by sending out invitations for the anniversary of the King's coronation. John Macarthur was not included and his four friends, Abbott, Minchin, and both Piper brothers, stuck by him, but William Paterson led the remainder to Government House.[21]

1801, A GATEWAY YEAR

Matters had been brought to a head just as the governor hoped. John Macarthur's hold on his fellow officers had been broken and he was generally supposed to have dishonoured the privacy of their colonel's wife. In revenge for that indignity, William Paterson demanded a duel. John Macarthur, who never aimed wide, hit his sometime friend in the right shoulder and Paterson fell, badly hurt.[22] The governor ordered the arrest of John Macarthur and both seconds, on a potential charge of murder. If Paterson recovered they were to be released, on a commitment to keep the peace, and John Macarthur was to take up duty on Norfolk Island. Paterson did recover but Macarthur refused to come out of arrest without a court martial to prove his perfect innocence. He was sure, as usual, that he could justify himself before the world. With no impartial trial possible on the spot, King ordered him to prepare for trial at the centre of power, on a charge of 'creating dissension' between the governor and his own commanding officer. As the jokers put it, John Macarthur was to be 'transported to England'.[23]

Edward was already there, at school. Their parents decided that the next two, John and Elizabeth, were old enough to follow him, under their father's care, so that they too could have the benefit of more advanced education. Why, then, should any of them come back? With four of the family gone it only remained for the rest – Elizabeth, Mary (aged six), James (nearly three) and the baby William – to follow when land and stock were finally sold.

Raising the stakes considerably, in November, just before he left, John Macarthur managed the single largest purchase he had ever made. Foveaux had already sold his cattle to Governor King but he was still waiting to hear about his sheep. His price was £2 a head. With a flock of 1350, that added up to £2700, but Foveaux needed the money straightaway. He was now on Norfolk Island but, presumably through an agent at Sydney Cove, John Macarthur offered him £2000 altogether for the sheep and the pasture they ran on (1770 acres, or 716 hectares), cash down. Foveaux agreed and John then informed Governor King that he had changed his mind about his livestock. He now wanted £37 each for his cattle and £2.10s for his sheep – his own, that is, combined with Foveaux's.[24]

It was checkmate. Foveaux had no stock left to sell and John dictated terms for the whole. King's great project, his hopes of seeing government spinners and weavers working wool from thousands of government sheep, now depended on John Macarthur. To justify the high cost to government, Elizabeth's eight samples were already on their way home and John Macarthur had more among his baggage. Here was hope of substantial profit from years of service at the earth's wrong end.

16

ANSWERS FROM THE EDGE OF EMPIRE

John Macarthur sailed from Sydney Cove with his two children, Elizabeth, nine, and John, seven, on 15 November 1801. Their ship, the *Hunter*, was bound for Calcutta (Kolkata), where they intended to change to another vessel for the rest of their journey.

For the children it was an extraordinary adventure. Not many their age had ever done anything like it. For their father the journey was to be useful beyond anything he could have expected. His horizons were now vastly expanded. The *Hunter* called first at Norfolk Island, where John Macarthur and Joseph Foveaux finalised the sale of flocks and land.[1] That done, the ship docked next – it was dismasted in a storm – at Ambon, or Amboyna, a small island at the centre of what was then called the Spice Islands, west of New Guinea, its air scented with nutmeg and cloves, its harbour a focal point for regional trade. Once Dutch, Ambon had lately been taken by the British and it was governed by a 'commercial and political resident' responsible to the East India Company's governor and council at Madras (Chennai).

Robert Farquhar, the resident, was the 25-year-old son of Sir Walter Farquhar, physician to Prime Minister William Pitt and to the Prince of Wales. The Farquhars were originally Scottish and included a number of Presbyterian ministers of liberal persuasion. John Farquhar, the sermoniser mentioned already, was Robert's uncle. His mother, on the other hand, came from a rich slave-owning family in Barbados, but he hated slavery – 'the greatest of all evils', he called it – and it was to be an issue that complicated his whole career.[2] Waiting with the children for another ship, John Macarthur became the young man's confidential advisor.

Aiming to forestall a rising threat to British control, Farquhar had lately organised a failed attack on Ternate, a place nearby still held by the Dutch. The authorities in Madras had told him not to try again but he had already done so and won. When the Macarthurs arrived, Robert Farquhar had just heard again from Madras. He was censured and demoted, and a new resident was on the way. Farquhar and John Macarthur put together a defiant letter in response. As the representative of British power Farquhar had to cope, they said, with 'the machinations of our *artful, indefatigable, and politic enemy* the Dutch', besides keeping local rulers in check. Only strong measures well timed could make British power safe.[3]

Robert Farquhar then resigned and appealed to the governor-general in Calcutta, Lord Wellesley. Wellesley, persuaded by his boldness, arranged new duties and promised him the government of Prince of Wales Island (Penang), the company's base in Malaya. Meanwhile, John Macarthur and his children transferred to a spice ship, reaching London in December 1802.[4] Staying first with the Thompsons in Castle Street, they then found rooms at 5 Great George Street, Westminster, within reach of Robert Farquhar's father in Mayfair.

Sir Walter Farquhar was deeply grateful for John Macarthur's advice to his son, and at his London house, as a Farquhar daughter later remembered, John was soon 'one of the valued additions to the family circle'. He built up a powerful circle of friends. Hugh Elliot, another Scot, was to keep in touch with him for years afterwards. Elliot was highly educated – including by the philosopher David Hume – and remarkably bold, with a colourful reputation as a senior European diplomat. As a governor in the West Indies he was to take the unusual step, in 1811, of hanging a man for murdering slaves. Elliot even played with the thought of getting himself appointed governor of New South Wales, or so John afterwards recalled, 'with a view to forward my plans'.[5]

When he said 'my plans' John Macarthur meant a raft of ideas for New South Wales emerging from this time in London, thanks to the people he met and the new thoughts they gave him. This was to be the most stimulating period of his life so far.

SUCH CONNECTIONS MADE FOR A DYNAMIC OVERLAP with those he already had. His kinsman John McArthur lived near Portman Square. It was a long walk from Great George Street, but since 1789–90, when Elizabeth and John saw him last, McArthur had been gathering influence of his own, just as useful as the Farquhars'.

This other John McArthur had grown up in Greenock, Glasgow's port town.[6] He seems to have trained for the law but as a young man he had spent time on the European mainland, perfecting his swordsmanship in Paris and picking up languages. He had also lived briefly in India, where he learnt Persian. Noticing similarities between Asian languages and his native Gaelic, he had mastered the new theory that European and Asian languages had a common root.[7] John McArthur loved big systems of knowledge. He was a man who hurried everything into neat patterns. He saw connectivity, but also counting and calculation, as keys to power.

At the outbreak of the American Revolution John McArthur had joined the navy as a ship's clerk. Then, as purser, he had been responsible for his ship's signalling at sea and he had drawn up a new signalling code, a 'numerary' or numbers system, which was used briefly by some squadrons. He had also acted as judge-advocate in naval courts martial and he had published a book on swordsmanship, theory and practice.[8] After the war he did more work on his signals code and he wrote a book on courts martial, which became a standard authority. His first book had been dedicated to the Duke of Argyll, the old family patron. This new one went to his commander at sea, Vice-Admiral Hood.

During the first years of the new war with France, Hood commanded the Mediterranean Fleet and John McArthur had gone with him as his multilingual secretary. He had also served as the fleet's commissary and prize agent. Ship's crews were entitled to share the money value of all captured enemy vessels and ordnance, and prize agents managed the legal and financial complexities, taking a percentage of the investment dividends while they did so. The returns could be enormous. Hood's capture of an entire French fleet at Toulon in 1793 brought in a quarter of a million pounds, a fund John McArthur managed for the next eight years.[9]

He made his fortune. He sent his son to Eton, bought a supposed Titian and had his portrait painted by a fashionable artist. He took a house in the country, which he filled with books and with naval and Highland relics, and he secured a family coat of arms – used also by the Elizabeth Farm Macarthurs. The house was Hinton Lodge, near Portsmouth, and to save confusion from now on I will call him 'Hinton McArthur'. He also bought a share in a sugar plantation in British Guiana – 'my colonial property' – though he seems to have believed in the gradual emancipation of the slaves.[10] How gradual is hard to know.

Admiral Hood's successor in the Mediterranean, the great Horatio Nelson, asked Hinton McArthur to go with him as his own secretary. Nelson was McArthur's hero but by that time the 'ingenious Highlander' had turned to a second life, in writing, publication and the manipulation of ideas.[11] However, he did work as Nelson's publicist and prize agent, and he made good use of such high connections in founding a monthly journal of history, essays and biography, the *Naval Chronicle*, with J.S. Clarke, the Prince of Wales's librarian. At the same time he returned to his roots by attaching himself to the eminent Scottish landowner Sir John Sinclair. Sinclair, another man of never-resting brain, was to be his mentor from this point.

Hinton McArthur did a good deal to shape the career of his kinsman from New South Wales. It is likely that John had already been sending him reports from afar, and it might have been Hinton McArthur's encouragement that led him to pit his 'theories' against Governor Hunter's attempts to use his own ideas in managing New South Wales. John's imagination was more fluid and fertile, but Hinton McArthur's was more learned – obsessively so. They fed each other's curiosity in highly constructive ways. All his life, John felt a deep debt to Hinton McArthur.

At this point, Hinton McArthur's ties with Sir John Sinclair were especially useful. During the 1780s Sinclair had written at least ten books and pamphlets, mainly about British public finance and military and naval power, but lately he had turned his attention to life and work on the land. During the 1790s he was responsible for the groundbreaking 21-volume *Statistical Account of Scotland*, a parish-by-parish compilation of economic, demographic, cultural, historical and topographical detail. He had aimed overall, he said, to measure the *'quantum of happiness'* enjoyed by the Scottish people – that is, their current well-being *'and the means of its future improvement'*.[12] This was happiness as Elizabeth Macarthur used the word. It was happiness drawn by labour from the soil.

HINTON MCARTHUR'S IDEAS ABOUT HAPPINESS WERE narrower than Sinclair's. They were also narrower than Elizabeth and John's. For McArthur, a country's happiness depended largely on its muscle-power, measurable in statistics and proved in war. That might explain his compromise with slavery. McArthur loved language and languages, including heroic verse, but he also loved numbers. He put naval signalling on a 'numerary' basis and he thought swordsmanship could probably be boiled down to 'proper mathematical demonstrations'. Now, trailing Sinclair, he made a 'numerary' effort with the national economy. '[E]very nation, taken collectively,' said Hinton McArthur, 'is happy in proportion to its industry.'[13] On a national scale, riches, power and happiness could be measured all at once.

Hinton McArthur was one of a new generation of scholars and writers who set themselves to measure the power of nations. Now he wanted to prove that Britain's material strength was enough to win the current war. He aimed, he said, to assess 'the various advantages this country intrinsically possesses over all others, in respect to the wealth, power, and resources of the nation'. Knowing those advantages, Britons would understand their duty, under God, to make use of them by all possible means.[14]

Hinton McArthur's next publication, *Financial Facts of the Eighteenth Century*, finished in 1801, went through three editions in that year alone, changing its name meanwhile and growing from a pamphlet to a large volume. Making war, McArthur said, was 'a science of money', but so in the end was the management of peace. A man of sober Calvinist sensibility, he wanted indirect taxes to be lessened for the working poor and increased for the idle rich. Above all, he wanted the government to make Britain and its empire more productive. He had a lot to say about Scotland. In his boyhood, he said, herring from Loch Fyne – McArthur ancestral territory – sold for twopence halfpenny a 100.[15] No wonder the Highlanders were poor.

However, Hinton McArthur, like John Macarthur in New South Wales, also thought that the security of power depended on trust. That included trust between government and people. The British national debt, crucial for every great government effort, was safe, he said, because of 'public credit'. In France, on the other hand, erratic fiscal policy had been the root cause of the recent revolution. That 'able writer', his fellow Scot Sir James Steuart, had predicted the revolution for that reason, he said, long before it happened.[16]

Sir John Sinclair, a wool-grower himself, in county Caithness, paid particular attention to home-grown fleece, and of the finest kind. Wool, for him, was a prime ingredient of national happiness. Even while he was busy with his *Statistical Account* he had started the Society for the Improvement of British Wool. He had also persuaded the government to set up a Board of Agriculture and Internal Improvement, managed by himself, to look for ways of making British soil more productive altogether. Over a number of years the board pooled expertise from every corner, gathered news of experiment and innovation – new machinery, new techniques, new breeds – and churned out publications. And though the focus was Britain itself, the project had a wider reach. To George Washington in America, Sinclair sent ideas about sheep-breeding, together with seeds of the native flax plant gathered on the far side of the world by Philip Gidley King.[17]

Sir John Sinclair was also a leading member of the Highland Society of London. Hinton McArthur joined the Highland Society in 1799 and together they set out to make it into a think tank – not the term used at the time – for their new understanding of national power, cultural and commercial, Scottish, British and Empire-wide. France under Napoleon Bonaparte was a nation armed and reborn. Britain had to be the same. Manhood itself was to be reimagined for a militarised nation. The Highland Society helped to lead the way in making England and Scotland together feel like the home of a single, invigorated people.[18]

The Highland Society was starting to gather power when John Macarthur arrived from New South Wales late in 1802. Hinton McArthur was its workhorse and his skill in pulling strings produced remarkable results. Royal patronage arrived in 1805 when the King's son, the Duke of Sussex, became a member.

Sir Walter Farquhar had already belonged to it for some years. So had dozens of Campbells, the McArthurs' kinsmen. Once in London, John Macarthur himself signed up almost as soon as he could. He might not have shared altogether in the society's point of view, especially its militarist gloss, but he was certainly ready to take advantage of it.[19]

17

A NEW STORY

Gaelic verse, shaped long ago in far-off wild places, was supposed to sum up the Highland spirit – 'all those manly virtues,' as Sinclair put it, 'those generous traits, and those noble qualities, which distinguish the Hero in war, and the Citizen in peace'. The Highland Society did what it could promote an understanding of Gaelic verse, and in particular the poetry of Ossian.

Ossian's verse, said to date from the third or fourth century, was in fact largely made up by a Scotsman, James Macpherson. How rich Mr Macpherson has made himself, remarked a lady friend, Anne Grant, by tuning up 'the mouldy harp of Ossian'. The message was powerful all the same. Anne Grant thought so, as much as anyone else. Echoing from Britain's ragged north-west edge, Ossian's verse seemed to show how men, violent, decisive but enlightened, might change the world.[1] They had a duty to do it, though the many thousands of unenlightened might stand in their way.

The story allegedly told by Ossian was straightforward. There were two heroes, Fingal, Ossian's father, who ruled in south-west Scotland, and Cuchullin, a prince across the narrow waters to the east, in Ulster. Cuchullin's country was invaded by a neighbour. Cuchullin, fighting back, seemed beaten, until Fingal arrived and together they won. It was a story about friendship between two brave men, and yet they were men of different types. Hugh Blair, one of the luminaries of the Scottish Enlightenment, explained.

'Cuchullin is a hero of the highest class; daring, magnanimous, and exquisitely sensible to honour.' He is, however, a little colourful, a little flash. Fingal is the greater man, a wartime leader, a loyal friend, a tender lover, a fond father, a kind master and a careful ruler.[2] Fingal is complete.

These two, in a life-and-death struggle at Britain's far edge, stood for manhood at its best, as newly understood. They parcelled up daring and duty. There were some readers, even with Ossian in mind, who thought that friendship between women could be finer than friendship between men. So said Anne Grant. 'Their [men's] way of shewing friendship,' she said, 'is to venture for each other those lives which they are so apt to squander in duels.' The virtues of men shone before the world in verse and story, 'while ours,' said Anne Grant, 'that flourish in the shade, are their consolation, and the chief blessing of society after all'.[3]

Manly glories, said Hugh Blair, unpersuaded by womanly irreverence, were best revealed in ancient verse like this. 'Irregular and unpolished we may expect the productions of uncultivated ages to be; but abounding, at the same time, with that enthusiasm, that vehemence and fire, which are the soul of poetry.' Among weather-beaten, heathered hills, far from the dense lives of today, he said, 'human nature shoots wild and free', and the end result, 'high exertions of fancy and passion', could be truly sublime.[4]

Stories of Ambon and Sydney Cove, on Britain's new outskirts, scented with nutmeg, eucalyptus or something else exotic, might carry a soupçon of that same glory. Entangled with real life, they could echo Ossian. In June 1801 Sir Joseph Banks, president of the Royal Society, had received from Governor King three boxes. In two were indigenous seeds, moss and other plants, with their own strange scent. In the third were the eight carefully differentiated samples of wool from Elizabeth Farm, with an oily wool-yolk smell, which King had been given by the Macarthurs in their effort to sell all they had to the government.[5]

A NEW STORY

These samples needed to be backed up by a persuasive story, so as to make their mark where it mattered. Usually, when Europeans made settlements in remote places they told stories in advance, predicting prosperity, so as to gather energy and capital. Most earlier settlements had relied on some joint-stock company publishing its ambition and raising funds at home. So the East India Company had exploited India. So the Dutch East India Company (Vereenigde Oost-Indische Compagnie, or VOC) had put down roots in various places abroad. The VOC had occupied the Cape of Good Hope until the British took over in 1795 and it was a VOC settlement at Ternate that Robert Farquhar had attacked just before John Macarthur landed at Ambon.

At the Cape, the VOC's vineyards had been valuable and famous. In that case the VOC had told its story so well that wine produced at its Constantia vineyard was bought by the rich all over Europe. Arthur Phillip, on the way to New South Wales in 1787–88, had gathered 8000 Constantia cuttings, which had been planted in the government garden at Parramatta. Surely, said Watkin Tench, NSW wine, as with Constantia, would one day become 'an indispensable article of luxury at European tables'. However, effort, funding and persuasion had all failed. With no good story, well broadcast, Phillip's wine project had withered on the vine.[6]

The VOC had followed up, also at the Cape, with plans for fine wool, but before it was available in any quantity Britain had taken over the settlement, the VOC was gone and there was no-one ready to make plausible promises to cloth-makers in Europe. It was therefore years before wool from the Cape mattered abroad.[7]

What stories, then, could be told of wool in New South Wales?

IN ENGLAND, IN DECEMBER 1802, ONE OF THE FIRST things John Macarthur and his two children had to look forward to was seeing Edward, who had left them when he was seven and who was now nearly 14. Edward, leaving his school at Chudleigh, in Devon, came to London so that he could be taught with his brother John, under their father's eye.

The boys' teacher in London was a Presbyterian minister in the Andrew Kinsman–John Farquhar mould, a Calvinist of the high Enlightenment. He was soon a family friend. James Lindsay was minister in charge of the Presbyterian meeting house in Monkwell Street, central London, and his school was at Newington Green, on the city's northern edge, though he moved it later to Grove Hall, in the east, and Edward and John were 'parlour boarders'. Among Lindsay's many influential friends was the Welsh dissenting minister Abraham Rees, who had just started putting together his 45-volume *Cyclopedia; or, Universal Dictionary of Arts, Sciences, and Literature*. This remarkable compendium of knowledge in time included the first published biography of John Macarthur, written by another of his friends, Robert Bakewell, an authority, not only on sheep and wool, but also on the way climate and terrain affected every form of organic life.[8]

With friends like these, during 1802–04, John Macarthur began to make himself part of a large, well-publicised understanding of European life abroad. 'His active spirit of inquiry and enterprise,' so the *Cyclopedia*'s readers were told, 'led him to direct his attention to the natural advantages which the soil and climate presented to the agriculturalist.'[9] John was lucky in such early storytellers. However, he also made his own luck. Elizabeth was, in fact, more alert to 'natural advantages' than he was. She more easily picked up details of vegetation and terrain, just as she saw how the First Nations peoples made their lives among Country. More completely than John, she saw the way tangible circumstances might shape human existence. He drew on that, however, and in London in 1802–04 he took their story to a larger circle.

18

THE GOLDEN FLEECE

The eight fleeces from Elizabeth Farm sent by Governor King to Sir Joseph Banks were inspected by Henry Laycock, a London wool-buyer. In Laycock's judgment the fleece from the Bengal ewe was not wool at all. It was '[h]air only fit for the bricklayers to mix amongst mortar to build their houses with in the colony'. The same ewe's offspring by a Spanish ram did much better, but the best of all came from a one-year-old ram, fully Merino, with both parents from the Cape.[1]

Laycock thought this last fleece '[n]early as good' as wool from the King's flock, 'quite free from hair, and of an excellent quality'. This fleece offered new possibilities altogether, not just for manufacture in New South Wales but also for export to Britain, where it might compete with the best of the best. '[C]ould the colony produce such kind of wools,' said Laycock, 'it would be a great acquisition to our manufactory in England.' Here was interesting information for Lord Hobart, the minister at the Colonial Office, as he looked for ways of making the colony pay for itself.[2]

The Paterson–King–Macarthur quarrel complicated this good news, however, and it was some months before Banks and Hobart wrote to King about it. Banks forwarded Laycock's remarks, which King immediately published verbatim and with 'great pleasure' in his new newspaper, the *Sydney Gazette*. Hobart complimented the governor on the 'highly creditable' efforts made by 'certain of the settlers'. Fleece of 'the finest quality', he said, should in future be set aside for the British market.³

The fineness of sheep's wool was currently an urgent question in Britain, and for the first time fineness seriously affected price. There were two great wool-growing regions in Britain, the West Riding of Yorkshire, and the English south-west. Fineness mattered especially in the south-west, though in far-off Cornwall prices still depended not on quality at all but on weight.⁴ John Macarthur, reaching England 18 months after the eight sample fleeces, might have had to learn very quickly, not only about Laycock's assessment but also what it meant in the great scheme of things. Whatever he remembered from the 1780s, including about the way wool had sold at Plymouth Dock, had changed a good deal.

In all this Hinton McArthur's friend Sir John Sinclair was a key figure. New South Wales had always counted among Sinclair's many interests. He had handled Norfolk Island flax very early. Then, in 1797, he had asked for details about farming in New South Wales during John Macarthur's years in charge. Now there was wool from that place and for Sinclair few things mattered more than wool. '[F]ine wool,' he had told his Wool Society, 'is of essential consequence to the manufactures of this country', and as much as possible should come from 'our own territories'. It was John Rickman, a Sinclair protégé, who first told the world about the Macarthurs' wool, in his *Agricultural Magazine*, February 1803.⁵

The future of British wool was currently troubling parliament itself. In the south-west, the Bath and West of England Agricultural Society was the leading institution of its kind anywhere, with powerful landowners making use of the best scientific expertise. Also, in the south-west the manufacturers were well informed and politically engaged, and their machinery was highly advanced. As a result, so it was said, fine woollen cloth from the south-west commanded 'the market of the world'.⁶ Its representatives also had a considerable voice in London.

The weavers and shearmen (artisans who trimmed the surface of woven cloth) in those parts lived in communities attached to the factories, which is partly why they were the first English working men of any kind to organise on a large scale. Now they made their voices heard too. They were afraid that new machinery would put them out of work, especially given the scarcity of home-grown wool, and because of the war, which threatened imports. In response, manufacturers were trying to reinforce their own power through new legislation, an effort led by Edward Sheppard, of Uley in Gloucestershire. Three parliamentary inquiries were held from March to May 1803, aiming to hear all sides, and manufacturers gathered in London to lobby and testify.

One early committee was chaired by Sinclair's friend Benjamin Hobhouse, and John Macarthur was able to meet with several of Hobhouse's witnesses. They included Edward Sheppard's neighbour John Wallington. Wallington was convinced that with enough wool there would be work for everyone, with or without machinery. He was therefore interested in the question of supply. It was Wallington who brought John Macarthur as a witness to the third committee. John had with him new samples of his own wool, which, he said, he had seen taken from the backs of his sheep shortly before he sailed.[7]

Meanwhile, something was starting to shift in John Macarthur's mind. Talk with Watkin Tench in Arthur Phillip's time had shaped the way he and Elizabeth had first imagined the whole experiment in the antipodes. Now, talk with his kinsman Hinton McArthur, with manufacturers such as Wallington, and possibly with Sinclair, moved him up another gear. His enthusiasm for political economy was in play. He began to see that wool-growing had its own political economy, its own history and its own geography. Here was a larger story than any he had used so far.

In May 1803, when he spoke to the House of Commons committee, John Macarthur said nothing about doing any more with

NSW wool himself. The current plan, provisionally endorsed by Lord Hobart, was for a government flock, with the best of its wool sent for sale in London and the rest processed at Parramatta for use on the spot. He was not an expert, John said. He had happened upon a useful thing and those who knew more than he did might make something of it. In New South Wales the sheep would quickly multiply, he said, so that 'the Settlers' would naturally turn their attention to the British market. '[E]very thing that is over the Freight would be Profit.' He said nothing about being among those settlers himself.[8]

That was at the end of May 1803. Within the next few weeks Hinton McArthur finalised a new edition of his 1801 book, with the expanded title *Political and Financial Facts of the Eighteenth and Present Century*. Most of the 1801 text was unchanged, but he now added an introduction with a detailed argument about NSW wool – the first explanation in print as to what it all meant, or might mean. First, he talked about the mortal threat Napoleon Bonaparte posed to Britain itself. Then he spoke of the wool trade, its importance for national power and its current difficulties. Finally, he came to the sheep currently grazing in the winter sunshine on Elizabeth Farm. The life-and-death challenge offered by the first was to be met, partly at least, so he suggested, by the promise of the last.[9]

With the picture thus clarified and the story thus laid out, during the following month, June 1803, John Macarthur decided that he should make this his life's work.

SO BEGAN THE SECOND PHASE OF THIS ENGLISH expedition. As a 21st-century writer says, for any new project to get traction in the wide world, 'there has to be a confluence between the ideas themselves, the spirit of the times, and the interests of powerful players who find the ideas congenial'.[10] The powerful players really matter, and they have to be not only powerful but active and obvious.

Several experts in England were impressed with what had been produced already in New South Wales. Benjamin Hobhouse's brother-in-law, Caleb Parry, a leading breeder of Merinos, called the Macarthurs' best fleece 'equal in fineness to almost any I have ever seen', although he doubted whether anything like perfection could be achieved in less than five sheep generations. Parry also questioned John Macarthur's forecast for future numbers.[11] However, neither of these doubts affected the main point.

Sir Joseph Banks, on the other hand, was definitely opposed. Banks went to the fundamental question of John Macarthur's character. A friend of the King and manager of the royal flock, he was also William Paterson's loyal patron and he held John Macarthur in deep distrust. He thought he had probably overlooked the cost of carrying wool over such a distance – he had not – and having seen the grass at Botany Bay himself in 1770, with Cook on the *Endeavour*, he was sure it was too coarse for sheep. Captain Macarthur wanted funds and encouragement for 'a crude theoretical speculation, unsupported by any decisive evidence in its favor, and of the success of which I confess I entertain no manner of hope'. The government should wait until the settlers sent home 'a few tons' of good wool before giving any help to anyone.[12]

John Macarthur bypassed Banks. He relied absolutely on the manufacturers and wool-buyers. Among those who had come to London to testify before the parliamentary committees was Abraham Lloyd Edridge, a Quaker manufacturer from Chippenham in Wiltshire, who used Merino wool. Chippenham was the parliamentary seat of John Maitland, London's leading trader in fine wool and a cousin of Sir John Sinclair's late wife. Edridge and another man from Yorkshire agreed to collect signatures in support of NSW wool from manufacturers and wool merchants, and their appeal went out in late July. At the same time John Macarthur handed in his own statement – argument and request – at the Colonial Office, for Lord Hobart.[13]

In this statement, no doubt taking copious advice from his cousin and others, he told a new story to fit his new ambition. Talk of happy accidents, and of knowing very little about wool and sheep, was put aside. He now said that he had acquired his sheep in the first place in the certain hope that their wool would be 'of the utmost consequence to this country'. Improvement, he said, had already surpassed his 'most sanguine expectations'. He was sure that in time output would meet all the needs of the mother country and he now proposed to devote his whole attention to making that happen. All government had to do was to make land available to him – he said nothing about legal title – together with convict men to work as shepherds.[14]

He would not ask for 'pecuniary aid', he said, though that left wide open the question as to how the shepherds would be fed and clothed, the land cleared, and buildings erected and maintained, while he waited to make a profit. No individual had ever taken it on themselves to do as he now aimed to do – all by themselves, to redirect such a vital aspect of the British national economy, let alone from such a distance. The risk he now took went beyond even the purchase from Joseph Foveaux in 1801.

John Macarthur's was an audacious appeal directed to government as a whole. The manufacturers and merchants had been asked to send their signed responses to Treasury and Macarthur's statement was addressed to 'His Majesty's Ministers'. Also, his network of support now reached into the central corridors of power. George Watson, a nephew of Sir Walter Farquhar's late wife, was private secretary to the president of the Board of Control – minister for Indian affairs – Lord Castlereagh. Watson was also a satirist, playwright and versifier, and a lively cynic adept at pulling strings. His manoeuvres were now crucial.

Treasury received 14 supporting letters with 394 signatures, some from individuals and some from firms, including John Maitland's firm in Basinghall Street. These letters were forwarded to the Board of Trade, which then consulted the former governor, John Hunter, and the naval captain and Macarthur family friend Henry Waterhouse, who had carried Mrs Gordon's Merinos from the Cape. During the same week more wool samples arrived from Elizabeth Macarthur, the even finer result of a more recent shearing. Elizabeth also sent the *Sydney Gazette* for 26 March 1803, with Henry Laycock's assessment of the first eight samples. It was filed at the board's office with the scribbled annotation 'Mrs McArthur'.[15] Far away, she could not know how the whole point of their effort had been transformed, though it promised her what she wanted – more time at Elizabeth Farm.

By Christmas 1803 a source of funding turned up. A number of wool-buyers and others, led by John Maitland, proposed a joint-stock operation, a company holding land in its own name with John Macarthur as agent on the spot, unpaid but with the right to sell unwanted sheep on his own account. Twenty years earlier Sir George Young and John Call had aimed to bring flax and timber from Norfolk Island using capital of £20 000. Maitland's target was £10 000, a large part of which would be needed straightaway to buy the Macarthurs' sheep. Instead of selling to the government he would sell to the company, at an even higher price.[16]

John Macarthur wrote to New South Wales, to his good friend John Piper, boasting he was 'up to the ears in papers for carrying on the war against our common enemy', Governor King. He looked forward, he said, to having everything settled by February 1804 and coming straight back. He might even bring a new governor with him, and if so 'I suspect you will all be in danger of turning idolators, and worship me.'[17] And why not? Returning as agent for a great London company he would be something like governor himself.

He had arrived in England technically under arrest, awaiting court martial on King's prosecution. That problem had been solved too. King had sent Neil MacKellar, under separate sail, to testify against Macarthur but MacKellar's ship had been lost, apparently, off the coast of South America. With no witnesses the case was closed, Macarthur sold his commission and was a soldier no more.[18] However, there were difficulties about the plan for a company, probably because it seemed to threaten both the governor's authority and the monopoly of the East India Company. In mid-May the government fell and George Watson, as Castlereagh's secretary, lost his post, but by providential coincidence he went to the same position with the new minister at the Colonial Office, Earl Camden. John Macarthur wrote again to the Board of Trade. As an alternative to a company he now suggested 10 000 acres (4047 hectares) for himself alone, as well as a guaranteed allowance of 30 convict shepherds.[19]

The new Board of Trade handed the whole matter over to Camden, and Camden took advice from George Watson. John Macarthur was to have his 10 000 acres, but, apparently at Sir Joseph Banks's urging, only half immediately and the rest when success seemed to justify it. He was also to have his convict shepherds. The Board of Trade had recommended a provisional land grant. Camden ordered absolute title, together with another 2000 acres for 18-year-old Walter Stevenson Davidson, Sir Walter Farquhar's nephew, who was to go with John Macarthur to New South Wales.[20]

New arrangements were put in place in London. John found a new agent, Thomas William Plummer, a merchant trading mainly to the West Indies, to replace his friend Thomas Thompson, who was ageing fast. Plummer was Thompson's son-in-law.[21] A firm was also found to take shipment of the wool and to partner in other efforts to get money together for the road ahead. Hullett Brothers, of Broad Street, London, were whalers in the south Atlantic. The

Hulletts, young men casting about for ways to be rich, came from fine-wool country themselves – Herefordshire – and had already been involved in John Maitland's plan for a company.[22]

The *Agricultural Magazine* now pronounced the fine-wool project to be of 'the greatest national importance' and John Macarthur drove that point home. He was exultant, a mood that made him almost giddy with self-importance. On 15 August 1804, 44 Merinos from the royal flock, supposed to be England's best, were auctioned at Kew, south of London. It was the first such auction by the King, it was widely publicised, and John Macarthur led the bidding. He spent £150, a fifth of the auctioneer's proceeds, and he brought away seven rams and three ewes.[23]

He had bought a share in one of the Hulletts' ships, which was fitted up to carry his sheep to New South Wales, and with the intention of bringing back whale oil for the British market. French-built, John Macarthur renamed it *Argo* and set on its bow a figurehead harking back to the Greek legend of the golden fleece. In Pindar's verse-story of the voyage of the *Argo*, Jason – like John Macarthur, a long way from home – is ordered to steal the golden fleece from a large serpent:

> This, Argonaut, thy task! who this defies,
> His be the splendors of th'eternal prize.

So went the translation that John himself might have read. It was a topical tale. In his story of the *Argo*, Pindar told of a great gamble and in Dublin, very lately, a group calling itself the Jason Club had deliberately outwitted chance in the Irish State Lottery, so as to net the vast sum of £30 000.[24] The prize in John's case had taken him two years but the tactical effort, stretched over two hemispheres, had been just as neat.

The lives of Elizabeth and John Macarthur were transformed. John had reattached their future to New South Wales, just as he had done in 1792 by appointment as paymaster. This time, however, the change meant much more. Their lives were to be antipodean.

The *Argo* left Portsmouth on 30 November 1804. Its voyage of hope was enlivened by youth. Besides young Elizabeth Macarthur, who was 12 when the ship set sail, and Walter Davidson, now 19, there was 16-year-old Hannibal Macarthur, John's brother's son from Plymouth Dock. Edward and John, his own older boys, stayed in England. Edward, a year younger than Hannibal, was to go into the army but his father imagined that he would eventually join them in New South Wales. Young John, more intellectually able, might follow his father's original ambition by going to the bar, with a fair chance of entering parliament.

Altogether, the horizon was alight with possibilities. John had made his own decisions. Even his earliest thoughts about their newly patterned future could not have reached Elizabeth until October 1803, by which time the business was well advanced. He could not have heard her thoughts until within six months of starting for home, but he must have understood that she was ready, even happy, to stay where she was.

PART 4

19
'OUR FIRST UNIVERSE'

Leap a long way forward in the story of the Macarthurs. One autumn day in 1870, when both parents were long dead, William Macarthur talked with his middle-aged niece about his childhood. She took notes. As he said, it had been a spartan upbringing, fraught with self-denial and self-control. John and Elizabeth Macarthur had avoided every hint of luxury. The family ate maize-meal bread when others like themselves had the fine wheaten sort. It was cheaper and, in John's opinion, 'exceedingly nutritious'. As for clothes, 'I never had more than two garments,' so William remembered, 'until I was seven years old – sometimes on winter evenings I used to feel it bitterly cold'. His only toy was a small wheelbarrow, probably a hand-me-down from his older brothers and sisters. 'I remember once taking a long walk with our nursemaid ... and returning home with this wheelbarrow wreathed in clematis [the dense, starry white *Clematis aristata*], suddenly the barrow broke – my grief was intense.'[1]

Through his tears 'little Billy' noticed that James and Mary, who were with him, cared less than he did about the wheelbarrow. Everyone, so it seemed, had their own feelings, a revelation for someone his age. Looking back, he also remembered how, for the first time, he grasped the thread in reading. He was four or five, a time of life when mystery attaches even to the opening and shutting of a drawer. Picking up a book with a poem in it about a rose, '[i]t suddenly flashed upon me,' William said, 'what it meant and I read it off.'

John Macarthur overshadowed his children's existence at least as much as most fathers, and his effect on all of them mattered to him deeply. He went to England when William was 11 months old and he came back – the *Argo* trip – on a winter evening in 1805, when his youngest son was four and a half, and sound asleep in bed. When William saw him for the first time next morning John Macarthur was a stranger. 'I distressed my father greatly,' so he recalled, 'by saying to him "You are so ugly I don't like you" (he was much pitted by small pox)'. But then, 'in the course of the day I told him "I liked him better now."'[2]

Such fragments aside, it is hard for us to know another family from within, its delicate fabric of feeling and its many-layered silences, just as it is to know another individual. Families have a self-regarding life of their own. Each has its own inner trust, a web of mysteries spoken and unspoken, its own humour and habits of mind – its own mix of smells, such as only its members might fully understand, pungent in the memory of children. Besides home-made tallow soap, in Sydney you could buy Castile, Bengal and other variously scented soap, each contributing in its own way to the inner character of well-off families.[3] Then and now, most people might understand their houses as specimens of geometry, jigsaws of squared spaces, but for littler children they can be more like a seashell, bulked out by larger lives. To outsiders too, houses are like seashells in suggesting only a little of the lives that have unfolded inside them. So the building at Elizabeth Farm, still standing, only hints at the world of feeling, sound, scent and self-awareness it once contained.

The Macarthurs' first antipodean home, for about six months, had been a hut of wattle and daub on the inland side of the Tank Stream, on Sydney Cove, apparently built for an officer of marines. At the beginning of 1791 they had moved from there to a brick cottage, also at Sydney Cove, where the younger Elizabeth was born in May 1792. In February 1793 John received his land grant at Parramatta, a larger house was built, a garden and orchard laid out, and the family moved in at the end of the year. This was Elizabeth Farm. It was part of the territory of the Burramattagal clan, and the Macarthurs' acreage spanned Duck River and Clay Cliff Creek – the invaders' names – freshwater sources of birdlife, shellfish and other sustenance until livestock destroyed the old abundance.[4]

During this last move Elizabeth was pregnant again. It was a boy, 'to whom', she told Bridget Kingdon, 'I have given his father's name John'. Their next – their fifth, counting the baby who was born and died at sea – was a girl, named after Elizabeth's stepsister Mary Isabella. Their sixth was James, in honour of John's brother, but he died at eleven months and his name was used again for their seventh, born in December 1798. William, their eighth, arrived exactly two years after that. Elizabeth and John were both then 34.[5]

John described their house in a letter to his brother at Plymouth Dock not long after it was finished. It was 'a most excellent' building, he said.

> It has no upper story, but consists of four rooms on the ground floor, a large hall, closets, cellar, etc.; adjoining is a kitchen, with servants' apartments, and other necessary offices. The house is surrounded by a vineyard and garden of about 3 acres, the former full of vines and fruit trees, and the latter abounding with most excellent vegetables.

The 'large hall' was a cross-passage, carrying breezes through the house. Halls of this sort were reception areas, designed for the protocol of receiving and farewelling visitors. This was a small house but deliberately decorous. Otherwise, family accommodation at

Elizabeth Farm was much the same as the old style of yeoman farm-houses in Cornwall – the house at Lodgeworthy, where Elizabeth had started life, or at Hampt, where her mother had lived with Edmund Leach.[6] The Kingdons' vicarage must have had a hall.

Parlour and dining room were in front, left and right of the hall, and the main bedroom and a skillion for the children behind the parlour, altogether an L-shape. Probably in the parlour, little William read the poem about the rose. The kitchen and servants' quarters were built apart, in a more expansive arrangement than English farmers usually had room for. From 1800 the main rooms were shaded by verandahs to the north and east.[7]

There were never more than five children living in the house at once, because while more were born others went to school in England, but it was crowded all the same. In 1800–01, as a baby, William might have slept with his parents, leaving, say, two children each in two beds in the skillion. In 1801–05, with their father, Edward, Elizabeth and John all gone, their mother was left with the three youngest: Mary, James and William. Then, in 1805 young Elizabeth came back with their father, adding up again to four children, aged four to 13. Imagine too the nameless creatures, imported and indigenous, their scuttling and squeaking from cellar and roof, numberless inhabitants audible from the children's beds at night.

A French writer, Gaston Bachelard, has said that 'our house … is our first universe.' That idea can be traced back to the lifetime of Elizabeth and John, to the philosophising of the Scot James Beattie, and to the poetry of the Englishman William Wordsworth. Our childhood home pulls together imagination and instils principles, feeling and conscience.[8] So it was with the Macarthurs at Elizabeth Farm, in one sense with the children and in another sense with the parents. John's career is hard to explain without thinking of this house as a rock on which everything

'OUR FIRST UNIVERSE'

rested, a 'cosmos', as Bachelard put it, on which his life centred. Aware of it or not, Elizabeth and John both remade themselves among its grammar of sound and silence.

THE HOUSE WAS HEADQUARTERS FOR A LARGE COLlection of properties, totalling 3500 acres (about 1420 hectares) when Elizabeth was left to manage alone, in 1801–05. John had bought various small parcels of land during the late 1790s, which he might have hoped to sell as consolidated estates, but half the current total, Joseph Foveaux's land at Seven Hills, near Toongabbie, was purchased in 1801. Foveaux's sheep still grazed there. A smaller outpost at Pennant Hills was also used for livestock. Besides Elizabeth Farm, enlarged since 1792, the rest included an assortment of small farms halfway to Sydney, at Cabramatta, and 55 vacant acres on Cockle Bay (afterwards Darling Harbour), next to Sydney Cove.[9] Some of the Cabramatta land was too rocky for cropping, but it might have been partly rented out all the same, even to previous owners.

As a whole, it was a miscellaneous scattering, all the more difficult to manage for its diversity. In 1798 the men employed to work it, free and unfree, totalled 30 or 40, but by the time Elizabeth took over there were less than that. Convict numbers overall were dwindling relative to demand and, counted in August 1802, the Macarthurs' numbered 16. Men came and went as they served their time but a few stayed on, some for many years.[10] The long-term employment of trusted men and women was key to the Macarthurs' success.

It is impossible to say much more than this about the way Elizabeth managed during 1801–05 because few records exist. One thing does appear. Richard Fitzgerald, one of John's overseers when he was inspector of public works, was now superintendent of the government farms at Toongabbie and he lent a hand. John always admired Fitzgerald's 'remarkable activity, regular conduct, and honesty', and their lives were long interwoven.[11]

There was reason to worry for the family's physical safety while John was away. There had been war between the invaders and the Indigenous peoples, on and off, since 1788. Raids on settlements were mainly in the south and west, but sometimes penetrated even within reach of Sydney Cove. During the most dangerous period for the settlers the Indigenous leader was the Bidjigal warrior Pemulwuy. His shooting death in June 1802, seven months after John Macarthur left for England, brought quiet for a while, but trouble flared again early in 1805. Elizabeth Farm was never directly threatened but settler deaths included two of Elizabeth Macarthur's stockmen, apparently at Cabramatta.[12]

John Macarthur had been a forthright defender of settlement, especially on the Hawkesbury frontier. As the acting-governor's right-hand man he had shared responsibility for the killings there in 1794–95, including the massacre called the Battle of Richmond Hill. Nevertheless, he and Elizabeth had always been sure of the friendship of Burramattagal men and women still living nearby and they had proof of it now. A man they called Bill, an outlaw from his own people because of a quarrel among them, found a lost cow and, as William remembered, came secretly at night to tell Elizabeth. He was seen and speared in front of the house – William, then four or five, remembered seeing him fall – and Elizabeth had him carried to a shed where his friends could look after him. 'We used to visit him every day,' so William recalled, until he died. Then it was, 'Good bye Missus. I shall never see you again'.[13]

The NSW Corps was their obvious protector. John Macarthur had broken with most of his fellow officers but the soldiers stuck by him and one of the last things he had done before he left was to order the distribution of meat, grain and rum, half a cup each, for them to drink his health. That gift was stopped, but the gesture was enough. Late on a Sunday in 1804 Elizabeth was visiting their neighbours, the Marsdens, with Mary and James, William being at home with his nurse, when the night exploded. Elizabeth told the story afterwards to their friend John Piper, at Norfolk Island.

They were sitting at supper, she said, when 'Old Joice [William Joyce, a small settler] burst into the parlour pale and in violent agitation. "Sir" says he looking wildly at Mr Marsden, "come with me", "And *you too Madam*" looking at me.' At the door, trembling and whispering, Joyce told them that the Irish convicts were up in arms, aiming to destroy all before them. Many of them were men who had joined in the great uprising in Ireland in 1798, an event ruthless in targeting homes and families.[14]

The rebels were already at Elizabeth's Seven Hills farm and some were headed for Parramatta. William and his nurse were fetched in haste, and 'Mrs Marsden myself and our children repaired to the [Parramatta] Barracks. We now learnt that Castle Hill was in flames.' Some of the Irish were dangerously close by the time boats were ready to take the women and children downriver to Sydney. Their 'hideous shouts' could be heard from somewhere around the Government House gates, but there they seemed to pause. Elizabeth found out afterwards that they were watching to the south-east for two fires as a signal to attack the town itself, and one of those fires was to be at Elizabeth Farm, in 'my house or some part of the premises'. The Irish understood, as everyone did, the bond between the Macarthurs and the soldiers of the Corps, and the fire at Elizabeth Farm was planned as a way of getting the Parramatta detachment to leave the town. '[M]y lonely situation and the attachment the soldiers had to my family would induce them [the soldiers] upon seeing the fire to repair instantly to my relief.' Parramatta would then be open to attack.[15]

The fugitives reached Sydney Cove at three in the morning and everyone there was up and active. The *Calcutta* was in port, fresh from landing convicts and guards at an intended new settlement at Port Phillip (soon moved south to Hobart), and Elizabeth had fortitude enough to notice how beautiful it was, lit up on the dark water. '[W]e and our little *frightened sleepy* tribe were escorted' to the Marsdens' house in town. Meanwhile, the two Parramatta fires had not happened, more troops had been sent from Sydney and the Irish were retreating to Castle Hill, where they were outwitted and betrayed. At least 15 were killed on the spot and nine were hanged.[16]

The rebels had chosen the Seven Hills farm and the Macarthurs' other outlying property at Pennant Hills to rendezvous, and the house at Elizabeth Farm was to be a bonfire signal. Altogether, it was '[n]o very flattering distinction', as Elizabeth said. However, it did prove John's celebrity and during the following summer, when a fire did indeed break out at Elizabeth Farm, in the kitchen, the soldiers came up to expectation. They must have seen the flames from their barracks and their quick response saved the house itself.[17]

Elizabeth Macarthur had an unmistakeable command over the men she came in contact with, including men of rank. John's fight with William Paterson had led, when John was gone, to the trial of John Piper, his second, and Elizabeth kept a close eye on the way Piper managed. 'One thing ... I cannot I think too much insist upon,' she told him, 'and that is that you will carefully avoid all offensive matter in your defence.' He had to appeal to the forbearance of his judges. 'It is useless my good friend to add fuel to the fire that has been blazing too long already.' She insisted that he show her what he had written down to say. Piper did as he was told and he was acquitted.[18] A thread of the same steel seems to have gone into her dealings with her husband, but with him she might have been more roundabout.

The *Calcutta*, a naval vessel, was three months in port and, as usual with such visiting ships, its officers paid their respects at Elizabeth Farm. Lieutenant John Houston came a number of times before the governor sent him to Norfolk Island to replace

Joseph Foveaux. Writing to Piper after Houston left, Elizabeth sent several messages. 'Mr Houstown cannot expect a letter from me having not written himself,' but remind him, she said, that she was looking after his little dog, 'an agreeable and lively companion to me when I travel in the woods'. She would send the dog if he liked. Meanwhile, '[t]he children join in love to yourself and Mr Houstown and the Colonel [Foveaux].'[19]

She had one or two long-term female servants to add to her sense of security. Sarah Richardson, the children's nurse, had come with her from England and in 1793 had married a soldier from John Macarthur's company, Zadoc Pettit. Zadoc and another man had 25 acres each as a single farm at the Field of Mars, to which 20 were added for Sarah herself, but it may be that she never slept away from her charges. Typically for good nursemaids, she was a skilled needlewoman. She stayed until William was seven, when she and Zadoc went back to England, where she made and sold lace.[20]

Elizabeth McDougall, or Evans, a convict – as a teenager she had stolen a bundle of clothes from a stagecoach – had been employed as a wet nurse for Mary, in 1795–96, and ever since she had kept in touch with the family, and with Mary especially. Elizabeth McDougall's own baby, suckled with Mary, was remembered at Elizabeth Farm, or at least by Elizabeth Macarthur, as the children's 'foster-brother'. William Buchan's popular handbook, *Domestic Medicine*, which the family had on hand, advised against wet nurses. 'Every mother who can,' said Buchan, 'ought … to perform so tender and agreeable an office [herself].'[21] How far Elizabeth agreed no-one now can say.

Elizabeth Macarthur's deeper friendships were for women educated like herself. These were still scarce in New South Wales. She and Betsy Marsden were close but they were different in faith, feeling and habits of mind. And then John's quarrel stopped communication with the wives of Governor King and Colonel

Paterson. During the Irish troubles of 1804, stranded in Sydney, Elizabeth found Anna King and both Patersons 'most attentive and kind' – afterwards several of the wives met for dinner – but relations were unsettled still.[22]

Bridget Kingdon was another matter. Though far away, Bridget tied Elizabeth to life's kindest memories. By the *Alexander*, arriving in October 1802, Elizabeth might have heard of Bridget's marriage to a neighbour, John Braddon, but then it was probably the *Glatton*, in March 1803, that brought news of her death, a six-months bride. Altogether then, uncertain friends on the spot, John's absence and now the loss of Bridget, added up to a deep disconnect during 1801–05, as with her time at sea, in 1790. Even John Piper, their dearest family friend, was nowhere within reach.

There was physical danger. There was loneliness. There was mourning. One visitor noticed Elizabeth's pain. The naval lieutenant Matthew Flinders had met the Macarthurs during an earlier tour of duty. Now he was back. During winter 1803 he completed the first circumnavigation of Australia, in HMS *Investigator*, and he then spent seven weeks in and around Sydney, not long after Elizabeth had heard of Bridget's death. In frequent visits he did his best for her, giving advice, for instance, when she was cheated in sales of pork, and in sending her his last farewells he called her his 'dearest friend'. 'I leave you,' he said, 'with anxious suspense, and borne down with the cares attendant upon the interests of a large family, the oppressive weight of which your single shoulders are at present left to bear.' God was her best support. She knew it. Trust to 'that Almighty Power whom you reverence and adore'. Only he could give 'such fortitude to your mind and health to your person as will enable you to discharge your various duties with the satisfaction that attends upon doing every thing well'.[23]

Besides the children she had about her, Mary, James and William, doing everything well was Elizabeth's chief consolation.

'OUR FIRST UNIVERSE'

Like John and like Flinders himself, she was uneasy with anything mediocre, but she was tired. The effort of managing alone, she told John Piper, was 'burthensome to me in the extreme'. 'God grant me health and patience for indeed my good friend, I have much need of both.'[24]

20

THE IMPORTANCE OF MISS LUCAS

In the evening of 9 June 1805 – cold on the water – the *Argo* anchored at last in Sydney Cove, and late at night John Macarthur and 13-year-old Elizabeth reached the front door at Elizabeth Farm. The older Elizabeth remembered the date all her life, or rather she misremembered it as the 7 June.[1] It was a sweet moment – triumph, reunion and relief combined.

William, at four and a half, was asleep in the bed he usually shared with Mary. However, Mary was staying with friends and it was his long-absent sister Elizabeth who crept in with him when teary greetings were over with her mother. He remembered many years afterwards feeling her presence. 'I woke and fancying it was Mary come home I said that I had broken so many tea cups.' Elizabeth threw herself into kissing him. 'Oh! Mary how kind you have grown.' Then he started to wonder. '[T]he voice is the voice of Mary but the tallness is not the tallness of Mary.'[2] Next morning he met his father, and so he took his first steps into a more complicated life.

William had been frightened when he first saw his father again. He did not say what he felt about another *Argo* passenger, a perfect stranger but from now on an intimate member of the household, sharing a bed, taking part in the parents' conversation and steadily making herself indispensable. This was Penelope

Lucas, aged 36. John Macarthur had listed her, on their leaving England, as his daughter's governess, but she was more than that. Penelope Lucas had her own inherited income. She had no need to work for a living and she was not paid at Elizabeth Farm.[3]

Penelope Lucas was to find her way into what I have called the grammar of the house, for Elizabeth Macarthur filling the gap left by Bridget Kingdon. John's success with fine wool was his most obvious achievement during 1802–04, but for their settled happiness his choice of Penelope Lucas mattered just as much. In her quiet friendship for his wife she made a new future possible at least as much as fine wool did.

Penelope Lucas, born in central London on 30 May 1769, was nearly three years younger than Elizabeth and John.[4] Hers was a family of wealthy London tradesmen, heirs to a soot and coal merchant named William Gordon, who had died when Penelope was little. Her mother, Gordon's granddaughter, had been married at 16 to her father, John Lucas, Gordon's nephew, and her father had then taken over Gordon's business. Tightly interconnected, it was also an argumentative family. On William Gordon's death Penelope's father's brother had sued Gordon's daughter and only child, Penelope's grandmother, over the inheritance. She was an imposter, he said, and should not be sole heir.[5]

During Penelope's girlhood John Lucas owned considerable property not far from their home, on and around two Thames-side wharves. Coal came to London by sea from northern England and coal merchants were common along this part of the river. Soot was coal's by-product. Constituent ammonia and nitrogen made it a valuable agricultural and garden fertiliser, and it was therefore shipped in turn upriver. John Lucas paid chimney sweeps to get him extra soot but he also bought it in.[6]

Among Lucas tenants on St Bride's wharf was Thomas Lowndes. Lowndes's father, Thomas senior, had pioneered lending libraries in England and the Lowndes library, with associated publishing house and bookshop, was only a step away in Fleet Street. There, for a guinea a year (£1.1s) subscribers could borrow six books at a time and with thousands of volumes – plays, poetry and novels, besides more obviously improving works – the library catered for families such as Penelope's. Lowndes senior had pioneered the book industry's focus on women as authors and readers. He published, for instance, Fanny Burney's celebrated *Evelina, or the History of a Young Lady's Entrance into the World* (1778).[7]

Penelope's mother died when she was eight and her father had married again, to Jane Lowndes, his tenant's sister. Another girl was born, 14 years younger than Penelope, but then John Lucas had also died, and his widow had married a naval officer, John Temple. Penelope seems to have lost her last Lucas relations, two uncles, about the same time. Quietly resilient, her first great achievement was emotional independence, even of the Temples.

Penelope Lucas might well have overseen the education of her half-sister. It is hard to say what other mentoring and/or teaching experience she could have had, but at some point during 1802–04 she took charge of John Macarthur's daughter Elizabeth. Young Elizabeth was destined not for school like her brothers but for a period living with a well-educated, well-ordered private family, where there was someone with the skill and time to oversee her studies. There is more to be said in another chapter about young Elizabeth's growing up.

Jane Lucas's second marriage had brought on another bitter argument about family property. John Lucas had died intestate. The inheritance was in dispute in the Court of Chancery, and Penelope was listed among the defendants.[8] Within the tangle of resentment she seems to have been largely on her own, but the Macarthur connection clearly made a difference. Hence her flight from the Temples to her new pupil's family and to New South Wales.

THE IMPORTANCE OF MISS LUCAS

We know the minute Penelope Lucas was born – 11.35 am – but her voice is hard to hear.[9] Very little she wrote has survived and very little, too, was ever said about her in other people's letters. There is a monument to her in St John's Cathedral, Parramatta, made of white marble and cut by the rising young English sculptor Richard Westmacott – expensive, pure and opaque. It is wonderfully symbolic. Clearly, Miss Lucas was revered by the friends she found in New South Wales. More than anything or anyone else, she represents the hidden heart of the Macarthur family, its secret engine, an economy of feeling unknowable now.

Before she decided to come, Penelope Lucas must have read about Australia, its endless forests, its bizarre creatures, its ancient peoples, probably in some of Lowndes's books. Now she saw it all for herself and, in particular, those mysteriously unfamiliar faces, darkly different, could come startlingly close. After the death of the warrior Pemulwuy his people had asked for peace and one of them, the boy Tjedboro, or Tedbury, said to be Pemulwuy's son, volunteered to identify the men who had killed the Macarthurs' two stockmen. The settlers saw in Tjedboro his father's 'diabolical' propensities and he was locked up all the same, but then freed on the understanding that he would keep the peace.[10]

This was about the time the *Argo* arrived and John Macarthur, as he settled back in, decided to see what he could do with Tjedboro. Penelope Lucas watched this educational experiment from the start, as Tjedboro became a familiar figure to them all, deeply attached to 'Master' – 'Boss' was a form of address yet to be invented – but also living as he liked in the bush. He was part of the world Penelope Lucas came to terms with in New South Wales, wondering, as she must have done, at his coming and going, largely naked, in and about the house. William remembered later on how Tjedboro had 'often chidden and restrained me in some of my boyish pranks'.[11] Miss Lucas might have wondered especially at that.

ELIZABETH & JOHN

Here were two strikingly different recruits to that crowded household, about the same time, but how Tjedboro and Penelope Lucas saw each other, how his particular sense of right met with her Fanny Burney manners, is beyond all measurement now.

21

TJEDBORO

Tjedboro's thoughts are hidden at least as thoroughly as the thoughts of Penelope Lucas. Why did he point out to the invaders the warriors who had killed the Macarthurs' stockmen? Was he familiar with Elizabeth Farm even before John Macarthur came home? Had Elizabeth Macarthur already won him over as she had done with other local people since 1790? Whatever the answers, John took an interest in him.

Many settlers tried to adopt Indigenous children. At this stage these were usually children left destitute by the disorder and death caused by invasion. They were usually given English names and persuaded by various means, such as regular meals and lack of any alternative, to become unpaid servants. Some were taught the rudiments of Christianity. There was kidnapping too, but more often in Van Diemen's Land, and a little later on.[1]

Elizabeth and John, and their children as they got older, took a more detached approach. They admired the way Indigenous people lived among themselves and if they could help it they were not inclined to get in their way. They understood that they had particular rules of conversation, as their daughter Elizabeth said, 'and perhaps they possess more native politeness than is found amongst any people'. According to William, they 'respected each other highly'. Except when moved by passion, greed or desire for a wife, they 'never interfered with each other', and usually, said

James, in dealing with White people, they have a habit of 'shrinking from an inadvertent intrusion'.²

Setting aside the mighty fact of invasion and theft of the land, the Macarthurs wanted to live and let live, and they could be generous when called on. According to one old Indigenous man, quoted long afterwards by William, his people had always found 'a home and food and shelter [at Elizabeth Farm] … when they needed it'.³

Tjedboro was the only Indigenous child the Macarthurs adopted in any sense. He seems to have been barely a teenager when the relationship started, 'a young child' or 'mere boy', according to William, and yet he was obviously old enough to take initiatives of his own among his people. To begin with, living at Elizabeth Farm after John's return, he was 'treated with kindness, and … was quite happy and docile', but the break soon came. As William described it, '[M]y father being out walking with the boy, and wishing to go in one direction while the boy wished to go in another, and finding persuasion of no avail, he [John] used the tone of command.' Tjedboro disappeared into the scrub and was gone for months. 'He then resumed his old habits, coming and going as he liked but always kindly treated, and without attempts to restrain him.'⁴

A remark nearly 200 years later by an Arnhem Land woman, her name unrecorded, helps to makes sense of Tjedboro's disappearance. It was a standard response. 'We Aborigines,' she said, 'we are different. If somebody growls at us and hurts our feelings, we don't like to stay.' John and Tjedboro, on other occasions, must have stepped around differences like this. What then did they talk about as they walked together? Did John pass on 'civilising' information? Did Tjedboro offer a little of the Dharug tongue? Kuñń = sun; durawai = grass; jirang = leaves; muru = pathway; jannawi = with me; paialla = talk; wilguja = whither; beal = no; kular = angry; wumerra = run; bulu = the silent shadow of the trees.⁵

TJEDBORO

Tjedboro seems to have been drawn to John Macarthur much as Bennelong, of the Eora people, had once been drawn to Governor Phillip. John's authority in family and household was obvious, just as Phillip's authority as governor had been obvious to Bennelong. Tjedboro 'used to say', so William recalled, 'he should "like to be as white man", that is civilized, that he might be a gentleman'. In chiding the Macarthur children he mimicked their father, and yet he would not bend to John's orders. 'He always called my father "master",' William said, 'but I do not think he would ever employ himself about any useful occupation … the idea of being controlled he could not endure.' For John Macarthur that was almost a plus. It proved his power to command the loyalty even of the unruly and to draw affection even from the wilderness of the antipodean bush. He loved that.

TJEDBORO'S PEOPLE, THE DHARUG, LIVED MAINLY ON the level country of the Cumberland Plain, between the Eora and Tharawal peoples along the coast, the Awabakal to the northeast, and, across the Hawkesbury–Nepean, the Wiradjuri and Gandangara. All the Macarthur pasture and farmland was within the territory of the Dharug, though the land to be granted to them by Lord Camden's order was on the far side of the Nepean to the south. That seems to have been the home country of Dharug and Gandangara combined.

When John Macarthur walked with Tjedboro he must have had some sense of Tjedboro's knowledge of Country and of the spirit world implicit in it. Since those early conversations with Watkin Tench, he and Elizabeth had heard of such things. How much, then, did the shadow of the dead warrior Pemulwuy, if he was indeed Tjedboro's father, walk between them?

With the arrival of the *Argo*, John Macarthur had suddenly appeared, as if from nowhere, not long after Pemulwuy's death.

Among his people any one of the invaders might be imagined – recreated in thought – as a reincarnation of the Indigenous past. And yet John Macarthur was to disappear again, just as completely, early in 1809, with disastrous consequences for Tjedboro, as a later chapter tells.

When John returned yet again, in 1817, Tjedboro was dead, but William remembered how a man they knew as Harry welcomed his father back. The family were at dinner when Harry suddenly appeared with a friend. The two were given seats at the table and glasses of wine. Harry, touching his glass, made a speech for his host, and 'I remember thinking', said William – he had been 17 at that point – 'I had never seen manner more graceful or heard expressions better turned than his.'[6]

His people had mourned John's absence, Harry said, 'as for a father'. He had some idea, he said, of the causes of his long absence and '[h]e … trusted that those things would never come again.' He hoped that 'he would never again depart, but dwell in peace and at length lay his bones amongst them'.[7] William struggled to remember exactly. However, if Harry did speak of John Macarthur as a father finding a place in the soil at his life's end it was a powerful indication of the impact he had made during the earlier period, while Tjedboro was alive.

Tjedboro's connection with John Macarthur might have shaped that of other local people, or vice versa. It was a world of feeling now lost, a buzzing universe of gossip and wonder, scorn and suspicion, in which Indigenous minds struggled to bring the new dispensation into line with the old. Certain Indigenous people had made that effort even from the beginning, hunting with extraordinary resilience among the roots of meaning so as to find new order, even while so much of the old one was under attack.

22

CURIOSITY

Each human mind is like each human body. However much it grows or dwindles, stays still or moves about, its basic patterning stays the same. John Macarthur's thinking was supercharged by his time away in 1801–05, but his deeper habits of mind did not change. Elizabeth's were settled too, within the life they had made for themselves in New South Wales, and beyond that by childhood in England's West Country. Elizabeth loved the 'retirement', as she called it, of life abroad but she must have felt with some pain the newer world of 19th-century Europe drawing away from her as she got older. In the same way her sons, all four of them, spent crucial years far beyond her hearing, sight and touch, returning, those that did return, 'grown quite out of my knowledge'.[1]

For anyone meeting them at intervals, what patterning made Elizabeth and John familiar and recognisable? When Penelope Lucas came to live with them in June 1805, suddenly seeing and hearing them together in their own home – married as they had been for nearly 17 years and in the same house for more than ten – how did she make sense of them? How far is it possible to do the same now, to know Elizabeth and John as they were known close-up? Within the method of each life, say to 1809, when John went again to England with the two younger boys, what changed? Even more, what stayed the same?

Take a better focused question – how did Elizabeth and John usually exercise their minds? Even curiosity follows pre-ordained patterns. What patterns shaped the curiosity of Elizabeth and John, each alone and both together? The family had books. Most of the books kept at Elizabeth Farm are now lost but a list survives of everything on the shelves in 1854, when the widowed Elizabeth was not long dead. Some were titles going back before 1809, in many cases a long way back. A few of those must have reached New South Wales very early. Given how hard it was for books to reach Sydney Cove during the first 20 or 25 years, a good number might have been brought with them at the very beginning.[2]

Considering the 1854 list as a whole, as reading matter for two generations, it is clear that the thoughts of Elizabeth and John must have been patterned by works of the Enlightenment. Their children, building on that, followed the postwar redirection of the European world. From about 1815 and the Battle of Waterloo, with large changes in book publishing in Britain – less regional, but more subject-specialised and enterprising – books were more abundant. With more shipping, many more books reached New South Wales.

Some of the older books at Elizabeth Farm might have been found in any good library during the first generation. Samuel Johnson's *Dictionary of the English Language*, Edmund Burke's *Origin of Our Ideas of the Sublime and Beautiful* and Adam Smith's *Theory of Moral Sentiments* were there. The imaginations of Elizabeth and John also fed on real-life adventure. They liked history, memoirs and travel. Roman history was John's favourite, and they owned at least half a dozen volumes of that – Cicero's *Letters*, Polybius's *Histories*, William Russell's *History of Ancient Europe* and others.

Another book on the list was *The Adventures of Gil Blas of Santillane*, Tobias Smollett's translation of the French original. Raucus, comic, even risqué, *Gil Blas* was apparently an Elizabeth

Farm favourite. Edward, the oldest of the Macarthur children, when he was grown up, quoted it to the others as if it were familiar to them all. 'I am happy', his quotation went, 'because I think myself so.'[3] Either parent, reading *Gil Blas* to the children, might have dwelt a moment on this dictum – especially Elizabeth, because it summed up her up attitude to life exactly. As a riveting story of young thieves wrestling with conscience, *Gil Blas* ought to have been a sort of Bible in New South Wales.

They must have owned English-origin novels too, but none survived to 1854 – no Henry Fielding, Samuel Richardson, Jane Austen or Charlotte Smith. Poetry and plays were certainly there, such as John Macarthur might have read aloud in declaiming to the children, including John Vanbrugh, George Farquhar and Joanna Baillie. John loved theatre, as this story has shown and will show again. He might have discovered Joanna Baillie's passionate work during his time in England in 1802–04, when it was newly popular. At that point too, Ben Jonson's *Every Man in His Humor* was playing at Covent Garden. It had its echo in a joke John made not long afterwards about the bouncing braggart Bobadil.[4]

The Macarthurs' older books on religion included nothing evangelical. They demonstrate instead a hunt for the foundations of faith, as in Isaac Barrow's *Sermons*, Robert Barclay's *Apology* and George Hume's *Letters on Infidelity*. Edward once mentioned to his mother the lessons both parents had taught him about the difference between essential and non-essential. That was a distinction taken from theology, between what really mattered in dealings with God and, on the other hand, what could be put aside. In other words, how do we disagree in ways useful to faith and human feeling?[5]

One book on their shelves, as listed in 1854, reveals a darker corner of John Macarthur's imagination. The *Secret Memoirs of the Late Mr Duncan Campbel* (spelt thus in the title) was published a long time beforehand, when John's father was young. It coincided with the McArthurs' Scottish past. In it Duncan Campbell, a man from Argyll but living in London, a sorcerer and fortune-teller – he did exist – told his life story. Many Scots, the book said, were '[what] they call *Second-Sighted*'. That is to say, they saw and talked with spirits, and they took from spirits power to tell the future. Duncan Campbell was famously second-sighted.[6]

Everyone, so Campbell said, was subject through life to particular spirits, good and evil, and to the fight between them. Some men and women gave themselves up to their evil spirit, because they saw no choice, or else because of 'the vile Satisfaction they take in doing mischief'. '[I]f Heaven had thought fit to give me what I want,' said one woman, quoted in the book, 'I should never have thought of having Recourse to Hell.'[7] The world was full of invisible spirits of both sorts.

It was in fact a common understanding. In Daniel Defoe's vivid story of *Moll Flanders* (1722), Moll tells of evil spirits drawing her over and over into sin. Even the learned David Hartley, in 1749, took for granted the existence of 'good and evil beings ... such as angels and devils', and the great Scottish philosopher Thomas Reid spoke of spirits (1764) as part of the 'the whole universe about me', though he did not see them as good and evil. In Germany, Johann Wolfgang von Goethe raised the sale-of-souls idea to sublime tragedy, in *Faust*. At a more palpable level, Duncan Campbell felt these beings cramming in upon him, almost fleshly, some ghastly, some joyful, pulling him to panic or to swooning delight.[8]

Duncan Campbell's was a world of belief that the Enlightenment was supposed to have abolished but, even in the lifetime of Elizabeth and John the spirit world remained very real. For many, there was no looking within themselves for the drama of conscience because it was roundabout, embodied in spirits. Cornwall especially – the rocks, the hills, the wells, the River Tamar – seemed full of spirits. Some were originally pre-Christian gods. In Cornwall and elsewhere, everyone knew about spirits, even if they did not believe in them. Watkin Tench said of the Indigenous people at Sydney Cove, 'They call a spirit, *Mawn.*' Spirits, Tench said, citing Cicero, played on imagination worldwide.[9]

Even the most enlightened men and women were tossed by impulses at least resembling spirits. John Macarthur felt himself driven by an 'indescribable fierceness of independence' and by an obstinacy beyond reason. He enjoyed the drama in that, the sense of sporting with tigers, though he was frightened to recognise the same impulse in John, his second son.[10] His interest in those who believed wholeheartedly in spirits, such as Tjedboro and the soldiers of the NSW Corps, made him half believe in them himself. With such adventures he shaped his own life, much like Duncan Campbell, as a morality play on a cosmic scale.

Men and women sold their services to the devil. Campbell's *Memoirs* said so. In England in 1802–04, John Macarthur entertained himself with thinking about the fate of two men who, in his mind, might have sold themselves in this way to 'his infernal Highness'. They were his current enemies William Paterson and Neil MacKellar, principal and second in the duel that had led to his arrest. John Macarthur shot to kill William Paterson and he speculated still on Paterson's chances of 'a furlough for the other world', serving his master, as he put it, in 'the regions of darkness'. MacKellar, 'that unfortunate apostate', had been sent to England to testify against him, but his ship had disappeared and MacKellar was probably dead, 'doomed', as John supposed, 'to prepare apartments in the lower regions for his infernal employer'.[11]

Apostates were traitors to faith. They were damnable in this world and the next. 'Depart from me, ye cursed,' says the Lord, 'into everlasting fire, prepared for the devil and his angels.' John Macarthur drew that terrifying injunction into his own life. So, in 1798, when he and William Balmain persuaded the 'officers of the settlement', military and civilian, to trade as a group, those officers were made to swear that any one of them who broke their self-imposed rules was to be shunned as 'an infamous character', in public, in private and for life.[12] Fully in step with God as he seemed to be, John Macarthur almost imagined that he could engineer real damnation.

AT HOME AT ELIZABETH FARM, MANY OF THE VISITORS, men and women, in their talking, fed the curiosity of Elizabeth and John, not to mention Penelope Lucas and the children. Post-1805, there was Tjedboro, already mentioned. There was John Oxley, still to be introduced. But for the present, imagine three others, all men. Imagine them sitting, one by one, in the Macarthurs' parlour. Imagine, with the mind's ear, the questions they induced, the small silences, the economy of conversation, the command used by John, interjections from Elizabeth, lapidary politeness from Penelope Lucas. Such conversation, Elizabeth once said, 'I am very fond of'.[13]

It was a pleasure she and John shared, and it points to the main secret of their life together. Both of them felt real joy in listening and talking, its surprise and ceremony, but also, even more deeply, both needed the bracing chill of isolation. Elizabeth Farm was well placed for both delights.

Of these three visitors, one came for a single evening. One made regular visits. One stayed for several days. John Fitzpatrick Jefferie has been mentioned already. A young man, acting purser of the *Earl Cornwallis*, he played a momentary part in the James Marshall affair of 1801. Jefferie, a Protestant, had Catholic relations in Ireland, among them Richard McCormick, a Dublin wool merchant and a key figure among the United Irishmen, the nationwide movement, Catholic and Protestant, fighting against British rule. The United Irish were inspired by Enlightenment ideas of shared humanity and by the revolution in France. Their 1798 uprising and its suppression cost at least 10 000 lives.[14]

Jefferie was staying with McCormick in Dublin when the rebellion started. Eighteen years old at that point, he was obsessed with the idea of human progress. His heroes included the revolutionaries in North America, sufferers, he said, 'under the lash of British power'. Now it was the Irish. Jefferie had been given command of a company of rebel Dubliners and he had afterwards fled with them to the mountains in rearguard resistance. He had then escaped to England. Arrested and questioned, he had been released as part of a general amnesty extended to all but the top men.[15]

In the Marshall affair Edward Abbott had treated Jefferie as less than a gentleman but John Macarthur saw more to him and asked him to an evening at Elizabeth Farm.[16] During his time at sea Jefferie was building up a collection of cleverly made objects, Māori, Tahitian, Philippine, Malay and colonial, and a few he might have brought that evening to show the Macarthurs, parents and children. Most beautiful of all in its symmetry, but possibly picked up later on, was a mourning mask from the Society Islands, an oval large enough to cover the face, half conch, half cowrie, pearly white matched with glossy mottled black, the two halves neatly joined and bound together with cording, an image of eternity, light and shadow, good and evil, drawn into unison. It still exists.[17]

The second visitor to Elizabeth Farm had also escaped a field of blood. Gabriel-Louis-Marie Huon came from a landowning family at Saint-Pol-de-Léon, a linen-weaving, Celtic-speaking town in western Brittany. Orphaned in childhood, Huon, or Huon de Kerilleau, was twenty at the outbreak of the French Revolution. Boats of all sizes took refugees across the channel to England and Gabriel Huon, as an 'ex-noble', had made his escape in February 1791.[18]

Some Huons, Gabriel's kin, did better. Under orders from the same regime, and in the same year, Jean-Michel Huon de Kermadec, a naval captain, sailed for the south seas with the great explorer Bruni d'Entrecasteaux. The Huon River in Tasmania and Kermadec Islands in New Zealand were named after him. In London, meanwhile, Huon de Kerilleau joined the NSW Corps as a private soldier. Calling himself simply Gabriel Louis, he arrived at Sydney Cove in October 1794. In Edward Abbott's company to start with, he moved over to John Macarthur's at Parramatta and in 1807 he was discharged. By then he was already tutor to the two Macarthur boys, James, who turned nine that year, and William, seven. They called him 'Mr Louis'.

Gabriel Huon loved books. He read them while taking walks, which could be dangerous. He had been a student at the Collège de Léon, founded by the Bishop of Léon, Jean-François de la Marche, another Huon kinsman. The bishop himself acknowledged that old attachment when he sent Gabriel Huon 45 Spanish dollars, entrusted to John Macarthur on the *Argo*. 'The poor fellow,' said Macarthur, 'was quite overcome with joy when he received them, more I really believe at such a proof of the bishop's affection than out of regard to the money.'[19]

The Bishop of Léon was a *philosophe* – an advocate of enlightenment, devoted to what he called 'the common rights of mankind' – and his college was organised to include the sons of the poor with no obvious discrimination. At the outbreak of revolution the boys had sung the great psalm of joy and hope, the 'Te Deum', and done military exercises with their own revolutionary flag. However, when the new regime began its attacks on the Church the teachers went into opposition, the students split for and against, the college closed and Gabriel Huon, with many others, fled.[20]

Teaching at Elizabeth Farm probably followed the Léon curriculum – French grammar, Latin, geography, secular history, classical mythology (taught as literature) and elementary mathematics. Church history must have been left out, though Huon himself remained a devoted Catholic. Two French grammar textbooks long survived on the Macarthurs' shelves, plus the

CURIOSITY

Chevalier de Mehegan's *Tableau de l'histoire moderne*, and various works of French literature, including a selection of *contes moraux* (moral tales) for children.[21]

At the Collège de Léon the boys had staged public performances – rhetoric, debating and plays – and at Elizabeth Farm the family might have gathered to watch its two do the same. Elizabeth and Mary might well have joined in. So they all learnt French. Their books also included the *Chef d'oeuvres dramatiques* and the three volumes of *The Theatre of Education,* a collection of dialogues for acting by children written by the celebrated Comtesse de Genlis. Acting, said Mme de Genlis, shapes memory and sensibility as nothing else can. But choose your scripts carefully, she said, because acting must teach virtue too.[22]

Gabriel Huon might be imagined coming daily for two or three years to Elizabeth Farm, his arrival triggering explosions of French conversation. He remembered his native Breton and, cheerfully curious himself, he liked to use Australian Indigenous words, probably Eora or Tharawal. In their conversation, therefore, various tongues might have been intermingled.[23] Over the years French language and habits of thought were to colour Macarthur attitudes to economic productivity, education and human difference. The ultimate cause might have been Catherine McArthur, John's mother, but the immediate one was Gabriel Huon.

THE THIRD VISITOR CAME FROM NEW ZEALAND. PHILIP Gidley King, the governor, had been interested in New Zealand since his time in charge on Norfolk Island. During 1805, as governor at Sydney Cove, he sent a present of pigs and goats to Te Pahi, a senior Māori chief at the Bay of Islands, as a diplomatic gesture to ease the way for ships' captains visiting that place, and in December the chief and his four sons came to Sydney on a thank you visit and study tour combined. Te Pahi caused a small sensation. He was tall, muscular and with a 'countenance', as the *Sydney Gazette* said, 'expressive and commanding, though much disfigured by his face being completely *tattooed*'. He was also deeply interested in European ways, including the management of sheep and the making of cloth. He spoke of importing sheep to the Bay of Islands, with shepherds to train his own people, but nothing came of it.[24]

The pigs and goats for Te Pahi had been carried to the Bay of Islands in three ships, among them the *Argo* and the *Venus*, Macarthur vessels, and soon after arriving at Sydney Cove the chief went with his sons upriver 'on a visit to Mr M'Arthur'. They stayed four days. Given his high rank – at Sydney Cove he lived at Government House and ate at Governor King's table – room must have been found for Te Pahi in the crowded homestead at Elizabeth Farm. During this visit, within those walls, the sense of human difference was visceral. Enlightenment, its mental and moral refinement, was truly challenged in the flesh – in skin, scent and timbre.

Everyone knew that some Polynesians, including Māori, were cannibals, and the very thought of cannibalism horrified most Christians. And yet, '[b]etter sleep with a sober cannibal than a drunken Christian', as Herman Melville says in his story of *Moby Dick*.[25] Much the same shift of thought might have taken place at Elizabeth Farm, one after another among those who sat at table with Te Pahi and who listened from their beds – children's whispered speculation – to his pre-sleep movements during those several summer nights.

Getting to know Te Pahi involved a leap of imagination large enough to transform invaders' ideas about this quarter of the globe. That leap subverted settled notions about Indigenous humanity, fixed so far by the Eora, Dharug and neighbouring peoples, who all seemed uninterested in things valued by Europeans. The

Macarthurs' neighbour, Samuel Marsden, talking with Te Pahi, glimpsed the possibility of taking the Christian faith across the Tasman Sea, which he later did, succeeding there as he had not succeeded among his Indigenous neighbours.

Te Pahi and his sons went back to New Zealand late in February. The *Argo*, following in March, failed to find them, but in May Te Pahi sent presents to named friends in New South Wales. So we might imagine some 'very fine' seed potatoes from New Zealand planted and watched, by Elizabeth especially, among the Macarthurs' kitchen vegetables.[26]

Māori men of standing had to provide well for their people and guests, giving and receiving with the grace that comes from genuine power, from *tapu* and *mana*. In Te Pahi's dealings with the invaders in New South Wales such grace made sense on both sides. And again, spirits (*kehua*), some of them terrifying, filled the Māori world too. They were the enemy that Christians such as Marsden wanted to root out and replace with the unadulterated love of the Christian God.

Not that either side really knew the other. Shared politeness and reciprocal ignorance – they were patterned within each point of view, like the shiny black and white of John Jefferie's funeral mask. Nothing thrilled John and Elizabeth more than treading the edge of difference as they did with Te Pahi.

23

EXACTITUDE

The whaler *Argo*, which sailed from London to Sydney Cove in 1804–05, carried another novelty. Among the men on board, variously packed into the passengers' cabins, was Edward Wood, a trained wool-sorter or, to use later terminology, a wool-classer. A first-class product called for first-class expertise, and John Macarthur trusted Edward Wood for that.

The work of the wool-sorter was rife with change and opportunity. Even titles were changing. There was a time when one man, called a wool-stapler, might buy, sort and sell, applying his own expertise at every point. However, sorting was now a more exacting skill. Wool-sorters were paid to divide the fleece more exactly than hitherto into types and grades. Fingers, eye and brain worked in more intricate combination, hunting with microscopic care for variations in the raw wool, because shades of difference imperceptible to a layman affected the finished cloth. The leading criteria were fineness and softness, and in judging fineness, exactitude was pushed to its human limit. The best sorters were already testing their wool to the thousandth of an inch (in micrometres or microns). Edward Wood, at 32, had seen skills intensify even since his time of training.[1]

Precise uniformity – exact similitude – mattered now too, for all sorts of goods. Statements of quantity had once varied from place to place and object to object – casks of this, bushels of that. Penelope Lucas's father had sold his soot in bushels. Now, everywhere, scientific communication, market pressure, and the sheer love of neat classification had as far as possible made its mark. Everything had to be measured and judged in the same way, using the same terms and standards. At Parramatta, Elizabeth Macarthur looked for tiny variations in the stamens and pistils of antipodean plants, fitting them into the comprehensive truth invented at Uppsala, in far-off Sweden, by Carl Linnaeus. For the first time, in Britain, the making of coins was precise and uniform, creating standard value nationwide. Mass armies meant the manufacture of firearms with strictly interchangeable parts. For the first time, with more accurate guns, it was useful to take careful aim.[2]

Taken altogether, trustworthy exactitude made a difference, even a neurological difference, to the way brains worked. For many, God's power was proved even more fully by the way exactitude could be applied to all of Creation. Edward Wood was especially devout. Tied up, however, in this mighty change was the risk of creating for human minds a new kind of providence, another deep certainty, systematic and eternal, and yet made by human beings themselves, so that God stood ever further back.[3]

Whatever the result, the passion for exactitude, like some peculiar virus, spread outwards, doubling back and doubling back, over and over, in an ever-thickening human web.

Edward Wood was born at Ross-on-Wye, a market town in Herefordshire, which was also the native place of the Hulletts, John Macarthur's London partners. All were young men on the make and such networks got things done. Edward's father belonged to a firm of wool-staplers – the Hulletts' father, owning sheep, might have been his client – and Herefordshire's wool, mainly Ryeland crossed with Merino, was said to be England's finest.[4] However, wool-milling in those parts happened mainly in nearby Gloucestershire, where the leading men included Edward Sheppard, who drove the 1803 parliamentary inquiry, and his neighbour John Wallington, who brought to that inquiry John Macarthur.

In Gloucestershire wool-sorters might have as many as 12 baskets about them, extending from the coarse wool used for blankets and broadcloth to the superfine. In Yorkshire, England's other great sheep-growing and wool-milling district, it was usually only two or three. Some of the very best Merino wool used in Gloucestershire came from Saxony, via an Anglo-German importer in London. Edward Wood's early experience had apparently included work, probably in Gloucestershire, with Saxon wool.[5]

In mid-1804 Edward Wood's father was bankrupt and within months he was at sea on the *Argo*, seeking a new future in New South Wales. However, John Macarthur intended first to make his expertise widely available among the settlers, so as to make wool-growing popular as soon as possible. On arrival a program was worked out with the help of Governor King, who was now onside, and a series of questions appeared in the *Sydney Gazette,* inviting flock-owners to detail their efforts, if any, in growing fine wool, and their experience with 'true bred Spanish Sheep'.[6]

Owners were then asked to bring their sheep to several central spots so that Edward Wood could see for himself. After consultations with the Macarthurs and Samuel Marsden, he made his report. Despite a 'very great improvement' from the declared original, there was, he told the governor, some way to go. The main obstacle was 'unaccountable prejudice' in favour of breeding for meat rather than wool. Flock-owners had yet to learn that Spanish Merinos of 'the pure breed' were good for both. John backed up this report with a new statement about the importance of producing as much wool as possible in New South Wales. He now recycled the concerns of John Wallington, the manufacturer who had introduced him to the Commons committee, affirmed by his own mathematical calculations. At present, mechanising the factories in England would throw thousands of labouring men out of work. However, 'if we can by our united efforts (as assuredly we can) raise in this colony any quantity of fine wool', that danger must disappear. There would be plenty of factory work whatever machinery was used. At the same time manufacturers would be able to sell their cloth so cheaply and so abundantly that they must win, even worldwide, 'the most complete monopoly that any people ever possessed'.[7]

Macarthur had always hoped that all the settlers keen to improve their wool would come to Edward Wood for advice, so as to get this dazzling process under way.[8] That never happened. As usual, possibilities crystal clear to himself were obscure to most others and interest fell away. Even government support failed. In April 1806 Governor King heard that his successor was imminent. William Bligh arrived in August and he brought with him an instinctive dislike for everything that wool-growing meant in a colony for convicts.

GOVERNOR KING GAVE EDWARD WOOD 300 ACRES ON South Creek and Wood named it Kingswood, but before long his original hopes dwindled and his ambitions changed. There were several American ships in the harbour – whalers from Nantucket, Massachusetts – and one of the captains, Daniel Whitney, stayed for some months. Wood followed him back to Nantucket, where he married and eventually, with Whitney's help, went back to wool-sorting. He was to be a key figure in the business of William Dickinson, who had his own flocks and factory in the Ohio valley and who was, in that country, a fine-wool pioneer.[9]

Wood's life was a life of exactitude. In it can be seen something of the vast transformation overtaking the world. The spread of Merino sheep beyond Europe, even to the far end of the earth, and the habits of precision that made such change possible, in navigation and gun-making, botanising and book-keeping, were all deeply interconnected and extraordinarily dynamic.

Elizabeth and John Macarthur knew that they were part of something big, and John aimed to go a long way beyond fine wool. To some extent, he had no choice. Thanks to the wool experiment their fortunes – costs and income – were out of balance, a problem that must get worse as their four sons passed through school in England and entered adult life. It all cost money. The Macarthurs needed other income until their wool experiment was a success, so as 'to prosecute the latter [object]', as John explained, 'with vigour and effect'.[10]

The solution was more far-flung exactitude. Back in New South Wales, John Macarthur informed Governor King of the projects he had in mind 'for the general Benefit of the Colony', apart from wool. With the Hullett brothers of London, he was already part-owner of the *Argo*, which from Sydney Cove went hunting whales, and during the second half of 1806 Hulletts sent out two more whalers under similar agreement, the *Parramatta* and the *Dart*. Backwards and forwards, by himself and others, it all meant improved communication between New South Wales and Europe. Export from Sydney Cove, whether whale oil or wool, would bring regular traffic in the other direction, with ships carrying '[a]rticles of use and Comfort to sell [to] the Inhabitants'. As John Macarthur also told the governor, it must help with the old problem of getting cheap, reliable supplies from abroad.[11]

He also had his eye on the islands of the western Pacific, looking for ways, as he said, 'to collect the various valuable articles of trade with which they are said to abound'. Pork from indigenous Tahitian pigs had already been brought to New South Wales under government contract when other food was short. On Fiji and elsewhere there was sandalwood, a sweetly scented timber exuding oil, and both wood and oil were in high demand in eastern Asia

EXACTITUDE

for use in Buddhist and Hindu ritual. Until it ran out, a Chinese market for sandalwood might be built up matching the British market for fine wool. Here, however, there was a problem. Only vessels based in India and registered with the East India Company could, in law, trade with China.[12]

The ex-convict merchant Simeon Lord, who had prospered mightily since the 1790s, had lately sent 120 tons of Fijian sandalwood to Canton (Guangzhou) on an American ship, the *Criterion*. It had sold well and Lord had brought back Chinese tea, but Governor King judged the import to be an infringement of the company monopoly. The *Criterion* arrived in Sydney Cove at the end of May 1806 and the governor, in duty bound, stopped it unloading. Into this stand-off John Macarthur stepped with marked precision. His family was now on good terms with the Kings, and Elizabeth and the two girls were staying at Government House. John had made a confidential friend of the governor's secretary, Garnham Blaxcell, so that it was altogether a hopeful moment.[13]

The *San Francisco y San Pablo*, a Spanish merchant brig captured off the coast of South America and now a prize of war, was also in port. For £700 John Macarthur suddenly bought it and renamed it *Elizabeth*, aiming to send it for sandalwood himself. King only insisted that no licence should be sought from the East India Company for trading further, a strange and roundabout prohibition in the circumstances. Reporting to London, King omitted to mention this new arrangement, and for good reason. It was underhand. King could not expect to continue in paid employment for much longer and he was worried about funding his family, including several young children, into the future. John Macarthur apparently suggested to him a joint investment, in sheep at least and possibly sandalwood too. In fact, nothing came of it.[14] Meanwhile, through bribery, or at least the suggestion of bribery, John Macarthur aimed to circumvent the dead weight of a 300-year-old ban.

Garnham Blaxcell, King's secretary, was young, bold and keen to make money, and with Blaxcell as manager in Sydney, after King left, plans quickly expanded. Their first creation was a multi-purpose trading fleet. To the Hullett vessels they added the *Venus* and *Hope*, both sloops built on the spot and, as small vessels, fit for taking government supplies to outlying settlements and bringing back local produce. Coal and cedar now came in bulk from the Hunter Valley, north of Sydney. On a much larger scale, the firm of Macarthur and Blaxcell put together a scheme for ocean trade, a vast circle reaching far beyond Fiji.

This new vision sprang from John Macarthur's urgent, long-term understanding that the settlement might develop its own skills and make its own money, without resort to Europe. There was to be a circle inscribed on waters still partly unknown to Europeans, with a possibility also of short-cutting from port to port. From Sydney to the mid-Pacific, supplies might go for barter with the 'natives' so as to pick up sandalwood for Canton. From Canton there was already an established trade with Calcutta (Kolkata). From Calcutta the circuit would be completed with supplies for Sydney Cove such as the settlement had taken from that place since the 1790s.[15]

Success depended on exactitude, on speedy interconnection at each point of exchange, on fitting in with local supply and demand, much of it seasonal, and on getting around the East India Company's monopoly. For much of this the partners looked to Walter Stevenson Davidson, another of the *Argo* passengers. Though barely 21, Davidson was highly capable and he had family connections with one of Calcutta's leading firms, Hogue, Davidson and Robertson, whose ships were already licensed by the company. Walter Davidson was to negotiate with his relations for a permanent connection with Macarthur and Blaxcell. However, the vessel they were to start with was the *Harrington*, owned by a firm in Madras (Chennai). It sailed from Sydney Cove late in January

1807, with Davidson on board, and was followed a month later by the *Argo* and *Elizabeth*, to help in gathering the sandalwood.[16]

The trade circle was itself part of an even larger scheme. On a summer afternoon, 18 December 1806, a 'select party' of men, women and children, attended by servants, arrived by boat on the peninsula immediately to the west of Sydney. On that high place, overlooking Cockle Bay (later Darling Harbour), was John Macarthur's allotment of 55 acres (22 hectares). Among the sandstone was a spring of fresh water, shining in the sun like the famous mineral waters of Europe. The party ate under a fig tree by the spring, and with a little ceremony this small estate was christened Pyrmont.[17] Pyrmont and Seltzer water, from spas in Germany, bottled for sale, was a familiar item in London shops.

Pyrmont was planned as the centre point of a great creative effort, with Garnham Blaxcell as manager on the spot. There were already men working on-site, seamen and boatbuilders busy among cedar planks, pitch, tar and tallow bought from another Spanish prize ship. Within a few weeks of the picnic, about the time the *Harrington* left, clearing and building began. A small shipyard was an early priority, including a sawpit, where timber might be cut, but in March operations started to multiply beyond that. Salt-making started. With four try-pots, designed for rendering whale blubber, a man named Taylor apparently produced about 1000 pounds (450 kg) of salt a week. Fish caught in Botany Bay and Broken Bay, again by their own men, could now be salted for crews at sea. Most elaborate of all, a very large flour mill took shape in spring.[18]

Hulletts of London remained an important part of John Macarthur's ambitions, and Hulletts's primary focus was still the Atlantic. That might be why, when Edward Wood the wool-sorter first reached the United States, in 1808–09, he set up as a wool-stapler, his father's trade, but also as 'agent for a merchant in New South Wales'.[19] He might have been intended as agent for the Pyrmont operation, not only importing NSW wool for sale in the

United States but otherwise building up American connections. That was before Edward Wood turned his mind to American-grown wool and went back to sorting.

Whatever John Macarthur might have hoped for exactly, this was certainly for him a time of blue-sky ambition. There was, of course, a possibility that the complications of the Pyrmont trade circle scheme were more than the local economy could yet bear. In earlier days Governor Hunter had seen a gap between John Macarthur's 'theoretical schemes' and 'real experience'.[20] So it might be this time, but then all ideals involve some fantasy and all ingenuity at least a little risk.

NAVIGATION FAR FROM LAND DEPENDED ON GOOD timepieces, which meant exactitude at its most refined. The best person for such work was the convict clockmaker Henry Lane, of Pitt's Row. Lane came from Bristol, England's oldest western port. With a shop on Bristol's quayside he had long catered for maritime traffic. His clocks were of the finest quality and beautifully decorated – calibrated, polished and gilded with the utmost care.

In Bristol, Lane had been caught making use of forged bank notes and he was charged with uttering with intention to defraud, a capital offence. He was sentenced to death and his daughter long remembered being fitted for a black dress for his hanging, but in the end he was transported instead. On arrival in New South Wales he opened a shop where he built, among other things, an eight-day grandfather clock featuring, under glass, a model ship 'in constant motion', surely the most elaborate machine made so far in this part of the world.[21]

European men and women were using time more carefully in their own lives than they had ever done before. Good watches were increasingly cheap, and it was easier for all ranks, apart from the very poor, to talk and think in exactly timed ways. Elizabeth

EXACTITUDE

Macarthur had a watch and chain tucked into her bodice, and she always spoke precisely about time. At Norfolk Island, so she once told Bridget Kingdon, the surf was so high that 'a spectator placed on the shore at an elevation of 10 or 12 feet will yet have the horizon frequently excluded from his view in the course of five minutes.' She and John shared in the new understanding that morning in England, for instance, coincided with evening in New South Wales. So at any moment, with a little calculation, you could imagine what friends were doing on the world's far side.[22]

Such were the habits of mind that governed life at Elizabeth Farm. Such were the habits of mind that John Macarthur hoped to project from his multipurpose base at Pyrmont. At the same time John let his thoughts loose on a scheme equally exact but with a deeper human dynamic. While in England in 1802–04, he had heard of large questions being asked about convict transportation and the integration of punishment with moral reform. For some years the jurist and philosopher Jeremy Bentham had argued in detail against transportation as barbaric, imprecise, unjust and wasteful. Bentham wanted to see a new prison built in London, a 'panopticon' as he called it, which would enforce solitary confinement and unceasing oversight, so as to end criminal behaviour altogether. He called it 'an iron cage, glazed'. Someone else called it 'a glass hive'.[23]

Caught in his panopticon as in a transparent engine, every prisoner – Bentham thought of men only – would live and work under an all-seeing eye. Forced to act with clockwork regularity, compelled to confront his own conscience, he would find his way back to virtue. Here, said Bentham, was '[a] new mode of obtaining power of mind over mind, in a quantity hitherto without example'.[24]

The shortcomings of the current system were well understood. According to one well-informed authority, many men sent to New South Wales came back again and were 'at this moment thieves on the town, or have been executed for new offences'. 'Mr Bentham's penitentiary' was talked about as a serious alternative for 20 years but shortly before John Macarthur reached England the government had decided against it. John aimed to fill the gap.

In 1806–08, besides Sydney and its hinterland, there were four settlements in New South Wales, one on Norfolk Island – though that was about to be abandoned – two in Van Diemen's Land and one at the mouth of the Hunter. John Macarthur's plan was as follows. The three or four smaller sites should all be places of punishment, but, he said, vary their harshness. Most transported convicts had seven-year sentences. Change the law in England so that more might be sentenced for life and then, in New South Wales, see that each went first to the settlement where 'the privations … [were] greatest and the labour hardest', before being moved successively through two more, conditional at every move on good behaviour. With a minimum of one year at each site the convict might hope to finish up at Sydney after three years. Despite his original life sentence, at Sydney, after four more years on probation he might be free in law.[25]

Bentham's scheme was designed to make the punishment fit the original crime. John Macarthur's made everything depend, but just as precisely, on the way convicts behaved when they got a new start. It was an interest he actively followed up all his life, as this story will show.

John's scheme for convicts also resembled the Macarthur–Blaxcell trade circle. Vessels were to pass from place to place, putting down each cargo of prisoners and picking up the next. In both cases, ships were to move like the hands in one of Henry Lane's clocks, in never-failing connection, around a central principle and a single point. So the antipodean seas might become a vast domain of skill and precision, a sheet-full of geometry alive with interacting minds. One thing, at least, he overlooked. He imagined this expanse of sea water as a vacancy – not 'terra nullius' but 'mare nullius' – on which he could draw his diagrams, and yet it was richly filled already. It had been patterned by other ideas about time, wrongdoing and redemption, livelihood and loss, for many thousands of years.[26]

PART 5

24

SUDDENLY LARGER LIMITS

In 1805, with everything else, John Macarthur had brought home a promise of more land – 5000 acres (2023 hectares) straightaway and 5000 more later on, if and when wool export was well established. Henry Waterhouse had suggested he look at a spot 70 kilometres south of Sydney Cove, at a place called the Cowpastures, an area bordered to the north and west by the Nepean River, which ran into the Hawkesbury. It was 40–45 kilometres inland from Elizabeth Farm – an easy afternoon on horseback. Government cattle had escaped and wandered to that place in Governor Phillip's time, two bulls and five cows, and there were now several thousand, grown wild. Treated as a precious resource, there were strict orders that they be left in peace, though there was also some careful culling.

Governor King was against any of the Cowpastures land passing into private hands. For five days, therefore, during spring 1805, John Macarthur rode with Walter Davidson over other possible sites. However, he came back in the end to the Cowpastures and King gave in. Two allotments were measured up for him and, sandwiched between them, one for Davidson, as instructed.[1] Altogether, this was a small fraction of the pasture used by the cattle but it lay along the river where they drank each day.

Flocks of sheep were immediately driven to these allotments, with Davidson in charge, while John Macarthur and Governor

King consulted about the cattle. King agreed that John Macarthur should cull the bulls, receiving for his effort one carcass in every three. However, John's ideas grew, as they usually did, into a jigsaw of shared advantage, with every detail quantified. He asked as well for all offal and other leftovers, and a quarter of the calves he could catch. In return he offered £30 000 worth of salted beef, new shoe leather from the hides and much quieter herds.[2]

At about the same time he had another idea, this one with reference to the sheep and wool, which he sent to his agent in London, Thomas Plummer, and which Plummer forwarded to the Board of Trade. Instead of 5000 extra acres when the fine wool experiment succeeded, there might be cumulative additions to both acreage and labour force as sheep numbers increased, subject to annual government inspections. Any exported wool might be taxed and at a certain point some of the best sheep might be handed over, at a pre-arranged price, as a 'public flock', or else for wider distribution, so that 'the breed might become disseminated over the whole colony'.[3]

Had these two ideas been accepted Elizabeth and John might have felt less on edge over the next few years. Governor King liked the proposal for the cattle but he was coming to the end of his time and he decided to leave the matter to his successor, expected any day. As for the sheep, the Board of Trade consulted Sir Joseph Banks, who gave his decided disapproval. John Macarthur, Banks said, was 'born a shopkeeper'. He could know nothing about sheep or cattle. His land at the Cowpastures was unfit for sheep but it was where the cattle came for water and he obviously wanted 'the privilege of killing them as trespassers'. Banks had been consulted in the same way about a new governor.[4] His nomination, his friend William Bligh, came primed with opinions of the same sort.

SUDDENLY LARGER LIMITS

THE GOVERNOR HAD BEEN TOLD TO LET JOHN Macarthur have 'a reasonable number' of convicts, and within a year of his return the convict workforce at Elizabeth Farm and the Cowpastures had tripled, totalling 42. Of those, a quarter had just arrived. Besides the convicts, the Macarthurs also employed six or seven men who had served their terms. Even then, John Macarthur wanted more, announcing in the *Sydney Gazette* that he would give work and ample rationing to 'any number' of free men who wanted it.[5]

They immediately lost six of their new additions, all Irish. With another newly arrived man, also Irish but with a different master, these six had taken to the bush, making a camp on Cabramatta Creek, raiding the Macarthurs' sheep and stealing muskets from the shepherds' huts. They also took a box of clothes belonging to the sheep overseer, Thomas Herbert. This was bushranging, which was a capital offence.

In his rush to expand, John Macarthur seems to have chosen badly – or were these men, beneath a promising exterior, principled rebels? Among the great mass of Irish convicts there were certainly many who were angry about oppression and their rights. Only one of these six, however, Patrick Cox, seems to have been 'desperate and dangerous'. Most of the others had been originally convicted as burglars and poultry thieves. Cox testified against the rest and it was partly due to him that two of them, men called Halfpenny from Tipperary, apparently brothers, were judged to be bushrangers of the worst kind and hanged.[6]

25

INSURRECTION

On the day John Macarthur and Walter Davidson officially received their large grants of land at the Cowpastures, 18 December 1805, 360 acres (145 hectares) were also allotted to Mary Macarthur, aged ten, at South Creek.[1] Unlike the other children of Elizabeth and John, any hopes Mary had of visiting England were disappearing fast. This gift of land, at her father's instigation, looks like a consolation prize. It also made her the first child born among the invading people to be given land of their own. Soon there were many more because families were putting down roots everywhere. The settlement included large numbers of unattached men – four-fifths of transported convicts were male – but there were already plenty of the new generation. The key to the future was very clearly the bustling household, in which all ages made a life together.

Long ago, Nathaniel Lucas, a native of Surrey, south of London (no relation to Penelope Lucas), had been tried for stealing clothes and sentenced to seven years transportation. He had arrived in January 1788, by the First Fleet, in the same ship with Olivia Gascoyne – armed robbery – and both were sent on to Norfolk Island. They had since had 13 children. At Norfolk, Nathaniel Lucas was the government's master carpenter, and he designed and built two windmills, but in 1805 the family moved back to Sydney, where they made their home on a town lease, one of a matching pair of allotments near St Phillip's church. The other allotment, still vacant, was John Macarthur's.

Nathaniel Lucas designed more mills – first, a small post mill for his own benefit, the whole structure turning on a single post to follow the wind, and then, for the government, a smock mill, whose roof, or cap, alone turned. Both were weatherboard. His third mill was for John Macarthur and Garnham Blaxcell at Pyrmont. By this time there were Lucas sons working with their father and learning the trade.

Work started on the Pyrmont mill during spring 1807. It was a stone tower with a turning cap and four floors, and it was the biggest mill so far in New South Wales. A sandstone quarry was opened up on the spot and Thomas Boulton, stonemason, directed the cutting, dressing and laying. Lucas and Boulton both worked under contract, with Lucas paid once (£224.7s.4d) as the designer and Boulton paid twice, in advance and on completion (total £182.2s).[2] The rest of the workforce were waged men, including a master carpenter, Charles Williams, and a master blacksmith, Thomas Hodgetts.

It was work for two generations. While it was underway Charles Williams, the master carpenter, married the millwright's eldest daughter, Ann. Afterwards the master blacksmith's son and assistant, John Hodgetts, married her sister Olivia. Building windmills, boats and so on, parents and children, the invaders matched their thoughts with local winds and water. They worked out how to see and feel the place in a masterly way. James Squire, father-in-law to one of Nathaniel Lucas's sons, discovered how to grow and brew hops in this strange soil. As with the Macarthurs, the soil, plus the winds and the water, gave such people homes and livelihoods.[3] Security meant self-respect. So their property, as property, became more than measurable.

ELIZABETH & JOHN

THIS INFRASTRUCTURE OF SETTLEMENT TOOK A HIT from the incoming governor. William Bligh arrived on 6 August 1806, in a two-vessel fleet with his second daughter Mary Putland and her husband, also a naval officer. The other ship carried Edward Macarthur, aged 17, on his first visit home. Bligh's wife Elizabeth, still in England, was able, strong-minded and well read, but she hated sea travel. She therefore stayed in London with their four unmarried daughters.[4]

The Blighs were not just a naval family. They also belonged to the London world of fashion and art. Mrs Bligh owned thousands of prints of work by European artists. A sixth daughter, Harriet, the eldest, was married to the well-known artist Henry Aston Barker, who, with his father, had invented panoramas, vast paintings that bent perspective and used curved surfaces, even to 360 degrees, so as to show entire cities, sea battles and so on, in a single sweeping view. These panoramas made spectators feel they were there, mid-city or mid-battle, embraced by colour, action and expansive sky. The Barkers' efforts in optical manipulation were among the sights of London, and Henry was busy with new ones – Constantinople, Copenhagen, the port of Malta. 'Panopticon' and 'panorama' were both new words and they were both about creating illusion. Jeremy Bentham's panopticon pretended to take the overseeing eye into individual souls. Barker's panoramas showed thousands at a glance.[5]

Panoramas also brought money and fame, and the Blighs carried with them a powerful sense of cultural superiority to New South Wales. Taste drawn from such fountainheads is authoritative and intractable. It cannot bend.

William Bligh, nearly 62 when he was named governor, had had a chequered career. He had sailed with Cook and fought in the French wars, including the great sea battles of Camperdown and Copenhagen. He had made his name as a maritime surveyor and as the naval captain who carried the breadfruit plant, a type of fig, from Tahiti to the West Indies as foodstuff for the enslaved workforce. There were two voyages because the first collapsed in mutiny. In April 1789 the men of the *Bounty* had put Bligh and 18 others into a small boat in mid-Pacific and only after an extraordinary trial of endurance, including nine weeks at sea, had they found safety at Timor.

Some of the *Bounty* mutineers were captured and court-martialled, but their trial deeply divided public opinion, including within the navy. For some Bligh was a tyrant, his cruelty and violent tongue unbearable to self-respecting Englishmen. Bligh, however, had a champion in Sir Joseph Banks. Meanwhile, New South Wales needed a strong governor because prosperity had created new problems of disorder. A few, the Macarthurs among them, thought that what it really needed was a larger legal and commercial foundation, but in London the authorities took the easier option – a governor who could make things work as first intended. Bligh was their answer.

As one of Banks's confidantes in New South Wales told him, Bligh soon proved that he did not understand what the place had become. For instance, propertied people started to arrive, with promises from the Colonial Office that they would be given large grants of land. The brothers John and Gregory Blaxland, farmers from Kent, were both disappointed thanks to Bligh. John and Robert Townson, also brothers, came with letters stating that they were to have 2000 acres each, but the governor insisted on getting further orders. Townsons and Blaxlands lost large sums while they waited.[6]

Bligh's abilities were too narrow and his imagination too slight. The only advisor he trusted fully, besides his daughter, Mary Putland, was his secretary, Edmund Griffin, who was honest, careful and astute, but only 18, a schoolmaster's son from Kent. Beyond that, he depended on old hands entangled in local affairs – Robert Campbell, an immigrant merchant, John Palmer, the commissary, and George Crossley, a perjured and transported attorney. It was a bad time for the governor of New South Wales to be using tools as blunt as these.

Then there was the Barker connection. If any site in the world proved the possibilities of panorama it was Port Jackson. The harbour offered glorious scenery and Mary Putland saw its possibilities. Government House was one vantage point, and teams of men were set to blowing up rock nearby and clearing trees and scrub so as to create more perfect views. Beyond the garden fence the challenge was more complicated. A new town plan was drawn up. It centred on two large spaces overlooking the water, one in front of the house and the other around St Phillip's church, with Bridge Street an elegant east–west line between the two.[7]

So Bligh and his daughter took Sydney in hand. No freehold title had ever been granted within the town boundary, thanks to orders issued by Governor Phillip. All private allotments were therefore held under lease or less formally. Bligh aimed to use this rule in pushing his own power to the law's limit.

It was therefore in Sydney, face to face with the governing family, that resentment gathered first. '[He] endeavoured to crush every person as much as possible,' Sarah Wills, shopkeeper, told her mother in England. 'From some he took good houses and gave them bad ones – from others he took their houses and turned them into the street and made them no recompense whatever. Some he stopped building.' Nathaniel Lucas's house was next to the church. He lost it to the governor and was forced to build a new one on another site. Richard Atkins, now judge-advocate, took Bligh's side whenever he could but, as he recalled, 'whenever I went along the streets, the people were talking about those houses having been pulled down by the Governor; and I have heard men say, "My turn will be the next".'[8]

John Macarthur had called at Government House, Parramatta, soon after Bligh arrived, to talk to him about sheep and wool.

INSURRECTION

Bligh was blunt, or so Macarthur recalled – 'What have I to do with your sheep, sir; what have I to do with your cattle?', and 'I have heard of your concerns, sir; you have got 5000 acres of land in the finest situation in the country; but by God you shan't keep it!' Soon afterwards Bligh set off for the Cowpastures to see for himself. The night before he left, the Macarthurs, undaunted, gave 'a splendid entertainment' at Elizabeth Farm in his honour. At the Cowpastures his host was Sir Walter Farquhar's nephew, 20-year-old Walter Davidson, who was managing for the Macarthurs on the spot. The governor stayed overnight with Davidson but by morning it was raining heavily, the Nepean was flooded and only after a week's confinement did he get across, in a boat built by 'a few obliging natives'.[9]

Bligh thought of most local trade as 'speculative', by which he meant risky and self-seeking. John Macarthur's scheme for the wild cattle – supplying government with copious beef – now vanished and any thoughts of the Pyrmont mill grinding government flour must have teetered too. As for maritime trade, there was everything to fear. John's coastal vessels mainly carried goods for government. Worst of all, he expected the completion of the first great trading circle, Sydney Cove–Fiji–Canton (Guangzhou)–Calcutta (Kolkata)–Sydney Cove, early in 1808. The voyage had not gone smoothly and profits depended on the way its last cargo was landed and sold. That rested entirely with Bligh.[10]

The governor himself was also in danger. There was the old question of the governor's legal authority over free settlers. The rule of law was fundamental to British ideas of governance and yet no act of parliament authorised the orders given to free people in New South Wales, or even, in fact, to convicts. In Governor King's day George Johnston of the NSW Corps remarked in a letter to England that the governor could not possibly have the right to impose any sort of tax on his own say-so. The convict lawyer George Crossley said that their ruler, apparently all-powerful, lacked authority to make any local laws at all. '[E]xcept in extraordinary cases,' said other settlers, '[he] is only an executive officer.' In England John Macarthur had heard of the detailed logic of Jeremy Bentham to the same effect, set out in print. He mentioned it to Governor King when he got back.[11]

This question had always hung over the settlement. With increasing riches, larger numbers of free and freed people, and new expertise of various sorts it was urgent.

As with the American Revolution, in New South Wales rights under law were mixed up with new ideas about the 'Rights of Man'. The mighty disturbances in France and Ireland had stunned British imagination with their blood and raw idealism. 'Read [Thomas] Paine's *Rights of Man*,' Neil MacKellar had said to John Piper, when they were still friends. Paine might be a dangerous democrat but 'he says many true things'. As for John Macarthur, he was intrigued by the Irish agitation. It has been noted already that he had asked John Fitzpatrick Jefferie, a captain of rebels in 1798, to dinner at Elizabeth Farm, and he felt especially for Matthew Sutton, a barrister who had fought on the same side in county Wexford, a storm centre of bloodshed, and had arrived as a convict. The same sympathies ran through the lesser ranks of the Corps.[12]

The governor's problems met and multiplied in the Corps because officers and men had family and property interwoven with the rest. That made his authority precarious. The soldiers swapped stories of the personal contempt he showed for them, while they also kept up their old attachment to John Macarthur, who had nourished their early hopes in this strange country. On the other hand, the small farmers, especially on the Hawkesbury, saw Bligh as their ally against the Sydney trading interest and everyone who hated the power of the Corps was loyal.

INSURRECTION

WORK WENT ON AT PYRMONT. AT ONE POINT IN 1807 Garnham Blaxcell bought a quantity of cherry and orange juice, which he mixed with spirits and water to produce weak forms of shrub (a popular type of punch) and cherry brandy. It sold for 40 shillings a gallon, double the cost, but it was a short-lived experiment.[13] The spirits had been bought from the government store, and must have been originally imported. Governor King had come down hard on private distillation, but at the end of his time he had agreed to think about a scheme that would allow him to ban all imports and rely on local distillation. In Britain brewing and distilling were central to the national economy and in the new United States the first president, George Washington, owned one of the largest distilleries in the country. In New South Wales there was a superabundance of peaches, and sometimes of grain. Under proper restrictions that might be used to replace the current random imports – so the settlers, including John Macarthur, had told King.[14]

King had promised to consult with London because at present he could do nothing, he said, without a 'stretch of power'. Thus encouraged, John had started to imagine a much greater stretch of power. Grain was a fundamental resource, its growers needed reliable demand and its buyers needed reliable supply. That had been obvious during his time as inspector of public works but it was doubly proved by severe flooding in the Hawkesbury River in March 1806, which destroyed much of the annual crop. The resulting scarcity led John Macarthur to argue fiercely about debt and money values, a story to be told later on. It also seems to have made him think again about distilling.

John Macarthur's solution to the problem of scarcity and abundance involved balancing good seasons with bad through careful storage from year to year. If that were done, the farmers, sure of continuing demand, would produce as much as they could every year and, as he now suggested, when there was too much in storage the excess might be made into spirits. Spirit import should be banned and the business should be entrusted to a private company accountable to government. In 1798, in a letter to Michael Hogan, John Macarthur had wondered about how to get farmers to produce up to their own limit without destroying local value, including land value.[15] Long thought through, storage and distillation were now his answer.

There was something else. John Macarthur imagined a system of distillery-and-storage as a kind of central bank. It would be a grain bank maintaining grain value. The promissory notes it issued in payment for grain might become local bank notes, like the navy bills circulating at Plymouth Dock, payable on demand and crowding out unstable currency. The political economist Sir James Steuart had already suggested 'meal-banks' and 'banks for grain' in certain rural areas of Britain and India, issuing 'paper credit' that might circulate roundabout. In the right circumstances – you needed strong government – money value might be made perfectly secure. Two hundred years later, grain banks were to be tried in parts of southern Asia with 'miraculous' effect. As a report from these latter days put it, 'nobody goes hungry.'[16] Why not New South Wales in 1806–08?

There is also some overlap with the idea of 'tradable energy quotas', developed in the 20th century as a possible way to regulate the use of fossil fuels worldwide. Currency might be linked to energy inputs through a centrally managed 'protocol', so that tradable units, as one writer says, could turn into a kind of currency themselves.[17]

This mix of ideas – grain storage, distillation and centralised currency – seems to have come together in John Macarthur's mind early in Governor Bligh's time. Earlier on, when he had argued only for a few private distilleries, he and Blaxcell had ordered a still – a large copper boiler with appropriate machinery – for themselves and another for John's friend Edward Abbott. The

INSURRECTION

two stills arrived from London in March 1807 and Blaxcell took delivery of both.

Here was 'speculation', anathema to Governor Bligh. He ordered the immediate reshipment of both stills and in October they were seized, or so John Macarthur argued, in a way far short of due process. John sued and a packed courthouse heard him denounce the governor's attempts to rule by personal diktat. Was this – his large voice rising with theatrical force – 'the tenor on which Englishmen hold their property in New South Wales?'[18]

This was his first public protest against Bligh's government. At the end of November, the *Parramatta*, which he owned jointly with Hulletts, got back to Sydney Cove from Tahiti. It had sailed in June, seeking pork for the Sydney market and taking local salt for that purpose. It brought back 65 casks. Constables had, as usual, scoured the ship before it left Sydney, looking for convicts trying to escape, but one man had evaded all eyes by hiding under firewood. Now the ship was back and Bligh decided that John Macarthur was responsible for the man's escape. No-one and nothing was allowed ashore, constables were posted on board and, again by mere personal order, a fine was set of £900.[19]

For John Macarthur this was, once again, palpable tyranny, which by temperament, principle and self-interest he was bound to resist. He told the *Parramatta's* captain that the ship had been confiscated by government and that the crew should therefore deal directly with the governor's officials. When they broke the governor's ban and came ashore Bligh again blamed John Macarthur and ordered his criminal trial. The warrant was brought to Elizabeth Farm late at night and John took it, or pretended to take it, as an order for his immediate arrest. He gave the constable a written statement – 'horrid Tyranny', 'Scorn and Contempt', 'I never will submit' – but next day, as the warrant required, he went to Sydney and was ordered to appear at the next session of the criminal court.[20]

William Bligh and John Macarthur were now seriously at odds. Bligh, angered by his enemy's language, ordered a new charge – treason, or sedition at the very least – while Macarthur stepped up his determination to bring Bligh to account for his arbitrary threats to property. Bligh now blundered. Governor King, in 1801, had managed to isolate John Macarthur. Bligh did the opposite, giving him room to bring much of the local population with him. John now looked to his own town lease, vacant as yet and adjoining Nathaniel Lucas's old home. Bligh had bullied soldiers and townspeople, such as Lucas, but so far he had kept clear of officers and gentlemen. John Macarthur aimed to end that distinction, so as to make himself one with men and women like Lucas.

On 13 January, 12 days before his trial in connection with the *Parramatta*, John Macarthur set labourers to work fencing in his allotment, digging postholes and placing posts. He saw to the work in person. Ordered to desist, he picked up a post and dropped it into one of the holes, at which Bligh's officer, the superintendent of convicts, got off his horse, pulled out the post and announced to the gathering crowd, 'When the axe is laid to the root, the tree must fall.' It was a deliberate reference, apparently, to the governor's plan for bringing down the whole 'speculative' system in New South Wales.[21]

With John Macarthur's trial came the crisis. At the meeting of the court the accused took immediate command. Usually, the townspeople might care very little about John Macarthur's fortunes. Now, his aim was to prove through public theatre that the rights of each were the rights of all.

The trial's presiding officer was the judge-advocate Richard Atkins. A few weeks beforehand Atkins had mentioned to John Macarthur his worries as to 'what was going on at Government House'. That might suggest that Atkins was now an ally. However, the moment proceedings began John Macarthur demanded

Atkins's removal. Atkins was prejudiced against him, he said, and he listed the reasons. Worse, Atkins was responsible for the present charge, which, he said, was obviously illegal, and he demanded impartial justice from the rest of the bench. These were all officers of the Corps. 'You have the eyes of an anxious Public upon you,' he told them, 'trembling for the safety of their *Property*, their *Liberty*, and their *Lives*. To you has fallen the lot of deciding a point which perhaps involves the happiness or misery of millions yet unborn.'[22]

This was an echo, and probably a deliberate one, of George Washington's public address at the end of the American Revolution – 'it is yet to be decided whether the revolution must ultimately be considered as a blessing or a curse … with our fate will the destiny of millions be involved.' The officers on the bench agreed, Atkins stormed from the room and proceedings collapsed.[23]

Bligh announced that he would charge all six officers with treason. The soldiers were thoroughly roused and on the following afternoon those stationed in Sydney marched on Government House, where, in his own drawing room, they put the governor under arrest. Among those who signed their names in support, high on the list, was the millwright Nathaniel Lucas.

Bligh had been unpopular from the start but the climax was sudden. His overreaction in the question of the *Parramatta* and at last his declaration against the officers, so different from King's careful handling, made some sort of violence hard to avoid. What John Macarthur intended was never clear. It might have been unclear even to himself. He had talked to very few – probably only to George Johnston, senior officer on the spot, who led the march, and to two on the bench, his old ally William Minchin and Anthony Fenn Kemp, who as a captain led the junior officers. Elizabeth, who was in the first months of her final pregnancy – she was 41 – was certainly surprised. '[I]t never entered my head,' she said, 'to imagine that the inhabitants would so effectively rouse themselves.'[24]

26

THE PARLOUR SCENE

The uprising against Governor Bligh included plenty of deliberate theatre, much of it orchestrated by John Macarthur, and, as an amateur dramatist, John himself seems to have valued most the scene in his own parlour at Elizabeth Farm late at night on 15 December 1807. There were only two players in this case, himself and Francis Oakes, Parramatta's chief constable, alone on a makeshift stage. This was stripped-down theatre. In its simplicity and punch it summed up, in John Macarthur's imagination, the whole extraordinary business.

He tried to make that scene live for posterity. Immediately after the uprising, on the same day, there began a detailed recording of evidence from the rebels' point of view, with lengthy hearings, shorthand transcriptions, multiple copies and careful collation for sending to England. For three days thereafter the governor's supporters, plus Richard Atkins, who tried to keep a strict impartiality, were questioned about events, including government corruption. After that, John Macarthur's trial, which had been instigated by Bligh, was restarted. That meant five more days of inquiry, all carefully transcribed. This last was a show trial in reverse. Every witness answered freely, but no amount of dissent stopped John Macarthur, as counsel for himself, from tracing out the reality he believed in. In doing so, he was intent on closing the gap between what he had done and said, and what, in the best of all possible worlds, he might have done and said.

THE PARLOUR SCENE

According to the American writer Joan Didion, 'We tell ourselves stories in order to live.'[1] The stories John Macarthur told himself during his life, and anyone else who would listen, were plays, and with the parlour scene of 15 December, he went to remarkable lengths. Through lengthy questioning of Francis Oakes, he tried to get Oakes to work with him in broadcasting this conversation as, he thought, it *should have been*. Seven weeks had passed. Oakes had his own straightforward recollection of what had been said in the parlour at Elizabeth Farm and it was not what John wanted to see recorded. Their disagreement could make no substantial difference. However, John Macarthur was one of those who spent a good deal of imaginative energy recalling and correcting words he had heard in his own mouth. With wishful thinking – that sounds much better, I wish I had said that – he recreated entire conversations.

Oakes was questioned first, not by John Macarthur as the accused, but by the prosecution. He had gone to Elizabeth Farm, Oakes said, late at night, bearing the warrant for John Macarthur's arrest on a criminal charge. Understanding that at that hour there would be no servant to answer the front door, he had gone first to the kitchen behind the house, and was then taken to see the master, who was sitting up alone. John Macarthur had brought Oakes into the parlour, got him a chair and mixed him a drink. He then read the warrant and told Oakes that it was illegal. If anyone but Oakes had brought it, John said, he would have thrown him out. The real criminals were the men who had robbed him, John Macarthur, of the ship *Parramatta*. However, he said, '[l]et them alone: they will soon make a Rope to hang themselves.'[2] That was Oakes's recollection.

John Macarthur, sitting in the parlour with Oakes – still Oakes's recollection – asked Oakes to take down a dictated reply, but Oakes refused. Macarthur therefore wrote it himself. Oakes pocketed it and made his exit, as he recalled, telling his host that 'it was a disagreeable business and I hoped he would not be angry with me.' In reply, John Macarthur said that Oakes had done his duty and that the note would prove it.³ Elizabeth, pregnant and headache-burdened, probably heard all this, or most of it, from her bed, but what she thought was not recorded.

As for John, from the raw material of this experience he built his own story. Standing to ask his own questions at the next stage of the interrogation, he offered that story to Oakes, but Oakes could only shake his head.

> [Macarthur:] Whilst I was copying this Paper, did you not say you was glad to have it, because it would prevent you making any mistake in repeating my words?
>
> [Oakes:] No.
>
> [Macarthur:] Did you not say, 'Do you think I can be hurt, Sir, for not serving this Warrant, for I w[oul]d on no acc[oun]t insult a Gentleman like you by taking him out of his house at this hour of the Night'?
>
> [Oakes:] I don't recollect.
>
> [Macarthur:] Do you not remember I said, 'Oakes, this Warrant can only be meant as an insult to me, and most probably they will be angry with you for disappointing their expectations; but you may tell them in your excuse that I am the sort of Gentleman you do not like forcing into anything, and that if they send you with another Warrant they had better provide you with an Armed Force for I looked in a desperate ill-humour'?
>
> [Oakes:] No.

THE PARLOUR SCENE

[Macarthur:] Did you not reply, 'I will tell them that I will take care not to expose my Life to danger, for I think there will be Blood Shed'?

[Oakes:] No.[4]

And so on. With manufactured recollection, John Macarthur was composing a play.

With the actual conversation over, Chief Constable Oakes was on his way home in the dark when he was overtaken by 18-year-old Edward Macarthur. As Oakes recalled, Edward told him that his father had decided to go to Sydney after all, next morning, in obedience to the warrant, and he therefore wanted the letter back. Oakes refused to give it up. 'I told him,' Oakes said, 'to deliver my compl[imen]ts to his father; that I could not deliver it with propriety.'[5]

Now, new fiction set in. Edward had not in fact been sent by John Macarthur, who was upset to learn that he had gone. John did not like looking irresolute. Who then had told him to run after Oakes? Next day, Hannibal Macarthur, apparently on John's instructions, told Oakes that it had been Nicholas Bayly, a lieutenant in the Corps. That seems improbable too. Most likely it was Elizabeth, who had good reason to be afraid of what the letter might do.[6] It was natural that the men should rally to keep her name out of it.

In that parlour scene, as recreated in the fertile mind of John Macarthur, the moral delicacy of home-and-family life was interwoven with high heroism. William Shakespeare used the same thing often and for John that was part of its charm. The hero in *Coriolanus*, his favourite Shakespeare play, is at home, for instance, among the intimacies of family life, when he is called to Rome's marketplace to confront those who aimed to destroy him. It is a pivotal scene in the play. Too proud to yield, Coriolanus is urged to go by his mother Volumnia. He must show the world his greatness, she says, apparent everyday to those who loved him. '[Y]ou can never be too noble, [b]ut when extremities speak.' At the same time, Volumnia says, he ought to bend and dissemble for the public good. A truly great man, after all, knows how to interweave honour and policy. Moved by his mother, Coriolanus goes.[7]

For present purposes, Sydney was John's Rome. Settling his mind to the next scene, he also went.

JOHN MACARTHUR HAD AIMED TO USE HIS OWN criminal trial to persuade the world to know him better, to know him as he was in his own parlour. For instance, he must have been only distantly acquainted with Edmund Griffin, Bligh's secretary, but that made persuading Edmund all the more urgent. Edmund, justifiably defensive, thought he heard John ridiculing his youth, although in fact the trust of the young was something John especially prized. It would be a blessing, indeed, at this point to be able to turn on the sound, so as to hear the 43-year-old voice and the 20-year-old voice talking past each other amid the murmurs of the courtroom. You must understand, John told Edmund, 'that I am an innocent and falsely accused man'. And again, in plaintive hope at the end, 'Do you know of a single Act of Injustice that I have ever committed against any human being?', to which Edmund, who had not even known him 18 months earlier, gave the baffled reply, 'I cannot say that I do.'[8]

From that question – am I just? – hung the whole drama, or so John Macarthur's imagination told him. Questioning Edmund Griffin also gave him the chance to retell an old story that had nothing to do with the trial and everything to do with the vital issue of his own character. Three years before, while John was on his way home from England, Richard Fitzgerald had sold some ewes for Elizabeth. Payment included a 'wheat note' stating the debt in bushels of grain, a settled currency, but the flooding of the Hawkesbury River had then destroyed most crops and the market value of wheat rose four-fold. The debt had been transferred to the Hawkesbury farmer Andrew Thompson and John Macarthur, in asking for payment, had insisted that Thompson repay it using current money value, as implied by the note and backed by common understanding. Instead, Thompson offered the original quantity of grain.

On three occasions thereafter, and as publicly as possible, John Macarthur explained why his own claim was just. Clearly the principle, moral and intellectual, mattered more to him than the debt itself. He had tried first in October–November 1806, when he took his case against Thompson to the Civil Court. He lost and in July–August 1807 he had appealed, the court of appeal being the governor. Bligh, though he heard Thompson, had refused to hear John Macarthur and at the same time the editor of the *Sydney Gazette*, the government paper, had set out the official point of view. To that John had replied with two letters, both signed 'Occulist' – mender of sight, opener of eyes. Thirdly and finally, at his post-insurrection trial, there was his exchange with Edmund Griffin.

Am I just? For a dozen years similar questions of currency value had been strenuously debated in England, as industrial and commercial revolutions, plus war, made their impact on prices. Did new thinking about political economy offer all the answers or did it make things worse? How did conscience sit with theory? How did conscience sit with profit? Sir James Steuart had said that it was the statesman's duty to ensure 'a certain fund of subsistence for all', but surely that could mean making men and women dependent on the vagaries of power.[9] Compassion and self-reliance had to work together in the weaving of justice – long-term and short-term justice – through human affairs.

Am I just? In the Occulist exchange, the *Sydney Gazette* spoke of settlers burdened with debts swollen beyond all expectation, but Occulist/John, so he said, knew of no 'unfortunate sufferers' forced to pay such debts. 'For the Credit of the Colony,' he added, 'I hope that no circumstance of the kind has happened.' Certainly, he went on, some settlers pretended to be 'unfortunate sufferers', aiming to escape their debts and exploit the truly unfortunate. No mercy was needed for these. 'Am I,' said Occulist/John, 'to forego my right with the man who has escaped the Calamity, and only resists my claim that he may sell his Wheat at a tenfold price[?].' John himself had forgiven debtors who had really suffered. However, he refused to forgive Andrew Thompson, who, whatever he pretended, was not among them. Thompson had debtors of his own. He also had other income. His material substance was more than enough, but his moral credit was nil.[10]

Be aware too of a larger principle, said this opener of eyes. Be aware of the 'pernicious Doctrine' that held that promises between ourselves – our honesty with each other – could be cancelled by the state. That doctrine undermined the power of conscience, on which we all depend. If that doctrine prevailed it would destroy 'all confidence in our mutual dealings with each other' so as to 'banish integrity and good faith from our Society'. The state ought to reinforce, not undermine, this rock on which everything else depended.[11] Hinton McArthur had said much the same in comparing Britain with pre-revolutionary France. When governments undermine common good faith apparently at random, they destroy that individual sense of right – the power of conscience – that was the foundation of true humanity.

John Macarthur expected everyone who heard him to be drawn inexorably into the light. The parlour scene, as concocted by himself, showed his honesty on an intimate scale, not just as a householder, host and citizen, but as husband and father, a man who *felt* truth, surrounded as he was by his sleeping children. The duties of family, as the poet Samuel Taylor Coleridge had said not long before, 'discipline the Heart'. 'Home-born feeling' leads directly to a larger sense of justice, which shows itself in all our dealings with the world.[12]

So John Macarthur asked Francis Oakes, 'During the whole time that you were at my house, did I treat you with any unkindness or incivility?' So he put it to Edmund Griffin, 'Do you know of a single Act of Injustice that I have ever committed against any human being?'

FOR JOHN MACARTHUR, THE REBELLION AGAINST Governor Bligh was life-defining. Years later he called it 'one of the most meritorious' things he had ever done. By implication, at least, he kept coming back to it, even as a way to laugh at himself. His was not an overflowing sense of humour but two of his jokes survive from the 1820s. Both echoed 1808. One was in a letter to his friend in Sydney, the physician James Mitchell, a native of county Fife, who was having trouble with interfering officialdom. He could give him good advice, John told Mitchell, on the business of 'trampling, with the high minded disdain of an honourable Scotchman, oppression and tyranny into the mire'.[13]

The other joke went by letter in the other direction, from Sydney to Elizabeth Farm. While staying with his daughter Mary in Sydney – she was married by this time – John spent days in bed with some unstated illness, 'confined', so he told Elizabeth, 'by the tyranny of two doctors'. Even 'a delightful stroll on the verandah' was forbidden him. 'But,' he told her, 'the cat will mew, the kittens play, and every dog will have his day, and depend upon it I will revenge my own, and the cause of all unhappy convalescents on them all.'[14]

27
VARIEGATED TRUTHS

'When shall I be known?', John Macarthur asked Elizabeth. No answer was possible. John made it hard for anyone to know him by the way he mixed up theatre, even melodrama, with what most understood to be the realities of daily life. His own realties were hard to translate. At certain levels he lacked skill in explaining himself. Though he was thoroughly literate, John Macarthur, as a friend remarked, was 'not very fond' of writing.[1] He liked talk better, but even that could be hard to get right.

It was a challenge characteristic of the Enlightenment, a by-product of the boom in self-awareness. The technology did not yet exist – could it ever exist? – which could take the inner truth for each individual without alteration to the world beyond. Elizabeth made some headway because of her habit of running one sentence into the next, as if in speech. She sometimes used full stops, but commas hardly at all. Over and over in each letter there recurs her characteristic all-purpose mini-dash, a dab of the pen, at which point her reader can hear her draw breath, as it were, between one thought and the next.[2]

Elizabeth watched herself as she wrote and read. Once in New South Wales she received a letter telling her about kindly visits made to her old mother in Bridgerule. Reading it, she felt 'my heart dilate', and that feeling, a feeling in the muscles of her chest, framed the way she wrote back. It was an old idea that the blood vessels around the heart expanded with certain kinds of human connection. In his *Theory of Moral Sentiments*, a book on the shelves at Elizabeth Farm, Adam Smith explained how the individual human being notices distant happiness. Learning of it, 'he feels his heart … instantly expanded and elated'. Elizabeth had that feeling, even while sketching her inner self. She sometimes wondered whether sensations of that sort could be premonitions of the future too.³

To work with pen in hand was to keep balance, as if on a high rope. Here I am, look at me. I draw my feeling from places no-one else can know and at the same instant I delicately set it down. This meticulous skill, this kind of balance, enlightened parents taught to their children. Track your feelings and show them off in agile ways. John, writing once to Elizabeth, had the two younger boys with him. 'I have asked James what I shall say for him to his dear Mama and sisters. With tears in his eyes he replied, "I do not know what to say". William interposes, "Send our loves Papa", oh but James explains I wish to say much more but cannot tell what.'⁴

Always, some of the most profound shifts in humanity come from new technology. During the late Enlightenment better roads, better vehicles, better sea navigation and so on, meant a more regular, reliable postal service. Chatting to and fro with pen and ink was more easily and speedily done. Getting used to new efficiency, the fingers of men and women became more nimble with their pens, so much so that at a certain point in their writing the message might take over from the medium. Thoughts flew and letter-writing was more fluid and more consistently intimate. Distance vanished. John might send to Elizabeth the boys' words, replete, almost, with lively breath. Someone more encumbered by distance than he was might have baulked at that.

Larger markets meant that new products, penetrating daily life, were drawn into day-to-day affection. Take pen nibs. In the experience of Elizabeth and John, nibs were usually made from goose feathers, although duck or crow were used too, even possibly in New South Wales, for finer work, and swan for flexibility. Skilled draftsmen had tried steel nibs but so far they were too rigid for ordinary writing. More flexible steel nibs were invented in 1803 but to start with they were expensive and too easily clogged with dry ink. It took a generation for those problems to be solved. When that happened love could speak more easily through steel.

Otherwise, of course, steel was found more often in the articulation of hostility. Steel was used in making swords and knives. Pistols had partly replaced swords in the protocols of hatred and so far pistols were made mainly of iron, but steel was used for trigger springs and for boring barrels.[5] Whether iron or steel, step by step such articles, like nibs, became artful instruments of feeling. The tip of a nib, the point of a sword, the touch of trigger and the slant of the pistol barrel, each became a nerve end in its own right.

Hinton McArthur, in his book about sword fighting, included advice for when the parties wanted to kill each other. Normally, at play, all sorts of movements could be tried with a sword, but, he said, '[i]n serious affairs few variations are practicable'. When there was no time for complications, he recommended two movements only, called 'carte' and 'tierce'. The swordsman, seeking to move more quickly than thought, needed some combination of the two and everything then depended on self-confidence and on 'the sensibility or feeling of your hand'.[6] With swords and pistols, as with pens, fingers made the final difference in closing the strange gap between thought and action – between the action of the mind, that is, and the mark made on others.

It was as if life was an ongoing re-run of Edmund Leach's efforts, in the 1780s, to have his canal, his newly invented machinery and his years of hard, determined work noticed by someone who could do something about it – anyone at all. Now, in 1808–09, John Macarthur felt a crucial urgency in closing the gap between his own self-understanding and what the world thought of him. Do I, my inner self, matter on the world's great stage?

Am I not just? At home with Elizabeth he was known as perfectly as he liked. However, the hopes of them both seemed to rest on something more than that – on the world knowing him too.

BLIGH'S SUPPORTERS CALLED THE EVENTS OF 26 JANUARY a 'mutiny', but his enemies, at least in their calmer moments, called it an 'arrest'. Bligh's enemies aimed to correct the injustice and inefficiency they saw in his government and for John Macarthur, at least, that meant putting the settlement on a new foundation altogether. From the first day George Johnston, the Corps' senior officer on the spot, called himself 'Lieutenant-Governor' and John Macarthur, his trial over, was added to the new establishment as 'Secretary to the Colony'. So he became virtual ruler again, as in 1793–95. Johnston had his own secretary too and the distribution of duties shows how these few at least saw the size of the task ahead.

John Macarthur was unpaid as secretary. It is impossible to be sure whether he made money in other ways from the insurrection, but there is no good evidence of it. He gave himself a good deal to do all the same. Besides getting the record straight, so as to tell the truth they themselves believed in, he was mainly concerned with government stores and livestock.

Within two months Johnston was able to report to the authorities in England that 300 individuals had been removed from the list of those fed and clothed by government, just the type of economy John Macarthur had always advocated. A few public officials had been replaced and new methods imposed, in an effort to cut back corruption. Large numbers of cattle, useless to government, had been given to settlers in exchange for grain, another significant economy. Finally, the public flocks and herds had been more minutely sorted and graded, so that the main principle of livestock management at Elizabeth Farm had been carried over to the government holdings.[7]

John Macarthur also put together a sketchy plan for larger change, which he sent to his agent in London, Thomas Plummer, for handing in wherever it might be most effective. A most remarkable document for its time and place, it called for a type of imaginative energy far beyond anything the British government could spare, at any time, on this strange spot.

The main points were as follows. Laws should be passed so as to remove all doubts about the legitimacy of public authority in New South Wales, and government should be strengthened and given deeper roots in public opinion with the appointment of a council. It might consist of five senior officials and two settlers, and it should be empowered to advise the governor, make laws and hear appeals from the courts. Convict punishment should be totally reformed, and the grain harvest should be better managed, with annual storage and a distillery working as a grain bank – two ideas that have been described already. However, both these reforms would depend on the first – a strong government in touch with thinking on the ground.[8] Typically, John Macarthur skipped over this last fundamental point. He was not good with the deeper logic of his own ideas.

Born of solitary thought, raw and untempered, all this died on exposure to the open air. Plummer seems to have been baffled by it. He divided it in half, and one half – an attempt to show that the insurrection was the result of deeply laid problems of settlement – he had printed, aiming to send it to the minister, Lord Castlereagh. It never went beyond proof stage. The other half, John Macarthur's suggestions for change, Plummer copied out, set up as a letter, signed with his own name and gave to the newly appointed governor, Lachlan Macquarie, Bligh's successor. Macquarie was on the point of sailing. He had much else on his mind so that John's suggestions, practicable or not, were put aside and forgotten.

VARIEGATED TRUTHS

IN THE MONTHS AFTER THE INSURRECTION ELIZABETH had been enduring her last pregnancy. She suffered a good deal. Emmeline Emily was born safely, at 9 pm on 2 June, but then the younger Elizabeth, aged 16, was ailing too, and there were fears for her life.[9] Soon after Bligh's arrest a meeting of townspeople had voted to send John to England to represent their grievances. It was also time for the two younger boys, James and William, to start the next stage of their schooling, as their brothers had done before them, which meant all three might go to England together. On the other hand, John had reason to wait, so as to see out the troubles of his wife and eldest daughter.

He also had work to do, in proving that their motivations in deposing Governor Bligh were of the purest. Governor Bligh and his friends, removed from power, sent back to London reports of an orgy of favouritism and waste, but one impartial witness, at least, told a different story. Robert Fitz, deputy commissary and a bystander in the great commotion, said that the new regime was in fact too austerely correct for the officers of the NSW Corps. They had expected rewards. John Macarthur said the same. The officers would not have been satisfied if, he said, 'the whole of the publick property' had been divided among them.[10]

However, that was not all that upset them. John Macarthur's aim was to show the difference between good government and bad. In his own mind he stood for high principle and moral purity, even beyond the law. Johnston was only third in command in the Corps. William Paterson, now commandant in northern Van Diemen's Land, and Joseph Foveaux, currently on his way back from leave in England, were both his seniors. Nevertheless, it was John Macarthur's intention that neither Paterson nor Foveaux should be allowed to take over unless they pledged total support. That idea, at least, he was forced to give up. It would have been mutiny, pure and simple.[11]

The soldiers were loyal, as ever, but they did not face the same consequences. At mid-year George Caley, Sir Joseph Banks's botanist on the spot, wrote to Banks in London. '[I]t will appear strange to you,' he said, 'to think that one man has overturned the government of the colony.' That man, he said, had always been unpopular among the people at large. Now he was detested. 'He has secured himself by the soldiers', and he had done that, so Caley implied, as he had always done it, by a kind of theatre. John Macarthur seemed all the time to live among extremes, to bring on risk, and the soldiers liked that. He was called clever, Caley said, but whether clever or not, he was dangerous. '[B]y his general behaviour I must reckon him only a bravado.'[12]

With all his moral certainty, John Macarthur was courting serious risk. According to Robert Fitz, Bligh had been a bad governor. Fitz thought there would certainly have been a popular uprising if the Corps had not acted first. That was the justifying argument the rebels depended on, but who could prove it? In London the minister consulted lawyers and they were not convinced, even by the evidence sent by the rebels. Bligh's faults seemed small to them and on the other hand they were struck with John Macarthur's boast, as reported by Bligh, that there never had been 'a *revolution* so completely effected, and with so much order and regularity' (my emphasis). This was not just an arrest, this was a deliberate attempt to overturn the King's government in New South Wales. According to the lawyers, all those involved who bore the King's commission should be court-martialled on a capital charge, with George Johnston bearing 'the highest degree of criminal responsibility'.[13] In other words, they were liable to be hanged.

John Macarthur, a civilian, had obviously 'excited the mutiny among the soldiers and ... instigated the arrest'. That was high treason, also a capital offence. The proposed courts martial could be held in England. However, procedural rules meant that John Macarthur's trial must be at the place of his offence.[14]

VARIEGATED TRUTHS

In July 1808 Joseph Foveaux arrived and took command. He refused to reinstate Bligh but he abolished John Macarthur's position and took all the government on himself. However, he continued John's reforms. In January 1809 William Paterson reached Sydney but Foveaux remained effectively in charge until the new governor, Lachlan Macquarie, arrived at the end of the year, and even Macquarie was guided by Foveaux to start with.

In other words, John Macarthur's reforms long outlasted his time in power, thanks to Foveaux. He was offended, all the same, by his summary removal and at the same time there was some jarring about money he owed to the government. In January 1809, with Foveaux no longer shielded by his rank as acting governor, John insisted on fighting him. He shot first, 'took very deliberate aim', according to Foveaux's second, 'and was perfectly cool'. He missed and Foveaux, a man of peace, did not shoot back.[15]

Two months later William Bligh was allowed to leave Sydney Cove on the naval ship *Porpoise*, having given his word that he would go straight back to England. Twelve days later again, on 29 March 1809, John Macarthur followed on the *Admiral Gambier* with his two boys, plus Johnston, Walter Davidson and others from the rebel side. Their purpose was straightforward and their hopes were high. With all the witnesses and documentation they needed, the truth must be obvious. For John Macarthur, all the same, optimism was laced with anxiety. 'In two months,' he wrote to Elizabeth, as the *Admiral Gambier* paused at Rio de Janeiro, and his cheerfulness sounds forced, 'I hope to be in England, and in three months after on my way back.'[16]

In firing at Foveaux, John Macarthur had missed. What happens when the nib breaks, the sword gets caught, the pistol jams or, in a duel, the other party refuses even to fire back? What happens when, after recitation and re-enactment enough to excite any ordinary imagination, your listener, like Francis Oakes, just says 'No'? Now it was Bligh himself who did not answer as expected.

Instead of going straight back to England, the late governor sailed southward. The settlement in southern Van Diemen's Land was under the command of David Collins, former judge-advocate of New South Wales and, as lieutenant-governor, subordinate to Bligh. Bligh seems to have looked forward to attacking and subduing Sydney with Collins's support, so as to enforce his own return, but Collins was politely uncooperative and Bligh sailed back to Sydney Cove. It was May 1810 before he finally set out for home.

So ended any chance of speedy resolution and so began a train of events during which, for John at least, hope was adjourned and determination failed. Elizabeth, on the other hand, persevered at home.

28

JOHN'S SELF-REFLECTION

For Elizabeth and John, friends in England were vital in all sorts of ways, acting for them, keeping them informed and reassuring them that they were not forgotten where it mattered. The children, during their English schooling, treated some of those friends as substitute parents. The Thompsons were always particularly close. In September 1808 Edward Macarthur, now 19, arrived back in England from New South Wales with news of the Bligh insurrection, and he was taken in straightaway by the Thompsons – 'to me,' he said, 'another father, mother, brother and sister'.[1] By now Thomas Thompson had retired from his army agency work, the original cause of the connection, and he and Margaret, his wife, had moved from the neighbourhood of Leicester Square to semi-rural Clapham.

John Macarthur and his two youngest boys, James and William, reached England in November 1809 and they were welcomed by the Thompsons in just the same spirit. 'Come, young kangaroo,' said Thomas Thompson to James, currently covered in mud, 'never mind your boots, they'll not hurt the carpet, so come along up stairs and let us see how you can hop.' It was obvious, however, that the Thompsons were ageing fast. They had kept an eye on the older boys but they could not safely do the same for James and William, and there was no-one to turn to instead.[2]

Also, there was no sign of Bligh and no way of knowing when he would arrive. John's hopes of a quick trip to and fro evaporated almost straightaway. Waiting became open-ended, but then he was forced to wait because of the boys. It was a 'dreary and comfortless' time, he said, worsened by nagging bad health, at this stage mainly indigestion, an old problem. There was also worry about young Elizabeth. When he left New South Wales her life had seemed to hang in the balance. Now, that 'excruciating subject' filled him with a brooding dread, enough to make him halt in the middle of a letter home, unable to go on. He was 'seized', he said, 'with violent spasms in my side'. Later he spoke of it as 'a complaint in my lungs', which over ten days got steadily worse. Then, when he heard that his child was much better, it lifted, but came back so severely that he was in bed for weeks. Even after that, he could not escape 'gloom' – a 'terrible nervous affliction' – which redoubled with news of his daughter's relapse. He heard that 'our sweet girl would probably never recover the use of her limbs again'. That news, he said, 'so shocked and affected my spirits that I have found it impossible … to tranquillise'.[3]

In May he heard that she was better again and, at last, as her health settled, he began to hope for 'the compleat recovery of my beloved girl'.[4] So the two, father and daughter, suffered together, in strange synchronisation on opposite sides of the world.

The London air was his enemy too. Within a few months of arrival he went to Bath and then to Cheltenham in Gloucestershire, resort towns with health-giving mineral waters for drinking and bathing. That did him some good. He then moved from lodgings in the West End to Clapham, near the Thompsons, where, he said, 'the air is excellent'. He and the boys could walk and run about Clapham Common, about 80 hectares of open country, still partly wild. Never a big eater, as a general cure-all John cut back meals to a minimum, with no meat.

> For my breakfast [he told Elizabeth] I eat bread and milk.
> My dinner consists of bread, potatoes and some times ripe

JOHN'S SELF-REFLECTION

currants or gooseberries. I drink no tea but when at home a basin of milk. In company I never deviate from my system and on no consideration ever touch beer, wine or spirits.

At Clapham he found himself stronger than he had been for years and for a time there was no more talk of indigestion. He had hitherto struggled to walk 2 kilometres. Now he did much better.[5]

At the same time, money worries mounted. The wool was still not bringing in much and hopes for Pyrmont and trade had been badly upset, only partly thanks to Bligh. Ventures by the *Dart* and then the *Elizabeth* – a final attempt to sell sandalwood – both failed, seriously affecting his London budget. The immediate solution was to call in debts. In New South Wales, the partnership with Garnham Blaxcell had ended and Blaxcell had leased Pyrmont on his own, buying the equipment, but money was owing there too. John had left that to Elizabeth, as also a dispute with the ex-convict merchant, Henry Kable, whose debt, over £2000, had been only partly paid. She must get back as much as possible, but without worrying herself overmuch. '[W]hatever may be the result,' he said, 'I shall be satisfied you have acted for the best.'[6]

Isolation, idleness, penny-pinching and worry weighed John down. Even when he felt physically strong he suffered from 'excessive nervousness'. When the business with Bligh was done, he hoped, his mind would be 'tranquillised'. Meanwhile, powerlessness, day after day, undermined his sense of self-control. He had always taken an interest in questions of physical health and stamina. Now he focused his mind more perhaps than he had ever done in his life on his physical and mental self – on pain, diet, exercise, the need to quieten his nerves and his losing battle with debilitating gloom.[7]

John Macarthur's feeling for his marriage and his home was turned inside-out while he lingered in England. His marriage was one of mutual accountability, each under the eye of the other.

Now he watched himself as Elizabeth might have done, but with idleness added in, and sent her anxious reports.

Anxiety was in the air. In Europe at large, Napoleon Bonaparte was at the height of his power and Britain was under serious threat of French invasion. Hope lay with the army and navy, and in this crisis the uprising in remote New South Wales looked like a criminal distraction. Bligh's friends stressed that point whenever they could. They also made an impact with their ingenious story of garrison officers knee-deep in the rum trade, who had rebelled at the governor's efforts to cut it back.[8]

The anti-Bligh network, on the other hand, had been boosted by the addition of George Johnston's patron, the Duke of Northumberland, one of England's richest men and a friend of the Prince Regent, afterwards George IV. The duke had wide interests and liberal-minded connections. His half-brother, James Smithson, endowed scientific research in the United States – the Smithsonian Institution was due to Smithson – and Northumberland himself experimented in New South Wales, by sending livestock and plants to George Johnston. These included, for instance, the Syrian silk tree, whose thread, shiny white in its seed pods, could be used to soften cotton and wool through interweaving.[9]

Northumberland had his own small group in the House of Commons, including Sir Samuel Romilly, a former solicitor-general who led reforms in the criminal law, and James Brogden, whom John Macarthur already knew.[10] Besides helping in the anti-Bligh campaign, these two were apparently consulted about reform in New South Wales – John's ideas for a council, convict reform, a grain bank and so on – and the legislation needed. Thus advised, John decided to sue Bligh on his own account, setting damages at £20 000. Consultation was well advanced when the governor finally arrived, in October 1810, opening the way for action. 'Be patient,' John told Elizabeth, 'and all will be well for I have formed a powerful body of friends in this country who are me their support to my endeavours past and *security* for *the future*.' been heard with flattering respect. d her, 'the colony will soon undergo a

he government moved first, charging George ny, as the law officers had advised at the start. ore shifted to a military footing, which was ssible outcome for the anti-Bligh party. Surely, said e, writing to Johnston, 'it was in your *civil* and not your *military* capacity that you superseded the gov[erno]r and the troops which accompanied you were for *his* protection against an enraged people.'[12] It was useless to say so.

Johnston's court-martial opened at Chelsea, a military hospital in London's west, on 7 May 1811 and his lawyers made the best of a wholly defensive position. They avoided any discussion of the governor's authority over free men and women, although that left the bench to conclude that it was a military government, in which the ruler's word ought to be law. They also tried to minimise the part played by John Macarthur. Johnston had simply done a soldier's duty, they said, and John Macarthur was nothing but 'an opulent and respectable settler' injured by tyranny.

The bench, however, soon decided that John was 'the mainspring of every thing'. In his own testimony, he was no help. He was ordered to make his answers more succinct – no inference, no hearsay, no lengthily quoted conversations – but his theatrical imagination would not be curtailed. Altogether Johnston's case did not hold up.[13]

Judgment came on 2 July and Johnston was only cashiered – dishonourably deprived of his rank and profession – when he could have been condemned to death. On the duke's advice, he appealed to the Prince Regent against even this sentence, with the argument that Bligh's deposition had been 'the means of saving the colony to H[is] M[ajesty] and this country'. However, his se[cretary?] Johnston, urged apparently by a desperate John Maca[rthur,] again, though the duke warned him not to. He failed aga[in and] were not believed.

FOR THE TIME BEING, THE INFLUENTIAL FRIENDS JO[HN] Macarthur had made during his previous spell in England ha[d] melted away. Hugh Elliot had come to see him when he first arrived, and had told him then that among the people he spoke to 'your conduct is a subject of much praise', but Elliot had since been absent, as governor of the Leeward Islands and then Madras (Chennai).[15] Robert Farquhar was also far away, as governor of Mauritius. Sir Walter Farquhar was old and frail. George Watson had married into a rich West Indian slave-owning family and was otherwise occupied. John McArthur of Hinton was compromised by other connections.

With John Macarthur, aimlessness fed aimlessness. James Brogden, who lived near him at Clapham, was his only ongoing source of encouragement. Brogden came from an English Presbyterian clerical family. In his youth he had owed part of his education to Joseph Priestley, the great intellectual leader of Dissent and a luminary of the English Enlightenment. Priestley was the first to notice, among other things, that plants somehow restore purity to the air. It was typical of his faith in continuous renewal, human and material. At least in his dealings with John Macarthur, Brogden showed the same sweeping, cheerful optimism.[16]

Even before the court-martial John Macarthur called Brogden 'amongst the forwardest and most active of our advocates'. Afterwards, Brogden urged him to offer his ideas to a parliamentary select committee newly formed to look into New South Wales and convict transportation. Chaired by Hugh Elliot's nephew, George Eden, it included Samuel Romilly, so that it ought to have been friendly, but John, moved by pride or petulance, refused.[17]

JOHN'S SELF-REFLECTION

About the same time Brogden became a junior minister at the Treasury, and concerned himself with the cost of funding New South Wales. Again John Macarthur refused to help. His plans, he told Elizabeth, if carried out – he did not say what they were now – would cut into their own income. No-one should be expected to make that sacrifice, 'more particularly one to whom they have displayed so much ill will'.[18]

GEORGE JOHNSTON'S MILITARY COURT-MARTIAL HAD been preceded by the naval court-martial of William Kent, the young commander of HMS *Porpoise*. Kent had been charged with disregarding Bligh's orders after he, Bligh, had been deposed. Kent was acquitted, but John Macarthur's involvement in that trial, on top of his larger anxieties, brought on his first serious mental collapse. 'I sunk into a state of mental despondency,' he told Elizabeth, 'for which I could in no manner account, that made existence a complete burthen to me.' Then Johnston's trial and its result 'sunk me still deeper and made life if possible still more hateful'. He said these things a year afterwards, having written nothing at all to her in the interim. Words had failed him. It had been too hard, he said, to let his pen dwell on events 'that must ever occasion the bitterest, the most disgusting feelings'.[19] One or more of their boys must have sent her news instead.

'There are a thousand things that I wish to say' – so he told her several times – 'but whenever I sit down to write to you my feelings are so overpowered that my recollection seems to forsake me.' Only in time did he work out a way to get the words down, which was 'to hurry on without either method or thought, for any attempt at either only tends to perplex and confuse me more.' '[W]ere I to ponder not a line could I write.'[20] In England, what he might have said at home at Elizabeth Farm, whether by word of mouth, glance or gesture, would not find form with pen and ink.

He played a part, as if on stage, all the same. He sent Elizabeth scant detail about trading ventures, guarding himself against her doubts in that direction, and he also told her less than he could have done about other important negotiations. Instead, he offered her a play of feeling.

Writing about George Eden's committee, he wove a small drama around the question of his own self-respect, as if nothing else mattered. 'I am too old,' he told her, 'to learn the lesson of advancing my interest or making friends by making my opinions always conform to the will of the most powerful.' He would have told the committee the truth, 'and that I am certain would have proved very offensive'.[21] Elizabeth might have guessed that there was some other, plainer reason. For one thing, his evidence might have affected Johnston's appeal against his sentence. John might have known she would guess but in such cases, the closest ties can be fraught with silent truces.

In his longing for her, John called Elizabeth his 'best beloved and most excellent creature', his 'dearest dearest', his 'dear dear dear'. He wanted to know about her health and he worried about her worrying. To be 'one flesh' as husband and wife were said to be, sanctified in the eye of God, was mystery and metaphor with real power. The authors of the *Book of Common Prayer* pointed out, quoting Paul's letter to the Ephesians, that 'no man ever yet hated his own flesh, but nourisheth and cherisheth it'.[22] No man ever wrote letters to his own flesh either, and it was not necessarily easy.

John's letters to Elizabeth, as to everyone else, were usually signed with his full name. Only sometimes, longing for her, he signed himself simply 'McArthur', her name for him and warmer in its way than 'dearest dearest' and 'beloved wife'. The lack of physical closeness was agonising. To start with he assured her that 'to hear what you are doing will be my chief consolation until we meet again'. Then as time passed, turning inward, he comforted himself more with the thought of being 'restored to your arms'. The

JOHN'S SELF-REFLECTION

point of perseverance lay in experiencing once again, eventually, 'those endearments to which I have been so long a stranger'.[23]

'Dear little Emmeline!' he said – Emmeline was three – 'What an interesting description do you give of her.' 'Interesting' meant 'engaging' or 'loveable'. At this distance, news of their children was the best way Elizabeth and John had of touching each other deeply. William was still only eight during the journey to England and while they were at anchor at Rio, he leapt about the ship as if it belonged to him.

> [He] sits on a yard arm [John told Elizabeth] or a top gallant masthead with as much apparent ease and satisfaction as if he were in an elbow chair. Coming onboard a few days since I saw him perched aloft like a bird, but before I could ascend the side the urchin had descended like lightning down one of the back stays, and was at the gang way before me.

At such detail they could smile together. There was pride in all John's news of his sons, and a glow in his telling her about it, as if he shared her thought that, in this world of men, their boys were their real reward. 'It is impossible,' he told her, 'to imagine better disposed young men … as free from vice, or any idle inclinations, as any human beings can be.'[24]

In March 1812 he wrote for the first time about being attacked by gout. It had come on during the northern winter. 'Startle not my beloved wife at the word gout for it has relieved me from the most dreadful the most insufferable of all maladies, the malady of the mind.' It was the same during the following winter. This time he called it 'flying gout' and 'wandering gout'. It came upon him when the frost set in, bringing 'such an irritable state of nerves that I feel myself unable to mix in any company or to pursue either business or amusement'. Even in summer, from 1813, there was its sudden appearance, usually in hands and feet, which was welcome only because it brought an end to mental depression, a misery deeper, he said, than anyone could imagine who had not known it themselves, and complicating everything was indigestion. Either he had given up his scanty diet or it no longer helped. He now tried saltwater bathing at Littlehampton, a resort on the south coast near Portsmouth.[25] Bathing, of one sort or other, was John Macarthur's cure-all.

He consulted Pelham Warren, a fashionable London doctor and supposedly an expert with gout, but he also experimented on himself. Elizabeth might have looked at her copy of William Buchan's *Domestic Medicine*, where there was vivid detail on gout. Before an attack, Buchan said, '[t]he patient complains of weariness and dejection of spirits'. That could be severe. The gout itself usually started at the coldest part of the night, and in the big toe or heel, with the pain spreading and increasing so that the sufferer feels 'stretched, burnt, squeezed, or torn in pieces', altogether an 'exquisite torture' lasting, perhaps, 24 hours. 'The paroxysms … [then] generally grow milder every day, till at length the disease is carried off by perspiration, urine, and other evacuations.' Buchan recommended wrapping the painful parts in wool, still in its oil if possible, to bring on sweating, and visits, such as John Macarthur had made already, to the waters at Bath.[26] Even when free of depression, John's was a three-part suffering, a loneliness of the flesh plus indigestion, itself a needling pain impossible to ignore, and gout.

His doctor, probably Warren, told him that his physical and mental troubles were partly a result of circumstances. Buchan's book said the same and John himself noticed that whenever he thought about recent failures and current frustration his pain got worse, while good news from home, especially about young Elizabeth, made it a little better. He missed all three daughters – 'Dear dear girls how do I desire to press you all to my bosom' – but most of all, he thought his suffering was due to his being so long

JOHN'S SELF-REFLECTION

away from his wife. '[B]elieve me my Elizabeth the period of my separation from you has been an almost uninterrupted scene of indescribable wretchedness.' Future happiness, if any, 'can only be in your society'.[27]

Absence made his emotional dependence all-consuming. Her letters do not survive, but if she felt the same for him she might have been less likely to admit it. She had already lived most of her life apart from her mother and she seemed likely to do the same from her two elder sons. She had learnt very early on not to think too much about the things she lacked. But it was a hard time for both.

The two younger boys, when they came to him on holiday, shared John's privations and watched his moods. Their liveliness, William's especially, was a happy distraction. So was the simple business of watching them pass on from childhood, for John Macarthur one of the most interesting events of human life. Pointing to the future, each in in his own way, the two boys were to be their father's salvation.

29

ELIZABETH'S JUDGMENT

When Elizabeth Macarthur was left alone in charge of all the family concerns in New South Wales, in March 1809, she already knew some of what to expect because of the experience of 1801–05. Some things were better this time but some were worse.

She was less completely alone. She had Penelope Lucas, and two of the girls were no longer little. In March 1809, young Elizabeth was 17 and Mary 13. On the other hand, family finances were much more complicated and holdings much larger, so that she shrank, as she said at first, from the 'accumulated weight of responsibility and care'.[1] There was now their investment in fine-woolled sheep, which needed particular vigilance – protection while grazing, judicious herding and breeding, shearing, and then sorting, packing and sending off the wool. Every stage had its complications and challenges. There were also the ocean trading concerns John had left behind. For these, Elizabeth was his accredited agent, authorised to deal with debtors and to keep an eye on the sale of incoming cargoes. Most challenging of all, young Elizabeth was seriously ill, sometimes apparently at death's door.

As mistress of house and farm, Elizabeth Macarthur also had her old, familiar duties. The household and outside staff had to be watched, directed, fed and clothed. There were crops of wheat, barley and oats to be managed from season to season. Cattle and sheep had to be fattened for butchers' meat, which was still the family's main source of income, and coarse wool, separated from the fine, had to be sent for spinning and weaving at Parramatta. Now too, there were the blood stallions, Percy and Hotspur, progeny of a horse the Duke of Northumberland had given to George Johnston, to be put to stud each year.[2]

She introduced improvements. She was the first settler in New South Wales to make hay for sale. The hay advertised as a novelty in the Sydney market, in June 1813, at £1 per hundredweight, was probably hers. Also, according to her children, she discovered a new method of removing the stumps after trees had been felled. Stumps hardly mattered with hoe farming but anyone using a plough, as the Macarthurs did, might break its blades against roots left in the ground. Again, details are obscure but the slow-burning method, with logs heaped around old, dry stumps, first publicised in 1816, was probably Elizabeth's invention.[3]

From the start, in 1793, the Macarthurs had worked within a barter economy, or rather barter-and-credit. For both Elizabeth and John, barter-and-credit was not an awkward substitute for real money because they had grown up with local versions of it at Bridgerule and at Plymouth Dock. In both places, more or less, as in New South Wales, coinage had been hard to come by and assets had depended on seasonal returns. The Macarthurs paid their various workers partly in kind, and returns from rental or mortgage seem to have come to them in the same way – in grain after harvest, for instance.

Coarse wool from the Macarthurs' sheep was made into yarn and so into blankets by the convict women in the Female Factory at Parramatta. Beginning in Governor King's time, its bulk had grown with the years. The 1815 clip resulted in 930 pounds (about 420 kilograms) of yarn, which converted to 160 yards (about 150 metres) of cloth and 32 blankets. No cash changed hands because blankets were returned in numbers equivalent to the raw wool sent in. At Elizabeth Farm some, at least, were then distributed to Indigenous people roundabout. With such gifts, issued each winter, the Macarthurs created allies among the invaded population so as to give themselves safety in this occupied land. The better known government system of blanket distribution seems to have begun in 1825–26.[4]

The distribution of blankets and other items to Indigenous people might explain why a man the family knew as Bill, in about 1803, risked his life to tell Elizabeth where she could find a missing cow, a story told earlier. More recently, at the Cowpastures (Camden), John Macarthur likewise dealt with some of the leading men of the Tharawal and Gandangara people, including the young man Budbury, called by the invaders 'Mr McArthur's Budbury'. Budbury was 'a brave man and a quiet one too', so William Macarthur recalled, who led by a type of intellectual authority, or what William called 'mental power'.[5] Gifts must have been part of the Cowpastures regime as well, within a to-and-fro continued by Elizabeth.

Some arrangements with Indigenous men were more complicated. One of Elizabeth's occasional workmen was listed in her memoranda with no family name. He was just 'Andrew', and he was probably the Cadigal man Nanbarry, who had been given that name by the First Fleet surgeon John White when, as a child, he had been orphaned during a smallpox epidemic. Taken in by White, Nanbarry/Andrew had since sailed with Henry Waterhouse. Over three months in the height of summer, 1811–12, Elizabeth paid him, if this was he, a total of £6.7s.6d. It was harvest time and a wage so good suggests that he was one of the reapers.[6]

Within the settlement there was also a growing cash economy, although it was mainly cash-and-credit. Early in 1810 Elizabeth paid the enormous sum of £85 for a second-hand piano for the older girls, while at about the same time John, short of money in London, urged her to hunt up money debts. He suggested that she take advice from the new judge-advocate, Ellis Bent, the settlement's first fully qualified, reputable lawyer, and this she

ELIZABETH'S JUDGMENT

did, giving Bent in return some hints on the local management of livestock. In January 1811 she sued Simeon Lord and Henry Kable, with complete success, although Kable took his case to appeal. This effort brought in £532.7s, plus costs, which, as she might have told herself, was over six times the cost of the piano.[7]

Of her own initiative Elizabeth also took on two lesser figures. Mary Chalker, an Irishwoman transported in 1793, had been a farmer on the Hawkesbury. She had suffered flooding, she had been seriously burnt in a house fire, she had parted from the man she lived with and her farm had been given to tenants too poor to pay the rent. She also had an old debt to the Macarthurs for 160 bushels of wheat. All the same, Elizabeth might have been aware of hidden resources just as John had been with Andrew Thompson in 1806, because Mary Chalker certainly had high connections. They settled for a quarter of the debt, and Elizabeth gave her two months to pay up.[8]

A NEW ARRIVAL SAID IN JULY 1810, WITHOUT EXAGGERating much, that 'the grazing farmer is the only really wealthy person' in New South Wales. The 'grazing farmer' produced fresh meat, which was in constant demand. '[T]he profit is certain, the expense and risk nothing.' At Elizabeth Farm income depended mainly on the sale of mutton. Here again it was barter-and-credit. During 1811–12, for instance, Elizabeth kept a list of promissory notes issued in payment for labour and supplies. There were generally 15 or 20 each week, an outlay totalling £25 or so, and in every case she used her credit with one or other of two Sydney butchers, Richard Cheers of George Street and Richard Tuckwell of Pitt Street. Later on George Cribb, of Cambridge Street, in the Rocks, was a third. Each had a slaughter yard, to which she sent her sheep – say, 40 at a time, mainly wethers – plus occasional cattle. With no banks – the Bank of New South Wales started in

1817 – these butchers were her bankers. The men and women to whom she gave her notes could trade on her accounts with them, so that no-one needed cash. For large sums she also used her credit with Garnham Blaxcell, who was her Sydney agent as he had been John's.[9]

During 1812 this arrangement took a more expansive turn. In March, John Macarthur sent home the news they had both been waiting for since June 1805, when, back from England after his first visit, he had detailed his hopes for fine wool. Now, he told her, that project seemed secure. '[T]he value of the wool is established beyond doubt.' This news was brought from England by John's nephew, his brother James's son, Hannibal Macarthur. Hannibal had arrived in New South Wales for the first time on the *Argo*, in 1805. Now, newly married to Maria King, daughter of the former governor, he was coming back to settle, enthusiastic about the wool and ready to tell Elizabeth whatever else she needed to know. A useful assistant, he had his limitations. 'Hannibal,' John told his wife, 'is as blunt, honest and *unsophisticated* as when he left Parramatta.' He had promised, John assured her, 'to regulate himself upon all occasions by your advice'.[10]

In his early enthusiasm Hannibal invented new machinery for compressing the wool in bales before it was loaded for sea. He found a large screw among ironwork brought out in the *Argo* and he had it fitted into a wooden framework so as to pack the fleece down more effectively than hitherto. It was the first screw press in New South Wales. Freight charges depended on bulk, not weight, so that the cost of carriage to England was in this way markedly reduced.[11]

John had decided, he said, to give Hannibal a share of the business but this never came to pass. Hannibal and Maria lived briefly at Elizabeth Farm, until his aunt found that 'inconvenient' and they moved to the Macarthurs' other house on Sydney Cove. Hannibal then bought land on the other side of Parramatta River and they made their home there.¹² Hannibal saw to the packing and shipment of Elizabeth's wool, but no more was heard of a formal connection.

In this and other ways Elizabeth's experience on the ground prevailed over John's planning in London. She chose to rely on her own confidantes, and it was among those few that she made her decisions. Penelope Lucas was one, 'a single lady', as Elizabeth called her, 'about my own age who shares all my cares'. In Penelope's own family her father had sold coal and soot, but she had uncles who were butchers in Leadenhall Market. Living where she did as a child, she could hardly have forgotten the noise of cattle, sheep and barking dogs forcing their way into the city's centre, and the stench of their slaughter. Penelope knew it all as part of her family's livelihood and in that respect at least she had been well prepared for her work in New South Wales. Already, the old animal and coaldust smells of her childhood had been overlaid by the smell of a gaslight company, new tenants on the Lucas estate, a taste in the air 'like copper to the mouth'.¹³ That she was spared.

Elizabeth was clearly in charge at Elizabeth Farm, but Penelope, with a far neater hand and fewer distractions, helped in tying up loose ends. Authorised to sign on behalf of the family, Penelope was also bookkeeper, translating rough notes into neat aggregate tables. She visited the Cowpastures with Elizabeth and she kept a detailed record of the livestock, down to the birth and death of each lamb. From New Year 1813, the whole fine wool business having been raised to a new level, she put this material into tabulated form in the back of an old ledger, making her entries fortnightly, with perfect uniformity and with hardly a break for five years.¹⁴

Elizabeth and her family shared Penelope's cares in return. During her years in New South Wales her family was still in dispute about her father's estate. Her stepmother's second husband, the naval captain John Temple, had looked after the accounts and a London friend, Elizabeth Wren, had used part of Penelope's income to send her books and clothes. It was probably Penelope who repaid Miss Wren with the gift of an emu's egg, a piece of exotica she was to prize all her life.[15]

However, John Temple went down with his ship in December 1808, and when John Macarthur arrived in England a year later, on top of the court case, estate finances were still being disentangled. In New South Wales, with no money arriving, Penelope was sharing Elizabeth's clothes, but Miss Wren was unhelpful. They should pay Penelope a salary, she said – 'that ought to provide her with every thing she could possibly want'. At last, in 1814, young John, now a law student, started working on the case. Penelope sent him her power of attorney and all issues were more or less quickly settled. She had about £1000 due, plus £235 in annual income. It was more than enough to live on if she stayed at Elizabeth Farm, John told Elizabeth, 'which tell her she will be most welcome to do as long as she shall find … herself comfortable and happy'.[16]

What was Elizabeth's feeling for Penelope? How much did the two learn from each other, as Elizabeth and John had learnt? How much did Penelope colour Elizabeth's habits and vice versa? How much were Elizabeth's ideas Penelope's ideas? One slight clue lies in the way John mentioned her in his letters home. Writing in step with her letters to him, at the start it was 'Remember me most kindly to Miss Lucas.' However, by the end 'most kindly' had turned into 'most affectionately' and 'Miss Lucas' into 'Mrs Lucas'. 'Mrs', an echo of 'Mistress', suggests an older woman, unmarried still but settling with some authority into middle age.[17]

Just occasionally, Elizabeth's thoughts escaped to another world altogether. Early in 1816 she was surprised to hear from Eliza Kingdon, the youngest of the Bridgerule family. She had been a baby when they left England. She was now in her late twenties and living with her brother's family in the vicarage. The sight of Eliza's handwriting reconnected Elizabeth, as nothing else could, to her childhood, and she could hardly find words, she said, to express her delight. An exchange of letters followed and each of Eliza's stirred deep feelings, a useful effect among all her worries, Elizabeth said, because of the 'salutary effect upon my mind'. 'How do I wish "that I had wings like a bird" that I might sit myself down beside you, at the bridge so often passed and repassed in my younger days, and there fondly embrace you.'[18]

FROM 1812–13 SUCCESS WITH THE WOOL BROUGHT NEW priorities. John Macarthur sent word that the fleece was arriving dirty. It could be washed on arrival, before sale, but it was cheaper and easier to wash the sheep before shearing. That was now done. Elizabeth also built a shed at Camden for short-term storage, and a slab cottage to replace her bark hut, and there was Hannibal's new press, so that altogether the work was raised to a higher level. The main thing lacking was a skilled wool-sorter. Only one man in New South Wales could do the work well and he was not always available. Sometimes, in London, half a dozen different degrees of fineness were found within a single bale, which damaged their standing in the market.[19]

At one end of the business everything depended on the arcane skills and obscure preferences of English buyers. At the other end, and just as important, were the shepherds. The best of the shepherds were old hands, who were committed to the work, who understood dingoes and could notice the early signs of scab – endemic mange. Each normally had his own hutkeeper, his wife or an older man who had otherwise outlived his usefulness. Old John Mortlock, for instance, lived for years with John Wade, until he collapsed into dementia. He ended his life in the Liverpool asylum. The shepherds also had their dogs, a type of mastiff, a breed used by shepherds in Spain, thickset and strong, capable of managing dingoes.[20]

When Penelope Lucas began her more formal listing of livestock at the beginning of 1813 one of the shepherds was William Baker. Baker came from Wiltshire, sheep country. Charged with stealing a silver teaspoon, he had arrived in New South Wales in 1791. Penelope's first tabulation showed him and three others at Camden with flocks of breeding ewes, 325 each, and a fifth man with 301. With other flocks of mixed breed, ewes and wethers, the shepherds at Camden numbered 11. A twelfth, with pure Merinos only, stayed at Elizabeth Farm, and the rams were sent out, four or five for each flock, at the right time for each year's breeding. While Elizabeth was in charge she kept the total number of sheep at about 4000, managing the annual increase by sending to the butchers her wethers plus all ewes with inferior fleece. At Camden there were also two herds of cattle, with one herdsman each. In January 1813, each man saw to 60 cows and three bulls, plus sundry heifers and calves.[21]

Besides their rations – grain, meat, tobacco – stockmen were given £1, more or less, every month, paid in notes on the butcher. Sometimes they were rewarded with a little more and in two cases, for long and superior service, with land. For Thomas Herbert and John Condron, in 1811, Elizabeth secured 100-acre grants – one each – near the Cowpastures, where they kept cattle, though they were still available to work for her. The money might be taken to the shepherds and others at their workplace. In August 1813, Elizabeth's black velvet wallet was lost somewhere on the road from Parramatta, with eight notes for various men on their payroll, each signed by Penelope Lucas.[22]

The Cowpastures, on the frontier of British occupation, was a hazardous place to work. John McCormick, in charge of one herd of cattle, disappeared briefly in 1811 and Elizabeth, anxious, as she said, that 'some accident may have befallen him', posted a £2 reward for information. He turned up safe, but William Baker was not so lucky. In January 1814, during a raid, apparently by

Gandangara, mountain people, he was killed at his hut, together with Mary Sullivan, possibly his hutkeeper. He was mourned as 'a faithful old servant', so Elizabeth recalled, 'who had lived with us since we first came to the colony'. He was John's 'old favourite'.[23]

30
COMMANDING THE LONG TERM

In a normal household, at least in theory, the wife left to her husband all the big practical questions, and that included decisions for the long term. That long-term authority, second only to the providential power of God, was all-important for the maintenance of patriarchy – the institutionalised power of men. Recall Elizabeth Macarthur's remark in 1798, when their sheep numbers had almost reached the point where they could afford to kill for mutton. 'Next year, Mr. Macarthur tells me, we may begin.'[1]

In dealing with such questions a woman might be hobbled not just by custom but by a lack of training. With daily housekeeping, for instance, she might record her dealings, say, in a daybook, as a simple list of things bought and sold, whereas men with equivalent responsibilities might use double-entry bookkeeping. With double-entry it was possible to reconcile debit and credit from page to page so as to carry through the balance for the long term, making it much easier to see how funding evolved over months and years. John Macarthur used double-entry, doubtless learnt at Plymouth Dock. However, double-entry required ruled stationery properly bound. The sheets must stay in order together. Because of a general shortage of paper, in New South Wales even cash accountancy might depend on memory and/or loose notes.

Double-entry carried assets from past to future. Lacking such skill, women's management was more likely than men's to be short-term and narrow-range. Elizabeth Macarthur had apparently never learnt double-entry. However, Penelope Lucas knew it well so that she was more useful than ever now, as they made their calculations for the long term.

This question of men and women, the long term and short term, was tackled in 1799, though in a roundabout way, in a book called *A Letter to the Women of England, on the Injustice of Mental Subordination*, by Mary Robinson. Robinson was Mary Wollstonecraft's friend and disciple, and her *Letter* came in the wake of Wollstonecraft's more famous *Vindication of the Rights of Woman* (1792). Known to London society as 'Perdita', Mary Robinson was also a celebrated actor and former mistress of the Prince of Wales, and she was besides a gifted writer. The poet Coleridge called her 'a woman of undoubted genius'.[2]

In her *Letter,* she pointed out a striking contradiction in the England of her day. On the one hand, with so much published writing by women there could be no doubt now that many of her sex possessed 'both energy of mind, and capability of acquiring most extensive knowledge'. And yet, women were still barred from making decisions of any large and long-term importance. 'Man is a despot by nature,' Robinson said, 'he can bear no equal, [and] he dreads the power of woman.'[3]

In 1789 Mary Robinson had interested herself in a young woman, Eleanor, or Nell, McDonald, lately sentenced to transportation to New South Wales. Nell had been convicted of theft, but Mary Robinson believed she was a young woman of 'virtuous education' and she mustered influence with the Home Office in an effort to save her. She had known Nell's mother, who was now dead. The girl was orphaned, destitute and ill, but she had friends, said Robinson, keen to see her 'restored to society'. Mary Robinson's eloquence had no effect, but she had connections in New South Wales.[4] Her current lover was Banastre Tarleton, cousin and correspondent of Watkin Tench. Her next step, almost certainly, was a letter to Tench, as Nell's passport to new friends at Sydney Cove.

This seems to explain Nell's early attachment to Elizabeth Macarthur, still keenly felt during Elizabeth's second time alone, in 1809–17. Twelve months after her arrival Nell had married the Macarthurs' overseer, the convict David Kilpack, and when he died she continued with her three girls as the Macarthurs' nominal tenant. She took another husband but still called herself Kilpack, which suggests that despite this second marriage she thought of herself now as an independent woman. To the Macarthurs she was Nelly. She grew wheat and maize, and bred pigs and sheep, running her ewes with a neighbour's Merino rams. Nell Kilpack appears again at the end of this story. Thanks probably to Mary Robinson, she and her family did well from the Macarthur connection.[5]

There is some small evidence that Nell came from a family of silk-weavers in London's East End, a type of aristocracy among the working class.[6] Hence her 'virtuous education'. In making her own decisions in New South Wales, she did not just manage from day to day. Though it was hard enough, she seems to have avoided all compromising contact with the convict world. Her girls, at least in their choice of husbands – married in 1810–18 – did the same. Nell's was a type of determination for the long haul that Mary Robinson might have warmed to.

THE MACARTHURS THEMSELVES, ELIZABETH AND JOHN, managed between themselves in the traditional way, and yet they also bent to the wind of circumstance. While he was away John sent Elizabeth scant advice or instruction because she already had most of what she needed, but he did insist on the need for extreme care in separating the finest wooled ewes from the rest, for breeding.[7] He might have worried about that in particular because it was so difficult to do. She had no skilled wool-sorter on hand to guide her in picking out the best ewes, so that she must have taught herself, with advice from trusted shepherds. And yet, it was all-important for the future of the flocks.

The other harrowing decision in this period, which was also Elizabeth's, concerned their own future. Would they stay at Elizabeth Farm or settle at last in England? John felt the tug of England, with its concentration of power and its large ideas. He delighted in clever and powerful friends, men and women who could engage with his more elaborate thoughts. He also wanted to be able to watch the achievements of all four sons, the pride of his life. On top of that, the government's reaction to the Bligh rebellion made it hard, even impossible, for him to go back to New South Wales, although it took a while for him to focus on that point.

At the same time, the possibilities of that remote place had taken root in his imagination. For both of them, New South Wales was the scene of their married life. More subtly and powerfully than England, it had become their home. They knew each other's feelings in that respect, but it may be that Elizabeth knew better than John how much his deeper energies were tied to the unfolding experiment of New South Wales.

Their thoughts went backwards and forwards across the globe. During 1811–12, the year following George Johnston's trial, John made up his mind that he could not go back. He felt too much damaged by defeat. By all received understanding, he was responsible for the long-term fortunes of his family so that the decision was his. However, there was an awkwardness in the way he told Elizabeth of his intentions for them all. They would be together again at some point, he assured her. 'But will not my Elizabeth sigh when she is told that this union … cannot take place in the country in which she has tasted so much prosperity and pleasure, and drunk so deeply of adversity and calamity?' They must all, he said, come back to England. It was for the good of their children, and he relied on her now, he told her, to put aside her own feelings, including her fear of the ocean journey. He would come for her, he said, if she had 'the smallest apprehension or dread of coming home alone'.[8]

Five months later, he was able to admit that the decision was really about himself and his own fears. Hers were beside the point. He was shocked by the way the new governor, Lachlan Macquarie, honoured men of doubtful honesty, ex-convicts such as Andrew Thompson and Simeon Lord. He had met Macquarie at Hinton McArthur's London house in 1803–04. He had always had a high opinion of him and he appreciated his kindness to Elizabeth. Macquarie and his wife had found her once at her base at Camden, a 'small miserable Hut', as Macquarie called it, where she ate and slept when she went, sometimes with Penelope, to look at her stock. It had two pieces of furniture, one made of rushes and the other of bark, on which the Macquaries were polite enough to sit for a while.[9]

Elizabeth Macarthur thought Elizabeth Macquarie 'a very good woman' and she was sure that the governor was their friend. John could not contradict her, but why then, John said, did Macquarie honour the dishonourable? He must have been duped. Whatever the reason, from top to bottom New South Wales had become a place of compromised integrity. 'A man of my known principles,' John told Elizabeth, 'must be hated and decried in self defence in such a colony.'[10] Returning from England to New South Wales, bearing the stigma of defeat, he would be at the mercy of men he despised.

They had to make their home in England, drawing income from New South Wales. Any number of West Indian plantation owners lived like that. They would need a reliable agent on the spot – so far, Hannibal was the only possibility – and they also would need to be sure, before they committed themselves, that their funds would hold up. He calculated that they would need £1600 a year, £800 for themselves and their daughters, and the same to set up their sons with creditable careers. She must do the sums herself, from what she knew about income and expenditure in New South Wales, so as to work out whether that was possible. He would rely, he said, on her conclusion. The final word was hers, 'on which it is probable the dark or bright hue of our future fortune will very materially depend'.[11]

The marriage of Elizabeth and John had already passed through two phases. They had been very happy in the 1790s but still he had divided his loyalties between his family and the regiment. So they had arrived at their mid-thirties. Then he had broken with the regiment and there had been years of rethinking. They had also aimed higher. That had been a time of risk and difficulty. Tensions might have cropped up between them, but there is no evidence of that one way or the other. Now they were both tired. He had less to prove, not only to her but also to his children. He understood, better than he had done in his twenties, how much, but also how little, he was needed – a useful revelation, such as only age can bring.

While in London he said very little to her about making money from ocean trading. He knew that she no longer had much faith in that. In her mind, for the time being, everything depended on the livestock she could send to the butchers in Sydney. For John, however, it was this part of their income that seemed most doubtful. The cloth-dealer's son argued with the farmer's daughter. In the late 1790s he had said that the value of their grain could not hold up and he said the same now about their meat. It was a question of political economy, of balancing supply and demand. With meat, as with grain in those earlier days, the current equilibrium could not last. '[D]epreciation must proceed,' he told her, 'and with increased rapidity until the price is brought down to the lowest point at which stock will pay for rearing.' The future value of their wool might help, but it was not yet enough.

The widening gap between what they earned and what they needed must be painful, 'unless,' he insisted, 'we can do something in the mercantile way'.[12]

The 'mercantile way' no longer meant Pyrmont, but John had other plans afoot. Sure of these, he used them to justify a home in England. During 1813, when he had not heard from Elizabeth for a very long time, he started to think that she had done what he wanted – handed over to Hannibal – and was on her way back. On a visit to Hinton McArthur in Hampshire he heard of a house with 142 acres (58 hectares) for sale nearby and he decided to buy it, as soon as funds arrived from a cargo sent lately to New South Wales. During March–June 1814 he was busily imagining his wife and daughters looking about and settling in when four vessels arrived with letters, some of them 18 months old. Hannibal told him that the cargo in question had completely failed. Elizabeth announced her decision that they must stay in New South Wales.[13]

With this decision, Elizabeth gave up all hope of bringing the family all together, leaving them instead scattered across two hemispheres. She took the risk of never seeing her two older sons again. In fact, during her lifetime Edward came home once more, for ten months in 1824–25, but her second son John, gone from her at seven years old, she never saw again.

On the other hand, the failure of the latest cargo, detailed by Hannibal, made her decision providential. Already John had thanked her several times for her fortitude and prudence. Now he was overcome. Thank God, he said, 'that your good sense enabled you to resist the temptation to coming to England'. What would have happened if she had decided otherwise! '[I]nto what an abyss of misery would you and my beloved children have been plunged – dearest best beloved woman, how great are my obligations to you!'[14]

ELIZABETH HAD ASKED HIM, IF HE COULD NOT COME back himself, to send one of the two younger boys to help. James, at 14, had finished school. He was the obvious choice but John hesitated to let him go.[15] His hopes for the children's education were more expansive and elaborate than Elizabeth's, and he was sure that the two boys needed more time before they buried themselves in New South Wales.

As for himself too, there was still reason to hesitate. It was usual for colonists of rank and property, before setting out, to call on the minister, to get his official blessing and other favours. George Johnston had slipped away, returning in disgrace, but John Macarthur refused to do the same. James Brogden did what he could to help. He was now chairman of Ways and Means in the House of Commons – presiding at budget debates – and with easy access to senior figures in government, he urged the minister at the Colonial Office, Lord Bathurst, to order John Macarthur a passage home. So far Bathurst had not budged.[16]

Midway through 1814, Brogden discovered an obstacle that neither he nor John Macarthur had known about. Governor Macquarie's initial instructions, issued five years earlier by Bathurst's predecessor, had included an order for John Macarthur's criminal trial, should he be found in New South Wales. That order still stood. If John went back now it would be up to the governor to decide whether or not to try him for his life, on a charge of high treason.[17] For the next six months, although he wrote to Elizabeth about other things, John kept back the news of this revelation, hoping that a solution would emerge. He broke the news only at the end of the year. In desperation he urged her to see if the governor could be persuaded to have the order withdrawn. The Macquaries might even be open to a shared investment, as Governor King had been at the end of his time. Of course, in exploring these possibilities she must be careful. Here again, he trusted to 'your own good sense'.[18] There is no evidence of her making any move at all.

He was more dictatorial on other matters. She was remiss in not sending him regular information. She should keep notes to remind herself what she had to tell him. In her latest letters she had complained about money lost on speculative imports to New South Wales. Failure so far, he said, had been Hannibal's fault. He was now sending another, which she must look after herself. 'I feel confident that if prudence and good sense can ensure success it will prove successful in your hands.'[19]

He knew what he owed her. God must surely bless and protect his 'best beloved and most excellent' wife. '[I]f it be his good will that I shall be restored to your arms it will be the study of my life to requite you for all you have suffered on my account.'[20] On the other hand, he also knew what she owed him, as his wife, in the great scheme of things that neither of them thought to question.

PART 6

31

THE SUPPOSED POINT OF INVASION

During the trouble with Governor Bligh in January 1808 the young man Tjedboro – his story, or what is known of it, has been told already – had suddenly turned up in Sydney. He said he was there to spear the governor. Tjedboro was no longer living at Elizabeth Farm, but he dropped in now and then, and was welcome there. Now, finding John Macarthur safe – this was William Macarthur's story, set down in writing much later – he 'expressed his joy in the most extravagant manner saying "master they told me you were in gaol".[1]

John Macarthur had entered Tjedboro's universe in 1805, when he came back from England on the *Argo*. In March 1809, 15 months after this post-rebellion episode, John left again for England, disappearing once more into the ocean void. A few months passed and Tjedboro returned to his warrior ways. He started with robbing travellers on the Parramatta–Sydney road, which was just a version of bushranging. Then he was seen with groups attacking farms at George's River and Cook's River. At the same time, he also spent time around Parramatta and in February 1810, partly drunk, he threw a spear at a little girl playing outside her house in town. He missed. The child's older brother ran out with a gun and his bullet hit Tjedboro in the mouth. The injury was superficial but now, more than ever, Tjedboro was at risk.

He was killed soon afterwards, probably in some incident of the same sort.²

Other boys and young men of various backgrounds were drawn to John Macarthur as Tjedboro was, and John in turn delighted in the drama and potential of young lives, and in being somehow part of them. That hands-off, hands-on connection with Tjedboro was typical, and its apparent tenuousness might have made attachment between man and boy all the stronger. James Byrnes, an apprentice carpenter-builder, met John Macarthur, probably in 1826, when building work was underway at Elizabeth Farm. What John told young Byrnes, walking as he had walked with Tjedboro, it is impossible to know, but according to Byrnes, much later on, he 'took great pains to infuse right principles in my mind and heart'. '[I]f I have anything at all,' he added, 'which qualifies me to look at the past and provide for the future', it was thanks to John Macarthur. '[B]y many persons [he] was not understood, by others not appreciated but by me admired.'³

Tjedboro ended up dead in his early twenties. James Byrnes ended up a cabinet minister in self-governing New South Wales. Byrnes was minister for public works in 1866–68 and 1870–72, adding to the infrastructure of settlement. That difference in their lives says something both obvious and complicated about the invasion process, and about the parts taken in it by both Elizabeth and John.

John Macarthur was away for eight years, 1809–17, with his two youngest boys, James and William. When all three came back, it was not just Tjedboro who had disappeared. Indigenous numbers roundabout were much reduced. William Macarthur was startled, he said, to find this essential part of his childhood greatly changed.⁴

At the same time, far away in the interior, invasion was proceeding apace. Thirty years earlier Governor Phillip had arrived with instructions to leave the Indigenous peoples alone, except where absolutely necessary. That made no sense now. British expeditions of discovery were heading off in all directions, beyond the mountains to the west, across the Southern Tablelands, up the Hunter Valley and along the coast, opening the way for new occupation. The invaders multiplied too. Tjedboro left no children, or at least none that anyone seems to have remembered. James Byrnes was survived by nine.

Occupation picked up pace from about the time the Macarthurs came back, partly because grants of land were often much bigger than before, as required for pasturing sheep and cattle, and the sheep and cattle themselves multiplied from year to year. Livestock penetrated the bush in random ways, crashing and trampling, destroying old sources of livelihood.

The pace of occupation meant less chance of mutual adjustment between Black and White, and for learning names and snippets of language. Risking their fortunes, often with families to provide for, the invaders were more impatient than they had been. Besides the conflict between old and new, Indigenous groups were pushed into each others' territories, so that violence multiplied on all sides. When Governor Macquarie took office in 1810, permanent settlement had reached little more than 60 kilometres from Sydney. By the time he left, in 1822, that distance had tripled, taking in great swathes of country belonging to clans and families of Wiradjuri, Geawegal, Wonnarua, Darkinjung, Gandangara and others, great nations 'time out of mind'.

The first invaders, like the government that sent them, had thought that they would not need much land at all. For 20 years that idea had lingered, though it was more and more obviously incorrect, and even as their methods shifted, the invaders continued to believe that the two populations might co-exist for the long term.

The fact that Tjedboro was left alone by police, even after robbing with violence, hints at how compromise might have worked, but also, of course, how it was bound to fail. Tjedboro's case illustrates what was already an established pattern, the interweaving of violence and adjustment – beginning with violence, ending with violence, framed by violence, but including a good deal of hypocrisy and genuine hope as well.

Some of the invaders believed in all sincerity that their presence would leave the Indigenous peoples better off in the end. After all, as emissaries from Enlightenment Europe, they had much to offer and these peoples seemed to be much in need. Here was a fragment of suffering humanity, said one early official, a people plunged in wretchedness, ignorance and want, so that their every day was misery.[5] Some, surely, must welcome the gifts now presented, whatever the pain involved for them.

William Macarthur, at 17 years old, was surprised to find Indigenous numbers so much thinned. That surprise might have drawn him to a clearer understanding as to what invasion really meant, because it was a clarity emerging for many from this time. Population was dwindling not only through violence, devastating though that was, but by new diseases and by deeper psychological–physical change, affecting childbirth and the will to live. The damage caused by the wholesale theft of land and the destruction of community was profound. And yet, even as they began to understand it better the invaders knew that they could not and would not stop. 'The blacks,' said one settler, 'cannot be conciliated unless by giving up their country.' Just to say so was to show how unlikely that was.

Note, in this statement, the reference to 'their country'.[6] It was an idea widely understood. Elizabeth, John and their children thought like that too. They knew that the country still belonged to the people who had lived there for countless generations. They could see that sense of possession expressed in a certain ancient civility. The third son, James, spoke of the politeness the old inhabitants used among themselves in small matters of territory, especially waterholes. Like gentlemen, he said, announcing themselves at a house by sending in visiting cards, Indigenous people called out as they approached new places, with a series of 'cooeys'. '[H]e should himself,' he said, 'hesitate in going suddenly amongst blacks, however well he might be known to them, without using this precaution.'[7]

If they admitted prior ownership, and of much more than a waterhole, how did the family at Elizabeth Farm justify sudden invasion and wholesale theft? They were all capable of making the effort demanded by Edmund Burke in 1785, in speaking to the House of Commons about India. Imagine, Burke had said, some brutal invader overrunning Britain as the men of the East India Company were doing in India. Imagine your own 'sweet and cheerful country … emptied and embowelled' by alien greed.[8] It was the same case, or very close, in New South Wales.

The point of the next few chapters in the story of Elizabeth and John is to sketch the energy, including an energy of mind, that overcame such questions of conscience. It is hard to disentangle genuine and special pleading, but there is no doubt that the invading people thought that their power was in some sense God-given and that God intended them to use it, for their own good first and foremost, but also, if possible, for the good of others. Again James summed it up:

> There could be no doubt that, in taking possession of their country, we committed what to the blacks appeared a gross outrage, and a violation of their rights; but we were only acting in conformity with the divine command which enjoined us to go forth and multiply – to occupy and cultivate the land, and to render it useful.[9]

At least in practice, the rule 'Might is right' was reshaped as Christian doctrine.

It was harder to believe that invasion was altogether a good thing as it became more obviously brutal and rapacious, as it did during the 1820s. The numbing of moral sensibility was as rapid as invasion itself. For the original 15 years of invasion, even for the first 25–30 years, hopes for some sort of co-existence prevailed. From then on such hopes were seriously contested. In the 1820s, for the first time, there were some among the invaders who publicly used the word 'extermination'. There must have been many more who used the word and dwelt on the idea only among themselves.[10]

Running close to the house at Elizabeth Farm were the streams and waterholes of Duck River and Clay Cliff Creek, rich sources of food for the Burramattagal people before their banks and beds were trodden down by the Macarthurs' livestock. These two watercourses must have been a constant reminder of old forms of sustenance and old ways replaced, suddenly and violently, by new. These large questions certainly troubled Elizabeth, John and their children, but how much and how painfully is a difficult question to answer. I can only come at it in a roundabout way.

32
INTRIGUED BY THE YOUNG

Europeans had various ancient theories about the stages of human life. In *As You Like It*, William Shakespeare set out the 'Seven Ages of Man', starting with 'the infant, Mewling and puking in the nurse's arms', and ending with 'second childishness and mere oblivion', toothless, eyeless, tasteless and at death's edge. According to the Old Testament (Psalms 90:10), the end comes at 'threescore years and ten', or 70. Living longer than that is pointless effort.

Seven, 14, 21 or 70, the number seven turned up often. Among boys, the first stage of learning supposedly ended at seven, but maybe in practice at eight or nine. At 14 boys might be bound to apprenticeships, normally until they were 21. For girls there was less numerical rigour. After 14 or thereabouts, the next thing they had to wait for was marriage.

The Macarthur children followed this regime, more or less, but what they did during each stage was more in tune with their own time. Jean-Jacques Rousseau affected everything at least a little. Rousseau's book, *Èmile, or On Education* (1762), at least in broad outline, was the final authority for most progressively minded parents, together with the work of other theorists following Rousseau's lead. There was a new concentration on the individual mind and inclinations of those taught, and more about the child positioned in nature and in touch with the material world. The manuals of the Comtesse de Genlis, on the shelves at

Elizabeth Farm, took this line. So did the work of Johann Heinrich Pestalozzi and Philipp Emanuel von Fellenberg, in Switzerland, and of George Jardine in Glasgow. They all belong in this story.

The rigours of childhood at Elizabeth Farm – scant clothes in winter, coarse food, very few toys – matched the regime set out by Rousseau. 'The child who has overcome hardships,' said Rousseau, 'has gained strength, and as soon as he can use his life he holds it more securely.'[1] The little wheelbarrow, William's only toy, might have done service with each of his older brothers and sisters, one after the other, falling apart at last during William's tenure. Rousseau thought that there should be no formal teaching at this early stage of life, nothing but running about, but the Macarthur children acquired some skill in writing and reading aloud when they were little. All of them might have begun with their mother, though Emmeline also had her older sisters and Penelope Lucas to guide her.

The second stage of schooling, roughly from seven to 14, was meant to open up young minds to the world beyond home, as well giving them method and discipline. In the 1790s there was nothing that made the older Elizabeth want to leave New South Wales, so she told Bridget Kingdon, except for 'the difficulty of educating our children'. As they got older, she said, 'it would be unjust towards them to confine them to so narrow a society'.[2] The problem was met by sending or taking them away.

Edward and John each went off to England at seven, and Elizabeth at nine. James, however, at about seven, started with Gabriel Louis Huon, and probably William, though two years younger, sat in some lessons with him. Three or four years later, when these two reached England with their father, James's handwriting was 'very fair'. William was still practising his downward strokes before going on to whole letters. James had not mastered multiplication, but both of them spoke good French, thanks to their acting and speech-making with Gabriel Louis.[3]

INTRIGUED BY THE YOUNG

Early writing exercises included family letters, with children copying out drafts made for them by someone else. So they also learnt composition and the protocols of politeness. Even at 11, James wrote home to his mother by copying from a draft his father made for him. At seven, in the same way, their youngest sister Emmeline was exchanging letters with a 'lover', as she called him, Sam Kingdon, twelve, far away at Bridgerule. One of Sam's letters arrived in March 1816. Emmeline would answer when she could, her mother said, but it was hard to know when. 'Her sisters indulge her to a very great degree and I am a very bad preceptress myself.'[4]

As a pedagogical parent, John Macarthur was much more careful than this. As a fundamental rule, for instance, he forced himself to be impartial among his children. Among the girls, young Elizabeth – cheerful, witty, well read but often ill – drew everyone's attention, while Mary was more withdrawn and unassuming, less inquisitive and, as her mother said, 'not very apt to be taken with strangers'. Their father fumbled to reassure Mary of his impartial affection. 'Let not my dear Mary imagine I have forgotten her', he said, writing home from London, though Mary could hardly be blamed if she did.[5]

Among the boys he could be firm in shutting down talk of preference. In one episode involving Edward and young John, Edward, 20 years old, wept at the suggestion that he had complained about John being preferred. The idea never occurred to him, he said. 'If you knew my father what my sentiments were on that head ... you would no longer even hint things which however delicately they may be expressed still touch me to the quick.'[6]

In England during 1809–17 their father kept a close eye on all four boys, but Edward was especially keen in claiming his affections, flourishing his feelings as his brothers never did. Having finished school in England, Edward had spent 18 months in New South Wales, in 1806–08, before carrying back to London the rebels' first announcement of their action against Governor Bligh.

His father then bought for him a commission in the 60th Regiment and he fought in the disastrous battle of Corunna in Spain, in January 1809, before moving with promotion to the 39th. He then served in Gibraltar, Malta and Sicily before returning to Spain. He was at the Battle of Vitoria, one of the turning points in the war against Napoleon, and then went with the 39th to North America, to protect Canada from American invasion. In 1815, Edward and his regiment were part of the army of occupation in conquered France.

As young men starting out, Edward and John both made use of old family connections, most of them Scottish – engineered by Hinton McArthur – and Edward had an introduction to Major-General James Campbell, adjutant-general of the British forces in the Mediterranean. Campbell promised straightaway, so Edward told his father, that 'he should take every opportunity of advancing my interests, [and] would be at all times happy to see me.'[7]

However, for all the boys such contacts could never replace John himself. Edward not only promised that in the ups and downs of army life he would rely on 'those principles which you [his father] have so carefully instilled into my mind'. His father thought that Edward was at risk from the humidity of the Mediterranean. Regulating perspiration and otherwise ventilating the skin was understood to be an important aspect of daily hygiene, and each morning, his father told him, he must get up early, go for a long walk and wash his feet and head in cold water. Omitting to wash the head too was said to cause an uprush of blood, bringing on headache, but Edward found, so he said, that head washing brought on a violent ache in his left temple. To get rid of that he spent a warm day climbing and walking. 'I threw myself into so great perspiration,' he said, 'that on my return to my room the pain was quite gone.'[8]

His father was convinced that good health was undermined by idleness. 'You will be greatly pleased I know to hear,' Edward wrote from Gibraltar, 'that I keep my hands full, and allow no time to pass without some occupations.' His father had imposed on him a large body of reading. 'When I open my great box of books,' Edward told him, 'I think I shall never get through with them, but I take courage on reflecting on what you have often repeated to me on similar occasions, that "Rome was not built in an hour".' With his father ever in mind, he worked on his French, in Gibraltar he took up Spanish, and in Sicily Italian, paying a tutor each time. He struggled with mathematics, he read history and drama, and he kept an eye out for relics of European history, art and architecture. His program made him a rarity in his regiment. If he managed to keep it up, he told his father, 'I shall during the greater part of my advancement, find myself a solitary traveller.' There was ridicule too, which he long remembered, but he did not mention that.[9]

In his letters Edward struggled at the same time to recapture the warmth of feeling and the chat, including family sayings, he remembered from Elizabeth Farm. Physically tough, never complaining about battle hardship, in his feeling for his parents he was remarkably soft, especially with his mother. Writing to her, he asked her to unite her mind with his so as to cancel the distance between them. 'When alone consider my dear mother, that I am with you, for into your presence my imagination is often conducting me. There I am ideally at this moment.' He read her letters as an evangelical Christian might read Scripture, saying each detail over and over so as to bring his mind to the right pitch. The reading, he said, 'gives birth to a variety of ideas, and creates in the mind a pleasing degree of tender melancholy, diffusing itself over the imagination, and rendering it susceptible of impressions lively and pure'. So they were together indeed, he told her, 'the tenderest of mothers' and 'the most affectionate of sons'.[10]

Edward, as his mother herself put it, was 'single hearted'. She might have been surprised by his intensity of feeling, but she liked it. With voice or pen, he seemed to offer undivided affection. In

May 1810, at Gibraltar, he was asked to form up his men on the parade ground. He told his mother how it felt. 'I had never exalted my voice before in the presence of so many people. I felt what I believe most do, when placed in an untried situation. My presence of mind however did not forsake me; and fortunately I did right.' The girls, of course, were listening as their mother read this out. 'I dare say,' Edward added, 'Sister Mary thinks it would be very funny to see Brother Edward giving the word of command, and Elizabeth would like much to quiz him to put on his red coat and sword and strut about the room.'[11]

To his father he happily admitted his failings, as if even those brought him closer to John's loving oversight. 'I greatly fear,' he told him on leaving England in 1810, 'I shall widely deviate from the path you have pointed out to me.' And then, from Sicily, 'how often I wish for your presence, to communicate the thoughts that arise in my mind, some of which perhaps I should cherish, and others probably that I ought to banish.' He had promised that 'there is no circumstance which concerns me, however minute, that I shall not communicate, and no thoughts that I shall hesitate to disclose or confide to you.'[12] In fact, the detail came from him in inconsequential lumps. At Gibraltar, thanks to General Campbell, he received invitations to Government House, where the governor, another Campbell, had a large family. 'I do not know how it is,' he told his father, 'but tho' I am always pleasant and comfortable when at their house, I yet feel an awkwardness in accepting their invitations, the same as I should experience from receiving a repetition of benefits from an unknown or strange hand.'[13]

In the same sort of detail he dwelt on the joys of staying busy:

> The pleasure I find in fully occupying my time is my dear father indescribable ... I am surprised often at the rapidity with which the hour floats away. By these means I enjoy security of mind, and place it in such state, as

to receive delight from amusement which by many are not considered as worthy seeking because the sensations which they create are not sufficiently strong.

And yet, failure was never far away. On the point of leaving Gibraltar for Sicily, '[t]he prospect of removing so soon renders me uneasy; my mind is like troubled water, in irregular motion. I feel a desire to do something without knowing what.'[14]

John gave back a steady flow of advice, plus all the physical paraphernalia his son, as a junior officer, could possibly need. Besides books, he loaded him with financial credit, on tap wherever he was, military accoutrements and an excellent watch, 'which,' Edward told him, 'far exceeds any thing I could have desired or could have expected'.[15] John had unbounded faith in all his children, but he admired Edward – handsome, cheerful, polite – even to idolatry. '[H]e is everything that can give pleasure to the breast of a parent,' he told Elizabeth, 'sober, discreet, sensible, active, intelligent, brave.' Men in authority who dealt with Edward seemed to think so too, as John proudly reported. The Duke of Northumberland did what he could for him. Hugh Elliot took to him straight away. James Brogden, busy though he was, wrote to Edward often, 'with as much warmth of affection as if he were his son'.[16]

In Sicily, Edward was introduced to a 19-year-old Englishman, Lord Malpas, who was travelling with his tutor, and the two discovered a shared love of 'polite literature'. Malpas came often to Edward's quarters to read his books. They spent a good deal of time together and the viscount's taste, according to Edward, was an education in itself. 'I assure [you] my dear father that until I heard him read I was unacquainted with the force and harmony of Shakespeare's language. Nothing can be more fortunate than my acquaintance with him.' In England, however, among his relations, Malpas was a disappointment. He was called 'effeminate' and he gave clear indications of wanting to turn Roman Catholic – he settled on Methodism – but of these unmanly propensities Edward said nothing.[17]

EDWARD MACARTHUR KNEW VERY WELL THAT HIS brother John was cleverer than he was. '[S]uch is his manner of reasoning,' he told their parents when John was ready to leave school, 'that he is beheld with astonishment, mixt with admiration.'[18] Already, at that point, young John looked forward to a career in the law. The Scottish universities took students much younger than the English ones and after school John spent 18 months at the University of Glasgow, before going on to Cambridge. While at Cambridge he was also admitted to Lincoln's Inn, one of the Inns of Court in London, to begin his legal training. In 1818, at 24, he graduated and was called to the English bar.

Settling in London, young John changed the spelling of his name from 'McArthur' to 'Macarthur', probably because of anti-Scottish prejudice among some Londoners he mixed with. The rest of the family then followed suit. And yet their Scottish connections had been crucial so far, for John as well as for Edward. At Glasgow, Archibald Campbell of Blythswood, a member of Hinton McArthur's Highland Society, was rector (that is, chancellor) of the university and he took young John under his wing. A member of parliament and a dabbler in agricultural innovation, Archibald Campbell's interest in the Macarthurs was to be long-term.[19]

John's professor at Glasgow, George Jardine, was influential in other ways. Jardine was a great and inspiring educational reformer, who took Rousseau's general approach – the mind of the student is all in all – to the university level. In his book, *Outlines of Philosophical Education*, written about this time, Jardine described several decades of teaching experiment with students John's age. The teacher, Jardine said, must be a figure of authority but he must also be the student's friend. Teaching was a form of conversation. There must be lively attention to and fro, an exchange 'of Looks and Feeling', 'intercourse between the Mind and the Eye', said Jardine – and not just between teacher and student. Students must attend to each other in the same way. Jardine made enthusiastic use of what was later to be called peer assessment. His students were asked to judge each other's work because, he said, that put everything above board, while also creating a finer sense of discrimination among the students themselves.[20]

Young John was said to have been the professor's favourite. Jardine even persuaded him, as a literary exercise, to invent a Gaelic legend, about Druids in the Isle of Man, for young John an unusual venture into whimsy. Each year Jardine asked for essays describing the ideal student, partly as an exercise in self-understanding, and young John won the prize for that. However, he seems to have thought in the end that he had grown beyond Jardine's methods, and he finished at Glasgow thinking that he should have been pushed harder.[21]

PROFESSOR JARDINE TOLD A STORY ABOUT HIS OWN time, many years before, as a Glasgow student, when he was taught by the great moral philosopher Thomas Reid. By Jardine's account, the class was working on Cicero's *De Finibus*. Reid was translating some sentences from his desk when he suddenly stopped. '"Gentlemen," said he, "I thought I had the Meaning of this Passage, but it has escaped me; I will therefore be obliged to any one of you who will translate it."' A student jumped up and offered a good translation, and Reid praised and thanked him. The effect of this small incident, so Jardine said, was profound. Reid's students were struck with the fact that their revered master could share his lapse so easily. They suddenly felt at one with him, as Jardine supposed, and worked all the harder. 'Powerful, indeed, and lasting, are the Impressions which such incidents make on Minds of ingenuous Youths.' The great teacher Socrates, as he pointed out, did the same sort of thing all the time.[22]

Jeremy Bentham had boasted that his panopticon would create 'power of mind over mind, in a quantity hitherto without example'.[23] However, when it came to 'mind over mind' methods like Jardine's were much more effective than a panopticon could have been. The experience of Elizabeth and John proved the same thing. That 'intercourse of Looks and Feeling' had an enormous cumulative energy, though at the same time it was vanishingly subtle, living and dying in a glance.

Shared feeling and shared duty meant that the children learnt not to voice their disagreements in writing – 'how necessary it is,' Edward said, 'to be cautious in the choice of words in letters.' We might be tempted to write as we would speak, but without voice, gestures and intonation we are easily misunderstood. In order not to offend, we need to realise, he said, '[w]hat a turn will the manner of reading give to a sentence.'[24] That sums up one of the main challenges in this story. We read, but we cannot see or hear, a sad gap when it was living talk and attentive listening that made the engine spin.

33

A DAUGHTER GROWS UP

Elizabeth and John thought slightly differently about questions of bodily health. John seems to have had more faith in self-regulation, by exercise, diet, cold and warm washing, early rising and so on. Her ideas were more passive, with echoes of a more old-fashioned logic. For Elizabeth, health and the lack of it depended on weather, climate and Providence. Preventative action was certainly possible all the same. To revive happy memories had a 'salutory effect' on the mind and, on the other hand, it was 'not healthy to the mind' to indulge gloomy thoughts, especially on rainy days. Mood could also be a predictor. 'I expected from my feelings,' she said once, 'that a change again in the weather was about to take place.'[1]

Elizabeth was sure that nothing could be more healthy, for body and for mind, than the climate in New South Wales. Their eldest girl, young Elizabeth, had been physically advanced as a small child, walking, led 'by one hand', her mother said, at ten months. However, when she returned from her first and only venture abroad, in June 1805, aged 12, she had grown weak, especially, it seems, in the legs. Her mother blamed the English climate. She said the problem was an 'aguish affliction'.[2]

And yet, at home young Elizabeth only got worse. She also suffered from more than the usual symptoms of ague, which were listlessness and fever. Whatever it was, by 1808–09 it had turned dangerous. Before he left the second time, in March 1809, her father saw to the building of a second home in Sydney, on his lease at the south-west corner of the cove, partly, we might suppose, to allow young Elizabeth a change of air. Staying in that house also put her within reach of her doctor, William Redfern, at the government hospital on Dawes Point. Redfern was a pardoned convict. His had been the sort of crime the government now wanted John Macarthur charged with – encouraging rebellion, as surgeon's mate during the great naval mutiny in the Thames estuary, in April 1797.[3]

Redfern's family was Irish and one of his brothers had been a local organiser for the United Irishmen, but in New South Wales he kept clear of politics. John Macarthur was sure – Elizabeth's opinion is unrecorded – that he had saved the life of their eldest daughter. It was Redfern, John said, who had succeeded at last in 'discovering and applying an efficacious remedy to her extraordinary disease'. Redfern's diagnosis is lost but his warning that Elizabeth, if she lived, would lose the use of her legs, suggests it was polio.[4]

Polio was a newly identified and as yet unnamed disease. Michael Underwood, London surgeon-accoucheur, had set out all that was known about its symptoms in his *Treatise on the Diseases of Children* (1789), a pioneering text that Redfern surely owned. The only remedies offered so far were blistering or caustics (sodium or potassium hydroxide) applied to the lower back or upper leg, and hard rubbing of legs and thighs. In short, if Redfern did make a difference with young Elizabeth it is impossible to know how. Her sister Mary was also briefly paralysed in her right leg when she was about ten, so that John thought the problem must be hereditary. 'I sometimes almost wonder they do not feel little gratitude towards parents who have entailed upon them so much positive evil.' The crisis passed for both, but young Elizabeth was never strong.[5]

A DAUGHTER GROWS UP

TEN YEARS LATER A FRENCH COUPLE, THE EXPLORER Louis de Freycinet and his young wife Rose, spent two nights at Elizabeth Farm. Rose de Freycinet, who had smuggled herself on board her husband's ship, kept her own record of the expedition. The Macarthurs' eldest daughter, she said, was 'witty, well educated and very kind'. She 'came to fetch us [from Sydney] in her father's carriage'. Rose was intrigued by this strong-minded young woman, a native of New South Wales. 'I wish', she said, 'I could have become better acquainted with her.'[6]

It is easy now to think the same. If only we could know young Elizabeth better. She seems to have inherited her mother's curiosity for the tangible world around her, but her intelligence was better stretched in youth. In her girlhood she had moved in higher circles than her mother ever did and it showed. Limited in her physical movements – this trip to Sydney must have been on one of her good days – she had the liveliest humour of them all, except for Edward, and Edward lacked her wit.

In England in 1802–04 young John, with Edward, had gone to James Lindsay's school, but Elizabeth, like most girls of her social rank, seems to have taken lessons within a family setting, probably using a plan of instruction mapped out by her father and women friends. The Thompsons, their closest friends in London, included a daughter-in-law, Sarah Margaretta, from a bookish, teaching, clerical family background, and she took a particular interest in young Elizabeth. It might have been Sarah Thompson who brought in Penelope Lucas, but there is no way of knowing in whose house they sat down together for lessons. From this time must date, among other things, young Elizabeth's acquaintance with Latin and also the 'large book' she kept for doing arithmetic – filled up later on with Edward's efforts to learn Italian.[7]

The connection with Sir Walter Farquhar's family took her into some distinguished drawing rooms. Charity Farquhar, the middle daughter, became a particular friend. Of Charity young

Elizabeth said years later, 'I have never ceased to love her.' Nor could she forget her kindness 'when kindness was so doubly needed'. She brought back to New South Wales one of Charity's gifts, *Adèle et Théodore*, a book on modern education by the Comtesse de Genlis.[8]

With men too she learnt to hold her own, as a bright teenager among cultivated grown-ups. John Matthew Williams, aged 29, another of her father's friends, teased her with talk of marrying one day, though he was married already. Williams was a 'very pleasant man', according to Edward – handsome, laughing, at home with all sorts. He spent lavishly and he used devious means to stay financially afloat. His wife had been the teenage widow of the rich and brilliant Earl of Barrymore and it was Williams, later on, who introduced Edward to Lord Malpas, a Barrymore kinsman. Later still he was a spy for the government in the affairs of the estranged wife of George IV. Williams led an aimless life but he was certainly clever. Elizabeth was in England, as her mother said, to broaden her experience of the world. Laughing with Williams, she certainly did that.[9]

She was 13 when she got back to her old home, and one of the first things she did was to send a sample of London wit to John Piper at Norfolk Island. She teased him as she might have teased Williams. Piper had just taken over as Norfolk's commandant and 'I know,' she said, 'that *you great people* seldom make any other use of your letters than to light your fires. However, as it is not very cold at Norfolk Island this letter may escape, and at last be read, to expect an answer would be presumption indeed!'[10]

FOR A WOMAN, EIGHTEEN WAS A DECENT AGE TO MARRY. Sarah Thompson had been a wife at 18. Young Elizabeth looked forward to the same. John Oxley, her first and only serious suitor, eight years her senior, had arrived in New South Wales in 1802

A DAUGHTER GROWS UP

as master's mate on HMS *Buffalo*. He stayed, probably making visits to Elizabeth Farm from the start, and he was on hand when the *Argo* brought young Elizabeth home in June 1805. He had just been promoted to acting lieutenant. Afterwards famous for his exploration of the west (1817–18) and north (1823–24) of New South Wales, Oxley was not especially well-read but he was a daring leader with a cheerful, active mind. He was soon one of John Macarthur's disciples and a family favourite.

Oxley went back to England on the *Buffalo* in February 1807. While he was there he and a younger friend, John Porteous, had themselves appointed to the command – Captain Porteous and Lieutenant Oxley – of HMS *Porpoise*, currently stationed in New South Wales. Porteous's father was one of George III's favourite retainers, which explains the rapid promotion. Riding high, the two young men announced their arrival in New South Wales with an expensive dinner on board the *Porpoise* for local officers, civil and military, and their wives, and a year later, their tour of duty ended, they staged a ball and supper in the same place and style. On this second occasion the older Elizabeth was there, unescorted herself because John had gone to England, but probably as chaperone for her eldest daughter. Young Elizabeth was on the point of turning 18 and this would have been her first ball, her coming-out.[11] When Oxley sailed a month later he left a proposal of marriage.

On duty in New South Wales, Oxley had seen a good deal of the two new settlements in the south, Hobart Town and Launceston, and on the way back to England, as a way of recommending himself to authority he wrote a detailed report on both. It was very much a Macarthurite document, driven by ideas of future prosperity. He might well have shown it to John Macarthur in England before handing it in.[12]

They certainly talked about young Elizabeth. No letters survive between father and daughter, though she certainly wrote to him during these years. He had been responsible for her schooling since the journey to England in 1801–02, he was tortured by thoughts of her dangerously bad health, and they seem on the whole to have been kindred spirits. Like her father, young Elizabeth knew she was clever, but she handled the knowledge better than he did, with self-mockery rather than uneasy conceit. He might have admired her for that.

He was not surprised by Oxley's proposal. The possibility might had been broached among them all long before. Mentioning only, in a letter home, 'the interesting event that had taken place in your little society', young Elizabeth's father busied himself with engineering Oxley's promotion and his return to duty in New South Wales.[13] Thus encouraged, she sent Oxley her consent. In Sicily her old friend, J.M. Williams, hearing about it, forwarded a joking message by her brother Edward. He was 'displeased you will not *wait* for him,' Edward teased. What did he mean? 'You perhaps my dear Elizabeth may comprehend him. I am quite in the dark.'[14]

John Macarthur imagined that Oxley would stay in the navy, with steady promotion and improving pay. However, Oxley suddenly secured appointment as surveyor-general of New South Wales. That meant the same pay level for life. Also, as John Macarthur now discovered, Oxley's English debts meant that even as surveyor-general he would struggle to live decently in Sydney, married or single. The young man was yieldingly good-natured but he had no inheritance, no skill in making money and obviously no sense in keeping it. John Macarthur lent him £300, but he feared for his daughter. '[F]rom her crazy health and shattered nerves,' he said, '[she] will never be able to bear with the privations to which she will be inevitably exposed should this marriage take place.'[15]

All the same, he said, if they were committed to each other it was no good getting in the way. '[A]n opposition on our parts,' he told Elizabeth, 'could only tend to make what appears to me a

A DAUGHTER GROWS UP

very unpromising connexion for our dear girl a still worse one.' He might have recalled the story of his parents' marriage many years before. As a bride around 1750, marrying 'in opposition to the wishes of her family', Catherine, John's mother, might have been no older than young Elizabeth was now.[16]

Oxley left Portsmouth for Sydney in June 1812 on board the convict ship *Minstrel*, and arrived in October. Meanwhile, more English debts kept turning up, as if from a bottomless pit. Still, if the marriage must go ahead, John Macarthur said, the couple might have £100 a year and the promise of something better when his own affairs were better settled. Then Oxley condemned himself. On board the *Minstrel* he struck up a liaison with one of the convict women, Charlotte Thorpe, and in Sydney the relationship continued. Babies were born. Young Elizabeth had not been put off by what she knew of Oxley's debts, but betrayal of this kind was another matter. Her feelings for him were deep and fixed, but now, obviously with painful regret, she drew the line.[17]

EVEN AS A GIRL YOUNG ELIZABETH HAD STARTED TO take over parts of the garden at Elizabeth Farm. 'What are the alterations made in the house and grounds[?],' Edward asked her, while her future with Oxley was still in suspense. Edward was at Coria, in Spain, where olives and olive oil were a specialty. 'I hope you endeavour to propagate the olive. When I learn that the tree [at Elizabeth Farm] bears fruit I will send you instructions how to produce the oil.' The tree in question had come on the *Argo* in 1805.[18]

During her post-Oxley existence, the garden came wholly under young Elizabeth's control, and she worked on it as a botanist, horticulturalist and landscaper. In terms of fruit alone, besides the olive tree, there were oranges, lemons, apples, apricots, peaches, plums, mulberries, nectarines, medlars, grapes, strawberries, cherries, almonds and walnuts, all familiar produce in England. Other trees came from the Mediterranean (pomegranate), from Central America (guava) and from China, India and south-east Asia (loquat, citron and shaddock, or pomelo). The shaddock was another citrus, its blossom highly scented and its fruit reddish inside and as big as a human head. Most of these were originally of her mother's planting – the mulberries were well-grown trees, dating from the 1790s – but young Elizabeth started adding more, including two red-flowering ironbarks, *Eucalyptus sideroxylon rosea*. With richly coarse bark and grey-green leaves, the stem growing with glacial slowness, these could reach 10 metres. They were plantings for the long term.[19]

From an early stage, young Elizabeth had real weight in the family counsels, including wool matters. Unceasingly cheerful, she was also responsible, or so Edward told her, for general morale. In 1816, at 23, her character was sketched by her mother. Already possessed of 'great powers of imagination', young Elizabeth's wide reading (in both English and French) had given her a good knowledge of the world and 'solidity of judgment'. 'Miss Livy', as the other children called her, was a highly useful combination of good nature, curiosity, ironical wit and common sense. Her only obvious flaw was handwriting even her family struggled to read.[20]

At her mother's suggestion she started exchanging letters with Eliza Kingdon, who had been the baby of the Bridgerule vicarage when the Macarthurs left in 1790. Legible or not, young Elizabeth was an easier writer than her mother at the same age, and she wrote as if she wanted to be known well all at once. Her first letter was mainly about the Indigenous people. They were largely unhoused and unclothed, she said, 'utterly ignorant of the arts' – it is not clear what she meant by that – and yet 'very intelligent'. 'They have great vivacity and a peculiar turn for mimickry,' she went on, 'acquiring our language, tones and expression with singular facility.' They moved beautifully – '[t]heir carriage is very graceful'

– and they had a striking delicacy of manner. '[P]erhaps,' she said, 'they possess more native politeness than is found amongst any people.'[21]

She ended on a joking note – 'Pray pardon the partiality of a native for native subjects' – but when she wrote a second time it was partly about the vegetation of her birthplace. The family spent a large part of each day in 'our woods' or else in the garden, she told Eliza, 'until the evening surprises us'. 'I wish it were possible to convey to you some of our flowering plants; their bright and varied colors would please you much; and their form so different from the productions of Europe.' It was winter, and many of their European trees were bare, though interspersed, as she put it, with 'luxuriant and beautiful orange trees' in full bearing, and also with native vegetation, original and transplanted. '[Y]ou would smile at the contrast.' In warmer seasons 'the beautiful green of the English trees far surpasses, particularly when the leaves are young, the verdure of our unchanging ever greens.' So, in their garden the two were deliberately mixed, 'and [we] enjoy the beauty of each in their season.'[22]

Her grasp of French might have led young Elizabeth to think of her garden as an interactive web of life, in *philosophe* style. Among the books she had on hand, for instance, was the *Ètudes de la nature* of Bernadin de Saint-Pierre (1773), including the memorable story of the strawberry plant that Saint-Pierre kept in a pot on his windowsill. Over three weeks, the author counted 37 varieties of winged insect gathering and dispersing on the strawberry's leaves, 'some of a golden hue, some silver, some bronze'. Snails, butterflies and beetles gathered, and spiders set up nearby to catch wanderers. This book sat on young Elizabeth's shelves beside the more businesslike annual *Le bon jardinier*, with its advice on salving insect bites and beating back garden pests.[23]

Her garden at Elizabeth Farm was a universe of limitless, interconnected knowledge, approachable at various levels of sophistication. So she could joke with Edward about her interest in 'strange and rare plants with long names … hard to be understood by the *uninitiated multitude*'. She had grown up in and with her garden – with the mulberry trees and, later on, the ironbarks – so that it had become imagination's outer skin. There is some evidence that she made a study of its insects too, as Saint-Pierre did with his.[24] She was a clever woman, well worth knowing better.

34
THE EXCELLENCE OF MADEIRA

If any one sensual delight could sum up the Enlightenment it would be the taste of wine made on the islands of Madeira, off the coast of Morocco. Constantia wines from the Cape were good. Madeira was better. Sweet or dry, Madeira, to contemporary taste, was exquisite. There were several varieties, and the quality of any one bottle depended on many things. The rolling motion of carriage by sea helped. So did heat, and bottles and casks were best stored in some warm place – an attic, for instance. Bibbers and collectors debated as to what otherwise mattered most. Madeira was all the rage among the cognoscenti of North America. 'I should prefer,' said Benjamin Franklin, 'to any ordinary death, the being immersed in a cask of Madeira wine.'[1]

Around August–September 1810, when John Macarthur had been nearly a year in London and was looking for some new source of income, Sir Walter Farquhar's son-in-law, Gilbert Mathison, came back from a two-year stay in Jamaica, in the West Indies. He had spent childhood years on that island and in the interim White settlers, slave-holders included, had yielded in significant numbers to a taste for Madeira wine. To that change Mathison attributed a dramatic improvement in the moral tone of White society, which in turn boded well, he thought, for the eventual abolition of West Indian slavery. 'A few years ago,' he said, 'it was the prevailing practice with young men to sit up to a very late hour in the night, drinking punch or spirits, and smoking segars.' Now, they drank

Madeira. They savoured it in moderation, went to bed early and rose better and kinder men, or so Mathison imagined.[2]

The political economist Adam Smith had said much the same about wine generally. Thanks largely to Smith it was now widely understood that, from both a moral and a physical point of view, wine was a far healthier beverage than spirits. Meeting in the Farquhar drawing room, Gilbert Mathison seems to have passed on his thoughts about Madeira wine to John Macarthur because John put his mind immediately to planning regular shipments of this wonderful liquor to New South Wales. If Madeira could be suddenly popular in that place too, its import would make money. Pyrmont and the western Pacific trade circle had largely failed. Madeira might fill some part of the gap. And then, a general delight in Madeira might also soften manners in New South Wales, which would be a boon for all concerned. John Macarthur had lately made elaborate plans for the local distillation of spirits. Now he turned to good wine, imported or, perhaps, home-grown.[3]

Purchase arrangements were made with Keir, Buxton and Co., a London firm that took wine direct from Madeira, and Hannibal Macarthur, who was about to return to New South Wales, was told to stop over at the islands to settle details with the agent and to take on the first shipment. If only it sold well John imagined his family settling at last in England, while Hannibal carried on in New South Wales, managing imports of wine and exports of wool.

Elizabeth took £20 worth of Hannibal's Madeira and £40 more later on, but in general it did not sell well. Again, John had asked too much of New South Wales, or else Hannibal – 'blunt, honest and *unsophisticated*', as John said himself – was not the man to give the uninitiated a taste for good wine.[4] And yet, 'in vino spe'. There was hope in wine, as later transpired.

THE EXCELLENCE OF MADEIRA

STRUGGLING TO MANAGE CHRONIC INDIGESTION, John Macarthur drank no wine himself. In London, sick, tired and sorry for himself, feeling his age – he was in his late forties – he began to transfer his hopes to his children. The two youngest boys, James and William, were currently part of their father's life in ways none of his other children had ever been. Their adolescence was interwoven with his suffering. 'Poor fellows – many an anxious thought do they give me as we sit together at our little solitary meal.' William, probably more than James, noticed their father's vulnerability. William was alert in that way; his mind moved quickly and his curiosity was touched by feeling. According to a woman in London, in conversation with his father, 'that boy always looks as if he were penetrating into your innermost soul.'[5]

At Grove Hall, James Lindsay educated boys to the age of 14, so that James was ready to leave at the end of 1812. He stayed until mid-1813 while his father thought about sending him to one of the great 'public' schools, where he could spend two or three years more, as his brother John had done at university in Glasgow. However, in the end James went to live with a merchant in the city, Charles Coles, so as to learn about the import business in Coles's office in Great Tower Street.[6] William, two years younger, stayed with Lindsay until the end of 1814.

These two were very close and they were to continue so all their lives. '[N]ever,' their father said, 'did brothers bear a more ardent affection for each other', and yet they were very different. Affection-plus-difference John found fascinating and on the stage set of his own imagination he often placed his two younger sons side by side. '[They] make an admirable mixture.' James was patient and persevering, 'orderly, correct, well disposed'. He was also more self-contained, hiding his feelings with unruffled courtesy and even, gentle accents, while William was cheerful and impulsive, even garrulous. James was hard to read. William was frank and open.[7]

Writing to their mother, John never hinted at impatience with either James or William. Even as children, they felt for his weakness and shared his troubles, and he admired them for that. When money was tight and they were living as frugally as possible the boys never flinched. '[T]hey are a couple of old men in prudence and as they are acquainted with the reverses I have sustained in money matters are as ready to practice any plan of economy or to submit to any self denial as I am to recommend it.'[8] His mind was healed somewhat by the quiet drama of their growing up, free of crisis. As intimate audience and mentor, he owned their moods.

Everything shifted gear at the end of 1814, when William in turn finished school. The question of their future home was now settled, thanks to Elizabeth. It was New South Wales and John started to plan accordingly. Their mother wanted James to come straightaway to help her but in December John informed her that he aimed to round off the education of both boys with a period in southern France. There, he said, he would find 'some enlightened French preceptor of established reputation', who might guide their reading in 'those sciences, particularly mineralogy, that may be useful to them in New South Wales'. He also wanted them to learn 'those exercises which give ease and gracefulness to the person', such as dancing and fencing.[9]

In much the same way, as very young men, his own father in the 1740s and Hinton McArthur in the 1770s had travelled from Scotland to mainland Europe. Such finishing might seem pretentious and unnecessary among families of the same rank – less than aristocratic – in England. Not so for Scots, who had long looked to the mainland for a polish and variety of experience beyond what Scotland could offer.[10]

The boys' need for mineralogy might have been urged by John Macarthur's London friend Robert Bakewell. Bakewell was a sometime dealer in wool who had studied the influence of the natural environment, including soil, on land use, and who offered expert advice to gentlemen on the mineralogical composition of their estates. The Macarthurs had a copy of Bakewell's *Introduction to Geology,* a popular pioneering text. Bakewell spoke of the slow-moving 'oeconomy of nature', through which Providence prepared the earth for the better support of life. Over ages, he said, mountains were worn down and the life-giving elements settled. It was our duty to work in concert with Providence, struggling to understand this vast process and, 'by imitating nature, and profiting by the instruction she affords … to acquire certain fixt principles to guide us in our attempts to bring barren lands into a state of profitable cultivation'.[11]

John Macarthur also hoped that this expedition to the Continent would give the boys a chance 'of seeing and studying the whole practice of the culture of the vine and the olive, and the making the wine and the oil'. In short, they were to learn to understand soil and vegetation altogether, in a way that was both useful and scientific, and they were to get that training in a climate like their own. The French *philosophes* had insisted on a unified web of life. Now France led the way in integrating science and labour on the land. It was agroecology, a modern science in pioneering form.[12]

In planning for this trip John found a sense of direction again, for himself as well as for James and William. His writing grew firmer and clearer, his health seemed to improve and his attention shifted a little from the boys so as to give himself a central role in what they aimed to do. He intended, he said, to make a thorough study of the ways in which the produce of the soil in southern Europe could be transplanted to New South Wales, concentrating mainly, but not entirely, on grapes and olives. The boys were now his necessary assistants. He looked forward to acquiring for himself a complete grasp of the subject, from planting to final manufacture, and on such a scale so as to give a new dimension altogether to settlement in New South Wales.

He must have been surprised to find himself looking forward once more. For a while depression had made him sluggish, even in some sense holding him back from the effort of going home. Now, crossing the English Channel, he would immerse himself in a strange language, the boys interpreting for him, in different ideas and in more expansive ways of knowing. So he regained some of the excitement, mental and physical, of 1803–04.

At the same time, hardship in London had taught father and sons to rely on each other. In this excursion 16-year-old James was to be manager of people and money. 'James,' his father said, 'is my accountant', the ever-present go-between, fluent with French and good with protocol. William, at 14, was more scientifically inclined. He was also happier to get his hands dirty. James liked the subtleties of human systems. William's instinct was for the tangible and organic. William was to be crucial for their putting to use all they found out.[13]

They sailed from Portsmouth at the end of February 1815, taking with them 15-year-old Frederick Thompson, son of young Elizabeth's mentor, Sarah Margaretta. Coming ashore at Le Havre they went straight on to Paris. Napoleon had been forced into exile 11 months earlier, making France safe for English travellers, but he had lately escaped and he reached Paris a few days after the Macarthurs did. They spent three weeks there all the same, certain, so John said, that the emperor would approve of their inquiries. At a Parisian jewellery shop, now or on the return trip, John spent largely on a diamond ring, a testimony of affection and thanks to take home.[14]

They hurried on to Geneva – French-speaking but across the Swiss border – to await events. The boys' language fluency led to conversation of all sorts on the way. Meeting a party of French soldiers, James asked them one by one 'whom they considered the best general in the world?' They all said Bonaparte, 'and that Wellington was the second'. Finally, a fellow traveller, Jacques-

THE EXCELLENCE OF MADEIRA

Dauphin Moulinié, the young son of one of Geneva's richest watchmaker-jewellers, introduced them to the city with a look around the fabulously bejewelled Moulinié workshop.[15]

Geneva's famous Academy, a type of university, offered public lecture courses. The boys seem to have made their choice of these and they were soon on familiar terms with at least two of the lecturers. In this way, almost by accident, they happened on one of the nerve centres of pan-European intellectual life. Antoine Duvillard, professor of Greek and Latin, was a stern republican who wanted a complete return to Geneva's 'ancient simplicity', so that his conversation echoed John Macarthur's self-training on 'the old Roman model' – highly principled, stoic, severe. Duvillard's 15-year-old son thought briefly of joining the Macarthurs in New South Wales.[16]

Marc-August Pictet, professor of natural philosophy, was a more important discovery. He and his brother Charles Pictet de Rochemont were well connected in England and their monthly *Bibliothèque Britannique* broadcast British science, literature and moral-intellectual life through Europe. Charles Pictet had an estate nearby where he ran Merino sheep from the flock of the late King of France. John Macarthur wondered about using his method of washing wool, after shearing, in New South Wales – but steam mechanised rather than Pictet's way, which was manual.[17]

The Academy's public lectures ended in late April. The Macarthurs then prepared to leave Geneva for Milan, where they could be closer to vineyards and olive groves. However, at the last minute they heard of the presence in Switzerland of Jean-Jacques Dufour, who had pioneered large-scale viticulture in the United States. Dufour was originally from Châtelard, near Montreux at the other end of Lake Geneva. He had come home on business but the war had forced him to stay and the Macarthurs, reaching Montreux, found him working among his ancestral vines. A little conversation was enough to persuade them, James said, 'to make a long stay'.[18]

Anxious, as ever, about first impressions, they rented the spacious chateau de Châtelard, before moving to something cheaper in Vevey, on the lake's edge. James, William and Frederick spent each morning at their books under John's eye. Edward, visiting from military duty in Paris, found his brothers remarkably changed. At first, he said, he did not recognise 'the two *kangaroos*' he had last seen five years before. 'James, whom I was once capable of instructing, has now the ability to repay ten fold whatever he acquired from me', and William was 'far more advanced than are generally found lads of the same age'.[19]

Their father had brought with him a run of the quarterly *Farmer's Magazine*, Britain's leading journal for the progressive farmer, and he now went through it making notes. More useful, however, was live instruction from Dufour, who offered advice on clearing new country and on various American crops. He also made suggestions for New South Wales. Maybe camels could be bred to carry wool from the distant inland? In his American vineyards, Dufour had so far used various species of grape already growing there, some of which were thought to be from Madeira. However, he was keen now to use cuttings fresh from the island soil, and so were the Macarthurs.[20]

They had come to this place well aware of its connection with Jean-Jacques Rousseau, and James transcribed on the spot, in French, some of his favourite lines from the master – 'walking along this beautiful shore, I abandoned myself to the sweetest melancholy ... I was filled with emotion, I sighed and wept like a child.' James was better than William at sitting still, turning over such thoughts. He liked to watch the sun going down over the lake, the golden brightness of the water fading into mountain shadows. 'It is impossible,' he said, 'to imagine a more tranquilizing scene.' Who could wonder at the way Rousseau had chosen it in his efforts to plumb the depths of human feeling?[21]

THE EXCELLENCE OF MADEIRA

It may be that from Vevey they visited the celebrated agricultural school run by Philipp Emanuel von Fellenberg at Hofwyl, about 100 kilometres away near Bern. Charles Pictet was a Fellenberg enthusiast, publicising the school wherever he could, and John must have heard him speak of it. One way or another, he took thoughts of Hofwyl back to London and so to New South Wales, a point for later.[22]

The Macarthurs left Vevey on 9 February 1816, stopping first for another week in Geneva. It was at this point, apparently, that James met the Pictets' Genevan friend, the historian J.C.L. Simonde de Sismondi, and heard him hold forth. In James's later thinking it is easy to find echoes of Sismondi, the Pictets and the intellectual novelty witnessed in this place.[23]

The south of France had been the Macarthurs' original destination, and by the time they left Switzerland Napoleon had been finally ousted, so that France was safe again for English travellers. On their way back they spent a couple of months looking at vineyards from Languedoc in the south to Burgundy and Champagne in the mid-east. The vignerons were generous with cuttings and they took away about 30 types, with as much as a dozen samples of each. Edward was now stationed in Brittany and William stayed with him there, but their father, James and Frederick Thompson, plus cargo, reached Dover in late April 1816.[24]

JAMES BROGDEN HAD MADE NO REAL PROGRESS IN persuading the Colonial Office to cancel the order for John Macarthur's criminal trial in New South Wales. It was therefore decided that James should go home by himself to help his mother. William, still only 15, his father thought 'too young to be removed from under my eye'. It was probably their Glasgow friend, Archibald Campbell of Blythswood, who suggested that William work for a time with 'an intelligent Scotch farmer'. However, as it turned out, both boys stayed with their father. When they did all go home Campbell sent after them, as a final gift, an iron plough.[25]

Campbell of Blythswood was among those amateur political economists who believed that in every country on earth, from Highland Scotland to newly invaded New South Wales, happiness depended on the clever use of the soil. That idea now drove the campaign to get John Macarthur home. Also, his active well-wishers now included George Watson Taylor, formerly George Watson. As Lord Camden's private secretary, Watson Taylor had engineered the Macarthur land grant at the Cowpastures (Camden) in 1804. Now, his artful manipulation was brought to bear again on John's behalf.

John Macarthur himself was still eager to remind the world about William Bligh. The complete story of Bligh's 'tyranny' had never been told and John now drafted a letter to the minister, Lord Bathurst, with a hinted threat to tell it to the world. He sent a copy first to Watson Taylor, who took it as it stood to Henry Goulburn, Bathurst's junior minister and, when Goulburn had cast his eye over it, invited him to think about how John Macarthur's 'powerful talents', instead of being wasted in argument, might be used for the good. Goulburn responded according to plan. He asked for a more conciliatory letter for Bathurst and John obliged. So far, he said, the fine wool experiment had been saved by his wife's careful management. Now, with his sons, he was ready to make a second experiment. They had together examined in France and Switzerland 'the different modes of cultivating those two sources of human enjoyment and wealth, the olive and the vine'. Now he wanted to take their findings home. His aim now was to be reunited with 'every thing that is most valuable to me in life', to keep clear of politics and to spend his days on this new work.[26]

Lord Bathurst yielded easily, except to insist that John admit the 'impropriety' of the part he had taken in 1808. John refused.

He had a long talk with Goulburn but in the end, as in the beginning, he could not give in. He could not gainsay 'one of the most meritorious [acts] in which I had ever been engaged'. So he retreated to his initial threat. He would petition parliament, he said, so as to expose 'the iniquities of Mr Bligh, of which I held in my possession abundant proofs'.[27]

At New Year 1817 nothing was settled, but in parliamentary circles there was talk of serious change in New South Wales, and such talk included an interest in the approach John Macarthur had long taken. 'I *positively know* that they *will be strongly pressed* to listen to my opinions,' so he told Elizabeth, 'and at all events to do me justice.'[28]

By February it was generally understood that John Macarthur's agricultural machinery might be sent out on a convict transport. In early March, with another letter to Bathurst, Brogden asked for confirmation that his plants might go too, 'under the care of his sons'. By this time, in fact, Bathurst was prepared to let them all go. Some lesser official, probably Henry Goulburn, seems to have got in the way, but on 23 March, after 'a train of the most vexatious, tho' petty obstructions', the order at last came through. They were all to sail by the convict ship *Lord Eldon*, with a greenhouse built on board and space in the hold for their machinery, all free of charge.[29] They were to go home after all in something like triumph.

The *Lord Eldon* sailed in April. Its itinerary included Madeira, but on arrival there it turned out to be the wrong time of year for cuttings. Orders were therefore given for sending some on. They could now look forward to a remarkable importation, with 35–40 varieties of grapes alone, plus olives, roses, camellias, figs and so on, together with a good deal of new equipment. They also had with them an overseer, Andrew Murray, another Scot, who had horticultural training with the celebrated London nurseryman Thomas Gibbs. Madeira was their reprise of Kew, where John had bought sheep from the King's flock in 1804. Murray was their new equivalent of the wool-sorter Edward Wood.[30]

On 30 September, anchored at last in Sydney Harbour, James and William went straight home. John followed more slowly. He was 51, exhausted and suffering again from gout. Now, at least, he could look forward to something like rejuvenation. *'[H]ome'*, he said, 'will do more for me than the doctor. How many dear associations does that word home create!' As for Elizabeth, the arrival of all three at once was so wonderful and so sudden, 'after a cruel separation of nine years', as to seem hardly real. Even ten weeks later, she said, with husband and boys all under her eye, 'I am yet scarcely sensible of the extent of my happiness.'[31]

35

MIND OVER MIND

When young Elizabeth was about 25 she had a second suitor keen to take John Oxley's place, though she did not know it. William Wentworth had been born in New South Wales about two years before her, his mother a convict woman, Catherine Crowley, and his reputed father the government surgeon, D'Arcy Wentworth. His mother died when he was nine or ten. He had then been sent to a good school in England. He arrived back in 1810 with uncertain prospects, although by this time D'Arcy had made a good deal of money as a landowner and public official.

This time William Wentworth had stayed in New South Wales for eight years. He helped to lead an expedition that opened up the country west of the Blue Mountains to British occupation and he sailed to Tonga on a ship looking for sandalwood.[1] In about 1815 he started to make frequent visits to Elizabeth Farm, so frequent that D'Arcy teased him about courting the younger Elizabeth. He was, in fact, doing so, at least in his own mind, but as he said later his hopes were 'cherished in secret'.[2]

Elizabeth and John Macarthur were on good terms with D'Arcy Wentworth and they took an interest in William. However the courtship did not prosper. William was not adept with educated women and in a moment of spite he wrote and handed around among his friends a piece of doggerel verse, unsigned, mocking the whole family. Among other cheap shots he reported on the arrival of a new carriage at Elizabeth Farm – he must have been visiting at the time – and, as he interpreted it, the 'exalting pride' of mother and daughters at the family coat of arms painted on the doors, certifying their gentility. John had sent the landau from London to replace an earlier vehicle and the heraldic decoration must have been the one granted to Hinton McArthur in 1797.[3]

Back in England during the first months of 1817, William Wentworth saw a good deal of John Macarthur and his sons. John encouraged his hopes of marriage, or so Wentworth believed, and he also shared with him his own thoughts on the future of New South Wales, much expanded by his recent tour of Switzerland and France. John and the two boys left for home in April, by which time Wentworth had begun training for the law, but he kept up a friendship with young John Macarthur, now a year short of being called to the bar.

William Wentworth hoped, as a barrister himself, to become a champion of British liberties, narrowly defined, in New South Wales. He believed that the free settlers were entitled to all the rights enjoyed by British subjects elsewhere throughout the empire, and by that he meant the right to make their own laws, to be free of taxes unless levied by their own consent, and to settle criminal cases through trial by jury. By marriage to young Elizabeth Macarthur he imagined their two families linked as a governing elite, the natural leaders of a free people, a model familiar in Britain, Ireland and any number of British settlements edging the Atlantic.[4]

At young John's suggestion, Wentworth set out to publish his thoughts about New South Wales in the quarterly *Edinburgh Review*. His essay soon grew to pamphlet size and ended up as a large volume, including an unacknowledged interpretation of the elder John's ideas. It appeared in London in 1819 as *A Statistical, Historical, and Political Description of the Colony of New South Wales, and Its Dependent Settlements in Van Diemen's Land*, and it sold remarkably well. In fact it was a turning point publication for the way men and women from Europe understood this little-visited place.

John Macarthur carried Wentworth's hopes of marriage to Elizabeth Farm and then, apparently, sent back his daughter's polite rebuff. Meanwhile, in London, Wentworth quarrelled with her brother John. Wentworth was chronically in debt and young John would not risk his own credit by getting involved.[5] This double rejection, as lover and borrower, brought the Wentworth–Macarthur family friendship to an end. William Wentworth did not return to New South Wales until 1824, but he was bitter when he did.

WENTWORTH'S BOOK MADE A DEEP IMPRESSION PARTLY because it was well timed. It was bought and read by people wanting to know about this distant place and what it might have to offer them, now the war with France was over. It was also an attractive book in the way it set out, for the first time, a long-term story of New South Wales, past, present and possible future. On top of that, Wentworth made full use of the settled language of Empire, of British power and individual opportunity. At the same time there was something about his barbed, no-nonsense tone bound to appeal, especially to young men.

The language of Empire took as its main point of reference the slave colonies of the West Indies. For Wentworth, it was time New South Wales matched more closely that old ideal. In those places local assemblies made their own laws. The free, in other words, made laws for the enslaved. And yet, in New South Wales at present, Wentworth said, 'the freeman and the slave are alike subjected to the uncontrolled authority of an individual [the governor]'.[6] By 'slave' he meant 'convict'. That, he said, must end. In New South Wales free men must be granted all the rights others of their kind enjoyed Empire-wide.

As for the convicts, their bondage must if anything be tightened. For instance, they were currently paid for working extra time, an arrangement that could plant in them seeds of independence and a sense of freedom. Such pay, Wentworth said, ought to be halved. Also, tickets of leave – certificates of probation awarded to convicts if they behaved well – ought to be harder to get. After all, the young man argued, these were not free people, whatever they might become in due course. These were 'a set of persons ... supposed to be smarting under the lash of the law'.[7]

The transatlantic slave trade had been banned for British ships in 1807. Humanitarians now looked forward to the end of slavery itself, but how and how quickly were vexed questions. Setting free tens of thousands of men, women and children was a major challenge in various ways. It involved the rights of property, as then understood, but it also involved the safety and security of the enslaved. Being cast adrift altogether in vast numbers, degraded and untrained, with no way of making a living, looked like a recipe for disaster. Mass violence seemed certain. So the humanitarians themselves believed.

The accepted answer was 'amelioration'. With the slave trade abolished, there would be no new arrivals from Africa. Masters in the West Indies would therefore have to pay more careful attention to the people they already had. They would have to look after them, making sure they survived and had families. If they did that, so the theory went, gradually slavery, individual by individual, must approximate to freedom. In due course, slavery as a system would in practice come to an end and might be abolished in law. Slave owners would begin to realise that free workmen, as Adam Smith said, were more productive than the enslaved. Gradually transferring the ownership of self, freeing minds as well as bodies, was the great agenda of the anti-slavery campaigners. How far they really understood what they were doing is hard to say.[8]

Just as leading educators argued about the relationship of teachers and taught, and about the exchange of 'Looks and Feeling' that could make that relationship most productive, so anti-slavery campaigners fastened on the connection between slave-masters and slaves. The great problem with slavery, said William Wilberforce, leader of the abolitionist movement, was 'utter forgetfulness of *mind* in the human subject'. It was as if the enslaved man or woman, 'like the vilest of the brute species', had 'no foresight or recollection', no memory, no ambition, no spiritual existence, and could only be persuaded by beating.[9] Slavery damaged the humanity of all concerned.

John Macarthur's friends, the Farquhars, drew a good deal of their inherited wealth from slavery, and the younger generation wrestled with that inheritance in various ways. Gilbert Mathison, Sir Walter Farquhar's son-in-law, had come into his Jamaican property, loaded with mortgages, as a child. He, most of all, was tortured by that legacy. Following the abolition of the slave trade Mathison started on a lifelong effort of amelioration backed up by a book in which he detailed his efforts in the hope that others would do the same. Discover your own true interests, he said, but also listen to the enslaved. Understand their needs and their sense of justice. Do everything possible to improve their lives. '*Feed abundantly, and give fair play.*' By creating security in mind and body – giving the enslaved a belief that their needs came before everything else – both parties must win in the end.

They had to be 'subdued', Mathison said, not with threats of flogging but 'with a thousand little kindnesses'. Most of all, you must work to end the '[h]abitual *distrust*' that was at the root of slavery – a seemingly impossible task. Reliable, assiduous medical care was its best antidote. Persuade them that their good health and freedom were your goal.[10] It is impossible to say how much real difference Mathison made but in 1824 he was bankrupted trying.

ELIZABETH & JOHN

Reading Gilbert Mathison's book, John Macarthur might have found some obvious echoes of his experience with convicts in New South Wales. Like Mathison, he wanted to see his own methods copied, but he was no writer of books. He had sent a plan for change to T.W. Plummer, his London agent, in 1808 (remember Chapter 22), but it was never heard of again. A new awareness of the problems of slavery must have helped as he refocused his mind on forced labour closer to home.

IN THE NORTHERN SPRING OF 1819, A FEW WEEKS BEFORE Wentworth's book made its appearance in London, a commissioner of inquiry, appointed by the British government, set sail for New South Wales. This was John Thomas Bigge, late chief judge in Trinidad. As commissioner of inquiry, Bigge had some large questions to answer. The end of the all-absorbing war with France had brought about serious unemployment of both men and money in Britain and Ireland. Much greater numbers of the poor, forced into crime, were sentenced to transportation and at the same time more moneyed families thought of taking their capital to New South Wales and Van Diemen's Land (Tasmania). As a result the government struggled with many new demands, including new questions of scale.[11]

Could New South Wales continue as a place of effective punishment without enormous cost and could it at the same time become a country of substantial free settlement? In seeking answers Commissioner Bigge spent 17 months in New South Wales and Van Diemen's Land and, returning to England in 1821, he made three lengthy reports. His solution was just as the government expected. Convicts were to be handed over in bulk to private employers, present and future settlers, as a workforce on the large estates now expected to take shape in both colonies.

Commissioner Bigge and his deputy and secretary, Thomas Hobbes Scott, had spoken to John Macarthur within their first months in New South Wales. Scott – his family called him by his second name, 'Hobbes' – had a letter of introduction from John's doctor in London, Pelham Warren. He had been especially friendly and John relayed to his son John in London his most encouraging remark. '[T]hey looked to my evidence', Scott had told him, 'as the key or touch stone of the truth of all they heard.' John Macarthur mattered as an obvious success story. If only more pastoralists modelled themselves on him, each making use of a tightly regulated, productive convict workforce, then the government's problems would surely be solved.[12]

More than Bigge, Hobbes Scott understood the Macarthurs' habits of thought. His feeling for the whole family, especially Elizabeth, John, young Elizabeth and James, and theirs for him, were to make a pivotal difference in years to come. Among other things, he paid attention to John's ideas about the way convicts ought to be managed in future in New South Wales, a point the commissioner largely ignored.[13] Strangely for a former judge, Bigge had no interest in making punishments more just and consistent, and even less in making the convict system an engine for reform.

John Macarthur was now provoked to give new thought to these questions. Everyone understood that a penal system must use force – 'coercion', as John put it. Also, employers in New South Wales must be able 'to compel their servants to perform a due quantity of work'. At the same time the system must be an improving one and it must reach to the minds of all concerned. We need to give 'extensive powers to intelligent and honorable men,' so John told Bigge, but they in turn must be under the eye of 'a vigilant government, prompt to correct abuses and ever ready to distinguish and reward merit'. It would then be reasonable to hope that 'a few of the unfortunate men sent hither for their crimes *might in time* be completely reformed.'[14]

He saw his own methods as the ultimate model. Each convict showing signs of reform could expect ongoing encouragement. 'I … feed them well,' he said, 'clothe them comfortably, and give sometimes extra rewards … To those who behave remarkably well I give gratuities, varying from £1 to £5.'[15] He did not mention the subtle exchanges and the vicissitudes of trust that gave meaning to those rewards. With each convict on the way to reform there also had to be 'a promise of speedy liberation from servitude'. That might start quite early with the ending of all obvious restraint. As John's son James put it, 'where a man behaves well … [we] make him forget, if possible, that he is a convict.' The ultimate reward was a ticket of leave, that form of freedom Wentworth wanted to trim back.[16]

In the larger penal system Bigge recommended, so John thought, rules would need to be more carefully codified – or rather, he thought they should have been from the beginning. The regulation of punishments was especially difficult. John Macarthur never recommended flogging. He sent men to the magistrates himself, he said, 'very reluctantly'. He now suggested a safer alternative. Employers, he told Bigge, might be authorised to make each convict's food ration depend on good behaviour.[17] Bigge took no notice, but John thought about it more when the commissioner was gone. An essay in the 1821 *Edinburgh Review* about rewards and punishments in British prisons caught his eye, including the dictum, 'The most vulnerable part of a thief is his belly.' In New South Wales, he said, why not make use of short periods on bread and water, as a summary punishment available to employers, with the proviso that they report each case to the magistrate and donate any savings on food to a fund for rural police.[18]

He turned over ideas on convict management until the arrival of Governor Macquarie's successor, Sir Thomas Brisbane, at the end of 1821. He then asked the new governor to authorise a committee, chaired by himself, to report on convict discipline. He listed as members his friend Charles Throsby, Hannibal Macarthur, John Oxley, Samuel Marsden and two others. Following a survey of well-informed landowners, he said, they might draw up a plan for reform, so as to give some certainty for government, employers and convicts alike.[19]

For reasons never explained the idea was blocked by Sir Thomas Brisbane's colonial secretary, or chief minister, Frederick Goulburn – a younger brother of Henry Goulburn, the junior minister in London.[20] In 1825, with Brisbane and Frederick Goulburn both about to leave, John tried again, and his committee was at last appointed in October.[21] Brisbane's successor, Lieutenant-General Ralph Darling, arrived two months later, bringing with him an order for a new legislative council, with John Macarthur among its members. That ought to have given him more power to act but among the tumult of the next few years the committee was heard of no more.

36

VICISSITUDES OF CONVICT REFORM

When John Macarthur came back with the two boys in 1817 he was not sure as to how well suited they were to the work they now had to do. James was 18 and William 16, and he could not see in either of them the 'hardness of character' he thought they would need for managing a convict workforce. In the event, they seem to have managed well enough, but they kept their distance more than he ever did, working through overseers instead of always face to face.[1]

James offered his own critique of his father. It was James who suggested that John Macarthur 'formed himself almost too much upon the old Roman model'. In other words, John tended to overplay the world-weary stoic, the great man hardened against ingratitude. He wore that character when he explained to Commissioner Bigge his way of managing convicts. He kept on trying, he said, but his efforts made little difference and produced 'no feeling of gratitude'. At the same time, he could not help boasting, also to Bigge, that none of his convicts had ever tried to run away.[2] He forgot the six Irishmen in 1806, but then they were gone before they knew what he was like.

From 1817, with fine wool export an obvious success, Camden was full of new ambition. Acreage multiplied. John's original grant had been 5000 acres and the family had had free use of Walter

VICISSITUDES OF CONVICT REFORM

Davidson's 2000. Now, new grants included 1000 each for James and William, together with several thousand more for John. This last was in exchange for land elsewhere and for a number of Merino rams that the government then sent to Van Diemen's Land for public auction. In 1825 more land was added in acknowledgment of their success with the wool, in line with Lord Camden's original promise. Counting leasehold, the final total was to be more than 25 000 acres (about 10 000 hectares).

The consignment of rams to Van Diemen's Land, thereby spreading the breed, was something John had wanted for some time. He sold them at a discount, although in New South Wales the best sires were already going at unprecedented prices. The Macarthur flocks multiplied as their acreage grew and at the same time, as James said, 'we are, every year, increasing our own knowledge and experience', improving the fleece and the shipment process, and matching the final product to precise demand, vicissitudes of fashion included. By the early 1820s, the Macarthurs' wool was at the top of the London market. With more of it and improved technique, from that alone they could be sure of £2000 a year, rising after ten years or so to £3500.[3] Despite the challenges offered by drought and short-term fluctuations in price, and despite John's early doubts about his sons, it was a story of considerable success.

In the new regime at Camden good order began partly with James's record keeping. Penelope Lucas struggled to keep up her monthly account of livestock under James's eye, first making her listing even more scrupulously neat but then finally giving it away.[4] The accounting methods James had learnt in London from Charles Coles set a new standard for a larger operation.

There was paper order and there was order on the ground. That included good fences. At Camden a vineyard and a garden were set aside for the cuttings brought from Switzerland and France, and in March 1818 a reserved area for the local Tharawal people was marked out by the government surveyor. Peter McGuire, an elderly Irishman, had long been a familiar figure, first at Elizabeth Farm and then at Camden. In May 1819 he was paid £1.15s for work described as 'Boodbury's fence', measuring 70 metres, part of what was to be called Budbury's paddock.[5]

During 1821–22 the slab cottage that Elizabeth Macarthur had built for herself was replaced with, or incorporated into, a rectangle of farm buildings, designed by a Sydney architect, Henry Kitchen, and including a cottage homestead of brick and weatherboard, positioned to catch the view. Housing otherwise was rudimentary. One hut, for instance, was occupied by another Irishman, John Mullen. Mullen had taken his first step towards New South Wales when he had put himself between the shafts of a jaunting car and run off with it at Dublin's Donnybrook Fair. Picked up naked – no-one said why – Mullen, now a cooper at Camden, was housed in bark and logs, his doorway blocked at night with a bark sheet, his window an unglazed open square.[6]

Finally, there was carefully managed human order. This was a community of mixed ages. There were several older men, living more or less as pensioners on the estate. Robert Higgins was one of them, once a sergeant in the NSW Corps, now possessed of a little land nearby, which he rented out. He had a son and daughter on the place, both married and starting families.[7]

Other men had arrived only lately, not much more than boys. Richard Boyd, convicted at 15 at Glasgow – fresh face, black hair – might have met John Macarthur on board the *Lord Eldon* on the way out in 1817. He was one of the few servants the family called by their first name – 'Dick'. Taught to manage the horses, he had been sent to Camden to look after the stud there. John Macarthur's projects included sending good horses en masse to India, realised at last in 1845.[8] Charles Heyles, or Hyles, a London chimneysweep, had also been convicted at 15, while Alexander Browne, another Scot, was 16. They too learnt their trade in the Macarthurs' stables. Both stayed on, Heyles, like Boyd, for many years.[9]

Learning skills was part of the business of finding freedom. Thomas Lowick had been a messenger or street-runner in London. On arrival he had gone straight to Camden, where he was taken into the kitchen. Years later, his term long expired, Elizabeth Macarthur found him there, 'administer[ing] the rites of hospitality'. She exclaimed at his skill 'in preparing a sallad, and sending a wild duck to table'.[10] Patrick Curry, from county Limerick, started as a shepherd but stayed as a tenant farmer. John Macarthur complained about the convicts' ingratitude. Curry, however, was quick to testify to the family's 'goodness'. They were Protestant gentlemen, he said, but 'kind to their Catholic servants and tenants'. '[T]hey seem to like me to get on.'[11]

OTHER CONVICTS SHUNNED SUCH 'GOODNESS'. NEW men were taken straight from the ships and, as James Macarthur explained some time later, 'after a certain trial, we threw out the exceptionable characters, and kept only the best.' '[W]e did not reject them,' he added, 'till we had tried every means of making them useful', and the method of testing might have varied a little with each case. Flogging was a last resort, useless for reform purposes, and James and William, like their father, tried to avoid it. In early summer of 1826, after something like a minor rebellion, cause unknown, William took several men to court and two were flogged. This looks like the brothers' first trial of corporal punishment. James had already tried his father's bread-and-water idea, with the shepherd Thomas Burton, but he did not repeat it.[12]

Their overseer at Camden, Malcolm Campbell, might have been struggling to stay in control when he had several more men flogged in 1827.[13] By this time, as the system overall grew more unwieldy and the language of a free society more pervasive, convicts grew harder to manage and at Elizabeth Farm and Camden the

Macarthurs tried a new approach. Among all the convict men sent to New South Wales, half were transported for seven years, the minimum sentence, and a little more than a quarter for life. Most of the rest were for 14 years. For a long time, as in most places, the Macarthurs' pattern matched that bigger picture. In choosing men, they took no notice of the period of their sentence. However, from about 1825 their seven-year men dwindled and they seem to have deliberately taken lifers instead. By 1828 lifers made up nearly half of all they had.[14]

John Macarthur had always thought that men with life sentences were the best material for genuine reform. Lifers had been central to his grand scheme of 1805–07, mentioned earlier. With a life sentence a convict could be more easily persuaded at the outset, during what the Macarthurs called the 'nursery' stage, to make a point of behaving well, because it was the only way out.

Certainly, some lifers were obdurate from the beginning. Joseph Moorbee was an Englishman sentenced for burglary. At Camden he milked the cows. He endured, unpunished and unrewarded, for several years. In England his accomplice had been hanged for their joint offence, but neither that nor the Camden experience made any obvious difference. In January 1830, with another Camden convict, he broke into three houses in nearby Campbelltown and this time both were hanged.[15]

The preference for lifers meant that in 1828 there were three murderers – or at least men convicted of murder – living at Elizabeth Farm and Camden. All three were Catholic and Irish, and two had taken part in organised protest. Richard Jones was one of a group of 'sky farmers' in county Limerick, men who lived by their wits on the land as brokers and small graziers, making an uncertain living in the rapidly changing rural economy. In 1824 he was involved in the fatal beating of an uncooperative farmer. Transported, he went straight to Camden, got his ticket of leave

(1834), married (1836), and was an employer himself, apparently, not far away, and with a conditional pardon, by 1841.[16]

Another man transported for murder, Martin Murphy, had joined in the Ireland-wide tithe warfare, the fight by Catholics against parochial taxes paid to Protestant clergy, and he had struck the fatal blow during an attack on a tithe collector in county Kilkenny. Condemned to transportation, Murphy left behind a wife, Mary, and four small children. Arriving in Sydney Cove, he was assigned straightaway to John Macarthur at Elizabeth Farm. There he found favour very quickly. Under new government policy, designed to build up family life in New South Wales, Irish convicts' wives and children were sent out free of charge. Murphy immediately applied for his and after a 20-month trial James Macarthur wrote to back him up 'most strongly', as he said, in light of his 'decent, sober, orderly and industrious conduct'. Murphy was quite able, he added, to support a family. Mary and the children arrived in April 1829, and two and a half years later Martin Murphy won a 'ticket of exemption', a ticket of leave issued early for deserving married men. Virtually free after six years, he did even better than Richard Jones.[17]

However, in the end all depended on that singular mystery, the workings of mind in the human subject. Minds might be guided and led, and the methods used at Camden and Elizabeth Farm were designed above all to do that. Ultimately, however, each mind was a universe to itself. Each mind was also shaped by individual strength of will and purpose, so that a man or woman easily guided in one direction might be just as easily shifted into another. Martin Murphy left the Macarthurs' service only to be charged and convicted, with another Irishman, an older man, with stealing and killing a heifer. He was sent away for life all over again, first to Norfolk Island and then to Van Diemen's Land.[18] Mary's fate is unrecorded.

THE WHOLE SYSTEM WAS VERY UNCERTAIN AND IT depended on a persevering faith in human nature such as newly constructed communities can hardly do without. John Macarthur might pretend pessimism – might be genuinely pessimistic at one level – but he and Elizabeth, and their children after them, liked to invest effort in the lives of others. There might be a certain romance in such lives, starting badly and finishing well. Elizabeth took a particular delight in that possibility, especially when Providence did more than usual to help. She was charmed, for instance, by the story of the convict Jane Mead, one of her own servants.

Jane was a harness-maker's daughter from Wiltshire. As a girl she had gone up to London and found work in a series of wealthy households. Well dressed and well mannered, as a young woman she had found a way of buying – in fact, stealing – goods from local tradesmen using her employers' credit, until she was caught and transported. Assigned to Elizabeth Farm, she stayed on as a house servant long after her term had expired. Eventually, however, she was informed by a newspaper notice, on English authority, that she had come into 'a handsome legacy' at home. Elizabeth paid for Jane Mead's passage back to England, adding £20 for her use on arrival, and then waited to hear how she had got on.[19] She had dug deep, after all, to hear the end of the story. However, Jane, apparently, never wrote back.

The story of Rose Richey was more prosaic. Rose was another Irish convict, born into a poor Catholic family at Baltinglass on the River Slaney, about 80 kilometres south-west of Dublin. As a little girl she might have witnessed the tumult of United Irishmen who gathered at Baltinglass during the uprising of 1798. During these troubles there were every night 'the most horrible murders' roundabout. A single day saw the hanging of eight convicted men.[20] On the other hand, Rose Richey also seems to have benefited from the efforts made by the local Catholic bishop for the education of his people. Bishop Delaney saw the schooling of both boys and girls, rich and poor, as the best way to free Ireland from lawless poverty. Happily for Rose, the parish priest at Baltinglass was of the same mind.[21]

Leaving as a young woman, Rose Richey found work in Dublin as cook-laundress for John McGloin, a rich grocer trading in Irish whiskey. One Sunday, when McGloin was out, she took £170 worth of gold, silver and banknotes and headed north. Discovering his loss, McGloin put a savagely worded portrait in the Dublin papers – 'a low fat Woman [Rose was 150 centimetres tall], with dark hair, a round face, large mouth and thick lips'. A second record later on added hazel eyes and smallpox scars, but McGloin's was enough to catch Rose almost straightaway. The money was found distributed about her person.[22]

Sentenced to seven years transportation, Rose Richey travelled to New South Wales with 81 other women, some with children. In transit, the ship's surgeon appointed her 'general school mistress to the children … as well as to those adults who were inclined to be taught'. She was also asked to take care of a little girl whose distraught mother threatened to kill her. On arrival she was assigned to Robert Cartwright, Protestant clergyman at Liverpool, who was on the lookout for elementary teachers and whose parish at that point included Camden. Within a year or two Rose Richey found herself assigned to the Macarthurs instead.[23]

At Camden there were three families of small children, with five boys and five girls of school age. Rose Richey seems to have been their first teacher. It is hard to assess her skills. She wrote clearly but not well, and how much she grasped of reading and arithmetic is hard to say, but it might have been her firm hand with children that best recommended her. She spent about two years at Camden. During that time she married William Oglethorpe, a free immigrant sawyer, employed, perhaps, on the new buildings. The evidence for Oglethorpe points to another wife in England and at least one son, but bigamous or not, her marriage made

Rose, though still a convict, a free agent. By 1828 Oglethorpe was dealing in timber on Darling Harbour, in Sydney. His wife, now calling herself Roseanna, ran a laundry in town.[24]

Rose Richey had no reason to be particularly grateful to the Macarthurs. Their methods of discipline passed her by. She did well enough. However, with other convicts, men and women, the path laid out by their masters was the only way forward. Some minds, at least, learnt over time to bend and conform.

PART 7

37

LA RÉVOLUTION MORALE

In May 1821 there arrived in New South Wales the convict ship *Speke*, carrying 19 Scotsmen transported for taking part in an insurrection near Falkirk. They had been fighting for fair working conditions and the vote. The clash of insurrectionists and Stirlingshire Yeomanry, brief enough, was called the Battle of Bonnymuir. The convicted men included Benjamin Moir, a Glasgow labourer. His family soon followed him. The Macarthurs took his daughter Margaret into their employment as soon as she arrived and when Benjamin Moir found himself in prison in Sydney for some trivial transgression, John Macarthur, suspecting 'scandalous oppression', did what he could to help. Moir, he said, was 'a Scotch radical, and I believe he is a decent character'.[1]

In 1805 he had made the same sort of statement about Matthew Sutton – an Irish insurrectionist 'and I have no doubt,' he said, 'a man of honor'. Some would have said, '*but* a decent character', '*but* a man of honor'. 'And', not 'but', made all the difference. A bold conscience was a noble thing. Elizabeth and John Macarthur taught their children to think well of individuals such as these, and of 'the high principle of genuine radicalism', as their son James called it.[2]

During the early part of their marriage, in their twenties and thirties, Elizabeth and John had watched from afar the great revolution in France. It had been hard to know what it all meant. Tom Kingdon, one of Bridget Kingdon's younger brothers, newly entered on his clerical career, had written a sermon about it, and Elizabeth, on reading what he had to say, was impressed. As children, with Bridget and the others, she and Tom Kingdon had both seen the Tamar in flood and the pain that came of it. In his sermon Tom seemed almost to draw on that memory. During these revolutionary years, he said, a torrent of novelty had burst upon us. '[F]lowing without intermission', it left us, like the Bridgerule villagers in flood-time – so he implied – 'confounded and overwhelmed'.[3]

What did God mean by these great and violent changes? For Tom Kingdon they were part of the Almighty's glorious plan for humankind. Thomas Hobbes Scott, once Commissioner Bigge's secretary, now a clergyman too, said the same. There might be still more to come, said Scott, 'strong convulsions … and many evils', but we might be sure it was all to the good. In the time appointed by Providence, as ever, 'the effervescence subsides and the dross is carried off', and with the storm over we live at last in the sunshine – the day of justice – our Father has in store for us.[4]

Now, two decades of war had been brought to an end with the Battle of Waterloo, so that during the 1820s – the children of Elizabeth and John were themselves grown up – the great transformation entered a new stage. 'It is the era for the emancipation of the human race,' declared a London radical in 1820. 'The revolutions hitherto have been solitary.' Now the tumult was to be more truly universal. A series of mighty storms gave way to the rising of a global tide. '[O]ne feeling,' said the same Londoner, 'seems to pervade all nations.'[5]

By 'all nations' he meant the European world. It was still hard for Europeans to avoid a Eurocentric view of humanity and yet the movement spoken of was vast enough. A single impulse for change, emancipation in various forms, had shown itself on either side of the Atlantic. In apparently inevitable steps, in all of the American colonies governed from Europe, slavery was abolished and nations were established on new bases, supposedly free, virtuous, inclusive and just.

In South America there were independence movements against the old monarchies of Spain and Portugal, so that by 1825 most of the colonies there were self-governing republics. In Europe itself civil rights were extended to new sections of the population, though men only. Men among minority groups, including British Catholics and French Jews, won nearly complete civil rights. In Britain a bloody uprising seemed possible during arguments about parliamentary reform, but compromise in the end, the Great Reform Bill of 1832, brought peace for a time.

In arguing against West Indian slavery William Wilberforce had spoken of its 'utter forgetfulness of *mind* in the human subject'. In fact, all the ancient structures of power had depended somehow on the same 'forgetfulness of mind' – of individual reasoning, forethought and memory. The family at Elizabeth Farm could sense that truth. Altogether, self-awareness and the life of the mind were central to their understanding of humanity and historical change.

William Wentworth, in his writing and speech-making, told a story of New South Wales that set its new inhabitants within the long trajectory of the British Empire. The family at Elizabeth Farm, well read in both English and French, were looking for a larger agenda, one that attached New South Wales to Europe, to the general emancipation as they understood it, and, as they thought, to humanity at its best. In the 1820s they found that agenda through various new friends and through two in particular, Hobbes Scott and Saxe Bannister.

HIGHER LEARNING THROUGHOUT EUROPE LOOKED TO the ancient literature of Greece and Rome. To be familiar with the classics, as the essayist William Hazlitt said, was to know 'that there is something really great and excellent in the world, surviving all the shocks of accident and fluctuations of opinion'. To know Latin, and even more to know Greek, was to be in touch with something beyond criticism, beyond shifts of opinion, beyond time, as Hazlitt said – beyond all 'present power and upstart authority'.[6] Only mathematics – numerical, spatial, quantitative and so on – could equal the pristine orthodoxy offered by the ancient European tongues.

There were attempts to add other early languages to the same canon, such as Anglo-Saxon and Scots Gaelic. The enthusiasm for the poetry of Ossian, mentioned earlier, was proof of that. A few scholars were even venturing beyond Europe, looking for an archetypal language for humanity as a whole. The possibilities of Sanskrit had been discussed since the 1780s. But still, Greek and Latin remained supreme in educated minds.

The history of ancient Greece and Rome was part of the education of every European child who went beyond elementary level. That included far more boys than girls, although most boys might progress no further than elementary Latin. John Macarthur must have remembered some Latin from school – he seems to have known the difference between 'minutia' and 'minutiae' – but almost certainly no Greek. There was a fair collection of ancient history at Elizabeth Farm, from Charles Rollin's *Ancient History* (translated from the French in 1700), to William Russell's *History of Ancient Europe* (1793), and John also read the verse of Pindar, who was called the greatest of the Greek poets. A new translation of Pindar had appeared while he was at school, which may be how he remembered Pindar's story of Jason and the golden fleece when in 1804 he renamed the *Argo*, the vessel he used to carry to New South Wales the King's sheep.[7]

As for Elizabeth, she knew no Latin. She might have read a little ancient history, but judging from the way she sometimes spelt 'Hannibal' – 'Hannible' or 'Hannable' – it was not familiar territory. Among the children, the boys and young Elizabeth learnt Latin, but only young John mastered Greek.[8] He won university prizes for it.

Of all the independence movements of the 1820s the one most potent in meaning for educated Europeans, especially learned Europeans, was the struggle of the Greeks against their Ottoman overlords in Istanbul. The Greeks, whose forebears had lit the light of free reason 2500 years before, were now pitted against a backward-looking, non-Christian autocracy. That was the general understanding. Therefore, to side with the Greeks, reminding them of their inheritance and arousing them to new effort, was to side with untrammelled intelligence against tradition – with the eternal summer of the Aegean against the still gloom of Hagia Sophia. So said Johann Wolfgang von Goethe, whose play, *Iphigenie auf Tauris (Iphigenia in Tauris)*, a remarkable tribute to the enlightened soul, was translated by German students into modern Greek for performance on the spot, in 1818.[9]

So said Lord Byron:

The mountains look on Marathon –
And Marathon looks on the sea;
And musing there an hour alone,
I dream'd that Greece might still be free;
For standing on the Persians' grave,
I could not deem myself a slave.

The freedom of the Greeks was a cause dear to the heart of highly educated Europeans because of all these large questions of mind and character, including the mind and character of the Greeks themselves. What was needed in Greece, said one such intellectual, was 'la révolution morale'.[10]

Hobbes Scott, exposed to the best of Greek scholarship as a child, was to be involved with the English movement for Greek independence from the start. Meanwhile, Saxe Bannister's younger brother Tom enlisted in a British force raised to help in the struggle. Tom Bannister distinguished himself on Syros and at Athens in 1827. '[B]rave but irresponsible', in the words of one historian, he was afterwards an overland explorer in Western Australia.[11]

In England the idealisation of the Greek cause was typical of the 'philosophical radicals', individuals keen to refashion national communities by awakening 'genius' and the godlike ability to do and make – the free intelligence of humankind, such as they found in what they knew of the ancient Greeks. The best way to uncover genius among national populations in the present was by universal education. So, they said, you empower whole peoples.

For Hobbes Scott and Saxe Bannister the opening of minds everywhere was something that had to happen, and soon, for the good of humankind. During the 1820s, conversation with Scott and Bannister made that idea fundamental at Elizabeth Farm. The urgent need to open minds, so as to instil the kind of clarity Hazlitt spoke of, certainly seemed to justify the European occupation of countries such as New South Wales. In Europe itself, including Britain, it might even mean education by force of law. Make schooling compulsory, said Hobbes Scott, and he was only halfjoking. *'D[am]n 'em, they sh[oul]d have it willy nilly!'*[12]

38

HOBBES SCOTT

Thomas Hobbes Scott was 36 when the Macarthurs first knew him. Over the years he and the family at Elizabeth Farm grew deeply attached. For young Elizabeth he was 'one of the dearest friends it has pleased God to bless us with'. Emmeline frankly said she loved him. The older Elizabeth, who called him 'dear T.H.S.', shared with him a reverence for Reginald Heber, Bishop of Calcutta, an endlessly inquiring Christian. Heber's published journal, recounting his travels in northern India, a present from Scott, was among her best-cherished possessions.[1]

Hobbes Scott taught James Macarthur, in particular, about the new variations of enlightenment. His first present to James was the complete works, 'handsomely bound', of the 17th-century writer Francis Bacon, a font of wisdom for philosophical radicals. His larger endowment was a deep and enduring sense of the way communities could be newly arranged from the bottom up.[2]

Hobbes Scott had grown up at Southampton on the English south coast, the son and grandson of clergymen. The Scotts were a close and clever family, familiar with the jostling of language and ideas. One particular friend during Hobbes's childhood was the Greek and Spanish scholar John Warner, a man remarkable, it was said, 'for his great conversational powers, his brilliant wit, inexhaustible anecdotes, and captivating hilarity'. Another, even closer friend was the lawyer and philologist John Horne Tooke, lover of classical Greek and Anglo-Saxon. Warner, as Hobbes recalled much later, was 'a warm and steady advocate ... for civil and religious liberty'. Tooke was a leading figure in the London Corresponding Society, an organisation dedicated to making everyone in England, rich and poor, into active, understanding citizens and voters.[3]

As a teenager – by then his father was dead – Hobbes Scott lived partly with his eldest brother William, a law student, not far from Horne Tooke's house at Wimbledon, near London. William and Hobbes were at Tooke's nearly every day, dining with English radicals as eminent as Tooke himself, including Mary Wollstonecraft, her husband William Godwin, and Thomas Paine. For a time Hobbes corresponded with Paine and he was at the Corresponding Society's first meeting in 1797, as he long remembered, when he donated a guinea and drank a toast to the Rights of Man. His brother William, already grown up, 'a d[amn] sharp little fellow' by one account, took a more prominent part.[4]

Both brothers saw a good deal of Godwin, who was currently preoccupied with questions of educational reform. Perhaps as a result, both thought of education and politics as two sides of the one coin. The people had to be freed from old methods of schooling, which left them powerless in every way. Society as currently organised, said Godwin, was 'the great slaughter-house of genius and of mind'. Horne Tooke thought the same. Genuine education was not about words alone, but about words in their connection with things and the real world. We can understand 'the nature of the *signs*', said Tooke, only after we 'consider and arrange the *things signified*'.[5]

According to Godwin, the main purpose of educating a child was not to teach anything in particular but to create a mind genuinely free, 'well regulated, active, and prepared to learn'. Also, Godwin believed that children learn from each other. George Jardine said the same of his own students at Glasgow. True learning was sympathetic. We learn by being with others and watching others learn. It was the polar opposite of Jeremy Bentham's panopticon, which relied on isolation. 'The social affections,' Godwin said, 'are the chief awakeners of man.'[6]

As a young man Hobbes Scott joined with Samuel Brown, another of the Horne Tooke circle, in a wine-and-hops business in central London. He also experimented with soil improvement on 220 acres (about 90 hectares) he bought near Southampton, planting it with young trees. Within five years he had 270 000 trees doing well, had raised the rental value of the land 12 times over and had won a gold medal from the Society for the Encouragement of Arts, Manufactures and Commerce. However, the wine business then collapsed and Scott gave up his land as well.[7]

Scott's friends from this period included Frederick North, fifth Earl of Guilford, another enthusiast for classical Greek – and for all things Greek. Guilford led efforts to raise educational standards in Greece, though mainland Greece was still ruled from Istanbul, and he was a pioneer in the international movement for Greek nationality and independence. On the Ionian Islands, then a British protectorate and not yet politically part of Greece, Guilford had already sketched a system of schools at elementary level together with a new university, the Ionian Academy on Corfu, which was to open in 1824.[8]

Even more important for tying education to spiritual life, always crucial from Scott's point of view, was his friendship with Joseph Blanco White, who, as José María Blanco y Crespo, had once been a Catholic priest in Spain. There, he had been the eager publicist of the Pestalozzian Institute, established under government auspices in Madrid in 1805, and modelled on Johann Heinrich Pestalozzi's experimental school at Neuhof, near Zurich. The institute was meant as a pilot for the wholesale reform of Spanish elementary schools. Its pupils, boys aged five to 14, made rapid progress in a very short time and teachers came in large numbers to learn the new ways, until Church opposition and

French invasion together brought the exercise to an end. Blanco White had then fled to England, seeking a freer form of religious faith and disgusted with what he called the 'mental slavery' of his native land.⁹

IN MAY 1817 ANOTHER OF HOBBES SCOTT'S OLDER brothers, Harry Scott, was appointed British consul at Bordeaux. Hobbes joined him there as vice-consul before moving to the same position in Venice, where an old acquaintance, Belgrave Hoppner, son of the eminent portraitist, John Hoppner, was consul. Venice was a gathering place for intellectual leaders of the Greek diaspora, men with connections all over Europe, who wove science, scholarship and educational innovation into the logic of Greek independence. Scott's acquaintance, Andreas Mustoxidis, for instance, pioneered the history of nationhood in Greece. Mustoxidis also mixed with the intellectual luminaries of Geneva, including those the Macarthurs had met there very lately.¹⁰

Venice was a crossroads for the booming tourist traffic of the eastern Mediterranean. The poet Byron's little daughter Allegra lived with the Hoppners and Byron himself spent some months there and roundabout. At Venice too, Scott was not far from Guilford's educational project on the Ionian Islands. In fact, Guilford seems to have been partly responsible for his getting the post with Hoppner. Scott found enlightenment with Guilford as he had found it with Horne Tooke, Godwin and others, learning all the time the language of emancipation, nation and mind.¹¹

HOBBES SCOTT WAS STILL VICE-CONSUL AT VENICE when he was invited to go with Commissioner Bigge, his sister's brother-in-law, to New South Wales. He had no official instructions but in the course of this forthcoming inquiry he was to fill up ten good-sized notebooks on his own account. Blanco

White was currently writing against the Portuguese slave trade, and Scott, stopping on the way out at Rio de Janeiro, explored that subject as far as time allowed. Everywhere on this trip he picked up ideas, made sketches and collected documents and natural history specimens. Interested especially in the make-up of the soil, in the Australian colonies he gathered hundreds of small rocks, which he passed on to English museums.[12]

Hobbes Scott's experience was multilingual and pan-European and his conversation was a sudden gift for Elizabeth Farm. He expanded and clarified for the Macarthurs their understanding that emancipation was a matter of mind and education. He also localised that idea. In this country too children might learn to read 'el gran libro de la naturaleza' – the great book of nature – as they had done in Madrid and as Guilford intended they do at Corfu, by observation, handling and experiment.[13] Trained to think for themselves, the new generation might be pioneers of genius and virtue – forerunners of a higher kind of nationality. It only needed faith in Providence, proper planning and good government support.

In principle, such visions looked to a kind of 'managed complexity' – hands-on and hands-off at the same time – such as John Macarthur, in his solitary, searching, self-taught way, had experimented with from his earliest years in New South Wales. John was never as warmly attached to Scott as others in his family were, but in this respect at least his mind and Scott's marched in step.[14]

John Macarthur himself had brought back from Switzerland detail on the educational institute founded by Philipp Emanuel von Fellenberg, a former colleague of Pestalozzi, on his estate at Hofwyl, in the canton of Bern. There Fellenberg had several loosely connected schools, from elementary to something like university level, and including an 'Agricultural Institute', using throughout his own version of Pestalozzian method. It was a famously successful experiment and Charles Pictet, one of the two Pictet brothers of Geneva, was among its keenest advocates, so that John Macarthur, whether he saw Hofwyl or not, might have been persuaded by Pictet. In London early in 1817 he was already imagining a type of agricultural school at Camden, and of one day offering as well 'the higher branches of education', just as Hofwyl did.[15]

The *Edinburgh Review*, an influential progressive quarterly, was taken at Elizabeth Farm, and while Bigge and Scott were in New South Wales two issues arrived with detailed accounts of Hofwyl. The author was Henry Brougham, a leading advocate of school reform in England. Brougham himself had found at Hofwyl an interconnected community, 'a great whole', as he said, with a single budget and a single sense of purpose, where the students, whatever their age, were treated as 'rational creatures', self-reliant in their thinking, and taught to be masters each in his own small field.[16]

When Bigge and Scott returned to England, in July 1821, young John Macarthur, now a barrister at Lincoln's Inn, moved straightaway to take full advantage of their findings. He saw them both often, in a concerted attempt to use the inquiry to his family's advantage and as a catalyst for his father's ideas. About the same time he also introduced himself to the new junior minister at the Colonial Office, Robert Wilmot, afterwards Wilmot-Horton, and succeeded in making himself Wilmot's trusted advisor on Australian affairs.[17]

By March 1823 Bigge had completed the last of his three reports. He had nothing to say about convict reform and very little to say about the future of education, but by this time Hobbes Scott had turned clergyman and, with Wilmot's approval, young John wrote to him about schools. Hobbes sent back his plan for fundamental change, 'drawn up', he said, 'in the colony', it was given official approval and he was asked to go to New South Wales to make it happen.[18] He was to be first archdeacon and as local head of the Church of England, the government church, he would be in charge of all government schools, which, as in England, were the business of the Church. The minister, Lord Bathurst, was Lord Guilford's first cousin. He had already approved Guilford's plan for the Ionian Islands. Why not something in the same spirit for New South Wales?

HOBBES SCOTT AIMED FOR A SINGLE EDUCATIONAL system for New South Wales, 'a great whole' like Hofwyl, and like Hofwyl it was to be anchored in the soil. Land was to be set aside for its endowment and as a teaching resource. Every elementary schoolhouse should be surrounded by two acres of vegetables, fruit trees and crops, but in the long term student energies were be tied mostly to livestock, and to their breeding and multiplying year by year. Some of the land should be measured up as farms for the best students to lease when their skills were perfected.

Again, Scott echoed Horne Tooke. The great aim in educational reform, he said, was to replace a system that 'instead of teaching *things* … has taught only *words*'. A free people, every one of them, must be made to realise that their happiness depended not just on possessing 'the right knowledge' – both practical knowledge and expectations of government – but also its 'true use'.[19]

To mark his appointment Scott put together a more detailed plan, more like Guilford's Ionian Islands than the Hofwyl ideal. Reform was now to be managed in stages and altogether in this new version there was less of the smell of grain and soil. On the other hand, ambition was now more sweeping. As a way of resettling both churches and schools Scott made demographic projections and he also asked for a new survey of the east coast and inland. He wanted a meticulous spatial pattern, with hints of a more finely grained civility and spiritual life – European, that is – than existed so far, etched on the antipodean landscape.[20]

William Godwin had told his readers and listeners about how important the 'social affections' were in the learning process. In that respect, Hobbes Scott had a working model ready to hand. The Madras or monitorial system, worked out by the clergyman-schoolteacher Andrew Bell and newly fashionable in England, made even young children into teachers, leading their fellows in the simpler parts of each lesson. According to Bell, children delighted in such work – 'being, in a great measure, their own masters'.[21]

Scott also hoped to see a new version of student teaching at secondary level, although as yet there was only one such school in England where it had been tried. This was Charterhouse, in London. John Russell, the current head, had also attempted to abolish flogging, and again, when he reached New South Wales, Hobbes Scott followed suit, at least in the two orphan schools, boys and girls, where he had, or thought he had, some kind of direct oversight.[22] Conversation to and fro, George Jardine's 'intercourse between the Mind and the Eye', a method as old as Socrates, was surely much more effective than the birch.

WIDELY READ AND MANY TALENTED, AND WITH HIS high rank in New South Wales, Hobbes Scott saw himself as a type of organising mind for the government as a whole. Young John seems to have thought in the same way. It was therefore vital for them both that Scott work in close liaison with his father. So it was agreed between them that Scott should be based at Parramatta, within easy reach of Elizabeth Farm.

It was an opportune idea. During 1821–22 the Macarthurs had built two cottages. Besides the one at Camden for James and William, there was another, 600 metres from their old house at Elizabeth Farm, across Clay Cliff Creek. This second cottage was partly paid for by Penelope Lucas, apparently with the idea that she should live in it some day.[23] Edward stayed there for ten months while he was on leave in 1824–25. Hobbes Scott arrived in May 1825, after Edward had left, and he made his home at this cottage, apparently rent-free.

He added stables, a coach-house and a garden with a great variety of flowers, 'beautiful and extraordinary', so Elizabeth said, including exotic flowering trees – the glorious *Bignonia catalpa* for one, from the southern United States. Among the bulbs he planted was Amaryllis Josephine, such as Napoleon's empress grew at Malmaison, though its scarlet bell flowers might take years to appear. With his own small staff, including a trained gardener, a convict from Wiltshire, Scott was apparently in the cottage to stay.[24] This building was much later called Hambledon, but it is not likely that anyone in the Macarthurs' day called it that.[25]

Within a few weeks of his arrival Hobbes Scott met 23-year-old James Busby, who had just started as manager of the Orphan School land at Cabramatta. On that property Busby was being paid to create a vineyard, using the boys from the school as unpaid trainee vignerons. He had toured vineyards in the south of France, living briefly near Bordeaux, where Scott had been vice-consul, and he had decided that vineyards would succeed in New South Wales. John Macarthur had lent him Jean-Jacques Dufour's notes about North America and he had also asked for government help. The Cabramatta appointment, with orphan-boy labour, was the government's response.[26]

Hobbes Scott might have been surprised to find something like John Macarthur's agricultural school already underway at Cabramatta. He asked Busby to rethink his efforts along the lines of Fellenberg's Hofwyl and in June, meeting at Scott's cottage, they settled the details. Teaching at Busby's establishment was to include trades skills and the careful management of the soil – Scott's great interest – and of sheep, using the best from the Macarthurs' flocks. A wheelwright, a carpenter and a blacksmith were to have their own teaching departments and others were to follow. As masters themselves, these men were to teach mastery. All instructors were to be free arrivals, not convicts – Scott insisted on that – and they were to be well paid so as to attract the best.[27]

So Hobbes Scott began the great project of his life, closely watched by the family at Elizabeth Farm. He was well prepared in some ways, but not in others. Loved by friends and parishioners – polite, kind, tactful – with subordinates in office he could be bullying and bad-tempered. So far Scott had always played second fiddle to someone else, from Horne Tooke to Commissioner Bigge. Now, in quick time, he had been ordained, named archdeacon and sent to create a new system of churches and schools in New South Wales. Normally modest but also impulsive, sometimes wonderfully diplomatic, at other times rash, Hobbes Scott fumbled his way. As with many of the philosophical radicals, his intellectual energies were too sharp-edged for the practical purpose in hand.

He was keen to make a difference – profound, complete, 'une révolution morale' – and he was sure he was right. He therefore pushed to the limit his authority as head of the church and as 'King's Visitor' of all government schools. Dedicated, scrupulous, hard-working, he hated apathy and dissent. He started his great work with problems inbuilt.[28]

39
JUSTICE AT EVERY STEP

In his book, published in 1819, William Wentworth pinpointed a 'faction' in New South Wales, a small group of individuals who, by his account, had an unfair, unprincipled, underhand grasp on power. He named no names, but these were settlers who had arrived free, gathered property and privilege, and kept aloof from former convicts. They aimed, he said, to perpetuate the immigrant–ex-convict distinction even beyond the present generation, so as to make criminal conviction into 'an hereditary deformity'.[1]

Commissioner Bigge, arriving in New South Wales not long after the book was published, agreed. However, for Bigge it was a good thing that New South Wales should have a group like that, men and women who had never offended against the law and who felt, as he said, 'a greater or less degree of repugnance' towards those who had. New South Wales was a penal colony. What could be more important than the difference between vice and virtue, and the perpetual shame of criminal conviction?[2]

When John Macarthur read Wentworth's 'hereditary' remark he scribbled in the margin, 'false [and the] young man knows it to be so'.[3] False or not, it was a poisonous idea, which reverberated through the 1820s and beyond. To begin with there was only one Sydney newspaper, the *Gazette*, but from 1824 others started publication and in a competitive market sales depended on polarising abuse. The stories told by Wentworth and Bigge, each from his own corner, were perpetuated by the papers for several years, blackening reputations and vitiating debate.

John Macarthur's opinion did not save him from being seen as the epitome of aristocratic conceit. His manner was often haughty, his temper could be sharp and there was plenty of evidence of him monopolising or trying to monopolise power. He had his own line of communication with the British government through his son John and the latter's friend Robert Wilmot-Horton at the Colonial Office. John Oxley, the surveyor-general, young Elizabeth's sometime suitor, was onside. For a long time John Macarthur had avoided him, but Oxley dealt with other members of the family on the question of land grants and then, in summer 1822–23, 'Mr Oxley,' as Elizabeth told Edward, 'has met your father again.' '[T]hey speak, and so forth.' After that, in November 1823, James Bowman, principal surgeon, married the Macarthurs' second daughter, Mary. Bowman was a highly efficient manager, capable, John Macarthur said, of 'miracles' in the management of public health, and a succession of governors thought much the same.[4] Finally, Hobbes Scott, who controlled church and schools, had taken up residence a step away from the homestead at Elizabeth Farm.

Taken altogether, here, certainly, was something like a faction. In August 1824, a nominated council of five began to meet in Sydney, authorised to pass laws for New South Wales, and Scott and Bowman both belonged by right of office. Next year, the council was increased to seven, leaving out Bowman but adding John Macarthur himself as one of three non-government members. What more could they want at Elizabeth Farm?

William Wentworth and his friend, Robert Wardell, both of them journalists and barristers, arrived from England in July 1824. Three months later they launched the weekly *Australian*, soon thrice-weekly, filling its pages with news and abuse of the faction. With a joint legal practice doing equally well, Wentworth and Wardell fought the same war in court. A particular target, because he was often in court and also an obvious visitor at Elizabeth Farm, was the attorney-general, Saxe Bannister.

SAXE BANNISTER WAS THE SON OF A TANNER IN SUSSEX, who had made himself into a landed gentleman. His mother was the daughter of a yeoman farmer and Bannister's original first name, Sex, was her family name. He changed it to 'Saxe' when he started at Oxford. As a young man, he learnt to make his way by his cleverness and moral enthusiasm, which explains why, later on, he found it hard to compromise with the practicalities of power. On graduating from Oxford he had enlisted in the regular army in order to help with the final push against Bonaparte, but his regiment was sent to North America before he could join it.[5] With the coming of peace he therefore started straightaway on his chosen career, the law.

Bannister thought of the law as an instrument of progressive civilisation, a civilisation duty-bound by the dictates of Providence to expand its benefits to all humankind. His first activist campaign focused on the old grammar school in his home town, moribund because its trustees had neglected their duties under the original endowment. Still a student in law, Saxe gathered signatures for a petition to force compliance. Then, during the three-year court battle, he carried out a nationwide survey of English grammar schools. He discovered that while benefactors had endowed these schools so as to educate the population at large, trustees all over England had lost sight of that original purpose. It was vital, he said, that this great system of schools, a 'mighty engine' for arming the people against superstition and lies, 'should be applied to its legitimate intent'.[6]

Saxe Bannister read voraciously on every subject that interested him. His thoughts were now beginning to settle especially around the question of law and trust. How does trust, the bedrock of community, work over the long term? In 1819 he published a book on *The Proper Use and the Reform of the Free Grammar Schools*, but then he produced another about the 17th-century English judge Orlando Bridgeman, a pioneer in the area of future interests – law securing property to a succession of interest holders.[7] Bannister's work so far proved to him that long-term trust went beyond black-letter law. The law itself was founded on trust. This insight led him to the question of what was afterwards called native title, or at least to that question's outer edge.[8]

The years 1822–23 were for Saxe Bannister highly exciting. His younger brother John William had returned to England from a period in Upper Canada (southern Ontario), also to train for the law. With him had come two leading men of the Mohawk people and Saxe involved himself in their arguments with the Colonial Office about land rights under the colonial government. Reading around this question he noticed the vast damage done by Europeans in their occupation of North America, and most of all its effect on individual lives among the old inhabitants. He shuddered, he said, 'with indignation and sorrow' at 'the barbarous personal tyranny exercised over these unfortunate people'.[9]

In Upper Canada his brother had come under the influence of Robert Gourlay, a passionate advocate of new forms of popular citizenship, through voting rights, land ownership and universal education. Throughout Britain postwar unemployment caused great suffering among the poor but if they could move to Upper Canada, Gourlay said, with their own land, good schools and all the rights of citizenship they might take control of their lives in ways hitherto impossible. In 1822 Gourlay published in London his *Statistical Account of Upper Canada*, in which he sketched 'a grand system of emigration' from Britain to the North American colonies, a vision so persuasive that within 20 years it led to the 'systematic colonisation', or wholesale occupation, even of South Australia and New Zealand.[10]

John William Bannister published his own *Sketch of a Plan for Settling in Upper Canada*. At this point he and Saxe were in touch with John Musgrave, a substantial landowner near Cork in southern Ireland, whose life study was poverty and unemployment among the Irish poor. John William extended his scheme to include the Irish, and Saxe, writing to the government in Dublin, offered to move to Ireland and make it work.[11]

Saxe Bannister was anxious to correct injustice on a large scale but he also needed employment. Failing with Dublin, he tried to persuade the Colonial Office to send him to Upper Canada to report on Indigenous rights under government, a subject now starting to dominate his thoughts, and at the same time, prodded by John William, he began writing a series of articles for London's *Retrospective Review*. His first article looked at emigration and the claims of the British poor and he aimed in the second to consider what might be done for the invaded peoples.[12] However, between the first and the second he was appointed attorney-general of New South Wales. He therefore carried the latter question with him, urgent and half-formed, even to the drawing room at Elizabeth Farm.

WRITING FROM LONDON, YOUNG JOHN MACARTHUR told his mother that Saxe Bannister's appointment was partly due to him. He had been informed, young John said, that Bannister was 'most *honorable, kind*, and *conscientious*', and he, John, had been anxious to head off the possible appointment of William Wentworth, or of Wentworth's friend Robert Wardell. Wilmot-Horton took his advice and it was done.[13] The new attorney-general sailed in November, with two of his five sisters, Mary Ann and Harriet.

Edward Macarthur, now a captain in the 19th Regiment, took the same ship, for a period at home on leave. Stopping at Cape Town, the two visited the vineyard at Constantia, though, as Edward said, 'Bannister … does not profess to be a wine drinker.'[14] They reached Sydney in April 1824 and the Bannisters rented a large house, Woolloomooloo, on Sydney's eastern edge.

Introduced by Edward, the attorney-general and his sisters came to think of Elizabeth Farm as an oasis in a moral and intellectual desert. 'A more estimable family,' Saxe said, 'in all its branches, does not live.' Mary Ann and Harriet took up with Emmeline, who told her mother that she liked them 'better and better every time she sees them'. Elizabeth herself found the Bannisters 'very eccentric'. However, Saxe was just what she liked – not interested in quarrelling, transparently honest and his conversation a tonic for John.[15]

The attorney-general was obviously clever, too clever for some people. He was also, in John Macarthur's opinion, 'unaffected, and just odd enough to make a pleasing companion'. In time John grew deeply fond of him and Bannister returned his friendship. '[O]n some points,' the younger man said, 'we think alike. In many we differ materially.' For John, a large part of Bannister's charm lay in the way he could carry the talk above local politics and beyond the need to take sides. They did not try to persuade each other of anything, or if they did, Bannister said, the effort went both ways.[16]

Bannister soon came to know all about John's jarring with governors past and present, from Hunter to Darling, and his explanation was more perceptive than most judgments of the colonial past. 'British Governors,' he said, 'ought to be able to control and act with, not against, or under clever, active men.' There was wisdom in knowing how to listen and learn, whatever foibles of personality might get in the way. 'Governors should possess this wisdom.'[17]

What did John Macarthur and Saxe Bannister talk about? Bannister's thoughts about justice ran in various directions and into some very knotty places, and it is likely that to some extent they went to those places together. The philosophical radicals believed that everyone was entitled to share fully in civilised life, however meagre their power and importance. In this light Bannister, even before leaving London, had started thinking about the lives of very small children. Experimental infant schools, using Pestalozzi's child-centred methods, had started very lately in London and Bannister brought promotional literature to New South Wales. As a result, an infant school was soon doing well in the crypt of St James's church, Sydney. The attorney-general dropped in often, the archdeacon secured government funding, and soon there were two more, also in town.[18]

Disordered family life was beginning to be a vexed question in England, including its effect on children. In New South Wales it was usual to blame the convict women and what John Macarthur called their 'promiscuous intercourse with the men', but Bannister brought a larger point of view. The problem for him was not the women but the men. Far more male convicts were transported than female, and the massive imbalance of the sexes, he said, gave a 'masculine character' to colonial society. That masculine character, brutal and lawless, affected the entire moral culture, from top to bottom, and did serious damage to family life.

Bannister attempted a rudimentary moral calculus for New South Wales by counting up crimes, and he discovered a deeply degraded people. Here was a community – as Hobbes Scott also thought – ripe for moral redirection. Criminal offences per head were much worse than Britain's and a careless attitude to children was indicated by the many drowning deaths among toddlers. Especially telling, he said, was the number of 'assaults on infant females'. Life was cheap, especially infant life, and Bannister was angered by the way children suffered from a social malaise created and kept up by men in power. 'I will not behold the poor children of the Colony,' he said, 'brought up as they are, in the midst of a convict population, without raising my feeble voice in their behalf.' The truth must be told, 'and as God shall judge me it shall be told.'[19]

There was another subject for conversation, just as difficult. Saxe Bannister and John Macarthur shared an interest in Roman history and Bannister's understanding of the British Empire was shaped by his understanding of the Roman. Or rather, Bannister justified his thoughts about the British Empire by looking for parallels in the ancient world. Talking to Bannister, John, possibly for the first time, was called to think about the larger rights and wrongs of British invasion in New South Wales.

The Roman Empire was ringed by 'barbarians', so Bannister argued, just as the British Empire was bordered by 'numerous uncivilized tribes'. And yet, how easily, even willingly, 'the manners of Rome', including Christianity, were adopted by those 'barbarians'. In the same way, 'the union of our neighbours with us', with late Enlightenment Britain, must result in 'general improvement'. That result, however, that great end of Empire, as he always insisted, must depend on the use of justice at every turn – not just generalised justice, but also personal, particular justice, justice in every aspect of every life.[20]

In earlier days Saxe Bannister had wanted to survey and report on Indigenous peoples 'in union or in alliance with us' in Upper Canada. Injustice of all sorts, he said, threatened the extinction of the 'Indians' and in making his offer he had included several preliminary suggestions for changes, all depending on Indigenous opinion and consent. Among other things the people might have schools staffed by their own, a veto on laws affecting them and even a part in making those laws. 'It is quite clear,' he had said at that point, 'they will approve of what is right.'[21] He had hoped in that way to create a new moral regime in Upper Canada.

That plan had had the active support of the Bishop of Quebec, Charles James Stewart, and now Bannister aimed to do much the same in New South Wales with Hobbes Scott, who as archdeacon was officially responsible for 'the Civilisation and Education of the Native Inhabitants'. However, as in Upper Canada, Bannister's 'general plan in regard to these people', as he called it, depended on a survey of their condition and opinions.[22]

Someone was needed to make such a survey in New South Wales. Richard Sadleir was an Irishman born into a network of landowners and industrialists around Cork, including the Bannisters' friend John Musgrave. Like Bannister's brother, John William, Sadleir had settled briefly in Upper Canada and on returning to Ireland he had helped in the gathering of over 2000 Irish poor as emigrants to the same place. In 1825 Sadleir had himself sailed with the first shipload of government-sponsored Irish emigrants to New South Wales, wives and children of convicts. In Sydney, he must have met promptly with Bannister and Scott, because in no time he was commissioned by Scott to visit and report on all the Indigenous peoples within reach.[23]

Richard Sadleir was gone five months, often travelling well beyond the frontier. Governor Macquarie's Native Institution had closed, but while Sadleir was away a new school was built for Indigenous children at Blacktown and it was part of his duty, while on his travels, to persuade parents to send their children in to take advantage of it. In this he completely failed. However, he arrived back with other ideas, which he included in his report and which were almost certainly adapted from Bannister's draft 'general plan'. Among other things, he suggested that 'stations' be formed beyond the frontier where volunteers from among the First Nations nearby might come to learn about European farming and otherwise take 'instruction', and where land might be reserved for them. So the Indigenous peoples of New South Wales might manage as the Mohawk people did in Upper

Canada, with 'their own places of worship, schools, saw-mills, farms, &c'.[24]

The school at Blacktown made a start with local children only, the boys learning carpentry and the girls needlework and spinning. There were hopes of an infant class too, if only parents roundabout would agree to give up their littler children for a few hours each day. And perhaps, it was said, the same parents and other relations might bring in possums' fur, taking tea, sugar and flour in return. 'When this is spun both boys and girls may be taught to knit stockings or other articles.'[25]

With how much confidence did Saxe Bannister look forward to watching little girls manipulate possums' fur onto their spinning wheels? Several generations later something similar was tried in New Zealand with great success, mixing possums' fur with sheep's wool – Merino cross – so as to create a valuable and marketable blend. In 1826–27 the idea might well have sprung from drawing room chat at Elizabeth Farm. It appealed to John Macarthur – so it appears later – but what Elizabeth thought is unrecorded.[26]

40
REBUILDING HOME

In August 1826 Elizabeth and John both turned 60. In the same year their youngest, Emmeline, was 18, while the four eldest were in their thirties. So they entered the last decade of the biblical 'three score years and ten', and according to current usage they could call themselves 'old'. John remained physically strong but Elizabeth began to have eye trouble – 'it ill agrees with my eyes to write by candle light' – though there is no evidence of her using glasses until 1833.[1] Keeping accounts and even writing letters became difficult. So began that sense of creeping disability that comes with advancing years.

Young Elizabeth, living with her parents at Elizabeth Farm, seems to have taken over the household as well as the garden. Her mother therefore had time on her hands, so that she could happily send her sons in England 'a proper old woman's gossiping letter'. Now, she said, 'when I take up my pen, I know not when to have done when addressing those that are dear to me'.[2] She also began to spend long periods away from home. She was in Sydney with Mary for about 12 months in 1826–27, at Camden with James and William for three months in 1830–31, and in Sydney again for more than a year from May 1832.

James, based at Camden but frequently on the move, acted more for his father, though that meant managing John's moods as well. Strong-minded but self-effacing, James knew how to appeal to his father's self-critical side, an important point in keeping affairs on track. At the same time, hunting for his own way forward, he wanted to give his family a more conciliatory public image. As a result, according to one Sydney paper, James was better liked generally – 'much more esteemed' – than John.[3]

James was the family's diplomat and businessman. At Camden, he also saw to the management and marketing of the cattle and horses. William, though they shared all important decisions, was more directly responsible for the sheep. William taught himself wool-classing, handling many thousands of fleeces throughout the 1820s, 'a nearly constant occupation', as he said, 'of a very irksome kind for two or three months each year', until a skilled wool-classer, Carl Koelz, was brought from Germany, to take over that part of the work.[4]

William was also a self-trained vigneron and horticulturalist. In 1816–17, while John Macarthur had waited in London for permission to go home, the cuttings gathered with so much trouble in Switzerland and France had been kept at a leading nursery, where they were apparently mixed up, deliberately or not, with second-rate equivalents – a fact discovered over the next few years as they failed to produce as expected. The cuttings sent from Madeira were no good either, so that the first decade of effort with grape-growing was largely wasted. In 1830 a second vineyard was laid out with new vines and entrusted to Antonis Manolis, a convict who knew about the work from an earlier life on the island of Hydra, in the Aegean. Produce then improved.[5]

The two elder sons, Edward and young John, lived on the other side of the world, and young John in particular was of crucial importance as the family's representative at the heart of affairs. Emotionally, Elizabeth admitted that with these two the gap was not just a matter of miles. 'I feel I can write more familiarly,' she said, 'and with a chance of being better understood, by those I have latest had the happiness of seeing.'[6]

At the same time, letter writing at that distance had its own value for both parents, as a type of release for things that could not be said easily at home.

Young John was for his father a type of second self. Distance encouraged that fantasy. It was with young John that the older man indulged his resentment of local critics and enemies, opinions he knew that his family did not always like to hear. In that way, differently nuanced stories reached London from different members of the family.

In June 1827 James was preparing to go to England again and their father, in a strangely weak moment, warned young John that 'on many points he [James] may be misinformed'. Therefore, he said – and it must have made young John wonder – 'do not act on what he says'.[7]

Altogether, Elizabeth and John were no longer a managing partnership. In some sense, as they discovered new kinds of friendship and comfort with their various children, a distance opened up between them. Elizabeth, as I say, spent long periods away from home. At the old house they still shared a bed, but it stood in what Elizabeth now called 'my bed room' and there was a couch in John's dressing room, where he could spend his more restless nights. It was another type of affection they had now.

DURING 1823–28, IN THE YEARS AFTER MARY'S MARRIAGE to James Bowman, John Macarthur finalised his will. That included decisions, not only about who should have what property but who should live where when he was gone. He talked it over with Elizabeth and, as she afterwards recalled, the business troubled him a good deal. She remembered him '*hoping* and *praying* as he conversed that our children would be satisfied with the disposition of his property'. Young John must stay in England, and James and William were settled at Camden. As for Edward, John and

Elizabeth had always expected that he would eventually make his home in New South Wales, ideally with an English-born wife. John made provision accordingly, without realising how much his eldest son needed the refinements of Europe. It was a bad mistake, with serious implications later on.[8]

Their daughters' future depended on whether or not they found husbands, and what sort of husbands. Mary's marriage was not a happy one. James Bowman, as Mary said herself – later on – was harsh and cruel, but at least as his wife she had a home of her own and children, some residual right to his property and room to hope, as she put it, that 'some day I might be free'.[9] Emmeline, still young, might be expected to marry too. That left the eldest, Elizabeth. Thirty-four in 1826, young Elizabeth was unlikely now to find a husband. Her future might seem to lie with Elizabeth Farm, where she had her all-important garden. Altogether, it was a turning point time, such as happens in any family when two generations become three and when the old must anticipate giving way to the young.

The homestead buildings at Elizabeth Farm, unpretentious and awkwardly set out, had been largely unchanged for many years. The main house was much too small. To begin with, in 1793, Elizabeth and John had had three small children, and the house had been designed accordingly. By 1820, there were five still at home, all grown up, plus Penelope Lucas. At that point, sleeping space was still limited to one good-sized bedroom and a couple of much smaller ones, while the building itself, as Elizabeth said, was tumbling down. '[I]t is quite a ruin.'[10]

When Commissioner Bigge and Hobbes Scott first saw the a house, only the book-lined walls and abundant garden might have suggested anything beyond the ordinary. Scott was interested in building and garden layout, and during this first period in New South Wales he seems to have talked with the Macarthurs about improvement. He urged James to read William Marshall's authoritative text, *Planting and Rural Ornament*, which explained in great detail how to combine horticultural skill and good taste, buildings and landscape, vistas and outlooks, within some 'great design'. Marshall was a pioneer of top-pruning, so as to save the roots during the transplanting of young trees.[11]

It seems to have been at Scott's suggestion that John Macarthur, in 1820, started to think in detail about a new house at Camden, Pyrmont or both. The Sydney architect Henry Kitchen was asked for plans, and his first drawings were modelled on a house in Scott's home territory near Southampton. That house had been built by a family of Greek scholars and its architectural style was Greek Revival. It was a style unfamiliar to Kitchen but for lovers of ancient Greece, such as Scott, it represented a purity of form much as the Greek language represented purity of thought.[12]

With Hobbes Scott gone in 1821, ambition lapsed, except that Kitchen was given two smaller projects, the homestead buildings at Camden, finished by September 1822, and the cottage at Elizabeth Farm, first used by Edward in April 1824. For the family, however, these were obviously not enough. According to Elizabeth, they now thought of moving altogether to Camden, which meant building a bigger house there. 'It is what we much want.'

Henry Kitchen had died, and James Smith, a Sydney builder, was entrusted with his designs, but nothing substantial was done until, in 1825, Hobbes Scott came back as archdeacon. Then there was movement again. Another builder-architect, Henry Cooper, had arrived from England and he was asked for new plans, once again Greek.[13]

Edward Macarthur had lately sent the Colonial Office a suggestion for a militia force in New South Wales, made up of locally born men but with an officer from England in charge. In such an establishment Edward might expect the senior appointment himself. With hopes that their eldest son was coming at last to live in New South Wales, John, giving up plans for Camden, ordered work to begin straightaway at Pyrmont.[14] So Edward might have a good house at the city's edge, while he, Elizabeth and their two so-far unmarried daughters might stay at Elizabeth Farm.

The Colonial Office referred the militia idea to Governor Darling and Darling's disapproval might have been clear enough by mid-1826. The plan for Pyrmont was then given up. Plans had already been made for refitting the old house at Parramatta, and work there went ahead, beginning apparently in July, when Elizabeth, at John's insistence, went to stay with their daughter Mary Bowman and her family in Sydney. 'I am told that if I return, your dear father will not proceed. I have lived so long in a ruin of a cottage that I think it best to stay where I am [with Mary], until I have a bedroom finished.'[15] That left, onsite, John himself, young Elizabeth, Emmeline and Penelope Lucas.

During the second half of 1826 house and garden were remodelled together, and much as William Marshall recommended in his book on planting. There must be 'unison' throughout, so Marshall ordained, so that much depended on the arrangement of garden walks, which drew the eye from point to point, and also on views from within the main building. This network of visual threads should bring the whole together. For the renovated building at Elizabeth Farm the architect was Henry Cooper, and for the garden they had 'a clever Scotch gardener', as John said, 29-year-old John Maclean, who had arrived in New South Wales five years before. Maclean was particularly good with visual effect. He was afterwards in charge of the government gardens in Sydney, where he cleared a new space by the water's edge and laid out a much admired system of visitors' paths.[16]

John Maclean had arrived with a Scottish couple, Annabella and John Campbell. He had been their gardener in county Argyll and he had settled with them on their large estate, Bungarribee, about 20 kilometres beyond Parramatta, where they built a house with three hectares of garden and orchard. There was much to and fro between Bungarribee and Elizabeth Farm. John Campbell borrowed over £1000 from John Macarthur, Annabella Campbell borrowed books from young Elizabeth, and the Macarthurs borrowed Maclean.[17] They also borrowed a key feature of Bungarribee for their altered house, namely its French doors opening onto stone-flagged verandahs and so to the airy spaces beyond.

By September the main bedroom at Elizabeth Farm had been enlarged and converted into what John called 'a handsome library'. The drawing room and dining room had been extended too, the floor had been lowered throughout, so as to give more height to the ceilings, and in all three rooms French doors drew in light and air from the north and east. Meanwhile, as her father put it, with Maclean's help 'Miss has regenerated the garden'. There is no record as to exactly what was done in the garden but it seems to have included new planting, also to the north and east, and the addition of a pond edged with native cypress and willow. 'Miss', otherwise 'Miss Livy' – young Elizabeth – also gave herself two small conservatories, or 'plant rooms', one at each end of the northern verandah, suitable for horticultural experiment.[18] Not only did the house now have better views into the garden – the garden was brought into the house.

Young Elizabeth had once spoken of the way trees and shrubbery were arranged about the house, indigenous and imported mixed together so that the family could, as she said, 'enjoy the beauty of each in their season'. That artistry was now taken to another level. Elizabeth, as her mother had said, possessed 'great powers of imagination'. The work she did with Maclean and her father in 1826 might be proof of that. Thomas Livingstone Mitchell, John Oxley's successor as surveyor-general, who saw it all when he visited Elizabeth Farm several years later, called the garden 'extensive and beautiful'. He was struck especially with the roses of all sorts, in beds and on trellises, scenting the air.[19] With the 1826 design that impression of roses might have been brought into every room.

All the same, it was the house, her father's achievement, that drew most praise. Hobbes Scott was 'not very encouraging when I commenced', John said, but he was persuaded by the result. James spoke of their old house 'transformed by our father's fertile genius'. With the creation of the library, there were fewer bedrooms, but a new wing planned for the eastern side was expected to take care of that.[20] In fact, that wing was never built.

Only the original roof was left intact, as a deliberate nod to family feeling. A completely new building on the same scale would have been cheaper and easier to bring about, so James admitted, but it was good to have the roof there still, 'under which was spent the happy hours of childhood'. The building team included the carpenter's apprentice James Byrnes, mentioned in Chapter 31, and it must have been during this work that Byrnes, an impressionable boy, met John Macarthur. John, as Byrnes long remembered, had taken him in hand, teaching him how 'to look at the past and provide for the future'.[21] There was an object lesson in the house itself.

41
NEMESIS WAS GREEK

Aonia, in the mountains of central Greece, was said to be the ancient home of the Muses, the spirits responsible for the genius of humankind. In New South Wales, the convict poet Laurence Hynes Halloran liked to think that he had felt the touch of the Muses when he first wrote verse as a young man:

> In happier days I woo'd their sacred shades,
> And owned the influence of th' Aonian maids.[1]

Halloran, transported for fraud in 1818, was probably the first teacher of Greek in New South Wales. He had led an eventful life, including an association years before with the Macarthurs' kinsman, whom I have called Hinton McArthur.

During the war with France, Halloran and his son had been present at the Battle of Trafalgar and his fine poem about that great clash of naval power had made him briefly famous. Action-packed and thick with firsthand detail, his lines conveyed hints of the free-minded heroism and bright celebrity of Homer's *Iliad*. So, of Horatio Nelson, Halloran said:

> His Genius, by no servile rules enslav'd,
> Grasp'd each event, and every danger brav'd.

In their patriotic, salt-sea detail, Halloran and Hinton McArthur were kindred spirits, and McArthur had made use of Halloran's biographical writing and verse in his *Naval Chronicle*.[2] Both had served as secretaries to senior naval commanders. Both took up their pens afterwards in the same great national cause, driving patriotism with the pen.

However, Laurence Halloran had several sides to him. He was a remarkable public writer and speaker, forceful, lucid, inspired, but salacious stories were told about his private life. He was given to vulgar abuse, in print if he could manage it, he often lied and his temper was fierce. For several years he had defrauded the Church of England itself by pretending to be a clergyman, performing even its holiest functions – the marriage ceremony, for instance – though his conviction was for a lesser crime. And yet, Halloran also understood the minds of children. Governor Macquarie called him the 'best and most admired' of Sydney's schoolmasters and Commissioner Bigge, well aware of his lying habits, said the same.[3]

Still a convict, Halloran followed up his teaching success with a sustained effort to get himself a pardon. Failing with the governor he wrote to England. One letter he sent to the lord chief justice, Lord Gifford, his pupil long ago in Devon. Did he send a second to John McArthur at Hinton? Did Hinton McArthur write in turn to Elizabeth Farm, which was all he could do, asking his kinsman to look out for Halloran? Certainly something made John Macarthur think differently about this unusual convict. Only lately he had spoken slightingly of 'the infamous Dr Halloran'.[4] Suddenly, he was one of his keenest supporters.

In mid-1825 Halloran found another way of recommending himself to authority, with a plan to make his school, currently his own property, into a public venture, managed by a board of trustees, funded by benefactions and government grant, but headed still by himself. Alerted to this scheme, John Macarthur made himself its principal benefactor, besides starting a fund to pay Halloran's debts. Gifts from his own pocket totalled at least £1600, an enormous sum, and he mustered donations as well from James, William and Hannibal. Other money came mainly from rich ex-convicts in Sydney and from public servants. The two judges, Francis Forbes and John Stephen, were leading names, and the outgoing governor, Sir Thomas Brisbane, committed land in town on which the trustees could build. Until that could happen the school, newly reconstituted, was to be in Halloran's old premises, starting in the new year, 1826.[5] It was all remarkably quick.

John Macarthur sat on the governing board, elected in December 1825. So did Simeon Lord and Samuel Terry, ex-convicts who both had boys with Halloran. Such men stood out among their kind, so Saxe Bannister said, in their care for their children's future. Bannister himself, with his enthusiasm for endowed grammar schools, might have helped in sparking John Macarthur's interest. He showed his own support by donating a set of Latin books, to be held under trust 'for the perpetual Use of the Head Master'.[6]

Many supporters were happy to overlook Halloran's weaknesses – he was elderly, scandal-ridden and might not last – because the school seemed such a good and timely idea. However, trouble started straightaway. Already in dispute with two newspapers, Halloran quarrelled with the board about his salary. At an angry meeting in April, John Macarthur, still his friend, was unable to contain himself, 'occasionally assisting, and as repeatedly interrupting', so that everyone spoke at once and the building rang with 'Order! Order!'. Halloran won that time, but week by week vitriol mounted, donations fell away and opinion gathered against him.

Hobbes Scott watched with interest. Scott had not yet found funds for a school of his own at this higher level and if Halloran failed he had reason to hope that he might inherit both the trust fund and the governing structure. He had his own plan ready – he showed it to the governor in May, as Halloran's troubles gathered – for a 'General Boarding School' for boys aged up to 16 or 17. Besides literacy, numeracy, history and geography, work was to include chemistry, mineralogy, botany and zoology, 'with specimens, as far as they can be obtained' and room for scientific experiment. There were also to be lessons on the wherewithal of bodily health, human and livestock, plus bookkeeping, surveying, astronomy and navigation. Scott did not want to train experts. As William Godwin had advised years before, he wanted to set minds free, by enabling them to engage with the world around them. Most boys, starting at seven, might leave at 12. A few of the cleverest might spend a year or two at the end preparing for specialist training in the learned professions.[7]

Scott must have hoped for help from John Macarthur, but John and his family now stepped back from the whole grammar school project. That left the leadership of the board to the two judges, Forbes and Stephen, Scott's mortal enemies, as he believed. Towards the end of the year Halloran was dismissed and the school closed, but while there were definite plans for reopening – it rose again as Sydney College – interest in Scott's radical vision was apparently nil.[8]

Something in this experience seems to have affected Scott's friendship with John Macarthur, though not with the rest of the family, and at the end of the year he moved from Elizabeth Farm to Sydney. In various ways his original plans were falling apart.

The archdeacon's dispute with the two judges had come to a head very lately. Scott's responsibilities included the two orphan schools, for boys and for girls, and late in 1825, on visiting the girls' school at Parramatta, he had found the children badly neglected. He demanded an explanation from the master but the master went to his own lawyer, William Wentworth. Wentworth advised him to fight, on the grounds that the archdeacon was pretending to an authority he did not possess. Forbes and Stephen presided together at the trial and they agreed with Wentworth. By some government oversight Hobbes Scott had no documented commission as 'King's Visitor' of New South Wales schools. As a result a large part of his authority was cast into doubt, at least until the right piece of paper could reach him.[9]

Scott's replica of Hofwyl, managed by James Busby, was also struggling. Busby's salary was fixed as a certain proportion of the school's proceeds, but the ratio was unrealistically high and in August 1826 steps were taken to cut back the whole experiment. Busby left and momentum failed.[10] This and his hopes for the grammar school were the two most obviously Pestalozzian parts of Scott's great plan. Both had now failed.

New South Wales was not Switzerland or the Ionian islands. Far away from the intellectual life of Europe, largely out of reach of well-informed public opinion, it was not a place for challenging experiments. The British government already baulked at the vast cost of convict transportation. In this remote and disreputable place, anything above and beyond that effort, any project needing high intelligence, consistent vision, good staff and a steady income, was impossible to sustain. Add to those problems the personal weaknesses of the archdeacon, already mentioned, and it could be said that his plans were bound to fail.

SAXE BANNISTER HAD HIS OWN BATTLES IN BRINGING radical enlightenment to New South Wales. Overshadowing everything for him was the question of invasion and the rule he always insisted on – 'we must be just at every step'. He knew that violence could not be avoided, but he was also sure that both invaders and invaded were rational beings, equally capable of understanding justice and sharing in the future of civilisation –

he meant European civilisation – in New South Wales. He was especially proud of the fact that during his time in this country, 'injured black people', even on the frontier, were heard to say that they would go for justice to the attorney-general.[11] That proved to him what might be done eventually overall.

Saxe Bannister did not think of the British occupation of New South Wales as theft. It did not occur to him that the original injury must bleed into every future act of attempted justice. In Bannister's mind the British had benefited mightily from Roman occupation, and the British themselves were now taking gifts of the same sort to the ends of the earth. That long-term vision gave another perspective altogether to notions of justice. Citizenship must be there for all, as with the Roman Empire – at least in theory. Using principles of perfect equity, government must 'take the lead', he said, and it must do so 'in a decisive manner and on a large scale, both in the coercion and in the improvement of the aborigines'.[12]

In case of lawlessness on the frontier the only answer was martial law, so as to guarantee equal control and protection to both sides, Black and White. In 1824 he had persuaded Governor Brisbane to use martial law near Bathurst, west of the mountains, together with a public declaration that bloodshed must be a last resort.

I will spell out again Saxe Bannister's line of argument. To his mind, invasion was ongoing and inevitable. It could not be stopped and it was, for him, clearly part of God's providential design. The invaders were therefore responsible to God for ensuring that the occupation of New South Wales was carried through for the ultimate benefit of humankind – 'benefit' as defined by enlightened Europeans. Also, all parties, invaders and invaded, must share equally in a single framework of law, order and beneficial government. The ongoing trouble around Bathurst was condemned by the Sydney press as 'an exterminating war', and so it was for some of the settlers.[13] Martial law, on the other hand, was designed to set a limit to damage on both sides. For Bannister at least, it also sent a powerful message, which the Indigenous people must, he thought, understand. Martial law was designed to show that the contending parties, invaders and invaded, could claim strictly equal rights under government. Gratuitous violence, by anyone, was therefore a criminal offence.

Governor Brisbane had followed his lead. However, late in 1825 Brisbane had been succeeded by Ralph Darling. In June 1826, when violence broke out in the Hunter Valley, to the north, Bannister urged the same on Darling, but Darling could not believe that legal process was justified, as he said, in putting down 'a few naked Savages'.[14]

Bannister was also busy at that point with a case of murder on the same frontier. Four men, all convicts, were charged with the premeditated killing of eight-year-old Tommy, of the Worimi people near Port Stephens, further to the north. It was 'as foul a murder,' Bannister said, 'as is possible to be conceived.' They were convicted and sentenced to death, but as Bannister bitterly noted, they were not hanged, at least for this crime.[15] The message this sent, to both invaders and invaded, was stark. It would have been very different had a Black man murdered a White.

Troubled with Bannister's punctiliousness, Darling wrote damning reports to London. 'His eccentricities would amuse,' he said, 'were it not for the impertinent style of his observations.' Worse, he said, Bannister cluttered up his own time and everyone else's with irrelevant 'projects and suggestions'. Of course he did. Justice at every step called for endless labour, patience and exactitude. It was costly and Bannister paid his own office expenses, so that he struggled to manage on his allotted salary. John Macarthur lent him money, with slender hope of getting it back, but Bannister also wrote home to ask for an increase in pay.[16]

He told the Colonial Office that he could not continue on his current pay. Primed by Darling's advice, the minister took him at his word. Without warning, he was removed. Bannister prepared to leave immediately. However, in the days before his departure the editor of the *Sydney Gazette* published a farewell, friendly enough but suggesting that the late attorney-general had been too much influenced by 'the faction'. For Bannister this was libel. He sued and in a long address to the Supreme Court told the whole story of his work in New South Wales. He had been scrupulously impartial, he said, from beginning to end. He was frank about his friends at Elizabeth Farm, but the court must understand that among men of high principle, friendship and subserviency were entirely different things.[17]

Saxe Bannister's transparent honesty, his mix of boldness and innocence, struck a chord at Elizabeth Farm, despite what James Macarthur called his 'flighty habits'. Elizabeth mourned his loss. '[H]e had a thousand amiable qualities,' she said, 'which insensibly wound round the heart.' James went to Sydney for the court hearing and, sitting through Bannister's five-hour speech, he was transfixed. It was 'luminous and clear', he said, and delivered 'with a force of eloquence that astonished even those who knew him best'. The jury, all the same, took five minutes to decide against him.[18]

From the court Bannister went straight to Elizabeth Farm, partly dismantled as it was for rebuilding. There he sat in long conversation at John Macarthur's bedside and there he spent his last night before boarding ship in Sydney Cove.[19]

On the same evening, in another room and unusually impassioned, James wrote to his brother John in England, asking him to do all he could to rescue Bannister's reputation. It was for their parents' sake especially. 'My father, all of us rather, beg of you to spare no means in your power.' Bannister, whenever he reached England, with his insight and judgment, 'can be of great assistance on N.S. Wales affairs'. The older John himself wrote too.[20]

For Elizabeth and John the loss of Saxe Bannister was deeply upsetting. It was 'so unexpected', Elizabeth said, 'and so sudden that I think of it as of a dream'. So too, like a dream, ended Bannister's 'general plan' for the Indigenous peoples in the age of invasion. Richard Sadleir gave his report of his travels beyond the frontier to Hobbes Scott, but his recommendations, probably a version of Bannister's plan, were too expensive altogether, when Scott was already struggling to fund his own reforms, and as a result nothing was done.[21]

Even in the short term, troubles multiplied in the Hunter Valley. On an officer's orders Jackey Jackey, a Wonnarua man, was murdered while in custody, exactly the type of crime that martial law might have prevented. 'Many things have happened,' Elizabeth told Edward, 'which Mr Bannister predicted … the Governor seems to me to be in difficulties very often.'[22]

Elizabeth was not hopeful about Hobbes Scott either. He was 'very low and dispirited', and apparently ready to give up. 'I endeavour to soothe his irritated feelings yet I am very sensible that he has been very ill used.' Scott was too honest, James added, and at the same time 'too simple and free, both in mind and conduct', to make his way in New South Wales. Having moved into the Bannisters' old house, the archdeacon hung on for another year before sending in his resignation. In one sense he had achieved a good deal. Besides reforming and expanding the orphan schools, he was well on his way to doubling the number of parish schools and of their enrolled pupils, while cutting overall expenses. Still he felt he had failed. 'I could have wished to have done some good here,' he told an English friend, 'but it is out of my power.' After all, what use were good enrolments when, thanks to press ridicule and consequent doubts among parents, such a small share of listed children turned up each morning?[23]

Even at the government level, Scott said, 'I have every impediment thrown in my way.' He had made no progress with the Madras method, with children teaching each other, so that all the old petty oppressions of school-learning lived on. He had therefore failed in his great aim, the creation of 'a better sort of school than the common primary parochial schools'. '[F]raud, injustice, and cruelty', he said, bedevilled New South Wales from top to bottom, and it was all too much for him.[24] He waited long enough for his successor to arrive and then, in October 1829, he too left.

PART 8

42
JOHN'S MISTED HORIZON

'I believe that at my season of life,' said Elizabeth, in April 1831, 'it is too late, to form new friendships.' She was 64. Having survived to that age, in her day, a woman might expect to live for another 12 years or so on average, a man rather less.[1] Within the human life span, among people of British descent, the mid-sixties in 1831 were like the mid-seventies two centuries later. Men and women of that age were more likely to live on the resources of the past — old friends, old ideas, capital gathered in more energetic days — than to look for anything or anyone new.

Pause here and go back to 1814. In that year, in London, James Macarthur, third son of Elizabeth and John, still a boy, had spent six months in the office of Charles Coles, East and West India merchant, in Great Tower Street, learning the intricacies of the import business. Charles Coles was 'a man of the first consequence' in the city, as James's father had said at the time, and it was apparently Coles who introduced James to the wealthy banker, philanthropist and MP John Smith.[2] If he was to be a man of business, James would need to know such people.

At that time John Smith was treasurer of Sir John Sinclair's Board of Agriculture. Sinclair, of course, had known about John Macarthur and New South Wales since the 1790s, which might be why, in 1814, Smith took a particular interest in James. The connection was one of mutual advantage, worth noticing in 1814 and, as it turned out, worth reviving later on. In 1817 James had gone back to New South Wales with his father and brother William, and a year later their elder brother John, writing home from London, told of meeting 'James's friend Mr Smith'. Smith, said young John, spoke to him about NSW wool. He would like to see more of it, Smith said, in the British market.[3]

When young John Macarthur thus met John Smith, 'James's friend', the wool market was booming and the struggle to sell in it, and to be ranked among quality suppliers, was severe. New suppliers were emerging all the time. The quantity of fine wool coming into Britain from the continent of Europe, for instance, especially from France and Hungary, had multiplied several times over. The leading breeder in Hungary, perhaps in Europe, was Prince Paul Esterházy, who from 1815 was also ambassador to Britain. Esterházy owned 300 000 sheep, most of them Merino or Merino-cross.[4] It was against such individuals, working on a new scale altogether, that the Macarthurs and New South Wales now had to compete.

Young John Macarthur had been elected to the Society for the Arts in 1816, not long after moving from Cambridge to London to begin his career in the law. John Smith was already a member and it might have been Smith who now persuaded the society to offer several medals for fine wool from New South Wales. The purpose was added publicity and increased sales. The Macarthurs' wool, and cloth made from it, won all of the medals when they were first awarded in 1822.[5]

These awards were noticed in British newspapers and, following as they did the second edition of Wentworth's book, they drew attention to New South Wales, as intended. For the next 20 years a good deal of British capital was sent in that direction. A continuous stream of emigrants arrived with money to invest, and some of them were keen to take advantage of old connections with Elizabeth and John at Elizabeth Farm. From the English West Country, John Boughton and Edward Cory – both newly

JOHN'S MISTED HORIZON

married and with family ties to the Kingdon and Veale network – called, seeking advice and encouragement. Both found land in the Hunter Valley and, as a gift from Elizabeth, Edward Cory's wife Frances took with her up-country 'a beautiful breed of fowls'.[6]

New arrivals wanting to connect up with John, usually Scots, were more numerous. They were also more demanding. Thomas Potter Macqueen was English-born but his family was from the Isle of Skye and he and his father were members of Hinton McArthur's Highland Society. Though still a young man, Macqueen had money and expansive ideas. He was already in parliament and he unsuccessfully angled to succeed Lachlan Macquarie as governor. He then chartered the *Hugh Crawford* as a shared investment with John Campbell of Bungarribee, and secured a grant of 20 000 acres (over 8000 hectares) in the Hunter Valley. He did not emigrate himself, yet, but he sent out an agent, 'a Highlander of the best repute', together with Highland shepherds and sheepdogs, artisans, first-class livestock and all necessary equipment, trusting that John Macarthur would keep an eye on it all.[7]

Time and useful friends had made John Macarthur into a deeply trusted resource, for funding as well as advice. John Campbell borrowed over £1000. Macqueen took £2000 in return for a mortgage on his new property. James Glennie, another emigrant of Scottish background, came recommended by Sir Thomas Farquhar, Robert Farquhar's brother and senior partner in Herries Farquhar, the family bank in London's West End, and Sir Thomas used John Macarthur's account with the bank to credit Glennie with £500 for use in New South Wales. At the same time he asked John to show the young man 'any attention in your power'.[8]

EVEN AT THIS POINT, AS A PLACE TO INVEST BRITISH money, New South Wales seemed remote, raw and a little risky.

Emigrating – going with the money – was one solution. Investment through chartered joint-stock companies based in London and, like Macqueen, using local agents was another. The planning of two companies, one each for New South Wales and Van Diemen's Land, started as soon as Commissioner Bigge had made his reports, and the NSW initiative was largely due to young John Macarthur. Afraid that Van Diemen's Land might draw money away from New South Wales, young John, with John Smith and others, moved quickly to get the New South Wales company started first. They secured government backing in April 1824, with a plan to gather funds from some of London's richest individuals and to run 20 000 sheep on a freehold grant of a million acres – double the Macarthurs' current stock and four times their acreage.[9] The Australian Agricultural Company was underway by the end of the year.

It was a complicated experiment. Fine wool was a highly variable product. Multiple issues in one hemisphere – soil, climate, labour and skills – had to mesh with the vicissitudes of market demand in the other. In dealing with these challenges, the founders had two models on hand and they aimed to use both at once. One was the system worked out, as they said, 'on the estates of the Esterhazy and other great [continental] families'. They would rely on a carefully organised hierarchy of skills and an intricate reporting system – on perfected paperwork. In Hungary, each of Esterházy's lambing ewes had its own small yard, every Esterházy mother and lamb were marked to record their connection, reports on printed forms were sent monthly from the various Esterházy estates to a central decision-making board, and so on.[10] Something of the same kind might ensure high efficiency and certain profits from the operation in New South Wales.

Secondly, the founders aimed to duplicate the achievement of Elizabeth and John. An agent or full-time manager was to be sent from England but there were also to be a good number of shareholders on the spot, together with a supervisory committee made up of Macarthur family members and a few trusted friends. In the end the committee had three effective members – James Macarthur, his brother-in-law James Bowman and his cousin Hannibal. The company directors in London did not want to burden John Macarthur with such work, but they agreed that everything the company aimed to do, even beyond growing fine wool, must benefit from John's 'general knowledge and long experience'.[11]

This last was at the suggestion of Robert Farquhar, now a baronet and one of the company's directors, who was convinced, he said, by 30 years' acquaintance, of John Macarthur's 'enlightened views, talents, and indefatigable perseverance'. No-one dissented. As young John told his mother, his father was imagined by its founders as the company's 'main spring'.[12] At least in theory, they hoped to interweave Macarthur aptitude with Esterházy magnificence.

The company's agent, Robert Dawson, arrived in November 1825 and, on the advice of the surveyor-general, John Oxley, he chose land at Port Stephens, north of the Hunter. There he settled with the men, women and children, livestock and equipment he had brought with him. He also took on more men and bought more stock, so that his establishment grew rapidly larger and more elaborate. Within two years Dawson was managing about 600 employees. Half were convicts, five or six times the number at Camden Park.[13]

For the Macarthurs in New South Wales the company was a mixed blessing. Local public opinion saw it as a perfect example of monopoly and privilege, typical of 'the faction', so that it sharpened enmity. Committee work was also time-consuming and invidious, and local flock-owners resented competition from the company in the purchase of Macarthur sheep, though every effort was made to prevent it. As a further complication, the Macarthurs already had a valuable market monopoly in the supply of good rams, and the company promised to be a damaging competitor.[14] They could see only two real advantages. This great initiative must help the British reputation of NSW wool. Also, Sir Robert Farquhar's tribute, publicly endorsed, was the most flattering John Macarthur had ever received.

Nevertheless, news of the company had taken John by surprise. Only when Dawson began making headway at Port Stephens did he start to imagine how he might live up to the compliment paid him. Even then, he almost seemed out of his depth. He now gathered ideas from various sources, old and new, but with little of the ingenuity and none of the interconnected vision of earlier days. He was showing his age.

Thomas Potter Macqueen had written to him lately about getting in alpacas from South America, as beasts of burden. John thought of that now for the company. John Campbell had started a dairy at Bungarribee. John Macarthur played with that idea too, aiming to use convict women just arrived from rural Ireland.[15] Robert Farquhar himself had once talked about skilled Chinese emigration to British colonies, including Australia. It ought to be encouraged, Farquhar had said, as long as it could be done with perfect justice to all concerned. Again, John Macarthur might have remembered that when he talked of travelling abroad to find labourers, Chinese included, for Port Stephens.[16]

These were his thoughts in 1826. Nothing came of any of them. A bitter winter, when his gout returned with a vengeance, made him think again about travelling anywhere. He was 60 and unwell, and no-one encouraged him to go. '[W]e none of us liked the thought,' Elizabeth said, 'and were exceedingly pleased when he abandoned the idea.'[17]

During 1827 and into 1828 he took on a different challenge but it is hard to know much about it. In April 1828 he appeared in Sydney among the onlookers at a military parade to mark the King's birthday and later in the day at a Government House ball, and both times he had with him several Indigenous men. A newspaper report called them his 'body-guard', apparently because they wore a 'uniform' – scarlet shirts, blue trousers and yellow neckerchiefs – and carried spears.[18] Who they were, where they came from, and why they had attached themselves to him, it is impossible to say, but there is more on this question a little later on.

The Australian Agricultural Company had become a complicated burden. In selling stock to Robert Dawson, John Macarthur now kept a careful distance, concerned by stories that his family were taking dishonest advantage of the company. According to Dawson, John began deliberately making sales difficult. He 'would sooner drown his sheep', Dawson said, than let tales of dishonesty affect his reputation in London. 'He is a very peculiar man.'[19]

James Macarthur was keen to disentangle family and company altogether. That meant a trip to England – he had several things to do there – so as to talk with the directors. He and the other committeemen were also worried about Dawson's management skills and even his honesty. During the summer of 1827–28, James spent a month at Port Stephens making a thorough inspection. He found late rising, wasted resources and poor discipline. Dawson, so promising to start with, seemed to lack the Macarthurs' key ingredient for success – skill in creating shared purpose. Under the right kind of authority even convicts should show a 'cheerful alacrity' in doing their best.[20] James could see none of that at Port Stephens under Dawson. The committee decided on Dawson's immediate dismissal and in April James took ship for London.

JOHN MACARTHUR NOW COMMITTED HIMSELF TO THE last great venture of his life, as Robert Dawson's successor at Port Stephens until the directors could decide what to do next. His first step was to call in all useful expertise. He asked the government botanist, Charles Fraser, to report on the local soil, he appointed a medical man, Alexander Nisbet, to oversee public health, and he converted one of the buildings to a hospital. He asked Laurence Halloran to come, presumably as chaplain and to teach the children, but Hobbes Scott, contemptuous of Halloran, blocked that. John Macarthur also found his own line of contact with the Indigenous people. Dawson had banished a young man the invaders called Wallace, the 'most influential native over a wide district', so John was told. John called him back, so that he might work with him as far as possible.[21]

He made a list of possible produce for sale in Sydney. Dawson had already started a dairy and planted some cotton. John began making up cargoes of firewood and, this being cedar country, he hoped to add timber for building. Livestock might be driven to Sydney for butchering, fish might be caught and salted, kitchen vegetables might be grown on a commercial scale and, if the soil was right, vine cuttings might be brought from Camden for a vineyard. Hay-making was another possibility. As for grain, nothing had yet been built for its storage and he suggested sealed underground silos, 'subterraneous granaries on an economical principle', where surplus from good seasons could be kept for bad.[22]

He thought again about his conversations with Saxe Bannister. Robert Dawson had shown an active interest in the Indigenous people, keen, as he said, to show them 'all the kindness in my power' so as to compensate somehow 'for our interference with their country'. Again, Dawson's methods jarred with the Macarthurs'. According to James, Dawson allowed too much familiarity between Black and White. A certain distance was needed, a certain mutual respect, so that each could go about their lives in their own way and without risk. John Macarthur made a particular effort to stop the convict men visiting the Worimi women at their camp, a 'disgraceful and pernicious intercourse', he said. The resulting disease, which had come originally with the invaders, not only disabled the men. It had already, he said, 'almost entirely put a stop to the further increase of the native population'.[23]

So far, these changes matched the Macarthurs' old ways. However, Saxe Bannister had taken John's thoughts in a new direction. Bannister had hoped to make the Indigenous peoples understand some of the core principles of European civilisation. Ill-disciplined mingling must be dangerous, but the two sides, according to Bannister, ought to be brought together in a conversation of trust, so as to build up a shared sense of right and wrong. It must depend on European initiative but, as Bannister had said of the Mohawk in Upper Canada, once trust was established invaded peoples 'will approve of what is right'.[24]

Moved, apparently, by Bannister's optimism John Macarthur persuaded some of the Worimi to dress 'comfortably and decently', much as he had done with his King's birthday 'body-guard' the year before. According to the *Sydney Gazette* – not a wholly reliable source – about 60 Worimi, in European dress, came to prayers each Sunday while John was in charge at Port Stephens, 'in failure of which they are mulcted of their flour for the week ensuing'. He also thought of trying the Blacktown possum fur experiment, but on a larger scale. Worimi might bring in fur for weaving, and be paid for it with tobacco, tea, sugar and clothes.[25] Finally, he planned a detailed report on the local population for Hobbes Scott. Richard Sadleir had not visited Port Stephens. John seems to have aimed to fill the gap.[26] So he fumbled with the little he understood of Saxe Bannister's vision.

AFTER ONLY FOUR MONTHS AT PORT STEPHENS, JOHN Macarthur collapsed and came home. He then called a meeting of the company's local shareholders and set out his conclusions. James had heaped blame on Dawson. John had once done much the same but now he found excuses for the agent. Instead, he blamed the directors in London. They had been wrong, he said, to send so many people and livestock all at once, even 'before the grant had been selected and their plans maturely considered'. Dawson had certainly made things worse by adding more of both on the spot, 'without being able to provide for the care of the stock or to regulate the employment of the servants in a useful manner'. However, on the whole he had done his best.[27]

This was partly self-vindication because John Macarthur himself had failed. And yet, addressing the shareholders, he also took on himself part of the larger blame, admitting, apparently for the first time, to his own serious error of judgment. The sheer magnificence of the original plan had seemed to guarantee success and he had shared, he said, in 'the general delusion'. He had forgotten the rule he had always followed – success in setting out depends on skill not numbers, on building slowly, on patience and forethought. At Port Stephens everything had been superabundant from the start and he had been led astray with everyone else. He should have known better.[28]

John Macarthur thought that the company could not survive, but it did. The directors dissolved the local committee and appointed a commissioner, with total authority in New South Wales. This was the arctic explorer Sir Edward Parry, son of Caleb Parry, the Merino wool expert mentioned earlier. Young John was already busied with other work. By change of government he had lost his connection with the Colonial Office but he had a friend in the new Lord Chancellor, Lord Lyndhurst, who appointed him a commissioner of bankrupts.[29] That at last gave him a good income, with hopes of better to come.

43
A TYPE OF DIVORCE

At Camden, a dozen years after planting, William Macarthur's garden had taken deep root and flourished. Elizabeth was there without John in spring 1830 and she sent her impressions to her daughter Elizabeth at home at Parramatta. The two women were very close.

> [T]here is a very fine iris, a dark blue or purple, much like the one just gone out of bloom [at Elizabeth Farm], but larger. The hydrangeas are exceedingly large, some lilac, some blue and some pink of various tints. I had no idea of their attaining such a size, but the pride of the garden just now is the magnolia. It has been in flower a week or ten days, the bud is about the size of an ostrich egg, pure white when it expands. I know not what to compare it to, the petals are thick and resemble white kid leather. The scent is a combination of sweetness and [of] fragrances something like essence of lemon, orange flower and bergamotte … William gathered a branch with a flower bud last week. It kept alive several days and perfumed the cottage.

It must have been after this that she and her daughter planted a magnolia grandiflora of their own at Elizabeth Farm. At springtime 11 years later she was to be cheered by a branch of its blooms in just the same way – 'very beautiful', she said – except that this time it was brought to her by grandchildren.[1]

Elizabeth was startled by the abundance of William's garden. There was a term she used, common in her own day – the novelist Charles Dickens used it – but obsolete by the 20th century. People and things, she said, 'grow out of my knowledge'. An arbutus or strawberry tree that Edward had given as a sapling to the botanical gardens in Sydney had 'grown out of my knowledge' when she saw it next. James and William, in England as boys, had 'grown quite out of my knowledge', coming back to her at last as young men.[2]

By 1830, with advancing years, she was herself transformed. She needed a new self-knowledge. Joking with her children, she started to call herself an old woman. So she could write to her sons in England 'a proper old woman's gossiping letter'. Indulging herself, she risked boring those she loved by rambling on 'with a repetition of uninteresting matter'. '[W]ill you not be tired of my scribbling?' There is no sign that idleness upset her, although it was not long since she had said that happiness consisted in having something useful to do – in 'health [and] industry with the blessing of God'.[3]

New South Wales, once her familiar home, had lately grown out of her knowledge too – 'such an altered place, full of strange faces'. The number of ships coming and going, and the traffic on the roads were extraordinary. At the beginning of the 1820s she had 'little thought', she said, that 'so many things predicted would so soon come to pass', but here they were, a mass of unfamiliarity pressing about her. 'It is so much changed, and so rapidly changing that I hardly feel myself at home in it. It is literally by keeping at home that I do feel at ease.'[4]

Even at home sometimes it might be hard to be at ease. Elizabeth's peace of mind depended on John's mood and on his health, physical and mental, which was now getting progressively worse. Almost as soon as he had returned from England in 1817, his bouts of misery had returned. Periods of 'dreadful gloom' had come and gone, interspersed with the agonies of gout, so that weeks had passed 'without one cheerful moment'. His handwriting from those years shows his ups and downs, sometimes trembling with pain, sometimes firm. His mood varied to match, arrogant bitterness alternating with expansive hope.[5]

Then, for a while, everything had improved. 'Your father,' Elizabeth reported to young John in spring 1824, 'has had better health and for a longer time together than I have known him to enjoy for a very long time.'[6] However, during autumn 1826, the crisis time already mentioned, there was a sudden reversal.

In these latter years, in her efforts to understand what was happening to him, Elizabeth spoke of 'the mind preying upon the body, and disturbing its proper functions'. To begin with, in 1826 he had 'given way', she said, 'to the most gloomy apprehensions', apparently provoked by drought in New South Wales and the poor British market for wool. And yet it was strangely sudden. He had started the year 'in excellent health and in exceeding good spirits'. Then just the opposite. She felt for him because she knew that he hid his worst pain. '[H]e suffers excessively,' she said, 'and even more than we can well judge.'[7]

By April 1827 he had begun to feel better again. She was still with Mary, until the house should be completely rebuilt, so that they were still separated, but he now went briefly to Sydney to stay with her. Returning to Elizabeth Farm, as she told their sons in England, he began 'to interest himself a little in the building again'.[8] He also entered with gusto into a dispute about water management nearby on the Parramatta River. The ex-convict millwright George Howell and his son had built a wind and water mill on the riverbank, but in doing so they had offended another mill owner, the free emigrant John Raine. John gave his support to the Howells, sending his own men to help them in what became an unedifying waterside struggle, and standing by to watch.

'[T]here is that young man [George junior],' he shouted, ' ... making five hundred pounds by his mill, and there is that fellow [Raine], not worth two-pence, wanting to ruin him – but I'll make him smart.'[9]

In May 1828 he went off to Port Stephens, as acting agent for the Australian Agricultural Company, so Elizabeth said, in 'very good health and ... cheerful spirits', but then he came home at the end gloomy and debilitated. He was apparently much the same on and off for the next two years. At the end of 1830, as summer came on and with Elizabeth admiring William's garden, he was feeling better. His firm writing hand proves it, and yet it was not long before he was '*low* and complaining' again, hardly venturing beyond the house.[10]

The family began to notice a frightening cycle of ups and downs. Repeatedly, a 'lowness of spirits', as Emmeline, his youngest, said, was followed by 'fearful fits of excitement'. The treadwheel regularity of it all made it painful for all who lived with him. Understanding the pattern as they now did, '[w]e have every reason to dread the death like calm which will inevitably succeed the *phrenzy* of the present moment'.[11]

'[B]ut yet,' said her mother, 'I am convinced it is not bodily ailment.' She was sure it was 'altogether hypochondria'. Hypochondria, according to Elizabeth's medical textbook, William Buchan's *Domestic Medicine*, was a mental disorder. Its causes included mental exhaustion, owing to 'long and serious attention to abstruse subjects', and it was said to show itself in depression and delicate nerves. To Elizabeth's mind that was John's case. '[H]e suffers severe rheumatic pains,' she said, 'particularly when the weather indicates change', but the source of his troubles was surely mental – 'too much deep thinking and great solicitude as to coming events'.[12]

For hypochondria, Buchan recommended exercise, cold baths and a change of scene. Also, he said, '[c]heerfulness and serenity of mind are by all means to be cultivated.' However, John's ailments grew more and more complicated. Elizabeth began to be puzzled – exactly when it struck her first is not clear – by the way he fell into small delusions, obvious to her but, so she thought, not to him or anyone else. It was as if he saw things through 'a disturbed medium', she said – through 'mists of the mind'.[13] Details that belonged to their joint existence no longer grasped in quite the same way. What could that mean?

MEANWHILE JAMES WAS STILL IN EUROPE. TOWARDS the end of his trip he had been with Edward in Germany, where they had called on the ageing polymath Johann Wolfgang von Goethe, at Weimar. The great man received many visitors but of these two he took particular note. They told him 'a lot of interesting things', he said, especially about the Indigenous peoples of their country. According to James, Goethe seemed glad to know that even in such a faraway place 'we had read some of his works'.[14]

When James arrived home in February 1831 he brought news that his brother John, in London, was seriously unwell. He suffered from 'water on the brain', afterwards called hydrocephalus. Beginning with headaches, nausea and giddiness, in young John's case it built up at last to a paralytic seizure. He died in his flat in Piccadilly on 19 April 1831, a month short of his 38th birthday. The announcement of his death, sent by Edward, reached his family on 19 September. Mary Bowman had just given birth to her third boy and Elizabeth, James and Emmeline were with her at home at Woolloomooloo, the house once occupied by the Bannisters and then by Hobbes Scott. James sent a message straightaway to William and early next morning all except Mary converged on Elizabeth Farm. James then broke the news to his father.[15]

Knowing already about his son's dangerous illness, John had given himself over to thoughts of losing him. Now, at this sudden family gathering, he feared the worst. Steeling himself, as William said afterwards, 'he received the details with … manly fortitude, blended with tenderness for his departed son, [and] tempered with … Christian resignation.' At that moment, so William confessed, 'I truly feel no words of mine can express how much I revered him.' Tears were shed all the same, before the bereaved father found relief in theatrical declaration, a loose quotation from a story in David Hume's *History of England*. 'Well may I say with the old earl of Crawford' – John's tear-ragged voice rang out – 'I thank God I would not exchange my dead son for many a living one.'[16]

There was a copy of Hume's *History* on the shelves nearby. John might have been mulling over the passage for weeks, waiting for the tragedy he felt must come – though in the moment misremembering the name of the noble father. In that way he managed his grief. As for Elizabeth, her method was to say little or nothing until her mind was settled. She waited a week, and then, 'I think,' she said, 'I have regained sufficient composure to address you, my beloved Edward, and therefore I seize the moment, when under the influence of that belief.' Even then she said more about others than herself. Mary could not remember her brother – he had left home when she was six – and with a new baby she had 'her little cares', so that she mourned little. '[I]t is well that it should be so.' James, on the other hand, had seen him only 12 months before. '[With] impressions vivid and fresh [he] naturally suffers the most, and he is under the necessity of keeping his sorrow in check.' He had his work and the feelings of others to look to.[17]

Over the next couple of days John talked about his son and read letters of condolence, including some from England, 'occasionally giving way to a burst of tears, which he declared gave him great relief'. A few days of silent and impenetrable mourning followed and Elizabeth stayed on until, as she thought, 'his mind [began] to right itself.' She then went back to Sydney to help Mary, weeping to herself, even six months later, but making little show of it.[18]

Young Elizabeth took over the care of her father when her mother left, although she too suffered. She and young John had always been close and the letters between them over the years – as their mother said, 'their sweet intercourse by sea and land' – had tightened the bond.[19] Now, staying with her father, she sent regular reports to Sydney. After a fortnight of mourning, '[h]e was shaved,' she said, 'dressed and sat up an hour yesterday, but did not leave his bed-room.' There had been a lengthy piece about his son in the *Sydney Herald*. 'He desired to see it and sitting up [in bed] read it himself, not without shedding tears but yet in such a frame of mind as you would most desire him to be.'[20]

For three or four months John Macarthur seems to have gone on much the same. Then, in January–February 1832, to his own surprise, he found himself much better, and during March, apparently improving all the time, he spent a week or two at Camden, 'in very good health, and in full activity'.[21] Then, back at Elizabeth Farm he threw himself into building again.

He was soon frantically active. On 26 March he sent Edward, now his only son in England, a sketch of the day's work. He had left his bed at four, he said, 'after a sound and refreshing sleep of four hours', and spent an hour or two in the darkness thinking over 'important affairs both public and private'. As day broke and the builders arrived, 'I sallied forth on foot to inspect the work of the preceding day and to give orders for the execution of other improvements.' All day he hurried about. The weather was only moderately warm, and yet '[f]our times,' he said, 'I was under the necessity of changing all my clothes, as they were nearly dripping wet.'[22]

He felt superhuman, 'enabled to attend to every minutia of our extended interests and to inspect the progress of all ordinary business', and on top of that 'to devote a large portion of my time to many great improvements', some already underway, others only planned. Elizabeth, writing herself to Edward, told a different story. There were endless plans, siting and re-siting, foundations dug and filled in, and still no building. The wet shirts were easily explained. '*[S]team engine power*', as she called it, 'is applied to the veriest trifle when in this excited state of mind.'[23]

In short, Elizabeth and John did not mourn their son together. Would they have done so, say, ten years earlier? It is impossible to say. Now, John busied himself, so he said, as a way of holding off 'a bitterness of grief which no language can describe' – all the more intense 'because I feel it necessary to conceal from your dear mother what I feel.' Elizabeth, however, knew that 'he grieved at heart *deeply*'. He showed it by endless talking about his dead son, '*continually* reading all the letters', and indulging his own feelings, she said, 'at the expence of ours'.[24]

JOHN MACARTHUR HAD RETREATED INTO HIS OWN world of super-heightened feeling. Self was disconnected and the feelings of others became a blank. He had all the symptoms of bipolar affective disorder, although that was not the name used at the time. Current medical theory spoke of this strange disease as a nervous disorder. Nerves were understood to be susceptible to 'irritability', something John himself had come to understand during his time in London. He had told Elizabeth then that he suffered from 'irritation of the nerves' and that the pain could be 'extraordinary' – 'beyond belief', he said. In 1815 he had gone to France and Switzerland partly because he had been informed that 'change of air, amusement and moderate exercise [were] … the best remedies for all disorders of the nerves'. So, briefly at least, they had proved to be.[25]

Now his self-diagnosis was very different. Now he talked of being the prey of 'conspirators' trying to destroy him. His daughters, he said, had robbed him. James and William had fled to some place in the mountains 'from which it would be necessary to dislodge them by force of arms'. Some of his enemies were even hidden in the house, and he got together an armoury of swords and pistols for the inevitable attack. '[O]f *me*', said Elizabeth, 'he has made the most fearful accusations', including even that she been unfaithful to him.[26]

She stopped talking about hypochondria. 'I cannot but consider,' she said early in May 1832, 'that he labours under a partial derangement of mind', and she admitted that they had all been afraid for some time 'that sooner or later, that mighty mind would break down, and give way'. The 39th Regiment had been stationed in New South Wales since 1826. Several of its officers knew the family well, and John trusted them. At the end of June the two senior officers, Patrick Lindesay and Donald McPherson, went to Elizabeth Farm, talked with the invalid and made separate reports. James and William then applied to the Supreme Court for a writ 'de lunatico inquirendo', or in other words a declaration that their father was insane in law. Commissioners of inquiry were appointed. They met in Parramatta on 3 August, and following their report James and William were empowered to manage their father and all his affairs.[27]

The family's local enemies were delighted. 'We never held the Hon. John's Attics to be in the most tenantable sort of order,' said the *Australian*, still the newspaper associated with William Wentworth. 'He is now mad in law – tho' not more crackbrained probably now than he was thought to be years ago.'[28]

The family read what they could about 'mental aberration' so as to have some understanding of what had happened to them all, and James took on the thankless task of looking after the invalid. His father counted him among the conspirators and he kept a certain distance, spending each night in the cottage across the creek. By mid-September he had been 'received ... again into favour [as Elizabeth put it] and at his [John's] request eats with him and sleeps at the house', but for the next seven months this kindness came and went. 'James devotes himself entirely to him,' Elizabeth told Edward, 'seldom leaving him an hour.' '[P]oor fellow ... he frets under the vehemence of your poor fathers expressions of wrath'; 'his feelings and affections [are] wrought upon to an excess.'²⁹

Stand now, in our own bright day, in that little corner room, John's dressing-room set up as a bedroom, and feel the pain of that time and place. Where was Coriolanus now? The grammar of sound and silence, as I call it, that had filled the house for so long, the happy productivity, the measured curiosity, the French declamations of Gabriel Louis, and so on and so on, were pushed aside, by savage delusions and bruised affection, over and over, father and son.

Change of scene was a general panacea for disordered nerves. Medical men urged John's move to Camden, where there were fewer difficult distractions and a number of positive things to interest him. A fine family home was at last being built there under William's supervision and the work was well advanced. However, John insisted on staying where he was, and with new enthusiasm took to the streets of Parramatta asking any officers he met home to dinner. James and William decided on forced removal and late in April, struggling and shouting, John was driven away.³⁰

He did seem to improve at Camden, living with his sons in the cottage homestead. He spoke rationally with visitors and he watched the building of the new house. He was pleased with the decision that a few rooms should be hurried so that he could take up residence early, and he asked the architect, John Verge, to put a bath in one of them.³¹ He might have used that even without moving in.

Bathing was self-medication. Over the years John Macarthur had tried a range of types of bathing, full or partial immersion, saltwater, mineral or plain, cold or warm, besides recommending it to his sons. When you bathed the shock to the skin was like a purgative. It must do good. The English philosopher David Hartley, very widely read, had thought so. 'When a Person goes into cold Water leisurely,' said Hartley, 'he is apt to sob, and to respire, in a convulsive manner, for a short time.' So the effect was usefully concentrated rather than dispersed and weakened. However, William Buchan, in his *Domestic Medicine*, the Macarthurs' family guide, warned against too sudden immersion in cold. Start with warm, Buchan said, and add cold slowly, 'by the most pleasing and gentle degrees'.[32] How gentle? Within such narrow latitudes did John Macarthur make his judgments now.

Despite the seeming improvement, John's shift to an even smaller and more perfectly separate world was for Elizabeth a sad and baffling blow. Her mind seemed paralysed. '[O]ne *great and overpowering* cause seems to enervate my faculties,' she said. 'I try to resist the influence but there are times when I can not rouse myself.' '[H]ow earnestly, how anxiously, I await the intelligence of every day.' She stopped going out. '[T]he apprehension of coming in contact with strangers I have not been able to combat.'[33]

She even found it hard to chat, as usual, with her surviving son in England – 'my dear Edward, you will not accuse me of forgetting to write' – and when she did force herself to make that effort, she skirted the great cause of misery, though it was in her mind all the time. '[T]o dwell on this harrassing subject will avail nothing but tend to distress you my dear Edward, and render me unfit to continue my letter.'[34]

Most painful of all was the bleak silence that now fell between husband and wife. 'I have had *no* immediate communication [from him],' she said. She asked people who saw him whether he ever mentioned her. After all, 20 years ago, in letter after letter from London, he had told her that she filled his heart and thoughts. She still had the diamond he had bought her in Paris. Now, nothing.

'[N]or can I learn that he has made but one enquiry about me.' That one was a passing question he had put to a visitor, the brother of a close friend, 'whether he had seen me'.[35] It was very hard.

44

THE BREACH MADE BY WIDOWHOOD

On 12 March 1834 Elizabeth was forced to report, in one of her letters to Edward, that while his father's physical health was still good, 'his mental aberration has again manifested itself, to the great grief of us all.' At Camden, James and William had to make new arrangements. John had to be more carefully watched.[1]

At Parramatta he had briefly had a paid companion, a newly arrived medical doctor. Now another man was brought in, William Wetherman, lately a clerk with the Australian Agricultural Company. However, Wetherman died of a stroke within a fortnight of reaching Camden. Another medical man was found to take his place but before he could arrive the final crisis came for the patient himself.[2]

John Macarthur died in the homestead cottage on Thursday, 10 April 1834, aged 67. His physical health had still seemed good and the end, when it came, was unexpected. Only William was on hand. James was at Elizabeth Farm and their mother was in Sydney, where Mary had lately given birth for the fourth time. William sent the news of their father's death to Parramatta, and from there James went straightaway to be with his brother while his sister Elizabeth, accompanied by their cousin Hannibal Macarthur, from across the river, took the news to Sydney.[3]

Burials among people of rank were not usually women's affairs because it was not thought decent for women to share in public expressions of feeling. For John Macarthur's burial, on Saturday the 12th, the men of the family – James, William, Hannibal and Hannibal's eldest son, another James, aged 20 – gathered at a spot John himself had chosen, on a hillside a little way from the house. Samuel Marsden, now an old man himself, took the service.[4]

Afterwards, James went to his mother in Sydney. William followed a week later and all three then returned to Elizabeth Farm, so that briefly the whole family, except for the Bowmans in Sydney and Edward in England, were there together. Elizabeth longed, as she said, to 'mingle her tears' with them all, Edward included. She seems to have missed her eldest son now more than ever, 'and yet,' she said, 'why should I have desired this. We ought not to expect our vain wishes to be accomplished.' Her husband was dead, 'the immortal spirit is, I humbly hope and trust, in a state of blessedness. Under this impression, my dearest Edward, I am resigned, and can look around me for sources of consolation.'[5]

She longed to be told that before he died John had been at peace with them all, but even William could not tell her that. And yet, '[t]hat he was restored to reason for a few minutes I have no doubt.' Again, there was no evidence for it but to Elizabeth's mind the goodness of God made it certain. '[M]ore was not granted.'[6]

Six months later she had not found the right time to go to Camden herself. 'I want to be quiet and alone with my family when I make this first visit, which must excite feelings I would *not forego,* but of too solemn a nature for publicity.' Finally, in January 1835, she went, accompanied by young Elizabeth, her best comforter. She wept and prayed at the grave, as she told Edward, and 'you may be sure … I thought of and prayed for you also my dear son'.[7]

THE BREACH MADE BY WIDOWHOOD

SO THEY ENTERED A NEW STAGE OF FAMILY LIFE. EVEN before her father's death, young Elizabeth had been doing a good deal at Elizabeth Farm. She and her mother were so much in step that it might have been hard to say whose word was final, but from day to day the house servants were Miss Macarthur's to manage and even beyond the house and garden it seems to have been understood that she was in charge. There survives at least one reference, in a Parramatta police report, to the farmland as 'Miss M'Arthur's Estate', though by her father's will it belonged in fact to Edward.[8]

Young Elizabeth was therefore very busy – too busy, she said, even to write family letters. Her other main responsibility was the early schooling of her sister Mary Bowman's little boys. She had started with the firstborn, Edward, when he was four or five. Whether she had ever taught before – say, in Sunday school – does not appear, but within a year or two, as her own mother put it, '*the aunt* is oracular with the nephew'. Edward then started at the new King's School, within walking distance of Elizabeth Farm, but he was asthmatic and often stayed at home, where he and his aunt read and gardened together. He became an enthusiast for plants and insects, and he was to be a collector all his life. At 13 he won medals for ranunculus and Cape bulbs at the annual horticultural exhibition in Sydney. At 16 he led the show with over 40 different garden flowers, and won ten prizes. The list of his exhibits – azalea, narcissus, polyanthus, gladioli and so on – mirrored the garden built up over 40 years by his grandmother and aunt.[9]

The younger boys, James and William Bowman, were less horticulturally minded, but they started in the same way, each when he was barely four. Edward, said their grandmother, was 'by no means deficient in mental acquirements', but the younger boys 'will not make bright scholars'. '[I]dle rogues', she called them, and yet 'well disposed'. William Bowman, 'our Parramatta Willy', was her daughter's favourite in the end.[10]

Besides the main house at Elizabeth Farm, there was the smaller building across the creek, 'the cottage on the plain', as Elizabeth called it, or 'Mrs Lucas's cottage'. Penelope Lucas had moved there altogether during the manic tumult of May 1832, Emmeline had joined her and the two households had been merged for most purposes. Emmeline, said her mother, 'rises early and is with us, sometimes at seven'. Penelope 'comes to us every day to dinner [a four o'clock meal, usually involving a change of dress] and remains according to circumstances, to sometimes ten o'clock'.[11]

A routine took shape. At the main house, sitting at table or in the drawing room, or walking in the garden after dinner, the four women talked about doings at Camden, about the Bowman children, about social gatherings and friends, and about the recently dead, brother/son and father/husband. 'I may truly say,' Elizabeth wrote, 'no day passes, and on many, scarcely an hour that my thoughts do not revert to the many excellencies and virtuous traits of character of both.' Memories of her husband of 45 years were all over the house. To her mind, they were all over occupied New South Wales. The China rose, for instance, 'a lovely plant', as she said, flowering through the year, had been grown first at Elizabeth Farm. He had brought it home for her in 1817. Now she could see its delicate red and pink on any number of garden fences. Surely, she said, 'the many benefits he bestowed on this community' must have brought him his heavenly reward.[12]

They talked about Edward in England, his distinguished friends and his rarified social life – 'how frequently,' his mother told him, 'you are the subject of our conversation, and particularly when we two old folks [she and Penelope] retire into a corner to "gossip".'[13] Edward was now a major on half-pay. His friend from Sicily, Lord Malpas, now Marquess of Cholmondeley, had taken over as Lord Great Chamberlain with Edward as his secretary, moderately paid but accommodated in the House of Lords. At

Elizabeth Farm they speculated about the forthcoming coronation of William IV. As chamberlain's secretary Edward would be distributing tickets. 'James and your sisters laugh at me,' Elizabeth told him, 'and say I am looking out for velvet and trappings!!'[14]

She had old friends within reach. Governor King's widow, Anna Josepha, lived across the Parramatta River with her daughter Maria, who had married Hannibal Macarthur. Mrs King came and sat for hours. Jane Bennett, one of the few friends in New South Wales Elizabeth called by her first name, lived in Parramatta. For several years, first young John and then Edward had worked to secure an English inheritance due to her husband and then, when he died, to Jane herself. '[D]ear good woman,' Elizabeth called her, ever 'the picture of meek resignation.' When her £536.5s.6d finally came through they walked together in the garden and young Elizabeth picked for Mrs Bennett 'a beautiful nosegay of flowers'.[15]

Mrs King and Mrs Bennett were 'two *ancients* like myself'. A third, Nell Kilpack, she had known longer than both. Twice widowed, Nell lived with her daughter, another Nell, and son-in-law Andrew Murray. Murray had come from England with John in 1817, to oversee the gardens and vineyards. Jane Bennett was one of Hobbes Scott's admirers and Nell Kilpack was another, often asking after Scott, bobbing a curtsy and with 'a blessing on his name'.[16]

In June 1836, in England, Elizabeth's mother died, aged 89. She had been living near Bridgerule with her other daughter, Isabella Hacker (born Leach), son-in-law and granddaughters. The news, though not surprising, '*saddened* me, I must allow'. The Hackers were poor and an annual allowance had been paid to Grace Bond from the Macarthur bank account in London, first £50 and then £75 a year. Elizabeth asked Edward to keep sending £50, at least, to Isabella.[17]

Penelope Lucas started to suffer badly from dropsy, a painful swelling of the lower legs and feet which a later generation was to call edema. Aware that her time might be short, she found a lawyer and with James Macarthur's help finalised her will. '[S]he told me,' Elizabeth said, 'she had arranged *all* in her own mind, some time [ago].' Whatever she owned in their cottage was to be Emmeline's. Continuing proceeds from the family property in London were to go to her English relations but she left money to each of the Macarthurs as well as setting aside £300 for 'a school or college at Camden'. The last looks like an echo of John Macarthur's plan for a colonial Hofwyl.[18] Penelope Lucas died on 2 October 1836, aged 67.

Emmeline seems to have moved back to the main house and the Murrays came to live, though briefly, in the vacated cottage, but Nell Kilpack was dead by that time too.[19] So the old world passed away.

FURTHER AFIELD, THROUGHOUT THE OCCUPIED PARTS of New South Wales, one great experiment had failed and another was beginning. The forced labour of convicts was a system whose days were numbered. In its place the assisted immigration of families was to create a free workforce and with it, in the minds of many, 'une révolution morale'. Saxe Bannister had pinpointed the 'masculine character' of settlement as the source of many evils. The hope now was that that should be stifled at its source.

Even before his father died, James Macarthur had begun to look like the public face of his family in New South Wales, and, thanks to Bannister and Scott, he had learnt to anticipate and plan for a new era. In October 1835, Governor Richard Bourke promised government subsidies for employers who wanted to bring free labouring families to New South Wales. James then prepared for another period abroad, aiming among other things to join with his brother Edward in finding people who might take the place of the old workforce at Camden.[20]

He soon had more to do there. There was talk of new laws for New South Wales, introducing some form of elected legislature and juries of a traditional kind in criminal trials, but one great question bedevilled the discussion. In British-origin communities criminal conviction often meant lifelong disqualification, at least from jury service. In New South Wales, how far then should former convicts share in these larger reforms? James Macarthur believed that everything should depend on individual character and on evidence of reform. He quoted a remark by Scott's mentor, Horne Tooke. The worst kinds of ignorance and selfishness – 'that mistaken selfishness which excludes all public sense' – justified the loss of some rights, said Tooke, and so did 'extreme criminality', which might be much the same thing.[21] It matched very closely the moral principles James and the others had learnt at home from the beginning.

As long as it lasted, however, the convict system in New South Wales should be tightened up, with local laws 'to control the conduct of masters towards their assigned servants, [and] with penalties for non-observance'. It had been faulty from the beginning. So James recycled the opinions of his father. If there was to be constitutional reform as well, then every aspect of convict emancipation, from transportation to freedom and the plenitude of rights thereafter, should depend on individual reform. However, as it turned out, there were to be no great emancipatory changes for the time being. Convict transportation was to end first and the British and NSW governments began to prepare for that instead.[22]

James and Edward together organised the shipment of 41 families to New South Wales. A few were vignerons from the Rhine valley near Frankfurt, but the rest were from southern England, chosen mainly from areas notorious as centres of violent agrarian protest some years before. John Macarthur, during his life, had trusted to his own abilities in taking on difficult convicts. His sons took the same self-confident approach. In choosing free labourers, they thought they could still the anger of England's rural poor – men and women victimised, as James said, by laws that 'fettered the labouring classes ... and chained them down'.[23]

In June 1838 James was married in London to Emily Stone. He was 39 and she 32. Emily had been born in India and educated in Scotland, and she had also since seen a good deal of Europe, travelling with women friends. A banker's daughter, related to all the great English banking families, she brought a dowry of £10 000. James had met her through George Warde Norman, her sister's husband, a director of the Bank of England, a leading writer on finance and economics, and an old family friend of Hobbes Scott. Scott came to London to preside at the marriage.

The new house at Camden had been finished in 1834 and was ready for a family. All the same, at Parramatta Elizabeth waited with some apprehension. Emily came from such a different world. 'I cannot but feel considerable anxiety lest the country and habits of the community may disappoint my daughter-in-law.'[24] James and Emily arrived in March 1839 and stayed briefly in Penelope Lucas's cottage before settling in the new house with William, and in spite of Elizabeth's fears, Emily, if anything, grew to like her new home, including colonial manners, more than she did England. Their only child, a third Elizabeth, was born at Camden in May the following year.

ELIZABETH DID NOT GO TO CAMDEN OFTEN. SHE WAS there about the time her granddaughter was born but she liked the summer better, when all the really interesting work was going on – the shearing and packing of the wool, the wheat harvest and the vintage – and when she could watch and understand the sort of networked energy that intrigued her most.

She was there again during the first months of 1842. On a late Tuesday afternoon in April – summer had given way to autumn

— she was alone in the house, except for servants. James, Emily, William and the little girl had all gone to the consecration of a new church at Cobbitty, across the Nepean River. She had been reading a book, newly published in England, that Edward had sent her. It was William Moorcroft's story of his travels in the Himalayas, an 'extraordinary country', she called it, which she longed to know more about.[25]

She sat in her room, upstairs in the new house. Her window looked across the lawn to the north-east, taking the eye beyond the river to a windmill in the distance. Young John, her now-dead son, had invented a way of showing his family how he lived in London, by sending with his letters home small bundles of his other correspondence, the to and fro of his daily life. Edward continued this method and Elizabeth now had a new bundle spread out before her. She had been reading those too. The moment was vacant enough, but scanning each item had brought Edward 'so forcibly before me', she said, that she had decided to write back.[26]

She had not gone with the others, she told him, because she found crowds oppressive and she had seen the church already. There was a second one nearly finished at Camden itself, and how thankful she was to Almighty God 'that I have lived to *see* two temples devoted to his worship' in these once wild places. Maybe this was the point of her letter — to muse on the impossibility, all those years ago, during 'my solitary rambles and excursions in the neighbouring forest', to have imagined a change so remarkable — so gratifying, of course, to the Christian soul.[27]

'Oh how I wish you could look in upon us.' After all, sitting at her writing table, 'I feel I have much to say, but what can a letter contain?' It was a strange, brief, dreaming missive, a reflection on the shifts of scene, impossible to sum up, that had characterised her long life. She ended as she had begun. 'The old notes and letters I before mentioned lie open on my table. It was these tempted me to write to you today. I will tie them up again for the present and relieve you from the perusal of a dull letter.'[28]

She went back to Elizabeth Farm, escorted by William, on the following Monday. Her first concern on reaching home was her daughter Elizabeth. During her absence they had written to each other nearly every day. It was their custom now, when they were both at home, to sleep in the same bed, so that if possible they were closer than they had ever been. Often unwell in earlier years, young Elizabeth had gained strength in middle age, thanks, her mother said, to 'a great deal of exercise in and about the garden'. Very lately, however, she had experienced 'palpitations of the heart'. They bothered her now.[29]

The two women walked in the paddocks beyond the garden, catching up – 'chatting chearfully', as Elizabeth senior put it, even as far as the hill beyond the cottage where Penelope Lucas had lived, now occupied by Matthew Anderson, a medical doctor and the closest of their family friends. 'We had observed Dr Anderson crossing the plain with a quick step and a paper in his hand, and guessing that he had some agreeable intelligence to communicate we waited under the shade of a tree until he should have ascended the hill, when our anticipations were gratified.' The newspaper was an English one, dated November 1839, announcing Edward's promotion from major to brevet lieutenant-colonel. 'Dear dear creature! she was quite rejoiced.'[30]

They went straight back to the house to tell Emmeline and all three were glad together. 'The scene is now vividly before me, little thinking it was to be so soon saddened.' The chest pain came and went for several days, but Anderson advised the sufferer to stay quiet and they were not apprehensive. 'Not to dwell upon this melancholy subject, I shall merely state that on the day week after my return from Camden dear Emmeline rushed into my room exclaiming frantickly, *She is gone, she is gone*!!'[31]

It was the anniversary of young John's death, 19 April, and it was evening. 'I was preparing to go to bed beside her.' Now 74, weakened by an accumulation of loss, Elizabeth found this death harder to manage than any in the past. Something in her was broken. Unlike every previous loss, she let herself dwell on the drama she had passed through and on what she had lost – 'a sweet, a sensible companion, an affectionate and dutiful child'. That term, 'sensible companion', newly fashionable – her reading kept Elizabeth up to date – had a wealth of meaning. A sensible companion echoed your own taste and feelings before you were sure of them yourself. So it was between mother and daughter – but, really, what a blessing that the younger woman had gone first! '[S]he would *ill* have sustained my loss!!'[32]

Six months later, 'still I mourn and tears will flow'. So sweet-tempered, so warmly affectionate, so prayerful – the virtues of the dead were told and retold, in thought and on paper, until once again she was overwhelmed. '[T]o me she was the most devoted of daughters. But I must not proceed in this strain and therefore for a few minutes I will lay down my pen.'[33]

45
OLD AGE

With Penelope Lucas and her eldest daughter both gone, Elizabeth was alone at Elizabeth Farm with her youngest, Emmeline. Emmeline, nearly 34 at her sister's death, had led a strangely isolated life so far. She had been born more than seven years after William, when her parents were both 42. Her father had left for Europe when she was nine months old and he had been gone for eight years. With her mother busy doing her father's work, it had fallen to her sisters, 16 and 13 years older than she was, to look after her. So she was brought up differently from the others. Altogether, said her mother at that time, 'she is in a fair way to be spoilt amongst us.'[1]

Emmeline had known none of her brothers until James and William came home when she was eight. Edward she first met when he took leave from the army in 1824–25. She was then 14, 'a tall girl ... fond of butterflies and flowers'. He was 35. Young John she never met at all. As she grew up she learnt to think of the two absentees, Edward and John, as ideal beings leading an ideal life. At 19, with some trepidation, she had started a correspondence with Edward. 'I certainly envy you,' she said, 'when I read your letters from Italy and Switzerland, so *interesting*, so captivating to an unsophisticated *Australian*!' What, she asked, could she possibly tell him in return? 'The mere every day occurrences of *this place* cannot possibly interest you.' '[T]he stupid monotonous life *we* lead would give *you* the *horrors*.'[2]

OLD AGE

There was something different about Emmeline that her mother never quite fathomed, though Penelope Lucas might have done. The management of feeling, an almost instinctive self-discipline Elizabeth had passed on to the other children, was lost on Emmeline. She had been impatient with her father's suffering – such a nuisance for them all – and yet when young John died in London she had been inconsolable. Her mother had been puzzled. '[Y]ou would scarcely credit how deeply she felt the loss of her brother,' she told Edward, 'although she had never known him.'[3]

With the death of her sister in April 1842, Emmeline confronted a lonely future. She seems to have found some consolation with visiting and receiving visits from Government House, Parramatta, where the current governor, Sir George Gipps, and his family spent a large part of each year. So she became 'entangled' – her mother's word – with the governor's private secretary, Henry Watson Parker, a nephew of Lady Gipps and a year older than she was. Within months of her sister's death they were engaged.[4]

It was an engagement, her mother told Edward, 'we have viewed with some distrust'. She was sure that the two were not well suited, so that the distrust targeted Emmeline as well as her intended. What could they want from each other? The 'entanglement' was one of fortune and feeling combined, because such a marriage necessarily also affected the family capital. Parker had no settled career. Married to Emmeline, he must be taken into the family counsels and he would have a moral claim on them all, even in hard times. They were not used to relying on Emmeline's judgment. Now it seemed dangerously suspect. Edward pointed out that she was old enough to decide for herself, 'or ought at least to be'.[5] That was obvious, but it hardly helped.

Writing to Edward as an ally, Emmeline blamed Emily, James's wife, for the opposition she met with. She was prejudiced, Emmeline said, against Parker. Worse, Emily had 'a cynical an[d] unbounded influence' over James and William. In short, Emmeline said the sort of things, even in writing, that none of the others would think of saying, things shocking to family solidarity. Edward himself had noticed long ago 'how necessary it is to be cautious in the choice of words in letters'.[6] Emmeline was unrestrained.

With regard to her marriage, Emmeline would not be dissuaded and during that year, 1842, Elizabeth spent many months in Sydney with her middle daughter, Mary Bowman, fearful of going home, thinking, as she said, of 'my *loss there* and of what further awaits me'.[7] There was loss with Mary too. James Bowman had built a house on Blackwattle Bay, one of Port Jackson's southern inlets, which they called Lyndhurst, and they had lived there for seven years. However, the colonial economy was now in serious trouble. The 1830s had been a boom time, but labour and good land were suddenly scarce, and lavish investments made when money was abundant left many merchants and woolgrowers financially exposed. To the surprise of his wife and her family, James Bowman was one. They already knew that Bowman was not a kind and gentle husband, but 'I thought,' so Mary told them in her despair, 'he would care for worldly things.'[8]

It was left to Mary's family to save the Bowmans from complete bankruptcy, which was eventually to cost them many thousands. And here was Emmeline's engagement to Henry Watson Parker. Why should Parker be safer than Bowman? In May 1843 the Bowmans gave up Lyndhurst. James Bowman was already at his sheep run near Singleton in the Hunter Valley, where there was a substantial stone cottage, with a good library and a large ornamental garden. Now Mary prepared to follow him. It was 'a sad breaking up', Elizabeth said, and 'quite time for me to force myself away [from Lyndhurst], for in truth I would be of no use'.[9] She came home to Parramatta and to Emmeline.

OLD AGE

SHE NOW THOUGHT OF MOVING TO CAMDEN, TO SAVE on household expenses, or so she said. Emmeline was married at Parramatta on 21 November, and while Elizabeth did not go to the wedding itself she sat with the others at the wedding breakfast afterwards, held at Elizabeth Farm. James's wife, 'dear Emily', was 'a great comfort to me'. Here, maybe, was the best hope for her future. Emily, clever and strong-minded, was a considerable addition to the family. 'The more intimately I have become acquainted with Emily the more she has risen in my estimation – affectionately attached to James, to his *interests* and to that of the family *generally*, hospitable and courteous to all, practising at the same time a laudable oeconomy.'[10] Emily was very willing to have Elizabeth at Camden.

It was a hard decision. Her oldest daughter's death had left Elizabeth emotionally frail. In its aftermath she felt for the first time the full vulnerability of old age, so that in pouring out her thoughts to Edward, despite lifetime habits, she let her sympathies turn to 'self'. In some sense she was casting about now for the kind of undivided affection she had had for so long from her eldest daughter. In fact, it was a lifelong need, traceable, maybe, to her uncertain childhood.

Her daughter Elizabeth had been her last safe harbour. Just as in 1790, during her great voyage to New South Wales, now in her old age she was alone at open sea. Edward, her eldest, still unmarried, was the only one who seemed to offer what she wanted. He was also the only one familiar with her old friends in England and with her early life – her deeper needs, her other self. 'How often, how often,' she told him, 'do I wish for a chat with you!' In all his adult life Edward had been home only twice, both times now long ago, but she still hoped to hold him again before she died. 'If not, I hope and pray we may meet in heaven!'[11]

He could not afford to come. As an army officer, he depended on paid work so far unavailable in New South Wales. He was no longer the Lord Great Chamberlain's secretary, which had paid little enough, but in 1843 he was given a position at army headquarters in Ireland. It was a time of great difficulty there, soon to include the Great Famine, the failure of the potato crop. Stationed mostly in western Ireland, Edward spent his spare time appealing for government-assisted emigration from Ireland to New South Wales. Elizabeth followed his movements in detail, with her mind, as she said, 'travelling and conjecturing respecting your occupations very very often!!' Shifting her curiosity from northern India, she now read all she could about Ireland – 'what an unhappy and may be an ill used country!!!'[12]

'I thank the Almighty,' she told him, 'I continue to have health' – still 'capable of quietly moving about and of enjoying conversation with any friend who is kind enough to visit me.' Her age, her robust conversation, her respectability and her reputation as one of the pioneers of settlement made her a distinguished figure in colonial society, and her house was visited as a matter of form by many. The explorer Ludwig Leichhardt was one caller, 'a very intelligent clever person', she said, 'active in body as well as in mind, and hardy withal'. Leichhardt came to see her before starting on his second expedition, from which, as it turned out, he never returned.[13]

With Emmeline married, Elizabeth stayed on at her old home, uncertain, and the newlyweds moved in with her. Parker took on all household expenses, although he spent most of each week on duty in Sydney, coming home by river steamer for a night mid-week and two at the weekends. Elizabeth began to feel settled with this new arrangement and she began to like Parker. 'I believe [him] to be well principled, and he is most attentive and kind to me, doing all he can to please.' She was surprised to notice 'a sincere attachment' between him and Emmeline. 'I trust it will be a lasting one.'[14]

OLD AGE

Emmeline needed her there. In September 1844 she had a baby, stillborn. Parker, Elizabeth deliberately pointed out, shared fully in her grief – '[n]othing can be more tender and affectionate than is his conduct.' It was the first of five pregnancies over four years, including only one live birth, a little girl, who soon died. So Elizabeth found herself working jointly with her son-in-law, attending to Emmeline in her suffering, mind and body, year by year.[15]

THE THOUGHTS OF JOHN MACARTHUR PENETRATED family feeling long after his death. He and Elizabeth had talked often together about the terms of his will and, as she recalled, he had been especially anxious that his lifework should continue. He had wanted none of their children, their sons especially, to use their part of the inheritance for 'individual or separate advantage'. He had wanted them to work together, even after his death, for 'the attainment of the objects he had through life ardently devoted himself to'. By that he meant not just the wool growing but all his later projects too, now concentrated mainly on Camden. It would have jarred with him to set conditions enforceable in law, but he had been confident that they were all 'strongly united in the bonds of mutual confidence and affection, and in the desire to carry out his plans for the general good'.[16] By 'general good' he had meant not just the good of the family. Public good was included. The two were, as ever in his mind, interwoven.

At that point Elizabeth and John had been sure that Edward would come back to live in New South Wales. Pyrmont and Elizabeth Farm were left to him for that reason, with James and William sharing Camden. Collaboration would be easy then. Edward, however, did not relish a life on the land, there was no army work for him in New South Wales and so he stayed in

England. Towards the end, in his lucid moments, John had begun to see the problem built into his will. He had wanted them to change it, but he was no longer capable in law.[17]

In the years after their father's death, problems had begun to emerge. By now, Edward had put aside the lightness and brightness of his youth, though it was never quite lost. William, especially, always insisted on the perfect equality of all three brothers, but Edward now thought of himself as head of the family. Stationed in England he must, in his own mind, have a larger view and a surer touch at the heart of affairs than his brothers could have in New South Wales. In writing to them he sometimes used a startlingly patronising, peremptory and accusatory tone, based partly on his belief that with regard to his own property they were his agents. He expected them to send him full and regular reports, to keep their debts separate from his and to follow his advice. 'What with you and the Irish,' he said, 'I have enough to think of. I wish I could settle your affairs with the same ease I can theirs.' Reading such language for the first time, Elizabeth said, 'was to me as an electrical shock'.[18]

He could have no idea, she told him, of the accumulating difficulties at Camden, the changes that had taken place in New South Wales since he had seen it last, and the priorities forcing themselves on his brothers. He did not understand the need to diversify and to keep folding in new improvements so as to stay ahead, methods learnt from their father. She urged him to come and see for himself. '[W]ere you present a few weeks [it] would dispel the mist.'[19] At the same time she flattered him, sure, as he was, of his importance as an advocate of New South Wales in England.

Elizabeth expressed herself differently with each of her children. With James and William she was easy and brief. With Edward, yearning across the ocean spaces created a kind of awkwardness. 'My pen is arrested from communicating a thousand things when

I recollect that you will not read them for four or five months.' In writing to Mary the main point was to cheer her up. However, in August 1846 James Bowman died and Mary moved to Camden. According to Emily, she was more cheerful then than she had been for years.[20]

From one to the other, Elizabeth shaped her language accordingly, so as to keep up a presence in their feelings. She was careful not to press too hard, not asking questions where she knew answers would be awkward; giving her opinions and then apologising, at least to Edward, for inflicting him with an 'old woman's prattle'. Understanding where her strengths still lay, she limited her efforts to the softening of differences among her children. Silence, as usual, was a useful tool. In a highly ordered life such as hers the spaces left for silence – saying nothing – might still have their weight.

46

THE END

In autumn 1843 Elizabeth suffered from an attack of erysipelas. Erysipelas was a disease, she said, 'to which I am I believe constitutionally subject', though there is no sign of her mentioning it before. It was a skin infection, a type of rash, accompanied by fever, headache and a general feeling of being unwell. Late in 1846 – she was now 80 – it came again more severely, leaving her very weak. About the same time Emmeline suffered the third of her failed pregnancies and, the better to recover their strength, early in January 1847 all three – Elizabeth and the Parkers – took a house near the South Head of Port Jackson belonging to Emmeline's cousin, Hannibal Macarthur, where they stayed for 11 weeks.[1]

This house, which Hannibal had christened Clovelly, was on a narrow neck of land between ocean and harbour. At the back it was an easy climb up to what was called the Gap, a high point with a wide view of the ocean. When she had been there three weeks Elizabeth sent Edward a full account. From the Gap, in an armchair placed there for her convenience, she looked down at the busy movement of vessels approaching the harbour. 'I can give you no adequate idea of the number of ships from various parts of the world that are constantly coming and going, to say nothing of the coasting vessels. It is a constant moving scene.'[2]

On the Port Jackson side, beside the little cove called Watson's Bay, she could test her own powers of movement. Emmeline and Henry Parker went for walks together by the water's edge and they

THE END

urged her to do that same. She tried it and with health improved by the sea air she had done well. 'I am now enabled to take short walks using a strong and light stick instead of the support of an arm. By this means I regulate my pace according to my ability of proceeding.'[3]

Elizabeth was an adventurer of sorts, and yet this was the first time in over 50 years that she had tried to make herself at home, mind and body, in a community quite new to her. The salt air was reminiscent of Bridgerule and of the sea winds that, in her recollection, had shaken the vicarage window frames there. There were sights everywhere that made her think too of her first years in New South Wales, the early 1790s, and she frequently now looked back at that time – looking down, as it were, from the height of the Gap, into the expanse of memory and the extent of years.

In that first letter to Edward from Clovelly she explained the workings of the scattered community roundabout, just as she had done half a century before for Bridget Kingdon, in describing the raw settlements at Sydney Cove and Norfolk Island. With the Parkers she went on boating excursions on the harbour and at her own particular request they went even as far as Manly Cove, across the harbour mouth to the north. There she wanted to see again a spot she and John had visited in spring 1791, with a party of picnickers.

Although it was her first return, she remembered well, she said, the 'fine capacious boat' they and their friends had used on that day, filled with 'all appliances of good cheer', their meeting with a group of officers who had been out shooting ducks, the boasting and banter, and the disposition, as she said, to be 'very very merry'. She had been pregnant – she remembered that too – a few months gone with her daughter Elizabeth. Anna King had been there with her husband, the future governor, pregnant too, and much closer to her time. It had been a risky, abundant moment and, as she had told Bridget then, she had never been more happy. As evening closed in on that picnic day the party had ventured back against a stiff wind and rough seas, a mast broke in transit but, she said – this was in her letter to Edward – 'we all reached home safely'.[4]

Some months later, when they were home again at Elizabeth Farm, Hannibal Macarthur joined the long list of local bankrupts. Clovelly and the big house on the other side of the Parramatta River were both sold, and Hannibal and Maria went to live with a daughter and son-in-law in the country to the south.

Governor Gipps had left, but Henry Watson Parker had stayed on and he was now chairman of committees in the Legislative Council. Safely salaried, Parker bought Clovelly for a fraction of the original cost – real estate prices had tumbled – as a home for the summer.

In the New Year, 1849, they all three moved again to 'this very pleasant abode', as Elizabeth called it, for a five-months stay.[5] She had not been well. She had never quite recovered from the attack of erysipelas two years earlier and a bout of influenza had since weakened her further. At home lately she had been unable to walk even into the garden.[6]

After a few weeks of sea air she felt stronger. Now, in her short walks she made a point of talking to the local fishermen, whose catch was sold in Sydney. An old couple, Billy and Bett Taylor, lived in a cave – it might have been just a rock overhang – by the beach, 'built up a little in the front', so Elizabeth said, 'and divided into two or three apartments, kept orderly and very clean. I can walk to this place and talk of "old times".' Billy Taylor, a long-term fisherman, had been born in Devon. He must have arrived as a child in New South Wales. '[B]less you Mrs Macarty,' he would say to her, 'why I've known you these fifty years and many's the five shilling orders I've had from you on Dick Cheers the butcher!! in payment for fish.'[7] Cheers had been one of the Sydney butchers who had taken Elizabeth's wethers and redundant ewes

THE END

when she was in charge at Elizabeth Farm, in 1809–17. With fish, apparently, Cheers had been a type of middle-man, paying Billy Taylor from Elizabeth's credit account.

'I gets my living by fishing still,' Billy Taylor told her. She enjoyed talking to him. 'He reminds me of many things.' Those many things might have included the fishermen she and Bridget Kingdon had seen on their walks to Bude, her work with Penelope Lucas while John was away, and the intricate network of debit, credit and decision-making, within which Billy Taylor had had his own small part. Many things. In that community she found another old acquaintance, Jane Siddins, a little girl long ago near Parramatta, now, Elizabeth said, 'a very respectable person, a widow'. '[H]er late husband kept the lighthouse [on South Head] many years and since his death her son.'[8]

During this second period at Clovelly more of the family came to take the sea air. In buying the house, Henry Watson Parker had obviously done a good thing. William Macarthur stayed for the fishing and boating, James and Emily came briefly with their little girl, and the Bowman children were 'very happy' in and about the water. By May 1849, when they were ready to go home, Elizabeth again felt the benefit of these few months. 'I have been enabled to rise from bed every morning so early as to be ready to join the breakfast table by 8 o'clock.' Walking during the day had got easier too, although 'the limbs are too feeble to walk long at a time'.[9]

At the end of May she wrote again to Edward from Parramatta. The house at Watson's Bay had given a new brightness to her life, but it could not replace in her heart her home at Elizabeth Farm, 'my abode [for] so many years and under a variety of circumstances, some indeed of a very painful nature and others of serene happiness'. During winter 1849, she suffered again from erysipelas and spent a fortnight in bed – still in the room John had once intended as a library – emerging at the end better, 'but of course more enfeebled'.[10]

She had always had a system, of sorts, for writing to Edward. Early on she had made a point of writing during the first week of every month, a regime she had imposed on herself, she said, with 'a rule in my own mind'. Then, from 1844, she had written so as to coincide with the new Sydney-to-London post office mail, also monthly. However, in May 1849 that service was discontinued, forcing her back to her own self-discipline. She tried it, but when she wrote next, on 23 November, she had already lost track. 'It is so long,' she said, 'since I took up my pen to address you that I hardly know how to begin.' Then, only a fortnight later, she managed five pages more for him, closely written and neatly set out, though her hand trembled and in the end, she said, fingers and eyes were weary. After that, nothing. Over the Christmas–New Year period all three went back to Watson's Bay for another summer spell. There, among those sea sounds, she died, on Saturday, 9 February 1850, aged 83.[11]

EPILOGUE: WHAT HAPPENED TO THE SURVIVING CHILDREN?

Edward Macarthur

In December 1851, less than two years after his mother's death, Edward finally came back to New South Wales, as deputy adjutant general of the forces. In 1854 military headquarters moved to Melbourne. In 1855 he took command of the troops there and for 12 months, in 1855–56, he was acting governor of Victoria. In 1858 his property in New South Wales was completely separated from his brothers'. He returned to England in 1860. In 1862 he was knighted and in the same year he married Sarah Neill. They had no children. Promoted to lieutenant-general, he died on 4 January 1872, aged 82.

Mary Bowman

Following her husband's death in 1846 Mary joined her daughter Isabella at Camden. She died there on 7 April 1852, aged 56. Isabella (Chisholm) and two of Mary's sons, William and Frederick, all married and left descendants.

James Macarthur

James was an elected member of the NSW Legislative Council in 1848–56 and of the new Legislative Assembly in 1856–59. He was one of the leading politicians of that period in New South Wales, one of the founders of Sydney University and a member of cabinet in the first responsible government. From 1859 to 1864 he was abroad with his wife Emily and daughter Elizabeth. In January 1866 he was appointed to the new Legislative Council (the upper house), but he died at Camden on 21 April 1867, aged 68. His daughter Elizabeth married Arthur Onslow and, as his only child, was the eventual heir to her father and both uncles, Edward and William. Of Elizabeth Macarthur-Onslow's eight children, James's grandchildren, three sons married and left descendants.

William Macarthur

William was an elected member of the Legislative Council in 1849–55. He represented New South Wales at the International Exhibition in Paris in 1855, when he was knighted and awarded the Légion d'honneur. He went away again for the London exhibition in 1862. By this time he was a trustee of the Australian Museum and of the Free Public Library, a member of the University Senate, vice-president of the Acclimatisation Society of NSW and an honorary member of the Société impériale zoologique d'acclimatation. He was a member of the new Legislative Council from 1864 until just before his death, at Camden, on 29 October 1882, aged 81.

EPILOGUE

Emmeline Parker

Emmeline's husband, Henry Watson Parker, was a member of the Legislative Council until 1856 and of the new Legislative Assembly in 1856–57, as premier of New South Wales. He was knighted in 1858. They then went to England and lived at Stawell House, near Richmond, in Surrey, where Henry Parker died on 2 February 1881. In spite of her mother's fears Emmeline loved him to the end. 'We were all the world to each other,' she said, 'and he was the dear light and guide of my life.' His death left her '[a]lone and friendless' in 'a strange country'. She died at Stawell, on 4 May 1888, aged 78.[1] There were no surviving children.

ACKNOWLEDGMENTS

This book has taken shape over about five years, during 2016–21, but it depends on work going back more than 50 years, to 1971, when I started a research thesis at Sydney University looking at John Macarthur and his family – mainly his sons – before 1842. That was followed by another thesis at the Australian National University on 'The political life of James Macarthur', the third son. Finally, there was a book, *Camden* (1988), about the community established by James and his brother William, near their headquarters at Camden Park from about 1840. The last was an experiment combining local history and new methods of historical demography, copied from abroad.[1]

Debts are acknowledged in all three efforts but here I need to remember again the kind support of the two scholars who supervised, respectively, my two theses, John Manning Ward (died 1990) and Allan Martin (died 2002), and the friendship during that period of the Sydney University historian Hazel King (died 1997). Hazel herself was a specialist in 'Macarthur studies', with two very useful monographs, one on Elizabeth and the other on the two eldest sons, Edward and the younger John Macarthur.[2] All three of these mentors, Ward, Martin and King, were kind, helpful and supportive. Allan Martin I knew best and last. As friend and exemplar, he made the discipline, for me, more genuinely human – more completely a matter of conscience and sensibility – so that he was a mentor in the richest sense.

Work for the Camden book also put me in touch with Annette Macarthur-Onslow. Annette's careful scholarship, her friendship

ACKNOWLEDGMENTS

and her unfailing encouragement have been crucial in reaching this final outcome. At Camden itself, my obligations to John and Julie Wrigley cover the same period. They have been wonderfully helpful with hospitality, advice and much else with regard to the historical material at Camden Park. And again, at Camden Park, first Quentin Macarthur-Stanham and more recently Edwina and John Macarthur-Stanham have been wonderfully kind and hospitable, in providing access to artefacts, papers and books belonging to the family from the earliest period, and for the copying of portraits. I am enormously grateful to them.

There has been some particularly useful research and writing about early Macarthurs during the last ten years or so, which has added depth to the older work by Malcolm Ellis, Hazel King and so on. I have gained a good deal from ongoing work at Elizabeth Farm, carried out under the auspices of Sydney Living Museums. I would mention especially SLM curator Scott Hill. Scott's 2016 doctoral thesis, on John Macarthur as amateur architect, has been a vital source of information and inspiration at several points in the story. Julie McIntyre, of the University of Newcastle, has also added significantly to our knowledge of the Macarthur family's role in establishing commercial vineyards in New South Wales, and I value her advice. Finally, Michelle Scott Tucker's new biography of Elizabeth Macarthur (2018) has helped in a variety of ways, in bringing our understanding of Elizabeth up to date.[3] I am also grateful to Michelle for her very keen and generous help with the pictures sourced at Camden Park.

Skilled research work has been done for me in various places, and large slabs of the book could not have been written without it, especially given travel problems associated with the Covid pandemic and the fact that I have been based in Western Australia. In Sydney, Patricia Curthoys has done innumerable jobs with marvellous efficiency, Jonathan Auld retrieved material for me from the NSW State Archives, and in Canberra, Jessica Urwin was equally thorough in getting what I wanted from the Noel Butlin Archives Centre.

In England, Hugh Alexander and Dave Annal located and sent material from the National Archives at Kew, and I am similarly grateful to Evelyn Watson at the Royal Society of Arts, in London, and Ralph McLean of the National Library of Scotland. In Finland, Kenneth Silver of the Fiskars Museum was very helpful, and in Switzerland, Catherine Forster-Bonhôte, of Geneva, took a good deal of trouble with detail about early members of her own family. In the United States, I received some crucial material from the Peabody Essex Museum, Salem, Massachusetts, thanks to Kathryn White, and from the Massillon Museum in Ohio, thanks to Mandy Altimus Stahl.

John Maynard, emeritus professor and director of Purai Global Indigenous History Centre, University of Newcastle, very kindly read over draft chapters relating to First Nations history.

The two institutions that have mattered most in the production of this book have been the Mitchell Library, part of the State Library of NSW, and NewSouth Publishing. The Mitchell, a vast repository of NSW non-government archives, has been a type of spiritual home for me since 1969. More recently, digitisation, especially of the Macarthur Family Papers, and in some cases transcription, have made it doubly valuable to the geographically disadvantaged. This book, in its final form, would have been perfectly impossible without digital access. The possibility of poring over material, turning and returning to the original, makes all the difference in work of this sort.

At NewSouth Publishing, an imprint of UNSW Press, the book has been steered with wonderful skill mainly by Elspeth Menzies, executive publisher, and project editors Emma Hutchinson and Joumana Awad. I am grateful to Alex Ross for the very fine cover, and to Tricia Dearborn for her exact and inspired copyediting.

ACKNOWLEDGMENTS

As I say once or twice in this story – especially in connection with the Macarthurs and Watkin Tench – books are typically the product of living conversation. Some of my oldest friends have been part of the long-term, multi-layered vocal and email chat that underlies the making of this book. I have already mentioned Annette Macarthur-Onslow. In that regard I also owe a particularly large debt to Marian Quartly in Melbourne and Stephen Foster in Canberra (when he was not somewhere else). Marian and Stephen also each read every word of this story, often in a fairly raw state, over the two years 2020–22. Their feedback, each in their own way, has made an enormous difference to the precision and coherence of the whole. I am extremely grateful.

Still on the subject of chat over the years, I need to acknowledge my late mother, Gwen Atkinson, my sisters Meg Vivers and Helen Heath, and my children Tom, Catherine – adept, like the Macarthurs, with sheep and raw wool – and Elizabeth. And then, largest of all, is my debt to Cathie Pound. A large part of the book was read aloud to her and with her from time to time, to its great benefit. Altogether this work rests on her many years of patience.

For the supply of illustrations and permission for their use I am grateful to:

Natural History Museum, London (Charlotte Gunvor Thorkildsen in particular), for Thomas Watling's portrait, 'Da-ring-ha, Colebee's Wife', 1792–95, from the First Fleet artwork collection.

National Galleries of Scotland (Alejandro Basterrechea in particular), for George Romney's portrait of John McArthur, 1795.

John and Edwina Macarthur-Stanham, for portraits of John Macarthur (unknown artist), Elizabeth Macarthur (by William Nicholas), Edward Macarthur (unknown artist), and James Macarthur (by R.B. Scanlan), all of which were copied for me by Joshua Morris.

State Library of NSW, for portraits of Watkin Tench (unknown artist), Elizabeth Paterson (by William Owen), and Elizabeth Macarthur the younger and Mary Macarthur (both by an unknown artist and identification of subjects not perfectly certain).

National Gallery of Victoria, for Joseph Lycett's landscape, 'The Residence of John McArthur Esqre', from his *Views in Australia or New South Wales and Van Diemen's Land* (London 1824–25).

University of Southern California Digital Library, Rare Books and Manuscripts Collection (Yuriy Shcherbina in particular), for Pierre-Joseph Redouté's picture of the Amaryllis Josephine at the Château de Malmaison, c. 1809–12.

SELECT BIBLIOGRAPHY

Books published before 1850

Anon., *The Plymouth-Dock Guide; or, An Authentic Account of the Rise and Progress of that Town, with the Dockyard* (E. Hoxland, Plymouth Dock 1796).
Anon., *The Secret Memoirs of the Late Mr Duncan Campbel, the Famous Deaf and Dumb Gentleman* (J. Millan, London 1732).
Atkinson, James, *An Account of the State of Agriculture and Grazing in New South Wales* (J. Cross, London 1826).
Bakewell, Robert, *Introduction to Geology* (J. Harding, London 1813).
Bannister, Saxe, *Statements and Documents Relating to Proceedings in New South Wales in 1824, 1825 and 1826* (W. Bridekirk, Capetown 1827).
——— *Humane Policy; or Justice to the Aborigines of New Settlements Essential to a Due Expenditure of British Money, and to the Best Interests of the Settlers* (T. & G. Underwood, London 1830).
Bentham, Jeremy, *Panopticon; or, The Inspection-House* (three volumes) (T. Payne, London 1791).
Bigge, J.T., *Report of the Commissioner of Inquiry into the State of the Colony of New South Wales* (House of Commons, London 1822).
——— *Report of the Commissioner of Inquiry, on the State of Agriculture and Trade in the Colony of New South Wales* (House of Commons, London 1823).
——— *Report of the Commissioner of Inquiry, on the Judicial Establishments of New South Wales, and Van Diemen's Land* (House of Commons, London 1823).
Blair, Hugh, *A Critical Dissertation on the Poems of Ossian* (T. Becket & P. A. De Hondt, London 1763).
Buchan, William, *Domestic Medicine; or, A Treatise on the Prevention and Cure of Diseases by Regimen and Simple Medicines* (A. Strachan, London 1790; first publ. 1772).
Busby, James, *A Treatise on the Culture of the Vine, and the Art of Making Wine* (R. Howe, Sydney 1825).
Cantillon, Richard, *The Analysis of Trade, Commerce, Coin, Bullion, Banks, and Foreign Exchanges* (ed. Philip Cantillon) (author, London 1759).
Clarke, E.D., *A Tour Through the South of England, Wales, and Part of Ireland, Made During the Summer of 1791* (R. Edwards, London 1793).
Collins, David, *An Account of the English Colony in New South Wales* (two volumes, ed. Brian H. Fletcher) (Reed, Sydney 1975), (vol. 1 first publ. 1798; vol. 2 first publ. 1802).
Dawson, Robert, *The Present State of Australia* (Smith, Elder, London 1830).
Farquhar, John, *Sermons on Various Subjects* (two volumes, ed. George Campbell & Alexander Gerard) (E. and C. Dilly, London 1772).

Farquhar, R.T., *Suggestions Arising from the Abolition of the African Slave Trade for Supplying the Demands of the West India Colonies with Agricultural Labourers* (J. Stockdale, London 1807).
Gilbert, C.S., *An Historical Survey of the County of Cornwall* (two volumes) (J. Congdon, Plymouth Dock 1820).
Gourlay, Robert, *A General Introduction to a Statistical Account of Upper Canada* (Simpkin & Marshall, London 1822).
Hartley, David, *Observations on Man, His Frame, His Duty, and His Expectations* (two volumes) (J. Leake & W. Frederick, London 1749).
Jardine, George, *Outlines of Philosophical Education* (A. & J. Duncan, Glasgow 1818).
Leach, Edmund, *A Treatise of Universal Inland Navigations, and the Use of all Sorts of Mines* (printed London [1785, but n.d. and apparently never publ.; the sole remaining copy, in the British Library, is wrongly listed as 1790]).
[Macarthur, James], *New South Wales, Its Present State and Future Prospects* (D. Walther, London 1837).
[McArthur, John], *Financial Facts of the Eighteenth Century* (J. Wright, London 1801).
McArthur, John, *Financial and Political Facts of the Eighteenth Century* (J. Wright, London 1801).
[Macarthur, William, writing as 'Maro'], *Letters on the Culture of the Vine, Fermentation, and the Management of Wine in the Cellar* (Statham & Forster, Sydney, 1844).
Marshall, William, *Planting and Rural Ornament* (two volumes) (G. Nicol, London 1796).
Mathison, Gilbert, *Notices Respecting Jamaica, in 1808–1809–1810* (J. Stockdale, London 1811).
Millar, John, *Observations Concerning the Distinction of Ranks in Society* (J. Murray, London 1773; first publ. 1771).
Parry, C.H., *An Essay on the Nature, Produce, Origin, and Extension of the Merino Breed of Sheep* (William Bulmer & Co., London 1807).
Robinson, Mary, writing as Anne Frances Randall, *A Letter to the Women of England, on the Injustice of Mental Subordination* (T.N. Longman & O. Rees, London 1799).
Rousseau, Jean-Jacques, *Émile, or On Education* (trans. Barbara Foxley) (Dent, London 1911; first publ. in French 1762).
Sinclair, Sir John, *Address to the Society for the Improvement of British Wool* (T. Cadell, London 1791).
——— *An Account of the Highland Society of London, from Its Establishment in May 1773, to the Commencement of the Year 1813* (Longman, London 1813).
Smith, Adam, *The Theory of Moral Sentiments* (A. Millar, London 1759).
——— *An Inquiry into the Nature and Causes of the Wealth of Nations* (two volumes) (W. Strahan & T. Cadell, London 1776).
Stephens, Alexander (ed.), *Memoirs of John Horne Tooke* (two volumes) (J. Johnson, London 1813).
Steuart, Sir James, *An Inquiry into the Principles of Political Oeconomy* (two volumes) (A. Millar & T. Cadell, London 1767).
Tench, Watkin, *A Narrative of the Expedition to Botany Bay* (J. Debrett, London 1789).
——— *A Complete Account of the Settlement at Port Jackson, in New South Wales* (G. Nicol, London 1793).

SELECT BIBLIOGRAPHY

——— *Letters Written in France, to a Friend in London, between the Month of November 1794, and the Month of May 1795* (J. Johnson, London 1796).
Vancouver, Charles, *General View of the Agriculture of the County of Devon* (R. Phillips, London 1808).
Wentworth, W.C., *A Statistical, Historical, and Political Description of the Colony of New South Wales* (G. & W.B. Whittaker, London 1819).
Thom, J.H. (ed.), *The Life of the Rev. Joseph Blanco White, Written by Himself* (three volumes) (J. Chapman, London 1845).
Worgan, G.B., *General View of the Agriculture of the County of Cornwall* (G. & W. Nicol, London 1811).

Books published since 1850

Adler, Jeremy, *Johann Wolfgang von Goethe* (Reaktion Books, London 2020).
Ahnert, Thomas, *The Moral Culture of the Scottish Enlightenment 1690–1805* (Yale University Press, New Haven, 2014).
Allbrook, Malcolm, and Sophie Scott-Brown (eds), *Related Histories: Family history and historians in Australia and New Zealand* (Routledge, New York 2021).
Aplin, Graeme (ed.), *A Difficult Infant: Sydney before Macquarie* (UNSW Press, Sydney 1988).
Atkinson, Alan, *Camden: Farm and village life in early New South Wales* (Oxford University Press, Melbourne 1988).
——— *The Europeans in Australia: A history* (three volumes) (UNSW Press, Sydney 2016; vols 1 and 2 first publ. by Oxford University Press, Melbourne 1997 and 2004).
Attwood, Bain, and S.G. Foster (eds), *Frontier Conflict: The Australian experience* (National Museum of Australia, Canberra 2003).
Bachelard, Gaston, *The Poetics of Space* (trans. Maria Jolas) (Penguin Books, London 2014: first publ. in French as *La poétique de l'espace*, Presses Universitaires de France, Paris 1957).
Bate, Jonathan, *Radical Wordsworth: The poet who changed the world* (William Collins, London 2020).
Belmessous, Saliha, *Assimilation and Empire: Uniformity in French and British colonies 1541–1954* (Oxford University Press, Oxford 2013).
Broadbent, James, *Elizabeth Farm Parramatta: A history and a guide* (Historic Houses Trust of NSW, Sydney 1995; first publ. Historic Houses Trust of NSW, Sydney 1984).
Butlin, S.J., *Foundations of the Australian Monetary System 1788–1851* (Sydney University Press, Sydney 1953).
Carter, H.B., *His Majesty's Spanish Flock: Sir Joseph Banks and the Merinos of George III of England* (Angus & Robertson, Sydney 1964).
Champion, Justin, et al. (eds), *Politics, Religion and Ideas in Seventeenth- and Eighteenth-Century Britain* (Boydell & Brewer, Woodbridge, UK, 2019).
Clark, Andy, *Supersizing the Mind: Embodiment, action, and cognitive extension* (Oxford University Press, Oxford 2011).
Clogg, Richard (ed.), *The Struggle for Greek Independence: Essays to mark the 150th anniversary of the Greek War of Independence* (Archon Books, Hamden, Connecticut, 1973).

Colley, Linda, *Britons: Forging the nation, 1707–1837* (Yale University Press, New Haven 2005; first publ. Yale University Press, New Haven 1992).
——— *The Gun, the Ship and the Pen: Warfare, constitutions, and the making of the modern world* (Profile Books, London 2021).
Dakin, Douglas, *British and American Philhellenes during the War of Greek Independence, 1821–1833* (Hetaireia Makedonikōn Spoudōn, Thessaloniki, Greece, 1955).
Dubinsky, Karen, Adele Perry, and Henry Yu (eds), *Within and Without the Nation: Canadian history as transnational history* (University of Toronto Press, Toronto 2015).
Dunér, David, and Christer Ahlberger (eds), *Cognitive History: Mind, space, and time* (De Gruyter, Oldenbourg, Germany, 2019).
Ellis, M.H., *John Macarthur* (Angus & Robertson, Sydney 1955).
Fletcher, Brian H., *Landed Enterprise and Penal Society: A history of farming and grazing in New South Wales before 1821* (Sydney University Press, Sydney 1976).
Flynn, Michael, *The Second Fleet: Britain's grim convict armada of 1790* (Library of Australian History, Sydney 1993).
Foster, Stephen, *A Private Empire* (Murdoch Books, Sydney 2010).
French, Henry, and Mark Rothery, *Man's Estate: Landed gentry masculinities, 1660–1900* (Oxford University Press, Oxford 2012).
Gapps, Stephen, *The Sydney Wars: Conflict in the early colony 1788–1817* (NewSouth Publishing, Sydney 2018).
Gillen, Mollie, *The Founders of Australia: A biographical dictionary of the First Fleet* (Library of Australian History, Sydney 1989).
Hainsworth, D.R., *The Sydney Traders: Simeon Lord and his contemporaries 1788–1821* (Cassell Australia, Melbourne 1972).
Harvey, Karen, *The Little Republic: Masculinity and domestic authority in eighteenth-century Britain* (Oxford Scholarship Online, Oxford University Press, Oxford 2012).
Hewitt, Rachel, *A Revolution of Feeling: The decade that forged the modern mind* (Granta Books, London 2018; first publ. Granta Books, London 2017).
Jennings, Judith, *The Business of Abolishing the British Slave Trade, 1783–1807* (F. Cass, Portland, Oregon, 1997).
Karskens, Grace, *The Colony: A history of early Sydney* (Allen & Unwin, Sydney 2009).
——— *People of the River: Lost worlds of early Australia* (Allen & Unwin, Sydney 2020).
King, Hazel, *Elizabeth Macarthur and Her World* (Sydney University Press, Sydney 1980).
——— *Colonial Expatriates: Edward and John Macarthur junior* (Kangaroo Press, Sydney 1989).
Macarthur Onslow, Sibella (ed.), *Some Early Records of the Macarthurs of Camden* (Angus & Robertson, Sydney 1914).
McGrath, W.J., *German Freedom and the Greek Ideal* (Palgrave Macmillan, New York 2013).
McIntyre, Julie, *First Vintage: Wine in colonial New South Wales* (UNSW Press, Sydney 2012).
Macquarie, Lachlan, *Lachlan Macquarie, Governor of New South Wales: Journey of his tours in New South Wales and Van Diemen's Land* (ed. Phyllis Mander-Jones) (Trustees of the Public Library of NSW, Sydney 1956).

SELECT BIBLIOGRAPHY

Malafouris, Lambros, *How Things Shape the Mind: A theory of material engagement* (MIT Press, Cambridge, Mass., 2016; first publ. 2013).

Marshall, P.J., and William B. Todd (eds), *The Writings and Speeches of Edmund Burke* (nine volumes) (Oxford University Press, Oxford 1981–2000).

Menudo, J.M. (ed.), *The Economic Thought of Sir James Steuart, First Economist of the Scottish Enlightenment* (Routledge, London 2020).

Murphy, A.E., *Richard Cantillon: Entrepreneur and economist* (Oxford Scholarship Online, Oxford University Press, Oxford 2003; first publ. Oxford University Press, Oxford 1989).

Pearson, Jacqueline, *Women's Reading in Britain, 1750–1835: A dangerous recreation* (Cambridge University Press, Cambridge 1999).

Pinney, Thomas, *A History of Wine in America: From the beginnings to Prohibition* (two volumes) (University of California Press, Berkeley, USA, 2007; first publ. University of California Press, Berkeley 1989).

Reece, Bob (ed.), *Exiles from Erin: Convict lives in Ireland and Australia* (Palgrave, Basingstoke, UK, 1991).

Rousseau, George S., *Nervous Acts: Essays on literature, culture and sensibility* (Palgrave Macmillan, Basingstoke, UK, 2004).

Satia, Priya, *Empire of Guns: The violent making of the Industrial Revolution* (Penguin, New York 2018).

Skinner, A.S., *A System of Social Science: Papers relating to Adam Smith* (Oxford Scholarship Online, Oxford University Press, Oxford 1996; first publ. Oxford University Press, Oxford 1979).

Stoekl, Allan, *The Three Sustainabilities: Energy, economy, time* (University of Minnesota Press, Minneapolis 2021).

Styles, Michael H., *Captain Hogan: Seaman, merchant, diplomat on six continents* (Six Continent Horizons, Fairfax Station, Virginia 2003).

Taylor, Charles, *Sources of the Self: The making of the modern identity* (Harvard University Press, Cambridge, Mass., 1989).

Tink, Andrew, *William Charles Wentworth: Australia's greatest native son* (Allen & Unwin, Sydney 2009).

Tomalin, Claire, *The Life and Death of Mary Wollstonecraft* (Penguin, London 1977; first publ. Weidenfeld and Nicolson, London 1974).

Tucker, Michelle Scott, *Elizabeth Macarthur: A life at the edge of the world* (Text Publishing, Melbourne 2018).

Walzer, Michael, *The Revolution of the Saints: A study in the origins of radical politics* (Harvard University Press, Cambridge, Mass., 1965).

Whitaker, Anne-Maree, *Unfinished Revolution: United Irishmen in New South Wales, 1800–1810* (Crossing Press, Sydney 1994).

―――― (ed.), *Distracted Settlement: New South Wales after Bligh* (Melbourne University Press, Melbourne 1998).

―――― *Joseph Foveaux: Power and patronage in early New South Wales* (UNSW Press, Sydney 2000).

Journal articles

Albree, Joe, and Scott H. Brown, '"A valuable monument of mathematical genius": The Ladies' Diary (1704–1840)', *Historia Mathematica*, vol. 36 (2009), pp. 10–47.

Allen, Matthew, 'Alcohol and authority in early New South Wales: The symbolic significance of the spirit trade, 1788–1808', *History Australia*, vol. 9, no. 3 (December 2012), pp. 7–26.

Allen, Richard B., 'Slaves, convicts, abolitionism and the global origins of the post-emancipation indentured labor system', *Slavery and Abolition: A journal of slave and post-slave studies*, vol. 35 (2014), pp. 328–48.

Atkinson, Alan, 'Whigs and Tories and Botany Bay', *Journal of the Royal Australian Historical Society*, vol. 62 (1976), pp. 73–90.

—— 'Jeremy Bentham and the Rum Rebellion', *Journal of the Royal Australian Historical Society*, vol. 64 (1978), pp. 1–13.

—— 'John Macarthur before Australia knew him', *Journal of Australian Studies*, no. 4 (June 1979), pp. 22–37.

—— 'Master and servant at Camden Park', *Push from the Bush*, no. 6 (May 1980), pp. 42–60.

—— 'The British Whigs and the Rum Rebellion', *Journal of the Royal Australian Historical Society*, vol. 66 (1980), pp. 73–90.

—— 'James Macarthur as author', *Journal of the Royal Australian Historical Society*, vol. 67, (1981), pp. 264–71.

—— 'A new John Macarthur', *Push from the Bush*, no. 17 (April 1984), pp. 43–56.

—— 'The little revolution in New South Wales, 1808', *International History Review*, vol. 12 (1990), pp. 65–75.

—— 'The multiple voices of John Macarthur', *Journal of Australian Colonial History*, vol. 23 (2021), pp. 21–38.

Baines, Edward, 'On the woollen manufactures of England: With special reference to the Leeds clothing district', *Quarterly Journal of the Statistical Society*, vol. 22 (1859), pp. 1–34.

Baugh, Daniel, 'Parliament, naval spending and the public: Contrasting financial legacies of two exhausting wars, 1689–1713', *Histoire et Mesure*, vol. 30, no. 2 (2015), pp. 23–50.

Blouet, O.M., 'Slavery and freedom in the British West Indies, 1823–33: The role of education', *History of Education Quarterly*, vol. 30 (1990), pp. 625–43.

Boud, R.C., 'Scottish agricultural improvement societies, 1723–1835', *Review of Scottish Culture*, no. 1 (1984), pp. 70–90.

Browne, S.E., '"A just and profitable commerce": Moral economy and the middle classes in eighteenth-century London', *Journal of British Studies*, vol. 32 (1993), pp. 305–32.

Chaves, K.K., '"A solemn judicial farce, the mere mockery of a trial": The acquittal of Lieutenant Lowe, 1827', *Aboriginal History*, vol. 31 (2007), pp. 122–40.

Cookson, J.E., 'The Napoleonic wars, military Scotland and Tory Highlandism in the early nineteenth century', *Scottish Historical Review*, vol. 7 (1999), pp. 60–75.

Dunbabin, Thomas, 'William Raven, R.N. and his Britannia, 1792–95', *Mariner's Mirror*, vol. 46 (1960), pp. 297–303.

Durie, Alastair J., 'The markets for Scottish linen, 1730–1775', *Scottish Historical Review*, vol. 52 (1973), pp. 30–49.

SELECT BIBLIOGRAPHY

Dwyer, John, 'Clio and ethics: Practical morality in enlightened Scotland', *Eighteenth Century*, vol. 30, no. 1 (1989), pp. 45–77.

Essary, Kirk, and Yasmin Haskell, 'Calm and violent passions: The genealogy of a distinction from Quintilian to Hume', *Erudition and the Republic of Letters*, vol. 3 (2018), pp. 55–81.

Fletcher, B.H., 'The development of small scale farming in New South Wales under Governor Hunter', *Journal of the Royal Australian Historical Society*, vol. 50 (1964), pp. 1–31.

Forster, H.C., '"Tyranny opression and fraud": Port Jackson, New South Wales, 1792–1794', *Journal of the Royal Australian Historical Society*, vol. 60 (1974), pp. 73–88.

Gaillet, Lynée Lewis, 'George Jardine: Champion of the Scottish philosophy of democratic intellect', *Rhetoric Society Quarterly*, vol. 28 (1998), pp. 37–53.

Gordon, Daniel, 'The dematerialization principle: Sociability, money and music in the eighteenth century', *Historical Reflections/Réflexions Historiques*, vol. 31 (2005), pp. 71–92.

Greenberg, Dolores, 'Energy, power, and perceptions of social change in the early nineteenth century', *American Historical Review*, vol. 95 (1990), pp. 693–714.

Guillou, Jean, 'Un émigré de la révolution Française aux antipodes', *Bulletin de la Société d'Études Historiques de la Nouvelle Calédonie*, no. 57 (1983), pp. 21–40.

Hearn, Mark, 'A single Australia? Alan Atkinson's narrative construction of late modernity', *History Australia*, vol. 19 (2022), pp. 1–16.

Hopkins, Darren, 'Governor King and the illicit distillers, 1800–1806', *Journal of the Royal Australian Historical Society*, vol. 105 (2019), pp. 159–79.

McIntyre, Julie, 'Camden to London and Paris: The role of the Macarthur family in the early New South Wales wine industry', *History Compass*, vol. 5 (2007), pp. 427–38.

—— 'Adam Smith and faith in the transformative qualities of wine in colonial New South Wales', *Australian Historical Studies*, vol. 42 (2011), pp. 194–211.

Mitchell, Adrian, 'Watkin Tench's sentimental enclosures: Original relations from the first settlement', *Australian and New Zealand Studies in Canada*, no. 11 (June 1994), pp. 29–33.

Randall, Adrian J., 'Peculiar perquisites and pernicious practices: Embezzlement in the west of England woollen industry, c. 1750–1840', *International Review of Social History*, vol. 35 (1990), pp. 193–219.

Schaffer, Simon, 'Ceremonies of measurement: Rethinking the world history of science', *Annales: Histoire, Sciences Sociales* (English edition), vol. 17 (2015), pp. 335–60.

Simpson, Ian, 'The imprint of India at Elizabeth Farm, Parramatta', *Journal of Australian Colonial History*, vol. 18 (2016), pp. 23–38.

Smail, John, 'The culture of credit in eighteenth-century commerce: The English textile industry', *Enterprise and Society*, vol. 4 (2003), pp. 299–325.

—— 'Credit, risk, and honor in eighteenth-century commerce', *Journal of British Studies*, vol. 44 (2005), pp. 439–56.

Stenning, Eve, 'Nothing but gum trees: Textile manufacturing in New South Wales 1788–1850', *Australasian Historical Archaeology*, vol. 11 (1993), pp. 76–87.

Ward, J.R., 'The amelioration of British West Indian slavery, 1750–1834: Technical change and the plough', *Nieuwe West-Indische Gids / New West Indian Guide*, vol. 63, no. 1/2 (1989), pp. 41–58.

Theses

Atkinson, Alan, 'The position of John Macarthur and his family in New South Wales before 1842', MA thesis, University of Sydney 1972.
—— 'The political life of James Macarthur', PhD thesis, Australian National University 1977.
Bramble, Christine, 'Relations between Aborigines and white settlers in Newcastle and the Hunter District, 1804–1841', BLitt thesis, University of New England 1961.
Bridges, B.J., 'The Sydney Orphan Schools 1800–1830', MEd thesis, University of Sydney 1973.
Broadbent, James, 'Aspects of domestic architecture in New South Wales 1788–1843', PhD thesis, Australian National University 1985 (three volumes).
Clarke, R.M., 'Vanguards of Empire: The lives of William Dawes, Watkin Tench and George Worgan', PhD thesis, Australian National University 2015.
Hill, S.E., '"Paper houses": John Macarthur and the 30-year design process of Camden Park', PhD thesis, University of Sydney 2016 (two volumes).
Mackillop, Andrew, 'Military recruiting in the Scottish Highlands 1739–1815: The political, social and economic context', PhD thesis, University of Glasgow 1995.
Paskins, Matthew, 'Sentimental industry: The Society of Arts and the encouragement of public useful knowledge, 1754–1848', PhD thesis, University College London 2014.
Pemberton, P.A., 'The London connection: The formation and early years of the Australian Agricultural Company', PhD thesis, Australian National University 1991.
Stenning, Eve, 'Textile manufacturing in New South Wales 1788–1851', MA thesis, University of Sydney 1986.

NOTES

Abbreviations
HRA   Historical Records of Australia
HRNSW   Historical Records of New South Wales
ML   Mitchell Library (State Library of New South Wales)
NL   National Library of Australia
NSWSR   New South Wales State Records
SG   Sydney Gazette
TNA   The National Archives, London

Edward   Edward Macarthur (1789–1872)
EM   Elizabeth Macarthur (1766–1850)
Elizabeth jr Elizabeth Macarthur (1792–1842), daughter of Elizabeth and John
Emmeline   Emmeline Macarthur (1808–88; from 1843 Emmeline Parker)
James   James Macarthur (1798–1867)
JM   John Macarthur (1766–1834)
John jr   John Macarthur (1794–1831), son of Elizabeth and John
Mary   Mary Macarthur (1795–1852; from 1823 Mary Bowman)
William   William Macarthur (1800–82)

Introduction
1   [James], 'Memorandum for life of the late John Macarthur, Esq.', n.d. (watermark 1841), ML A2897; James, 'Memoir of John Macarthur', n.d. [post 1852], ML A2897; J.O. McWilliam, 'Macarthur, John', *Imperial Dictionary of Universal Biography* (3 vols) (1857–63), vol. 3 (1863), pp. 257–58 (virtually a transcript of James's memorandum).
2   Notes by Elizabeth Macarthur-Onslow, n.d., ML A2910; F.M. Bladen (ed.), *Historical Records of New South Wales*, vol. 2 (Sydney 1983), pp. xxv, 487–512; Elizabeth Macarthur-Onslow, notes, n.d., ML A2910; Sibella Macarthur Onslow (ed.), *Some Early Records of the Macarthurs of Camden* (Sydney 1914), p. 4.
3   *Sydney Morning Herald*, 3 February 1843; *Port Phillip Gazette*, 22 February 1843.
4   M. Barnard Eldershaw, 'The happy pioneer, Elizabeth Macarthur', in Flora Eldershaw (ed.), *The Peaceful Army: A memorial to the pioneer women of Australia, 1788–1938* (Sydney 1938), pp. 3–25.
5   Robert Murray, journal, 1793, mfm ML (New England Microfilming Project; original in Peabody Museum of Salem, Massachusetts); Thomas Dunbabin, review of Vance Palmer, *National Portraits*, in *Australian Quarterly*, March 1941, p. 111.
6   M.H. Ellis, *John Macarthur* (Sydney 1955), pp. 8–9, 57.

7   Ellis, *John Macarthur*, p. 484.
8   Margaret Steven, 'Macarthur, John (1767–1834)', *Australian Dictionary of Biography*, adb.anu.edu.au/biography/macarthur-john-2390/text3153, publ. first in hardcopy 1967.
9   Kate Grenville, *A Room Made of Leaves: A novel* (Melbourne 2020), pp. 2–3; 'A room made of leaves', kategrenville.com.au/books/a-room-made-of-leaves; *Guardian* (Australia), 3, 31 July 2020.
10 Ellis, *John Macarthur*, p. xiv; Michelle Scott Tucker, *Elizabeth Macarthur: A life at the edge of the world* (Melbourne 2018).
11 Ellis, *John Macarthur*, p. xiv.

PART 1
1   The first border
1   A.G. Brown, *Alluvial Geoarchaeology: Floodplain archaeology and environmental change* (Cambridge 1997), p. 334; Peter Ackroyd, *Thames: Sacred river* (London 2008), p. 23.
2   Daniel Defoe, *A Tour Thro' the Whole Island of Great Britain* (4 vols) (London 1761; first publ. 1724–27), vol. 2, p. 8; Anna Eliza Bray, *A Description of the Part of Devonshire Bordering on the Tamar and the Tavy* (3 vols) (London 1836), vol. 3, p. 266.
3   [E.D. Clark], *A Tour Through the South of England, Wales, and Part of Ireland, Made During the Summer of 1791* (London 1793), p. 72; Priya Satia, *Empire of Guns: The violent making of the Industrial Revolution* (New York 2018), pp. 205–10.
4   [Clark], *A Tour*, pp. 91–98, 117–18; George Lipscomb, *A Journey into Cornwall* (Warwick 1799), p. 262; A.K. Hamilton Jenkin, quoting an unidentified traveller in 1775, *Western Morning News* (Plymouth), 1 February 1928; Bernard Deacon, 'The reformulation of territorial identity: Cornwall in the late eighteenth and nineteenth centuries', PhD thesis, Open University, UK, 2001, pp. 68–79.
5   Adrian J. Randall, 'Peculiar perquisites and pernicious practices: Embezzlement in the west of England woollen industry, c. 1750–1840', *International Review of Social History*, vol. 35 (1990), pp. 194–96.
6   Charles Vancouver, *General View of the Agriculture of the County of Devon* (London 1808), pp. 338–52.
7   Satia, *Empire of Guns*, pp. 66–145.
8   Sarah Irving-Stonebraker, 'The surprising lineage of useful knowledge', in Justin Champion et al. (eds), *Politics, Religion and Ideas in Seventeenth- and Eighteenth-Century Britain* (Woodbridge, UK, 2019), pp. 286–87.
9   EM to Edward, 5 April 1842, and to James, 11–18 November 1848, ML A2907; Allan Stoekl, *The Three Sustainabilities: Energy, economy, time* (Minneapolis 2021), pp. 172–74.
10 Baron von Grimm, July 1782, quoted in Leo Damrosch, *Jean-Jacques Rousseau: Restless genius* (Boston 2005), pp. 445–46.
11 Charles Taylor, *Sources of the Self: The making of the modern identity* (Cambridge, Mass., 1989), pp. 130–36.

2   The stepfather
1   H.D. Love, *Vestiges of Old Madras, 1640–1800* (4 vols) (Delhi 1913), vol. 2, pp. 413, pp. 599–600; Alistair Forsyth, 'Sir John Call (1732–1801)', addendum

Notes to pages 21-28

    to Peter Herring, 'A folly on Kit Hill', *Cornish Archaeology*, no. 28, 1989, p. 257; Sudip Bhattacharya, *The Strange Case of Lord Pigot* (Newcastle-upon-Tyne 2013), p. 183.
2   Love, *Vestiges*, vol. 2, pp. 159, 589–90, and vol. 3, pp. 43–44, 65; Kent Archaeological Society, 'St Margaret's Churchyard, Lee', Discovering History in Kent, www.kentarchaeology.org.uk/research/monumental-inscriptions/lee.
3   Herring, 'A folly on Kit Hill', pp. 253–58.
4   John Howard, *The State of the Prisons in England and Wales* (London 1784; first publ. 1777), p. 395; Simon Devereaux, 'Convicts and the state: The administration of criminal justice in Great Britain during the reign of George III', PhD thesis, University of Toronto, 1997, pp. 130–36.
5   Edmund Leach to Samuel More, 6 December 1785, RSA/PR/MC/101/10/1513, Royal Society of Arts Archive, London (thanks to Evelyn Watson for help with this); Edmund Leach, *A Treatise of Universal Inland Navigations, and the Use of All Sorts of Mines* (London 1791), p. 24.
6   Leach to the Society for the Encouragement of Arts etc., 26 November 1780, RSA/PR/MC/101/10/956.
7   Leach, *A Treatise*, p. v.
8   Matthew Paskins, 'Sentimental industry: The Society of Arts and the encouragement of public useful knowledge, 1754–1848', PhD thesis, University College London, 2014, pp. 87–88.
9   Leach to Society for the Encouragement of the Arts etc., 16 November 1785; Leach, *A Treatise*, pp. 189–90; *A Catalogue of the Machines, Models, and Other Articles, in the Repository of the Society Instituted for the Encouragement of Arts, Manufactures, and Commerce* (London 1814), p. 13.
10   Leach to Society for the Encouragement of the Arts etc., 16 November 1785; *Critical Review* (London), December 1790, pp. 701–702; *Analytical Review* (London), May–Aug 1791, pp. 334–36; *Monthly Review* (London), August 1791, pp. 400–403, and September 1791, pp. 119–20.
11   *Monthly Review*, August 1791, p. 403.
12   Margaret Steven, 'Macarthur, John (1767–1834)', *Australian Dictionary of Biography*, adb.anu.edu.au/biography/macarthur-john-2390/text3153, publ. first in hardcopy 1967.
13   David Stagg, 'Silviculture inclosure in the New Forest from 1780 to 1850', *Proceedings of the Hampshire Field Club and Archaeological Society*, vol. 46 (1990), pp. 131–33.

3 Elizabeth

1   Jocelyn Lloyd, 'The Gilberts of Tackbeare', in *The Corys of Paterson's Plains*, www.thomasl.com/cory/index.html.
2   Richard Veale and Grace Hatherly, prenuptial settlement, 3 July 1764, X355/353, Kresen Kernow (Cornwall Record Office); James to Roger Therry (draft), 24 February 1859, ML A2897.
3   Veale and Hatherly, prenuptial settlement.
4   Edward to EM, 13 February 1809, 11 July 1812, ML A2912.
5   John Veale 'of Lugworthy', possibly Richard's brother, died in 1763, apparently leaving a son John, aged four. John Veale's will and Richard Veale's intestate estate are listed in E.A. Fry (ed.), *Calendars of Wills and Administrations Relating to the Counties of Devon and Cornwall* (London 1908), but were themselves destroyed in World War II.

6   Sir Thomas Edlyne Tomlins, *The Law-Dictionary* (ed. T.C. Granger) (London 1835; first publ. 1797), vol. 1, n.p.; Grace Leach, release of dower, February 1791: 1038M/T/1/1,2, Cornwall Record Office (thanks to Di Gibbs for advice on dowry rights).
7   Edward to EM, 15 February 1809, ML A2912; EM to Edward, 29 September 1833, ML A2906; Elizabeth Macarthur-Onslow, note, n.d., ML A2906.
8   EM to Edward, 23 March, 26 November 1832, ML A2906; EM to Edward, 7 October 1843, 7 February 1845, ML A2907; [Laetitia Matilda Hawkins], *Annaline; or, Motive-Hunting* (3 vols) (London 1824), vol. 1, p. 40.
9   Bridget Kingdon to EM, 23 August 1796, 15 September 1799, and EM to Eliza Kingdon, March 1816, ML A2908.
10 EM to Bridget Kingdon, 7 March 1791, ML A2908; Joseph Conrad, *Under Western Eyes* (New York 2001; first publ. 1911), p. 216.
11 EM to Eliza Kingdon, 4 September 1822, ML A2908; Griselda Kingdon's monument, St Bridget's church Bridgerule, quoted [Frank Allaben], in *Arms and Pedigree of Kingdon-Gould of New York and Georgian Court*, Lakewood, New Jersey (New York 1906), pp. 24–25.
12 T.H. Kingdon to EM, 6 July1841, ML A2917.
13 Richard Polwhele, *The History of Devonshire* (3 vols), vol. 3 (Exeter 1806), pp. 432–23.
14 Bridget Kingdon to EM, 15 September 1799, ML A2908; John Kingdon, will, dated 10 November 1806, proved 4 May 1809, PROB 11/1497/41, TNA.
15 *Exeter Flying Post*, 31 March 1808; Nicholas Carlisle, *A Concise Description of the Endowed Grammar Schools in England* (2 vols) (London 1818), vol. 1, p. 248; information kindly supplied by Penelope Baker, archivist, Exeter College, Oxford.
16 EM to Edward, 28 January 1843, ML A2907; Lynda Mugglestone, *Speaking Proper: The rise and fall of the English accent as a social symbol* (Oxford 2003; first publ. 1995), pp. 17–34.
17 James to EM, 7 April 1829 (using lengthy French without apology but apologising for Latin), ML A2931.
18 C.S. Gilbert, *An Historical Survey of the County of Cornwall* (2 vols) (Plymouth Dock 1820), vol. 2, pp. 159–60.
19 Bridget Kingdon to EM, 23 August 1796, ML A2908; C.E. Byles, *The Life and Letters of R.S. Hawker (Sometime Vicar of Morwenstow)* (London 1905), pp. 14–16, 19–20, 483–84; M.D. Jeune, *Pages from the Diary of an Oxford Lady 1843–1862* (Oxford 1932), p. 9; Henry French and Mark Rothery, *Man's Estate: Landed gentry masculinities, 1660–1900* (Oxford 2012), p. 110.
20 Daniel Lysons and Samuel Lysons, *Cornwall* (Magna Britannia, vol. 3) (London 1814), p. 6; G.B. Worgan, *General View of the Agriculture of the County of Cornwall* (London 1815), pp. 94–97.
21 William Albert, 'The turnpike trusts', in Derek H. Aldcroft and Michael J. Freeman (eds), *Transport in the Industrial Revolution* (Manchester 1983), pp. 34–44; Jacqueline Pearson, *Women's Reading in Britain, 1750–1835: A dangerous recreation* (Cambridge 1999), p. 12; Temma Berg, *The Lives and Letters of an Eighteenth-Century Circle of Acquaintance* (Aldershot, UK, 2006), p. 17; Leslie Ritchie, *Women Writing Music in Late Eighteenth-Century England: Social harmony in literature and performance* (Abingdon, UK, 2008), p. 75.
22 Joe Albree and Scott H. Brown, '"A valuable monument of mathematical genius": The Ladies' Diary (1704–1840)', *Historia Mathematica*, vol. 36 (2009),

p. 13; James Raven, *The Business of Books: Booksellers and the English book trade 1450–1850* (New Haven 2007), p. 246.
23   Karen Halttunen, 'Humanitarianism and the pornography of pain in Anglo-American culture', *American Historical Review*, vol. 100 (1995), pp. 303–307.
24   Jane Austen to Cassandra Austen, 20 November 1808, in Deirdre Le Faye (ed.), *Jane Austen's Letters* (Oxford 2011; first publ. 1932), p. 159.

4   A locomotive disposition
1   Jeremiah 48:11 (King James Version); Anthony Purver, *A New and Literal Translation of All the Books of the Old and New Testament* (2 vols) (London 1764), vol. 2, p. 119; Thomas Gray to Norton Nicholls, 26 January 1771, in Thomas Gray, *The Poems of Mr Gray* (ed. William Mason) (2 vols) (Dublin 1775), vol. 2, p. 147.
2   Alexander McArthur, claim for losses incurred by Jacobite raids, June–July 1685: Land Tax Roll, Argyll, 1684–88, E016/3/1/14V, National Records of Scotland; Anon., *An Account of the Depredations Committed on the Clan Campbell, and Their Followers, during the Years 1685 and 168*6 (Edinburgh 1816), p. 47.
3   Alexander McArthur to Earl of Argyll, two letters, 1679, GD/40/9/80 (fragile; not seen), Hearth Tax Roll, Argyll, 1691–95, E69/3/1, and 'Accompt of the hearth-money of the shires of Argyle and Bute collected by Alexr. McArthur in Feorlyne', 1694, GD 26/7/386, all National Records of Scotland; Alan Atkinson, 'John Macarthur before Australia knew him', *Journal of Australian Studies*, no. 4 (June 1979), pp. 22–25.
4   Grant of Arms to John McArthur, 14 January 1797, Public Register of Arms, vol. 1, f. 575, Court of the Lord Lyon (copy from Max Marcus, Secretary to Lyon Office); G.F. Macarthur, n.d. (author died 1890; detail gathered pre-1855), 'Genealogical map of the MacArthurs of Strachur', ML D80; copy of a family tree sketched by Gen. Charles McArthur, died 1904, provenance lost (copy in my possession).
5   T.P. Macqueen to JM, 29 December 1824, ML A 2911.
6   James, 'Memoir of John Macarthur', n.d. [post 1852], ML A2897; Andrew Mackillop, 'Military recruiting in the Scottish Highlands 1739–1815: The political, social and economic context', PhD thesis, University of Glasgow, 1995, pp. 16–29.
7   Thomas Reid, *Essays on the Active Powers of Man* (Glasgow 1788), p. 385.
8   Matthew 19:21 (King James Version).
9   George Whitefield to 'Mr S.', 20 November 1750, and to 'Mr L.', 13 January 1751, in *The Works of the Reverend George Whitefield, M.A.* (2 vols) (London 1771), vol. 2, pp. 387, 392; Thomas Timpson, *Church History of Kent* (London 1859), p. 309; Anon., 'Academical discipline in the 18th Century', *Transactions of the Congregational Historical Society*, vol. 3 (1907–08), pp. 67–68.
10   Baptismal register, 20 January 1752, Guildhall Street Independent Chapel, Canterbury, RG 4/2426, TNA; J.A. Marusek, A Chronological Listing of Early Weather Events, 2010, wattsupwiththat.files.wordpress.com/2011/09/weather1.pdf, p. 230.
11   William, her youngest son, was baptised on 27 August 1770, Stoke Damerel; Catherine McArthur was buried on 31 August 1777, Stoke Damerel. Her gravestone, no longer extant, gave 40 as her age at death: 453/5 Stoke Damerel Parish Church, Devonport, undated monumental inscriptions, Plymouth

Archives, The Box (thanks to Alan Barclay for this). However that age at death makes her too young to have given birth in January 1752. She might have been, say, 44.
12 G.F. Macarthur, 'Genealogical map of the MacArthurs of Strachur'; H.C. Allport, 'Catalogue of the library at Elizabeth Farm, the property of Col'l Macarthur', May 1854, ML A2919/4; James to Roger Therry, 24 February 1859 (draft), ML A2897.
13 'Genealogical map of the Macarthurs of Strachur'.
14 JM to EM, 22 July 1816, ML A2898; Michael Walzer, *The Revolution of the Saints: A study in the origins of radical politics* (Cambridge, Mass., 1965), pp. 2–4, 9–65; Charles Taylor, *Sources of the Self: The making of modern identity* (Cambridge, Mass., 1989), pp. 213–33.
15 Anon., 'On the linen, muslin, and cotton manufactures in the canton of Appenzell', *Tradesman: or, Commercial Magazine*, vol. 3 (November 1809), pp. 432–33; J.G. Zellweger, 'Appenzell', in John Bowring, *Report on the Commerce and Manufactures of Switzerland* (London 1836), pp. 17–18.
16 *Weekly Register* (Sydney), 10 February 1844; *Argus* (Melbourne), 16 May 1931.
17 Emmeline de Falbe to Elizabeth Macarthur-Onslow, 'Wed.' [1890–95?], ML A2910; A.J. Durie, 'The markets for Scottish linen, 1730–1775', *Scottish Historical Review*, vol. 52 (1973), pp. 39–47; A.L. Karras, *Sojourners in the Sun: Scottish migrants in Jamaica and the Chesapeake, 1740–1800* (Ithaca, NY, 1992), pp. 3–4, 11–12, 21–22, 83–106; S.D. Smith, 'The market for manufactures in the thirteen continental colonies, 1698–1776', *Economic History Review*, new series, vol. 51 (1998), pp. 676–708.
18 Bernard Le Bovier de Fontenelle, *A Conversation on the Plurality of Worlds* (trans. William Gardiner) (Edinburgh 1753; first publ. in French 1686), pp. 33–34. The listed works by Fontenelle at Elizabeth Farm were *Entretiens sur la pluralité des mondes*, *Éloges* and *Histoire des oracles*: Allport, 'Catalogue of the library at Elizabeth Farm'.

5 John

1 [James], 'Memorandum for life of the late John Macarthur, Esq.', n.d. (watermark 1841), ML A2897; Alan Atkinson, 'John Macarthur before Australia knew him', *Journal of Australian Studies*, no. 4 (June 1979), pp. 28–29.
2 *Spectator*, vol. 1 (London 1713) pp. 22–23 (no. 6, 7 March 1711); James to Roger Therry (draft), 24 February 1859, ML A2897; Edward to JM, 14 May 1809, ML A2912; Stephen Miller, 'The strange career of Joseph Addison', *Sewanee Review*, vol. 122 (2014), pp. 650–60.
3 James to Therry (draft), 24 February 1859.
4 Various documents re David Jardine, 1761–91, Cornwall Record Office, Devon Heritage Centre and TNA.
5 William Burt, *Review of the Mercantile, Trading, and Manufacturing State, Interests, and Capability of the Port of Plymouth* (Plymouth 1816), pp. 131, 241–42; R.N. Worth, *The History of Plymouth, from the Earliest Period to the Present Time* (Plymouth 1873), pp. 249–51.
6 R.N. Worth, *History of the Town and Borough of Devonport, sometime Plymouth Dock* (Plymouth 1870), p. 93.
7 Frederick Rogers to Navy Board, 3 January 1766, ADM 174/114, TNA; Edward Lecras to Navy Board, 16 January 1783, ADM 174/118, TNA; John Smail, 'Credit, risk, and honor in eighteenth-century commerce', *Journal of*

British Studies, vol. 44 (2005), pp. 449–50; Daniel Baugh, 'Parliament, naval spending and the public: Contrasting financial legacies of two exhausting wars, 1689–1713', *Histoire et Mesure*, vol. 30, no. 2 (2015), pp. 24–25.

8   Andrew Kinsman, *The Christian Warrior Finishing His Course* (ed. John Hughes) (London 1768), p. 13.

9   Luke 12:48 (King James Version); Burt, *Review*, p. 175; Worth, *History of Plymouth*, p. 250.

10 John Britton and E.W. Brayley, *The Beauties of England and Wales* (4 vols), vol. 4 (London 1803), pp. 177–78.

11 James Spry, 'Liberty Street', *Western Antiquary*, December 1881, p. 149; Worth, *History of the Town and Borough of Devonport*, pp. 89–93; James M. Haas, 'The introduction of task work into the royal dockyards, 1775', *Journal of British Studies*, vol. 8, no. 2 (1969), pp. 52–64.

12 Land tax assessments, parish of Stoke Damerel, Devon Heritage Centre; St Aubyn Estate Rentals, Plymouth Archives; Anon., *The Plymouth-Dock Guide; or, An Authentic Account of the Rise and Progress of That Town, with the Dockyard* (Plymouth Dock 1796), p. 8; Atkinson, 'John Macarthur before Australian knew him', pp. 25–26.

13 Rogers to Navy Board, 3 January 1766; Lecras to Navy Board, 16 January 1783; Baugh, 'Parliament, naval spending and the public', pp. 24–25, 37.

14 John Law, 'Histoire des finances pendant la Régence', n.d., quoted in Daniel Gordon, 'The dematerialization principle: Sociability, money and music in the eighteenth century', *Historical Reflections/Réflexions Historiques*, vol. 31 (2005), p. 87.

15 Jeremy Adler, *Johan Wolfgang von Goethe* (London 2020), pp. 165–80, 211–13.

16 Anon., *The Plymouth-Dock Guide*, pp. 19–22; J.S. Attwood, 'Booksellers and printers in Devon and Cornwall in the seventeenth and eighteenth centuries', *Devon and Cornwall Notes and Queries*, vol. 9 (1916–17), p. 130; Richard Findlater, *Joe Grimaldi: His life and theatre* (Cambridge 1978; first publ. 1955), pp. 68–69.

17 Ella Stewart-Peters, 'From "ignorant mothers" to "conscientious fathers": Cornwall and the Vaccination Act, 1840–1907', PhD thesis, Flinders University, 2018, p. 63 (quoting *West Briton* [Truro], 28 October 1836); Elizabeth Onslow, notes on Sir William Macarthur's reminiscences, 18 March 1870, ML A2935.

18 James to Therry (draft), 24 February 1859; Nicholas Carlisle, *A Concise Description of the Endowed Grammar Schools of England* (2 vols) (London 1818), vol. 1, pp. 250–53. JM's son Edward and nephew Hannibal both went to Chudleigh: Edward to Hannibal Macarthur, 30 September 1808, ML 2912.

19 Thomas Kerr to the War Office, 28 June 1792, WO 1/1053, TNA (kindly shown to me by Michael Durey, the writer possibly identical with Thomas Kerr, who wrote to the Navy Board, 7 June 1788: ADM 106/1296/235, TNA). William McArthur was baptised on 27 August 1770, and buried on 24 November 1772, Stoke Damerel.

20 James to Therry (draft), 24 February 1859; 'Excerpts from Pitt's Secret Service accounts, 1784–1793', *English Historical Documents*, 1783–1832 (ed. A. Aspinall and E. Anthony Smith) (London 1959), pp. 321–22.

21 Andrew Kinsman to Ann Kinsman, 26 July 1757, in Anon., 'Life of Rev. Andrew Kinsman', *Evangelical Magazine* (August 1793), pp. 54, 59.

22 *Australian* (Sydney), 25 May 1832.

6 The joint design

1. Jane Austen, *Mansfield Park* (New York 2010; first publ. 1814), pp. 49–50.
2. Sir George Yonge to Thomas Townshend, 10 December 1782, WO 25/152, pp. 149–50, TNA.
3. Hannibal Hawkins, will, signed 11 August 1800 (codicil 24 April 1802), proved 27 October 1803, PROB 11/1399/833, TNA.
4. Yonge to Isaac Barré, 5 October 1782, WO 4/119, and Thomas Taylor to Yonge, 31 January 1783, WO 1/1019, both TNA; Edward Houndle, mayor, and two aldermen, Barnstaple, to War Office, 11 March 1783, WO 1/1018, Muster roll, 17 March 1783, papers of the 4th Corps of Infantry, WO 12/10707, and Benjamin Fish, memorandum, n.d., with the final return of his corps, 10 April 1783, WO 17/234, all TNA.
5. James, 'Memoir of John Macarthur', n.d. [1853?], ML A2897.
6. EM to Eliza Kingdon, March 1816, ML A2908; EM to Edward, 5 November 1846, ML A2907.
7. John Watkins, *An Essay Towards a History of Bideford in the County of Devon* (Exeter 1792), p. 270; Documents re Edward Bound, 1783–1807, Devon Heritage Centre.
8. Charles Vancouver, *General View of the Agriculture of the County of Devon* (London 1808), p. 342.
9. Bridget Kingdon to EM, 15 September 1799, ML A2908; James to William, 23–24 May 1864, ML A2932.
10. EM to Bridget Kingdon, 1 September 1795, ML A2908.
11. Elizabeth Veale, articles of agreement with James Vowler, 24 June 1788, 1038M/T/1/1, Devon Record Office; EM to Eliza Kingdon, 21 September 1822, ML A2908.
12. EM to Eliza Kingdon, March 1816, 11 December 1817, ML A2908.
13. Yonge to Charles O'Hara, 6 May, 26 August 1788, and Yonge to John Lambton, 10 March 1789, WO 4/990, TNA.
14. Yonge to JM, 4, 16 April 1789, WO 4/990, and Yonge to JM, 25 April 1789, WO 4/138, both TNA. Edward's birthday is given in the *Australian Dictionary of Biography* (vol. 5, p. 122) as 16 March. That makes the timing of events extremely tight. His mother remembered it as 18 March: EM to Edward, 18 March 1841, 25–26 July 1844, ML A2907.

PART 2
7 The far side of the earth

1. Edmund Burke, 'Speech on Fox's East India Bill', 1 December 1783, in P.J. Marshall and W.B. Todd (eds), *The Writings and Speeches of Edmund Burke*, vol. 5 (Oxford 1981), p. 402.
2. Edmund Burke, 'Speech on the Nawab of Arcot's Debts', 28 February 1785, in Marshall and Todd, *The Writings and Speeches of Edmund Burke*, vol. 5, p. 520; Edmund Burke, 'Opening of the impeachment of Warren Hastings', 15 and 19 February 1788, in P.J. Marshall and William B. Todd (eds), *The Writings and Speeches of Edmund Burke* (nine volumes), vol. 6 (Oxford 1991), pp. 304–305.
3. Warren Hastings to Nathaniel Smith, 4 October 1784, foreword to Charles Wilkins (translator), *The Bhagavat Geeta, or Dialogues of Kreeshna and Arjoon* (London 1785), pp. 12–13.
4. J.M. Matra to Evan Nepean, 1 October [November] 1784, *HRNSW*, vol. 1, pt 1, p. 8.

5   W.H. Blumenthal, *Brides from Bridewell: Female felons sent to colonial America* (Rutland, Vermont, 1962), pp. 15–16, 35–7; Alan Atkinson, 'Whigs and Tories and Botany Bay', *Journal of the Royal Australian Historical Society*, vol. 62 (1976), pp. 294–98.
6   Sir George Young to Alexander Davison, 3 February 1793, and enclosed 'Sir George Young's Observations on Madagascar', [1783–84], *HRNSW*, vol. 2 (Sydney 1893), pp. 9–12; Thomas Rowcroft to T.B. Thompson, 4 August 1810, papers of Sir Robin Mackworth-Young, Sutton Montis, UK; Atkinson, 'Whigs and Tories and Botany Bay', pp. 192–97; Alan Frost, 'Thomas Rowcroft's Testimony and the "Botany Bay" Debate', *Labour History*, no. 37 (November 1979), pp. 101–107; D.L. Prior, 'Call, Sir John, first baronet (1732–1801)', *Oxford Dictionary of National Biography*.
7   Governor's instructions, 25 April 1787, *HRA*, series 1, vol. 1, pp. 11–16.
8   *Morning Herald* (London), 23 September 1786; *Public Advertiser* (London), 28 September 1786; Alan Atkinson, 'The ethics of conquest', *Aboriginal History*, vol. 6 (1982), pp. 82–91; David Andrew Roberts, '"They would speedily abandon the country to the new comers": The denial of Aboriginal rights', in Martin Crotty and D.A. Roberts (eds), *The Great Mistakes of Australian History* (Sydney 2006), pp. 14–18.
9   *Morning Chronicle*, 3 November 1786; Governor's instructions, 25 April 1787, pp. 15–16.
10 Watkin Tench, *A Narrative of the Expedition to Botany Bay* (London 1789).
11 Sir George Yonge to Treasury, 20 May 1789, *HRNSW*, vol. 1, pt 2, p. 232; W.W. Grenville to Phillip, 19 June 1789, *HRA*, series 1, vol. 1, pp. 122–23; EM to Grace Leach, 18 March 1791, ML A2908.
12 EM to Leach, 8 October 1789, 18 March 1791, ML A2908.
13 Matthew Lewis to JM, 29 June 1789, and Yonge to Francis Grose, 25 July 1789, WO 4/990, TNA; EM to Leach, 8 October 1789, and EM to Eliza Kingdon, March 1816, ML A2908.
14 EM, journal, 1789–90, ML A2908.
15 EM, journal, 1789–90, and EM to Leach, 20 April 1790, ML A2908.
16 EM, journal, 1789–90.
17 EM, journal, 1789–90; James to Roger Therry, 24 February 1859, ML A2897. Sibella Macarthur Onslow mentions 'Mrs Abbott' on board the *Scarborough*, but this is a misreading of EM's journal, 19 February 1790, ML A2908: Sibella Macarthur Onslow (ed.), *Some Early Records of the Macarthurs of Camden* (Sydney 1914), p. 13.
18 EM to Leach, 20 April 1790, and to Bridget Kingdon, 7 March 1791, ML A2908.
19 EM to Bridget Kingdon, 7 March 1791.
20 EM to Bridget Kingdon, 7 March 1791.
21 EM to Bridget Kingdon, 7 March 1791; Watkin Tench, *A Complete Account of the Settlement at Port Jackson, in New South Wales* (London 1793), p. 200.
22 EM to Bridget Kingdon, 7 March 1791.

8   Everyone thinks
1   *English Chronicle*, 7–10 October 1786; Alan Atkinson, 'The pioneers who left early', *Push from the Bush*, no. 29 (1991), pp. 110–15.
2   Mary Guyatt, 'The Wedgwood slave medallion: Values in eighteenth-century design', *Journal of Design History*, vol. 13 (2000), pp. 93–105; Martha J. Cutter,

The Illustrated Slave: Empathy, graphic narrative, and the visual culture of the transatlantic abolition movement, 1800–1852 (Athens, Georgia, 2017), pp. 1–11.

3   Adam Smith, *The Theory of Moral Sentiments* (London 1759), p. 3; Judith Jennings, *The Business of Abolishing the British Slave Trade, 1783–1807* (London 1997), p. 54; Martyn Hudson, *The Slave Ship, Memory and the Origin of Modernity* (London and New York 2016), pp. 29–30, 82–83; Cutter, *The Illustrated Slave*, p. 13.

4   Adam Smith, *An Inquiry into the Nature and Causes of the Wealth of Nations* (2 vols) (London 1776), vol. 1, pp. 415–16; A.O. Hirschman, *Essays in Trespassing: Economics to politics and beyond* (Cambridge 1981), p. 288.

5   Alan Atkinson, 'The free-born Englishman transported: Convict rights as a measure of eighteenth-century Empire', *Past and Present*, no. 144 (August 1994), pp. 88–115.

6   Edmund Leach, *A Treatise of Universal Inland Navigations, and the Use of All Sorts of Mines* (London 1791), pp. 184–86; J.M. Beattie, *Crime and the Courts in England 1660–1800* (Oxford 1986), pp. 540–59.

7   Arthur Phillip, 'Phillip's suggestions on the conduct of the expedition and the treatment of convicts', n.d. [about February 1787], *HRNSW*, vol. 1, pt 2, p. 53; Alan Atkinson, *The Europeans in Australia: A history*, vol. 1 (Melbourne 1997), pp. 150–54.

8   Governor Phillip's Instructions, 25 April 1787, HRA, series 1, vol. 1, pp. 11, 12, 14; Arthur Phillip, 'Instructions for Philip Gidley King, Esq., Superintendant and Commandant of Norfolk Island', 12 February 1788, *HRA*, series 1, vol. 1, p. 34; Atkinson, 'The free-born Englishman transported', pp. 88–115.

9   Robert Ross to W.W. Grenville, 29 August 1790, and 'Remarks and observations on Norfolk Island by Major Ross', n.d. [about December 1790], *HRNSW*, vol. 1, part 2, pp. 402–403, 416–20; General Orders at Norfolk Island, 8 January, 9 February 1791, *HRA*, series 1, vol. 1, pp. 241–45; Atkinson, *The Europeans in Australia*, vol. 1, pp. 98–101.

10 R.C. Boud, 'Scottish agricultural improvement societies, 1723–1835', *Review of Scottish Culture*, no. 1 (1984), pp. 79–82; T.C. Smout, 'A new look at the Scottish improvers', *Scottish Historical Review*, vol. 91 (2012), pp. 125–49.

11 Various letters, 1778–83 (trans. Duncan Bull), in *Robert Jacob Gordon: His verbal and visual descriptions of South Africa (1775–1795)*, www.robertjacobgordon.nl; various letters, 1779–83 (trans. Anna Böeseken), in G.J. Schutte (ed.), Hendrik Swellengrebel jr, *Briefwisseling oor Kaapse sake 1778–1792* (Cape Town 1982) pp. 309, 363; G.J. Schutte (ed.), *Hendrik Cloete, Groot Constantia and the VOC 1778–1799: Documents from the Swellengrebel Archive* (English trans. N.O. van Gylswyk and D. Sleigh) (Cape Town 2003), pp. 19–23; B.F. von Bouchenroeder, *Beknopt Berigt Nopens de Volkplanting de Kaap de Goede Hoop* (Amsterdam 1806), p. 23 (but incorrect as to date for the original import of the sheep and the initiating body). I am very grateful to Duncan Bull, Rijksmuseum Amsterdam, for help with this detail.

12 Dirk Helbing and Alan Kirman, 'Rethinking economics using complexity theory', *Real-World Economics Review*, issue 64 (2013), n.p.; Christopher Berry, 'James Steuart on the public good', in J.M. Menudo (ed.), *The Economic Thought of Sir James Steuart, First Economist of the Scottish Enlightenment* (Oxford 2020), pp. 7–12; Giulio Bocaletti, 'The new land economy', *Project Syndicate*, 11 February 2022.

13 Richard Cantillon, *The Analysis of Trade, Commerce, Coin, Bullion, Banks, and Foreign Exchange* (ed. Philip Cantillon) (London 1759), pp. 10–12; Antoin E. Murphy, 'Bernard Cantillon's expedition to Louisiana, 1719', in his *Richard Cantillon: Entrepreneur and economist* (Oxford 1986), pp. 88–104.
14 Sir James Steuart, *An Inquiry Into the Principles of Political Oeconomy* (2 vols), vol. 1 (1767), pp. 2, 72–73, 233, 320, 457–69, 512–13; David Williams, *Lessons to a Young Prince, by an Old Statesman, on the Present Disposition in Europe to a General Revolution* (London 1790), pp. 56–57; A.S. Skinner, 'Sir James Steuart: Principles of political economy', in A.S. Skinner, *A System of Social Science: Papers relating to Adam Smith* (Oxford 1996; first publ. 1980), pp. 256–84.
15 Cantillon, *The Analysis of Trade*, p. xiv.

9 Ginger group

1 EM to Bridget Kingdon, 7 March 1791, ML A2908.
2 EM to Grace Leach, 18 March 1791, ML A2908; JM to EM, 26 June 1816, ML A2898; John Allen, *The History of the Borough of Liskeard and Its Vicinity* (London 1856), p. 526.
3 C. Julius Caesar, *Commentaries of His Wars in Gaul, and Civil War with Pompey* (trans. Martin Bladen) (London 1719; first publ. in this translation 1705; Camden Park copy inscribed [in EM's hand?] 'Captain W. Tench of the Marines'); Samuel Johnson, *The Works of the English Poets* (59 vols) (London 1779–80; Camden Park copy inscribed 'Thos. Timmins Decr. 21st 1782'); Cassandra Pybus, '"not fit for your protection or an honest man's company"; A transnational perspective on the saintly William Dawes', *History Australia*, vol. 6, no. 1, 2009), pp. 1–7; R.M. Clarke, 'Vanguards of Empire: The lives of William Dawes, Watkin Tench and George Worgan', PhD thesis, Australian National University, 2015, pp. 177–79. I am very grateful to Bob Clarke for his help here.
4 The *Australian Dictionary of Biography* is doubtful about Tench's birthday but he was born 6 October 1758 (baptised 10 November): parish register, St Mary's, Chester.
5 Watkin Tench, *Letters Written in France, to a Friend in London, between the Month of November 1794, and the Month of May 1795* (London 1796); editor's introduction, in L.F. Fitzhardinge, *Sydney's First Four Years, Being a Reprint of a Narrative of the Expedition to Botany Bay and a Complete Account of the Settlement at Port Jackson* (Sydney 1979), pp. xv, xxi; Adrian Mitchell, 'Watkin Tench's sentimental enclosures: Original relations from the first settlement', *Australian and New Zealand Studies in Canada*, no. 11 (June 1994), pp. 23–33; Gavin Edwards, *Narrative Order, 1789–1819: Life and story in an age of revolution* (London 2006), pp. 11–14, 56–80.
6 Watkin Tench, *A Narrative of the Expedition to Botany Bay* (London 1789), pp. 129–30; EM to Bridget Kingdon, 7 March 1791; Watkin Tench, *A Complete Account of the Settlement at Port Jackson, in New South Wale*s (London 1793), p. 203; Tench, *Letters Written in France*, p. 180. The 'perish' quotation comes from a speech in the House of Commons, quoted in a book review in the *Critical Review*, vol. 8 (1793), p. 331.
7 David Hartley, *Observations on Man, His Frame, His Duty, and His Expectations* (2 vols) (London 1749), vol. 1, pp. 114, 486–92; EM to Bridget Kingdon, 7 March 1791; Tench, *A Complete Account*, pp. 105, 178–204.

8   Tench, *A Narrative*, pp. vi, 120, 140–41.
9   Tench, *A Complete Account*, pp. 163–64, 212.
10 Banastre Tarleton, speech, 21 February 1791, *European Magazine*, vol. 19 (January–June 1791), p. 218.
11 EM to Bridget Kingdon, 7 March 1791, 21 December 1793, ML A2908.
12 Banastre Tarleton to Thomas Cadell, 10 February 1791, extract of letter offered for sale by Hordern House Rare Books, September 1914; Tarleton, speech, 21 February 1791; Pay lists and muster rolls, NSW Corps 1798–99, ML A2998.
13 Francis Grose to Henry Dundas, 3 September 1793, *HRA*, series 1, vol. 1, p. 447; EM to Eliza Kingdon, 21 September 1822, ML A2908. Alexander McArthur was buried at Plymouth Dock, 23 September 1790; Grace Leach married John Bond at Bridgerule, 27 March 1792.
14 Richard Cantillon, *The Analysis of Trade, Commerce, Coin, Bullion, Banks, and Foreign Exchanges* (ed. Philip Cantillon) (London 1759), pp. 10–12.
15 Henry Dundas to Hunter, 1 July 1794, *HRA*, series 1, vol. 1, pp. 467–76; David Collins, *An Account of the English Colony in New South Wales* (2 vols, ed. Brian H. Fletcher) (Sydney 1975), vol. 1 (first publ. 1798), p. 224; Hunter to Duke of Portland, 25 July 1798, *HRA*, series 1, vol. 2, pp. 160–88.
16 Grose to King, 25 February 1794, *HRNSW*, vol. 2, pp. 125–27; Hunter to Portland, 25 July 1798, pp. 162–64.

10   Inspector of public works

1   Evan Nepean, budget for NSW settlement, rough and fair copies, n.d. [August 1796], HO 42/7, ff. 23, 24, TNA.
2   David Collins, *An Account of the English Colony in New South Wales* (2 vols, ed. Brian H. Fletcher) (Sydney 1975), vol. 1 (first publ. 1798), pp. 209–10; Alan Atkinson, *The Europeans in Australia* (3 vols), vol. 1 (Sydney 2016; first publ. Melbourne 1997), pp. 94–5.
3   John Hunter to Duke of Portland, 12 November 1796, *HRA*, series 1, vol. 1, p. 667; Brian H. Fletcher, *Landed Enterprise and Penal Society: A history of farming and grazing in New South Wales before 1821* (Sydney 1976), pp. 27–30. The calculations (not counting Norfolk Island) are drawn from detail in R.J. Ryan (ed.), *Land Grants 1788–1809: A record of registered grants and leases in New South Wales, Van Diemen's Land and Norfolk Island* (Sydney 1974). See also A.G.L. Shaw, 'Missing land grants in New South Wales, 1792–1800', *Historical Studies*, no. 17 (1951), pp. 68–78.
4   Hunter to Henry Dundas, 11 September 1795, *HRA*, series 1, vol. 1, p. 528; Hunter to Sir Joseph Banks, 12 October 1795, ML SAFE/Banks Papers/Series 38; Collins, *An Account of the English Colony in New South Wales*, vol. 1, pp. 228, 266.
5   EM to Bridget Kingdon, 7 March 1791, ML A2908; Collins, *An Account of the English Colony in New South Wales*, vol. 1, pp. 108, 157; M.N. McConnell, *Army and Empire: British soldiers on the American frontier, 1758–1775* (Lincoln, Nebraska, 2004), pp. 104–106.
6   Collins, *An Account of the English Colony in New South Wales*, vol. 1, pp. 263, 277; Atkinson, *The Europeans in Australia*, vol. 1 (Melbourne 2007), pp. 203–204 (quoting Richard Roome and Stephen Smith, soldiers, 7 August 1804).
7   Joseph Addison, *Dialogues upon the Usefulness of Ancient Medals, Especially in Relation to the Latin and Greek Poets* (London 1726), pp. 38–39; John

Adams, *The Flowers of Ancient History; Comprehending on a New Plan, the Most Remarkable and Interesting Events, as Well as Characters, of Antiquity* (Dublin 1789), p. 223.
8   EM to Bridget Kingdon, 1 September [1798]; S.J. Butlin, *Foundations of the Australian Monetary System* 1788–1851 (Sydney 1953), pp. 12–15, 30–31.
9   Portland to Hunter, 10 June 1795, and Hunter to Portland, 27 August 1796 (enclosing civil officers to Hunter, 25 February 1796, and his undated response), *HRA*, series 1, vol. 1, pp. 494–95, 646–48; JM to Hunter, 15 August 1796, *HRA*, series 1, vol. 2, pp. 97–98.
10 Alan Finkel, *Getting to Zero: Australia's energy transition* (*Quarterly Essay*, issue 81) (Melbourne 2021), p. 44; Allan Stoekl, *The Three Sustainabilities: Energy, economy, time* (Minneapolis 2021), pp. 183–88; Adam Frank, David Grinspoon and Sara Walker, 'Intelligence as a planetary scale process', *International Journal of Astrobiology*, vol. 21 (2022), pp. 1–15.
11 Hunter to Portland, 28 April 1796, *HRA*, series 1, vol. 1, pp. 556–57; JM to Portland, 15 September 1796, HRA, series 1, vol. 2, p. 92; James to Roger Therry (draft), 24 February 1859, ML A2897.
12 JM to Hunter, 24 February 1796, and Hunter to Portland, 28 April, 14 September 1796, *HRA*, series 1, vol. 1, pp. 95, 560, 661–62, 689; Hunter to Portland, 25 July 1798, *HRA*, series 1, vol. 2, pp. 160–63.
13 Sir James Steuart, *An Inquiry into the Principles of Political Oeconomy* (2 vols), vol. 1 (London 1767), pp. 26–35; JM to Portland, 15 September 1796, *HRA*, series 1, vol. 2, pp. 91–92.
14 JM to Portland, 15 September 1796, pp. 91–92.
15 Portland to Hunter, 30 August 1797, *HRA*, series 1, vol. 2, p. 89.
16 JM to Hunter, 15 August 1796, *HRA*, series 1, vol. 2, pp. 97–98.
17 Hunter to Portland, 10 June 1796, Hunter to JM, 18 August 1796, JM to Hunter, 19 August 1796, and JM to Portland, 15 September 1796, *HRA*, series 1, vol. 2, pp. 91, 99–100, 115.

11 'A maneuvering business'

1   EM to Bridget Kingdon, 7 March 1791, ML A2908; Geoffrey Lancaster, *The First Fleet Piano* (2 vols) (Canberra 2015), vol. 1, pp. 475–91.
2   EM to Bridget Kingdon, 7 March 1791; diagram on title page, n.d. [1790–92], ML A 2903/1. The Camden Park library still holds Dawes's copy of John Bonnycastle, *An Introduction to Algebra* (London 1782).
3   EM to Bridget Kingdon, 7 March 1791.
4   James Lee, *An Introduction to Botany* (London 1776; first publ. 1760), pp. vi–xiv, 11–13 (Dawes's copy, now at Camden Park); EM to Bridget Kingdon, 7 March 1791; Peter Moore, *Endeavour: The ship and the attitude that changed the world* (Sydney 2018), pp. 133–36.
5   EM, journal, 1789–90, and EM to Bridget Kingdon, 7 March 1791, ML A2908.
6   John White, *Journal of a Voyage to New South Wales* (London 1790), pp. 90–91; Wrey J'Ans, n.d., quoted in G.B. Worgan, *General View of the Agriculture of the County of Cornwall* (London 1811), pp. 93–97; L.C. Rookmaaker, *The Zoological Exploration of Southern Africa 1650–1790* (Rotterdam 1989), p. 64.
7   William Paterson, *A Narrative of Four Journeys into the Country of the Hottentots, and Caffraria* (London 1789), p. 3; William Paterson to Sir Joseph Banks, 23 August 1794, 26 October 1795, ML SAFE/Banks Papers/Series 27.07,

27.11; EM to Edward, 28 January 1834, ML A2906; John M. MacKenzie, *The Scots in South Africa: Ethnicity, identity, gender and race, 1772–1914* (Manchester, UK, 2007), pp. 33–35; Council of Heads of Australian Herbaria, 'William Paterson, (1755–1810)', biographical notes, *Australian National Herbarium*, www.anbg.gov.au/biography/paterson-william.html.
8   EM to Bridget Kingdon, 7 March 1791, 1 September [1798], Elizabeth jr to Eliza Kingdon, 15 July 1818, ML A2908; EM to Edward, 13 September 1832, ML A2906; Ian Simpson, 'The imprint of India at Elizabeth Farm, Parramatta', *Journal of Australian Colonial History*, vol. 18 (2016), pp. 32–34.
9   EM to Bridget Kingdon, 1 September [1798].
10 JM to EM, various letters 1809–17, ML A2898.
11 JM to James McArthur, n.d., quoted EM to Bridget Kingdon, 23 August 1794, ML A2908.
12 JM to James McArthur, quoted 23 August 1794.
13 EM to Bridget Kingdon, 21 December 1793, 1 September [1798]; Henry Waterhouse to JM, 12 March 1804, ML SAFE/Banks Papers/23.30; Worgan, *General View of the Agriculture of the County of Cornwall*, p. 83.
14 J'Ans, n.d., quoted in Worgan, *General View of the Agriculture of the County of Cornwall*, pp. 93–97.
15 P.G. King, comments (n.d.) on JM to King, 30 September 1800, *HRA*, series 1, vol. 2, p. 538; JM, evidence given to J.T. Bigge, n.d. [1822], CO 201/120, f. 132, TNA.
16 Richard Bradley, *The Country Housewife, and Lady's Director, for Every Month of the Year* (London, 1762; first publ. 1727), pp. 3–4; EM to Bridget Kingdon, 1 September [1798] (emphasis added); Nicola Verdon, '" ... Subjects deserving of the highest praise": Farmers' wives and the farm economy in England, c. 1700–1850', *Agricultural History Review*, vol. 51 (2003), pp. 23–39.
17 EM to Bridget Kingdon, 1 September [1798].
18 John Millar, *Observations Concerning the Distinction of Ranks in Society* (London 1773; first publ. 1771), p. 86; Karen Harvey, *The Little Republic: Masculinity and domestic authority in eighteenth-century Britain* (Oxford Scholarship Online 2012), pp. 78–87; Jane Austen, *Mansfield Park* (New York 2010; first publ. 1814), pp. 49–50.

12   Cloth, a family concern
1   George III, instructions to Arthur Phillip, 25 April 1787, *HRA*, series 1, vol. 1, 13; Henry Dundas to Francis Grose, 15 November 1793, *HRA*, series 1, vol. 1, p. 456; David Collins, *An Account of the English Colony in New South Wales* (2 vols, ed. Brian H. Fletcher) (Sydney 1975), vol. 1 (first publ. 1798), pp. 426–29.
2   P.G. King to Lord Hobart, 30 October 1802, *HRA*, series 1, vol. 3, pp. 589, 596; King to Hobart, 9 May, 7 August 1803, *HRA*, series 1, vol. 4, pp. 107, 312; T.A. Coghlan, *Labour and Industry in Australia: From the first settlement in 1788 to the establishment of the Commonwealth in 1901* (4 vols) (Cambridge 1918), vol. 1, pp. 129–30; Eve Stenning, 'Textile manufacturing in New South Wales 1788–1851', MA thesis, University of Sydney, 1986, pp. 25–36; Eve Stenning, 'Nothing but gum trees: Textile manufacturing in New South Wales 1788–1850', *Australasian Historical Archaeology*, vol. 11 (1993), pp. 76–78; Paul Moon, 'King's 1793 vocabulary: The culture, politics and linguistics behind the development of an early Māori lexicon', *History Australia*, vol. 15 (2018), pp. 78–88.

Notes to pages 112–116

3   William Berlase, *The Natural History of Cornwall* (Oxford 1758), p. 286; Mary Wright, *Cornish Guernseys and Knitfrocks* (Clifton-upon-Teme, UK, 2008), n.p.; Adrian J. Randall, 'Peculiar perquisites and pernicious practices: Embezzlement in the west of England woollen industry, c. 1750–1840', *International Review of Social History*, vol. 35 (1990), pp. 194–96, 205.
4   John Hunter to a friend (name unrecorded), 16 October 1795, *Northampton Mercury*, 20 August 1796.
5   Michael Hogan, memo, 3 January 1794, ML MSS7359 (I am very grateful to Page and Kathleen Styles for help with the Hogan material); D.R. Hainsworth, *The Sydney Traders: Simeon Lord and his contemporaries* (Melbourne 1972), p. 225; Michael H. Styles, *Captain Hogan: Seaman, merchant, diplomat on six continents* (Fairfax Station, Virginia, 2003), p. 8 (suggesting that Hogan's family, living at Stone Hall, Co. Clare, being Catholic, must have been tenant farmers, despite good literacy and high connections; in fact the estate as a whole was leased to a series of gentry families, Catholics included); Ellis Wasson, *The British and Irish Ruling Class 1660–1945* (2 vols), vol. 2 (ebook 2017), p. 158.
6   EM to Edward, 25 December 1842–20 January 1843, ML A2907.
7   Hunter to John King, 30 April 1796, *HRA*, series 1, vol. 1, pp. 565–66; James McArthur to Hogan, 13 August 1797, JM to Hogan, 16 November 1798 and 28 October 1798, with enclosed paper no. 2 ('Statement of Cornwallis Place'), ML MSS7359; J.C. Garran and Les White, *Merinos, Myths and Macarthurs: Australian graziers and their sheep, 1788–1900* (Sydney 1985), pp. 95–96; Styles, *Captain Hogan*, pp. 62–67. Thanks to Catherine Atkinson for the detail on lambs' wool.
8   JM to Duke of Portland, 15 September 1796, and enclosed 'Observations', *HRA*, series 1, vol. 2, pp. 89–95; Hunter to Portland, 25 July 1798, *HRA*, series 1, vol. 2, p. 166.
9   EM to Bridget Kingdon, 1 September [1798], ML A2908; JM to Hogan, 16 November 1798.
10 JM to Hogan, 16 November 1798.
11 Hendrik Cloete to Hendrik Swellengrebel jr, 15 March 1787, in G.J. Schutte (ed.), Hendrik Swellengrebel jr, *Briefwisseling oor Kaapse sake 1778–1792* (English trans. Anna Böeseken) (Cape Town 1982), p. 390; Paterson, *A Narrative of Four Journeys*, p. 125; Lord Somerville, *The System Followed During the Two Last Years by the Board of Agriculture Further Illustrated* (London 1800), pp. 81–82.
12 P.G. King to Portland, 10 March, 21 August 1801, 1 March 1802, P.G. King to John King, 21 August 1801, P.G. King to Hobart, 9 November 1802, *HRA*, series 1, vol. 3, pp. 13, 247, 347, 405, 433–34, 439, 636; JM, evidence before the House of Commons select committee on bill respecting laws relating to woollen trade, 31 May 1803, *House of Commons Papers*, 1802–03, vol. 7, p. 819.
13 Hunter to Evan Nepean, 31 August 1796, *HRA*, series 1, vol. 1, p. 649; Henry Waterhouse to JM, 12 March 1894, ML SAFE/Banks Papers/23.30; JM, evidence given to J.T. Bigge, n.d. [1822], CO 201/120, ff. 133–34; Ian M. Parsonson, *The Australian Ark: A history of domesticated animals in Australia* (Melbourne 2000; first publ. 1998), pp. 15, 17–18, 23–24.
14 JM, evidence before the House of Commons select committee on bill respecting laws relating to woollen trade, p. 819; Paterson, *A Narrative of Four Journeys*, p. 125; Henry Waterhouse, draft answer, n.d., to Sir Joseph Banks to Waterhouse, 8 July 1806, ML MSS6544.

15 JM to Hogan, 16 November 1798; Waterhouse to JM, 12 March 1804.
16 Hunter to Portland, 10 July 1799, *HRA*, series 1, vol. 2, pp. 373–74; P.G. King, 'Nature of employments', n.d., enclosed with King to Portland, 10 March 1801, and King to Portland, 14 November 1801, 1 March 1802, *HRA*, series 1, vol. 3, pp. 27, 328–29, 405, 433–34; Stenning, 'Textile manufacturing in New South Wales 1788–1851', pp. 40–44, 49–50, 52–53.
17 EM to Bridget Kingdon, 1 September [1798]; Edward to Hannibal Macarthur, 30 September 1808, ML A2912.
18 Bridget Kingdon to EM, 15 September [1798], ML A2908.

13 The meaning of happiness
1 EM to Bridget Kingdon, 7 March 1791, 1 September [1798], ML A2908.
2 EM to Bridget Kingdon, 1 September [1798].
3 Samuel Johnson, *A Dictionary of the English Language* (Dublin 1768; first publ. 1755), no pagination; EM to Bridget Kingdon, 7 March 1791.
4 John Farquhar, *Sermons on Various Subjects* (2 vols, ed. George Campbell and Alexander Gerard) (London 1772), vol. 1, p. 102; EM to Eliza Kingdon, March 1816, ML A2908.
5 George Ogle, *Gualtherus and Griselda; or, The Clerk of Oxford's tale* (London 1739), pp. 60–62.
6 Charlotte Smith, *Emmeline, the Orphan of the Castle* (4 vols) (London 1788), vol. 2, p. 11.
7 William Godwin, *St Leon: A tale of the sixteenth century* (4 vols) (London 1799), vol. 1, pp. 102, 104; Claire Tomalin, *The Life and Death of Mary Wollstonecraft* (London 1977; first publ. 1974), pp. 262–63.
8 EM to Bridget Kingdon, 1 September [1798].
9 George Worgan to Richard Worgan, 12–18 June 1788, in George Worgan, *Journal of a First Fleet Surgeon 1788* (Sydney 1978), p. 22; EM to Bridget Kingdon, 7 March 1791; John Grant, 'Ideas awakened before day-break by a terrible storm', December 1805, ML FM4/1141.
10 William Henry to London Missionary Society, 10 August 1799, *HRNSW*, vol. 3, pp. 714–15.
11 Hugh Blair, *Sermons* (London 1780), p. 260; Thomas Ahnert, *The Moral Culture of the Scottish Enlightenment 1690–1805* (New Haven 2014), pp. 96–121.
12 EM to Grace Leach, 20 April 1790, 18 March 1791, ML A2908; T.H. Kingdon, *A Sermon, Preached at St Mary's, Guildford, on Wednesday, March 12, 1800; Being the Day Appointed for a General Fast* (London 1800), pp. 3–4, 7–8. John Hatherly, yeoman, was buried at Bridgerule on 16 August 1792.
13 EM, journal, 1789–90, ML A2908; [Samuel Taylor Coleridge], 'The Rime of the Ancyent Marinere', in [William Wordsworth and Samuel Taylor Coleridge], *Lyrical Ballads, with a Few Other Poems* (Bristol 1798), p. 21 (the wording differs in later versions of this poem); Alan Atkinson, *The Europeans in Australia* (3 vols), vol. 1 (Melbourne 1997), pp. 292–94.
14 EM to Bridget Kingdon, 7 March 1791.
15 [John Perkins], *Theory of Agency; or, An Essay on the Nature, Source, and Extent of Moral Freedom* (Boston 1771), p. 21; James Lee, *An Introduction to Botany* (London 1776; first publ. 760), p. iii; Caleb Alexander, *The Young Ladies' and Gentlemen's Spelling Book* (London 1799), p. 125; EM to Eliza Kingdon, March 1827, ML A2908.

16 Edward to EM, 15 November [1809], and Edward to JM, 21 June 1811, ML A2912.
17 Farquhar, *Sermons on Various Subjects*, vol. 1, p. 102; T.H. Kingdon, *A Sermon*, p. 10; T.H. Kingdon, *The Sacrament of Baptism Considered, with Especial Reference to the Church of England* (London 1834), pp. 143–44; [James Anderson], in *Bee* (Edinburgh weekly), 1791, quoted John Dwyer, 'Clio and Ethics: Practical morality in Enlightened Scotland', *Eighteenth Century*, vol. 30, no. 1 (1989), p. 48; Watkin Tench, *Letters Written in France, to a Friend in London, between the Month of November 1794, and the Month of May 1795* (London 1796), pp. 208–209.
18 EM to Leach, 8 October 1789, and EM to Bridget Kingdon, 23 August 1794, ML A2908.
19 John Kingdon, 'Sermons "On Death" [the first only is on death] preached at Marhamchurch and Whitstone', 1797–1802, X 956, Cornwall Record Office; EM to Eliza Kingdon, March 1816, ML A2908.
20 George Carr, *Sermons: By the Late Reverend George Carr, Senior Clergyman of the English Episcopal Congregation in Edinburgh* (3 vols) (Edinburgh 1777), vol. 1, pp. 76–80; John Kingdon, 'Sermons preached at Marhamchurch and Whitstone'; Ahnert, *The Moral Culture of the Scottish Enlightenment*, pp. 60–65.
21 EM to Bridget Kingdon, 1 September [1798].
22 EM to Bridget Kingdon, 7 March 1791, ML A2908; Watkin Tench, *A Complete Account of the Settlement at Port Jackson, in New South Wales* (London 1793), pp. 35, 190.

PART 3
14 Trust and lack of trust
1 JM to EM, 19 August 1816, ML A2898.
2 P.G. King, comments (n.d.) on JM to P.G. King, 30 September 1800, *HRA*, series 1, vol. 2, p. 538.
3 JM to John Piper, 4 December 1801, ML A254-1; EM to Bridget Kingdon, 1 September [1798], ML A2908; JM to EM, 31 August 1813, 22 July 1816, ML A2898; Thomas Dunbabin, review of *National Portraits* by Vance Palmer, *Australian Quarterly*, March 1941, p. 111.
4 Anon., letter to editor, *Morning Post* (London), 13 October 1803.
5 EM, journal, 10 February 1790, ML A2908.
6 Alan Atkinson, *The Europeans in Australia: A history* (3 vols), vol. 1 (Melbourne 2007), pp. 203–204 (quoting Richard Roome and Stephen Smith, soldiers, 7 August 1804).
7 Robert Hamilton, *The Duties of a Regimental Surgeon Considered* (2 vols) (London 1787), vol. 1, pp. 127–31.
8 Robert Murray, journal, September–October 1792, mfm ML (New England Microfilming Project; original in Peabody Museum of Salem, Massachusetts); Joseph Foveaux (in JM's hand) to Cox and Greenwood, 14 April 1793 – 16 December 1794, and associated paymaster's accounts, ML A2988/2; NSW Corps paymasters' bills and receipts, 1792–98, ML A2903/1; Cash book, NSW Corps, 1789–94, ML A2999; D.R. Hainsworth, *The Sydney Traders: Simeon Lord and his contemporaries 1788–1821* (Melbourne 1972), pp. 26, 28–29, 225. The paymasters' bills, cited by Hainsworth, do not include the first cargo by the *Experiment*, arrived December 1794, though the officers bought it all: William Paterson to Sir Joseph Banks, 17 March 1795, ML SAFE/Banks Papers/27.09.

9   Murray, journal, September–October 1792; Thomas Dunbabin, 'William Raven, R.N. and his Britannia, 1792–95', *Mariner's Mirror*, vol. 46 (1960), pp. 297–98; John Smail, 'The culture of credit in eighteenth–century commerce: The English textile industry', *Enterprise and Society*, vol. 4 (2003), pp. 304, 307–12.
10 P.G. King to Henry Dundas, 10 March 1794, *HRNSW*, vol. 2, pp. 162–63.
11 Murray, journal, September–October 1792.
12 Murray, journal, September–October 1792; S.E. Browne, '"A just and profitable commerce": Moral economy and the middle classes in eighteenth-century London', *Journal of British Studies*, vol. 32 (1993), pp. 313–19. I assume that Murray, who was certainly very young, was the son of Giles Murray, shipwright/lighterman, and baptised St Dunstan, Stepney, 16 August 1775.
13 Murray, journal, September–October 1792; EM to Bridget Kingdon, 1 September 1795, ML A2908; William Balmain, 'Courts of Justice', enclosed with Balmain to Sir Joseph Banks, 24 May 1802, ML SAFE/Banks Papers/23.03.
14 William Shakespeare, *The Tragedy of Coriolanus*, Act 3, sc. 2.
15 Paterson to Banks, 17 March 1795; Henry Waterhouse to Banks, 10 June 1806, ML SAFE/Banks Papers/Series 23.42; Hainsworth, *The Sydney Traders*, pp. 31, 37–38.
16 B.H. Fletcher, 'The development of small scale farming in New South Wales under Governor Hunter', *Journal of the Royal Australian Historical Society*, vol. 50 (1964), pp. 8–10; Hainsworth, *The Sydney Traders*, p. 226.
17 David Collins, *An Account of the English Colony in New South Wales* (2 vols, ed. Brian H. Fletcher) (Sydney 1975), vol. 1 (first publ. 1798), p. 383; Atkinson, *The Europeans in Australia*, vol. 1 (Melbourne 2007), p. 437.
18 Hunter to John King, 30 April 1796, *HRA*, series 1, vol. 1, pp. 565–66; Portland to Hunter, September 1797, Transport Commissioners to Hunter, 3 October 1797, and Portland to Hunter, 18 September 1798, 3 December 1798 and 5 November 1799, *HRA*, series 1, vol. 2, pp. 110–11, 227, 239–40, 387; David Collins to Michael Hogan, n.d. [March 1797], ML MSS7359; Collins, *An Account*, vol. 1, pp. 415–16; M.H. Styles, *Captain Hogan: Seaman, merchant, diplomat on six continents* (Fairfax Station, Virginia, 2003), pp. 53–84.
19 Government and General Orders, 11, 25 June 1798, *HRA*, series 1, vol. 2, pp. 216–17; Agreement by officers and others, 18 June 1798, *HRNSW*, vol. 3, pp. 405–406.
20 Hogan to P.G. King, 22 March 1796, ML MSS7359; EM to Bridget Kingdon, 1 September [1798]; JM to Hogan, 29 November 1798, ML MSS7359.
21 JM to Hogan, 29 November 1798, ML MSS7359; Settlers to Portland, 9 January 1800, *HRA*, series 1, vol. 2, pp. 442–43; William Smith, *Journal of a Voyage in the Missionary Ship Duff to the Pacific Ocean in the Years 1796, 7, 8, 9, 1800, 1, 2, &c* (New York 1813), pp. 129, 130–31.
22 JM and others to Hunter, 13 January 1800, *HRA*, series 1, vol. 1, p. 438; P.G. King to John King, 8 November 1801, *HRA*, series 1, vol. 3, p. 323.

15   1801, a gateway year

1   John Hunter to Duke of Portland, 10 August 1796, and enclosures, *HRA*, series 1, vol. 1, pp. 573–79; David Collins, *An Account of the English Colony in New South Wales* (2 vols, ed. Brian H. Fletcher) (Sydney 1975), vol. 1 (first publ. 1798), pp. 379–80.

Notes to pages 139-146

2   Hunter to Portland, 10 August 1796, and enclosures; William Balmain to Hunter, 18 June 1798, Hunter to William Balmain, 19 June 1798, and Balmain, memorandum, n.d., *HRA*, series 1, vol. 2, pp. 174–77.
3   Balmain to Hunter, 18 June 1798, and Balmain, memorandum, n.d.
4   Richard Atkins to JM, 17, 18 July 1796, JM to Hunter, 18 July 1796, *HRA*, series 1, vol. 2, pp. 101–102; Alan Atkinson, 'Richard Atkins, the women's judge', *Journal of Australian Colonial History*, vol. 1, no. 1 (April 1999), pp. 115–42.
5   Correspondence relating to JM and Richard Atkins, 18 July – 23 August 1796, *HRA*, series 1, vol. 2, pp. 101–106; Hunter to Portland, 12 November 1796, *HRA*, series 1, vol. 1, pp. 672–74; Atkinson, 'Richard Atkins, the women's judge', pp. 125–26.
6   Edward to EM, 25 April 1811, ML A2912; EM to Edward, 23 January 1834, ML A2906.
7   Jane Kelso, 'The first Government House', *Sydney Journal*, vol. 5, no. 1 (2017), p. 61.
8   *London World*, 10 December 1787; Paul L. Stevens, 'To keep the Indians of the Wabache in His Majesty's interest': The Indian diplomacy of Edward Abbott, British Lieutenant Governor of Vincennes, 1776–1778', *Indiana Magazine of History*, vol. 83 (1987), p. 172.
9   P.G. King to Portland, 8 July 1801, and Lord Hobart to P.G. King, 29 August 1802, *HRA*, series 1, vol. 3, pp. 111–12, 562; Hobart to P.G. King, 24 February 1803, P.G. King to Hobart, 9 May 1803, 1 March 1804, P.G. King to Evan Nepean, 9 May 1803, *HRA*, series 1, vol. 4, pp. 37, 246, 460.
10 James Tennant, Evidence in the trial of Marshall, 17 August 1801, *HRA*, series 1, vol. 3, pp. 196–98.
11 Edward Abbott, Evidence in trial of James Marshall, 29 July 1801, *HRA*, series 1, vol. 3, p. 200.
12 Two trials of Marshall, and P.G. King to Portland, 5 November 1801, *HRA*, series 1, vol. 3, pp. 188–242, 274–77.
13 Two trials of Marshall, and P.G. King, Statement of reasons for sending JM to England, 25 September 1801, *HRA*, series 1, vol. 3, pp. 212–15, 278–79.
14 Paterson to P.G. King, 25 September 1801, *HRA*, series 1, vol. 3, pp. 316–17; Thomas Rowley to Henry Waterhouse, 4 October 1801, *HRNSW*, vol. 4, pp. 588–89.
15 P.G. King to John King, 21 August 1801, and Paterson to Robert Brownrigg, 24 August 1801, and P.G. King's comments thereon, n.d., *HRA*, series 1, vol. 3, pp. 245–46, 289, 292.
16 P.G. King to John King, 21 August 1801, and Paterson to Brownrigg, 24 August 1801, and P.G. King's comments thereon, n.d.
17 P.G. King to Portland, 9 September 1800, enclosing JM to P.G. King, 30 September 1800, and P.G. King's comments thereon (n.d.), *HRA*, series 1, vol. 2, pp. 533–34, 538; P.G. King to Sir Joseph Banks, 28 September 1800, ML SAFE/Banks Papers/39.60; K.R. Binney, *Horsemen of the First Frontier (1788–1900) and the Serpent's Legacy* (Sydney 2005), p. 10.
18 P.G. King to Treasury, 7 July 1800, and P.G. King to Portland, 9 September 1800, *HRA*, series 1, vol. 2, pp. 525–26, 533–34; P.G. King to Portland, 21 August 1801, and P.G. King to Hobart, 30 October 1802, *HRA*, series 1, vol. 3, pp. 124, 589, 596; *SG*, 26 March 1803; Anne-Maree Whitaker, *Joseph Foveaux: Power and Patronage in Early New South Wales* (Sydney 2000), p. 65.

19 Neil MacKellar, statement, 15 September 1801, and Paterson to P.G. King, 29 September 1801, *HRA*, series 1, vol. 3, pp. 296–97, 301–302.
20 P.G. King to Portland, 9 November 1801, 2 November 1802, P.G. King, Statement of reasons for sending JM to England, 25 September 1801, *HRA*, series 1, vol. 3, pp. 279–80, 649–50.
21 JM to William Minchin, 21 September 1801, Samuel Marsden to P.G. King, 24 September 1801, Neil MacKellar to P.G. King, 29 September 1801, and P.G. King to Portland, 5, 9 November 1801, *HRA*, series 1, vol. 3, pp. 279–80, 308–309, 311–12, 315–16, 650.
22 Neil MacKellar's statement, 15 September 1801, *HRA*, series 1, vol. 3, pp. 296–97.
23 Anon., letter to editor, *Morning Post* (London), 13 October 1803.
24 P.G. King to John King, 14 November 1801, *HRA*, series 1, vol. 3, pp. 345–46; Joseph Foveaux, two receipts for JM, for sheep and for land, 5 December 1801, ML A2967; Whitaker, *Joseph Foveaux*, pp. 65–66.

16 Answers from the edge of Empire

1 Joseph Foveaux, two receipts for JM, for sheep and for land, 5 December 1801, ML A2967; Anne-Maree Whitaker, *Joseph Foveaux: Power and patronage in early New South Wales* (Sydney 2000), pp. 65–66.
2 Robert Farquhar, report (n.d.), enclosed with Robert Farquhar to John Lumsden, 30 September 1805, quoted in R.B. Allen, 'New perspectives on the origins of the "new system of slavery"', in Maurits S. Hassankhan, Lomarsh Roopnarine, Hans Ramsoedh (eds), *The Legacy of Indian Indenture: Historical and contemporary aspects of migration and diaspora* (London 2017), p. 50; Earl Bathurst to George IV, 28 September 1823, in Arthur Aspinall (ed.), *The Letters of King George IV, 1812–1830* (3 vols), (Cambridge 1938), vol. 3, p. 23; R.B. Allen, 'Slaves, convicts, abolitionism and the global origins of the post-emancipation indentured labor system', *Slavery and Abolition: A journal of slave and post-slave studies*, vol. 35 (2014), pp. 333, 334, 336.
3 Robert Farquhar to Lord Clive, 22 February 1802, British Library Add MSS 13869; James to Roger Therry, 24 February 1859 (draft), ML A2897 (the best surviving account of JM's involvement but in places inconsistent with contemporary evidence); Muridan Widjojo, *The Revolt of Prince Nuku: Cross-cultural alliance-making in Maluku, c. 1780–1810* (Leiden, Netherlands, 2009), pp. 193–202.
4 P.G. King to Duke of Portland, 14 November 1801, *HRA*, series 1, vol. 4, p. 331; Robert Farquhar to Clive, 22 February 1802, and to Marquess Wellesley, 1 October 1802, and enclosures, British Library Add MSS 13869; Wellesley to Clive, 7 January 1803, British Library Add MSS 13622, ff. 9–11; Anthony Webster, 'British expansion in South-East Asia and the role of Robert Farquhar, Lieutenant-Governor of Penang, 1804–05', *Journal of Imperial and Commonwealth History*, vol. 23 (1995), pp. 1–25.
5 Edward to JM, 26 October 1808, 3 March 1810, ML A2912; Sir Walter Farquhar to Wellesley, 25 September 1810, British Library Add MSS 37292; JM to EM, 8 December 1814, ML A2898; Charity Hamilton to William, 28 September 1859, ML A2936; Countess of Minto, *Life and Letters of Sir Gilbert Elliot, First Earl of Minto, from 1751 to 1806* (3 vols) (London 1874), vol. 1, p. 385.
6 He was said to be in his 85th year when he died, on 29 July 1840; his own family record says he was born at Strachur on 3 April 1756: *Nautical Magazine*, vol. 9

(1840), p. 679; Anon., 'McArthurs of Strachur', n.d. [c. 1890], typescript copy of a family tree sketched by his grand-nephew, General Charles McArthur (in my possession, provenance lost).

7   John McArthur, 'Supplemental observations on the authenticity of Ossian's poems', in Sir John Sinclair and John McArthur (eds), *The Poems of Ossian in the Original Gaelic, with a Literal Translation into Latin by the Late Robert Macfarlan, A.M.* (3 vols) (London 1807), vol. 3, pp. 405–31.

8   John McArthur, *The Army and Navy Gentleman's Companion; or A New and Complete Treatise on the Theory and Practice of Fencing* (London 1780; second edition 1784); Julian S. Corbett, 'General introduction', in Julian S. Corbett (ed.), *Signals and Instructions 1776–1794* (London 1908), pp. 58–59, 62–63, 67–68.

9   Elizabeth Wynne, diary 17 May 1805, in Anne Fremantle (ed.), *The Wynne Diaries 1789–1920* (London 1952), p. 386; [John McArthur], 'Biographical memoir of the Right Honourable Samuel, Lord Viscount Hood', *Naval Chronicle*, vol. 2 (July–December 1799), pp. 24–25; 'Abstract of proceedings respecting Lord Hood's claim to prize money taken at Toulon', presented to the House of Commons, 23 March 1804, *Cobbett's Parliamentary Debates*, vol. 1 (November 1803 – March 1804), col. 1169; Brian Lavery, *Nelson's Victory: 250 Years of war and peace* (Barnsley, UK, 2015), pp. 82–86; Evan Wilson, *A Social History of British Naval Officers, 1775–1815* (Woodbridge, UK, 2017), pp. 145–46.

10 Grant of Arms to John McArthur, 14 January 1797, Court of the Lord Lyon, Public Register of Arms, vol. 1, f. 575; John McArthur, will, signed 2 October 1829 and proved 24 October 1840, PROB 11/1935/126, TNA.

11 J.S. Clarke, 'Biographical memoir of William Falconer', in William Falconer, *The Shipwreck: A poem* (London 1804), p. xv; Lavery, *Nelson's Victory*, p. 110.

12 Sir John Sinclair (ed.), *The Statistical Account of Scotland* (21 vols) (Edinburgh 1798), vol. 20, p. xiii.

13 [John McArthur], *Financial Facts of the Eighteenth Century* (London 1801), p. 247.

14 [McArthur], *Financial Facts of the Eighteenth Century*, pp. 50–51; Dolores Greenberg, 'Energy, power, and perceptions of social change in the early nineteenth century', *American Historical Review*, vol. 95 (1990), pp. 697–99.

15 [McArthur], *Financial Facts of the Eighteenth Century*; John McArthur, *Financial and Political Facts of the Eighteenth Century* (London 1801; third edition; no copy seems to survive of the second edition), p. 91, 101–102 (quoting William Eden to Lord Carlisle, 24 October 1779, but not an exact quote; see William Eden, *Four Letters to the Earl of Carlisle, from William Eden, Esq.* [London 1779], pp. 52, 54, 214, 247.

16 Sir James Steuart, *Inquiry into the Principles of Political Oeconomy* (2 vols) (London 1767), vol. 2, p. 378; McArthur, *Financial and Political Facts of the Eighteenth Century*, p. 172; Nesrine Bentemessek and Rebecca Betancourt, 'James Steuart: A modern approach to the liquidity and solvency of public debt', in J.M. Menudo (ed.), *The Economic Thought of Sir James Steuart, First Economist of the Scottish Enlightenment* (Oxford 2020), pp. 123–31.

17 George Washington to Sir John Sinclair, 20 July 1794, 10 July 1795, 10 December 1796, in Sir John Sinclair (ed), *The Correspondence of the Right Honourable Sir John Sinclair, Bart.* (2 vols) (London 1831), vol. 2, pp. 18–20, 21, 25; G.E. Fussell, 'Impressions of Sir John Sinclair, Bart., first president

of the Board of Agriculture', *Agricultural History*, vol. 25 (1951), pp. 162–63; Rosalind Mitchison, 'The old Board of Agriculture (1793–1822)', *English Historical Review*, vol. 74 (1959), pp. 41–43.
18 Linda Colley, *Britons: Forging the nation, 1707–1837* (New Haven 2005; first publ. 1994), pp. 11–24; Priya Satia, *Empire of Guns: The violent making of the Industrial Revolution* (New York 2018), pp. 136–42, 247–48.
19 Sir John Sinclair, *An Account of the Highland Society of London, from Its Establishment in May 1773, to the Commencement of the Year 1813* (London 1813), pp. 48, 55, 62; J.E. Cookson, 'The Napoleonic Wars, military Scotland and Tory Highlandism in the early nineteenth century', *Scottish Historical Review*, vol. 7 (1999), pp. 65–68.

17 A new story

1 Anne Grant to Jane Brown, 10 October 1788, in Anne Grant, *Letters from the Mountains: Being the real correspondence of a lady between the years 1773 and 1807* (3 vols) (London 1806), vol. 1, pp. 264–65; John McArthur, 'Supplemental observations on the authenticity of Ossian's Poems', in Sir John Sinclair and John McArthur (eds), *The Poems of Ossian in the Original Gaelic, with a Literal Translation into Latin by the Late Robert Macfarlan, A.M.* (3 vols) (London 1807), vol. 3, p. 461; Sir John Sinclair, *An Account of the Highland Society of London, from Its Establishment in May 1773, to the Commencement of the Year 1813* (London 1813), pp. 1–4, 5–7.
2 Hugh Blair, *A Critical Dissertation on the Poems of Ossian* (London 1763), pp. 30–31.
3 Anne Grant to Isabella Ewing, 18 April 1779, in Anne Grant, *Letters from the Mountains*, vol. 2, pp. 63–66.
4 Blair, *A Critical Dissertation on the Poems of Ossian*, pp. 1–2.
5 P.G. King to Sir Joseph Banks, 28 September 1800, ML SAFE/Banks Papers/Series 39.60; H.B. Carter, *His Majesty's Spanish Flock: Sir Joseph Banks and the Merinos of George III of England* (Sydney 1964), pp. 184–85.
6 Watkin Tench, *A Complete Account of the Settlement at Port Jackson, in New South Wales* (London 1793), p. 165; Julie McIntyre, *First Vintage: Wine in colonial New South Wales* (Sydney 2012), pp. 47–57, 75–80.
7 Lord Somerville, *The System Followed During the Two Last Years by the Board of Agriculture Further Illustrated* (London 1800), pp. 81–82; C.H. Parry, *An Essay on the Nature, Produce, Origin, and Extension of the Merino Breed of Sheep* (London 1807), pp. 89–90; Marian George, 'John Bardwell Ebden, his business and political career at the Cape 1806–1849', MA thesis, University of Cape Town, 1980, pp. 117–20.
8 Robert Bakewell, 'Wool', in Abraham Rees (ed.), *The Cyclopaedia; or, Universal Dictionary of Arts, Sciences, and Literature* (45 vols) (London 1819), vol. 38, n.p.; W.R. Mead, *An Experience of Finland* (London 1993), p. 81.
9 Bakewell, 'Wool'.

18 The golden fleece

1 *SG*, 26 March 1803; H.B. Carter, *His Majesty's Spanish Flock: Sir Joseph Banks and the Merinos of George III of England* (Sydney 1964), pp. 261–69.
2 Lord Hobart to P.G. King, 29 August 1802, *HRA*, series 1, vol. 3, pp. 565, 568.
3 Hobart to King, 29 August 1802, p. 563; *SG*, 26 March 1803.
4 G.B. Worgan, *General View of the Agriculture of the County of Cornwall* (London 1811), pp. 148–49.

5 Sir John Sinclair to Duke of Portland, 20 May 1797, *HRNSW*, vol. 3, p. 209; Sir John Sinclair, *Address to the Society for the Improvement of British Wool* (London 1791), p. 25; *Agricultural Magazine*, vol. 8, no. 43 (February 1803), p. 148; *Manchester Mercury* and *Cumberland Pacquet* (Whitehaven), both 1 February 1803.

6 Thomas Fowle, evidence before the House of Commons select committee on the woollen trade bill, 14 May 1803, *House of Commons Papers*, 1802–03, vol. 7, p. 635; Edward Baines, 'On the woollen manufactures of England, with special reference to the Leeds clothing district', *Quarterly Journal of the Statistical Society*, vol. 22 (1859), pp. 14–16.

7 JM, evidence before the House of Commons select committee on bill respecting laws relating to woollen trade, 31 May 1803, *House of Commons Papers*, 1802–03, vol. 7, pp. 817–21; John McArthur, *Financial and Political Facts of the Eighteenth and Present Century* (London 1803), pp. lx–lxi. Hobhouse presented to Treasury the letter from Bradford (Wiltshire) manufacturers supporting Macarthur's effort (received 5 August 1803), suggesting that he was part of the opinion-gathering: BT 1/24, f. 43, TNA.

8 JM, evidence before the House of Commons select committee on bill respecting laws relating to woollen trade, 31 May 1803, pp. 817–21.

9 McArthur, *Financial and Political Facts of the Eighteenth and Present Century*, pp. liii–lxiii.

10 Nicholas Lemann, *Transaction Man: The rise of the deal and the decline of the American dream* (New York 2019), quoted in Sebastian Mallaby, 'How the dismal science broke America', *Atlantic* (Boston, Mass.), 1 September 2019, p. 33.

11 John Lawrence, *A General Treatise on Cattle, the Ox, the Sheep, and the Swine* (London 1805), pp. 457–67; C.H. Parry, *An Essay on the Nature, Produce, Origin, and Extension of the Merino Breed of Sheep* (London 1807), pp. 89–90, 92–93, 98–99, 102.

12 William Fawkener to Sir Joseph Banks, 21 September 1803, British Library Add MSS 32439; Banks to Fawkener, 23 September 1803, and Prinsep, Saunders and Co. to JM, 29 October 1803, BT 1/24, TNA; James to Roger Therry, 24 February 1859 (draft), ML A2897.

13 Thomas Atkinson and A.L. Edridge, form letter to wool manufacturers, 20 July 1803, ML A2964.

14 JM to John Sullivan, 26 July 1803, with enclosed 'Statement of the improvements and progress of the breed of fine wool'd sheep in New South Wales', CO 201/ ff. 11, 13–16, TNA (published in *Philosophical Magazine*, 31 August 1803, pp. 363–65, and *Universal Magazine of Knowledge and Pleasure*, October 1803, pp. 267–68).

15 *SG*, 26 March 1803, copy at BT 1/24, ff. 91–92.

16 JM, 'Proposal for establishing a company to encourage the encrease of fine woolled sheep in New South Wales', 3 January 1804, and JM to Nicholas Vansittart, 2 February 1804, and endorsement, 6 July 1804, BT 1/24; Banks to unknown correspondent, 31 March 1804, ML A78-2, p. 319 (draft) (Carter says Banks's recipient was John Maitland, but the letter was clearly written for someone who knew nothing so far: *His Majesty's Spanish Flock*, pp. 432, 497); *SG*, 24 June 1804; *Agricultural Magazine*, vol. 10 (June–July 1804), pp. 243–44; Stephen Quinn, 'Money, finance and capital markets', in Roderick Floud and Paul Johnson (eds), *Cambridge Economic History of Modern Britain* (3 vols) (Cambridge 2004), vol. 1, p. 158.

17 JM to John Piper, 9 November 1803, ML A254-1.
18 *London Gazette*, 8 May 1804, p. 591.
19 John Sargent to Sullivan, 8 February 1804, T 28/42, TNA; Sargent to Fawkener, 22 February 1804, and JM to Board of Trade, 4 May 1824, BT 1/24; James to Therry, 24 February 1859 (draft).
20 Banks to unknown correspondent, 31 March 1804; Banks to Maitland, 31 March 1804, ML A78-3; Cottrell to Cooke, 14 July 1804, BT 3/7, TNA; Banks to P.G. King, 29 August 1804, *HRNSW*, vol. 5, p. 459; Earl Camden to King, 31 October 1804 (two letters), *HRA*, series 1, vol. 5, pp. 161, 162; JM to John jr, 20 February 1820, ML A2899.
21 'Plummer, Thomas William (d. 1817)', in *The History of Parliament*, www.historyofparliamentonline.org/volume/1790-1820/member/plummer-thomas-william-1817.
22 *Agricultural Magazine*, June–July 1804, pp. 243–44.
23 *Agricultural Magazine*, August 1804, pp. 143–47; Carter, *His Majesty's Spanish Flock*, pp. 295–96, 447.
24 Pindar, *The Pythian, Nemean, and Isthmian Odes of Pindar* (trans. E.B. Greene) (London 1778), p. 55; *Saunders's News-Letter* (Dublin), 2, 5 December 1795; Bernard Shillman, 'Benjamin Disraell', *Dublin Historical Record*, vol. 3 (1941), pp. 116–17.

PART 4
19 'Our first universe'
1 *Macarthur v. Thompson*, October–November 1806, Court of Civil Jurisdiction, 'Decisions of the superior courts of New South Wales, 1788–1899', *Colonial Case Law* (Macquarie University), www.law.mq.edu.au/research/colonial_case_law/nsw/cases/case_index/1806/macarthur_v_thompson_1806_nswkr_3_1806_nswsupc_3/; Edward to JM, 6 January 1813, ML A2912; JM to J.T. Bigge, 7 February 1821, ML BT1, pp. 222–23; Elizabeth Onslow, notes on William's reminiscences, 18 March 1870, ML A2935.
2 Eliza Thompson to JM, 24 August 1820, ML A2900; Onslow, notes on William's reminiscences.
3 *SG*, 28 April 1805.
4 Applied Ecology Pty Ltd, *Upper Duck River Wetlands and Riparian Plan of Management*, 25 October 2012, prepared for Parramatta City Council, p. 46, www.cumberland.nsw.gov.au/sites/default/files/inline-files/plan-of-management-upper-duck-river-wetlands-riparian-plan.pdf.
5 EM to Bridget Kingdon, 21 December 1793 (but substantially written in March 1793), and EM to Grace Bond, 23 August 1794, ML A2908; Onslow, notes on William's reminiscences.
6 JM to James McArthur, [1794], quoted in EM to Bridget Kingdon, 23 August 1794, ML A2908; R.W. Brunskill, *Houses and Cottages of Britain: Origins and development of traditional buildings* (London 1997), pp. 206–10; V.M. and F.J. Chesher, *The Cornishman's House: An introduction to the history of traditional domestic architecture in Cornwall* (Truro, UK, 1968). pp. 101–106.
7 JM to J.T. Bigge, 7 February 1821, ML BT 1, pp. 222–24; S.E. Hill, '"Paper houses": John Macarthur and the 30-year design process of Camden Park', PhD thesis, University of Sydney, 2016 (2 vols), vol. 1, pp. 44–45.
8 James Beattie, *Dissertations Moral and Critical* (London 1783), p. 87; Gaston Bachelard, *The Poetics of Space* (trans. Maria Jolas) (London 2014: first publ.

Notes to pages 176–185

        in French as *La poétique de l'espace* 1957), pp. 26–29; Jonathan Bate, *Radical Wordsworth: The poet who changed the world* (London 2020), pp. 86–87.
9   Returns of agriculture and livestock, 17–27 July 1804, *HRA*, series 1, vol. 5, pp. 34–37. I am grateful to Roderick Best, of the Beecroft Cheltenham History Group, for help with this detail.
10   EM to Bridget Kingdon, 1 September [1798], ML A2908; Muster of 1802, in C.J. Baxter (ed.), *Musters and Lists, New South Wales and Norfolk Island, 1800–1802* (Sydney 1988), pp. 37–52.
11   JM to Bigge, 7 February 1821.
12   *SG*, 28 April, 5 May 1805; P.G. King to Earl Camden, 30 April 1805, and Richard Atkins, 'Opinion on the treatment of the natives', 8 July 1805, *HRA*, series 1, vol. 5, pp. 306–307, 503.
13   William, 'A few memoranda respecting the Aboriginal natives', [1835?], ML A2935; Grace Karskens, *People of the River: Lost worlds of early Australia* (Sydney 2020), pp. 133–45.
14   P.G. King, Statement of reasons for sending JM to England, 25 September 1801, John Hobby to P.G. King, 5 October 1801, and William Moore to P.G. King, 7 October 1801, *HRA*, series 1, vol. 3, pp. 295, 298–300; EM to John Piper, 15 April 1804, ML A256.
15   EM to Piper, 15 April 1804.
16   EM to Piper, 15 April 1804; Lynette Ramsay Silver, *The Battle of Vinegar Hill: Australia's Irish rebellion, 1804* (Sydney 1989), pp. 132–33.
17   EM to Piper, 15 April 1804; *SG*, 27 January 1805; Hill, '"Paper Houses"', vol. 1, p. 72.
18   EM to Piper, n.d. [January–February 1802], ML A256; Sir Charles Morgan to P.G. King, 11 December 1802, *HRA*, series 1, vol. 3, pp. 744–45.
19   EM to Piper, 15 April 1804; 'Alexander Houstoun or Houston of Clerkington', *Legacies of British Slave-ownership*, database, wwwdepts-live.ucl.ac.uk/lbs/person/view/2146640465.
20   John jr to Elizabeth jr, 7 December 1822, ML A2911; Michael Flynn, *The Second Fleet: Britain's grim convict armada of 1790* (Sydney 1993), pp. 477–78.
21   William Buchan, *Domestic Medicine: or, A Treatise on the Prevention and Cure of Diseases by Regimen and Simple Medicines* (London 1790; first publ. 1772), p. 3; EM to Edward, 30 April 1846, ML A2907.
22   EM to Piper, 15 April 1804; Eliza Marsden to Piper, 15 August 1804, ML C244.
23   Matthew Flinders to EM, 6, 28 July 1803, ML Safe 1/55.
24   EM to Piper, 15 April 1804.

20   The importance of Miss Lucas
1   EM to Edward, 1 August 1849, ML A2907.
2   Elizabeth Onslow, notes on William's reminiscences, 18 March 1870, ML A2935.
3   JM to William Chapman, 3 October 1804, CO 201/34, f. 243, TNA; JM to EM, 6 April 1811, ML A2898.
4   William Gordon, memorandum, n.d. (c. May 1769), with Henry Gostling (counsel), narrative of life and family of William Gordon, in *Caporn v. Lucas*, 17 February 1775, PROB 18/86/43, TNA; Baptismal register, St Bride's, Fleet Street (baptised 11 June 1769).
5   Gostling, narrative of life and family of William Gordon.

6   *R. v. William Westwood and George Wilson*, Old Bailey trials, 15 July 1767, www.oldbaileyonline.org/browse.jsp?id=t17670715-48-defend501&div=t17670715-48#highlight; *Abstract of the Premiums Offered by the Society Instituted at London for the Encouragement of Arts, Manufactures, and Commerce* (London 1785), p. 8; John Johnson, 'Strong wet land', in *Communications to the Board of Agriculture* (7 vols) (London 1797), vol. 4, p. 70.
7   Norbert Schürer, 'Four catalogues of the Lowndes Circulating Library, 1755–66', *Papers of the Bibliographical Society of America*, vol. 101 (2007), pp. 329–57; Edward H. Jacobs, 'Eighteenth-Century British circulating libraries and cultural book history', *Book History*, vol. 6 (2003), pp. 1–22.
8   *Lucas v Temple*, accounts, and associated cases, 1795–1811, C101/2914, TNA; *Times* (London), 9 April 1807.
9   Gordon, memorandum.
10 *SG*, 19 May, 4 August 1805.
11 William, 'A few memoranda respecting the Aboriginal natives', [1835?], ML A2935.

21 Tjedboro
1   Lyndall Ryan, *The Aboriginal Tasmanians* (Brisbane 1981), p. 78.
2   Elizabeth jr to Eliza Kingdon, 8 March 1817, ML A2908; James, journal kept at Port Stephens, December 1827 – January 1828, Noel Butlin Archives 78/1/6, Australian National University, p. 52; Elizabeth Onslow, notes on Sir William Macarthur's reminiscences, 18 March 1870, ML A2935.
3   William, 'A few memoranda respecting the Aboriginal natives', [1835?], ML A2935.
4   William, 'A few memoranda'.
5   R.H. Mathews, 'The Thurrawal language' (Appendix), *Journal and Proceedings of the Royal Society of New South Wales*, vol. 35 (1901), pp. 155–60; F.R. Myers, *Pintupi Country, Pintupi Self: Sentiment, place, and politics among Western Desert Aborigines* (Berkeley, USA, 1991; first publ. 1986), pp. 123–25; V.K. Burbank, *Fighting Women: Anger and aggression in Aboriginal Australia* (Berkeley, USA, 1994), pp. 82–84.
6   William, 'A few memoranda'.
7   William, 'A few memoranda'; Keith Vincent Smith, 'Corrangie/Harry', *Eora People: Saltwater People of the Sydney Area*, www.eorapeople.com.au.

22 Curiosity
1   EM to Eliza Kingdon, May 1818, ML A2908.
2   H.C. Allport, 'Catalogue of the library at Elizabeth Farm, the property of Col'l Macarthur', May 1854, ML A2919/4. In most cases the list does not include dates of publication, but some could have been published only before 1809, and of those a few were so old as to make it unlikely that they were acquired after that date.
3   Edward to EM, 19 May 1810, ML A2912 (quoting from Alain-René Lesage, *The Adventures of Gil Blas of Santillane* [4 vols; trans. Tobias Smollett] [London 1749; first publ. in three volumes 1715–35], vol. 3, p. 91).
4   Joanna Baillie, *A Series of Plays* (London 1798).
5   Edward to EM, n.d. [1809], ML A2912.
6   Anon., *The Secret Memoirs of the Late Mr Duncan Campbel, the Famous Deaf and Dumb Gentleman* (London 1732), pp. 186–87; T.F. Henderson, rev. David

Turner, 'Campbell, Duncan (c. 1680–1730)', *Oxford Dictionary of National Biography*.
7   *The Secret Memoirs*, pp. 46, 145–46.
8   *The Secret Memoirs*, pp. 118–28; David Hartley, *Observations on Man, His Frame, His Duty, and His Expectations* (2 vols) (London 1749), vol. 1, pp. 354, 492; Thomas Reid, *An Inquiry into the Human Mind, on the Principles of Common Sense* (London 1764), pp. viii, 23–24, 526–27.
9   Watkin Tench, *A Complete Account of the Settlement at Port Jackson, in New South Wales* (London 1793), pp. 103, 186. M.A. Courtney, 'Cornish folk-lore', *Folk-Lore Journal*, vol. 5 (1887), p. 27.
10 JM to EM, 28 November 1809, ML A2898.
11 JM to John Piper, 4 December 1801, 9 November 1803, ML AA254-1; Brian P. Levack, *The Devil Within: Possession and exorcism in the Christian West* (New Haven 2013), pp. 62–63.
12 Matthew 25:41 (King James Version); Agreement between officers and others, 18 June 1798, *HRNSW*, vol. 3, pp. 405–406.
13 EM to Edward, 4 March 1827, ML A2906.
14 R.R. Madden, *The United Irishmen, Their Life and Times* (Dublin 1857; first publ. 1842), p. 389.
15 *Morning Post Gazetteer* (London), 10 September 1798; J.F. Jefferie to William Wickham, 28 October 1798, HO 42/45/131, ff. 517–18, TNA; Ruan O'Donnell, *Robert Emmet and the Rebellion of 1798* (Dublin 2003), p. 91.
16 JM to Jefferie, invitation, 25 September 1801, *HRA*, series 1, vol. 3, p. 320.
17 Jefferie to Salem East India Museum Society, December 1802, in Ernest S. Dodge, 'An early letter to the Salem East India Marine Society', *Essex Institute Historical Collections*, vol. 77 (1941), pp. 260–61; Mary Malloy, 'Capturing the Pacific world: Sailor collections and New England museums', in Patricia Johnston and Caroline Frank (eds), *Global Trade and Visual Arts in Federal New England* (Durham, New Hampshire, 2014), p. 242. Thanks to Kathryn White of the Peabody Essex Museum, Salem, Massachusetts, for advice and for an object list of museum holdings.
18 Abbé J. Tanguy, *Une Ville Bretonne sous la Révolution: Saint-Pol-de-Léon* (Brest, France, 1903), p. 352; Jean Guillou, 'Un émigré de la révolution Française aux antipodes', *Bulletin de la Société d'Études Historiques de la Nouvelle Calédonie*, no. 57 (1983), pp. 24–25; K. Carpenter, *Refugees of the French Revolution: Émigrés in London, 1789–1802* (Basingstoke, UK, 1999), pp. 45–46.
19 JM to James Chapman, 20 July 1805, CO 201/38, f. 239; Abbé Louis Kerbiriou, *Jean-François de la Marche: Évêque-Comte de Leon (1729–1806)* (Quimper, France, 1924), p. 217; Guillou, 'Un émigré de la révolution Française aux antipodes', pp. 23–25, 35.
20 J.-F. de La Marche, *Letter of the Right Reverend John Francis de La Marche, Bishop of Leon, Addressed to the French Clergymen Refugees in England* (London 1793), p. 3; Kerbiriou, *Jean-François de la Marche*, pp. 304–307; Nicolas Déplanche, 'From young people to young citizens: The emergence of a revolutionary youth in France, 1788–1790', *Journal of Social History*, vol. 45 (2011), pp. 225–37.
21 Allport, 'Catalogue of the library at Elizabeth Farm, the property of Col'l Macarthur'.
22 Kerbiriou, *Jean-Francois de la Marche*, pp. 216–17.
23 Guillou, 'Un émigré de la révolution Française aux antipodes', pp. 29, 35.
24 *SG*, 1, 8 December 1805; P.G. King to Earl Camden, 15 March 1806, *HRA*,

series 1, vol. 5, pp. 658–60; Angela Ballara, 'Te Pahi', *Dictionary of New Zealand Biography*, teara.govt.nz/en/biographies/1t53/te-pahi; Mark Stocker, 'A silver slice of Māori history: The Te Pahi Medal', *Tuhinga: Records of the Museum of New Zealand Te Papa Tongarewa*, no. 26 (2015), pp. 35–37.
25   *SG*, 1 December 1805, 13 April, 15 June 1806; P.G. King to Camden, 15 March 1806, *HRA*, series 1, vol. 5, pp. 658–60; Herman Melville, *Moby Dick, or The White Whale* (Boston 1920; first publ. 1851), pp. 25–29; Ann Salmond, 'Self and other in contemporary anthropology', in Richard Fardo (ed.) *Counterworks: Managing the Diversity of Knowledge* (London 1995), pp. 35–38.
26   *SG*, 15 June 1806; Angela Ballara, 'Te Pahi'.

23   Exactitude
1   Benjamin Graf von Rumford, *Essays, Political, Economical, and Philosophical* (3 vols) (London 1797), vol. 1, p. 80; C.H. Parry, *An Essay on the Nature, Produce, Origin, and Extension of the Merino Breed of Sheep* (London 1807), pp. 193–95.
2   Priya Satia, *Empire of Guns: The violent making of the Industrial Revolution* (New York 2018), pp. 199–206, 249–50, 353–55.
3   Simon Schaffer, 'Ceremonies of measurement: Rethinking the world history of science', *Annales: Histoire, Sciences Sociales* (English edition), vol. 17 (2015), pp. 352–60; David Dunér, 'The axiomatic-deductive ideal in early modern thinking: A cognitive history of human rationality', in David Dunér and Christer Ahlberger (eds), *Cognitive History: Mind, space, and time* (Oldenbourg, Germany, 2019), pp. 99–104.
4   Edward Wood's gravestone, Steubenville, Ohio (stating birth, 19 March 1773, and death, 17 September 1851); W.H. Hunter, 'The pathfinders of Jefferson County', *Ohio Archaeological and Historical Quarterly*, vol. 6 (1898), p. 262.
5   James Malcolm, *A Compendium of Modern Husbandry* (3 vols) (London 1805), vol. 1, p. 374; Edward Sheppard to Sir John Sinclair, 31 December 1806, in Thomas Rudge, *General View of the Agriculture of the County of Gloucester* (London 1807), pp. 398–400; William R. Dickinson, evidence before congressional Committee on Manufactures, 1827–28, 25 January 1828, *American State Papers: On finance*, vol. 5 (Washington 1859), p. 802; Adrian Randall, *Before the Luddites: Custom, community and machinery in the English woollen industry 1776–1809* (Cambridge 1991), p. 16.
6   Earl Camden to P.G. King, with enclosure, 31 October 1804, answers to governor's questions on sheep breeding, 5–10 August, and agricultural returns, August 1805, *HRA*, series 1, vol. 5, pp. 163, 559–63, 604–607; *SG*, 28 July, 4 August 1805.
7   Edward Wood to P.G. King, 3 September 1805, and JM, 'Report on the state of Mr McArthur's flocks of sheep', 2 October 1805, *HRA*, series 1, vol. 5, pp. 565–68.
8   JM to William Chapman, 3 October 1804, CO 201/34, f. 243.
9   *SG*, 17, 24 August 1806; Daniel Whitney to Thomas Rotch, 1 September 1810, Thomas and Charity Rotch Manuscripts A-367, and Wood to Rotch, 30 June 1817, same, A-381, Massillon Public Library, Massillon, Ohio, (Mandy Altimus Stahl of Massillon Museum kindly helped with this material); William R. Dickinson, evidence before congressional Committee on Manufactures, 25 January 1828, *American State Papers: On finance*, vol. 5, p. 802; Anon., *Portrait and Biographical Record of Stark County, Ohio* (Chicago 1892): pp. 121–22.

10 JM to P.G. King, 10 June 1806, *HRNSW*, vol. 6, p. 92.
11 P.G. King to Camden, 20 July 1805, *HRA*, series 1, vol. 5, p. 510; P.G. King to Camden, 15 March 1806, p. 658; JM to P.G. King, 10 June 1806, *HRNSW*, vol. 6, pp. 92–93; *Public Ledger* (London), 21 July 1806; *SG*, 15 March, 5 April 1807.
12 P.G. King to Camden, 20 July 1805, *HRA*, series 1, vol. 5, p. 510; P.G. King to Camden, 15 March 1806, p. 658; JM to P.G. King, 10 June 1806, pp. 92–93; William Bligh to William Windham, 21 October 1807, *HRA*, series 1, vol. 6, p. 152.
13 William Ramsay to Sir Stephen Cottrell, 6 June 1805, BT 6/88; A.J. King to John Piper, 22 June 1806, ML A256-1; P.G. King to Viscount Castlereagh, and enclosures, 30 June 1806, *HRA*, series 1, vol. 5, pp. 719–20, 733–39.
14 *SG*, 1, 15 June 1806, 1 March 1807; JM to P.G. King, 10 June 1806; P.G. King to JM, 14 June 1806, NSWSR 4/1720; JM to EM, 8 December 1814, ML A2898.
15 Macarthur and Blaxcell to W.S. Davidson, 12 January 1807, NRS 2652/X1986, pp. 4–7; D.R. Hainsworth, *The Sydney Traders: Simeon Lord and his contemporaries 1788–1821* (Melbourne 1972), pp. 67–69.
16 *SG*, 1 February, 1 March 1807; Hainsworth, *The Sydney Traders*, pp. 67–69.
17 *SG*, 21 December 1806, 11 January 1807 (Blaxcell advertisement); JM cash book, 1807–08, ML A2903/1, pp. 17–20.
18 *SG*, 23 November, 7 December 1806, 4, 11 January 1807; JM cash book, 1807–08, pp. 17–34; Brian Rogers, 'Derivation of technologies employed in some pre-1900 salt works in eastern Australia', *Journal of Australian Historical Archaeology*, vol. 8 (1990), p. 38.
19 Daniel Whitney to Thomas Rotch, 1 September 1810.
20 John Hunter to Duke of Portland, 25 July 1798, *HRA*, series 1, vol. 2, p. 161; JM to Chapman, 3 October 1804.
21 Anon., *The Only Genuine Trial, of Henry Lane, Who Was Tried Before Vicary Gibbs Esq., Recorder…* (Bristol [1800]); *SG*, 29 May 1807, 5 November 1809, 14 April 1810; Thomas Earnshaw, '"This excellent timekeeper"', in National Library of Australia (exhibition catalogue), *Mapping Our World: Terra Incognita to Australia* (Canberra 2013), p. 213.
22 *Exeter Flying Post*, 30 June – 7 July 1769; EM to Bridget Kingdon, 7 March 1791, ML A2906; JM to EM, 3 August 1810, ML A2898; Morgan Kelly and Cormac Ó Gráda, 'Adam Smith, watch prices, and the Industrial Revolution', *Quarterly Journal of Economics*, vol. 131 (2016), pp. 1731–38.
23 Jeremy Bentham, 'A proposal for a new and less expensive mode of employing and reforming convicts', n.d., in Twenty-Eighth Report from the Select Committee on Finance, *House of Commons Papers*, 1797–98, vol. 13, p. 363; William Hazlitt, *The Plain Speaker: Opinions on books, men, and things* (2 vols) (London 1826), vol. 2, p. 130.
24 Jeremy Bentham, *Panopticon: or, The Inspection-House* (Dublin 1791), p. ii.
25 T.W. Plummer to Lachlan Macquarie, 4 May 1809, *HRA*, series 1, vol. 7, pp. 204–208 (for authorship of this letter, see Alan Atkinson, 'The multiple voices of John Macarthur', *Journal of Australian Colonial History*, vol. 23 (2021), pp. 21–38).
26 Monica Mulrennan and Colin Scott, 'Indigenous rights and control of the sea in the Torres Strait', *Indigenous Law Bulletin*, vol. 2, issue 5 (January 2001), pp. 11–15.

PART 5
24 Sudddenly larger limits
1. Earl Camden to P.G. King, 31 October 1804, King to Camden, 20 July, 1805, King to Edward Cooke, 9 September 1805, and King to Camden, 1 November 1805, with enclosures, *HRA*, series 1, vol. 5, pp. 161–62, 510–13, 552–53, 576–95.
2. King to Camden, 1 November 1805, King to Cooke, note 6, January 1806, JM to King, 2 March 1806, with enclosure, and King to Camden, 15 March 1806, *HRA*, series 1, vol. 5, pp. 577, 632, 675–76, 681–84.
3. King to Camden, 15 March 1806, *HRA*, series 1, vol. 5, p. 676; T.W. Plummer to Board of Trade, 1 July 1806, BT 1/29, TNA.
4. Plummer to Board of Trade, 1 July 1806; Sir Joseph Banks to [Lord Auckland], 22 August 1806, and Banks to [Auckland], 22 August 1806, BT 6/88, TNA; Sir Stephen Cottrell to Plummer, 29 August 1806, BT 3/8, TNA.
5. Camden to King, 31 October 1804, p. 161; *SG*, 19 October 1806.
6. *Saunders's News-Letter* (Dublin), 2 September, 4 October 1803, 5 January 1804; *SG*, 12 October, 16 November, 21 December 1806, 17 May 1817, 21 March 1818, 17 March 1832; J.T. Campbell to James Wallis, 10 May 1818, NSWSR 4/3498, p. 217.

25 Insurrection
1. R.J. Ryan (ed.), *Land Grants 1788–1809: A record of registered grants and leases in New South Wales, Van Diemen's Land and Norfolk Island* (Sydney 1974), pp. 181, 182, 183.
2. JM's cash book, 1807–08, ML A2903/1, pp. 17–34.
3. P.G. King to Camden, 20 July 1805, *HRA*, series 1, vol. 5, p. 510.
4. William Bligh to Sir Joseph Banks, 21–30 March 1805, ML SAFE/Banks Papers/58.29; Greg Dening, *Mr Bligh's Bad Language: Passion, power and theatre on the Bounty* (Cambridge 1994; first publ. 1992), pp. 12, 54.
5. 'The panorama: With memoirs of its inventor, Robert Barker, and his son, the late Henry Aston Barker', *Art Journal*, new series, vol. 3 (1857), pp. 46–47. The *Australian Dictionary of Biography* wrongly says that Mary was the eldest, overlooking Harriet Barker.
6. George Caley to Banks, 7 July 1808, ML SAFE/Banks Papers/18.072.
7. John Harris to A.J. King, 25 October 1807, *HRNSW*, vol. 6, p. 347; Alan Atkinson, 'Taking possession: Sydney's first householders', in Graeme Aplin (ed.), *A Difficult Infant: Sydney before Macquarie* (Sydney 1988), pp. 86–87.
8. Sarah Wills to Elizabeth Harding, 1 May 1808, quoted Alan Atkinson, *The Europeans in Australia: A history* (3 vols) (Sydney 2016; first publ. 2004), vol. 1, p. 383; Caley to Banks, 7 July 1808; Bligh, evidence, 9 May 1811, and Richard Atkins, evidence, 23 May 1811, *Proceedings of a General Court-martial Held at Chelsea Hospital* (London 1811), pp. 59, 175.
9. *SG*, 19, 26 October 1806; JM, evidence, 23 May 1811, *Proceedings of a General Court-martial*, pp. 178–79.
10. Bligh to William Windham, 31 October 1807, *HRA*, series 1, vol. 6, pp. 149, 154; D.R. Hainsworth, *The Sydney Traders: Simeon Lord and his contemporaries 1788–1821* (Melbourne 1972), pp. 69–70.
11. George Johnston to John Schank, 8 August 1803, Percy Family Letters and Papers (Alnwick, UK), vol. 61 (thanks to the tenth Duke of Northumberland for permission to see this material, and to his staff for their help); Anon.,

'Extract of a letter from Sydney (Botany Bay), May 3', *Morning Post* (London), 13 October 1803; Alan Atkinson, 'Jeremy Bentham and the Rum Rebellion', *Journal of the Royal Australian Historical Society*, vol. 64 (1978), pp. 1–13; Atkinson, *The Europeans in Australia*, vol. 1, pp. 367–68.

12   Neil MacKellar to John Piper, 29 December 1793, ML A256; Sir Richard Musgrave, *Memoirs of the Different Rebellions in Ireland* (2 vols) (Dublin 1802; first publ. 1801), vol. 1, p. 457; JM to Piper, 29 September 1805, Eliza Marsden to Piper, 30 September 1805, ML A254-1; Thomas Whittle, evidence, *Proceedings of a General Court–martial*, pp. 367–68; Alan Atkinson, 'The little revolution in New South Wales, 1808', *International History Review*, vol. 12 (1990), pp. 74–75; Atkinson, *The Europeans in Australia*, vol. 1, pp. 390–93.

13   Spirits account, May 1807, JM cash book, 1807–08, pp. 41–42 ('Baker' is almost certainly John Bader, master of the *Argo*); Hainsworth, *The Sydney Traders*, pp. 56–57.

14   P.G. King, memorandum, 2 January 1806, *HRNSW*, vol. 6, p. 1; Bligh to William Windham, 31 October 1807, and enclosure JM v. Robert Campbell jr, report of proceedings, 24 October 1807, *HRA*, series 1, vol. 6, pp. 160, 174–78; [Plummer] to Viscount Castlereagh, [October] 1808, ML C475, pp. 23–24 (thanks to Patricia Curthoys for help with this material; for dating and authorship see Alan Atkinson, 'The multiple voices of John Macarthur', *Journal of Australian Colonial History*, vol. 23 (2021), pp. 22–38); Matthew Allen, 'Alcohol and authority in early New South Wales: The symbolic significance of the spirit trade, 1788–1808', *History Australia*, vol. 9, no. 3 (December 2012), pp. 18–21; Darren Hopkins, 'Governor King and the illicit distillers, 1800–1806', *Journal of the Royal Australian Historical Society*, vol. 105 (2019), pp. 159–79.

15   JM to Michael Hogan, 16 November 1798, ML MSS7359; Plummer to Lachlan Macquarie, 4 May 1809, *HRA*, series 1, vol. 7, pp. 200–204; Atkinson, 'The multiple voices of John Macarthur'.

16   Sir James Steuart, *Considerations on the Interest of the County of Lanark* (Glasgow 1769), pp. 67–74; Sir James Steuart, *The Principles of Money Applied to the Present State of the Coin of Bengal* (London 1772), pp. 74, 79; Plummer to Macquarie, 4 May 1809, pp. 200–204; Purabi Patnaik, 'Grain banking', *Outlook* (New Delhi), 19 October 1998; Jean Cartelier, 'James Steuart on John Law's system: The beginnings of a rational monetary analysis?', in J.M. Menudo (ed.), *The Economic Thought of Sir James Steuart, First Economist of the Scottish Enlightenment* (London 2020), pp. 91–96.

17   Allan Stoekl, *The Three Sustainabilities: Energy, economy, time* (Minneapolis 2021), pp. 116–17.

18   JM v. Robert Campbell jr, report of proceedings, 24 October 1807, pp. 174–78; Atkins, indictment of JM, 2 February 1808, *HRA*, series 1, vol. 6, pp. 292–95; [Plummer] to Castlereagh, [October] 1808, pp. 24–31.

19   Cargoes of departing vessels, January–June 1807, *HRA*, series 1, vol. 6, p. 194, Atkins, indictment of JM, 2 February 1808, pp. 295–301; JM cash book 1807–08, pp. 51–52; JM, evidence, 24 May 1811, in Ritchie, *A Charge of Mutiny*, pp. 190–91.

20   Francis Oakes, evidence at the trial of JM, 6 February 1808, *HRA*, series 1, vol. 6, pp. 347–52; Oakes, evidence, 10 May 1811, *Proceedings of a General Court-martial*, pp. 91–92.

21   William Gore to Castlereagh, 27 March 1808, *HRNSW*, vol. 6, p. 552; JM, evidence, 24 May 1811, *Proceedings of a General Court-martial*, p. 183.

22 JM, declaration to court at his own trial, 25 January 1808, *HRA*, series 1, vol. 6, p. 227.
23 George Washington, *A Circular Letter from His Excellency General Washington, to the Several States, Called His Legacy, Being His Last Public Communication* (London 1783), p. 7.
24 EM to Piper, 5 February 1808, ML A254-1; Atkinson, *The Europeans in Australia*, vol. 1, pp. 403–405.

26 The parlour scene

1 Joan Didion, *The White Album* (New York 1979), p. 1.
2 Francis Oakes, evidence at the trial of JM, 6 February 1808, *HRA*, series 1, vol. 6, pp. 347–52; Francis Oakes, evidence, 10 May 1811, in *Proceedings of a General Court-martial Held at Chelsea Hospital* (London 1811), pp. 91–94.
3 JM to EM, 'Sat. 5 OClock' [30 January 1808?], ML A2898; Oakes, evidence at the trial of JM, pp. 347–49.
4 Oakes, evidence, 6 February 1808, *HRA*, series 1, vol. 6, p. 350.
5 Oakes, evidence, 6 February 1808, *HRA*, series 1, vol. 6, p. 348.
6 Oakes, evidence, 6 February 1808, *HRA*, series 1, vol. 6, pp. 348, 350.
7 William Shakespeare, *The Tragedy of Coriolanus*, Act 3, sc. 2; JM to EM, 1 October 1816, ML A2898.
8 Edmund Griffin, evidence at the trial of JM, 4 February 1808, and William Bligh to Viscount Castlereagh, 30 April 1808, *HRA*, series 1, vol. 6, pp. 322–32, 431.
9 Sir James Steuart, *An Inquiry into the Principles of Political Oeconomy* (2 vols) (London 1767), vol. 1, pp. 2, 320; S.E. Browne, '"A just and profitable commerce": Moral economy and the middle classes in eighteenth-century London', *Journal of British Studies*, vol. 32 (1993), pp. 305–32.
10 *Macarthur v. Thompson*, October–November 1806, Court of Civil Jurisdiction, 'Decisions of the superior courts of New South Wales, 1788–1899', *Colonial Case Law* (Macquarie University), www.law.mq.edu.au/research/colonial_case_law/nsw/cases/case_index/1806/macarthur_v_thompson_1806_nswkr_3_1806_nswsupc_3/; *SG*, 5, 12, 19, 26 July, 2 August 1807; Griffin, evidence at the trial of JM, pp. 323–28; JM to EM, 21 April 1811, ML A2898.
11 *SG*, 2 August 1807.
12 S.T. Coleridge, *Conciones ad Populum: or, Addresses to the People* (no place of publication recorded, 1795), pp. 29–30.
13 JM to James Mitchell, Wednesday morning [1824?], ML A2026.
14 JM to EM, 1 October 1816, and 'Thursday Evg' [1824?], ML A2898.

27 Variegated truths

1 John Hunter to Duke of Portland, 25 July 1798, *HRA*, series 1, vol. 2, p. 161; JM to EM, 11 November 1810, ML A2898; S.M. Thompson to JM, 4 October 1823, ML A2900.
2 This sometimes makes her meaning hard to follow, and in this book I have taken the considerable liberty, when quoting her, of punctuating her sentences in an orthodox way.
3 Adam Smith, *The Theory of Moral Sentiments* (London 1759), p. 75; EM to Eliza Kingdon, 15 July 1818, 4 February 1826, ML A2908; EM to Edward, 4 May, 2 June 1832, ML A2906; Kirk Essary and Yasmin Haskell, 'Calm and violent passions: The genealogy of a distinction from Quintilian to Hume', *Erudition*

and the Republic of Letters, vol. 3 (2018), p. 73 (thanks to Yasmin Haskell for this reference).
4   JM to EM, 3 August 1810, ML A2898.
5   Priya Satia, *Empire of Guns: The violent making of the Industrial Revolution* (New York 2018), pp. 68, 74.
6   John McArthur, *The Army and Navy Gentleman's Companion; or, A New and Complete Treatise on the Theory and Practice of Fencing* (London 1780), pp. 146–54.
7   George Johnston to Viscount Castlereagh, 11 April 1808, *HRA*, series 1, vol. 6, pp. 219–20; JM to John Piper, 24 May 1808, ML A256-1; JM, evidence, 23 May 1811, in *Proceedings of a General Court-martial Held at Chelsea Hospital* (London 1811), p. 177.
8   [T.W. Plummer] to Castlereagh, [October] 1808, ML C475; Plummer to Lachlan Macquarie, 4 May 1809, *HRA*, series 1, vol. 7, pp. 197–210; John Blaxland, 'Remarks on the state of the colony of New South Wales', 26 October 1809, CO 201/50, TNA; Alan Atkinson, 'The multiple voices of John Macarthur', *Journal of Australian Colonial History*, vol. 23 (2021), pp. 22–38.
9   JM to Piper, 24 May 1808; Emmeline to Edward, 2 June 1832, ML A2959.
10 JM to Piper, 24 May 1808; Robert Fitz to James Chapman, 9 April 1808, CO 201/48, TNA.
11 Fitz to Chapman, 9 April 1808; JM to John Piper, 24 May 1808, ML A256-1.
12 George Caley to Sir Joseph Banks, 7 July 1808 ML SAFE/Banks Papers/18.072.
13 Fitz to Chapman, 9 April 1808; William Bligh to Castlereagh, 30 April 1808, *HRA*, series 1, vol. 6, p. 431; T.G. Harris, report on correspondence from NSW, 12 September 1809, and Sir Vicary Gibbs and Sir Thomas Plumer to Castlereagh, 17 November 1809, *HRNSW*, vol. 7, pp. 209–14, 229–30.
14 John Webb and William Brumlow/Bremlow/Barlow, evidence enclosed with Bligh to Charles Manners Sutton, 30 April 1811, WO 72/35, TNA.
15 James Finucane, journal, 19 January 1809, in Anne-Maree Whitaker (ed.), *Distracted Settlement: New South Wales after Bligh* (Melbourne 1998), pp. 73–74; Anne-Maree Whitaker, *Joseph Foveaux: Power and patronage in early New South Wales* (Sydney 2000), pp. 104–18.
16 *SG*, 26 March 1809; JM to EM, 30 July 1809, ML A2898.

28   John's self-reflection
1   Edward to JM, 1 October 1808, ML A2912.
2   JM to EM, 3 August 1810, ML A2898; James to EM, 7 April 1829, ML A2931.
3   JM to EM, 30 July, 28 November – 11 December 1809, 14 February, 16 March, 3 August 1810, 6 April 1811, ML A2898.
4   JM to EM, 6 April 1811.
5   JM to EM, 3 May 1810, 3 August 1810, ML A2898.
6   JM (but in EM's hand), memorandum, n.d. [1809], ML A2902, pp. 148–49; JM to EM, 3 May, 20 July, 11 November 1810, 6 April 1811, ML A2898; D.R. Hainsworth, *The Sydney Traders: Simeon Lord and his contemporaries 1788–1821* (Melbourne 1972), pp. 173–75.
7   JM to EM, 3 May 1810, 6 April 1811.
8   H.J. Washington [fictional name?] to Sir Joseph Banks, 21 Sept 1808, ML SAFE/Banks Papers/43.02, and published, *National Register* (London), 2 October 1808.

Notes to pages 254-261

9   George Johnston to John Schank, 8 August 1803, *Percy Family Letters and Papers*, vol. 61, Alnwick Castle, UK; Anon., review of J.A. Möller, 'On the cultivation and use of the Syrian silk-plant', *Philosophical Magazine*, vol. 8 (1800), pp. 150–51.
10 David Sekers (ed.), 'The diary of Hannah Lightbody 1786–90', *Enlightenment and Dissent*, no. 24 (2008), p. 51 (10 December 1787); Johnston to Schank, 8 August 1803; Northumberland to Thomas Stirling, 10 November 1808, Duke of Northumberland's letter book 1807–09, Alnwick Castle.
11 Sir Samuel Romilly, speech, 5 June 1810, *House of Commons Debates (Hansard)*, series 1, vol. 17, cc. 338–40; JM to EM, 11 November 1810.
12 Robert Fitz to William Chapman, 9 April 1808; T.G. Harris, report on correspondence from NSW, 12 September 1809, and Sir Vicary Gibbs and Sir Thomas Plumer to Viscount Castlereagh, 17 November 1809, *HRNSW*, vol. 7, pp. 209–14, 229–30; Northumberland to Johnston, 5 July 1811, Duke of Northumberland's letter book 1809–12.
13 Johnston, speech, 23 May, JM, evidence, 23, 24 May 1811, in *Proceedings of a General Court-martial Held at Chelsea Hospital* (London 1811), pp. 148, 176–216.
14 Northumberland to Johnston, 5 July, 10, 24 December 1811, 14 January 1812, Duke of Northumberland's letter book 1809–12; Northumberland to Johnston, 11 April, 20 July 1812, Duke of Northumberland's letter book 1812–13.
15 JM to EM, 14 February 1810.
16 *Mining Magazine*, vol. 3 (July–December 1854), p. 563; Jack Fruchtman jr, 'The apocalyptic politics of Richard Price and Joseph Priestley: A study in late eighteenth-century English republican millennialism', *Transactions of the American Philosophical Society*, vol. 73, no. 4 (1983), pp. 25–62, 82–93.
17 JM to EM, 28 November 1809, 18 November 1812.
18 JM to EM, 9 December 1812.
19 *Naval Chronicle*, vol. 25 (January–July 1811), pp. 79–80; Kent's evidence, 31 May 1811, in *Proceedings of a General Court-martial,* p. 337; JM to EM, 4 March 1812.
20 JM to EM, 3 August 1810, 18 November 1812, 26 July 1814, 9 December 1816, ML A2898.
21 JM to EM, 18 November 1812.
22 Ephesians 5:31 (King James Version); 'The solemnization of matrimony', *The Book of Common Prayer* (Oxford 1796), n.p.
23 JM to John Piper, [17 September 1801], 'Friday evng', 'Wed mng' (both September 1801), ML A254-1; JM to EM, 30 July 1809, 8 December 1814, 22 July 1816, 24 March 1817, ML A2898.
24 JM to EM, 30 July 1809, 14 May 1812, 22 July 1816.
25 JM to EM, 30 4 March, 18 November 1812, 31 August 1813, 21 September 1814, 16–17 February 1815.
26 William Buchan, *Domestic Medicine; or, A Treatise on the Prevention and Cure of Diseases by Regimen and Simple Medicines* (London 1790; first publ. 1772), pp. 381–88; JM to John jr, 20 February 1820, ML A2899; 'Dr Pelham Warren', *Lancet*, 2 January 1836, pp. 550, 551.
27 JM to EM, 26 July 1814, 26 September 1814, 8 December 1814, 16–17 February 1815, 9 December 1816.

29 Elizabeth's judgment

1. EM to Garnham Blaxcell, 30 May 1809, ML A2906.
2. *SG*, 19 December 1812, 4 September 1813, 9 October 1819.
3. *SG*, 12 June 1813, 7 September 1816, 1 October 1829; EM to Eliza Kingdon, March 1816, ML A2908; James Atkinson, *An Account of the State of Agriculture and Grazing in New South Wales* (London 1826), pp. 85–87; James, evidence before the House of Commons select committee on transportation, 23 May 1837, *House of Commons Papers*, 1837, vol. 19, p. 191.
4. Francis Oakes, in account with EM, 12 October 1815, ML A2964; Elizabeth Farm day book, 20 December 1819, ML A2903/3; *Australian* (Sydney), 28 June 1826; *SG*, 7 January 1828; R.H.W. Reece, 'Feasts and blankets: The history of some early attempts to establish relations with the Aborigines of New South Wales, 1814–1846', *Archaeology and Physical Anthropology in Oceania*, vol. 2 (1967), pp. 195–99.
5. *SG*, 23 March 1816; William, 'A few memoranda respecting the Aboriginal natives', [1835?], and his recollections of Aborigines, [1870], ML A2935.
6. EM, memorandum of promissory notes, 1811–12, ML A2999; Keith Vincent Smith, 'Nanbarry', *Dictionary of Sydney*, dictionaryofsydney.org.
7. *SG*, 31 Dec 1809; David Bevan, invoice, 7 January 1810, ML A2909; Ellis Bent to J.H. Bent, 30 July 1810; *John Macarthur represented by Elizabeth Macarthur v. Simeon Lord and Henry Kable*, 21 January 1811, *John Macarthur v. Henry Kable*, 21 January 1811, and *John Macarthur represented by Elizabeth Macarthur v. Henry Kable*, 23 January 1811, Court of Civil Jurisdiction, NRS 2659/5/1104, case nos 167, 168, 173, NSWSR; *John Macarthur represented by Elizabeth Macarthur v. Henry Kable the Elder*, 30 April 1811, Governor's Court, NRS 2659/5/1106, case no. 25, NSWSR. I am grateful to Jonathan Auld and Michelle Nichols for help with this material.
8. *John Macarthur represented by Elizabeth Macarthur v. Mary Chalker*, 28 January 1811, Court of Civil Jurisdiction, NRS 2659/5/1104, case no. 189, NSWSR.
9. Ellis Bent to Hannah Bent, 27 July 1810, NL MS195/3 (thanks to Stephen Foster for this reference); EM, memorandum of promissory notes, 1811–12.
10. JM to EM, 4 March 1812, ML A2898.
11. Hannibal Macarthur to JM, 3 July 1812, ML A2901; *Weekly Register* (Sydney), 10 February 1844.
12. Hannibal Macarthur to JM, 4 July 1813, ML A2901.
13. Henry Gostling (counsel), narrative of life and family of William Gordon, in Caporn v. Lucas, 17 February 1775, PROB 18/86/43, TNA; *Star* (London), 20 November 1815; EM to Eliza Kingdon, March 1816, ML A2908; *Farmer's Magazine* (London), vol. 19 (January–June 1849), p. 142; Leslie Tomory, 'The environmental history of the early British gas industry, 1812–1830', *Environmental History*, vol. 17 (2012), pp. 36–37.
14. Livestock returns, Camden and Elizabeth Farm, 1813–19, ML A2999; EM to Edward, 11 September 1835, ML A2906.
15. Elizabeth Wren, will signed 28 January 1841, proved 25 March 1845, PROB 11/2015/81, TNA.
16. JM to EM, 6 April 1811, 1 October 1816, ML A2898.
17. JM to EM, 11 December 1809, 18 Feb 1817, ML A2898; EM to Eliza Kingdon, March 1816.
18. EM to Eliza Kingdon, March 1816, 4 September 1822, 4 February 1826, ML A2908.

19 Hannibal Macarthur to JM, 3 July 1813, 16 May 1814, ML A2901; JM to EM, 26 July 1814, ML A2898; S.E. Hill, '"Paper Houses": John Macarthur and the 30-year design process of Camden Park', PhD thesis, University of Sydney, 2016 (2 vols), vol. 1, pp. 210–16.
20 Robert Bakewell, 'Wool', in Abraham Rees (ed.), *The Cyclopaedia; or, Universal Dictionary of Arts, Sciences, and Literature* (45 volumes), vol. 38 (London 1819), n.p.; Toby Raeburn, Carol Liston, Jarrad Hickmott and Michelle Cleary, 'Liverpool "lunatic asylum": A forgotten chapter in the history of Australian health care', *Collegian* (Australian College of Nursing), no. 25 (2018), p. 350.
21 Ellis Bent to J.H. Bent, 30 July 1810, NL MS195/3; EM to Edward, 27 December 1830, 27 April 1838, ML A2906.
22 Lachlan Macquarie, order for land grants, 12 June 1811, NSWSR 9/2652; *SG*, 7 August 1813.
23 *SG*, 7 December 1811, 14 May 1814; Hannibal Macarthur to JM, 16 May 1814, ML A2901; EM to Eliza Kingdon, March 1816.

30 Commanding the long term
1 EM to Bridget Kingdon, 1 September [1798], ML A2908.
2 Eugene Stelzig, '"Spirit Divine! With Thee I'll wander": Mary Robinson and Coleridge in poetic dialogue', *Wordsworth Circle*, vol. 35 (2004), pp. 118–22.
3 Mary Robinson, *A Letter to the Women of England, on the Injustice of Mental Subordination* (London 1799), pp. 63–65, 72–73, 90–91.
4 Mary Robinson to Home Office, 14 July 1789, HO 42/14, TNA.
5 Rowland Hassall, answers to sheep questionnaire, 10 August 1805, *HRA*, series 1, vol. 5, p. 560; *SG*, 28 April 1810; Beecroft and Cheltenham History Group, 'Small farms to subdivision', bchg.org.au/index.php/en/changing-times/earlysettlement/small-farms-to-subdivision/43-small-farms-to-subdivision.
6 One Eleanor McDonald was born 17 March 1766 into a large family of Spitalfields weavers and baptised at Shoreditch, 2 June 1766. In spite of later evidence, she must have been still a 'girl', as Robinson said, and not far into her twenties when transported.
7 G.B. Worgan, *General View of the Agriculture of the County of Cornwall* (London 1811), pp. 148–49; JM to EM, 26 July 1814, 16–17 February 1815, ML A2898.
8 JM to EM, 4 March 1812, ML A2898.
9 Edward to JM, 14 May 1809, ML A2912; JM to EM, 22 July 1809, ML A2898; EM to Eliza Kingdon, March 1816, ML A2908; Lachlan Macquarie, *Lachlan Macquarie, Governor of New South Wales: Journey of his tours in New South Wales and Van Diemen's Land* (Phyllis Mander-Jones, ed.) (Sydney 1956), pp. 5–12.
10 JM to EM, 16 October 1812, ML A2898.
11 JM to EM, 16 October, 18 November 1812, ML A2898.
12 JM to EM, 16 October 1812, 8 December 1814, ML A2898.
13 JM to EM, 21 May 1813, ML A2898.
14 JM to EM, 26 July 1814, ML A2898.
15 JM to EM, 30 June, 26 July 1814, ML A2898.
16 JM to EM, 26 July 1814.
17 Viscount Castlereagh to Lachlan Macquarie, 14 May 1809, *HRA*, series 1, vol. 7, p. 81; JM to EM, 8 December 1814, ML A2898.
18 JM to EM, 8 December 1814.

19 JM to EM, 8 December 1814.
20 JM to EM, 8 December 1814.

PART 6
31 The supposed point of invasion
1   William, 'A few memoranda respecting the Aboriginal natives', [1835?], ML A2935; James Byrnes to Edward, 29 November 1856, ML A2917.
2   *SG*, 3 September, 1, 15 October 1809, 24 February 1810; *R. v. Luttrell*, 13 March 1810, Court of Criminal Jurisdiction, 'Decisions of the superior courts of New South Wales, 1788–1899', *Colonial Case Law* (Macquarie University), www.law.mq.edu.au/research/colonial_case_law/nsw/cases/case_index/1810/r_v_luttrell; Stephen Gapps, *The Sydney Wars: Conflict in the early colony 1788–1817* (Sydney 2018) pp. 190–96.
3   James Byrnes to Edward, 29 November 1856.
4   William, 'A few memoranda respecting the Aboriginal natives', [1835?], ML A2935.
5   David Collins, *An Account of the English Colony in New South Wales* (2 vols, ed. Brian H. Fletcher) (Sydney 1975), vol. 1 (first publ. 1798), pp. 16, 296–97, 460–61.
6   [Alexander Harris], *Settlers and Convicts; or, Recollections of Sixteen Years' Labour in the Australian Backwoods* (London 1847), p. 400.
7   James, speech, *Australian*, 26 August 1842.
8   Edmund Burke, 'Speech on the Nawab of Arcot's debts', 28 February 1785, in P.J. Marshall and W.B. Todd (eds), *The Writings and Speeches of Edmund Burke*, vol. 5 (India: Madras and Bengal: 1774–1785) (Oxford 1981), p. 520.
9   James, speech, *Sydney Morning Herald*, 24 August 1842.
10 Henry Reynolds, *An Indelible Stain?: The question of genocide in Australia's history* (Melbourne 2001), pp. 52–56; Alan Atkinson, 'Historians and moral disgust', in Bain Attwood and S.G. Foster (eds), *Frontier Conflict: The Australian experience* (Canberra 2003), pp. 115–19.

32 Intrigued by the young
1   Jean-Jacques Rousseau, *Émile, or On Education* (trans. Barbara Foxley) (London 1911; first publ. in French 1762), pp. 14–16, 57–77.
2   EM to Bridget Kingdon, 1 September [1798], A2908.
3   Edward to JM, 19 November 1809, ML A2912.
4   Edward to JM, 19 November 1809; JM to EM, 3 August 1810, ML A2898; EM to Eliza Kingdon, March 1816, ML A2908.
5   JM to EM, 3 May 1810, ML A2898; EM to Edward, n.d. [October 1834], ML A2906.
6   Edward to JM, 29 November 1809, ML A2912.
7   John jr to EM, 30 September 1808, ML A2912; Edward to JM, Friday morning [March 1810], 22 September, 5 November 1810, ML A2912.
8   William Buchan, *Domestic Medicine; or, A Treatise on the Prevention and Cure of Diseases by Regimen and Simple Medicines* (London 1790; first publ. 1772), p. 639; Edward to JM, 25 April, 22 September 1810, ML A2912.
9   Edward to JM, Sunday morning [January 1810], Friday morning [2 March 1810], 14, 25 April, 23 October 1810, ML A2912; Hazel King, *Colonial Expatriates: Edward and John Macarthur junior* (Sydney 1989), p. 59.
10 Edward to EM, 19 May 1810, ML A2912.

11 Edward to EM, 19 May 1810; EM to Elizabeth jr, Friday [November 1830], ML A2906.
12 Edward to JM, Friday morning [March 1810], 24 December 1810, ML A2912.
13 Edward to JM, 7 December 1809, 25 April 1810, ML A2912.
14 JM to EM, 28 November 1809, 25 April, 30 May 1810, 12 August 1810, ML A2898.
15 Edward to JM, 26 October 1808, ML A2912; JM to EM, 17, 28 November 1809, 12 January 1810, ML A2898.
16 JM to EM, 28 November 1809, 31 August 1813, 8 December 1814, ML A2898.
17 Edward to JM, 21 June 1811, ML A2912; 'Cholmondeley, George Horatio, Earl of Rocksavage (1792–1870)', *The History of Parliament; the House of Commons, 1790–1820 – Members*, www.historyofparliamentonline.org/volume/1790-1820/member/cholmondeley-george-horatio-1792-1870.
18 Edward to EM, 30 September 1808, ML A2912.
19 JM to EM, 1 December 1810, 21 April 1811, ML A2898; C.D. Donald (ed.), *Minute Book of the Board of Green Cloth, 1809–20* (Glasgow 1891), p. 127.
20 George Jardine, *Outlines of Philosophical Education* (Glasgow 1818), pp. 277–78, 355–56, 394–98; Anon., 'Memoir of John Macarthur, Esq. of Lincoln's Inn, London', *Sydney Herald*, 3 October 1831.
21 Edward to JM, 18 February 1810, and Edward to Elizabeth jr, 18 February 1810, ML A2912; Anon., 'Memoir of John Macarthur, Esq. of Lincoln's Inn, London'; W. Innes Addison (ed.), *Prize Lists of the University of Glasgow, from Session 1777–78 to Session 1832–33* (Glasgow 1902), pp. 135, 139–40; Lynée Lewis Gaillet, 'George Jardine: Champion of the Scottish philosophy of democratic intellect', *Rhetoric Society Quarterly*, vol. 28 (1998), pp. 42–43.
22 Jardine, *Outlines of Philosophical Education*, pp. 274–75, 419.
23 Jeremy Bentham, *Panopticon; or, The Inspection-House* (Dublin 1791), p. ii.
24 Edward to JM, 29 November 1809.

33 A daughter grows up
1 EM to Bridget Kingdon, 1 September [1798], ML A2908; EM to JM, Friday [November 1830], ML A2906; EM to Eliza Kingdon, 4 February 1826, ML A2908; EM to Edward, 21 April 1845, ML A2907.
2 EM to Eliza Kingdon, March 1816, ML A2908.
3 EM to Grace Bond, 21 December 1793, ML A2908; EM to John Piper, 13 November 1811, ML A254-1.
4 JM to EM, 3 May 1810, ML A2898; R.R. Madden, *The United Irishmen: Their lives and times* (4 vols) (Dublin 1858; first publ. 1842), vol. 1, pp. 545, 582; Michelle Scott Tucker, *Elizabeth Macarthur: A life at the edge of the world* (Melbourne 2018), pp. 173–74.
5 Michael Underwood, *A Treatise on the Diseases of Children* (2 vols) (London 1789; first publ. 1784), vol. 2, pp. 53–57; JM to EM, 22 July 1816, ML A2898; EM to Edward, 29 October – 2 November 1848, ML A2907; M.R. Smallman-Raynor, A.D. Cliff, and others, *Poliomyelitis: Emergence to eradication* (Oxford 2006), pp. 71–74.
6 Hannibal Macarthur to JM, 3 July 1813, ML A2901; EM to Eliza Kingdon, March 1816, ML A2908; Rose Marie de Freycinet, *A Woman of Courage: The journal of Rose de Freycinet on her voyage around the world, 1817–1820* (ed. and trans. M.S. Rivière) (Canberra 2003), p. 119.

7   Edward to Elizabeth jr, 23 April 1811, ML A2912; James to EM, 7 April 1829, ML A2931; Michele Cohen, 'A mother's dilemma: Where best to educate a daughter, at home or at a school?', *Gaskell Journal*, vol. 28 (2014), pp. 35–52.
8   Stéphanie-Félicité de Genlis, *Adèle et Théodore: Lettres sur l'éducation* (Maastricht 1782) (inscribed copy, now at Camden Park); Elizabeth jr to Edward, 4 October 1831, ML A2906.
9   EM to Bridget Kingdon, 7 March 1791, 1 September [1798], ML A2908; Edward to Elizabeth jr, 23 April 1811.
10 Elizabeth jr to Piper, n.d. [June 1805], and JM to Piper, 10 June 1805, ML A254.
11 *SG*, 19 February 1809, 14 April, 28 April 1810; *Naval Chronicle*, vol. 38 (July–December 1817), p. 348.
12 John Oxley, 'Remarks on the country and settlements formed in Van Diemen's Land', and 'Remarks on settlement at Port Dalrymple', both n.d., *HRA*, series 3, vol. 1, pp. 569–80, 758–77.
13 *SG*, 14 April 1810; JM to EM, 11 November 1810.
14 Edward to Elizabeth jr, 23 April 1811.
15 JM to EM, 11 November 1810, 6 April 1811, ML A2898; JM to John jr, 18 February 1824, ML A2899.
16 G.F. Macarthur, n.d., 'Genealogical map of the MacArthurs of Strachur', ML D80; JM to EM, 14 May 1812, ML A2899.
17 JM to EM, 14 May, 18 November 1812, 15 January, 21 May 1813, 26 July, 8 December 1814, ML A2898; EM to Edward, 31 May 1828, ML A2906. The *Minstrel* arrived on October 1812; daughters were born August 1813 and January 1815.
18 JM to James Chapman, 20 July 1805, CO 201/38, f. 239; Edward to Elizabeth jr, 12 February 1813, ML A2912; *Quarterly Review*, vol. 24 (1821), p. 60.
19 EM to Eliza Kingdon, March, 1816, ML A2908; T.L. Mitchell, *Three Expeditions in the Interior of Eastern Australia* (London 1839), pp. 5–6; William Woolls, *A Contribution to the Flora of Australia* (Sydney 1867), p. 220; William Woolls, 'Eucalypts of the County of Cumberland', *Sydney Mail*, 20 August 1881.
20 EM to Eliza Kingdon, March 1816, ML A2908; EM to Edward, 1 May 1833, 5 April 1840, and Elizabeth jr to Edward, [18 December 1840], ML A2906; Rose de Freycinet, *A Woman of Courage*, p. 119.
21 Elizabeth jr to Eliza Kingdon, 8 March 1817, ML A2908/2.
22 Elizabeth jr to Eliza Kingdon, 15 July 1818, ML A2908/2.
23 H.C. Allport, 'Catalogue of the library at Elizabeth Farm, the property of Col'l Macarthur', May 1854, ML A2919/4; Woolls, *A Contribution to the Flora of Australia*, p. 220; Woolls, 'Eucalypts of the County of Cumberland'; William Woolls, 'Parramatta and the early naturalists of the colony', *Cumberland Mercury*, 20 March 1886; Arvède Barine, *Bernadin de Saint-Pierre* (trans. J.E. Gordon) (London 1893), pp. 91–95 (Saint-Pierre's French also trans. by Gordon).
24 Elizabeth jr to Edward, 18 March 1841, ML A2917; Woolls, 'Parramatta and the early naturalists of the colony'.

34 The excellence of Madeira

1. Benjamin Franklin to Jacques Barbeu-Dubourg, n.d. [May–June 1773?], *The Complete Works in Philosophy, Politics and Morals of the late Dr Benjamin Franklin* (3 vols), (London 1806), vol. 2, pp. 223–24.
2. Gilbert Mathison, *Notices Respecting Jamaica, in 1808–1809–1810* (London 1811), pp. 4–7.
3. Papers re investment by *Isabella*, 1810–13, ML A2902, pp. 152–85; JM, suggestions to J.T. Bigge, no. 1 (this item crossed out in ms), 7 February 1821, ML A2897; Julie McIntyre, 'Adam Smith and faith in the transformative qualities of wine in colonial New South Wales', *Australian Historical Studies*, vol. 42 (2011), pp. 194–206.
4. JM to EM, 4 March 1812, ML A2898; Hannibal Macarthur, invoices for EM, 7 September 1812, 15 May 1814, ML A2909.
5. JM to EM, 3 August 1810, 26 December 1814, 9 December 1816, 24 March 1817, ML A2898.
6. JM to EM, 18 November 1812, 31 August 1813, 26 July 1814, ML A2898.
7. JM to EM, 3 August 1810, 6 April 1811, ML A2898; EM to Edward, 15 November 1842, ML A2907; [G.F. Macarthur], 'Harry the king of Kissing Point', *Sydney Morning Herald*, 17 July 1880.
8. JM to EM, 26 December 1814.
9. JM to EM, 26 December 1814.
10. Siân Reynolds, *Paris-Edinburgh: Cultural connections in the Belle Epoque* (London 2016; first publ. 2007), pp. 5–11; Elisabeth Jay, *British Writers and Paris 1830–75* (Oxford 2016), p. 5.
11. Robert Bakewell, *Introduction to Geology* (London 1813), pp. 190–94; H.C. Allport, 'Catalogue of the library at Elizabeth Farm, the property of Col'l Macarthur', May 1854, ML A2919/4.
12. JM to EM, 26 December 1814, ML A2898; Isabelle Laboulais, 'Serving science and the state: Mining science in France, 1794–1810', *Minerva*, vol. 46 (2008), pp. 27–36.
13. JM to EM, 26 December 1814.
14. EM, memorandum, 23 December 1843, ML A2907.
15. James, Journal of a tour in France and Switzerland, March 1815–April 1816, ML A2929/1.
16. Antoine Duvillard, *Quelques réflexions sur les moeurs républicaines et sur l'établissement d'un theatre a Genève* (Geneva 1814); James to Roger Therry (draft), 24 February 1859, ML A2897; W.R.W. Stephens (ed.), *Memoir of the Right Hon. William Page Wood, Baron Hatherley* (2 vols) (London 1883), vol. 1, pp. 28–29, 118–19; Cyprian Blamires, *The French Revolution and the Creation of Benthamism* (Basingstoke, UK, 2008), pp. 112–13; Marc Lerner, *A Laboratory of Liberty: The transformation of political culture in republican Switzerland, 1750–1848* (Leiden, Netherlands, 2011), pp. 51–73.
17. JM, Notebook kept in Switzerland, 1815–16, ML A2951/4; JM to John jr, 20 February 1820, ML A2899; *Archives de la famille Roget* (Bibliothèque de Genève: Catalogue des manuscrits) (Geneva 2010), p. 92; Nicolas Eyguesier, 'Owen as read by Marc-Auguste Pictet (1752–1825) and J.C.L. Simonde de Sismondi (1773–1842)', *History of European Ideas*, vol. 46 (2020), pp. 1–4.
18. James, Journal of a tour in France and Switzerland; JM to EM, 29 April 1815, ML A2898; Thomas Pinney, *A History of Wine in America: From the beginnings to Prohibition* (2 vols) (Berkeley, USA, 2007; first publ. 1989), vol. 1, pp. 117–26.

Notes to pages 316–323

19   JM to EM, 29 April 1815; Edward to EM, 9 December 1815, ML A2912.
20   JM, Notebook kept in Switzerland, 1815–16; Pinney, *A History of Wine in America*, vol. 1, pp. 119–20.
21   James, Journal of a tour in France and Switzerland; Lord Byron, *Childe Harold's Pilgrimage* (London 1837), p. 274, supposedly quoting Jean-Jacques Rousseau, *Les Confessions de J.J. Rousseau, suivies des Rêveries du Promeneurs Solitaires* (2 vols) (Lausanne 1782), p. 274; David Ellis, *Byron in Geneva: That summer of 1816* (Liverpool, UK, 2011), pp. 3–12, 63–66.
22   A.D. Bache, *Report on Education in Europe to the Trustees of the Girard College for Orphans* (Philadelphia 1839), pp. 621–22.
23   James, Journal of a tour in France and Switzerland; *Sydney Morning Herald*, 1 September 1853; Ross E. Stewart, 'Sismondi's forgotten ethical critique of early capitalism', *Journal of Business Ethics*, vol. 3 (1984), pp. 227–34; Adrien Lutz, 'On commercial gluts, or when the Saint-Simonians adopted Jean-Baptiste Say's view', *Journal of the History of Economic Thought*, vol. 41 (2019), p. 216.
24   'Maro' [William], *Letters on the Culture of the Vine, Fermentation, and the Management of Wine in the Cellar* (Sydney, 1844), pp. v, vii, 20; Eyguesier, 'Owen as read by Marc-Auguste Pictet (1752–1825) and J.C.L. Simonde de Sismondi (1773–1842)', pp. 2–5.
25   JM to EM, 1 December 1810, 21 April 1811, 19 August 1816, ML A2898; JM to John jr, 20 February 1820, ML A2899; Alan Atkinson, 'The political life of James Macarthur', PhD thesis, Australian National University, 1977, pp. 85–87, 163.
26   JM to Earl Bathurst, 1 August 1816, and JM to EM, 28 July – 3 August 1816, ML A2898; G. Watson Taylor to R.J. Wilmot-Horton, 2 August 1822, D3155/C/6046, Derbyshire Record Office.
27   JM to EM, 19 August, 1 October 1816, and Henry Goulburn to JM, 2 August 1816 (copy), ML A2898.
28   JM to EM, 22, 23 July 1816, 19 August, 6 December 1816, ML A2898.
29   James Brogden to Bathurst, 4 March 1817, CO 201/88, ff. 34–35, TNA.
30   *Morning Post* (London), 23 April 1817; 'Maro', *Letters on the Culture of the Vine*, p. vi; Ralph Hawkins, 'Andrew Murray (1793–1858)', *Pick of the Great North Road*, vol. 3.9, www.convicttrail.com.au/uploads/8/7/1/9/87196654/pick_vol_3.9_andrew_murray.pdf.
31   JM to EM, 'Tuesday morng' [30 September 1817], ML A2898; EM to Eliza Kingdon, 11 December 1817, ML A2908.

35   Mind over mind

1   D'Arcy Wentworth to Earl Fitzwilliam, draft, n.d. [1809], ML A752; *SG*, 22 October 1814.
2   W.C. Wentworth to D'Arcy Wentworth, 10 April 1817, ML A756.
3   Hannibal Macarthur to JM, [4 July 1813], ML A2901; W.C. Wentworth, lampoon on the Macarthurs, c. 1815, ML A4073 (date between apparent arrival of the landau, June 1815, and Wentworth's departure, March 1816); Hazel King, *Elizabeth Macarthur and Her World* (Sydney 1980), pp. 89–91.
4   W.C. Wentworth to D'Arcy Wentworth, 10 April 1817, ML A756; Andrew Tink, *William Charles Wentworth: Australia's greatest native son* (Sydney 2009), p. 43.
5   W.C. Wentworth to Fitzwilliam, 15 January 1817, and to W.C. Wentworth to D'Arcy Wentworth, 25 May, 10 November 1818, ML A756; Tink, *William Charles Wentworth*, pp. 42–43.

6   W.C. Wentworth, *A Statistical, Historical, and Political Description of the Colony of New South Wales, and Its Dependent Settlements in Van Diemen's Land* (London 1819), p. 215.
7   Wentworth, *A Statistical, Historical, and Political Description of the Colony of New South Wales*, pp. 394–96.
8   J.R. Ward, 'The amelioration of British West Indian slavery, 1750–1834: Technical change and the plough', *Nieuwe West-Indische Gids / New West Indian Guide*, vol. 63, no. 1/2 (1989), pp. 41–58; O.M. Blouet, 'Slavery and freedom in the British West Indies, 1823–33: The role of education', *History of Education Quarterly*, vol. 30 (1990), pp. 625–43; Claudius Fergus, '"Dread of insurrection": Abolitionism, security, and labor in Britain's West Indian colonies, 1760–1823', *William and Mary Quarterly*, 3rd series, vol. 66 (2009), pp. 757–80.
9   William Wilberforce, A *Letter on the Abolition of the Slave Trade* (London 1807), pp. 143–44.
10 Gilbert Mathison, *Notices Respecting Jamaica, in 1808–1809–1810* (London 1811), pp. 99–103, 111–12.
11 Earl Bathurst to Viscount Sidmouth, 23 April 1817, HO 142/64, TNA; Hamish Maxwell-Stewart, 'Convict transportation from Britain and Ireland 1615–1870', *History Compass*, vol. 8 (2010), pp. 1230–32.
12 JM to John jr, 20 February 1820; J.T. Bigge, *Report of the Commissioner of Inquiry into the State of the Colony of New South Wales* (London 1822), p. 161.
13 T.H. Scott, Notes 'respectg New S. Wales, 1822', encl. with Scott to William Ord, 29 April 1822, NRO 324/A/32, Northumberland Archives.
14 JM to Bigge, 7 February 1821, ML BT 1, pp. 222–24.
15 JM, evidence to Bigge, n.d. [1822], CO 201/120, ff. 130–32, TNA; JM, 'Suggestions relative to the employment, discipline and ultimate reformation of the convicts in New South Wales', [December 1821?], ML A2897.
16 JM, evidence to J.T. Bigge, n.d. [1822], ff. 130–32; James, evidence before the House of Commons select committee on transportation, 19 May 1837, *House of Commons Papers*, 1837, vol. 19, p. 164.
17 JM to Bigge, 7 February 1821; JM, evidence to J.T. Bigge, n.d. [1822], ff. 130–33.
18 JM, evidence to Bigge, n.d. [1822], f. 131; [Sydney Smith], 'State of prisons', *Edinburgh Review*, July 1821, p. 290; JM, 'Suggestions relative to the employment, discipline and ultimate reformation of the convicts in New South Wales'.
19 JM, 'Suggestions'.
20 JM, note on 'Suggestions', n.d.
21 *SG*, 10 October 1825.

36 Vicissitudes of convict reform

1   JM to EM, 22 May 1816, ML A2898; JM to W.S. Davidson, 3 September 1818, ML A2897.
2   JM, 'Suggestions relative to the employment, discipline and ultimate reformation of the convicts in New South Wales', [December 1821?], ML A2897; JM, evidence to J.T. Bigge, n.d. [1822], CO 201/120, f. 132; James, journal kept at Port Stephens, December 1827 – January 1828, p. 37, Noel Butlin Archives 78/1/6, Australian National University; James to Roger Therry (draft), 24 February 1859, ML A2897.

3   T.W. Plummer to Board of Trade, 1 July 1806, BT 1/29, TNA; Wool sales accounts, 1818–32, William to John jr, 16–30 January 1824, James to John jr, 31 January 1824, ML A2965; JM to John jr, 20 February 1820; Lachlan Macquarie to Earl Bathurst, 28 February 1820, *HRA*, series 1, vol. 10, pp. 288–89; James, memoranda, 8 May 1832, ML A2971, William to Edward, 20 January 1858, ML A2933; Jill Ker, 'The wool industry in New South Wales, 1803–1830', pt 2, *Business Archives and History*, vol. 2 (1962), pp. 26–28.
4   Livestock returns, Camden and Elizabeth Farm, 1813–19, ML A2999.
5   Elizabeth Farm daybook, 4 May 1819, ML A2903/3; Anne-Maree Whitaker, *Unfinished Revolution: United Irishmen in New South Wales, 1800–1810* (Sydney 1994), pp. 67–68; Carol Liston, 'The Dharawal and Gandangara in colonial Campbelltown, New South Wales, 1788–1830', *Aboriginal History*, vol. 12 (1988) p. 55; Niklas Frykman, 'The mutiny on the Hermione: Warfare, revolution, and treason in the Royal Navy', *Journal of Social History*, vol. 44, (2010), pp. 159–87.
6   *Saunders's News-Letter* (Dublin), 28 August, 5 September 1823; *Sydney Monitor*, 27 September 1828; S.E. Hill, '"Paper houses": John Macarthur and the 30-year design process of Camden Park', PhD thesis, University of Sydney, 2016 (2 vols), vol. 1, pp. 210–43.
7   'Return of persons in the employ of John MacArthur Esq, Septr 23d 1824', CO 201/167, ff 320–21, TNA; Alan Atkinson, *Camden: Farm and village life in early New South Wales* (Melbourne 1988), pp. 29–30.
8   *Caledonian Mercury* (Edinburgh), 3 October 1816, 14 July 1821; EM to Edward, 21 April 1845, 7–8 September 1845, ML A2907. Biographical detail on Boyd and other convicts mentioned in this chapter has been pieced together from NSW censuses and convict musters to be found on the Ancestry family history website (ancestry.com.au), and numerous similar sources.
9   JM, evidence given to J.T. Bigge, f. 139; *SG*, 8 September 1821, 18 January 1822; James to JM, 17 February 1824, ML A2962.
10 EM to Elizabeth jr, [November 1830], and to Edward, 23 March 1832, 27 April 1838, ML A2906.
11 Patrick Curry, statement to Caroline Chisholm, 6 January 1846, *Sydney Morning Herald*, 6 June 1848.
12 Trial of Thomas Burton, 15, 22 August 1825, Cawdor bench book, 1825–26, 4/7567, NSWSR; trials of James Herbert, John Halloran, John Wilkinson and James Sparks, 23 November 1826, Cawdor bench book, 1826–28, 4/7568, NSWSR.
13 Trials of William Carroll, Robert Smith and John Edmunds, 18 June 1827, Cawdor bench book, 1826–28.
14 James to John jr, 17 May 1827, ML A2931. This appears from a comparison of the 1824 list ('Return of persons in the employ of John MacArthur Esq') with the NSW census of 1828, and a survey of convict transport indentures for 1826–28.
15 *Lancaster Gazette*, 26 May, 15, 22 September 1821; *SG*, 2 February 1830.
16 *Southern Reporter* (Cork), 4 October 1823; *Morning Post* (London), 16 October 1824; *Waterford Mail*, 23 October 1824. This is presuming he was the Richard Jones listed at Oatland, Picton, in the NSW census, 1841; the detail matches as far as it goes.
17 Martin Murphy, petition, 25 October 1825, and James, testimonial, 15 May 1827, NRS 898, 4/1112.1A, pp. 233–37, NSWSR; Hans Caulfield to

W.H. Gregory, 3 January 1826, CSO/RP/1825/1745 (catalogue summary only seen), National Archives of Ireland; *Sydney Monitor*, 21 November 1835; J.S. Donnelly, *Captain Rock: The Irish agrarian rebellion of 1821–1824* (Madison, Wisconsin, 2009), p. 417.
18 *Sydney Monitor*, 21 November 1835.
19 *Sydney Herald*, 9 January 1832; EM to Edward, 30 June 1832, 29 September 1833, ML A2906.
20 *True Briton* (London), 31 May 1798, 1 January 1799; *London Observer*, 30 September 1798, 17 March 1799.
21 Michael Comerford (ed.), *Collections Relating to the Dioceses of Kildare and Leighlin* (Dublin 1883), pp. 149, 159–61.
22 *Saunders's News-Letter*, 26 March 1821; *Freeman's Journal* (Dublin), 30 March 1821; Rose Richey, certificate of freedom, 2 September 1828, 28/0795, NSWSR.
23 William Elyard, surgeon's journal, 25 July, 3 November 1821, ADM 101/38/7/1, TNA (extract at convictrecords.com.au/convicts/richey/rose/136081); NSW musters and censuses, 1822, 1824, 1825, 1828, ancestry.com.au.
24 *SG*, 20 April 1827; NSW census, 1828; *Currency Lad* (Sydney), 10 November 1832.

PART 7
37 La révolution morale
1   JM to James Mitchell, 25 November [listed as October] 1824, ML A2026; Margaret and Alastair Macfarlane, *The Scottish Radicals: Tried and transported to Australia for treason in 1820* (Sydney 1975), pp. 11, 46–47.
2   JM to John Piper, 29 September 1805, ML A254-1; James to Emily Macarthur, 4 March 1857, Macarthur Papers at Camden Park.
3   T.H. Kingdon, *A Sermon, Preached at St Mary's, Guildford, on Wednesday, March 12, 1800; Being the Day Appointed for a General Fast* (London 1800), pp. 3–4, 7–8; EM to Edward, 20 July 1836, ML A2906.
4   T.H. Scott to G.W. Norman, 25 February 1832, C200, Kent Archives Office.
5   [Richard Carlile], 'Completion of the revolution in Portugal – Where are we to look next?', *Republican* (London), vol. 4 (1830), pp. 227–32; Linda Colley, *The Gun, the Ship and the Pen: Warfare, constitutions, and the making of the modern world* (London 2021), pp. 139–54.
6   William Hazlitt, *The Round Table: A collection of essays on literature, men, and manners* (2 vols) (Edinburgh 1817), vol. 1, p. 27.
7   Pindar, *The Pythian, Nemean, and Isthmian Odes of Pindar* (trans. E.B. Greene) (London 1778), pp. 27–63; JM to Edward, 5 June 1832, ML A2899; M.L. Clarke, *Greek Studies in England, 1700–1830* (Cambridge 1945), pp. 146–47, 162–63, 239.
8   James to EM, 7 April 1829, ML A2931.
9   *St James's Chronicle* (London), 15 August 1818; W.J. McGrath, *German Freedom and the Greek Ideal* (New York 2013), pp. 13–41; Jeremy Adler, *Johann Wolfgang von Goethe* (London 2020), pp. 120–26.
10 Adamantios Korais, *Mémoire sur l'état actuel de la civilisation dans la Grèce* (Paris 1803), pp. 14–17; Lord Byron, 'The isles of Greece', in Hardin Craig (ed.), *Byron's Childe Harold, Cantos III and IV, The Prisoner of Chillon, and Other Poems* (New York 1913), pp. 161–62; Catherine Koumarianou, 'The contribution of

the intelligentsia towards the Greek independence movement, 1798–1821', in Richard Clogg (ed.), *The Struggle for Greek Independence: Essays to mark the 150th anniversary of the Greek War of Independence* (London 1973), pp. 79–81.
11 Scott to Earl of Guilford, 25 March 1819, 1 September [1822], British Library Add MSS 88900/1/54; *Monitor* (Sydney), 30 April 1828; Douglas Dakin, *British and American Philhellenes during the War of Greek Independence, 1821–1833* (Thessaloniki, Greece, 1955), p. 148; Elizabeth Elbourne, 'The Bannisters and their colonial world: Family networks and colonialism in the early nineteenth century', in Karen Dubinsky, Adele Perry, and Henry Yu (eds), *Within and Without the Nation: Canadian history as transnational history* (Toronto 2015), p. 64.
12 Scott to Norman, 22 December 1834, C200, Kent Archives Office.

38 Hobbes Scott
1 Elizabeth jr to Edward, 4 October 1831, ML A2906; EM, memorandum, 23 December 1843, and EM to Edward, 30 September 1847, ML A2907.
2 John jr to James, 21 September 1821, ML A2911; Elizabeth jr to Edward, 4 October 1831, and EM to Edward, 23 January 1834, ML A2906; Emmeline to Edward, 7 January 1832, ML A2959; EM, memorandum. The Heber book must have been Amelia Heber (ed.), *Narrative of a Journey through the Upper Provinces of India from Calcutta to Bombay 1824–25* (London 1827, or later edition). The Bacon book might have been *The Works of Francis Bacon, Baron of Verulam, Viscount St Alban, and Lord High Chancellor of England* (London 1819), now at Camden Park.
3 John Warner, will, signed 18 January 1800, proved 28 January 1800, PROB 11/1336/157, TNA; Richard Warner, *Literary Recollections* (2 vols) (London 1830), vol. 1, pp. 102–105; T.H. Scott to William Ord, 27 January 1844, NRO 324/A/32, Northumberland Archives.
4 *Star* (London), 19 May 1797; Scott to Thomas Jefferson, 8 February 1803, *Founders Online*, National Archives, founders.archives.gov/documents/Jefferson/01-39-02-0416; Frank Hamel, *Lady Hester Lucy Stanhope: A new light on her life and love affairs* (London 1913), pp. 24–25, 315; M.T. Davis (ed.), *The London Corresponding Society, 1792–1799* (6 vols) (London 2016; first publ. 2002), vol. 4, pp. 152–56, 220–28, 246; D.V. Erdman, 'Lord Byron and the genteel reformers', *Publications of the Modern Language Association*, vol. 56 (1941), pp. 1066–94.
5 William Godwin, *The Enquirer: Reflections on education, manners, and literature* (London 1797), p. 17; Alexander Stephens, *Memoirs of John Horne Tooke* (2 vols) (London 1813), vol. 2, pp. 325–26; Tilottama Rajan, 'Uncertain futures: History and genealogy in William Godwin's *The Lives of Edward and John Philips, Nephews and Pupils of Milton*', *Milton Quarterly*, vol. 32 (1998), p. 80; Victoria Myers, David O'Shaughnessy and Mark Philp (eds), *The Diary of William Godwin* (Oxford: Oxford Digital Library, 2010), godwindiary.bodleian.ox.ac.uk/search.html?q=scott&domain=diary&queryType=and&action=Search&prev=; John Horne Tooke, *Epea pteroenta; or, The Diversions of Purley* (2 pts) (London 1786), pt. 1, p. 21.
6 Godwin, *The Enquirer*, pp. 4–6, 56–58, 78–82, 329–36; Rajan, 'Uncertain futures', p. 80.
7 *London Gazette*, 16 March 1805; *Transactions of the Society, Instituted at London, for the Encouragement of Arts, Manufactures and Commerce*, vol. 32 (1814), pp. 34–38.

8   Deborah Harlan, 'British Lancastrian schools of nineteenth-century Kythera', *Annual of the British School at Athens*, vol. 106 (2011), pp. 328–33.
9   [Joseph Blanco White?], *Noticia de las Providencias Tomadas por el Gobierno para Observar el Nuevo Método de la Enseñanza Primaria de Enrique Pestalozzi* (Madrid 1807), pp. 25–28; J.H. Thom (ed.), *The Life of the Rev. Joseph Blanco White, Written by Himself* (3 vols) (London 1845), vol. 1, pp. 50, 132–37, 140, 363; Sir Henry Holland, *Recollections of Past Life* (London 1872), p. 255; M. Consolación Calderón España and M. Isabel Corts Giner, 'Los principios educativos Pestalozzianos y su influencia en la educaciónón Española', *Revista Panamericana de Pedagogía*, no. 3 (2002), pp. 37–39.
10 Scott to Earl of Guilford, 1 September [1822], British Library Add MS 88900/1/54; Konstantina Zanou, *Transnational Patriotism in the Mediterranean, 1800–1850: Stammering the nation* (Oxford 2018), pp. 173–76.
11 *London Gazette*, 10 May 1817; Lord Byron to John Cam Hobhouse, 25 June 1818, in Richard Lansdown (ed.), *Byron's Letters and Journals: A new selection* (Oxford 2015), p. 295; Scott to Guilford, 1 September [1822]; John Mitford, 'Conversations of Lord Byron and Lady Blessington', *Gentleman's Magazine*, vol. 155 (January–June 1834), p. 585; Catherine Koumarianou, 'The contribution of the intelligentsia towards the Greek independence movement, 1798–1821', in Richard Clogg (ed.), *The Struggle for Greek Independence: Essays to mark the 150th anniversary of the Greek War of Independence* (London 1973), pp. 74–75.
12 [J.M. Blanco White], *Bosquexo del comercio en esclavos y reflexiones sobre este tráfico considerado moral, politica, y cristianamente* (London 1814; edition in Portuguese, London 1821); Scott to Ord, 29 April 1822, NRO 324/A/32, Northumberland Archives; D.F. Branagan, 'The geological society on the other side of the world', in C.S.E. Lewis and S.J. Knell (eds), *The Making of the Geological Society of London* (London 2009), pp. 342–43.
13 Heleni Antjoulatou and Helena Maniati, 'The physical sciences in higher education in Greece during the 19th century', paper presented at the 19th International Congress of Historical Sciences, 18 August 2000, Oslo, Norway, pp. 1–4, www.oslo2000.uio.no/AIO/AIO16/group%205/maniati.pdf.
14 Allan Stoekl, *The Three Sustainabilities: Energy, economy, time* (Minneapolis 2021), pp. 183–88.
15 W.C. Wentworth, *A Statistical, Historical, and Political Description of the Colony of New South Wales, and its Dependent Settlements in Van Diemen's Land* (London 1819), pp. 279–87; JM to John jr, 20 February 1820, ML A2899; John jr to R.J. Wilmot-Horton, 16 April 1823, Derbyshire Record Office, D3155/WH/2834; JM to J.D. Lang, 17 November 1831, ML A2900.
16 [Henry Brougham], review of five publications, *Edinburgh Review*, vol. 31 (1818–19), pp. 150–65, and review of fifteen publications, vol. 32 (1819), pp. 487–507.
17 John jr to JM, 27 July 1821, 22 September 1821, 18 August 1822, and to James, 21 September 1821, 24 March 1822, ML A2911; Bathurst to Sir Thomas Brisbane, *HRA*, series 1, vol. 10, p. 655.
18 Scott to R.J. Wilmot-Horton, 4 September 1823, CO 201/147, ff 343–53, TNA; Scott to Bathurst, 1 March 1824, CO 201/157, f. 157, TNA.
19 Scott to Bathurst, 1, 30 March 1824, CO 201/157, ff. 156–85, TNA; Scott to G.W. Norman, 22 December 1834, C200, Kent Archives Office.
20 Scott to Bathurst, 1, 30 March 1824, ff. 156–85.

21 Andrew Bell, *The Madras School; or, Elements of Tuition* (London 1808), p. 310; Scott to James, 11 April, 1831, ML A2955; Scott to Norman, 22 December 1834.
22 W.H. Brown, *Charterhouse Past and Present* (Godalming, UK, 1879), pp. 149–51; Harlan, 'British Lancastrian schools', pp. 328–33.
23 JM to John jr, 20 February 1820; S.E. Hill, '"Paper houses": John Macarthur and the 30-year design process of Camden Park', PhD thesis, University of Sydney, 2016 (2 vols), vol. 1, pp. 156–99, 251–84, vol. 2, pp. 110–11.
24 EM to Edward, 31 May 31 1828, 26 November 1832, ML A2906; the gardener was Isaac Horton, who came by the *Sesostris*, March 1826.
25 The only recorded 19th-century use of the name Hambledon was by the *Australian*, 10 August 1832, in a report stating that 'a Commission [de lunatico inquirendo] sat last week, at Hambledon Cottage, the seat of Mr John Macarthur'. However JM's 'seat' was the main homestead at Elizabeth Farm, the number who met for the inquiry (at least 25) would not have fitted into either house, and in fact they met at the Red Cow Inn, Parramatta: Writ de lunatico inquirendo, 24 July 1832, signed by James Dowling, and report of inquiry, 3 August 1832, NRS-13524, NSWSR. The reporter was probably thinking of the property of the former commissary, John Palmer, called Hambledon, 18 kilometres away on the Windsor Road.
26 James Busby, *A Treatise on the Culture of the Vine, and the Art of Making Wine* (Sydney 1825), pp. xxxiii, 49–50; B.J. Bridges, 'The Sydney orphan schools 1800–1830', MEd thesis, University of Sydney, 1973, pp. 685–93.
27 James Busby to committee of Church and School Corporation, n.d., received 28 August 1826, 4/7502, *NSWSR*; Bridges, 'The Sydney orphan schools 1800–1830', pp. 685–93.
28 Scott to James, 10 March 1837, ML A2955; Brown, *Charterhouse Past and Present*, p. 154; Bridges, 'The Sydney orphan schools 1800–1830', pp. 574–75, 579.

39 Justice at every step

1 W.C. Wentworth, *A Statistical, Historical, and Political Description of the Colony of New South Wales, and Its Dependent Settlements in Van Diemen's Land* (London 1819), pp. 346–51.
2 J.T. Bigge, *Report of the Commissioner of Inquiry into the State of the Colony of New South Wales* (London 1822), p. 40.
3 JM, marginal note, n.d., in his copy of Wentworth, *A Statistical, Historical, and Political Description*, p. 350, now at Camden Park.
4 JM to John jr, 20 February 1820, ML A2899; EM to Edward, 12 February 1823, 7 June 1824, 31 May 1828, ML A2906.
5 *London Gazette*, 5, 29 March 1814; W.O. Hughes-Hughes, *The Register of Tonbridge School, from 1820 to 1886* ([Tonbridge, UK] 1886), p. 15.
6 *London Gazette*, 5, 29 March 1814; Saxe Bannister, Notice to the inhabitants of the parish of Steyning, 13 October 1815, E/183/5/2, West Sussex Record Office (not seen); [Saxe Bannister], 'A letter to Henry Brougham, Esq. M.P.', *Pamphleteer*, vol. 25 (1819), p. 278; Saxe Bannister, *Mr Bannister's Claims* (London 1853), p. 11; W.P. Breach, 'Wm. Holland, alderman of Chichester, and the Steyning Grammar School', *Sussex Archaeological Collections*, vol. 43 (1900), pp. 67–68.
7 Saxe Bannister, *Essays on the Proper Use and the Reform of the Free Grammar Schools* (London 1819); Saxe Bannister, *Reports of Judgements Delivered by Sir Orlando Bridgman* (London 1823); Saxe Bannister (ed.), *Some Revelations in Irish History;*

or, Old Elements of Creed and Class Conciliation in Ireland (London 1870), unpaginated postscript; Saxe Bannister, *Classical and Pre-Historic Influences on British History* (London 1871), pp. 32–33; David Sugarman, 'Law, economy, and the state in England, 1750–1914: Some major issues', in David Sugarman (ed.), *Legality, Ideology, and the State* (London 1983), pp. 216–17.

8 Bain Attwood, *Possession: Batman's treaty and the matter of history* (Melbourne 2009), pp. 36–38; Saliha Belmessous, *Assimilation and Empire: Uniformity in French and British colonies 1541–1954* (Oxford 2013), pp. 89, 102–103.

9 'Philadelphus' [Saxe Bannister], *Remarks on the Indians of North America, in a Letter to an Edinburgh Reviewer* (London 1822), pp. 3, 31.

10 J.W. Bannister, petition for land, [November 1819], no. 210, bundle B12, vol. 42 (and three later petitions), Land Petitions of Upper Canada, 1763–1865, Canada National Archives; Robert Gourlay, *A General Introduction to a Statistical Account of Upper Canada* (London 1822), p. ccclxvi; Elizabeth Elbourne, 'The Bannisters and their colonial world: Family networks and colonialism in the early nineteenth century', in Karen Dubinsky, Adele Perry, and Henry Yu (eds), *Within and Without the Nation: Canadian History as transnational history* (Toronto 2015), pp. 52–54.

11 'A Settler' [J.W. Bannister], *Sketch of a Plan for Settling in Upper Canada, a Portion of the Unemployed Labourers of England* (London 1821); Gourlay, *General Introduction*, pp. cccxiii–cccxiv; Saxe Bannister to Henry Goulburn, 25 October 1822, CSORP1822/2597, National Archives, Ireland (not seen); J.W. Bannister to R.J. Wilmot-Horton, 23 June, 5 November 1823, D3155/WH/2744, Derbyshire Record Office; Bannister (ed.), *Some Revelations in Irish History*, p. xxxix.

12 J.W. Bannister to T. Spring Rice, 23 June 1823, and Saxe Bannister to Wilmot-Horton, 21 August 1823, D3155/WH/2744; Elbourne, 'The Bannisters and their colonial world', pp. 54–56; [Saxe Bannister], review of William Wood, *New England's Prospect* (1634), *Retrospective Review*, vol. 8 (1823), pp. 55–71 (for authorship, see Bannister, *Claims*, p. 12).

13 John jr to EM, 12 April 1825, ML A 2911; Saxe Bannister to Wilmot-Horton, 16 September 1823, D3155/WH/2744.

14 Edward to John jr, 29 January 1824, ML A2913.

15 EM to John jr, 7 June 1824, and to Edward, 4 March 1827, ML A2906; Saxe Bannister, *Statements and Documents Relating to Proceedings in New South Wales in 1824, 1825 and 1826* (Cape Town 1827), pt 1, p. 13.

16 JM to John jr, 17 April 1824, ML A2899; *SG*, 25 October 1826; Saxe Bannister to E.S. Hall, 8 December 1826, in Bannister, *Statements and Documents*, pt 1, pp. 72–73.

17 G. Watson Taylor to Wilmot-Horton, 2 August 1822, D3155/C/6046, Derbyshire Record Office; Saxe Bannister, *Statements and Documents*, pt 1, pp. 210–12.

18 *SG*, 16 December 1824; T.H. Scott to Ralph Darling, 1 May 1826, *HRA*, series 1, vol. 12, p. 315; *Monitor* (Sydney), 1 September 1826; Scott to Darling, 25 September 1857, *HRA*, series 1, vol. 14, p. 52.

19 *SG*, 25 October 1826; Saxe Bannister, *Statements and Documents*, pt 2, p. 19, and pt 3, pp. 49–55.

20 Saxe Bannister, *Humane Policy; or, Justice to the Aborigines of New Settlements: Essential to a Due Expenditure of British Money, and to the Best Interests of the Settlers* (London 1830), pp. vi, 2–3.

21 J.W. Bannister to Spring Rice, 23 June 1823, and Saxe Bannister to Wilmot-Horton, 21 August 1823, D3155/WH/2744; Elbourne, 'The Bannisters and their colonial world', pp. 54–56.
22 Saxe Bannister to Darling, 6 April 1826, in Bannister, *New South Wales*, pt 1, pp. 130–1.
23 Richard Sadleir, petition for land, 21 July 1821, RG 5 A1, vol. 53, pp. 26425–58, Land Petitions in Upper Canada Sundries, Canada National Archives; *Southern Reporter* (Cork), 31 March 1825; Scott to Darling, 1 August 1827, enclosing Scott to Sadleir, 29 July 1826, *HRA*, series 1, vol. 14, pp. 56–57, 63–64; Sadleir, memoir, *Australian Town and Country Journal*, 2 April 1887; L.J. Smith, 'Unsettled settlers: Irish Catholics, Irish Catholicism, and British loyalty in Upper Canada, 1819–1840', PhD thesis, University of Toronto, 2017, pp. 19–21.
24 EM to Eliza Kingdon, March 1816, ML A2908; Scott to Darling, 1 August 1827, pp. 59–60; Richard Sadleir, *The Aborigines of Australia* (Sydney 1883), pp. 5, 38.
25 Scott to William Hall, 6 February 1827, ML A850; Larry Prochner, *A History of Early Childhood Education in Australia, Canada, and New Zealand* (Vancouver 2010), p. 66.
26 JM to directors of Australian Agricultural Company, 26 May 1828 (official), Noel Butlin Archives 78/1/6/17, Australian National University; 'The perfect combination', McDonald New Zealand, 'Possum merino', mcdonaldtextiles.com/collections/possum-merino.

40 Rebuilding home
1 EM to John, [1824? letter no. 179], 16 December 1826, and to Edward, 17 December 1826, 4 March 1827, ML A2899.
2 EM to Edward, 4 March 1827.
3 James to JM, 17 February 1824, ML A2962; *SG*, 18 February 1828.
4 EM to JM, [November 1830?], ML A2906; William to Edward, 4 July 1840, and EM to Edward, 5 October 1840, ML A2935.
5 James Busby, *A Manual of Plain Directions for Planting and Cultivating Vineyards, and for Making Wine, in New South Wales* (Sydney 1830), p. 21; 'Maro' [William], *Letters on the Culture of the Vine, Fermentation, and the Management of Wine in the Cellar* (Sydney, 1844), pp. vi–vii; EM to Edward, 17 October 1845, ML A2907; Julie McIntyre, 'Camden to London and Paris: The role of the Macarthur family in the early New South Wales wine industry', *History Compass*, vol. 5 (2007), pp. 432–33.
6 EM to Edward, 31 May 1828.
7 JM to John jr, 1 June 1827, ML A2899.
8 JM to Edward, 8 April 1828, ML A2899; EM to Edward, 31 May 1828, Tuesday [November 1830], 23 April 1831, ML A2906; James to JM, 7–8 April 1829, ML A2931; William to Edward, 4 July 1840, and EM to Edward, 5 October 1840, ML A2935.
9 Mary to James, 14 January 1847, ML A4285; EM to Edward, 3 July 1848, ML A2907.
10 EM to Grace Leach, 20 April 1790, ML A2908; EM to Eliza Kingdon, 4 September 1822, ML A2908.
11 William Marshall, *Planting and Rural Ornament* (2 vols) (London 1796), vol. 1, pp. xxiii–xxiv; John jr to James, 21 September 1821, ML A2911;

EM to Edward, 29 October 1848, ML A2907; Mark Johnston, *The Tree Experts: A history of professional arboriculture in Britain* (Oxford 2021), p. 238.
12 S.E. Hill, '"Paper houses": John Macarthur and the 30-year design process of Camden Park', PhD thesis, University of Sydney, 2016 (2 vols), vol. 1, pp. 172–74, 177–78, 456–62; A.L. Boyington, 'Maids, wives and widows: Female architectural patronage in eighteenth-century Britain', PhD thesis, University of Cambridge, 2017, pp. 196–201.
13 EM to Eliza Kingdon, 4 September 1822, ML A2908; Hill, '"Paper houses"', vol.1, pp. 345–76.
14 *Australian* (Sydney), 7 June 1826; Hazel King, *Colonial Expatriates: Edward and John Macarthur junior* (Sydney 1989), pp. 31–33.
15 EM to Edward, 17 December 1826, ML A2906 (saying she had been five months in Sydney).
16 Marshall, *Planting*, vol. 1, pp. 260–61, 285; JM to Edward, 12 September 1826, ML A2899; EM to Edward, 26 May 1832, ML A2906; *Sydney Herald*, 16 July 1832, 10 January 1833. By November 1828 Maclean had moved altogether to Elizabeth Farm: NSW census, 1828.
17 John Campbell to JM, 8 April 1824, 31 March, 3, 5 July, 21 August, 20 September 1824; James Norton to JM, 23 February 1825, ML A2900; *SG*, 11 August 1828; Carolyn Williams, *The Travelling Table* (Woodford, NSW, 2017; first publ. 2016), pp. 8–10, 21–22, 30–31, www.hawkesburyaustralia.com.au/_eventimages/imagesDB/events/The-Travelling-Table-Carolyn-Williams-updated.pdf.
18 EM to Edward, 31 May 1828.
19 Elizabeth jr to Eliza Kingdon, 15 July 1818; T.L. Mitchell, *Three Expeditions in the Interior of Eastern Australia* (London 1839), pp. 5–6.
20 JM to Edward, 12 September 1826; James to John jr, 17 May 1827, ML A2931; EM to Edward, 31 May 1828, ML A2906; James Broadbent, 'Aspects of domestic architecture in New South Wales 1788–1843', PhD thesis, ANU, 1985 (3 vols), vol. 1, pp. 229–34; Hill, '"Paper houses"', vol. 1, pp. 389–97.
21 James to John jr, 17 May 1827, ML A2931; James Byrnes to Edward, 29 November 1856, ML A2917.

41 Nemesis was Greek
1 L.H. Halloran, *The Battle of Trafalgar, a Poem* (London 1806), pp. 2, 5.
2 Halloran, *The Battle of Trafalgar*, p. 5; *Naval Chronicle*, vol. 15 (1806), pp. 441–49, and vol. 17 (1807), pp. 113, 415–16; *SG*, 1 December 1825; Kelvin Grose, 'A letter from Trafalgar 1805', *Naval Historical Review*, vol. 26 (2005), www.navyhistory.org.au/a-letter-from-trafalgar-1805/.
3 Lachlan Macquarie to Earl Bathurst, 20 March 1821, *HRA*, series 1, vol. 10, p. 478; J.T. Bigge, *Report of the Commissioner of Inquiry into the State of the Colony of New South Wales* (London 1822), pp. 126–27; Richard Warner, *Literary Recollections* (2 vols) (London 1830), vol. 2, pp. 292–98; Kelvin Grose, '"A strange compound of good and ill": 'Laurence Hynes Halloran', in Bob Reece (ed.), *Exiles from Erin: Convict lives in Ireland and Australia* (Basingstoke, UK, 1991), pp. 85–111.
4 JM to John jr, 31 January 1824, ML A2899; L.H. Halloran to Bathurst, 27 January 1825, enclosing Halloran to Lord Gifford, 31 October 1824, CO 201/167, ff. 4–12, TNA; R.W. Hay to Ralph Darling, 22 July 1825, *HRA*, series 1, vol. 12, p. 36.

5   *Scourge* (London), 1 April 1812; L.H. Halloran, *Proposals for the Foundation and Support of a Public Free Grammar School in the Town of Sydney* (Sydney 1825); *SG*, 20 October, 1, 5 December 1825, 5 April 1826; JM, bank pass book, 10 November 1825, ML A2903/5.

6   *SG*, 20 October, November 1825, 8, 16 January 1827; EM to Edward, 17 December, 1826, 4 March 1827, ML A2906; Saxe Bannister, *Statements and Documents Relating to Proceedings in New South Wales in 1824, 1825 and 1826* (Cape Town 1827), pt 1, p. 35.

7   [Joseph Blanco White?], *Noticia de las Providencias Tomadas por el Gobierno para Observar el Nuevo Método de la Enseñanza Primaria de Enrique Pestalozzi* (Madrid 1807), p. 28; T.H. Scott to Darling, 1 May 1826, and his enclosed 'Plan for a general boarding school', *HRA*, series 1, vol. 12, pp. 316, 319–20.

8   *SG*, 22 April 1826; *Monitor* (Sydney), 27 October 1826; Scott, 'Plan for a general boarding school', enclosed with Scott to Darling, 1 May 1826, *HRA*, series 1, vol. 12, pp. 319–20; Halloran to James Norton, 27 August 1828, *HRA*, series 1, vol. 14, pp. 393–94. Note the otherwise mysterious reference to 'original endowment' in 'Plan for a general boarding school', p. 320, and to the apparently endowed 'grammar school' in Scott to Darling, 25 September 1827, *HRA*, vol. 14, pp. 49–50.

9   *SG*, 26 December 1825, 26 January, 1 February 1826; *Australian*, 2 February 1826; JM to directors of the Australian Agricultural Company, 26 May 1828 (official), 78/1/6, Noel Butlin Archives, Canberra; B.J. Bridges, 'The Sydney orphan schools 1800–1830', MEd thesis, University of Sydney, 1973, pp. 168–95.

10 Bridges, 'The Sydney orphan schools 1800–1830', pp. 709–34.

11 Bannister, *Statements and Documents*, pt 1, p. 131; Saxe Bannister (ed.), *Some Revelations in Irish History; or, Old Elements of Creed and Class Conciliation in Ireland* (London 1870), p. viii.

12 Bannister, *Statements and Documents*, pt 1, pp. 92–101, 125–7; Saliha Belmessous, *Assimilation and Empire: Uniformity in French and British colonies, 1541–1954* (Oxford 2013), pp. 69–79; Elizabeth Elbourne, 'The Bannisters and their colonial world: Family networks and colonialism in the early nineteenth century', in Karen Dubinsky, Adele Perry, and Henry Yu (eds), *Within and Without the Nation: Canadian history as transnational history* (Toronto 2015), pp. 57–58.

13 *SG*, 14 October 1824 (thanks to Tricia Dearborn for this); Michael Pearson, 'Bathurst Plains and beyond: European colonisation and Aboriginal resistance', *Aboriginal History*, vol. 8 (1984), pp. 72–76.

14 *SG*, 26 August 1824; Darling to R.W. Hay, 11 September 1826, *HRA*, series 1, vol. 11, pp. 574–75; K.K. Chaves, '"A solemn judicial farce, the mere mockery of a trial": The acquittal of Lieutenant Lowe, 1827', *Aboriginal History*, vol. 31 (2007), pp. 130–35.

15 *SG*, 23 September 1826; Saxe Bannister, *Humane Policy; or, Justice to the Aborigines of New Settlements: Essential to a due expenditure of British money, and to the best interests of the settlers* (London 1830), p. ccxl; Robert Dawson, *The Present State of Australia* (London 1830), pp. 43–44; Christine Bramble, 'Relations between Aborigines and White settlers in Newcastle and the Hunter district, 1804–1841', BLitt thesis, University of New England, 1961, pp. 71–74; Sydney, Australia Coroner's Inquests, 1788–1853, 1826, pp. 20–24 (separate pagination for each year), cjrc.osu.edu/sites/default/files/Sydney%20Australia%20inquests%201826.pdf.

Notes to pages 381–389

16   JM, bank pass book, 22 February, 4 July 1826; Bathurst to Darling, 7 April 1826, Darling to Hay, 25 July, 11 September 1826, *HRA*, series 1, vol. 12, pp. 227, 445–46, 575–76; Bannister, *Statements and Documents*, pt 1, pp. 38–9, 72–3.
17   *SG*, 14, 25 October 1826; Bannister, *Statements and Documents*, pt 1, pp. 12–13.
18   James to John jr, 20 October 1826, 17 May 1827, ML A2899; *SG*, 25 October 1826; EM to Edward, 17 December 1826, ML A2906.
19   James to John jr, 20 October 1826.
20   JM to John jr, 16–20 October 1826, cross-written by James to John jr, 20 October 1826, ML A2899.
21   EM to Edward, 17 December 1826, ML A 2906; Darling to Bathurst, 22 December 1826, encl. Scott to Darling, 9 December 1826, *HRA*, series 1, vol. 12, pp. 795–97; Viscount Goderich to Darling, 6 July 1827, *HRA*, series 1, vol. 13, pp. 433–34; Darling to William Huskisson, 27 March 1828, with enclosures, *HRA*, series 1, vol. 14, pp. 54–64.
22   EM to Edward, 4 March 1827, ML A2906; Chaves, '"A solemn judicial farce, the mere mockery of a trial"', pp. 130–35.
23   Scott to Darling, 1 May 1826, pp. 312–15; EM to Edward, 17 December 1826, to John jr, 15 March 1827, and to Edward and John jr, 25 March 1827, ML A2906; James to John jr, 17 May 1827; Scott to G.W. Norman, 27 December 1827, C200, Kent Archives Office.
24   Darling to R.J. Wilmot-Horton, 26 March 1827, *HRA*, series 1, vol. 13, pp. 190–91; Scott to Norman, 27 December 1827; Horace Twiss to Scott, 14 November 1828, *HRA*, series 1, vol. 14, p. 461; [Scott], 'New South Wales', and Scott to editor, *Times* (London), 12, 22 October 1833.

PART 8
42   John's misted horizon

1   EM to John jr, 23 April 1831 (young John had died on 19 April 1831), ML A2906; Office for National Statistics (UK), 'How has life expectancy changed over time?', 9 September 2015, www.ons.gov.uk/peoplepopulationand community/birthsdeathsandmarriages/lifeexpectancies/articles/howhaslife expectancychangedovertime/2015-09-09.
2   JM to EM, 26 July 1814, ML A2898.
3   John jr to EM, 5 March 1818, ML A2911.
4   *Report of the Earl of Sheffield to the Meeting at Lewes Wool Fair, 26th July, 1816* (Dublin 1816), pp. 2–9; Richard Bright, *Travels from Vienna Through Lower Hungary* (Edinburgh 1818), pp. 373–75; J.S.C. Abbott, *Kings and Queens; or, Life in the Palace* (New York 1848), pp. 136–37.
5   *Transactions of the Society for the Encouragement of Arts, Manufactures, and Commerce*, vol. 43 (1824), p. xliii; P.A. Pemberton, 'The London connection: The formation and early years of the Australian Agricultural Company', PhD thesis, ANU, 1991, pp. 49, 141–45.
6   James to EM, 7 April 1829, ML A2931; EM to Edward, 12 May 1831, 29 September 1833, ML A2906.
7   T.P. Macqueen to JM, 5 February 1822, 12 July [1824], 10 October, 29 December 1824, ML A2900; John jr to James, 14–17 November 1824, ML A2911; Macqueen to R.W. Hay, 19 December 1826, *HRA*, series 1, vol. 12, p. 795.

8   Sir Thomas Farquhar to JM, 28 July 1823, and James Glennie to JM, 13, 29 April, 2 November 1825, ML A2900.
9   Anon., 'Plan for establishing a company', [1824], CO 280/2, TNA; *SG*, 11 November 1824; Pemberton, 'The London connection', pp. 53–56, 165.
10 Bright, *Travels from Vienna*, pp. 373–75; Anon., 'Plan for establishing a company'.
11 *SG*, 11 November 1824; Pemberton, 'The London connection', pp. 53–56, 165.
12 *SG*, 11 November 1824; John jr to EM, 12 April 1825, ML A2911; Pemberton, 'The London connection', pp. 43–44, 189–91.
13 P.A. Pemberton, *Pure Merinos and Others: The 'shipping lists' of the Australian Agricultural Company* (Canberra 1986), p. 98.
14 James to John jr, 17 May 1827, ML A2899.
15 *SG*, 27 May 1826 (stating that the woman convicts were for Camden, but it is hard to see how they could have been wanted there); Convict indents for transport *Lady Rowena*, arrived 16 January 1826, ancestry.com.au.
16 R.T. Farquhar, *Suggestions Arising from the Abolition of the African Slave Trade for Supplying the Demands of the West India Colonies with Agricultural Labourers* (London 1807), pp. 18–19, 52–61; William Walton, *Historical and Descriptive Account of the Peruvian Sheep* (London 1811), pp. 31–32, 163–83 (there was a copy at Elizabeth Farm in 1854); Macqueen to JM, 10 October 1824; Ralph Darling to Hay, 2 September 1826, *HRA*, series 1, vol. 12, p. 523.
17 EM to Edward, 4 March 1827, ML A2908.
18 *SG*, 25 April 1828.
19 Robert Dawson to J.S. Brickwood, April 1827, Dawson to JM, 11 October 1827, and JM to Dawson, 16 October 1827, ML A4318.
20 James, journal kept at Port Stephens, December 1827 – January 1828, Noel Butlin Archives 78/1/6, Australian National University; James to John jr, 28 May 1827, ML A2931; JM to Darling, 16 May 1828, ML A4314; JM to directors of the A.A. Company, 26 May 1828 (private and confidential), Noel Butlin Archives 78/1/6.
21 JM to directors, 26 May 1828 (official) and John Armstrong, testimony, 13 August 1828, Noel Butlin Archives 78/1/6.
22 JM to directors, 26 May 1828 (official), Noel Butlin Archives 78/1/6, Australian National University; Robert Dawson, *The Present State of Australia* (London 1830), p. 410.
23 Saxe Bannister to R.J. Wilmot-Horton, 21 August 1823, D3155/WH/2744, Derbyshire Record Office; James, journal kept at Port Stephens, December 1827 – January 1828; JM to directors, 26 May 1828 (official); Saxe Bannister, *Humane Policy; or Justice to the Aborigines of New Settlements: Essential to a Due Expenditure of British Money, and to the Best Interests of the Settlers* (London 1830), pp. ccxli–ccxlii; Dawson, *The Present State of Australia*, p. 157; Christine Bramble, 'Relations between Aborigines and White settlers in Newcastle and the Hunter district, 1804–1841', BLitt thesis, University of New England, 1961, pp. 25–26, 58–59, 72–75.
24 J.W. Bannister to T. Spring Rice, 23 June 1823, and Saxe Bannister to Wilmot-Horton, 21 August 1823, D3155/WH/2744; Elizabeth Elbourne, 'The Bannisters and their colonial world: Family networks and colonialism in the early nineteenth century', in Karen Dubinsky, Adele Perry, and Henry Yu (eds), *Within and Without the Nation: Canadian history as transnational history* (Toronto 2015), pp. 54–56.

25   JM to directors, 26 May 1828 (official).
26   Order no. 12, 10 May 1828, and JM to directors, 26 May 1828 (official), Noel Butlin Archives 78/1/6.
27   Minutes of a general meeting of proprietors of the A.A. Company, 12 December 1828, Noel Butlin Archives 78/1/6.
28   Minutes of a general meeting, 12 December 1828.
29   Hazel King, *Colonial Expatriates: Edward and John Macarthur junior* (Sydney 1989), pp. 36–37; Pemberton, 'The London connection', pp. 280–89.

43   A type of divorce
1   EM to Elizabeth jr, 'Friday morng', November [1830], and to Edward, 27 December 1830, 10 November 1834, ML A2906; EM to Edward, 15 November 1842, ML A2907.
2   EM to Eliza Kingdon, May 1818, ML A2908; EM to Edward, 26 May 1832, ML A2906; Charles Dickens to W.H. Wills, 10 December 1867, in Jenny Hartley (ed.), *The Selected Letters of Charles Dickens* (Oxford 2012), p. 416.
3   EM to Eliza Kingdon, March 1816, and EM to Edward, 4 March 1827, 2 June 1832, ML A2906.
4   EM to John, and to Edward, 23 April, 12 May 1831, 23 March 1834, 27 April 1838, ML A2906.
5   JM to W.S. Davidson, 3 September 1818, ML A2897.
6   EM to John jr, 26 March 1824, ML A2906.
7   EM to Edward, 4 March 1827, ML A2906.
8   EM to Edward and John jr, 25 March 1827, ML A2906.
9   *SG*, 15, 18 February 1828; *Australian* (Sydney), 28 March 1828.
10   EM to Edward, 31 May 1828, ML A2906; T.H. Scott to G.W. Norman, 27 June 1828, C200, Kent Archives Office; Patrick Hill to Campbell France, 22 March, 1833, ML MSS 8000, quoted in S.E. Hill, '"Paper houses": John Macarthur and the 30-year design process of Camden Park', PhD thesis, University of Sydney, 2016 (2 vols), vol. 1, p. 89.
11   EM to Edward, 4 March 1827, ML A2906; Emmeline to Edward, 2 June 1832, ML A2959.
12   William Buchan, *Domestic Medicine; or, A Treatise on the Prevention and Cure of Diseases by Regimen and Simple Medicines* (London 1790; first publ. 1772), pp. 451–52; EM to Edward, 27 December 1830, EM to Edward and John, 19 Feb 1831, EM to Edward, 23 Apr 1831, ML A2906.
13   Buchan, *Domestic Medicine*, p. 452; EM to Edward, 4 May 1832, ML A2906.
14   James, diary, 15 December 1829, of a tour through Belgium and Germany, ML A2929/B; K.S. Guthke, *Exploring the Interior: Essays on literary and cultural history* (Cambridge 2018), p. 133 (quoting Goethe's diary for 15 December 1829).
15   EM to Edward, 26 September 1831; *Sydney Herald*, 3 October 1831; Hazel King, *Colonial Expatriates: Edward and John Macarthur junior* (Sydney 1989), p. 39.
16   David Hume, *The History of England, from the Invasion of Julius Caesar to the Revolution in 1688* (6 vols) (London 1762), vol. 6, p. 340; William to Edward, 23 September 1831, ML A2935; JM to Edward, 23 February 1832, ML A2899; H.C. Allport, 'Catalogue of the library at Elizabeth Farm, the property of Col'l Macarthur', May 1854, ML A2919/4.
17   EM to Edward, 26 September 1831, ML A2906. John, according to William,

said 'Earl of Crawford', while Hume says 'Duke of Ormonde' – but William might also have misremembered his father's exact words.
18   EM to Edward, 26 September, 1 October 1831, 12 May 1832, ML A2906.
19   EM to Edward, 26 September 1831.
20   Anon., 'Memoir of John Macarthur, Esq. of Lincoln's Inn, London', *Sydney Herald*, 3 October 1831; EM to Edward, 5 October 1831, quoting Elizabeth jr to EM, same day, ML A2906.
21   JM to Edward, 23 February, 23 March 1832, and EM to Edward, 23 March 1832, ML A2906.
22   JM to Edward, 26 March 1832, ML A2899; weekly meteorological table, *Sydney Herald*, 2 April 1832.
23   JM to Edward, 5 June 1832, ML A2899; EM to Edward, 5 June 1832, ML A2906.
24   JM to Edward, 26 March 1832.
25   JM to EM, 18 November 1812, 26 July, 21 September 1814, 16–17 February, 29 April 1815, 23 July 1816, ML A2898; Andreas Marneros, 'Origin and development of concepts of bipolar mixed states', *Journal of Affective Disorders*, vol. 67 (2001), pp. 229–35; Sean Dyde, 'Cullen, a cautionary tale', *Medical History*, vol. 59 (2015), pp. 225–30; Hubert Steinke, *Irritating Experiments: Haller's concept and the European controversy on irritability and sensibility, 1750–90* (Leiden 2005), pp. 212–16.
26   EM to Edward, 30 June 1832, 3 July [1832], ML A2906.
27   EM to Edward, 4 May, 30 June, 3 July 1832, ML A2906; Affidavits of Patrick Lindesay, Donald McPherson, Arthur Hamilton, all 17 July 1832, and other documents relating to the committal of JM for lunacy, 1832–33, NRS 13524, NSWSR.
28   *Australian* (Sydney), 10 August 1832.
29   EM to Edward, 13 September 1832, 6 January, 10 April, 25 May 1833, 28 January 1834, ML A2906; Emmeline to Edward, 18 March 1833.
30   EM to Edward, 3, 10 March, 1 May 1833, ML A2906; *Australian*, 17 May 1833.
31   EM to Edward, 25 May 1833, ML A2906.
32   David Hartley, *Observations on Man, His Frame, His Duty, and His Expectations* (2 vols) (London 1749), p. 124; Buchan, *Domestic Medicine*, pp. 633–46; JM to EM, 3 May 1810, 3 August 1810, 31 August 1813, ML A2898; EM to Edward, 25 May 1833; Hill, '"Paper houses", vol. 1, pp. 519–20, 563–65, 578.
33   EM to Edward, 13 September, 2 November 1832, 28 January 1834, ML A2906.
34   EM to Edward, 13, 25 September, 26 November 1832, 6 January 1833, 28 January 1834, ML A2906.
35   EM to Edward, 29 September 1833, ML A2906.

44   The breach made by widowhood
1   EM to Edward, 12 March, 17 May 1834, ML A2906.
2   *SG*, 1 April 1834; EM to Edward, 17 May 1834.
3   EM to Edward, 17 May 1834. M.H. Ellis makes the date 11 April, and most subsequent sources, including the *Australian Dictionary of Biography*, say the same. However, this date, given in the first Sydney newspaper reports, was corrected after a few days with a family notice in the *Sydney Herald*, and afterwards by the inscription on his gravestone: *Australian* (Sydney) 14 April

1834; *SG*, 15 April 1834; *Sydney Herald*, 17 April 1834; M.H. Ellis, *John Macarthur* (Sydney 1955), pp. 530, 585–86. He was buried on 12 April (Cobbitty–Narellan parish register) and two days between death and burial is much more likely than one. Thanks very much to Tony Stephenson of the Camden Area Family History Society for prompt assistance with the parish register.

4 EM to Edward, 23 March, 17 May 1834, ML A2906; William to Edward, 20 January 1858, ML A2933.
5 EM to Edward, 17 May 1834, ML A2906.
6 EM to Edward, 17 May 1834.
7 EM to Edward, [24?] October 1834, ML A2906.
8 *Commercial Journal* (Sydney), 13 June 1838; EM to Edward, 12 January 1841, ML A2907.
9 EM to Edward, 26 September 1831, 2 June 1832, late March – 1 May [1833], 9 May 1833, 11 September 1835, 16 December 1836, ML A2906; *Australian*, 21 September 1839, 19 September 1840; *Australasian Chronicle* (Sydney), 23 September 1841; EM to Edward, January 1842, ML A2907; *Sydney Morning Herald*, 15 September 1842; William Woolls, 'Parramatta and the early naturalists of the colony', *Cumberland Mercury* (Parramatta), 20 March 1886; Anthony R. Bean, 'The life and botany of Edward Macarthur Bowman (1826–1872)', *Historical Records of Australian Science*, vol. 30 (2019), pp. 12–18.
10 EM to Edward, 15–20 August 1843, 13 January 1846, 1 July 1847, 2 September, 29 October – 2 November 7 December 1848, ML A2907.
11 EM to Edward, 29 September 1833, 23 January 1834, ML A2906.
12 EM to Edward, 10 November 1834, 11 September 1835, ML A2906; EM to Edward, 29 October – 2 November 1848, ML A2907.
13 EM to Edward, 29 September 1833.
14 EM to Edward, 23 April 1831, ML A2906.
15 John jr to Elizabeth jr, 4 June 1825, ML A2911; Papers re Jane Bennett's legacy, 1826–33, ML A2990; EM to Edward, 4 May 1832, 13 September 1832, 26 November 1832, 29 September 1833; EM to Edward, 27 January 1845.
16 EM to Edward, 2 June 1832, 29 September 1833.
17 EM to Edward, 29 September 1833, 23 January 1834, 20 July, 16 December 1836, ML A2906. Mary Isabella Leach married Thomas Hacker on 22 January 1801, at Poundstock, near Bridgerule. Grace Bond, living at Pyworthy, died on 22 June and was buried on 27 June 1836, at Bridgerule. John Bond, her third husband, was buried on 16 July 1824, at Bridgerule.
18 EM to Edward, 20 March, 20 July 1836, ML A2906; Penelope Lucas, her will; signed 23 July 1836, and administration granted 19 June 1840, ML A2990. Penelope Lucas died 2 October 1836.
19 EM to Edward, 23 March, 27 April 1838, ML A2906. Eleanor Kilpack died on 28 September 1835.
20 Alan Atkinson, 'The political life of James Macarthur', PhD thesis, Australian National University, 1977, pp. 151–54, 158–68.
21 Adamantios Korais, *Mémoire sur l'état actuel de la civilisation dans la Grèce* (Paris 1803), pp. 14–17; Alexander Stephens (ed.), *Memoirs of John Horne Tooke* (2 vols) (London 1813), vol. 2, p. 37; James, speech, *Report of the Proceedings of the General Meeting of the Supporters of the Petitions to His Majesty and the House of Commons, Held at the Committee Rooms, May 30, 1856* (Sydney 1836), pp. 14–18; Atkinson, 'The political life of James Macarthur', pp. 162–65.

Notes to pages 415-425

22 [James Macarthur], *New South Wales, Its Present State and Future Prospects* (London 1837), pp. 47–61 (for the authorship of this book, see Alan Atkinson, 'James Macarthur as author', *Journal of the Royal Australian Historical Society*, vol. 67 (1981), pp. 264–71; Atkinson, 'The political life of James Macarthur', pp. 184–87, 189–92.
23 James Macarthur, speech, *Sydney Morning Herald*, 8 July 1855; Alan Atkinson, *Camden: Farm and village life in early New South Wales* (Melbourne 1988), pp. 36–41.
24 EM to Edward, 21 November 1838, 6 March 1839.
25 William Moorcroft, *Travels in the Himalayan Provinces of Hindustan and the Panjab, in Ladakh and Kashmir, in Peshawar, Kabul, Kunduz, and Bokhara from 1819 to 1825* (London 1841); EM to Edward, 15 October 1842, 24–26 February 1847, ML A2907.
26 EM to Edward, 5 April 1842, ML A2907.
27 EM to Edward, 5 April 1842.
28 EM to Edward, 5 April 1842.
29 EM to Edward, 28 August 1842, ML A2907.
30 *London Gazette*, 24 November 1841; EM to Edward, 28 August 1842.
31 EM to Edward, 28 August 1842.
32 EM to Edward, 31 August 1842, ML A2907.
33 EM to Edward, 28 August, 31 August – 1 September, 12 October 1842, ML A2907.

45 Old age

1 EM to Eliza Kingdon, March 1816, ML A2908.
2 EM to Eliza Kingdon, 4 September 1822, ML A2908; Emmeline to Edward, 25 February 1829, ML A2959.
3 EM to Edward, 26 September 1831, ML A2906; Emmeline to Edward, 7 January 1832, ML A2959.
4 EM to Edward, 19 November 1842, ML A2907.
5 EM to Edward, 12 October, 19 November, 16 December 1842, ML A2907; Edward to James, 15 May 1843, ML A2915.
6 Edward to JM, 29 November 1809, ML A2912; Emmeline to Edward, 9 September 1844, ML A2959.
7 EM to Edward, 15 October, 19 November, 16 December 1842, ML A2907.
8 Mary to James, 14 January 1847, ML A4285; EM to Edward, 3 July 1848, ML A2907.
9 EM to Edward, 4 March, 4 May 1843, 5 June 1845, ML A2907; Sir Edward Parry, journal, 6 March 1832, quoted in Gordon Bennett, 'Early days of Port Stephens', *Dungog Chronicle*, 18 February 1927; Hazel King, *Elizabeth Macarthur and Her World* (Sydney 1980), pp. 18–87.
10 EM to Edward, 6 June 1841, January 1842, 7 October, 29 November 1843, ML A2907.
11 EM to Edward, 7 October 1843, 3 June 1844, 18 September 1845, ML A2907.
12 EM to Edward, 3 June 1844, 2 September 1848, 7 March 1849, ML A2907; Hazel King, *Colonial Expatriates: Edward and John Macarthur junior* (Sydney 1989), pp. 57–63.
13 EM to Edward, 8 September 1844, 30 August 1846, ML A2907.
14 EM to Edward, 22 January, 2 April 1844, ML A2907.
15 EM to Edward, 6 October, 16 December 1844, 7 February, 17 March 1845,

27 February 1846, 24–26 February 1847, 4 June, 3 July 1848, ML A2907; *Sydney Morning Herald*, 27 September 1844.
16 EM to Edward, 5 October 1840, ML A2935.
17 William to Edward, 4 July 1840, ML A2935.
18 William to Edward, 4 July 1840, and EM to Edward, 5 October 1840, ML A2935; Edward to James and William, various letters, 26 September 1841 to 10 December 1854, ML A2915 (quotation 18 November [1843]); William to Edward, 20 January 1858, ML A2933; James, statement for the information of Edward, 25 February 1858, ML A2928; King, *Colonial Expatriates*, pp. 46, 63–65, 87–88.
19 EM to Edward, 5 November 1846, ML A2907.
20 EM to Edward, 5 June, 18 September 1845, 4 June 1848, ML A2907.

46 The end
1   EM to Edward, [1–2 February 1847], ML A2907.
2   EM to Edward, [1–2 February 1847].
3   EM to Edward, [1–2 February 1847].
4   EM to Bridget Kingdon, 7 March 1791, ML A2908; EM to Edward, 2 April 1847, ML A2907.
5   EM to Edward, 29 October – 2 November 1848, 4–5 January 1849, ML A2907.
6   EM to Edward, 29 October – 2 November, 7 December 1848, 4–5 January 1849, ML A2907.
7   EM to Edward, 30 January 1849, ML A2907; Michelle Scott Tucker, *Elizabeth Macarthur: A Life at the edge of the world* (Melbourne 2018), p. 326.
8   EM to Edward, 30 January 1849, ML A2907.
9   EM to Edward, 30 April 1849, ML A2907.
10 EM to Edward, 31 May, 1 August 1849, ML A2907.
11 EM to Edward, 6 February 1848, 31 May, 1 August 1849, ML A2907; *Sydney Morning Herald*, 18 February 1850.

Epilogue
1   Emmeline, notes on her bereavement, [1881?], ML A2959.

Acknowledgments
1   Alan Atkinson, 'The position of John Macarthur and his family in New South Wales before 1842', MA thesis, University of Sydney, 1972; Alan Atkinson, 'The political life of James Macarthur', PhD thesis, Australian National University, 1977; Alan Atkinson, *Camden: Farm and village life in early New South Wales* (Melbourne 1988).
2   Hazel King, *Elizabeth Macarthur and Her World* (Sydney 1980); Hazel King, *Colonial Expatriates: Edward and John Macarthur junior* (Sydney 1989).
3   M.H. Ellis, *John Macarthur* (Sydney 1955); Julie McIntyre, 'Camden to London and Paris: The role of the Macarthur family in the early New South Wales wine industry', *History Compass*, vol. 5 (2007), pp. 427–38; Julie McIntyre, *First Vintage: Wine in Colonial New South Wales* (Sydney 2012); S.E. Hill, '"Paper houses": John Macarthur and the 30-year design process of Camden Park', PhD thesis, University of Sydney, 2016 (2 vols); Michelle Scott Tucker, *Elizabeth Macarthur: A life at the edge of the world* (Melbourne 2018).

INDEX

Abbott, Edward 74, 141–44, 146, 199–200, 230
accounting and book-keeping 1, 31, 208, 331, 270
    credit accounts 263, 264, 389, 413, 431
    double-entry 272–73
    records of livestock and produce 109, 270, 331
    see also banking, commercial exchange
Addison, Joseph 46, 97
Agricultural Magazine 162, 169
America, Central 306
America, North 109
    British forces 71, 96, 142, 359
    emigration to 360
    Revolution 56, 57, 68, 80, 151, 199, 228, 233
    trade 43, 48, 207, 209, 212
    wine 309, 316
    see also Canada, Washington, West Indies
America, South 168, 209, 343, 392
Anderson, James 123
Anderson, Matthew 418
Anglo-Saxon language 344, 347
architectural design 21, 293, 332, 370–73, 406
Argyll, first Duke of 36, 38
Argyll, fifth Duke of 152
astronomy 104, 378
Atkins, Richard 140–41, 143, 226, 232–33, 234
Austen, Jane 34, 56, 110, 195
Australian, Sydney newspaper 358, 405
Australian Agricultural Company 393, 400, 409

Bachelard, Gaston 176–77
Bacon, Francis, Viscount St Alban 347
Baillie, Joanna 195
Baker, William 270–71
Bakewell, Robert 160, 312–13
Balmain, William 130, 137–38, 197
    Baughan case 139–41
    opinions 135, 144–45
banking 18, 51–52, 265
    Bank of England 51, 416
    Bank of NSW 265–66
    grain banks 230, 246, 254
    Herries Farquhar 389
    see also accounting, commercial exchange, grain
Banks, Sir Joseph 68, 70, 158, 161, 165, 168, 220, 225, 248
Bannister, John William 360–61, 365
Bannister, Mary Ann and Harriet 361–62
Bannister, Saxe 343, 361, 362–63, 381–83, 401, 414
    early life 359–60
    educational ideas 346, 359, 363–64, 366, 377
    invasion and justice 359–61, 364–65, 379–81, 383, 394–95
    see also First Nations (martial law), infant schools, Macarthur (John)
Bannister, Thomas 346
Barclay, Robert 195
Barker, Harriet and Henry Aston 224
Barrow, Isaac 195
Barrymore, seventh Earl of 302
Bath and West of England Agricultural Society 162
Bathurst, third Earl 279, 318–19, 353
Baughan, John and Mary 139
Bayly, Nicholas 237
Beattie, James 176
Bell, Andrew 354
Bennelong, Wangal man 75, 78, 125, 191
Bennett, Jane 413

Bent, Ellis 264–65
Bentham, Jeremy 213–24, 224, 228, 298, 349
Bible 39, 120, 289
Bill, Burramattagal man 178, 264
Bigge, John Thomas 326–27, 350, 352, 357, 370, 376, 390
    JM remarks to 327, 328, 330
Blair, Hugh 121, 123, 124, 157–58
Blaxcell, Garnham 266
    partnership with JM 209–10, 211, 214, 223, 253
    spirits 229, 230–31
Blaxland, John and Gregory 225
Bligh, Elizabeth 224
Bligh, William 134, 224
    early life 224–25
    enterprise 207, 220, 227
    insurrection Sydney 1808 228, 231–33, 234, 239, 241, 245–49, 251–55, 257, 318–19
    support for 226, 228, 245, 247, 254
    Sydney 226–27, 228, 231–32, 248, 250
    see also insurrection 1808, New South Wales (executive authority)
Bloodsworth, James 94
Board of Agriculture, British 101, 155, 387
Board of Trade, British 167, 168, 220
boatbuilding 23, 71, 201, 215
Bonhôte, Jean-Louis 43
Bonnymuir, Battle of 341
botany 86, 104–105, 123, 378
    indigenous plants 104, 106, 165, 306–307, 373
    see also gardens
Boughton, John 388
Boulton, Thomas 223
Bound, Edward 59
Bourke, Sir Richard 414
Bowman, James 358, 369, 370, 391, 422, 427
Bowman children 370, 401, 410–11, 412, 431, 433
Boyd, Richard 332
Braddon, John 182
Bridgeman, Sir Orlando 360
Brisbane, Sir Thomas 328–29, 377, 380–81
British Empire 6, 154, 155, 343, 364
    constitutional rights 322–23, 364, 380, 415

    see also invasion, slavery
Brogden, James 254, 256–57, 279, 295, 317, 319
Brown, Samuel 349
Browne, Alexander 332
Buchan, William 181, 260, 400–401, 407
Budbury, Gandangara man 264, 332
Burke, Edmund 65–66, 194, 287
Busby, James 355, 379
bushranging 221, 283
Butler, Samuel 46
Byrnes, James 284–85, 374
Byron, George Gordon, Lord 345, 350

Caley, George 248
Call, Sir John 21–23, 25, 65, 69, 72, 112, 167
Calvinism 38–39, 42, 47, 49–50, 123
    see also God, Enlightenment (Scottish), Presbyterianism
Cambridge University 38, 296
Camden, second Earl 168, 191, 318, 331
Camden and Cowpastures 264, 269, 270, 276, 318, 330–35, 337, 352, 354, 367–71, 397, 406, 409, 412, 414, 416–17, 425–26
    see also architectural design, convicts, gardens, livestock, Nepean River, vineyards
Campbell, Annabella 372–73
Campbell, Archibald 296, 317–18
Campbell, Duncan 196–97
Campbell, James 292, 294
Campbell, John 372–73, 389, 392
Campbell, Malcolm 333
Campbell, Robert 225
Campbell clan network 36, 156
Canada 292, 360–61, 364–66, 395
canals 21–24, 32, 80, 244
Cantillon, Richard 83–84, 91, 94
Cape of Good Hope 65, 74–75, 105, 159
    gardens and vineyards 106, 159, 309, 362
    sheep 81–82, 112, 115, 116, 145, 159, 161, 167
Carr, George 124
Castlereagh, Viscount 166, 168, 246
Celtic language and belief 15, 36, 151, 297, 344
    Gaelic 36, 151, 157, 344

INDEX

see also spirits
Chalker, Mary 265
Cheers, Richard 265, 430–31
China
    labourers 392
    market 209
Church of England 38, 55, 352–53, 376
Cicero, Marcus Tullius 194, 197, 297
Clark, Edward Daniel 16, 19
Clarke, James Stanier 152
cloth and clothing 17–18, 37, 42–43, 49, 111–12, 115, 132, 388
Coham, William Holland 59
Coleridge, Samuel Taylor 121, 241, 273
Colebee, Cadigal man 75–76, 78
Coles, Charles 311, 331, 387
Collins, David 95, 96, 136–37, 250
commercial exchange 51, 83, 98, 133, 230, 265
    barter 51, 98, 210, 263, 265
    coinage 16, 133, 205, 263
    notes 98, 133, 230, 265, 270
    see also accounting, banking, trust
Condron, John 270
Conrad, Joseph 29
conversation 25, 189, 198, 314–15, 347, 351, 362, 364, 394–95, 424
    scripted 235–37, 255
    and teaching 297, 354
    and writing 101
    see also letter writing
convicts and ex-convicts 114, 120, 131, 139, 207, 212, 222, 227, 254, 276, 323, 334, 352, 357, 375–77, 415
    at Camden and Elizabeth Farm 177, 181, 221, 273–74, 330, 332–34, 336, 355, 368, 414, 415
    children 337, 363, 364–65
    clothing 110, 112, 132
    as dealers and merchants 134–37, 209, 253
    diet and provisioning 80, 93, 96, 110, 114, 132, 328
    discipline 324, 328, 333–34, 393, 415
    English 80, 114
    escape 77, 231, 330
    First Fleet 70–71
    and First Nations 381, 394–95
    Irish 80, 113, 179–80, 221, 228, 300, 330, 335, 336
    JM's ideas about 326–29, 330
    labour (men) 77, 80, 89, 91, 93, 97, 102, 109–10, 117, 166, 168, 391, 414
    labour (women) 112, 117, 141, 181, 263, 336, 392
    punishment 246, 328, 333, 381
    Scots 80, 341
    as settlers 7–8, 91, 94–95, 97, 135
    transportation 68–69, 72–74, 112–13, 213–14, 256, 305, 319, 334, 379, 415
    see also Bigge, Elizabeth Farm, Macarthur (John), New South Wales, punishment, slavery, *and individual names*
Cook, James 68, 70, 165, 224
Cookworthy, William 48
Cooper, Henry 371, 372
Coriolanus, Caius Martius 47, 135, 237–38
Corunna, Battle of 292
Cory, Edward Gostwyck and Frances 388–89
courts of law
    England 55, 58, 68, 186
    martial 147, 151, 168, 248, 255–57
    NSW 143–44, 231–33, 239, 246, 333, 359, 382, 405
Cox, Patrick 221
Cox and Greenwood 133
Crawford, Henry 142–43
Cribb, George 265
Crossley, George 226, 227
Crowley, Catherine 321
Culloden, Battle of 2, 38
Curry, Patrick 333

Daringa, Cadigal woman 76
Darling, Ralph 329, 362, 372, 381–82
Davidson, Walter Stevenson 168, 170, 210–11, 249
    at Cowpastures 219–20, 222, 227, 330–31
Dawes, William 86–87, 104
Dawson, Robert 391–96
Defoe, Daniel 16, 196
Delaney, Daniel, Bishop of Kildare and Leighlin 336
Dickens, Charles 398
Dickinson, William 207

509

Didion, Joan 235
duelling 73, 140, 143, 158, 249
   Macarthur–Paterson 147, 197
   see also Macarthur (John)
Dufour, Jean-Jacques 315–16, 355
Duvillard, Antoine 315

East India Company (Dutch) 81, 106, 159
   see also Cape of Good Hope
East India Company (English) 21, 65, 149
   exploitation 70, 77, 88, 159, 287
   monopoly 65, 69, 70, 136, 168, 209, 210
Eden, George 256
Edinburgh Review 322, 328, 352
Edridge, Abraham Lloyd 165–66
Elizabeth Farm
   buildings 174–76, 284, 332, 354–55, 370–74, 403–404, 412
   convicts 102, 110, 177, 179–81, 221, 273–74, 330, 332–35, 336, 355, 415
   farm labour 332, 110
   fires 179–80
   First Nations 178, 189–92, 263–64, 283, 287–88
   garden 105, 106–108, 129, 145, 175, 305–308, 355, 367, 370, 372–73, 397, 411–13, 418
   hospitality 125, 141, 142, 143, 180, 198–201, 202, 227, 301, 303, 321, 347, 359, 362, 388–89
   house servants 175, 176, 181, 235, 336, 411
   land 95
   library 86, 194–95, 243, 289–90, 344, 373, 374
   livestock 107–109, 113, 115, 136, 145, 245, 270
   orchard 105–106, 108, 129, 175
   poultry 108, 389
   potential sale 114–15, 117, 145, 275
   produce 107–109, 265
   sense of place 107, 125, 175–77, 290, 293, 431
   sheep and wool 107, 145, 158, 161, 164
   sleeping arrangements 176, 184, 369, 370, 373, 374, 406, 418, 431
   see also architecture, Lucas (Penelope)
Elliot, Hugh 150–51, 256, 295

Ellis, M.H. 4–5, 6, 8
Enlightenment 10–11, 17–19, 20, 21, 22, 25, 47, 49, 51, 59, 67, 82, 120, 198, 202–203, 256, 286, 309
   literature 194–96, 347, 350
   Scottish 36, 39, 78–79, 157–58
   technology 242–43
   trust 129
   see also Industrial Revolution, political economy, schooling
Esterházy, Prince Paul 388, 390, 391
Europe
   pan-Europeanism 315, 351
   travel 38, 312–13, 350, 401
   see also French

Farmer's Magazine 316
farming 99, 365
   cooperative 96–98
   government 89, 91, 93–94
   machinery 18, 109, 263, 318
   progressive 59, 81, 101, 109, 162, 263, 316
   tenant 27, 116, 265, 274, 333
   see also convicts, grain, political economy, schooling
Farquhar, Charity (later Hamilton) 301–302
Farquhar, George 195
Farquhar, John 119, 123, 149–50, 160
Farquhar, (Sir) Robert 149–50, 159, 256, 389, 391–92
Farquhar, Sir Thomas 389
Farquhar, Sir Walter 149, 150, 156, 166, 168, 227, 256, 301, 309–10, 325
Farquhar family 149, 151, 301, 325, 389
Fellenberg, Philipp Emanuel von, and Hofwyl 290, 317, 351, 355
Fielding, Henry 195
Fiji 208–209, 227
First Fleet 70, 77, 103, 122, 222
First Nations
   Awabakal 191
   Burramattagal 175, 178, 288
   children 189, 190, 365
   clothing 111, 187, 306, 393, 395
   conflict with colonists 177, 284–86, 380–81, 394–95
   Darkinjung 285
   Dharug 190, 191, 202

INDEX

diet 75, 174
disease 286, 394–95
economic activity 75, 125, 365, 395
Eora 68, 125, 191, 201, 202
Gandangara 191, 264, 271, 285
Geawegal 285
languages 75, 201, 285, 306
protocol 189, 190, 192, 202–203, 286–87, 306–307
spirituality 191–92, 197
Tharawal 68, 191, 201, 264, 331
Wiradjuri 191, 285
Wonnarua 285, 383
Worimi 381, 394–95
see also Bannister (Saxe), invasion, weapons, *and individual names*
fish and fishermen 15–16, 48, 211, 394, 430–31
Fish, Benjamin, and Fish's Corps 57, 58
Fitz, Robert 247, 248
Fitzgerald, Richard 177–78, 238
Flinders, Matthew 182
flour-milling 95, 99, 211, 223, 227, 399
Fontenelle, Bernard Le Bovier de 44
Forbes, (Sir) Francis 377, 378–79
Foveaux, Joseph 143, 166, 247
acting governor 181, 249
livestock 145–46, 147–48, 149, 177
see also duelling
Fraser, Charles 394
French
educational method 200–201, 312
intellectual life 41, 44, 82–83, 176, 194–95, 313, 316, 343
language 39, 200–201, 290, 306–307, 314
Revolution 86, 134, 154–55, 198–200, 240, 254, 341
see also Huon de Kerilleau, Rousseau
Freycinet, Louis de 301
Freycinet, Rose de 301

Gaelic language, *see* Celtic language and belief
gardens 105
Camden 331, 397–98
government 106, 140, 159, 398
regimental 96
see also Elizabeth Farm
Garrett, John and Mary 53
Geneva 42, 314–15, 317, 350, 352, 438
Genlis, Stéphanie-Félicité, Comtesse de 201, 289, 302
Gascoyne, Olivia (later Lucas) 222
George I, King 36
George II, King 38
George III, King 169, 303
sheep 161, 165, 169, 320
George, Prince of Wales (later George IV) 149, 152, 254, 273, 302
Gibbs, Thomas 319
Gifford, first Lord 376
Gilbert, Thomas 73
Gipps, Sir George and Lady (Elizabeth) 421, 430
Glasgow 151, 317
commerce 36–37, 43, 79
University 78, 290, 296–97, 311, 348
Glennie, James 389
God
Creator 18, 87, 123, 205
duty to 39, 123, 154, 195, 380, 417
favour of 39, 42, 47, 49, 67, 280, 287, 410
protection of 73, 121, 122–23, 124, 182, 198, 203, 258
providential design 67, 73, 119, 121, 124, 272, 287, 342
see also marriage, patriarchy
Godwin, William 120, 348–49, 350, 354, 378
Goethe, Johann Wolfgang von 52, 196, 345, 401
Golden Rule 67
Gordon, Robert Jacob 106, 115
Gordon, Susanna 115, 117, 167
Gordon, William 185
Goulburn, Frederick 329
Goulburn, Henry 318–19, 329
Government House, Sydney 202, 209, 232–33
building 94, 226
social centre 141, 142, 144, 146, 294, 393
Government House, Parramatta 179, 226, 421
grain
crops and harvest 91, 95, 98–99, 109
price 100, 102, 115, 134, 136, 230, 239, 277

rations 102, 178, 263, 270
storage 230, 246, 394
supply 91, 93, 229
surplus 100–101, 114
see also banking, political economy
Grant, Anne 157, 158
Grant, John 120
Gray, Thomas 35
Greek
  independence movement 345–46, 349, 350
  language 53, 344–45, 347, 349, 371, 375
  myth 54, 169
  see also architectural design
Grenville, Kate 7
Griffin, Edmund 225, 238–39, 241
Grose, Francis 71, 90–92, 108
Guilford, fifth Earl of 349–51, 353

Halfpenny, Stephen and James 221
Halloran, Laurence Hynes 375–78, 394
Hambledon Cottage, see Lucas (Penelope)
happiness 47
  national 153–55, 318, 353
  personal 118–20, 124–25, 243, 398
Harry, Burramattagal(?) man 192
Hartley, David 196, 407
Hastings, Warren 65–66, 77
Hatherly, John 27, 121, 122, 123
Hawke, Richard 28, 29
Hazlitt, William 343–44, 346
Heber, Reginald, Bishop of Calcutta 347
Henry, William 120
Herbert, Thomas 221, 270
Hewett, Daniel 28
Heyles, or Hyles, Charles 332
Higgins, Robert 332
Highlands, Scotland 36–37, 38, 152, 154, 157, 318, 389
  Highland Society (London) 155, 157, 296, 389
Hobart, Lord (later Earl of Buckinghamshire) 161, 164, 166
Hobhouse, Benjamin 163, 165
Hodgetts, Thomas and John 223
Hogan, Michael 113, 114–15, 116, 136–37, 142, 230
Hogue, Davidson and Robertson 210

Homer 375
Hood, first Viscount 152
Hoppner, Belgrave and John 350
Horne Tooke, John 347–49, 350, 353, 356, 415
Houston, John 180–81
Howard, John, prison reformer 22
Howell, George and George jr 399
Hullett, John and Thomas 168–69, 205, 208, 210–11, 231
Hume, David 150, 402
Hume, George 195
Hunter, John 99, 115, 117, 132, 136, 139, 141, 153, 167, 362
  opinions 95, 100, 112, 212
Hunter River and Valley 210, 214, 285, 381, 383, 389, 391, 422
Huon de Kerilleau, Gabriel-Louis-Marie (also known as Gabriel Louis and Gabriel Huon) 199–201, 290, 406
Huon de Kermadec, Jean-Michel 199–200

Indigenous people, *see* First Nations
Industrial Revolution 17–18, 111, 239
Inns of Court 58, 296
insurrection Sydney 1808 233, 234–39, 245–46
  aftermath (NSW) 239–41, 247–50
  aftermath (England) 251–56, 257
internet 8–9, 18
invasion 1, 10, 88, 96–97, 189–90
  British Empire generally 25–26
  Canada 292, 364
  changing impact 284–88
  contemporary justification 284–88, 364, 379–80
  genocidal intent 286, 288
  India 65–67, 70, 287
  see also Bannister (Saxe), Burke, First Nations, Hastings
Ionian Islands 349, 350, 353, 379
Irish
  convicts 113, 179–80, 221, 300, 330, 332, 335, 336–37
  emigrants 361, 365
  uprising 1798 179, 198–99, 228
  uprising 1804 182, 341
  see also convicts
Italian language 293, 301

INDEX

Jackey Jackey, Wonnarua man 383
James II, King 36
J'Ans, Wrey 22–23, 32, 60, 106, 109
Jardine, David 48
Jardine, George 290, 296–98, 348, 354
Jefferie, John Fitzpatrick 143, 198–99, 203, 228
Jeremiah, prophet 35
Jesus Christ 39
Johnson, Richard 132
Johnson, Samuel 86, 118, 194
Johnston, George 227, 247, 249, 263, 279
    court martial 255–58
    insurrection 1808 233, 245, 248, 254
Jones, Richard 334, 335
Jonson, Ben 195
Josephine, Empress 355
Joyce, William 179

Kable, Henry 253, 265
Keir, Buxton and Co. 310
Kelly, Benedictus Marwood 59
Kemp, Anthony Fenn 233
Kent, William 115–17, 257
Kerr, Thomas 53
Kilpack, David 274
Kilpack, Eleanor 'Nell' (McDonald) 273–74, 413, 414
King, Anna Josepha 115, 141, 181–82, 249, 413
King, Philip Gidley 115, 129, 134, 141, 142, 147–48, 202, 207, 219–21, 228, 229, 232
    disputes 167, 209
    interest in cloth 112, 117, 158, 161, 206, 263
King, Maria (later Macarthur) 266, 413, 430
King's School, Parramatta 411
Kingdon, Bridget (later Braddon) 182, 341
    closeness to EM 29, 60, 182, 185, 431
    girlhood 29–32, 85
    letters from 117
    letters to 75, 85, 87, 98, 104, 105, 107–108, 109, 110, 114, 117, 118, 122, 137, 175, 213, 290, 429
Kingdon, Charles 29
Kingdon, Eliza 30–31, 61, 268–69, 306–307
Kingdon, Griselda 30, 119
Kingdon, Jane 30
Kingdon, John (1735–1808) 22–23, 30–32, 55, 119
Kingdon, John (1768–1843) 29, 124
Kingdon, Roger 29
Kingdon, Samuel 291
Kingdon, Thomas Hockin 58, 59, 60, 121, 123, 124, 341–42
Kinsman, Andrew 49, 54, 123, 160
Kitchen, Henry 332, 371
Koelz, Carl 368

Lambton, John 60–61
Lane, Henry 212, 214
Latin language 53, 200, 301, 344–45
Law, John 51–52
Laycock, Henry 161–62, 167
Leach, Edmund 22, 24, 27, 28, 31, 66, 90, 176
    canal project 22–25, 32, 80, 244
Leach, Mary Isabella (later Hacker) 23, 58, 175, 413
Lee, James 104–105
Leichhardt, Ludwig 424
letter writing 33, 242–44, 268–69, 291, 298, 306, 367–69, 426–27, 432
Lindesay, Patrick 405
Lindsay, James 160, 301, 311
linen 17, 38, 42–43, 199
    drapers 37, 52, 59, 112
    duck 112, 115
    sailcloth 26, 48, 37, 68, 112
Linnaeus, Carl 104–105, 116, 205
livestock 93, 95, 101, 108, 109, 113, 133, 177, 245, 254, 277, 353, 394
    alpacas 392
    beef cattle 1, 114, 115, 145, 147–48, 219–20, 227, 262, 265, 267, 285, 368
    camels 316
    dairying 107, 108–109, 392, 394
    destruction by 1, 175, 285, 288
    distribution by government 81, 93, 245, 396
    horses 108, 109, 145, 263, 332, 368
    hunting dogs 108
    management 18, 109, 129, 265, 267, 270, 331
    numbers 95, 108
    pigs 81, 100, 201–202

see also Elizabeth Farm, sheep, wool
Lord, Simeon 135, 209, 265, 276, 377
Lowick, Thomas 333
Lowndes, Thomas 185–86, 187
Lowndes, Thomas snr 185, 186
Lucas, Jane (Lowndes, later Temple) 186
Lucas, John 185–86, 204
Lucas, Nathaniel 222–23, 226, 232–33
    daughters Ann and Olivia 223
Lucas, Penelope 198, 267, 268, 370, 372, 420, 421
    early life and arrival 185–88, 193
    cottage 354–55, 412, 416, 418
    old age and death 413–14
    work 262, 270, 273, 290, 301, 331, 431
Luke, St 49
Lyndhurst, Lord 396

McArthur, Alexander (fl. 1680s–90s) 36–37
McArthur, Alexander (Glasgow) 37
McArthur, Alexander (d. 1790) 36
    death 90
    early life 37–38, 40–43, 312
    at Plymouth Dock 47–49, 50–52
McArthur, Catherine (d. 1777) 40–42, 201
McArthur, Catherine (Hawkins) 57
Macarthur, (Sir) Edward 2, 176, 296, 302, 398
    birth and infancy 61, 71, 72–73, 74, 90, 122, 123, 125
    career 170, 292–93, 294–95, 317, 362, 412–13, 418, 425–26
    character 291, 293, 301
    education 113, 117, 147, 160, 290, 301
    emigration projects 414–16, 424
    and his father 292–93, 295, 298
    and his mother 2, 195, 368, 369–70, 417, 423, 425, 426–27, 428–32
    letters to 402, 403, 404, 406, 407, 409, 410, 412, 413, 417, 420–22, 423, 426–27, 428–32
    and his sisters 294, 304, 305, 306, 308, 358, 420–22
    and his brothers 292, 296, 316, 401, 414, 415
    inheritance 371–72, 411, 426
    later life 433
    visits NSW 224, 237, 251, 278, 291–92, 355, 371, 383, 423

and see Malpas
Macarthur, Elizabeth (Veale) (1766–1850)
    ageing 194, 422–23
    agricultural ingenuity 203, 263
    attachment to NSW 103, 124–25, 167, 170, 193, 275, 278–80, 290
    attitude to work 107, 119, 124, 153, 262, 416, 421
    biographical accounts 3–8
    birth and childhood 1, 23–24, 28–30, 268–69
    book-keeping 267, 272–73
    breast feeding 181
    character 3, 29, 41, 74, 118–19, 180, 402
    curiosity and sense of adventure 32–33, 66, 71–72, 75, 79, 98–99, 118, 124, 194, 198, 416, 424, 429
    death 432
    education 31, 72, 103–104, 121, 344
    family background 2, 15–16, 23, 27–28, 35, 176
    feeling for her children 113, 182, 184, 252, 259, 278, 290, 299, 320, 368, 397, 402, 404, 410, 412, 417, 418–19, 423, 424–25, 426–27
    First Nations 75–76, 78, 87, 125, 160, 178, 189–92, 263–64, 284, 286–88
    flowers and nature 75, 104–106, 160, 355, 397–98, 412
    friends 28–30, 32, 98, 106, 117, 180–82, 185, 198, 209, 251, 268–69, 276, 372–73, 382–83, 387, 413, 414
    health 299, 423, 428, 430, 431
    and her mother 72, 85, 90, 413
    inheritance 28, 56, 60
    journal 3, 122
    letters and writing 3, 9, 46, 75, 98, 107–108, 122–23, 417, 418, 426, 431–32
    management when alone 176–83, 250, 253, 262, 264–65, 270–71, 274–75, 332, 397, 420, 430–31
    mourning 410, 411–13, 420, 422
    pregnancies and childbirth 61, 71, 72, 90, 123, 175, 233, 236, 247, 429
    reading 9, 104–105, 417
    record keeping and orderliness 109, 129, 145, 158
    religion 121–24

INDEX

scientific interests 104–106, 116, 205, 213
self-understanding 10–11, 19, 33, 242–43
sensibility 19–20
see also Elizabeth Farm
Macarthur, Elizabeth and John 1, 4–5, 8, 26, 34, 61
  affection 110, 118, 120, 241, 245, 258–59, 314, 392, 398–99, 407, 410, 412
  collaboration 52, 110, 167, 425–26
  differences 73, 107, 110, 119, 160, 237, 260–61, 404
  early homes in NSW 85, 95, 124, 176–77
  friends and sociability 25, 85, 86–87, 88, 103, 125, 198–201, 358–59
  income 60, 114, 116, 137, 148, 158, 167, 169, 208, 220
  journey to New South Wales 72–74
  mutual confidence 52, 72, 103, 110, 129, 245, 253–54, 274, 278
  negotiation 274–75
  phases in marriage 272, 277–78, 341–42, 367, 369, 398–99, 400–401, 402, 404–405
  shared effort 105, 106–107, 262, 267, 336
  wedding 55, 60–61
  see also Macarthur (Elizabeth), Macarthur (John), Elizabeth Farm
Macarthur, Elizabeth (1792–1842) 262, 327
  authority 367, 370, 373, 411
  birth and childhood 90, 149, 170, 175, 290
  character 291, 301, 373
  death 418–19
  education 185, 186, 195, 201, 301–302, 307, 314, 345
  First Nations 189–90
  friends 347
  health 247, 252, 260, 262, 291, 299–300, 418–19
  and her father 300, 303–304, 403, 409
  and her mother 302, 303, 410, 418–19, 423
  horticulture 305–306, 306–307, 373
  inheritance 370, 411
  letter writing 303–304, 306–307, 418
  return to NSW 1805 176,184
  suitors 302–305, 321–32, 358, 370
  teaching 411
  see also Elizabeth Farm
Macarthur, Elizabeth (later Onslow) 2–3, 416, 417, 434
Macarthur, Emily (Stone) 416, 417, 421, 423, 427, 431, 434
Macarthur, Emmeline Emily (later Parker) 3, 362, 367, 370
  childbirth 425, 428
  childhood 247, 259, 291, 347
  education 290, 291
  feeling 421, 422
  and her father 372, 400
  and her mother 372, 401, 412, 418, 420–23, 425, 428–29
  later life 435
  marriage 421–23, 423
  and Penelope Lucas 290, 372, 412, 414, 421
Macarthur, Hannibal 170, 328, 377, 391, 413
  agent and assistant 237, 266–67, 276, 278, 280, 310
  Clovelly 428–31
  JM's death 409–10
McArthur, James (1752–1824) 40, 41, 43, 53, 54, 57, 68, 108, 113, 266
Macarthur, James (b. 1796–97; d. 1797) 175
Macarthur, James (1798–1867) 317, 320, 331, 354, 377, 391, 393, 394–95, 413, 420, 425
  and S. Bannister 382
  birth and childhood 123, 125, 147, 173, 175, 176, 179, 182
  character 311–12, 316, 330, 367–68, 401–402, 414–16
  convict management 328, 333, 335, 341
  education 200, 247, 279, 290–91, 311, 312, 316, 317, 331, 387
  First Nations 190, 286–87
  and his father 2, 243, 251, 284, 311–14, 316, 330, 341, 367, 369, 374, 405–406, 409–10
  and his mother 291, 312, 317, 398, 410, 426

inheritance 354
land grants 331
later life 434
marriage 416–17, 421–23, 431
skills and interests 314–16, 331, 387–88, 393, 401
and T.H. Scott 327, 347, 370, 374, 383
see also Australian Agricultural Company, Macarthur (Emily), Macarthur family papers

McArthur, John (of Hinton) (1755–1840) 101, 322
advice to JM 71, 153, 163, 165, 278
employment 151–52
and L.H. Halloran 375–76
origins 37, 151, 312
patronage network 151, 153, 155–56, 162, 256, 276, 376, 292, 296, 389
writing and scholarship 151–52, 153–54, 155, 165, 240, 244

Macarthur, John (1766–1834)
army career 60–62, 65, 71–72, 90–92, 93, 108, 115, 130–31
attachment to NSW Corps 98, 131, 132–35, 136–38, 139–40, 141, 143, 146–47, 178, 197–98, 228, 247–48
and S. Bannister 362–64, 366, 377, 381, 382, 395
bathing 252, 260, 299, 406–407
biographical accounts 3–6
birth and childhood 46–47, 53–54, 65
change of direction 1803–04 163–64, 165–70, 193
character 46–47, 60, 92, 129, 130, 140, 165, 173, 197, 200, 315, 330, 336
convict reform 213–15, 246, 254, 325, 327–29, 332–35, 341, 415–16
death and burial 1, 409–10
departure for England 1801 149–51, 159, 162, 176, 197, 238
departure for England 1809 247, 249–50, 251, 283, 284
debt to 'Hinton' McArthur 37, 71, 151, 153, 163, 292, 296
diet 252–53, 260, 299, 311
duels 73, 140–41, 142–44, 147, 180, 197, 249
education 53–54, 66, 272, 344
educational priorities 58, 99, 279, 291, 312–13, 317, 351–52, 355, 376–78
expedition 1815–16 314–17, 404
family background 15–16, 35–38, 40–41, 47–54, 108, 111–12, 201
feeling for his children 174, 291, 295, 304, 311, 401–404, 425
First Nations 87, 178, 189–92, 264, 283–84, 286, 288, 394–95
friends 25, 74, 150, 160, 198–200, 209, 251, 254, 256, 275, 318, 326–27
health 53, 74, 122, 241, 252–53, 257, 260–61, 299, 300, 311, 367, 395, 399, 403–407, 409
honour/pride 60, 73, 129–30, 135, 140, 169, 191, 197, 231, 239–41, 248–49, 256, 318–19
inspector of public works 91–92, 93–95, 96–98, 99–100, 108, 109–10, 131, 132, 177–78
intellect 18, 47–48, 51–52, 94, 99, 114, 144, 153, 160, 246, 275
jokes 195, 241
land grants 94–95, 96, 113, 168, 175, 211, 219, 222, 330–31
mentoring 303–305, 332–35, 374, 376–77, 388–89, 399–400
plans to return to England 72, 114, 115, 117, 124–25, 145, 275–76
quarrels with governors 99–102, 146–47, 167–68, 181–82, 231–33, 234, 241, 248, 254–55, 279, 317–18
radicalism and revolution 228, 341–42
reading 9, 46–47, 82, 84, 97, 194–96, 325–26, 344, 355, 357, 373, 402
religion 42, 120–21, 198
reputation 3, 4, 6–8, 10, 100, 135, 165, 220, 227, 238, 244–45, 276, 358, 391–93
return from England 1805 174, 176, 184, 187, 191–92, 219
return from England 1817 192, 319–20, 413
secretary to the colony 245–46
self-understanding 6, 10–11, 19, 129
theatrical display 54, 60, 107, 144, 195, 232, 234–41, 242, 248, 255
trade 208–209, 210–12, 213, 220–21, 223, 227, 262, 277–78, 310, 330–31
and W.C. Wentworth 321–23
will 369–70, 425–26

INDEX

see also Australian Agricultural Company, Camden, Elizabeth Farm, political economy, Pyrmont, Tjedboro
Macarthur, John (1794–1831) 327, 354, 382, 399, 413, 417, 420
   birth and childhood 175
   career 352, 368–69, 425
   death 401–403, 421
   education 268, 290, 296–97, 301, 311, 345
   and his father 197, 292, 311, 369
   and his mother 278, 368
   and W.C. Wentworth 322–23, 361
   work for NSW in London 358, 361, 388, 390–91, 396
   see also Australian Agricultural Company
Macarthur, Mary Isabella (later Bowman) 291, 402
   childhood 125, 147, 173, 179, 182, 184, 201, 262, 291, 300
   education 201
   and her father 222, 241, 291, 372
   infancy 175–76, 181
   later life 422, 427, 433
   marriage 358, 367, 370, 399, 401, 409, 411
   see also Bowman (James), Bowman children
McArthur, William (1770–72) 53
Macarthur, (Sir) William (1800–82) 320, 367, 369, 377, 388, 401, 405, 416, 417
   birth and childhood 147, 173–74, 175, 176, 179, 181, 184, 251, 290, 420
   character 259, 261, 311, 314
   convict management 330, 333
   education 200–201, 247, 290–91, 311, 312, 316, 317–18, 397
   First Nations 178, 187, 189–91, 192, 264, 283, 284, 286
   and his father 174, 176, 184, 243, 251, 259, 261, 311, 312, 317, 402, 405, 406, 409–10
   and his mother 182, 243, 397, 418, 426
   inheritance 354, 405, 425–26
   land grants 331
   later recollections 173–74, 187, 192, 264, 283, 402
   later life 434
   skills 314, 368, 397–98, 400

see also gardens, vineyards
Macarthur/McArthur family
   coat of arms 152, 322
   papers 1–3
   sept or clan 36
   slavery 79
   spelling of name ix, 36, 296
Macarthur sibling ties
   Edward and Emmeline 420–22
   Elizabeth and John 403
   James and William 354, 367, 369, 398, 401, 405–406
McCormick, John 270
McCormick, Richard 198–99
McDougall, or Evans, Elizabeth 181
MacKellar, Neil 146, 168, 197, 228
Maclean, John 372–73
McPherson, Donald 405
Macpherson, James 157
Macquarie, Elizabeth Henrietta 276
Macquarie, Lachlan 246, 249, 279, 285, 328, 389
   and EM 276, 279
   First Nations 285–86, 365
Macqueen, Thomas Potter 389–90, 392
Maitland, John 165, 167, 169
Malpas, Viscount (later Marquess of Cholmondeley) 296–97, 302, 412
manhood 155, 157, 158, 295–96
   see also New South Wales Corps, patriarchy
Manolis, Antonis 368
Māori 201–203
   flax 112
   language 203
   spirituality 199, 203
Marche, Jean-François de la, Bishop of Léon 200
marriage
   ceremonies 55, 123, 376
   settlements 23, 27, 28, 55, 56, 305, 421
   see also Macarthur (Elizabeth and John), patriarchy
Marsden, Betsy 179–80, 181
Marsden, Samuel 116, 146, 179, 203, 206, 328, 410
Marshall, James 142–44, 146, 198–99
Marshall, William 370–71, 372
mathematics 22–23, 31, 86, 104, 154, 200, 293, 344

Mathison, Gilbert 309–10, 325–26
Matra, James 68–69
Maurice, Patrick Ferdinand 52
Mead, Jane 336
Mehegan, Guillaume Alexandre, Chevalier de 201
Melville, Herman 202
Millar, John 110
Milton, John 46
Minchin, William and Ann 141, 142, 146, 233
mineralogy and geology 16, 312, 313, 378
mining
    coal 18, 185, 210
    copper and tin 16, 19
Mitchell, James 241
Mitchell, Thomas Livingstone 373
Mohawk people 360, 365–66, 395
Moir, Benjamin and Margaret 341
Moorbee, Joseph 334
Moorcroft, William 417
Mortlock, John 269
Moulinié, Jacques-Dauphin 314–15
Mudge, John 53
Mullen, John 332
Murphy, Martin and Mary 335
Murray, Andrew 319–20, 413, 414
Murray, Robert 134–35
Musgrave, John 361, 365
music 33, 103–104
Mustoxidis, Andreas 350

Nanbarry, Cadigal man (Andrew) 264
Napoleon I, Emperor 155, 164, 254, 292, 314, 317, 355
natural environment
    agroecology 313
    economy of nature 313, 307
    romantic appreciation 19–20, 29, 75, 106, 351
naval dockyards 47, 48–49, 50–51
navy, British 25, 47, 51, 52, 68, 99, 112, 254
    signalling 151–52, 154
needlework 111, 181, 366
Nelson, Horatio, Lord 37, 152, 375
Nelson, Richard 52
Nepean, (Sir) Evan 54, 68, 69, 93
Nepean, Nicholas 71, 73, 96
Nepean River 191, 219, 227, 417

New South Wales
    constitutional reform 249, 254–55, 415
    executive authority 70, 88, 132, 144, 168, 191, 225, 227, 231, 245
    experiment of settlement 69, 84, 89, 91, 97–98, 163, 275, 414
    factional politics 357–58, 381–82, 391
    masculine character 222, 363, 414
New South Wales Corps 71, 131, 141, 178–79
    funds 95, 132–33, 137
    men 95, 96–97, 228
    officers (and civilian officials) 90–91, 99, 106, 130, 141–42, 233, 247
    officers (differences among) 134–35
    see also insurrection Sydney 1808, *and individual names*
Nisbet, Alexander 394
Norman, George Warde 416
Northumberland, second Duke of 254, 263, 295

Oakes, Francis 234–37, 241, 249
Oglethorpe, William 337–38
olives 305, 313, 315, 318, 319
Onslow, Arthur Alexander Walton 434
Onslow, Sibella Macarthur 3
Ossian, mythical bard 157–58, 344
Oxford University 38, 359
Oxley, John 198, 303, 328, 358, 373, 391
    and Elizabeth jr 302–305, 321

Paine, Thomas 50, 228, 348
Palmer, John 132–33, 136, 225–26
Parker, Henry Watson 421–22, 424–25, 428–30, 431, 435
parliament, British 23, 54, 56, 89, 162, 227, 319, 343
    Commons 65, 89, 254
    inquiries 163, 165, 205, 256
    Lords 412
Parry, Caleb Hillier 165, 396
Parry, Sir Edward 396
Paterson, Elizabeth 106, 115, 141, 142, 146–47, 182
Paterson, William 91, 106, 115, 141, 142–43, 144, 165, 247
    acting governor 91, 249
    quarrel with JM 142, 146–47, 161, 180, 181–82, 197

INDEX

patriarchy 3–4, 76, 272–73, 330, 343, 410
see also manhood, marriage, womanhood
Paul, St 258
Pemulwuy, Bidjigal man 178, 187, 191–92
Persian language 151
Pestalozzi, Johann Heinrich 290, 349, 351, 363, 379
Pettit, Zadoc 181
Phillip, Arthur 70, 80, 90–91, 141, 159
    First Nations 76, 191, 284–85
    governing method 84, 88, 94–95, 99, 132–34, 226
    see also vineyards (government NSW)
Pictet, Marc-August and Charles 315, 317, 352
Pindar 169, 344
Piper, Hugh 143, 146
Piper, John 228
    letters from Macarthurs 129, 167, 179, 180, 183, 302
    Macarthurs' friendship for 143, 146, 182
Pitt, William 149
Plummer, Thomas William 168, 220, 246, 326
Polybius 194
political economy 47, 51, 82, 88–89, 98, 100, 163, 277
    leading writers 82–83, 239
    networked effort 18, 107, 416
    see also Cantillon, happiness, Smith (Adam), Steuart
Porteous, John 303
Portland, third Duke of 100–101
Prater, William 49
Presbyterianism 36, 38–39, 160
Priestley, Joseph 256
punishment
    capital 180, 212, 221, 248, 255, 281, 334, 336, 381
    corporal 325, 328, 333, 354
    see also convicts
Putland, Mary 224, 225–26
Pyrmont
    early state 211
    mercantile project 211–12, 213, 223, 227, 229, 253, 278, 310
    planned house 371–72, 425

Raine, John 399–400

Rawleigh, Fanny (J'Ans) 32
Redfern, William 300
Rees, Abraham 160
Reform Bill 1832 343
Reid, Thomas 39, 196, 297
Richardson, Samuel 195
Richardson, Sarah (later Pettit) 72, 181
Richey, Rose (later Oglethorpe) 336–38
Rickman, John 162
Robinson, Mary 273–74
Roman history 98, 194, 364
    Empire 364, 380
    republic 47, 97, 315, 330
    see also Latin language
Romilly, Sir Samuel 254, 256
Ross, Robert 81–82
Rousseau, Jean-Jacques 20, 25, 33, 289–90, 296, 316
Russell, John 354
Russell, William 194, 344

Sadleir, Richard 365, 383, 395
Saint-Pierre, Jacques-Henri Bernadin de 307–308
salt-making 211, 231
sandalwood 208–209, 210–11, 253, 321
Sanskrit 15, 344
schooling
    grammar schools 31, 53, 58, 113, 359–60, 377–79
    infant schools 363–64, 366
    Madras method 383
    social 247, 312–13, 348
    stages 247, 290–91
    student centred 289, 348, 352, 354, 363
    things not words 348, 353
    universal education 346, 360
Scipio Africanus, Publius Cornelius 47
Scott, Harry Harmood 350
Scott, Thomas Hobbes 326–27, 343, 347, 363, 394–95, 413, 414, 416
    and Bigge 326–27, 342, 352, 370
    buildings and landscape 355, 370–71, 374
    educational ideas 345, 346, 352–56, 358, 377–79, 383–84
    First Nations 365, 383
    radical connections 348–49
Scott, William 348

Second Fleet 72–74
self-awareness 11, 19, 35, 242, 343, 398
sermons 49, 54, 119, 121, 124, 195, 342
Shakespeare, William 135, 237, 289, 295
sheep
    Bengal 112–13
    breeding 155, 165–66, 206
    butchering 265–66
    Cape of Good Hope 81–82, 112, 115–17
    English breeds 17–18, 59, 112, 113, 205
    impact on environment and First Nations 1, 175, 285, 288
    Irish 113
    management 2, 202, 318, 355
    Macarthurs' 107, 109, 116, 136, 145, 158, 161, 164, 166, 219–20, 221, 262, 263, 270
    Merinos 59, 81–82, 169, 205–207, 315, 388
    mutton 107, 145, 262
    numbers 107, 109, 145, 263, 270
    other settlers 115–17, 145–46, 147, 177, 206, 390, 422
    purchases by JM 147–48, 169, 320, 344
    shepherds 109, 166, 168, 202, 221, 269–70, 389
    sheepdogs 269, 389
    see also livestock, wool
Sheldon, John 39–40, 42, 43
Shepherd, William 48–50
Sheppard, Edward 163, 205
ships
    Admiral Gambier, convict transport 249
    Argo, whaling vessel 200, 202, 203, 208, 211; arrival 170, 174, 184, 187, 191; naming 169, 344; in NSW 211, passengers 1804–05 200, 204, 206, 210, 266, 283, 303, 305
    Bounty, HMS 225
    Britannia, storeship 133–34
    Buffalo, HMS 303
    Calcutta, convict transport 179, 180
    Criterion, American trading vessel 209
    Dart, trading vessel 208, 253
    Earl Cornwallis, convict transport 142–43, 198
    Endeavour HMS 68, 70, 165
    Elizabeth, trading vessel 211, 253
    Harrington, trading vessel 210, 211
    Hope, trading vessel 210
    Hugh Crawford, trading vessel 389
    Hunter, trading vessel 137, 149
    Investigator, HMS 182
    Lord Eldon, convict transport 319, 332
    Marquis Cornwallis, convict transport 113, 136, 142
    Minstrel, convict transport 305
    Neptune, convict transport 72–74, 130
    Parramatta, trading vessel 208, 231
    Porpoise, HMS 249, 257, 303
    Scarborough, convict transport 74
    Venus, trading vessel 202, 210
Siddins, Jane 431
Siddons, Sarah 53
Simonde de Sismondi, Jean-Charles-Léonard 317
Sinclair, Sir John 101, 153–55, 157, 162–63, 387
slavery 19,
    abolition 77–78, 79, 87, 150, 309, 342–43
    amelioration 324–25
    and convicts 80–81, 132
    Portuguese 351
Smith, Adam 78–79, 82–83, 194, 243, 310, 324
Smith, Charlotte 119, 195
Smith, James, builder 371
Smith, John, banker 387–88, 390
Smithson, James 254
Smollett, Tobias 194–95
Society for the Encouragement of Arts, Manufactures and Commerce 23, 349
Socrates 298, 354
Spanish
    language 103, 293, 347
    school reform 349–50
Spenser, Edmund 46
spirits (alcohol) 37, 142, 229–30, 253, 309–11
spirits (supernatural) 196–97, 203, 375
Stanhope, third Earl 24
Stephen, John 377–79,
Steuart, Sir James 82–84, 91, 94, 100, 155, 230, 239
Steven, Margaret 6
Stewart, Charles James, Bishop of Quebec 365

INDEX

Stuart, Prince Charles Edward 38, 56
Sullivan, Mary 271
Sussex, Duke of 155
Sutton, Matthew 228, 341
Switzerland 37, 38, 39, 40, 42, 290, 315, 317, 318, 322, 331, 368, 404
Sydney, first Viscount 68–69
Sydney Gazette 161, 167, 202, 206, 221, 240, 395
    editorial opinion 239, 382

Tamar River 15–16, 21, 22, 24, 27, 30, 46, 67, 85, 196, 342
Tarleton, (Sir) Banastre 87, 89, 273
Taylor, Billy and Bett 430–31
Te Pahi, of the Bay of Islands 201–203
Temple, John 68, 88, 89, 95, 186, 267
Tench, Watkin 86–87, 124, 159, 163, 191, 273–74
    books 71, 86–87, 89
    First Nations 76, 125, 197
Terry, Samuel 377
theatrical productions 53, 195
    see also Shakespeare
Thompson, Andrew 265, 276
Thompson, Frederick 314, 317
Thompson, Sarah Margaretta 301, 302, 314
Thompson, Thomas and Margaret 251, 252, 301
Thorpe, Charlotte 305
Throsby, Charles 328
time, attention to 84, 205, 208, 212–13
Timins, Thomas 86
Tjedboro, Bidjigal man 187–88, 190–92, 197, 198, 283–86
Tommy, Worimi boy 381
Townson, John and Robert 225
Trafalgar, Battle of 375
Trail, Donald 73
trust 49, 129, 200, 225, 389
    collaboration 25, 113
    community 32, 48, 98–99, 129, 132
    confianza 103
    convicts 328
    employer–employee 109–10, 116, 177, 204, 275
    family 28, 29, 174, 238, 280
    First Nations 395
    in God 49, 182, 205
    and law 18, 136, 359–60, 376–77

monetary credit 18, 50, 52, 133, 378
public authority 51, 132, 136, 154, 376
slavery 325
soldiers 51, 129, 138, 405
    see also marriage
Tuckwell, Richard 265

Underwood, Michael 300

Van Diemen's Land (Tasmania) 189, 214, 326, 331, 335, 390
    Hobart Town 250, 303
    Launceston 247, 303
Vanbrugh, John 195
Vattel, Emer de 43
Veale, Grace (later Leach, then Bond; 1747–1836) 23–25, 27–28, 90
    EM's letters to 72, 85, 121–22, 124
    income 28, 90, 413
Veale, Grace (1769–72) 28
Verge, John 406
vineyards
    American 316
    Camden 331, 368, 394, 413
    Constantia 159, 362
    Elizabeth Farm 175
    European 315, 317
    government NSW 355
    see also wine
Vitoria, Battle of 292
VOC (Vereenigde Oost-Indische Compagnie) *see* East India Company (Dutch)
voices 1, 46
    accent 24, 31, 32
    rhetoric 53, 54, 57–58, 201
    see also conversation

Wade, John 269
Wallace, Worimi man 394
Wallington, John 163, 206
Walter, William 31, 58–69, 60
Wardell, Robert 358–59, 361
Warner, John 347–48
Warren, Pelham 260, 327
Washington, George 155, 229, 233
Waterhouse, Henry 115–16, 117, 167, 219, 264
Waterloo, Battle of 194, 342

Watson, George (later Watson Taylor) 166, 168, 256, 318
weapons
    firearms 18, 73, 139, 205, 208, 221, 244
    spears 75, 125, 178, 283, 393
    swords 56–57, 151, 154, 244, 405
Wellesley, first Marquess 150
Wellington, first Duke of 314
Wentworth, D'Arcy 321
Wentworth, William Charles 321–23
    his book 322, 323–24, 326, 328, 357, 388
    politics 343, 358–59, 361, 378–79, 405
Westmacott, Richard 187
White, John 85, 86, 264
White, Joseph Blanco 349–51
Whitney, Daniel 207
Wilberforce, William 325, 343
Wilkinson, James 95
William IV, King 413
Williams, Charles 223
Williams, John Matthew 302, 304
Wills, Sarah 226
Wilmot-Horton, (Sir) Robert 352, 358, 361
wine 35, 37, 159, 192, 253, 310–11, 313, 349
    Madeira 309–10
    see also vineyards
Wollstonecraft, Mary 120, 273, 348
womanhood 33, 66, 76, 85, 110, 111, 119, 272–73

female ties 106, 267, 273–74, 276, 413, 419
    see also patriarchy
Wood, Edward 204–205, 206–207, 211–12, 320
wool 1–2, 3, 17–18, 43, 111, 112–13, 155
    blankets 115, 117, 206, 263–64
    blend 254, 366
    coarse 117, 161, 165, 206, 262, 263
    export from NSW (early efforts) 253, 262
    export from NSW (proposed) 162, 164–67, 168, 208, 211, 219
    export from NSW (realised) 266–67, 269, 310, 330–31
    fine 158–59, 161–62, 165, 169, 185, 206–207, 267, 318, 388, 390–91
    industrial trouble 163
    manufacture 17, 48, 148, 163, 205–206
    sorting 204, 206, 207, 212, 262, 269, 274–75, 320
    technology 17, 266
    see also Australian Agricultural Company, cloth
Wordsworth, William 25, 176
Worgan, George 85, 86, 103–104, 109, 120
Wren, Elizabeth 268

York, Duke of 144
Young, Sir George 69, 112, 167

Milton Keynes UK
Ingram Content Group UK Ltd.
UKHW020412101024
449483UK00018BB/121

9 781761 170317